THE MANAGEMENT OF SPORT

ITS FOUNDATION AND APPLICATION

SECOND EDITION

THE MANAGEMENT OF SPORT

ITS FOUNDATION AND APPLICATION

SECOND EDITION

BONNIE L. PARKHOUSE, Ph.D.
Professor, Temple University
Department of Sport Management & Leisure Studies
Philadelphia, Pennsylvania

EDITOR

With the Endorsement of
The National Association for Sport and Physical Education (NASPE)
an association of the American Alliance for Health,
Physical Education, Recreation and Dance (AAHPERD)

National
Association
for Sport &
Physical Education

Mosby

St. Louis Baltimore Boston Carlsbad Chicago Naples New York Philadelphia Portland
London Madrid Mexico City Singapore Sydney Tokyo Toronto Wiesbaden

Mosby
Dedicated to Publishing Excellence

A Times Mirror
Company

Vice President and Publisher: James M. Smith
Senior Acquisitions Editor: Vicki Malinee
Developmental Editor: Brian Morovitz
Project Manager: Carol Sullivan Weis
Production: Carlisle Publishers Services
Manufacturing Manager: David Graybill

SECOND EDITION
Copyright © 1996 by The McGraw-Hill Companies, Inc.

Previous edition copyrighted 1991

Printed in the United States of America

Composition by Carlisle Communications, Ltd.
Printing/binding by Courier Companies, Inc.

19303882

Library of Congress Cataloging-in-Publication Data

The management of sport : its foundation and application / Bonnie L.
   Parkhouse, editor.—2nd ed.
        p.   cm.
   Includes bibliographical references and index.
   ISBN 0-8151-6620-6
   1. Sports administration—Study and teaching—United States.
 I. Parkhouse, Bonnie L. II. National Association for Sport and
 Physical Education.
 GV713.M35   1996
 796'.06—dc20
                                          95-35404
                                          CIP

 96 97 98 99 00 / 9 8 7 6 5 4 3 2 1

Preface

This book represents a "labor of love" for me personally. When approached by Mosby-Year Book, Inc. and officials of the National Association for Sport and Physical Education (NASPE) to serve as editor of this project initially, I immediately accepted the challenge. Although it is virtually impossible to exhaustively describe the body of knowledge that constitutes a profession in one volume, *The Management of Sport: Its Foundation and Application,* 2nd Edition, reestablishes the precedent set by the first edition, serving as the most comprehensive and current entry in its market. This edition is tailored around the informational needs of the sport manager and benefits from new contributors in the specialty areas of experiential learning, organizational theory, group decision making and labor relations.

In the era of the fitness entrepreneur, sport has become even more significant (especially financially) and pervasive in our society. This multibillion-dollar industry places unique demands on its personnel and increasingly requires specialized training. Jobs in the sport industry involve myriad skills applicable to the sport setting and specific to the increasingly complex and multifaceted areas it represents. As a result, a new breed of specialists has emerged. Sport management is now recognized as a legitimate field of study in colleges and universities throughout the United States, Canada, and other countries. Lacking has been textbooks and related resources in this endeavor. *The Management of Sport: Its Foundation and Application,* 2nd Edition, is the most compre-

hensive compilation of subject matter published to date for the sport management profession.

AUDIENCE

In increasing numbers, students with a wide variety of backgrounds are choosing a course of study in sport management. Our intention with this book is to cater to this changing and rapidly growing audience.

Also, although this book was primarily written for third- and fourth-year undergraduate and postgraduate students, instructors at other levels are encouraged to review its content for potential use as well. **Practitioners will also find it to be a valuable resource.**

FEATURES

Organization

This book uses a unique approach in addressing the substantive aspects of the profession by presenting both the theoretical foundations and subsequent application of these principles.

Content

Topics never before addressed in a text of this nature include: Experiential Learning (Chapter 3), which explains how internships add to the student's educational experience by providing real-world experience.

Organizational Theory and the Study of Sport (Chapter 5), which links organization theory, the politics of specific power structures, and a variety of organizational designs.

Group Decision Making (Chapter 6), which presents ideas for fostering involvement, dealing with polarized factions, and keeping groups focused on the task at hand.

Labor Relations (Chapter 8), which presents a history of employer-employee relationships in four major professional team sports, and also outlines crisis situations, their influence on the industry, and how opposing sides work through differences.

A chapter on Sport Licensing (Chapter 16) details the licensing recruitment, application, and review process and provides information on license distribution, royalties, and counterfeit detection.

Case Studies included throughout the book, offers the student an opportunity to apply new concepts by working through practical examples.

Pedagogy

This text uses many pedagogical features to aid students' comprehension of many diverse topics.

- Each author has indicated **key terms** with which the student will become familiar while reading the chapter. These terms are located at the beginning of each chapter, as well as in bold face type either in headings or text when they are discussed within the chapter.
- Each major section ends with a **Concept Check** that highlights the main discussion.
- A succinct enumerated **Summary** emphasizes the key points in each chapter.
- Each chapter includes a complete list of **References.** It is recommended that students read these references carefully for supplemental information.
- **Review Questions and Issues, Case Studies,** and **Exercises** give students further insight as to how to apply the theoretical principles.

ACKNOWLEDGEMENTS

I would like to express my gratitude to all who contributed to *The Management of Sport: Its Foundation and Application,* 2nd Edition. Brian Morovitz, Developmental Editor, made an invaluable contribution to this work. His tireless effort, expertise, and professionalism is greatly appreciated. He single-handedly kept all of us on schedule under very challenging circumstances. I'd also like to thank Andrea Bednar, Associate Editor at Carlisle Publishers Services, for her attention to detail and troubleshooting.

The ultimate success of a book is contingent on the quality of subject matter presented. Drawing on the expertise of a "Who's Who" list of authors and contributors, this work—as forementioned—is the most comprehensive compilation of subject matter ever published for the sport management profession. Without question, the authors made a commitment to excellence and set other priorities aside to meet extremely demanding deadlines.

I am also grateful to Stan Brassie, University of Georgia, for significant input that enhanced the quality of several individual chapters.

Special thanks to the reviewers of the second edition. Their feedback helped strengthen this edition:

Joseph Brownholz, University of Miami
Timothy Domke, Wayne State University
Bonnie S. Hamryka, University of North Carolina
Thomas H. Sawyer, Indiana State University
Marcia L. Walker, University of Northern Colorado
Roy E. Yarbrough, Liberty University

Many thanks to everyone who contributed to this book. In my opinion, it's an accomplishment we can all be proud of.

Bonnie L. Parkhouse, Editor

Editor

BONNIE L. PARKHOUSE
Temple University

Bonnie L. Parkhouse, Professor, received a Ph.D. in Administration from the University of Minnesota. Previous faculty appointments include the University of Southern California and California State University, Fullerton. Over 15 of her studies have been published in distinguished research journals. Numerous articles she has written have appeared in trade and commercial publications, and she is the senior author of previous books and the editor of the 1st Edition of this revision.

Dr. Parkhouse is a member of the editorial boards for the *Journal of Sport Management* and *Quest.* She is also one of seven members who serves on the Sport Management Program Review Council (SMPRC), which acts as an entity for the purpose of reviewing sport management programs in the United States. On invitation, she has served as a consultant in sport management curricular matters at numerous institutions in the United States, as well as in England and Australia. Dr. Parkhouse is recognized as a progenitor of sport management curricula and theory; her publications are frequently cited in related articles by other authors.

Contributing Authors

JOHN AMIS
University of Alberta

John Amis is a doctoral student at the University of Alberta. He earned an undergraduate honors degree in mathematics and physical education from the University of Birmingham and a Master of Arts degree from Dalhousie University in Nova Scotia. John was the 1994 NASSM student essay award winner. He has published articles in *Leisure Studies* and the *Journal of Sport Management.*

ELIZABETH BARBER
Temple University

Betsy Barber, Associate Professor, received her Ph.D. from the University of Iowa in 1987. Prior to teaching six years at Temple University, Dr. Barber taught at Southern Connecticut State University.

Her teaching experience is in recreation and leisure studies, commercial recreation and tourism. She has given numerous presentations on customer service and published in a variety of research journals.

TIM BERRETT
University of Alberta

Tim Berrett is a doctoral candidate in the Faculty of Physical Education and Recreation where he holds Killam, Seinhauer, and SSHRC Doctoral Fellowships. He received a Master's degree in Economics from Queen's University at Kingston, Ontario, and a Master's degree in Public Administration from the same university. Mr. Berrett has taught as a sessional lecturer at the University of Alberta in the Faculty of Physical Education and Recreation, and at the University of Saskatchewan in the Department of Economics. He has authored, or co-authored, a variety of articles on sport and leisure management in journals such as the *Journal of Sport Management, Leisure Studies,* and *Loisir et Societe.* In addition, Mr. Berrett is an international athlete in the sport of track and field athletics, having competed for Canada in the 1992 Olympic Games and 1995 Pan-American Games. He also serves as an athlete representative for athletics in the Canadian Olympic Association.

SCOTT BRANVOLD
Robert Morris College

Scott Branvold is an Associate Professor in the Department of Sport Administration at Robert Morris College in Pittsburgh, PA. His teaching experience at Robert Morris and the University of Oklahoma has involved both graduate and undergraduate programs and includes sport marketing, sport sociology, and legal issues in sport. He has been involved in sport as an athlete, coach, sports information director, and facility manager. A charter member in the North American Society for Sport Management (NASSM), he has presented several papers at NASSM, the American Alliance for Health, Physical Education, Recreation, and Dance (AAHPERD), and the International Sports Business Conference. He also has had articles published in the *Journal of Sport Management,* the *Journal of Sport Marketing,* and has written a chapter in *Sport Business: Operational and Theoretical Aspects.*

LAURENCE CHALIP
Griffith University

Laurence Chalip is a Senior Lecturer with the Faculty of Business and Hotel Management at Griffith University's Gold Coast Campus in Queensland, Australia. He has worked internationally in sport as an administrator, coach, and researcher, including working as an executive member of research teams at the Los Angeles and Seoul Olympics. He has held faculty positions at the University of Chicago, the University of Waikato, and the University of Maryland. He twice served as a lecturer for the International Olympic Academy in Greece. He earned his Ph.D. in policy analysis from the University of Chicago.

PACKIANATHAN CHELLADURAI
Ohio State University

Dr. Chelladurai, Professor, is a recognized scholar of management science, specializing in organizational theory and organizational behavior in the context of sport. Dr. Chelladurai has authored 3 books and contributed over 70 articles to sport management literature. He is a corresponding Fellow in the prestigious American Academy of Physical Education and the first recipient of the Earle F. Zeigler Award from the North American Society for Sport Management. He is the former editor of the *Journal of Sport Management* and current member of its Editorial Board. Dr. Chelladurai also serves as a guest reviewer for the *Journal of Sport and Exercise Psychology, and Perceptual and Motor Skills*. He has been invited to lecture and/or teach in France, India, Japan, Korea, Portugal, Scotland, and South Africa. Dr. Chelladurai delivered the opening keynote address at the First Conference of the European Association of Sport Management in 1993.

ANNIE CLEMENT
Cleveland State University

Annie Clement, Professor and Director of Sport Management, holds a Ph.D. from the University of Iowa and a J.D. from Cleveland State University. She is a member of the Ohio Supreme Court.

Dr. Clement is author of *Law in Sport and Physical Activity*, co-author of *The Teaching of Physical Activity*, and *Equity in Physical Education*. A sought-after speaker and writer, she has over eighty published works and one hundred and fifty presentations.

In 1992 Annie Clement received the American Alliance for Health, Physical Education, Recreation and Dance Honor Award and the Aquatic Council Award; the OAHPERD Merit Award; and the Council for National Cooperation in Aquatics Merit Award. She has also received the NASPE Joy of Effort Award, American Jurisprudence Award for Achievement in Business Associations, and was among the first twenty women selected by the American Council on Education in its Identification of Women Leaders in Higher Education. She was recently named a Fellow of the American Bar Association Foundation, an award given to only one half of one percent of the membership. Dr. Clement was the 1988-1989 President of the National Association for Sport and Physical Education (NASPE).

PETER J. FARMER
Guilford College

Peter Farmer, Assistant Professor and Director of the Sport Management Studies program, Guilford College, holds a Ph.D. from the University of New Mexico, M.B.A. from the University of Phoenix, and a M.Ed and B.S. from the University of Texas at El Paso. He currently teaches undergraduate sport management courses in the areas of sport marketing, sport and facility management. Dr. Farmer is currently completing a book in facility management and a publication on international sport policy. He has presented extensively in the areas of facility management and sport marketing. Dr. Farmer was a former Olympian for Australia.

WENDY M. FRISBY
The University of British Columbia

Wendy Frisby, Associate Professor, teaches courses on entrepreneurship, research methods, and organizational theory at the undergraduate and graduate levels of the Leisure and Sport Management Program. She has received numerous research grants and has published articles in the areas of organizational structure, organizational culture, organizational theory, and gender relations. Dr. Frisby has served on the editorial boards of several journals including the *Journal of Sport Management*.

HARMON GALLANT
Member of the Illinois Bar

Harmon Gallant is a sports lawyer in Chicago. He received a B.A. in philosophy from Northwestern University, and a J.D. from Illinois Institute of Technology/Chicago-Kent College of Law. His radio commentaries on legal and business issues in sport were syndicated by the American Radio networks, and for the past three years he has written a regular column for *College and Pro Football Newsweekly*. His recent writings include law review articles on baseball's antitrust exemption and the problem of professional sports franchise relocation. Mr. Gallant is a member of the American Bar Association Forum Committee on Entertainment and Sports Law.

DIANNA P. GRAY
University of Northern Colorado

Dianna P. Gray, Associate Professor, received her Ph.D. from The Ohio State University, and has held faculty positions at Kent State and Indiana Universities. Her research and teaching areas include sport marketing, management, and media relations, and she is published in a variety of trade and scholarly journals. The Indiana Pacers, Cleveland Indians, Cleveland Force, Women's Basketball Coaches Association, and Gus Macker Basketball are among the various sport organizations for which she has served as a consultant. Dr. Gray is also on the Advisory Board of the Women's Sports Foundation and has served as a sport management curriculum consultant.

SUE INGLIS
McMaster University

Sue Inglis is an Associate Professor in the Department of Kinesiology. She earned her Ph.D. from The Ohio State University, and M.A. and B.P.E. from the University of Alberta. Sue's experience includes 9 years varsity tennis coaching, 7 years chair of McMaster's women's athletic program, leadership positions in NASSM (North American Society for Sport Management) including president 1993-94, member of the NASPE-NASSM Sport Management Task Force 1989-92 and the Sport Management Program Review Council 1992-95, and numerous years teaching and research in sport management. Dr. Inglis' interests and published work focuses on governance issues in sport and intercollegiate athletic environments and women's involvement in organizational life.

RICHARD IRWIN
University of Memphis

Dr. Irwin (Ed.D., 1990, University of Northern Colorado) is currently the Director of the University of Memphis Bureau of Sport & Leisure Commerce which is housed within the Department of Human Movement Sciences and Education. In addition to his university responsibilities Dr. Irwin has conducted extensive research in the area of sport marketing with specific foci on spectator assessments and the management of sponsorship and licensing programs. Dr. Irwin is also a market research consultant for several major sport organizations and a member of the *Sport Marketing Quarterly* Editorial Board.

LISA M. KIKULIS
University of Saskatchewan

Lisa M. Kikulis, Associate Professor, received a Ph.D. from the University of Alberta with a specialization in Sport Administration and Organizational Theory. Lisa's research focuses on understanding organizational change and strategic decision making in voluntary sport organizations. She also studies the impact of the government-nonprofit partnership on the delivery of amateur sport programs.

AARON MULROONEY
Kent State University

Aaron L. Mulrooney is currently an Assistant Professor in the School of Exercise, Leisure and Sport. He holds an M.B.A. in Finance and a J.D. from the University of Akron and currently teaches graduate courses in sport law, finance, and facility management as well as coordinating the sport administration program at Kent. His primary publications have been in facility management and law, and he has developed presentations for various audiences at state, national, and international conferences. Along with Peter Farmer and Rob Ammon, he is currently completing a text specifically devoted to the topic of facility planning and management.

THOMAS H. REGAN
University of South Carolina

Tom H. Regan is an Assistant Professor of Sports Business at the University of South Carolina in the College of Professional Sciences. He brings with him a wealth of experience in the areas of regional economic impact analysis and event development in sports and entertainment. His research emphasis is regional economics and sports and entertainment event development. His recent accomplishments include a leading research study on the "Economic Impact of the Denver Broncos on the Denver Colorado Metropolitan Area," and a business/marketing plan proposed for luxury box seating at Notre Dame Stadium in South Bend, Indiana. Dr. Regan recently completed a comprehensive economic impact study on Golf Course Operations in the State of South Carolina. His work experience includes working as a staff accountant for Fox & Co., CPAs, and eight years as a comptroller for a fully integrated oil and gas company. He is currently working on a text book relative to "Managing Sport and Special Events." He holds bachelor and master of Accounting degrees from the University of Wyoming and a Doctorate degree in Sports Administration at the University of Northern Colorado.

LINDA A. SHARP
Consultant, Fort Collins, Colorado

Linda A. Sharp received her B.A. from Baldwin-Wallace College and her J.D. from Cleveland-Marshall College of Law. She taught sport law, administrative theory, and public relations to both undergraduate and graduate students. In addition to her teaching responsibilities, Ms. Sharp lectures extensively in the area of sport law. She has presented at six National Organization on Legal Problems of Education National Conventions. In 1991, she was a presenter at the Legal Quadrivium at AAHPERD's National Convention. Ms. Sharp published a monograph entitled *Sport Law* in 1990 and has written the chapter on "Sport Law" for NOLPE's *Yearbook of Education Law* for the years 1989 through 1994. Most recently, she prepared the supplemental material for the chapter on Tort Liability found in the *Legal Deskbook for Administrators of Independent Colleges and Universities* (2nd Edition). She is currently a writer and consultant in Fort Collins, Colorado.

TREVOR SLACK
University of Alberta

Trevor Slack is Professor and Associate Dean (Graduate Programs and Research) in the Faculty of Physical Education and Recreation at the University of Alberta. He also holds a position as an Adjunct Professor in the Faculty of Business. Dr. Slack has worked in the Center for Corporate Strategy and Change, a research center at Warwick Business School in England. He has also taught at Aston Business School in England and on the European Sport Management program at the Univesidade Tecnica de Lisboa in Portugal. Dr. Slack is the Associate Editor of the *Journal of Sport Management* and a member of the editorial boards of the *European Journal of Sport Management*, the *International Review for the Sociology of Sports*, and the *Scandinavian Journal of Medicine & Science in Sports*. His research interests are in the areas of organizational strategy and change in sport and leisure organizations. His latest book is entitled *Sport Organizations: Structure, Process, and Design.* Dr. Slack's work has been published in such journals as the *Journal of Sport Management, International Review for the Sociology of Sport, Leisure Studies, Quest, Organization Studies, Journal of Management Studies,* and *Human Relations.*

DAVID K. STOTLAR
University of Northern Colorado

Dr. David K. Stotlar has a Doctor of Education degree from the University of Utah and serves as the Director of the School of Kinesiology & Physical Education at the University of Northern Colorado. He teaches on the faculty in the areas of sport management and sport law. He has had more than forty articles published in professional journals and has written several textbooks and book chapters in sport, fitness, and physical education. He has made numerous presentations at national and international professional conferences. On several occasions, he has served as a consultant to fitness and sport professionals; and in the area of sport law, to attorneys and international sport administrators. He was selected by the USOC as a delegate to the International Olympic Academy in Greece and the World University Games Forum in Italy. He has conducted international seminars in sport management for the Hong Kong Olympic Committee, the National Sports Council of Malaysia, Mauritius National Sports Council, the National Sports Council of Zimbabwe, the Singapore Sports Council, the Chinese Taipei University Sport Federation, the Bahrain Sport Institute, the government of Saudi Arabia, the South African National Sports Congress, and the Association of Sport Sciences in South Africa. Dr. Stotlar's contribution to the profession includes having served as President of the North American Society for Sport Management.

BETTY VAN DER SMISSEN
Michigan State University

Dr. van der Smissen has the unique background of holding a doctorate in recreation, as well as a law degree. She is a member of the bar. Professionally, she has combined her legal and sport/physical activity interests in both her teaching and research, as well as organizational involvements. Dr. van der Smissen has taught both undergraduate and graduate level courses in the Legal Aspects of Sport and Leisure Services. For close to ten years she was Director of the School of Health, Physical Education, and Recreation at Bowling Green State University, with its extensive Sport Management program.

Her research is in the legal field. She has authored a 3-volume reference on Legal Liability and Risk Management for Public and Private Entities.

M. ELIZABETH VERNER
Illinois State University

M. Elizabeth (Beth) Verner, Associate Professor in the Department of Health, Physical Education and Recreation at Illinois State University, teaches fitness management at the undergraduate level, athletic administration at the graduate level, and coordinates the professional practice (senior field experience) program for undergraduate exercise science and athletic training students. She has authored articles and given presentations related to experiential learning, curriculum design, administration, and gender equity in sport. Dr. Verner is currently exploring a model based on social cognitive theory to study factors which influence the contribution patterns and preferences of those who financially donate to intercollegiate athletics.

Contents in Brief

Contents

PART VI   *ECONOMICS AND FINANCE*

PART VII   *CONCLUSION*

THE MANAGEMENT OF SPORT

ITS FOUNDATION AND APPLICATION

SECOND EDITION

Fundamentals

Definition, Evolution, and Curriculum

Bonnie L. Parkhouse

In this chapter, you will become familiar with the following terms:

Sport management

Sport administration

Athletic administration

Sport vs. sports

Sport business

Sport management program
    review council

Core content for the
    undergraduate program

Core content for the master's
    degree and doctoral degree

Overview

Sport has become a dominant influence in American society. No single aspect of our culture receives the media attention given to sport. Although Super Bowl Sunday has been viewed as media hype, it can be argued that it is also a celebration of the masses, rendering it a type of secular religion in our society. The highest television ratings each year are typically associated with such sporting events as the Super Bowl, the NCAA Final Four, golf's Masters tournament, and Wimbledon; the World Series has even preempted news coverage of major world crises. Sport demands its own section in newspapers and is often the political platform for defectors, ter-

rorists, and dissidents. "Sports talk" is common in corporate boardroom negotiations and coffee-break conversation. Sport often provides the visibility for athletes to enter politics or become entertainers or entrepreneurs. Recreational participation in sport also continues to gain popularity each year because individuals in our society have more time for leisure activities and more money to spend on their own fitness pursuits.

Sport is big business. The growth of the sport industry in the last half-century has been phenomenal. According to a study done by *The Sporting News* and Wharton Econometric Forecasting Associates Group, if all of the elements of the sport industry were combined—from the manufacturing of sporting goods, to the umpiring of softball games,

_____

P. Stanley Brassie, University of Georgia, contributed to this chapter.

to the televising of the Super Bowl—sport is a 63.1 billion dollar a year business, making it the twenty-second largest industry in the United States. When compared with other industrial giants, sport is bigger than the automobile, petroleum, lumber, and air transportation sectors of the U.S. economy (Comte and Stogel, 1990).

As mind boggling as the numbers are today, the estimates for the gross national sports product (GNSP) for the next century are even more amazing. By the year 2000, the GNSP will have increased 141% to 121.1 billion dollars (Rosner, 1989). Furthermore, these figures reflect the business of sport solely in the United States; this market is expanding internationally also. And, with dynamic changes in Eastern Europe and elsewhere, even greater sums of money will eventually be invested in this industry.

This multibillion-dollar industry also places unique demands on its management personnel. Management positions require management, marketing, communications, accounting, finance and economics, and legal skills applicable to the sport setting and specific to the increasingly complex and multifaceted areas it represents. Hence a new breed of specialists has emerged from the sport management arena.

DEFINITION OF SPORT MANAGEMENT

From an *applied* perspective, sport management has existed since the time of the ancient Greeks, when combat among gladiators or animals attracted crowds of spectators. Herod, King of Judaea, was honorary president of the eleventh-century Olympics. A magnificient ceremony opened the Games, followed by athletic competition where thousands of spectators were entertained lavishly (Frank, 1984). According to Parks and Olafson (1987), given the magnitude of such events, there must have been purveyors of food and drink, promoters, purchasing agents, marketing personnel, and management directors. Today, all of these individuals are known as *practitioners;* this term includes all persons employed in the applied field of sport management.

Although the terms **sport(s) management, sport(s) administration,** and **athletic administration** are often used interchangeably, the first most accurately describes this field from a universal, or global, perspective. That is, *management* is all-encompassing and represents the myriad sport-

related areas identified by DeSensi et al. (1990), including facilities, hotels and resorts, public and private fitness and racquet clubs, merchandizing, and collegiate and professional sports. The term *administration* is limiting and suggests a school-related focus, particularly at the interscholastic and collegiate levels. However, Parkhouse (1987) found that a significant number of programs with offerings in such areas as retail sales, fitness and racquet club management, and professional sport management title their curricular programs "Sport Administration" or "Sports Administration." In contrast, those limiting their focus to the study of school-related sports use the term "Sport Management" or "Sports Management" (see chapter 2).

Obviously, this distinction is not applied universally. Because the labeling of existing programs is inconsistent, the title often does not accurately describe the curricular focus and content. According to Milewski and Bryant (1985), some programs are titled "Health Promotion and Wellness," "Corporate Recreation," or "Facility Management." This is acceptable only when the content is limited to these specific areas.

The terms *sport* and *sports* are also used interchangeably. According to Parks and Zanger (1990), **sports** is singular in nature, whereas **sport** is a more all-encompassing term. The North American Society for Sport Management (NASSM) has elected to use the collective noun "sport" and encourages its use.

As previously mentioned, *sport* has several definitions (Loy, 1968; Snyder and Spreitzer, 1989; vander Zwaag, 1988); however, a workable definition for our purpose categorizes it as (1) spectator and (2) participant sport. Note that neither category is mutually exclusive. Often consumers of participant sports also want to be entertained, and spectators frequently like the opportunity to demonstrate their physical prowess; however, these are secondary motives. An example of the former is health and fitness clubs that offer members closed-circuit television viewing of special sporting events. An example of the latter includes "audience participation," in which selected fans are invited on the court at halftime to shoot baskets or to return a Chris Evert serve at the end of a celebrity match.

Technically, the term *sport management* is also misleading. Management is limited to subject matter that focuses on the functions of planning, organizing, directing, and controlling. It constitutes only one area of study within business schools. For this reason, business schools have been careful to label themselves as schools of business administration rather than those of business management. Other areas of study in business administration include accounting, marketing, economics, finance, organizational behavior, risk management, and legal studies. These are also legitimate areas of study within quality sport management programs.

Sport business is perhaps a more accurate term to describe both the applied and academic aspects of this industry. Unfortunately, "business" to many, particularly those involved in school-related sports, suggests entrepreneurial, for-profit, and exploitive motives.

Sport management is composed of two basic elements—sport and management. Getting things done with and through other people via planning, organizing, leading (directing), and evaluating (controlling) is the contemporary definition of management. Mullin (1980) defined sport management as including the functions of planning, organizing, leading, and evaluating within the context of an organization with the primary objective of providing sport- or fitness-related activities, products, and/or services. For our purpose, sport is defined as "you watch," or spectator activities primarily at the collegiate and professional levels. Fitness is defined as "you do," or participation activities such as those available in health and fitness clubs or corporate fitness programs, or such special events as marathons and 10-kilometer runs. Products are tangible and include such items as fitness equipment, shoes, and clothing. Services are intangible and include installation and repair of fitness equipment, and entertainment, which is the major focus of spectator sport. Practitioners seeking employment in spectator sport will primarily find positions in college and university athletics, professional sport, and arena and stadium management. Opportunities in participant sport can be found in corporations, public and private fitness or racquet clubs, hotels and resorts, retail sales, and the travel and cruise industry (see Chapter 2).

Hardy (1987) described the politics and frustration in attempting to accurately define and label this profession:

The term *sport management* is not always used to describe the domain, although it has probably become the preferred term. Relatively older programs have undergone several name changes in an effort to match title with curriculum. For instance, Robert Morris College began a management major option in Athletic Administration in 1978. By 1981 the college had a separate department of Sports Management. And in 1984, after many debates with the provost over proper usage, an *s* was dropped, resulting in Sport Management. Colleagues ask which letter will be dropped next. One suspects that many old hands in this field have suffered similar queries of curiosity or disdain.

The department of physical education at a university on the West Coast had recently developed a sport management program. When the course prospectus for a class, appropriately titled "Sport Marketing," was sent to the university curriculum committee for review, a territorial-rights "red flag" went up on behalf of the business school. The content of the course was fine, but the word *marketing* had to be replaced by a more innocuous term. As a result, a less-descriptive title for this course, "Sport Consumer Behavior," was reluctantly substituted for the initial title so the course could be approved. Clearly, it is most desirable that names have some discrete and widely understood meaning (Mullin, 1980).

CONCEPT CHECK

From an applied perspective, sport management has been in existence for centuries. Only recently, however, has sport management been acknowledged as an academic pursuit. This field shares two basic elements— sport and business administration, or management. The business component includes not only such management functions as planning, organizing, directing, and controlling, but also such areas as accounting, marketing, economics and finance, and law. From a sport management perspective, the term sport *includes the spectator sport industry, which focuses on consumer entertainment, and the fitness industry, which concentrates on consumer participation in fitness-related activities. Although the terms* sport management, sport administration, *and* athletic administration *are frequently used interchangeably, the first most accurately describes this field from a universal, or global, perspective.*

AN EVOLUTION IN SPORT MANAGEMENT

Although sport management is indeed a relatively new concept in academe, its acceptance as a legitimate area of study is well documented in the literature (Gleason, 1986; Hardy, 1987; Parkhouse, 1987; Parkhouse and Ulrich, 1979; Parks and Zanger, 1990; van der Smissen, 1984). It is also the topic of numerous trade articles and several published textbooks and has been featured in such popular publications as *USA Today* and *Time*.

The first university-sponsored sport management curriculum was established in 1966 at Ohio University. The Sports Administration Program at Ohio University was a master's offering that actually had its roots at the University of Miami in Coral Gables, Florida. James G. Mason, a physical education professor there, prepared a curriculum for a proposed program in sport management at the encouragement of Walter O'Malley, then president of the Brooklyn (soon to become Los Angeles) Dodgers. O'Malley first approached Mason in 1957 with the idea. Although it was never implemented, this curriculum became the basis of the Ohio University program (Mason et al., 1981). A few years later, Biscayne College (now St. Thomas University) and St. John's University became the first institutions granting baccalaureate degrees in sport management. The second master's program was established in 1971 at the University of Massachusetts.

In 1980, 20 colleges and universities in the United States offered graduate programs in sport management (Parkhouse, 1980). By 1985, this number had grown to 83 programs in the United States (40 undergraduate, 32 graduate, and 11 at both levels), as identified by the National Association for Sport and Physical Education (NASPE). The May 23, 1988, issue of *Sports, Inc.* published a compendium of 109 colleges and universities with programs in sport management. Of the 109 institutions identified, 51 offered undergraduate degrees, 33 were master's level, and 25 sponsored both undergraduate and master's programs (Brassie, 1989). A follow-up survey of colleges and universities in the United States conducted by NASPE in 1993 identified 201 sport management programs including six doctoral programs.

Although the first sport management program was established in 1966, the significant proliferation in curricular development was not observed until the mid-1980s. As a result, by 1988 only 10% of the programs had been in existence for more than 5 years.

Unlike the United States, the number of programs in Canada has not changed significantly in the past 10 years. In 1980 Bedecki and Soucie reported that 10 undergraduate, 9 master's, and 2 doctoral programs existed there. Eight years later, Soucie (1988) reported 6 undergraduate, 9 master's and 2 doctoral programs. By 1990 one additional doctoral program had been established.

Present programs in the United States are more applied in nature, focusing on such areas as collegiate and professional sports, facility, and health and fitness club management, whereas those in Canada are more theoretical. That is, the focus is on such subdisciplines as historical and cultural perspectives of sport and physical activity, psychological and sociological dimensions, and physiological and biomechanical aspects. I believe that as accreditation standards are adapted (discussed in the section "Curriculum,") a balance of applied and theoretical content will occur in programs in both the United States and Canada.

Sport management also has international appeal. In addition to Canada, West Germany, Korea, France, and the United Kingdom have all implemented programs. In 1990 the Bowater Faculty of Business at Victoria College established Australia's first bachelor of business program in sport management. This specialization consists of a core of business courses, a required core of sport studies, and offerings that combine the concepts of sport and management, such as sport marketing and sport law. *The Guidelines for Programs Preparing Undergraduate and Graduate Studies for Careers in Sport Management*, published by NASPE in 1987, were especially instrumental in the development of the Australian model.

The National College of Physical Education and Sports in the Republic of China (Taiwan) also has established a curriculum in sport management. As of 1992 graduates of this program are prepared to assume leadership roles in sport management in Taiwan. Again, the U.S. model was influential in shaping this program, although other Asian models—notably that found in Korea—were also examined. The curriculum in Taiwan includes a business core, a sport studies core, an integrated core, and a variety of field experiences.

Recently the Japanese physical education curriculum has also undergone a significant transformation. The major reason is the decreasing demand for physical education teachers and the increasing need for personnel in the commercial sport sector. Specifically, the demand in the driving range industry is unique to Japan. Unlike the United States and other European countries, Japan has had tremendous growth in this area; more than 100 million people use driving range facilities there each year. These facilities require personnel that have exceptional management skills. Management of spectator sports has also become increasingly important because this particular industry continues to grow rapidly not only in Japan but worldwide as well.

Two professional associations in North America serve the sport management profession. The North American Society for Sport Management (NASSM) and the National Association for Sport and Physical Education (NASPE) have monitored the rapid growth in this profession.

In 1985 NASSM was established to promote, stimulate, and encourage study, research, scholarly writing, and professional development in sport management (Zeigler, 1987). NASSM is the successor of the Sport Management Arts and Science Society (SMARTS), which was conceived in the 1970s by faculty at the University of Massachusetts. Like the members of SMARTS, those of NASSM focus on the theory, applications, and practice of management specifically related to sport, exercise (fitness), dance, and play. In addition to an annual conference, NASSM sponsors the *Journal of Sport Management* (JSM). JSM publishes refereed articles relative to the theory and applications of sport management. Published since January 1987, this journal has become the major resource for disseminating significant knowledge in the field.

NASPE, an association of the American Alliance for Health, Physical Education, Recreation, and Dance (AAHPERD), approved a sport management task force in 1986 to meet the needs of its members who were involved in sport management curricula. The NASPE task force included five professors and four practitioners. In an attempt to avoid duplication of the services offered by NASSM, the task force identified three agenda items: (1) curricular guidelines, (2) student guide-

lines for selecting programs, and (3) a directory of college programs preparing professionals in sport management. The task force drafted curricular guidelines and disseminated them to those directors of sport management programs identified by NASPE for input. Suggestions were then incorporated into the final document. In the fall of 1987, the NASPE Cabinet approved this document as NASPE's official curricular guidelines and published it as *Guidelines for Programs Preparing Undergraduate and Graduate Students for Careers in Sport Management* (Brassie, 1989a).

In the November/December 1989 issue of the *Journal of Physical Education, Recreation, and Dance* (JOPERD), an article titled "A Student Buyer's Guide to Sport Management Programs" appeared. Included in this article were the guidance questions developed for prospective sport management students seeking a suitable program of study (Brassie, 1989b).

When NASPE published its 1987 guidelines for programs preparing undergraduate and graduate students for careers in sport management, NASSM was invited to endorse the guidelines. Many members of NASSM believed the NASPE guidelines were too limited, which led to a discussion of developing curricular standards endorsed jointly by NASPE and NASSM. A joint task force of five NASPE and five NASSM members was appointed by the respective associations to develop standards that could shape the preparation of prospective sport management students. The joint task force was also mandated to investigate the feasibility of accrediting sport management curricula as a means to provide an incentive for institutions to upgrade their respective programs. The members of the task force agreed that program review and approval was an approach that could help assure students and potential employers that graduates of an approved program had been prepared in content areas that would result in the development of appropriate knowledge and skills required of an effective professional. The joint task force convened in 1989 to begin identifying the essential curricular content areas, establishing standards, and developing a program approval protocol that could evaluate programs for compliance with the standards.

The curricular standards were approved by the NASSM Board of Directors in 1990 after discussion by the entire membership in attendance at both its 1989 and 1990 conferences. NASPE conducted presentations at its conventions in 1990 and 1991. After the presentation at the 1991 convention, a referendum card and descriptive documents were sent to the 181 institutions with sport management programs, and a vote was taken. The NASPE Cabinet, as a result of the positive vote, approved the standards in 1992.

After the adoption of the standards, the joint task force continued working on a protocol that could be used to evaluate an institution's sport management program. Both associations agreed on a protocol and decided to adopt a voluntary "program review" procedure rather than an "accreditation process" so that the evaluation would be viewed more positively and less threateningly by an institution. The **Sport Management Program Review Council** (SPMRC) was created to govern the review process, which officially began in 1994.

CONCEPT CHECK

Although the number of programs in Canada has not changed much in the past 15 years, a significant proliferation in sport management curricula has occurred since the mid-1980s in the United States. Several other countries have also begun offering academic programs in sport management.

CURRICULUM

Curriculum in sport management has changed dramatically over the past 25 years. Historically sport management has had a strong physical education orientation. Required courses for the sport management student 20 years ago typically included physiology of exercise, motor learning, and measurement in physical education. Electives often included sociology or psychology of sport and perhaps a course in the history or philosophy of physical education and sport. A course in the organization and administration of physical education and sport was about the only course with a managerial focus available. Sometimes electives were available in business or journalism, and the more sophisticated programs may have created internship opportunities. Sport management was often promoted as a nonteaching option in physical education, which physical education faculty tolerated primarily to offset the declining enrollment in teaching and coaching.

Unfortunately many schools during this early period merely repackaged an existing physical education curriculum and added some catchy course titles to create a sport management curriculum (Berg, 1989). Parkhouse (1987) reported that a significant number of sport management programs still included physical education-related coursework that is questionable in meeting the educational or job-related needs of this industry. In 1989 Berg reported that only a handful of programs were sufficiently developed in terms of faculty and curriculum to produce qualified graduates.

The NASPE task force, which published the *Guidelines for Programs Preparing Undergraduate and Graduate Students for Careers in Sport Management* in 1987, made the first successful attempt to obtain a consensus of sport management faculty and practitioners on what coursework would constitute a sound sport management curriculum. The task force identified three components of a curriculum: (1) the foundation areas of study, (2) the application areas of study, and (3) the field experiences. Many colleges and universities, seeking to develop their sport management curriculum, eagerly embraced the guidelines. Slowly curricula began to shift from a physical education emphasis to a business management emphasis. The foundational areas of study included courses in management, marketing, economics, accounting, finance, computer science, public relations, communication, advertising and promotion, business law, and labor relations. These courses are typically offered through business and journalism schools on college and university campuses.

The foundational areas of study were specific to sport (Brassie, 1989a; and Parkhouse, 1984). At the undergraduate level, background content included such courses as history and philosophy of sport, sport culture, sociology of sport, and sport psychology. Specific applied content included such courses as sport law, sport marketing, sport administration, facility design and management, and sport finance and economics. Graduate students were encouraged to complete advanced courses in these areas. The guidelines also encouraged that only qualified faculty teach the applied courses. For example, a faculty member teaching a course in sport marketing should have background in such areas as basic marketing, consumer and buyer behavior, and marketing research. In addition, the instructor must have the knowledge or field experiences necessary to distinguish between traditional marketing and the unique marketing techniques employed in the sport industry.

The field experience component included part-time work experiences (practica) and full-time work experiences (internships). The task force (Brassie, 1989a) recommended practica and internship experiences at both the undergraduate and master's levels.

In 1989 NASPE and NASSM created a joint task force to further develop curricular standards for the preparation of students for the sport management profession. The approach differed from the NASPE Guidelines approved in 1987. Rather than identifying specific courses, content areas were developed that could be met in a single course or in multiple courses in the curriculum. Rather than identifying foundational and applied areas of the curriculum, each content area included a body of knowledge needed by those preparing for careers in sport management. The standards were divided into the core content required at the baccalaureate, master's, and doctoral levels.

UNDERGRADUATE CORE CONTENT AREAS

The **core content for the undergraduate program** includes the following 10 aspects: (1) behavioral dimensions in sport, (2) management and organizational skills in sport, (3) ethics in sport management, (4) marketing in sport, (5) communication in sport, (6) finance in sport, (7) economics in sport, (8) legal aspects of sport, (9) governance in sport, and (10) field experience in sport management.

In addition to the content areas, the standards mandate that 20%, exclusive of the field experience credit, of the total number of credit hours required for a baccalaureate degree must be sport management coursework offered in the home unit. Furthermore, there must be a minimum of two full-time faculty assigned at least one-half workload in sport management over an academic year available to staff the program.

MASTER'S DEGREE CORE CONTENT AREAS

The **core content for the master's degree** includes the following eight aspects: (1) management, leadership, and organization in sport, (2) research in sport, (3) legal aspects of sport, (4) marketing in sport, (5) sport business in the social context, (6) financial management in sport, (7) ethics in sport management, and (8) field experiences in sport management.

At least two full-time faculty assigned at least one-half workload in sport management over an academic year are required to meet the standards.

DOCTORAL DEGREE CONTENT AREAS

The **doctoral degree** is granted in recognition of proficiency in research, breadth and soundness of scholarship, and through acquaintance with sport management as a field of study. As the student's individual program of study is planned, the doctoral degree builds on previous graduate experiences. Therefore, the curriculum for a doctoral student in sport management is individualized and may vary considerably from one student to another. The Ph.D. or Ed.D. is of particular interest to individuals pursuing an academic career in sport management and administrators seeking tenure-track faculty in this field. The NASPE and NASSM standards require a strong research orientation and intensive study in one of the core content areas found in sport management curricular standards.

Currently the small number of full-time faculty available to staff more than 200 sport management programs in the United States and Canada is a major concern. It is impossible for one or two faculty at one university to have the expertise or time required to teach all of the content areas identified in the curricular standards. Yet, sport management programs with more than two full-time faculty are rare. To fill this void, many institutions are hiring sport management practitioners as part-time or adjunct faculty to teach one or two courses in their area of expertise. Although these part-time faculty members may be qualified in the content area in which they teach, their first obligation is to their employer, which may create conflicts with a scheduled course. Only in rare cases do these practitioners have the time; expertise; or interest in advising students, arranging and supervising internships, participating in curricular revision, or producing research and scholarly writing. Few have the expertise or interest to advise master's or doctoral students in their theses or dissertations. In summary, part-time and adjunct faculty can be a source of program enrichment, but should not be used to provide program stability.

Given its nature, sport management is a multidisciplinary field of study. It requires the integration of knowledge found in several disciplines, especially the business areas of management, finance, economics, and marketing, the journalism components of public relations, advertising, and mass communication, and the area of sport. None of these areas can accomplish this task single-handedly; collectively, however, they can contribute to an understanding of the management of sport.

A large portion of this book is devoted to major principles from each of the business and journalism areas. These principles form the foundation that sport managers apply to the sport setting. Subsequently, this book also describes how these foundational principles are applied.

The future of sport management has great potential although major hurdles must be confronted. First, although sport management is becoming increasingly more accepted as a profession—an appropriate prerequisite for employment in the sport industry—it will become legitimate only when graduates of sport management programs are able to demonstrate that they have the knowledge necessary to be successful in the marketplace, are able to perform the functions expected of a manager, and qualify for advancement through the ranks of the organization. NASPE and NASSM are working collectively to encourage all sport management programs to submit their curriculum for evaluation through the program review process so that every sport management student is subjected to the rigor of those content areas that are necessary for successful management.

Second, the potential of sport management will be influenced by the quality of its faculties. The new doctoral graduates of sport management programs compose the faculties of tomorrow. Many more talented and energetic students are needed in our doctoral programs to supply these faculty with quality pedagogy and scholarship, which is imperative for more than 200 current programs in this profession.

Lastly, sport management must continue its development as an area of scholarship. Considerable research predicated on management theories that are specific to sport need to be developed. The extent to which the latter is accomplished will largely determine whether sport management will take its place among the widely accepted professions or decline as an area with little substance.

CONCEPT CHECK

Historically, sport management has had a strong physical education orientation. Today the focus is on foundation areas of study, with a strong emphasis on business courses, application areas of study that build on foundation subject matter and are specific to the sport industry, and field experiences. Given its nature, sport management is a multidisciplinary field of study. It requires the cooperation of several disciplines, especially business administration (management) and physical education (now commonly referred to as "sport studies," "exercise and sport sciences," or similar titles that more accurately describe the academic components of physical education).

SUMMARY

1. Although sport management is relatively new to academia, its acceptance as a legitimate area of study is well documented in the literature.

2. Although the terms *sport management, sport administration,* and *athletic administration* are often used interchangeably, the first most accurately describes this field from a universal, or global, perspective.

3. There is a general agreement that the basic components of sport management curriculum should include foundation areas of study, application courses, and field experiences. A large portion of this book is devoted to the foundation and application components.

4. The North American Society for Sport Management (NASSM) and the National Association for Sport and Physical Education (NASPE) Task Force on Sport Management corroborate a rapid growth in this profession. NASSM was established to promote, stimulate, and encourage research, scholarly writing, and professional development in the area of sport management. The Task Force focuses on curricular needs. The *Journal of Sport Management* is the major resource for disseminating significant knowledge in this field.

5. This relatively new field has great potential, but its destiny is still in question. It is imperative that those responsible for the curricular development of sport management programs at both the national and institutional levels

accept this responsibility for ensuring quality professional preparation. At the institutional level, proliferation in the interest of increasing student enrollment must give way to a commitment to excellence.

6. Quality control is currently a major concern of academicians and practitioners in this field. In this endeavor, an "accrediting" agency comparable to those in business administration and communications is presently being operationalized in sport management.

REVIEW QUESTIONS AND ISSUES

1. Foundation and application courses, as well as field experiences, are necessary to meet the job-related needs of the sport management industry. What is the difference between a foundation and application offering? Cite an example of a field experience.
2. What is the purpose of accreditation? What is the difference between accreditation and program approval? How can program approval resolve the quality control problem that currently exists in sport management programs? Why have some academicians been reluctant to support "accreditation?"
3. Why does the term *sport management* more accurately describe this field than *sport administration* or *athletic administration?*
4. Why is the term *sport management* misleading? Why is *sport business* perhaps a more accurate term to describe both the academic and applied aspects of this industry? Explain why the latter term has not been adopted.
5. How has the sport management curriculum changed over the past 25 years?

REFERENCES

Bedecki, T., and Soucie, D. (1980). Trends in physical education, sport, and athletic administration in Canadian universities and colleges. Paper presented at the 26th Annual Conference of the Canadian Association for Health, Physical Education, and Recreation. St. John's New Foundland.

Berg, R. (1989). The quest for credibility. *Athletic Business*, 13(11), 44-48.

Brassie, S. (1989a). Guidelines for programs preparing undergraduate and graduate students for careers in sport management. *Journal of Sport Management*, 3(2), 158-164.

Brassie, S. (1989b). A student buyer's guide to sport management programs. *Journal of Physical Education, Recreation, and Dance*, 60(9), 25-28.

Comte, E., and Stogel, C. (1990). Sports: a $63.1 billion industry. *The Sporting News* (January 1), 60-61.

DeSensi, J., Kelley, D., Blanton, M., and Beitel, P. (1990). Sport management curricular evaluation and needs assessment: a multifaceted approach. *Journal of Sport Management*, 4(1), 31-58.

Frank, R. (1984). Olympic myths and realities. *Arete: The Journal of Sport Literature*, 1(2), 155-161.

Gleason, T. (1986). Sport administration degrees: growing to fill a need/supply overwhelms demand. *Athletic Administration* (February), 9-10.

Goodwin, M. (1986). When the cash register is the scoreboard. *The New York Times* (June 8), 27-28.

Hardy, S. (1987). Graduate curriculums in sport management: the need for a business orientation. *Quest*, 39, 207-216.

Loy, J. (1968). The nature of sport: a definitional effort. *Quest*, 10, 1-15.

Mason, J., Higgins, C., and Owen, J. (1981). Sport administration education 15 years later. *Athletic Purchasing and Facilities* (January), 44, 45.

Milewski, J., and Bryant, J. (1985). A survey of institutions offering sport administration, sport management, or related sport studies programs. Unpublished study; Western Carolina University.

Mullin, B. (1980). Sport management: the nature and utility of the concept. *Arena Review*, 4(3), 1-11.

Parkhouse, B. (1980). Analysis of graduate professional preparation in sport management. *Athletic Administration*, 14(2), 11-14.

Parkhouse, B. (1984). Shaping up to climb a new corporate ladder . . . sport management. *Journal of Physical Education, Recreation and Dance*, 55(6), 12-14.

Parkhouse, B. (1987). Sport management curricula: current status and design implications for future development. *Journal of Sport Management*, 1(2), 93-115.

Parkhouse, B., and Ulrich, D. (1979). Sport management as a potential cross-discipline: a paradigm for theoretical application. *Quest*, 31(2), 264-276.

Parks, J., and Olafson, G. (1987). Sport management and a new journal. *Journal of Sport Management*, 1(1), 1-3.

Parks, J., and Quain, R. (1986). Curriculum perspectives. *Journal of Physical Education, Recreation and Dance*, 57(4), 22-26.

Parks, J., and Zanger, B. (Eds.) (1990). *Sport and fitness management: career strategies and professional content.* Champaign, Illinois: Human Kinetics.

Rosner, D. (1989). The world plays catch-up. *Sports Inc.* (January 2).

Sandomir, R. (1988). The $50 billion sport industry. *Sports Inc.* (November 14).

Snyder, E., and Sprietzer, E. (1989). *Social aspects of sport.* Englewood Cliffs, N.J.: Prentice-Hall.

Soucie, D. (1988). Promotion of sport management programs in Canada. Paper presented to the North American Society for Sport Management. Champaign, Illinois.

van der Smissen, B. (1984). A process for success: sport management curricula—an idea whose time has come! In B.

Zanger and J. Parks (Eds.), *Sport management curricula: the business and education nexus.* Bowling Green, Ohio: Bowling Green State University, School of Health, Physical Education and Recreation, 5-18.

vander Zwaag, H. (1988). *Policy development in sport management.* Indianapolis: Benchmark Press.

Zeigler, E. (1987). Sport management: past, present, future. *Journal of Sport Management,* 1(1), 4-24.

2

Sport Management: Its Scope and Career Opportunities

Packianathan Chelladurai

In this chapter, you will become familiar with the following terms:

Sport industry
Sport products and services
Participant services
Spectator services and
  sponsorship services

Consumer services and human
  services
Human resources
Technologies
Support units

Context, or situational
  contingencies
Job dimensions

Overview

Most of the students in sport management degree programs have a professional career in mind just like students in accounting, engineering, and nursing. Although the career options in other professional preparation programs are more clearly defined that is not the case with sport management. This should not be surprising because the field of sport management is relatively new compared with other fields. It is an offshoot of the older field called *physical education*. In earlier days, a specialized field within physical education was called *administration of physical education*, which was concerned with management of physical education and sport in educational institutions. Subsequently, as the intercollegiate athletic programs and intramural programs grew in size and stature, specializations were developed to address the concerns of these programs.

Sport management, as it is taught and practiced, now encompasses all of these focuses, and, in addition, has been expanded to include professional sports. On a different level, sport management has been broadened to emphasize specialties within management such as facility management, event management, marketing, sponsorship, and sport law. The growth of sport management has been impressive indeed.

In an attempt to define the career opportunities within sport management, the scope of sport management as practiced today is first described. After this description, the organizational contexts in which sport management is practiced is presented. Finally, some guidelines for students who seek a career in sport management are outlined.

SCOPE OF SPORT MANAGEMENT

Many students are likely to be bewildered by the various terms used to describe the field of sport management. First, the use of the term *sport* engenders some confusion. The term has been used in a generic sense to denote those kinds of physical activities that concern those of us in the field, including competitive sports, recreational sports, exercise, and dance. For instance, the constitution of the North American Society for Sport Management (NASSM) defines the field as "the theoretical and applied aspects of management theory and practice specifically related to sport, exercise, dance, and play as these enterprises are pursued by all sectors of the population." Others use the term to refer to a specific form of physical activity. For instance, Snyder and Spreitzer (1989) implicitly distinguish between sport and other forms of physical activity when they state:

> We define sport as (1) a competitive, (2) human physical activity that requires skill and exertion, (3) governed by institutionalized rules. With this definition in mind, it is clear that some activities can be classified as sport under some conditions but not under others.

In our own field, Mullin's (1980) view of sport management is confined to an activity that "is playlike in nature, is based on physical prowess, involves physical skill, strategy or chance, is uncertain of outcome, is governed by rules and has specialized equipment and facilities." From this perspective, although sport is a form of physical activity, not all physical activities are sport. For the purpose of this text, I will follow the lead of NASSM and use the term sport in a global sense covering various forms of physical activities.

Yet another term that might confuse the reader is **sport industry.** Many scholars and practitioners tend to use the term in its singular form. Considering that an industry is a group of organizations that produce the same or similar products that are substitutable for each other, the question arises whether we are indeed a single industry. From this perspective, Mullin (1980) noted that "we have a collection of sport management occupations. The sports industry is fragmented. It is in fact a number of sports industries." In a similar vein, the NASPE-NASSM Joint Task Force on Sport Management Curriculum and Accreditation (1993) defined sport management as "the field of study offering the specialized training and education necessary for individuals seeking careers in any of the many segments of the industry."

Dialogue continues about the terms *management* and *administration.* Although some authors would distinguish between the two terms as referring to two different sets of activities of those charged with directing an organization. For example, administration is said to be concerned with setting the goals and policies, whereas management is concerned with executing those policies. However a majority of scholars and practitioners have accepted the two terms as synonymous. So it is not uncommon to see schools/colleges of business management and schools/colleges of business administration. The two leading journals, which cover the same topics and issues in the general field of management, are the *Administrative Science Quarterly* and the *Academy of Management Journal.* In the specialized field of sport management, we tend to use the term *management.* For instance, there are the North American Society for *Sport Management, NASSM,* and the *Journal of Sport Management.* Accordingly, the term *sport management* will be used throughout this textbook.

CONCEPT CHECK

*The term **sport** is used to refer to all recreational and competitive sports, exercise and fitness activities, and dance. Management encompasses the activities associated with administration, supervision, and leadership.*

The above view of sport management as dealing with different products and different industries suggests that the best way to define the field is to catalogue and describe its various products. This approach is consistent with the modern view that (1) all organizations are mechanisms that have evolved to facilitate the process of exchange of products, and (2) the types of organizational arrangements needed to support any particular exchange will depend on the inherent characteristics of the exchange (Hesterly et al, 1990). As noted elsewhere, "if we can define, describe, and classify the products of exchange within the context of sport, then we should be able to capture the essential nature of the field and its boundaries" (Chelladurai, 1994). Based on this view, sport management was defined as "a field concerned with the coordination of limited human and material resources, relevant technologies, and situational contingencies for the efficient production and exchange of sport services." This definition incorporates the notions of (1) **sport products (services),** (2) the production and exchange of those products, and (3) the coordination of the processes of such production and exchange.

SPORT PRODUCTS AND SERVICES

Products can be either goods or services. Goods within the context of sport are tangible things such as golf clubs, tennis balls, soccer shoes, weight training sets, basketball boards, and volleyball uprights. In many instances, sports equipment is needed to engage in sporting activities. Typically, however, sport management has not been concerned with goods per se except in their purchase, care, and maintenance. The production of these goods has been left to conventional manufacturing industries. On the other hand, most products are services, which are intangible, perishable, heterogenous, and simultaneous (Table 2-1 for a description of these characteristics).

An earlier elaborate classification of sport products (Chelladurai, 1992, 1994) can be meaningfully collapsed into fewer classes as shown in Figure 2-1. The major classes of sport products and services are **participant services, spectator services,** and **sponsorship services.** These services can be broken down into smaller categories as described below.

Participant services

Participant services are broken down on the basis of two criteria: (1) the distinctions among **consumer, professional,** and **human services** (Table 2-2), and (2) the client motives for participation in sport and physical activity (Table 2-3).

Consumer-pleasure and health services. Consumer-pleasure and health services involve the scheduling or reserving facilities and/or equipment as requested by clients who seek pleasure in

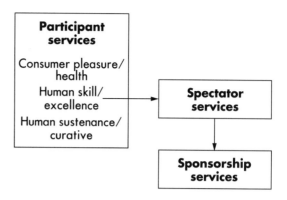

FIGURE 2-1 A classification of sport products.

physical activity. This class of service includes organizing and conducting different kinds of competitions for clients. Bowling alleys are prime examples of this service. The same type of service also can be provided to those who engage in physical activity for fitness and health reasons. For example, an enterprise may allow clients to use its fitness equipment and facilities for a membership or user fee.

Human skills and excellence. This class of service requires expert application of teaching technology and leadership in developing the skills (including techniques and strategies) of clients in various forms of sport and physical activity. Clients may be satisfied with developing their skills to a level where they enjoy the activity. When clients want to excel in an activity, expert guidance and coaching needs to be provided. In our culture, pursuit of excellence in sports is highly valued and practiced, thus the importance attached to coaching various age groups at various educational and professional levels.

Human sustenance and curative. Human sustenance and curative services requires organizing and conducting exercise and fitness programs on a regular basis under the guidance and supervision of experts. When healthy individuals want to participate in this class of service, their intention is to maintain and sustain present levels of fitness and health. This form of service also can be extended to rehabilitate those deficient in fitness, health, and/or physical appearance (e.g., cardiac rehabilitation, relaxation and stress reduction, and weight

TABLE 2-1 *Characteristics of a service*

Characteristic	Service
Intangibility	A service is intangible because the client or customer cannot judge its quality before experiencing it. Also, because the sensual and psychological benefits (feelings such as comfort, status, and a sense of well-being) are individualistic, the services offered will remain intangible.
Perishability	A fitness consultant cannot produce services without customers, nor can services be stored for future use. In contrast, a manufacturer can continue to produce fitness equipment and inventory it for future sales.
Heterogeneity	Services are likely to be heterogenous because (1) two clients with different psyches may perceive the quality of the service and the same fitness instructor differently, (2) one client may perceive the service differently at different times because of changes in frame of mind or mood, (3) two fitness instructors with different education, experience, expertise, and leadership style may not provide the same quality of service, and (4) the same instructor may not provide the same quality services at different times. Students should be familiar with variations of the quality of lectures by different professors or by the same professor at different times.
Simultaneity	Because a service is perishable, it has to be used as it is produced, and because of this simultaneity of production and usage, the interface between the employee (the producer) and the client (the consumer) becomes critical. In contrast, a tennis racket is produced at one point and sold to a customer at another.

From Chelladurai, P. (1992). A classification of sport and physical activity services: implications for sport management. *Journal of Sport Management*, 6, 38-51.

loss programs). This latter form of service is more curative and requires careful attention to scientific knowledge relevant to these clients.

The above classification covers only those services where clients actively participate in an activity. Sport management is concerned with much more than these participant services. We need to consider spectator services, sponsorship services, donor services, and social ideas to more clearly delineate the boundaries of sport management (Chelladurai, 1994).

Spectator services

First note that spectator services are fundamentally an offshoot of the pursuit of excellence, a participant service as described earlier. The second caveat is that spectator services also entail entertainment. These spectator/entertainment services are based on (1) the contest, (2) the spectacle, and (3) the notion of third place.

A contest is when two opponents (individuals or teams) strive to demonstrate excellence by win-

ning an event. The excitement and entertainment generated in a contest are derived from the excellence of the contestants; the unpredictability of the outcome; and fans' loyalty to the sport, team, and/or athlete.

Spectacle refers to the sight and splendor of opening parades, half-time shows, and closing ceremonies provided by the organization presenting the contest. These may be considered product extensions of the contest itself. Spectacle also includes the grandeur and vastness of the stadium, gymnasium, or playing surface; the ambience of the total setting—the large number of spectators, their colorful outfits, and their antics.

The concept of third place in the context of a sport contest was highlighted by Melnick (1993) who argued that modern life, both at home and work, is characterized by reduced and tenuous primary social ties with family and friends. Therefore individuals seek the satisfaction of their social needs in less personal ways in "casual encounters with strangers of a quasi-primary kind" (Melnick,

TABLE 2-2 *Description of consumer, professional, and human services*

Service	Description
Consumer	Consumer services are largely based on renting facilities or retailing goods. For example, when a university permits its students to use its gymnasia and playing fields on a drop-in basis, it is offering a consumer service. A racquetball club may restrict its operations to renting its courts and selling sporting goods. Such services require very little expertise on the part of the first-line operators. For instance, the clerk in the front office need only to know the appropriate reservation procedures for the facilities or equipment and guidelines for their use.
Professional	Professional services are largely based on knowledge, expertise, and special competencies of the employee, the service provider (e.g., lawyer, accountant, architect). Direct and active leadership is provided by the service worker in assessing clients' needs and making appropriate decisions.
Human	Application of knowledge can transform *people's* view to enhance personal well being (e.g., educating the child, coaching the athletes, and enhancing the spiritual life). The input in these services are people; the output are people whose attributes have been changed in a predetermined manner.

From Chelladurai, P. (1992). A classification of sport and physical activity services: implications for sport management. *Journal of Sport Management,* 6, 38-51.

TABLE 2-3 *Client motives for participation in physical activity*

Motive	Description
Pursuit of pleasure	People may participate to enjoy the kinesthetic sensations experienced in a physical activity or the competition posed by certain activities (e.g., a game of squash). The pleasures they seek can be enjoyed only during participation.
Pursuit of skill	The desire to acquire physical skills may compel people to participate in physical activity. That is, individuals may focus on perfecting their skills through continued vigorous physical activity.
Pursuit of excellence	People may participate in a form of physical activity with a desire to excel in that or another activity. A basketball player and a discus thrower may train with weights to enhance performance capability in their respective sport.
Pursuit of health and fitness	People may participate in vigorous physical activity mainly for health-related benefits (e.g., fitness, stress reduction, longevity) that accrue as a consequence of such participation.

From Chelladurai, P. (1992). A classification of sport and physical activity services: implications for sport management. *Journal of Sport Management,* 6, 38-51.

1993). And the places where such casual encounters can take place are called *third places* (in contrast to the home and workplace).

Although there are several examples of third places (e.g., bars), "sports spectating has emerged as a major urban structure where spectators come together not only to be entertained [by the contest] but to enrich their social psychological lives through the sociable, quasi-intimate relationships available" (Melnick, 1993). In essence, spectator services include the excitement of a contest and the offering of the stadium or gymnasium as third place for the spectator.

The third place as just defined also serves as a forum for BIRGing—*basking in reflected glory* (Cialdini et al, 1976; Wann and Branscombe, 1990)—and CORFing—*cutting off reflected failure* (Snyder et al, 1986; Wann and Branscombe, 1990). It is argued here that the presence of quasi-intimate relationships in a third place permits unmitigated expression of reflected glory and distancing from reflected failure.

Sponsorship services

There are two elements in the sponsorship services. First is the market access. The organization that seeks sponsorship offers the sponsor, in return, access to a market of their own; that is, the access to communication with the direct and indirect consumers of a sport. For example, for those who sponsor the Olympic Games, the payoff is access to the billions of people who watch the event. In some cases the sponsor seeks association with excellence related to an athlete, team, or event. Sponsors of the Olympic Games emphasize their association with the best and biggest sporting event in the world. Similarly, for those who sponsor Michael Jordan or seek his endorsements, the return is association with perhaps the most talented and accomplished basketball player of all time. In these cases, such association projects the sponsoring organization as excellent in its own right.

From a different perspective, some sponsors may wish to be associated with a worthy cause such as special sports events organized by community and charitable organizations. In this case, the sponsor is projected as a socially responsible enterprise.

CONCEPT CHECK

The services in sport management include participant services (consumer-pleasure and health, human skill and excellence, and human-sustenance and curative services), spectator and entertainment services, and sponsorship services.

PRODUCTION AND MARKETING

The next essential thrust in the definition of sport management is the inclusion of both the production and marketing of services. That is, manage-

ment is seen as the coordination of the factors and processes of both production and exchange, i.e., marketing is seen as one, albeit a major, function of management.

The distinction between the production of a service and the marketing of that service is clearly evidenced in the case of certain services. Take, for example, the spectator services where the production of entertainment largely rests with the players and the coaches of both contesting teams. The marketing of the players, the teams, and the contests can be carried out by others independent of the production of that entertainment. Similarly, sponsorship services can be independent of a team cultivating its fans and its own market. Along the same vein, it can be argued that the consumer-pleasure and health services, which involve only the renting of facilities and/or equipment, can be marketed independently of the production of these services. In this case, the producers of the service are separated from the consumers of the service.

On the other hand, the distinction between production and marketing is not so clear in the case of human services. This is because the production of human services requires the simultaneous involvement of the client and the service provider. Moreover, client involvement in the production of human services is physical and at times agonistic, as in the case of human-excellence services. In other words, the client is at least partially responsible for the production of that service. The interface between the employee and the client in a human service is the forum for both the production and exchange of a service, that is, the service provider is simultaneously the producer and marketeer of that service. Even in these cases, it is useful to keep the distinction between production and marketing in mind for analytical purposes.

CONCEPT CHECK

Although most services are produced and consumed simultaneously, the marketing of some services can be separated from the production of them, as in the case of spectator services.

MANAGEMENT AS COORDINATION

The third significant element in the definition is coordination of those factors associated with the

CHAPTER 2 *Sport Management: Its Scope and Career Opportunities* **19**

production and marketing of products. Management has been described from various perspectives, e.g., the functions a manager has to carry out (Fayol, 1949), the skills a manager has to have (Katz, 1974), and/or the roles one has to play as a manager (Mintzberg, 1975). When these descriptions are analyzed, we notice that the central thrust of each of them is the idea of coordinating the activities of individuals and groups toward the attainment of organizational goals within limited resources. For example, the managerial functions of planning, organizing, leading, and evaluating are all focused on coordination of human and material resources. In summary, coordination is the name of the game managers play.

The significant factors that need coordination for the production of sport services can be grouped into (1) **human resources** (e.g., paid employees, volunteer workers, and the clients themselves), (2) **technologies** (e.g., exercise physiology, sport psychology, pedagogy, coach education, and sport nutrition), (3) **support units** (e.g., the units dealing with facilities, events, ticket sales, legal affairs, finance, public relations), and (4) **context or situational contingencies** (e.g., organizational types, interorganizational networks, gov-

ernment regulations, cultural norms, and community expectations). The various factors that need to be coordinated in sport management are illustrated in Figure 2-2.

HUMAN RESOURCES

Although human resources management is a fundamental task in every organization producing any form of product, the task is made onerous in the case of human services, where clients also must be managed. The human resources of any venture offering sport and physical activity service should involve the clients of that service, since service cannot be produced without active client participation (Chelladurai, 1992). Clients may vary in their orientation toward sport and physical activity (pursuit of pleasure, health, and or excellence) and in the degree of commitment to such programs. Motivating clients and gaining their compliance is a challenge to service providers.

Paid employees may be further classified into consumer service or professional service employees. Consumer service employees engage in simple routine activities requiring little training, whereas professional service employees provide complex knowledge-based, and individualized service to clients.

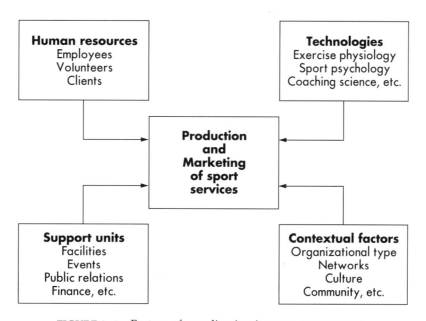

FIGURE 2-2 Factors of coordination in sport management.

Sport organizations also are characterized by heavy involvement of volunteers. These volunteers are the mainstay of projects such as the Special Olympics and youth sport organized by city recreation departments. The conventional approaches to managing paid workers have to be considerably modified in the case of volunteers. The coordination of volunteer contribution with those of paid employees is a critical area of sport management. In summary, motivating these different types of employees and coordinating their activities is a highly significant component of sport management, which offers both challenge and opportunity for sport managers.

TECHNOLOGIES

Technology refers to *the processes that transform organizational inputs into desired outputs* (Pierce and Dunham, 1990). Technology includes all equipment used, techniques employed, and knowledge units derived from different subject areas. For example, fitness assessment and exercise prescription involve sophisticated equipment, specific organizational arrangements for the production of this service, and the knowledge derived from physiology, nutrition, and psychology. Coaching a high pole vaulter would entail the modern fiberglass poles, and the knowledge units derived from biomechanics, sports medicine, and coaching science, for example. The more critical component of technology as defined above is the knowledge units that are generated in other allied fields. Those who use these knowledge units are professional people. Coordinating their activities with those of other organizational activities is the essence of sport management.

The relative significance of these technologies obviously vary from service to service (and with quality levels expected of a service). For example, human services aimed at enhancing excellence and/or health entails greater application of relevant knowledge as compared with consumer services. Following this argument, we can expect a high school coach to be more highly trained in the application of knowledge than a volunteer youth coach.

SUPPORT UNITS

In a small enterprise, all of the necessary activities can be carried out by a few individuals. For ex-

ample, there may be only one physical educator or coach in a small rural school. That person, apart from coaching the school team, may also carry out all arrangements for a game to be played on Saturday afternoon. Of course, a coach may recruit some students to assist in the process. However, as the organization grows in size and scope, several subunits may have to be created. Take the case of a Division I university athletic department. In this case, the coaches are assigned only coaching duties. All other necessary activities are assigned to specialized units. Thus we are likely to find separate units for facility management, event management, ticket sales, media relations, legal affairs, compliance to rules, etc. Coordinating the activities of these units is the responsibility of the top manager, the athletic director.

The term *support units* may be misleading. It is used here to emphasize that these units do support the fundamental purpose and activities of the department, i.e., to provide student athletes the opportunity to pursue excellence. However the term does not minimize their importance. That is why nearly every sport management degree program includes specialized courses in these areas.

CONTEXT

No organization operates in a vacuum. A host of environmental factors have an impact on the organization and its activities. These external forces may facilitate or constrain the organization in the production and marketing of its services. A successful sport manager would effectively coordinate the activities of the organization with the demands and constraints of these external factors. These factors may be classified as organizational types, interorganizational networks, market conditions, government, culture, and community.

Sport organizations differ in their profit orientation (e.g., a high school athletic department vs. a professional sport franchise). The emphasis on profit orientation imposes a different set of demands and constraints on managers of professional sports than it does on a high school athletic director.

A funding source is another factor that may affect the coordination process. In private organizations, which are sustained by membership fees, donations, and/or shares, the manager will be more influenced by the needs and desires of the members, clients, and donors. In contrast, the manager in a public organization such as the city recreation department will have to coordinate the departments' activities with not only the preferences of tax payers, but also the pressures exerted by city politicians.

Interorganizational networks such as the National Collegiate Athletic Association (NCAA) and the U.S. Olympic Committee link those organizations producing the same services. Other examples are the professional leagues such as the National Football League (NFL) and the National Hockey League, national and international sports federations such as the U.S. Tennis Association (USTA) and the International Federation of Basketball Associations (FIBA), and industry associations such as the Aerobic and Fitness Association of America (AFAA) and Club Managers Association of America (CMAA). These networks, or governing bodies, control member organizations and their operations to varying degrees.

The context would also include market conditions such as the rise and decline in the demand for services, and the organizations competing for clients and customers and resources. Thus a professional sport franchise has to coordinate its own activities, tactics, and strategies to counteract those of the competitors, which provide the same or similar services.

By the same token, operations should be consistent with government regulations, cultural norms, and societal expectations. For instance, the recent societal thrusts in favor of diversity and gender equity have affected the practice of management in general, and sport management in particular. The growing sport management literature on considerations of gender equity is a case in point, emphasizing the need for sport managers to alter their employment practices.

The need to coordinate the operations of a sport organization with a local community's interests and desires is best illustrated by the influence exerted by alumni associations in intercollegiate athletics. Similarly, professional sport franchises depend on local governments for building and/or renting stadiums and arenas (Johnson, 1993). Even smaller sport organizations look up to local communities for concessions and tax exemptions.

CONCEPT CHECK

Sport management is concerned with the coordination of material and human resources (clients, paid and volunteer workers); technologies (facilities, equipment, process, and knowledge units underlying the production process); support units dealing with facilities, events, legal affairs, etc.; and contextual factors such as organizational type, interorganizational networks, government regulations and community expectations).

CAREER PLANNING

Many who read this text will step into the world of organizations and work related to sport and physical activity. Career opportunities in this field are well described in Parks and Zanger's (1990) *Sport and Fitness Management: Career Strategies and Professional Content.* Several authors contributing to this text have discussed careers in intercollegiate athletics and professional sport, facility management, campus recreation programs, community-based sport, sports information, sport marketing, sports journalism, sports club management, physical fitness industry, athletic training and sports medicine, and consulting and entrepreneurship. Kelley et al, (1991) have elaborated on sport and fitness management careers clustered according to similarity of objectives and profit orientation. In addition, other authors have discussed issues of career patterns in sport management (Fitzgerald et al, 1994); gender and careers in sport management (Cuneen and Sidwell, 1993; Inglis, 1988; Lovett and Lowry, 1988, 1994; Pastore, 1991, 1992; Pastore and Meacci, 1994); roles, responsibilities, and stress associated with jobs in sport and recreation (Cuskelly and Auld, 1991; Danylchuk, 1993; Hatfield et al, 1987; Quarterman, 1994); and employment status of sport management graduates (Kjeldsen, 1990; Parks, 1991; Parks and Parra, 1994). This list does not exhaust all relevant information pertaining to careers in sport management. Students should consult other sources including trade journals. The following sections outline some general concerns in selecting a job or career.

Once students enter the work world, they are likely to move from one job to another. This movement may be vertical in the sense that they get promoted to higher level jobs in the same line of work. Consider the careers of May and June reported in the case study at the end of this chapter. Both women joined an intercollegiate athletic program as clerks. In time, May was promoted to the position of assistant director of the ticket office. In contrast, June left that athletic department to become a coach in a smaller four-year college. This progression through various jobs in one or several organizations is known as *one's career*. But every career begins with a first job, which is where our interests lie at the moment.

The descriptions of the jobs in these two organizational contexts contain information available to everyone. Also, the progression through various jobs to higher positions in each organization is known to everybody (or can be gleaned from the records). This aspect of one's career is rightfully known as the *objective* or *external career* (Johns, 1988).

What is not evident to observers is the personal experiences and reactions felt by two individuals in their career tracks. It is not clear to others why Person Y chose to leave athletics altogether and enter the field of parks and recreation. It may be presumed that Person Y did not like the experiences with the athletic program, and therefore preferred to move to another field where the experiences were more acceptable. However, the meanings Person Y had attached to the experiences in the two fields, and the reactions to those experiences were personal, and imperceptible or misunderstood by others. This aspect is called *subjective* or *internal career*.

CONCEPT CHECK

Career refers to one's progress from the first job to the final job before retirement. Such jobs may involve the same or different organizations. The objective aspect of the career is what external observers gather from written job descriptions, whereas the subjective career is what the incumbent of a job internally experiences.

Focus on external career

In making decisions about a job in sport management, the graduate has to consider several factors. Some of them, as noted earlier, would be objective factors such as job description, organizational type, and geographical location. Many questions related to these factors can be verified through objective analysis.

Job descriptions should contain information on organizational philosophy and policies; organizational type and size; tasks and activities associated with the job, working conditions, including supervision, salary, and fringe benefits; and promotional opportunities. The prospective applicant should carefully peruse all of this information. If necessary, the student may write or call the prospective employer for more information.

Although written job descriptions are useful, a one- or two-day visit to the organization may provide additional information. It may also be useful to interview one or more employees of the organization to get their personal feelings about the organization and their jobs. Such visits and interviews will assist the applicant in verifying the job description, and in assessing the mood and spirit of the organization. An institution may advertise its employment practices as equal opportunity, but the student may find that all employees of the organization are of one race or gender. Again, the working conditions such as room size, lighting, ventilation, seating arrangements, and parking facilities may not be as good as advertized. In summary, a thorough analysis of the job description and the organization would be worthwhile.

Organizational type. Consider that you are contemplating a job as manager of a racquetball club. Such a club may be operated by a branch of the YMCA; a city recreation department; a university intramural department; a private, exclusive nonprofit organization; or a private profit-oriented commercial firm. Although the same tasks need to be carried out in all these organizational forms, there are other factors that affect the employees.

Some differences among organizations were discussed earlier. To extend that discussion, city recreation department personnel are likely to enjoy relatively greater job security and higher salaries than those in a private profit-oriented commercial club. On the other hand, there are probably many levels of hierarchy through which a proposal has to be processed, which may impede the decision-making process. This is known as *red tape* in governments.

As another example, personnel working in a university intramural department may have higher social status than those carrying out the same activities in a commercial club. After all, the university is the ivory tower! Also, the university department personnel are exposed to students' youthful, energetic, and carefree life-style. Some may feel that is a reward in itself. Similarly, those who work in a Division I university athletic department or a professional club may gain satisfaction from the association with excellence in sport irrespective of the nature of their jobs or their remunerations.

Geographical location. Individuals have preferences for particular geographic locations. Preferences may be based on the proximity of family and friends, or even health. Some may prefer an urban center, whereas others may enjoy life in a less thickly populated locale. These are important considerations inasmuch as they will enhance the quality of life for an individual. After all, a job is only a tool to enjoy one's life.

Focus on internal career
The internal career simply implies a fit between the job and its context, and the personal characteristics of the individual. The job and the context refers to what the individual is required to do in a job and the parameters of a particular organization including its policies, procedures, working conditions, supervision, and work group. The personal characteristics include the person's personality, needs, values, beliefs, and preferences, along with abilities, skills, and talents. Abilities, skills, and specialized knowledge required for a successful job performance can be increased through general education and specialized professional preparation programs. Personality, needs, values, and preferences are relatively more stable.

The central issue for people who desire a job in sport management is to assess the fit between their personal characteristics and the characteristics of the job as well as those of the organization offering the job. Let us consider job characteristics. Obviously, salary, fringe benefits, chance for advancement, and the location are important considerations. Salary may be the primary consideration for a student who has incurred enormous expenditure and debt while in college. If only one job were available, such a student might be forced to take it without any consideration of the other job characteristics. On the other hand, if more than one job were available, it would be advisable that the

applicant evaluate the jobs in terms of their characteristics and choose the one that matches one's personal attributes.

It is not this chapter's intent to discuss individual difference variables. It will be useful, however, to point out some dimensions in which jobs differ. Consider the differences and decide whether those **job dimensions** are consistent with personal needs, values, and preferences.

Job dimensions. There are several schemes to define and describe the attributes of job dimensions (Campion and Thayer, 1985; Hackman and Oldham, 1980; Stone and Gueutal, 1985). The following section outlines some of the more significant dimensions of a job.

In discussing the differences between consumer services vs. the professional and human services (see Table 2-2), I alluded to the differences in the degree to which jobs may be simple or complex. The complexity of a job increases as the job's variety of the activities increase. For example, a secretary in an athletic department may be assigned only the task of typing, whereas another secretary may be involved in typing, answering telephones, and taking notes in departmental meetings. The latter person enjoys a variety of tasks, and, therefore, a relatively more complex job. The more important element in complexity is the variability of the tasks, that is, an employee is required to make different decisions based on different pieces of information. A coach may use different techniques to motivate athletes based on individual differences among those athletes. Similarly, the director of a city recreation department may use varying approaches when dealing with politicians, taxpayers, or participants. In contrast, the job of locker room attendant is not as complex as that of a coach. Consider a racquetball club that simply rents its premises and equipment to its clients. The necessary tasks in such a club may relate to keeping the courts and equipment in good repair, reserving the courts according to some specified criteria, budgeting and accounting, legal affairs, and marketing the club and its activities. As you can see, the activities in the first two tasks can be clearly specified and made routine.

From a different perspective, simpler jobs can be made routine and standardized. Everything required of the job may be specified by rules and regulations. What is to be done, when it is to be done, how it should be done, and who should do it can be stated in advance in the first two tasks. Also, monitoring and controlling these activities are easily carried out. On the other hand, the activities in the next three tasks are more complex in that every situation may entail different information, and therefore different decisions.

It must be noted that a job may contain some tasks that are routine and others that are more complex. Therefore the prospective applicant would do well to verify if the degree of simplicity or complexity in the job is consistent with personal preferences. There are those who prefer a structured and orderly setting. Others may feel restricted in such jobs, and prefer more flexibility, autonomy, and challenge of deciding how the job should be carried out.

The degree of interaction with other people required may vary from job to job. Take two individuals in the athletic department's public relations office. One individual may be involved in collating all the department's media coverage. The same individual may also engage in preparing advance material for the media. In all these activities, the individual may not be required to interact with the media people or other clients to any great extent. On the other hand, the second individual's job may require both contact with the media, and response to queries on a regular basis. Some people would like a job that requires interaction with people, whereas others may be uncomfortable in that position.

There is also the question of feedback. Some jobs provide clear and immediate feedback, and others delayed feedback. For example, when a fitness club employee sets out to recruit more members, feedback is likely on a daily, weekly, or monthly basis relative to the success rate. It is immediate and clear in terms of the exact number of new members recruited. Consider the same individual who is also in charge of a program of weight loss through physical activity. Feedback is going to be delayed because weight loss takes time. Also, feedback may not be clear-cut in the sense that some of the clients may lose weight, others may not. In addition, the weight one loses or gains is a function of many other factors such as diet and activity patterns away from the club.

In some jobs, one can identify the outcome of his or her efforts. If a marketing specialist in a university athletic department garners a few rich sponsorships, that particular outcome is attributable to that individual's efforts. On the other hand, if a person is one of several employees in charge of crowd control in a game, personal contribution to the total effort cannot be identified easily.

In the previous example, those in charge of crowd control realize and enjoy the significance of their jobs. Can you imagine what would happen if their collective responsibility falters in a game with 80,000 or so spectators? Some of you might have heard some of the gruesome tales of tragedies during sporting events in other parts of the world. Their job is so significant because peoples' welfare and lives are at stake. From this perspective, other jobs may not be so significant.

CONCEPT CHECK

A job can be evaluated on its relative complexity, requirement of interaction with other people, feedback available from the job itself, the possibility of identifying one's own contribution, and its significance.

After careful analysis of the job and the organization that offers the job, the student has to evaluate the extent to which the characteristics of the job and the organization matches his or her personal skills and abilities, needs, and values. In this assessment the student should consider the various higher level jobs one may move through in one's career. It is conceivable that the first job may be quite routine and devoid of any autonomy. Although this situation may not be acceptable immediately, subsequent promotions may land that person in a more complex and autonomous job. For example, the first job in a professional sport club may involve simply selling tickets at the counter. Although this may not be very appealing to a person, the opportunity exists for that person to move up in the hierarchy to a job such as the marketing director. That position may offer considerable flexibility and freedom of operation for the incumbent. Therefore students are well advised to consider not only the immediate job that is offered but also the other jobs that the present one may lead to.

SUMMARY

1. The products (i.e., the services) with which sport management is concerned are varied. Some of them are *participant services* wherein clients participate vigorously in some form of sport and physical activity. The other services labeled *spectator* and *sponsorship services* are nonparticipant services.

2. Sport management was defined as "a field concerned with the coordination of limited human and material resources, relevant technologies, and situational contingencies for the efficient production and exchange of sport services" (Chelladurai, 1994).

3. The coordination was said to involve human resources (clients, paid employees, and volunteer workers), technologies (the processes and knowledge units employed in the production of a service), support units (dealing with facility management, event management, legal affairs, public relations), and contextual factors (organizational type, interorganizational networks, government rules and regulations, community expectations, and social norms).

4. The objective and subjective aspects of a career were described. It was emphasized that a match between one's personal characteristics and the characteristics of the job and the organization is the critical factor that a student should consider before accepting a job. In this regard some of the job and organizational characteristics were outlined.

CASE STUDY

May Baxter and June Armstrong were good friends. They both went to the same school in a rural setting and graduated with good standing. Both played on the high school basketball team and were members of the school track team. They went to the same university and graduated with degrees in sport management. They were lucky to get jobs in the athletic department of a neighboring university.

May's first job was as a ticket office clerk. Her superiors, noting her diligent work and her interpersonal skills, promoted her to the position of supervisor of clerks. The same hard work and positive attitude in successive jobs facilitated her promotion to the position of assistant director of the ticket office within 6 years. She enjoyed her work very much and took great pride in being associated with the organization that had a high profile within the university and the community. She looked forward to possible promotions such as the assistant or associate athletic director either in the same university or in another. To equip herself better for the future, she enrolled part time in an MBA program.

June's first job was as a clerk in the media relations office. Like May, June impressed her bosses with her work effectiveness and pleasant manner. She was promoted to a supervisory position within her department. Everybody assumed she was happy in her job and had expectations that she would quickly move up the in her career. However, June was becoming restless with her current job and future prospects. She felt that she was removed from where the action was, that is, she realized that she was not directly involved in the production of the fundamental service of the department—the production of excellence in sports. She perceived her own job and those in her department as only supplementary to that fundamental task. In short, she felt that her own abilities, interests, needs, and values would be best served if she were to become a coach. With this in mind, she volunteered to assist the coach of the women's basketball team. In that role, she assiduously learned everything she could from the coach. In addition, she began taking courses such as sport psychology and coaching science. Subsequently, she applied for and got a job coaching the women's basketball team at a four-year college. She soon proved to be an effective coach with a winning tradition. She enjoyed her present status and was looking forward to being a coach at a big university. The media and the community began noticing her achievements and winning ways.

1. Compare and contrast the careers of May Baxter and June Armstrong.
2. What are the differences between the first job of May (ticket office clerk) and June (media relations clerk)?
3. How would you distinguish between May's present job (assistant director of the ticket office) and June's present job (coach in a four-year college)?
4. In this chapter, sport management was defined in terms of various services. Discuss the services in which May and June are currently engaged.

REVIEW QUESTIONS AND ISSUES

1. Define the field of sport management. Describe the various categories of services produced and marketed in the field. Explain the significance of defining the field from the perspective of its products.
2. Select a service (e.g., fitness service, youth soccer) offered by an organization (e.g., commercial fitness club, local YMCA, city recreation department). Describe the human resources, technologies, support units, and contextual factors associated with the production and marketing of the chosen service.
3. Distinguish between objective and subjective careers.
4. Consider any sport-related job. Describe it in terms of the job dimensions referred to in the chapter.
5. Evaluate the job in terms of how it matches your abilities, education, needs, and values.

REFERENCES

Campion, M. A., and Thayer, P. W. (1985). Development and field evaluation of an interdisciplinary measure of job design. *Journal of Applied Psychology, 70,* 29-43.

Chelladurai, P. (1992). A classification of sport and physical activity services: implications for sport management. *Journal of Sport Management, 6,* 38-51.

Chelladurai, P. (1994). Sport management: defining the field. *European Journal for Sport Management, 1,* 7-21.

Cialdini, R. B., et al. (1976). Basking in reflected glory: three (football) field studies. *Journal of Personality and Social Psychology, 34,* 366-375.

Cuneen, J., and Sidwell, M. J. (1993). Effect of applicant gender on rating and selection of undergraduate sport management interns. *Journal of Sport Management, 7,* 216-227.

Cuskelly, G., and Auld, C. J. (1991). Perceived importance of selected job responsibilities of sport and recreation managers: an Australian perspective. *Journal of Sport Management, 5,* 34-46.

Danylchuk, K. E. (1993). Occupational stressors in physical education faculties. *Journal of Sport Management, 7,* 7-24.

Fayol, H. (1940). *General and industrial management.* London: Pitman. First published in French in 1916.

Fitzgerald, M. P., Sagaria, M. A. D. and Nelson, B. (1994). Career patterns of athletic directors: challenging the conventional wisdom. *Journal of Sport Management, 8,* 14-26.

Hackman, J.R., and Oldham, G.R. (1980). *Work designed.* Reading, Massachusetts: Addison Wesley.

Hatfield, B. D., Wrenn, J. P., and Bretting, M. M. (1987). Comparison of job responsibilities of intercollegiate athletic directors and professional sport general managers. *Journal of Sport Management, 1,* 129-145.

Hesterly, W. S., Liebeskind, J., and Zenger T. R. (1990) Organizational economics: an impending revolution in organization theory? *Academy of Management Review, 15* (3), 402-420.

Inglis, S. E. (1988). The representation of women in university athletic programs. *Journal of Sport Management, 2,* 14-25.

Johns, G. (1988). *Organizational behavior: understanding life at work* (2nd Edition). Glenview, Illinois: Scott, Foresman.

Johnson, A. T. (1993). Rethinking the sport-city relationship: in search of partnership. *Journal of Sport Management, 7,* 61-70.

Katz, R. L. (1974). Skills of an effective administrator. *Harvard Business Review, 52,* 90-102.

Kelley, D. R., Beitel, P. A., DeSensi, J. T., and Blanton, M. D. (1991). In B. L. Parkhouse (Ed.)., *The management of sport (pp. 12-26).* St. Louis: Mosby.

Kjeldsen, E. K. M. (1990). Sport management careers: a descriptive analysis. *Journal of Sport Management, 4,* 121-132.

Lovett, D. J., and Lowry, C. D. (1994). "Good old boys" and "good old girls" clubs: myth or reality. *Journal of Sport Management, 8,* 27-35.

Lovett, D. J., and Lowry, C. D. (1988). The role of gender in leadership positions in female sport programs in Texas college. *Journal of Sport Management, 2,* 106-117.

Melnick, M. J. (1993). Searching for sociability in the stands: a theory of sport spectating. *Journal of Sport Management, 7* (1), 44-60.

Mintzberg, H. (1975). The manager's job: folklore and fact. *Harvard Business Review, 53,* 49-61.

Mullin, B. J. (1980). Sport management: the nature and utility of the concept. *Arena Review, 4* (3), 1-11.

NASPE-NASSM Joint Task Force on Sport Management Curriculum and Accreditation. (1993). Standards for curriculum and voluntary accreditation of sport management education programs. *Journal of Sport Management, 7,* 159-170.

Parks, J. B. (1991). Employment status of alumni of an undergraduate sport management program. *Journal of Sport Management, 5,* 100-110.

Parks, J. B., and Parra, L. F. (1994). Job satisfaction of sport management alumni. *Journal of Sport Management, 8,* 49-56.

Parks, J. B., and Zanger, B. R. K. (1990). Definition and direction. In J. B. Parks and B. R. K. Zanger (Eds.), *Sport and fitness management: career strategies and professional content* (pp. 1-4). Champaign, Illinois: Human Kinetics.

Pastore, D. L. (1991). Male and female coaches of women's athletic teams: reasons for entering and leaving the profession. *Journal of Sport Management, 5,* 128-143.

Pastore, D. L. (1992). Two-year college coaches of women's teams: gender differences in coaching career selections. *Journal of Sport Management, 6,* 179-190.

Pastore, D. L., and Meacci, W. G. (1994). Employment process for NCAA female coaches. *Journal of Sport Management, 8,* 115-128.

Pierce, J. L., and Dunham, R. B. (1990). *Managing.* Glenview, Illinois: Scott, Foresman/Little, Brown Higher Education.

Quarterman, J. Managerial role profiles of intercollegiate athletic conference commissioners. *Journal of Sport Management, 8,* 129-139.

Sage, G. H. (1974). The coach as management: organizational leadership in American sport. In G. H. Sage (Ed.), *Sport and American society.* Reading, Massachusetts: Addison-Wesley.

Snyder, C. R., Lassegard, M. A., and Ford, C. E. (1986). Distancing after group success and failure: basking in reflected glory and cutting off reflected failure. *Journal of Personality and Social Psychology, 51,* 382-388.

Snyder, E. E., and Spreitzer, E. A. (1989). *Sociological aspects of sport* (3rd Edition). Englewood Cliffs, New Jersey: Prentice-Hall.

Stone, E. E., and Gueutal, H. G. (1985). An empirical derivation of the dimensions along which characteristics of jobs are perceived. *Academy of Management Journal, 28,* 376-396.

Wann, D.L., and Branscombe, N.R. (1990). Die-hard and fair weather fans: effects of identification on BIRGing and CORFing tendencies. *Journal of Sport and Social Issues, 14* (2), 103-117.

SUGGESTED READINGS

Betz, N. E., and Fitzgerald, L. F. (1987). *The career psychology of women.* Orlando, Florida: Academic Press.

Bridges, J. S. (1989). Sex Differences in Occupational Values. *Sex Roles, 20*(4), 353-366.

Hackett, G., and Betz, N. E. (1981). A self-efficacy approach to the career development of women. *Journal of Vocational Behavior, 18,* 326-339.

NCAA (1991). Perceived barriers of women in intercollegiate athletics careers. Official publication of the NCAA. Overland Park, Kansas.

Weiss, D. J., Dawis, R. V., and Lofquist, L. H. (1973). Minnesota Importance Questionnaire. *Vocational Psychology Research,* Minneapolis.

CHAPTER 3

Experiential Learning Through Field Experiences: Internships and Practica

M. Elizabeth Verner

In this chapter, you will become familiar with the following terms:

Experiential learning	Field experience	Parallel/extended day
Experiential education	Internship	cooperative education
Pedagogical approach	Practicum/Practica	Vocational self-concept
Discrete experiential education	Cooperative education	Formal sources
Nondiscrete experiential	Alternating cooperative	Informal sources
education	education	

Overview

As students reach the point in their plan of study where they begin to consider a field experience, it is helpful for them to think about *how* they learn through an understanding of the learning process and the relationship between theoretical and experiential learning. An overview of the historical development of experiential education provides students with an awareness of why field experiences are important and how they have become an integral part of the curriculum designed to prepare professionals in various walks of life. Likewise,

recognition of the importance of internships and practica in the sport management curriculum is beneficial to students when they contemplate the value of experiential learning as a component of their own professional preparation.

This chapter provides information regarding the value of field experiences for the student, the sponsoring agency, and the university. Research pertaining to desirable intern characteristics is summarized to guide students in assessing their potential *fit* for a sport management internship.

Practical suggestions are offered relative to how to secure an internship. Additionally, a case study, written by a successful intern, willing to share his experience with other students, is included as a means of encouraging students to be diligent and persistent in the pursuit of an internship.

CONCEPTUAL BACKGROUND
Learning theory
In her keynote address during the 22nd annual National Society for Experiential Education Conference in the fall of 1993, Dr. K. Patricia Cross described learning as an active, dynamic process in which new material interacts with what is already known to transform and deepen meaning. New information results in meaningful learning when it connects with what already exists in the mind of the learner. Therefore learning is transformational rather than additive. This assumption promotes the concept of mental structures that store and organize learned material in the schema of a multidimensional map of interrelated ideas, with all sorts of connections among stored material. "The excitement of learning comes when new connections are made, sometimes transforming the structure, pulling apart some connections and making new ones" (Cross, 1944).

Experiential and academic approaches to learning become natural allies in the process of constantly changing and reformatting thought structures. For example, enlightenment occurs when something read in a textbook comes to life as the learner makes the connection between the idea and its execution. Likewise, revelation is apparent when the learner comprehends the textbook explanation for phenomena previously observed but never understood (Cross, 1994).

One of the most sophisticated combinations of learning theory and learning styles research is authored by Dr. David Kolb. He posits that learning is a social process based on experience and defines learning as "the process whereby knowledge is created through the transformation of experience" (Kolb, 1984). Kolb's learning theory synthesizes the work of Dewey, Lewin, and Piaget; it emphasizes adapting, creating, and re-creating, as well as insight and application (Hesser, 1990).

Experiential learning is frequently explained by reference to Kolb's experiential learning cycle (see Figure 3-1 for a graphic representation). According to this model, the learner proceeds from the actual experience itself through a process of reflection about the experience; conceptualization or generalization that relates

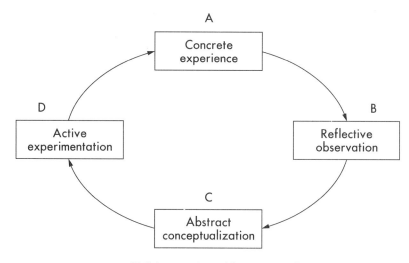

FIGURE 3-1 Kolb's experiential learning cycle.
From Kolb, D.A. (1976). *Learning style inventory technical manual.*

the experience to theories and to other experiences; and active experimentation with changed practice, based on these considerations.

Kolb's perspective on learning is called "experiential" because it "differentiates experiential learning theory from rationalist and other cognitive theories of learning that tend to give primary emphasis to acquisition, manipulation, and recall of abstract symbols and from behavioral learning theories that deny any role for consciousness and subjective experience in the learning process" (Kolb, 1984). The intent of Kolb's work "is not to pose experiential learning theory as a third alternative to behavioral and cognitive learning theories, but rather to suggest through experiential learning theory, a holistic, integrative perspective on learning that combines experience, perception, cognition, and behavior" (Kolb 1984).

Experiential learning and experiential education

Experiential learning refers to learning in which the learner is directly in touch with the realities being studied. It is contrasted with learning in which the learner only reads about, hears about, talks about, or writes about these realities, but never comes into contact with them as part of the learning process (Keeton & Tate, 1978).

Experiential education is a form of pedagogy, or teaching methodology, employed to facilitate experiential learning. Therefore " 'Experiential education' refers to learning activities that engage the learner directly in the phenomena being studied. This learning can be in all types of work or service settings by undergraduate and graduate students of all ages. . . [Experiential education is] carefully monitored, experience-based learning" (Kendall et al, 1986).

There are two basic categories of **experiential education activities: discrete and nondiscrete.** Discrete activities are those that are self-contained and constitute a separate entity. Examples of discrete experiential education activities include field study, internships, practica, student teaching, clinical experiences, cooperative education, and service-learning.

Nondiscrete experiential education activities are more often than not extensions or components of a course or program. As such they are not self-contained, separate entities. Many of the nondiscrete experiential education activities are considered to be innovative classroom instruction techniques. Examples of nondiscrete experiential education activities include: field trips, simulation/games, group process, role play, laboratory work, oral interviews, and participatory observations. The box below provides a more complete list of the most common types of experiential education activities.

No matter which activity becomes the vehicle, experiential learning is that transformation which

---

Types and forms of experiential education

1. Discrete experiential education courses or programs	2. Experiential education as one or more components of a course or program	3. Other experiential techniques incorporated into a course or program
Cooperative education	Field projects	Role playing
Field study, fieldwork, field research	Field trips	Laboratory work
Independent study	Participatory observations	Simulation games and exercises
Internships	Oral interviews	Student-led class sessions (presentations or discussions)
Practica	Site visits/field observations	Group learning activites
Service-learning	Use of primary source or raw data	Other active forms of learning
Work-learn	Others	
Others		

From *Strengthening Experiential Education Within Your Institution* by Kendall, J.C., Duley, J.S., Little, T.C., Permal, J.S., Rubin, S. National Society for Experiential Education, 3509 Haworth Drive, Suite 207, Raleigh, North Carolina 27609, 1986, page 31.

"occurs when changes in judgments, feelings, knowledge, or skills result for a particular person from living through an event or events" (Chickering, 1976). The value inherent in learning through experience is amply expressed in the adages: "No man's knowledge here can go beyond his experience," John Locke, 1690, *Essay Concerning Human Understanding,* and "The great difficulty in education is to get experience out of ideas," George Santayana, 1863-1952.

Field experiences, internships, practica, and cooperative education

Experiential learning in the form of field experiences, defined more specifically as practica and internships, are the types of experiential education activities that will be discussed in this chapter. **Field experience** is "an off campus learning activity, generally for credit, in which a student accepts a large share of the responsibility for his/her own learning" (Davis et al, 1978).

Internships are a type of field experience. They are "structured and career-relevant work experiences obtained by students prior to graduation from an academic program" (Taylor, 1988). Because they are most often pursued during the later stages of an academic degree program, internships are frequently the culminating experience for the plan of study. As such, they provide the student with an opportunity to experience the fusion of principles and theories with the solution of practical problems (Hoekstra, 1975; Rex, 1961).

Similar to internships, **practica** are "academically credited field experiences designed to meet specific academic objectives. They may be general and interdisciplinary in nature or oriented toward specific preprofessional training. These experiences are often degree requirements" (Stanton and Ali, 1987). Practica, however, are typically shorter than internships and frequently occur earlier in the academic degree plan of study.

On occasion, internships, and to an even lesser degree practica, are sometimes classified as **cooperative education** (co-op) experiences. To qualify as cooperative education, the field experiences must be "paid work experiences closely related to [the student's] academic and career pursuits" (U.S. Department of Education, 1991).

Cooperative education typically subscribes to one of two basic formats. The first is **alternating cooperative education,** which is a "plan of providing full-time, paid periods of work, balanced with full-time periods of study in institutions of higher education" (Gould, 1987). The second is **parallel or extended-day cooperative education,** which is a pattern allowing "attendance in classes, day or night, concurrent to a co-op placement" (Sheppard, 1987). Whether or not the experience is alternating or parallel/extended-day, receipt of payment in some form is usually necessary for the endeavor to be considered a cooperative education experience.

CONCEPT CHECK

*Both contexts, experiential and academic, are important as allies in the cyclic process whereby knowledge is created through the transformation of experience. Experiential education as a **pedagogical approach** refers to learning activities that engage the learner directly in the phenomena being studied. Field experiences are a type of experiential education and are often defined in terms of internships and practica. For a field experience to qualify as a co-op experience, the intern is typically paid.*

Application to sport management curriculum

Within the context of sport management, experiential learning is broadly interpreted as field experience. This concept is then more narrowly defined in terms of internships and practica in an attempt to operationalize curricular expectations. For example:

Internships are self-contained for academic credit. They involve actual work in a sport management setting subsequent to the junior year, in which management practices are applied. Final arrangement(s) for the internship are completed by a member of the faculty. The internship is a full-time (40 hr/week) work experience for a minimum of 400 hr. It must be directed and evaluated by a qualified faculty member with appropriate supervision by an on-site professional (NASPE-NASSM 1993).

Practica are similar to internships in terms of direction, evaluation, supervision, and the intent that they be career-relevant. Practica differ from internships in that they are not necessarily self-contained or offered for academic credit. Practica may assume various forms and may be extensions of a course. They are frequently pursued along with other course work, close to campus, and on a part-time basis, since they are less time consuming than internships. Some practica yield academic credit, whereas others may not (NASPE-NASSM, 1993).

A practicum and an internship are required by the "Standards for Curriculum and Voluntary Accreditation of Sport Management Education Programs" (NASPE-NASSM, 1993). The internship is a core component and the most commonly found element among undergraduate sport management programs in the United States (Parkhouse, 1987). Field experience plays an essential role and is highly valued in the preparation of both graduate and undergraduate sport management students (Brassie, 1989; Cuneen, 1992; Cuneen and Sidwell, 1993; DeSensi et al, 1990; Li et al, 1994; Parks and Quain, 1986; Sutton, 1989; Ulrich and Parkhouse, 1982).

As cornerstones of the curriculum, practica and internships take students beyond the classroom by placing them in a real work environment, thus providing the opportunity to bridge theory and practice. Participation in these activities helps students develop professional attitudes, behaviors, and values while providing the opportunity to problem solve and link theory with actuality. At the heart of these activities is *learning by doing.* Because they take place in the "real" workplace, practica and internships ensure opportunities to "practice the profession" while being immersed in the work behaviors and social culture of the host organization (Verner, 1993).

HISTORICAL OVERVIEW
From on-campus laboratories to off-campus work experiences
Learning experiences that take place outside the traditional classroom have not always been endorsed as a part of college and university study. Acceptance of experiential learning, and thus internships, as a part of higher education curricula has evolved in recent years.

According to Keeton and Tate (1978), experiential learning has been documented in American higher education as far back as the 1830s, when skepticism and serious debate preceded the introduction of laboratory sciences at Yale University. Not until the late nineteenth century did laboratory sciences gain respectability as collegiate courses. Applied studies became an accepted part of the curriculum in land-grant institutions after the Civil War. Medical students at Johns Hopkins University began to engage in clinical experiences during the 1870s, when performing autopsies and visiting hospital wards became a part of their training (Houle, 1976).

Cooperative education became a component in the plan of study for many technically oriented programs in the early twentieth century. More recently, studio arts have become recognized as credit-bearing activities in many higher education institutions. Field studies are now commonplace in the sciences of botany, anthropology, and archaeology. Several "professional and applied fields—medicine, architecture, clinical and counseling psychology, social work, and elementary and secondary education—have accepted experiential learning as a regular part of professional preparation" (Kendall et al, 1986). Therefore it is from well-established precedence that field experience in the form of a practicum and an internship be endorsed as experiential learning components by the NASPE-NASSM Joint Task Force, which developed the sport management curricular guidelines.

CONCEPT CHECK

American institutions of higher learning have not historically endorsed experiential learning as an accepted element of the credit-bearing curriculum. However, throughout the last century, experiential education as a pedagogical approach that directly engages the student in learning by doing has increasingly become a requirement in a number of professional preparation programs. Following this trend, the NASPE-NASSM Curricular Standards require a practicum and an internship in the professional preparation of sport managers.

BENEFITS OF THE INTERNSHIP EXPERIENCE
The internship is a triangular relationship entered into by three principal parties. These include the student, university, and sponsoring organization. Each one of the three helps to define the internship expectations. As a result, each has the potential to benefit from the unique educational opportunity that can develop. Students most notably desire to accomplish academic, personal, and career-related

goals. The university and sponsoring organization desire to provide practical, on-the-job experience for students to help them meet their goals (Lanese and Fitch, 1983). Additionally, the university can help students reinforce the connection between theory and practice. Further, the sponsoring organization can help to strengthen the profession by enhancing the work force through development of more capable entry-level employees. Following are benefits of specific value to the student, university, and sponsoring organization that can evolve from the internship relationship.

Value for students

Inherent in an internship experience for students is the opportunity to function as a professional and to become a part of the organization's culture through experiential awareness not only of its structure, resources, and purpose, but also the other internal and external factors that shape the organization (see Chapters 5-7). This includes becoming emersed in the behaviors, attitudes, beliefs, and values of the organization, an occurrence that can happen only when the internship experience duplicates or approximates that which is experienced by a full-time employee. Therefore outside commitments such as coursework or other employment should not be pursued during the internship (Sutton, 1989). Interns should expect to follow all rules, regulations, and policies of the sponsoring organization to acquire the values, behaviors, and attitudes that constitute the culture of a professional in the organization. Granted, students pursuing full-time internships who are totally involved with the host organization may be making a considerable sacrifice. However, tremendous benefits can be realized by those who accept the challenge (Verner, 1993). Detailed below are some of the benefits that may be realized by students.

A new learning environment. Knowledge and skills are acquired in different ways by different people. The practical settings that internships offer may be more effective learning environments for some students than the traditional classroom. Problem solving associated with an internship occurs in the "real world." The circumstances are not fictitious or contrived. Therefore lessons learned from the decision process can have a greater impact when experienced during an internship. For

many students, the implications of problem solving and decision making have greater meaning and are longer lasting when associated with an internship rather than a simulated situation within the classroom.

Realization of the meaning of professional commitment. Misconceptions often exist related to the totality of a career. It is not uncommon for the enjoyable and interesting parts of the job to be amplified at the expense of diminishing the less desirable tasks. A full-time internship places students in organizations where they are confronted daily with both the positive and negative sides of their career choice.

Assessment of skills and abilities by practitioners. Because of the environment in which they function, practicing professionals often view things from a more pragmatic and realistic perspective than college professors do. As a result, practitioners' assessment of interns' strengths and weaknesses can provide additional insight into the interns' potential for that particular career. This may help students progress toward greater crystallization of **vocational self-concept** and work values by facilitating the identification of vocationally relevant abilities, interests, and values (Taylor, 1988).

"Experience" as a category on the resume. One of the most frustrating obstacles for neophyte professionals to overcome is lack of experience. Internships provide the opportunity to gain invaluable work experience and as a result create another entry on the resume. Researchers have documented the value of work experience and internships in securing a job. Evaluation of resumes, including background as well as presence or absence of an internship for six college women graduates, indicated that the most common reasons for success in being selected for a job was relevant work experience and completion of an internship related to the job (Avis and Trice, 1991).

Two-way screening process. Students can determine whether they feel suited for the career choice during the internship, and those with whom they work can evaluate the performance of interns within the context of the real work environment. This is not to say that interns should expect to be hired by the host organization, although this does happen on occasion. Evaluation of an intern's potential is more valuable when based on how the student performed on the job rather than on the evaluator's perceptions of how the student *may* function on the job.

New mentor/mentee relationships. New relationships develop as a result of contact with people encountered during the internship. These new relationships can help interns learn more about themselves, both professionally and personally. Through guidance, direction, and suggestion, mentors can help interns develop attitudes and behaviors necessary for success in their career. Many insights can be gained when interns learn from the mistakes and successes of those who have preceded them. Administrators advocate that all young professionals seek to establish mentor/mentee relationships (Young, 1990). Quality internships in sport management provide a forum for the development of strong mentor/mentee relationships (Brassie, 1989; Parks and Quain, 1986).

Networking. Being on the inside of the organization allows interns to be a part of the informal employee network. Students can learn of potential job openings before they are advertised, and they can develop important contacts as well as possible references for future career opportunities. Young (1990) found "administrators agreed that recommendations by network contacts often take precedence over a candidate's experience in a job search [which] reinforces the adage 'it's *who* you know that counts.' "

Information regarding vacancies or job availability can be from formal or informal sources. **Formal sources** are the traditional mechanisms for attaining job information such as placement office bulletins and employment ads. **Informal sources** include friends and professional contacts. Greater access to informal sources of information regarding the job search is available to students who complete an internship (Parks, 1991; Taylor, 1988). According to Taylor (1984), the use of informal, as opposed to formal, sources of job information produces more satisfying job opportunities. Parks (1991) found the job placement strategy most frequently used by sport management majors was personal contact.

Mirror feedback and evaluation. Internships offer students the chance to discover whether theoretical ideas and textbook principles work in actual situations. The resulting successes and failures help establish a personal, critical assessment of how effective different strategies may be in a realistic environment.

Dealing with crises and critical decisions. In the real work world, daily incidences are not always predictable, and some situations may occur in which interns have had no experience. The conditions of the moment may not allow for consultation with mentors, the university supervisor, or textbooks. Action and decision making in such realistic dilemmas can accelerate the maturation process. Professional growth and development become evident as interns move away from reacting as students and assume the posture of young professionals.

Springboard for a career. An internship is the intermediate step between being a student and being a full-time professional. Depending on what the intern makes of the opportunity, it can be either a springboard or a barrier to a valued career position. A successful internship experience provides the basis for an excellent reference for future employment.

Value to university

Keeping in touch with the "real world." As new techniques and technology are developed and incorporated into the profession, it is helpful for university faculty to have exposure to what is and is not working in real-life situations. As visits and contacts are made with professionals who supervise student interns, faculty have the opportunity to discuss and witness both the effective and the ineffective procedures, equipment, and methodologies. This allows faculty to remain closer to the cutting edge of the profession. (Verner, 1990)

Updating curriculum. Sport management educators believe one of the most valued characteristics of an effective graduate program is that the program is "updated to include current areas of subject matter in sport management" (Li et al, 1994). The university may improve its educational programs and test "its curricula through feedback" associated with the internship (McCaffrey, 1979).

Faculty who supervise interns have tremendous opportunity to remain abreast of current developments in the profession. Additionally, feedback can be gained not only from student interns but also from sponsoring organization supervisors. Based on their exposure during the field experience, interns can inform faculty of the strengths and weaknesses of the curriculum. Likewise, feedback can be provided by supervisors in sponsoring organizations regarding how well prepared the intern was to accept responsibility and function in the organization (Konsky, 1976). Information from all of these sources can be useful to faculty as they update their lectures and revise the curriculum. Enriched by feedback from the field and subsequent reformulation of the curriculum, professional preparation programs will remain in step with the industry, and better prepared students will emerge to join the work force.

Exposing students to new equipment. Even though it is relatively inexpensive to update the curriculum based on various forms of feedback, at a time when technology is changing so rapidly, it is quite expensive to keep college/university teaching laboratories up to date. Higher education institutions often experience financial limitations, prohibiting replacement or addition of new equipment so that students can be exposed to the latest available. It is particularly difficult to remain current with the most advanced equipment in the fitness industry because manufacturers are constantly designing and producing updated cardiovascular and resistive weight training apparatus. Internship experiences can provide students with the opportunity to work with equipment that may not be available on the campus.

Enriching classroom instruction. Classroom instruction can be enriched through the process of students relating their field experiences to the content being discussed (Gryski et al., 1992). Because they have been a part of the organization and have experienced what happens there on a day-to-day basis, the relationship between theory and practice may be more apparent for a student who has completed or is enrolled in a practicum or internship. Students who have not yet completed a field experience can become enlightened when students who have share their experiences and relate them to topics of instruction.

Developing research contacts. Faculty who supervise interns network with professionals in the field. Extensions of these relationships may lead to developing new ideas or strategies for research, as well as solidifying contacts that may be valuable in other endeavors (Cottrell and Wagner, 1990). Particularly enhanced through these faculty/practitioner relationships are opportunities related to applied research. Interaction with practicing professionals can provide faculty the opportunity to engage in research, possibly using the organization, its clients, or employees as the population to be studied. A few examples of applied research opportunities that may promote collaboration among the intern, faculty advisor, and sponsoring organization supervisor include study related to the following: (1) fan recognition of identified advertising displays in a sports venue, which may influence an advertiser's marketing approach; (2) client preference for cardiovascular equipment in a fitness environment, which may influence management's purchasing pattern; (3) donor motivation characteristics of those who, through gift-giving, financially support the organization, which may help the fundraiser better relate to current donors as well as know how to approach new donors.

Enhancing public relations. Through interaction with sponsoring organizations, universities can disseminate information about the strength of their programs and the capabilities of their graduates (Gryski et al, 1992). This interaction provides a valuable basis upon which to build relationships between the university and potential employers for graduates. It may also increase the likelihood that future interns may be placed with the sponsoring organization (Sink and Sari, 1984).

Value to sponsoring organization

Expanding the available work force. It should not be expected that motivation on the part of an organization for hosting an intern is completely altruistic. In return for the time and energy invested in helping students advance their knowledge, skill, and ability, sponsoring organizations with an effective intern will gain an additional staff member. This aspect can be particularly appealing when budget constraints have inhibited hiring practices (Bjorklund, 1974; Conklin-Fread, 1990).

Even in the beginning of the experience, when interns would not be expected to be full contributors, simple tasks and responsibilities can be assigned, thus allowing regular employees to direct their attention to higher order tasks. As the interns become acclimated to the agency, greater responsibility can be assumed (Verner, 1990).

Bringing new ideas into the organization. Periodically introducing new ideas into the organization promotes variety and vitality. With each change in staff, new ideas are introduced to the agency. Such is also the case when hosting interns. "Students may sometimes serve as agents of change as they bring some of the latest information and innovation from the academic world into the field" (Gryski et al 1992). Though they often have not had the opportunity to try many of their ideas, interns can offer a new perspective and a fresh outlook on tradition-laden policies and procedures. Because of their recent classroom exposure to literature and theories, interns are an excellent source of creative ideas. (Verner, 1990)

Evaluating potential employees. Throughout the internship experience, personnel within the agency have the opportunity to evaluate the intern's capability to become a regular employee. Agency personnel can preview, with "no strings attached," preprofessionals who may be candidates for future job vacancies. Thus the internship can provide assistance in identifying talent among potential employees.

Assisting higher education develop more qualified employees. Through sponsorship of internship opportunities, organizations blend their efforts with those of academic institutions to develop a more qualified work force. The value of field experiences in accomplishing this goal was substantiated by DeSensi, et al (1990) when business or agency personnel in sport management organizations "indicated that both practica and internship experiences were very important." No doubt sport management curricular improvements since the late 1970s have narrowed the gap between employer expectations and entry level employee abilities, but at that time Parkhouse and Ulrich (1979) found employers believed that "on-the-job training rather than formal preparation, better serves the organization's needs."

CONCEPT CHECK

Internships and practica can benefit everyone involved in the triangular relationship—the student, university, and sponsoring organization. However, the student probably gains the most.

POTENTIAL INTERNSHIP INVOLVEMENT FOR SPORT MANAGEMENT STUDENTS

Before evaluating and selecting an internship site, students can narrow the search by creating a list of objectives they hope to accomplish during the internship experience. This process will enhance self-direction, which, according to Shipton and Steltenpohl (1980), promotes higher quality in experiential learning endeavors. By clarifying goals and planning a program to attain those goals, essential skills in self-direction are developed. Becoming self-directed related to one's education requires the following: (1) "learning how to plan"; (2) "learning how to assess personal values, interests, skills, aptitudes, and developmental needs [that contribute] to goal setting"; and (3) "knowing how to identify alternative learning activities and resources in relation to purposes." Having an environment in which to practice what is expected to be learned is requisite to developing ability in self-direction. Determining the most appropriate environment can be accomplished, in part, by subscribing to sound evaluation and selection criteria.

When considering potential organizations, it is helpful to be both creative and futuristic. Rather than being restrained by considering only typical placement sites, students should also look for organizations that could benefit from the knowledge, skill, and experience the intern could provide. Conversely, interns should evaluate whether potential organizations offer appropriate opportunities to fulfill their internship objectives. The following possibilities may meet the objectives of interns in fitness, leisure, and sport management (refer to Chapter 2 for additional opportunities):

1. Fitness
   a. Corporate fitness/wellness programs
   b. Hospital fitness/wellness programs—both for rehabilitation and for apparently healthy populations

c. YMCA/YWCA and park district fitness/wellness programs for community residents

d. Resort and cruise ship fitness/wellness programs

2. Leisure

a. Park districts and YMCA/YWCAs

b. Cruise ships, resorts, and hotels

c. National parks, amusement and theme parks

d. Hospitals and rehabilitation clinics for therapeutic populations

3. Sport Management

a. Collegiate athletic departments

b. Professional sport organizations

c. Youth sport associations

d. Governing organizations for all levels of sport

CONCEPT CHECK

Prospective interns should create a list of objectives to help define what they hope to accomplish during the internship. The process of developing objectives will assist in self-direction by clarifying goals and assist in planning to accomplish those goals. As a result, prospective interns should not be hesitant to make known their desires related to the type of internship placement.

COMPETENCIES DESIRED OF INTERNS

Two recent research studies documented potential employers' perceptions of desired competencies for sport management interns. Cuneen and Sidwell (1993) surveyed personnel who interview and select interns in major and minor league professional sports, college and university athletics, associations and conferences, resorts and clubs, event management, and the media. The respondents ($N=215$) reacted to six fictitious potential intern resumes providing a rank order and identifying the one they would select for placement in their organization. From this assessment, nine intern qualifications emerged as the most desirable. In order of preference, the desired competencies were "(1) marketing/promotion experience, (2) evidence of computer skills, (3) evidence of writing skills, (4) sales experience, (5) internship goal, (6) practical/work experience,

(7) athletic/sport background, (8) well-rounded, and (9) sports reporting experience."

Klein (1994) completed doctoral dissertation research, which led to the development of a "top 10" list of criteria for sport management interns as perceived by college athletic internship supervisors, nonprofit organization internship site supervisors, and sport management faculty advisors ($N=143$). From an initial group of 20 knowledge competencies, eight technical skills, 17 personal qualities, and 7 selection criteria (52 possible qualifications), the "top 10" list evolved and included seven personal qualities, two knowledge competencies, and one technical skill. The "top 10" criteria (actually there were 11 because of a tie for tenth place) for sport management interns emerging from this study in rank order were "(1) reliable, (2) responsible, (3) willing to learn, (4) positive attitude, (5) verbal skills, (6) ethics, (7) communications, (8) cooperative, (9) adaptable to situations, (10) attention to detail, (11) demonstrates initiative."

The two lists of competencies differ considerably in the items identified, most likely because of the differences in populations surveyed and the methodologies employed for the studies. Nonetheless, the results provide a point of departure for determining desirable intern characteristics.

CONCEPT CHECK

Sport management intern competencies have been identified in recent research and include as the top three work-related skills: marketing/promotion experience, computer skills, and writing skills. The top three personal qualities include reliability, responsibility, and willingness to learn.

SECURING AN INTERNSHIP

There are four basic steps to securing an internship: (1) identifying potential internship organizations; (2) contacting those of greatest interest; (3) interviewing with several organizations to find out more about their offerings; and (4) selecting the organization best suited for personal objectives. Before embarking on the process of securing an internship, students should become familiar with the expectations, resources, and requirements at their universities. By working closely with a university adviser or internship coordinator, the student will benefit by suggestions and become aware of approved university procedures.

Awareness of potential sites

Internship opportunities are advertised in numerous ways, most commonly in publications distributed to professionals in the field. Following are potential site sources categorized by career option.

1. Fitness
   a. Association for Worksite Health Promotion *Who's Who in Employee Health and Fitness*
   b. American College of Sports Medicine *Career Services Bulletin*
   c. University Internship Services *Directory of Internships*
2. Leisure
   a. National Recreation and Park Association *Park and Recreation Opportunities Bulletin*
   b. Resort and Commercial Recreation Association *Internship Directory*
   c. *Resource Sharing: Recreation Intern Programs within the Armed Forces*
   d. *YMCA Directory*
3. Sport Management
   a. National Collegiate Athletic Association's *The NCAA News*
   b. University Internship Services *Internship Directory* (available from University Internship Services, 2609 West 49½ St., Suite 100, Austin, TX 38731)
   c. *Sports Fan's Connection*

Initial contact

After targeting potential organizations, prospective interns should submit a resumé and cover letter. These materials should look professional because they are the first impression given by the potential intern. Make the cover letter concise and well constructed with correct grammar, punctuation, spelling, and appropriate word choice. The resumé should provide all information that will help the agency staff become familiar with the individual, including contact information, educational background, experiences related to the internship, and previous employment and volunteer experiences. According to Cuneen and Sidwell (1993), specific-

ity regarding work-related skills is of tremendous value. For example, it is preferable for the resumé to identify the type of computer hardware and software used by the incumbent rather than simply indicating that the incumbent is computer literate. Professional organization memberships, as well as school affiliations, should be listed. Leadership positions held in professional organizations and school affiliations should be highlighted.

After initial contact has been made with the preferred organizations, allow approximately 10 working days to receive a response. If no response is received, follow up the initial contact with a phone call. During this conversation, students can provide additional information or arrange to meet with someone from the agency to discuss the possibility of an internship.

Interview

The purpose of the initial contact is to arrange for an interview or to discuss the possibility for an internship. Try to obtain interviews with different agencies to compare the various opportunities. When visiting these organizations, tour the facilities and meet as many staff members as possible to evaluate the organizational culture and climate. Questions should be asked by both the interviewer and the interviewee to provide the information needed to help each make the appropriate choice to facilitate a good fit between the intern and the agency. Expectations held by the student, the agency, and the university should be discussed.

Selection

An internship site selection should occur only after the student has given considerable thought to the information collected during the interview, as well as from conversations with previous interns and the university internship supervisor. Information from these sources should be balanced against students' objectives for the internship experience. Factors to consider when making the selection should include the following:

Position identity. The agency selected for the internship should be similar to that desired for an entry-level position. If that is not possible, the agency should be one that will provide the experience needed to be competitive for the desired entry-level position. The anticipated tasks and responsibilities should be transferable. At a minimum, the skills used in the internship should be similar to those required by the desired entry-level position (Sutton, 1989).

Compensation. Remuneration, or the lack thereof, should be the pivotal point for site selection only if financial compensation is absolutely required to be able to pursue the internship. However, significant financial compensation is not typical; in most internship situations, there is no remuneration.

Time span. The length of the internship will be determined in part by university and organizational requirements. Typically, internships occur within the semester; however, some are 6 months to 1 year in duration. The time of year should be considered, since organizations may be involved in cyclic work patterns and may only accept interns during specific times of the year.

Location. Students seeking permanent residence in particular parts of the country may want to consider obtaining internships in the desired regions. This not only provides the opportunity to learn more about a selected area but also can help students make professional contacts with knowledge of future job opportunities.

New experience. Internships are perfect times to try something unfamiliar and challenging. During this period, experiment and explore new aspects of the profession. There is little risk on the part of either the intern or the host organization in terms of an extended commitment or obligation.

Compatibility. By taking initiative and being proactive, students can assume responsibility for making the internship experience happen "for" them, not "to" them. Prospective interns should define the parameters that are acceptable to them and identify their needs and desires, thus taking an active role in shaping the experience. An internship is a three-way agreement, with the student's part being most important. While students need to be aware of the constraints of the agency and its bottom-line necessity to serve clientele, within those parameters students should be articulate in

defining what they would like the experience to include. (Verner, 1993)

CONCEPT CHECK

There are recommended steps to be followed in seeking an internship placement. However, before embarking on the search process, potential interns should contact the university internship coordinator or academic adviser who coordinates the internship program to become familiar with university policies, procedures, expectations, and resources.

SOLIDIFYING INTERNSHIP EXPECTATIONS

After the intern, university representative, and supervisor from the sponsoring organization have concurred that the internship can take place, an agreement should be developed to solidify the parameters and expectations of the internship experience. A document signed by the three parties is often used for this purpose. Although many universities and sponsoring organizations have used the term "Learning Contract" to refer to this document, there is reason to believe that "Learning Agreement" or other terminology that excludes the term "contract" might be a better choice. The preference for refraining from using "contract" is to avoid any legal implications that may be inherent in the term. The intent to identify expectations related to the internship can be accomplished without using the term "contract"; so as a measure of caution, the document specifying these conditions should not include this term.

Items covered by the learning agreement include anything that aids in clarifying the intentions and expectations of the student, university, and sponsoring organization supervisor. These include, but are not limited to, criteria related to educational goals, work-related objectives, learning activities, evaluation and grading techniques, academic credit, supervision support, and insurance coverage. Often, organizations that sponsor internship programs require some type of learning agreement before the experience can begin. This ensures that all parties clearly understand and agree to the role each will play in the internship relationship (Stanton and Ali, 1987). (Figure 3-2 provides an example of a learning agreement.)

Illinois State University
Department of Health, Physical Education, Recreation and Dance
Professional Practice – Cooperative Education & Internship
LEARNING AGREEMENT

PART I

A. NAME	SOCIAL SECURITY NO.

CAMPUS ADDRESS *Street*	HOME ADDRESS *Street*

City *State* *Zip*	*City* *State* *Zip*

PHONE	PHONE

ADDRESS WHILE DOING CO-OP/INTERNSHIP *Street*

City *State* *Zip*	PHONE *(include area code)*

DATE CO-OP/INTERNSHIP COMMENCES	*DATE CO-OP/INTERNSHIP TERMINATES*

B. CO-OP/INTERNSHIP ORGANIZATION

ADDRESS *Street*

City *State* *Zip*	PHONE *(include area code)*

NAME OF AGENCY SUPERVISOR

STUDENT POSITION

STUDENT POSITION IS –
☐ Paid *or* ☐ Unpaid

C. FACULTY SPONSOR/ADVISER

PROGRAM

ADDRESS *Street*

City *State* *Zip*	PHONE *(include area code)*

CREDITS TO BE AWARDED

PROGRAM	COURSE NO.	NO. OF CREDITS

Copies: White - *Faculty Adviser*
Canary - *Agency Supervisor*
Pink - *Dept. P.P. Coordinator*
Gold - *Student*

For Graduate Use: Green - *Coordinator*

FIGURE 3-2 Sample learning agreement.
Adapted by Illinois State University from Stanton, T., and Ali, K.: *The experienced hand: a student manual for making the most of an internship.* National Society for Experiential Education, 3509 Haworth Drive, Suite 207, Raleigh, North Carolina 27609, 1987, p. 63-65. Reprinted with permission.

Professional Practice Learning Agreement

PART II. The Professional Practice Co-op/ Internship Experience

A. Job Description: Describe in as much detail as possible your role and responsibilities while on your internship or co-op. List duties, projects to be completed, deadlines, etc., if revelant.

B. Supervision: Describe in as much detail as possible the supervision to be provided. What kind of instruction, assistance, consultation, etc., you will receive from whom, etc.

C. Evaluation: How will your work performance be evaluated? By whom? When?

PART III. Learning Objectives/ Learning Activities/ Evaluation

A. Learning Objectives: What do you intend to learn through this experience? Be specific. Try to use concrete, measurable terms.

FIGURE 3-2, cont'd Sample learning agreement.

B. Learning Activities

(1) On-the-Job: Describe how your internship/Co-op activities will enable you to meet your learning objectives. Include projects, research, report writing, conversation, etc., which you will do while working, relating them to what you intend to learn.

(2) Off-the-Job: List reading, writing, contact with faculty sponsor, peer group, discussion, field trips, observations, etc., you will make and carry out that will help you meet your learning objectives.

C. Evaluation: How will you know what you have learned, or that you have achieved your learning objectives? How do you wish to evaluate your progress toward meeting these objectives? Who will evaluate? When? How will a grade be determined? By whom? When?

PART IV. Agreement

This agreement may be terminated or amended by student, faculty supervisor, or worksite supervisor at any time upon written notice, which is received and agreed to by the other two parties.

STUDENT SIGNATURE	DATE
FACULTY ADVISER	DATE
AGENCY SUPERVISOR	DATE

FIGURE 3-2, cont'd   Sample learning agreement.

SUMMARY

1. Historically, experiential learning endeavors have not been considered viable educational activities worthy of academic credit in American colleges and universities. However, over the last few decades, there has been considerable growth in the endorsement of field experiences as valuable components in the academic degree preparation for a number of professions. Curricular standards developed by the NASPE-NASSM Task Force require both a practicum and an internship experience in the preparation of sport managers.

2. The internship represents a three-way agreement. Tremendous benefits can be gained by each of the three principle parties involved in the internship experience—the intern, university, and sponsoring organization.

3. Desirable competencies of sport management interns have been identified in recent research. After considering these competencies, prospective interns should consult with their university internship program coordinator, and begin the process to select an internship site. There are recommended steps in the search, selection, and solidification of an internship placement.

4. When acknowledgment has occurred that an internship will be pursued, a document should be generated to specify the expectations and intent for the internship. It is advisable that this document not be called a "learning contract"; a better title may be "learning agreement."

The following case study was written by a student during the first few weeks of his internship experience. It is offered as a testimonial for fellow students who may be confronted with similar thoughts, fears, circumstances, and joys. As you read about John's situation, try to put yourself in his place. Would you make similar choices?

CASE STUDY

The field of sports management has to be one of the hardest fields to get into, but the thrill of sports can make it seem so inviting. Personally, it has been a long and difficult process. When I was growing up, my dream was to be a professional athlete. After realizing that I would never make it on my physical abilities, the dream of working in professional sports continued. At one point the dream almost became a nightmare. This is my experience of trying to find an internship in the sports management area.

My name is John Davila, and currently I am a senior physical education major at Illinois State University. My pursuit of an internship began in February of 1993. Between February and the end of the semester in May, I sent cover letters and resumés to the following professional sports organizations: the Chicago Bears, San Diego Chargers, Tampa Bay Buccaneers, Atlanta Falcons, Pittsburgh Steelers, Minnesota Vikings, Indianapolis Colts, Miami Dolphins, Kansas City Chiefs, Chicago Cubs, San Antonio Spurs, San Antonio Missions (a minor league baseball team), Quad City Thunder (Continental basketball team), Peoria Chiefs (minor league baseball), and the New England Patriots. Amateur agencies contacted included the National Collegiate Athletic Association (NCAA), the National Athletic Intercollegiate Association (NAIA), and the United States Olympic Committee. Universities and colleges included Illinois State University, University of Maryland, North Park College, and the Big Ten Conference Office.

With a few exceptions, all responses came back negative. Of the few positive responses, though, none were for the immediate future. All that remained for me to qualify for graduation was the internship and, as the end of the semester approached with no internship in hand, frustration set in.

A couple of weeks before the end of the semester, I did have positive contact with an Athletic Coast Conference school. There was interest in having me as an intern for the fall semester. At the end of April and early in the summer I was in constant contact with this university concerning the internship, which would have been in the athletic department. Things seemed positive, and I began making plans as though the internship were in hand.

This was a mistake. I had counted on getting the internship and had closed off pursuit of other opportunities. A few weeks into the summer, communication broke down. Feeling "brushed off" by the school, I was becoming pessimistic about finding an internship for the fall. The whole experience of finding an internship was becoming very frustrating—so frustrating, in fact, that self-doubt entered my mind. I started to wonder if I had made the right career choice. I love sports; it is the only thing I ever wanted to be a part of, but I began to think about other career options.

Just before the 1993 fall semester began, I spoke with my high school athletic director about doing an internship with the school. He was positive and extended the offer. I talked it over with my intern coordinator who wasn't thrilled about the idea. She told me that starting at the high school level would make it very difficult to advance to the next level. I knew what she was saying was true, but my situation was becoming more complex.

Financially, it made more sense to live at home and take the high school internship. Even though it was not my preference, I would be completing my degree and could move on to graduate school. On the other hand, I had completed four years of school, had been active in the campus community, maintained a good GPA, and felt I had done as much as possible to balance the two without sacrificing one for the other. At this point my resumé was about as good as I could get it. Finally, why wait any longer? I had been searching for 8 months and found nothing. Another couple of months wasn't going to make a difference. To top it all off, I had an "incomplete" in the seminar class preparing for an internship, which would become an F if I didn't have an internship secured by the end of the spring semester (May 1994).

I talked about the situation with my parents, family, and friends, and finally reached a decision. Against the hopes and expectations of those around me, I decided to wait. It was one of the toughest choices I ever made. I was burned out from school, frustrated by the search, and the degree was just out of my reach, contingent on the internship. I started second guessing myself again.

After turning down the high school internship, I worked part time as an assistant women's basketball coach at Knox College, a Division III school in Galesburg, Illinois. The experience was enjoyable, and it opened my eyes to another possible career choice—coaching. Had the present opportunity not arisen, I might have pursued coaching.

About a month into the Knox College job, one of my college program coordinators contacted me. One of the coordinator's former students, who now works for the Chicago Cubs, was looking for someone interested in doing an internship in the Cubs' marketing department. Fortunately, my coordinator gave him my name and then contacted me with the news. The Knox College team was about to leave for Memphis, Tennessee, to play in a tournament. As soon as we returned, I called the contact person, and we discussed the possibility of an interview.

A few weeks later the date was set for my first interview. After so long, I was thrilled to have the opportunity to interview. I was thinking positively but not banking on getting the internship. At the same time I was filling out an application for the NCAA, which has internships on a yearly basis at their national headquarters in Overland Park, Kansas. The Cubs internship was exciting, but I did not want to close myself off to other opportunities.

My first interview with the Cubs was mid-February 1994. It went smoothly. Representatives from both human resources and marketing interviewed me. The session with the human resources representative was the more difficult. She asked me to describe myself—a hard question to answer. I tried to relate myself to the kind of qualities they could expect from me as an employee. She also asked some general questions like what are my hobbies and what are my future goals. The session only lasted about 5 minutes. When we were finished, Phil, the coordinator of Broadcasting Services and Mezzanine Boxes, talked with me. He was very easy to talk to. He described the internship and was honest about the long hours expected of an intern. I would have to work all games, which would mean being at the park for 14-15 days at times. He did not "sugar coat" the job. After about 30 minutes, he told me he had interviews throughout the week and would be in contact with me about a second interview.

The second interview was at the end of February. This time it was with Phil and the Cubs' vice-president of marketing. The interview was short—about 10 minutes—and they did most of the talking. There was a lot of joking and, by the time I left, I felt confident of my chances. Phil told me that he would call in about a week and give me his decision.

A week came and went. I became aggressive and started calling him. I did not want to be pushy or get on his nerves, but I did call at least once a day and sometimes twice and left messages on his answering machine.

On March 2, 1994, the answer came. I was chosen to be an intern for the Chicago Cubs for the upcoming season! After waiting so long, the feelings were relief and satisfaction in addition to happiness. I am a very self-confident person, but the whole internship process had taken a little of that away. With the internship in hand, all of that confidence came back. You always hear that the hardest thing to do is to get your foot in the door, but once that foot is in the door, many other doors will open for you.

I have been with the Cubs for more than 2 months now. My responsibilities include supervision of the Leaf Candies batboy/batgirl program, a cosponsored program designed to give kids a dream day at Wrigley Field; the operation of Wrigley Vision, the in-stadium television network; helping with pre-game promotions and events; obtaining autographs from players for sponsors and charity events; working with community relations to choose which charitable organizations receive tickets through our special group program; going with players to school appearances; and a variety of other activities (Figure 3-3). It is a great learning experience. I have already learned so much about what goes on within the department—what kinds of

working habits are successful and which ones can put you behind in your work.

I hope there is a possibility for me to stay with the Cubs on a permanent basis. If that cannot happen, I will take some time off to relax before going to graduate school to pursue a master's in either sports management or business administration. As I said before, there are many options once I have finished with the internship.

My advice for anyone going into the field of sports management is simple: be aggressive and patient. The process is difficult. If you want to get into professional sports badly enough, you have to be willing to hear the words "no" and "sorry." But be patient. Persistence will pay off eventually. I believe my internship is the best I could possibly get; it took me a year to get it, but it was worth it. If I had to do it all over again, knowing what I know now, I would not change many things because the internship was worth the wait. As bad as things seemed at times, things are good now. I understand that for others it may be more important to get a degree instead of waiting for that special internship opportunity, which may never come along. There are short-term goals and long-term goals that we set for ourselves. My long-term goal was more

FIGURE 3-3 One of John Davila's responsibilities as an intern was to oversee a number of community relations efforts.

important to me. By waiting, I was able to achieve both goals. I hope everyone in search of the same dream achieves the opportunity I now have.

Having read John's case study, if you were confronted with the same or similar conditions, would you:

1. Choose to wait a year to try for a particular internship placement?
2. Be as selective as John regarding the type of internship?
3. Be more or less aggressive in pursuing the placement?

On June 23, 1994, John Davila was offered and accepted the position of Cubs Care and Community Relations Assistant. This is a prime example of how patience and perseverence can successfully be played out (no pun intended) in the real world—the marketplace.

REVIEW QUESTIONS AND ISSUES

1. What role do experiential and academic learning play in the process of creating knowledge through transformation?
2. Describe Kolb's experiential learning theory in terms of its structure and relate the four components to one another.
3. What are the two field experience components required by the NASPE-NASSM curriculum standards? How do they differ and how are they similar?
4. Identify and describe three possible benefits for the intern that can result from an internship experience.
5. What are three university/faculty benefits that can be realized from an internship experience? Name and describe them.
6. An organization that sponsors internship opportunities can benefit in numerous ways. List and describe three possible benefits that can result from hosting an intern.
7. Competencies desired by sport management interns have been documented in two recent research studies (Cuneen and Sidwell, 1993; Klein, 1994). Name any six of the desired competencies identified among the top five on either of the two lists generated by these two studies.
8. What term is *not* recommended for use in the document that specifies arrangements and ex-

pectations for the internship? Why should this term not be associated with the document that solidifies the internship relationship?

REFERENCES

Avis, R. K., and Trice, A. D. (1991). The influence of major and internship on the evaluation of undergraduate women's resumes. *College Student Journal, 25,* 536-538.

Bjorklund, C. (1974). *A feasibility study of internships in educational management and innovation.* Boulder, Colorado: Western Interstate Commission for Higher Education.

Brassie, P. S. (1989). Guidelines for programs preparing undergraduate and graduate students for careers in sport management. *Journal of Sport Management, 3* (2), 158-164.

Chickering, A. W. (1976). Developmental change as a major outcome. In M. T. Keeton (Ed.), *Experiential learning: rationale, characteristics, and assessment* (pp. 62-109). San Francisco: Jossey-Bass.

Conklin-Fread, M. T. (1990). An investigation of the direct, indirect, and intangible benefits which accrued to hospital dietetic departments sponsoring an internship for student dietitians (Doctoral dissertation, New York University, 1990). *Dissertation Abstracts International, 51/08B, 3785.*

Cottrell, R. R., and Wagner, D. I. (1990). Internships in community health education/promotion professional preparation programs. *Health Education, 21* (1), 30-33.

Cross, K. P. (1994). The coming of age of experiential education. *NSEE Quarterly, 19* (3), 1, 22-24.

Cuneen, J. (1992). Graduate level professional preparation for athletic directors. *Journal of Sport Management, 6* (1), 15-26.

Cuneen, J., and Sidwell, M. J. (1993). Sport management interns: selection qualifications. *Journal of Physical Education, Recreation and Dance, 64* (1), 91-95.

Davis, R. H., Duley, J. S., and Alexander, L. T. (1978). *Field experience.* East Lansing, Michigan: Instructional Media Center.

DeSensi, J. T., Kelley, D. R., Blanton, M. D., and Beitel, P. A. (1990). Sport management curricular evaluation and needs assessment: a multifaceted approach. *Journal of Sport Management, 5,* 31-58.

Gould, P. (1987). Alternating cooperative education programs. In D. C. Hunt (Ed.), *Fifty views of cooperative education* (5th ed.). Detroit: University of Detroit.

Gryski, G. S., Johnson, G. W., and O'Toole, L. J. (1992). Undergraduate internships: an empirical review. In A. Ciofalo (Ed.), *Internships: perspectives in experiential learning* (pp. 195-210). Malabar, Florida: Krieger Publishing.

Hesser, G. (1990). *Experiential education as a liberating art.* Raleigh, North Carolina: National Society for Experiential Education.

Hoekstra, R. B. (1975). *Internships as a means of training educational leaders: an historical and contextural perspective.* (ERIC Document Reproduction Service No. ED 103 999).

Houle, C. O. (1976). Deep traditions of experiential learning. In M. T. Keeton (Ed.), *Experiential learning: rationale, characteristics, and assessment* (pp. 19-33). San Francisco: Jossey-Bass.

Keeton, M. T., and Tate, P. J. (1978). *Editor's notes:* The bloom in experiential learning. In M. T. Keeton and P. J. Tate (Eds.), *New directions for experiential learning: learning by experience—what, why, how* (pp. 1-8). San Francisco: Jossey-Bass.

Kendall, J. C., et al. (1986). *Strengthening experiential education within your institution.* Raleigh, NC: National Society for Experiential Education.

Klein, D. C. (1994). *Knowledge, technical skills, personal qualities, and related selection criteria for sport management internships* (Doctoral dissertation, University of New Mexico, 1994).

Kolb, D. A. (1984). *Experiential education: experience as the source of learning and development.* Englewood Cliffs, New Jersey: Prentice-Hall.

Konsky, C. (1976). Practical guide to development and administration of an internship program: issues, procedures, and forms. Normal, Illinois: Illinois State University. (ERIC Document Reproduction Service No. ED 249 539).

Lanese, L. D., and Fitch, W. C. (1983). How to get an intern off and running: a model. *Performance and Instruction Journal, 22,* (1), 30-32.

Li, M., Cobb, P., and Sawyer, L. (1994). Sport management graduate programs: characteristics of effectiveness. *Journal of Physical Education, Recreation and Dance, 65* (5), 57-61.

McCaffrey, J. T. (1979). Perceptions of satisfaction and dissatisfaction in the internship experience. *Public Administration Review, 39,* 241-244.

NASPE-NASSM Joint Task Force on Sport Management Curriculum and Accreditation. (1993). Standards for curriculum and voluntary accreditation of sport management education programs. *Journal of Sport Management, 7,* 159-170.

Parks, J. B., and Quain, R. J. (1986). Sport management survey: employment perspectives. *Journal of Physical Education, Recreation and Dance, 57* (4), 22-26.

Parks, J. B. (1991). Employment status of alumni of an undergraduate sport management program. *Journal of Sport Management, 5* (2), 100-110.

Parkhouse, B. L. (1987). Sport management curricula: current status and design implications for future development. *Journal of Sport Management, 1* (2), 93-115.

Parkhouse, B. L., and Ulrich, D. O. (1979). Sport management as a potential cross-discipline: a paradigm for theoretical development, scientific inquiry, and professional application. *Quest, 31* (2), 264-276.

Rex, R. G. (1961). A theory of the internship in professional training. (Doctoral dissertation, Michigan State University, 1961). *Dissertation Abstracts International, 23/02.*

Sheppard, J. (1987). Parallel and extended-day cooperative education programs. In D. C. Hunt (Ed.), *Fifty views of cooperative education* (5th ed.). Detroit: University of Detroit.

Shipton, J., and Steltenpohl, E. (1980). Self-directedness of the learner as a key to quality assurance. In M. T. Keeton (Ed.), *New directions for experiential learning: defining and assuring quality in experiential learning* (pp. 11-27). San Francisco: Jossey-Bass.

Sink, K. E. and Sari, I. F. (1984). Internships: a mutually beneficial relationship. *Performance and Instruction Journal, 23* (10), 23-25.

Stanton, T., and Ali, K. (1987). *The experienced hand: a student manual for making the most of an internship* (2nd ed.). Cranston, Rhode Island: Carroll Press.

Sutton, W. A. (1989). The role of internships in sport management curricula: a model for development. *Journal of Physical Education, Recreation and Dance, 60* (7), 20-24.

Taylor, M. S. (1988). Effects of college internships on individual participants. *Journal of Applied Psychology, 73* (3), 393-401.

Taylor, M. S. (1984). Strategies and sources in the student job search. *Journal of College Placement, 45* (1), 40-45.

Ulrich, D., and Parkhouse, B. L. (1982). An alumni-oriented approach to sport management curriculum design using performance ratings and a regression model. *Research Quarterly, 53*(1), 64-72.

U.S. Department of Education. (1991). *Cooperative education program: guide for the preparation of applications fiscal year 1992.* Washington, DC: U.S. Department of Education.

Verner, M. E. (1993). Developing professionalism through experiential learning. *Journal of Physical Education, Recreation and Dance, 64* (7), 45-52.

Verner, M. E. (1990, September). The internship advantage. *Fitness Management,* pp. 34-35.

Young, D. (1990). Mentoring and networking: perceptions by athletic administrators. *Journal of Sport Management, 4,* 71-79.

SUGGESTED READINGS

Cuneen, J., and Sidwell, M. J. (1994). *Sport management field experiences.* Morgantown, West Virginia: Fitness Information Technology, Inc.

Morgan, B. J. (Ed.) (1992). *Sport fan's connection.* Detroit: Gale Research, Inc.

Stanton, T., and Ali, K. (1987). *The experienced hand: a student manual for making the most of an internship* (2nd ed.). Cranston, Rhode Island: Carroll Press.

4

Research and Inquiry

Sue Inglis

In this chapter, you will become familiar with the following terms:

Organizational behavior	Deductive reasoning	Qualitative
Organizational theory	Inductive reasoning	Quantitative
Organizational science	Validity	Participant observation
Work-related functions	Content validity	Direct observation
Theory	Face validity	Focus groups
Internal consistency	Construct validity	Triangulation
External consistency	Predictive validity	Survey research
Scientific parsimony	Catalytic validity	Experimental designs
Generalizability	Reliability	Peer review
Verification	Paradigm	Human ethics

Overview

As long as sport has existed, so has its management. The citizens of Elis, Greece, for example, managed the Ancient Olympic Games (Harris, 1967; Kyle, 1987). In the nineteenth and twentieth centuries professional organizations emerged to manage amateur and professional sport (Hardy, 1986; Hardy and Berryman, 1983). The study of sport and its management, however, is a relatively new field in contemporary society and is character-ized by emerging specializations and refined ways of conducting inquiry and research. The purpose of inquiry and research is to understand sport management and to allow for a meaningful contri-bution to the practical side or "the doing" of the management of sport.

This chapter begins with an organizational be-havior and theory and work-related functions framework that is helpful in understanding relevant topics within sport management. A major portion of the chapter is concerned with knowledge development in the field of sport management. Within knowledge development the concepts of theory and deductive and inductive reasoning are pertinent. Also introduced are the foundations of sport management, including sport and business administration and areas such as sociology and psychology from which theory can be derived. The importance of working with theory as the field of sport management develops is a theme stressed throughout the chapter.

Various types of validity and reliability are introduced as important concepts in conducting research and in evaluating published research. Next, qualitative and quantitative approaches to research design are outlined. Within the qualitative approach, direct and participant observation, focus group and social action research, and within the quantitative approach survey research (the most popular design used in sport management research) and experimental designs are presented.

Guidelines for evaluating various types of published research are included. These should be helpful in identifying a variety of sources including books and peer-reviewed journal articles, as well as understanding key questions to ask in assessing published work.

Individuals engaged in research have an obligation to adhere to ethical guidelines. The reader is introduced to some of the ethical areas through practical examples of communication between the researcher and respondents. The final section provides ideas on new directions for research in sport management. Some of the best scholars in the field have contributed their ideas to this section.

Although the topics and concepts cannot be fully explored in one chapter, hopefully the chapter will serve as an introduction for the reader and inspire more reading and application of sound research in this field of study.

FRAMEWORK FOR SPORT MANAGEMENT

A useful way of depicting some of the topics in sport management follows the organizational behavior and organizational theory framework used in the management literature (Daft and Steers, 1986; Johns, 1992). **Organizational behavior** includes areas such as individual perceptions, indi-

vidual differences, learning styles, motivation, communication, leadership, decision making, conflict, and work group behavior. Organizational behavior helps us understand why people behave the way they do in their organizational life and is thought of as taking a micro perspective, that is, a concern with individuals and groups as basic components for analysis of work behavior. Questions such as "How do individual differences affect the way we perceive others?", "What factors are involved with motivating individuals to perform on the job?", "How do group norms affect work behavior?", "What leadership styles are most prominent in the managing of change?", and "How do conflict management strategies apply to sport management?" are the types of questions typical of the organizational behavior perspective.

Organizational theory includes the study of areas such as the design, technology, and environment of organizations. Organizational theory takes a macro perspective with the organization as the unit of analysis. Questions and areas include "What are useful ways of describing the structures of our sport organizations?", "What effect does size have on the design and function of the organization?", "What role does a turbulent environment have on the design and operations of our work sites?", and "How do similar organizations compete for scarce resources?"

Organizational behavior and organizational theory fit under the umbrella term of **organizational science.** Organizational behavior and theory provide a useful way of understanding organizational life. Introductions to a number of organizational behavior and theory topics are provided in this textbook. The other range of topics actively pursued by researchers and writers of sport management include **work-related functions** of marketing (including advertising, sponsorship, and promotions), facility management, finance, computer application in sport environments, product development, and case law and its application to sport environments. These are just a few examples of the range of topics of interest to scholars in sport management. The inquiry and research into these topics will advance the understanding of how sport is managed and can be most effectively delivered to the benefit of the participants, spectators and communities. How knowledge is acquired and, the meaning of theory is also important to understand and is the focus of the next section.

CONCEPT CHECK

An organizational science framework for understanding specializations within sport management includes organizational behavior with an emphasis on the individual and group, and organizational theory with an emphasis on the organization as the unit of analysis. A number of work-related functions (e.g., marketing, legal liability, and facility management) are also important areas within sport management.

DEVELOPING KNOWLEDGE

Developing knowledge through research and inquiry in the field of sport management is concerned with creating theory and testing theory. In simple terms a **theory** is an explanation of how concepts are related. For researchers, a theory will be a series of statements that capture what is presently known about related concepts and assumptions about the concepts. The theory may be derived from the "field," that is, where the theory is played out in practice and may be tested and explored in various types of studies. Managers use theories too. Although a manager may not formally write down the ideas he or she has about particular concepts, his or her behavior at work often reflects trial and error attempts related to different theories they hold.

Using theories in research helps in three important ways (Hamner and Organ, 1978). First, theories provide a practical way of organizing knowledge and therefore provide a structure for understanding. Second, a good theory will summarize or capture a great deal of information into a few critical propositions. Third, theories help direct future study and practice. Good theories help to explain real behavior in real organizational settings, thus good theory development is inextricably linked to practice. Daft and Steers (1986) offer the well known quote of Kurt Lewin, "There is nothing so practical as a good theory." This is true for sport management.

To evaluate what makes a good theory, Kaplan's (1964) framework can be used.

1. **Internal consistency.** Are the concepts and relationships between the concepts in the theory free from contradiction? Do the concepts and relationships make sense?
2. **External consistency.** Does the theory seem to make sense when viewed in relation to real life examples?
3. **Scientific parsimony.** Is the theory simple? Does the theory include only the main concepts that explain a phenomena?
4. **Generalizability.** Does the theory apply to a variety of situations? For example, if we have a theory about why there are so few women in management positions at a particular organization, does the theory hold true for other situations of few women in management?
5. **Verification.** Can we test the theory? For the theory to be useful, it would need to be tested or explored in a research setting.

When a theory satisfies these characteristics, it has greater meaning and usefulness to both researchers and managers.

The work of Thibault et al (1993) is a good example of a research program reflecting Kaplan's framework for good theory. These authors were interested in understanding how sport organizations develop strategies to anticipate change and environmental challenges. They developed a relatively simple and meaningful theory, of value to sport managers and theorists, that explains how different nonprofit amateur sport organizations develop different strategies and plans for their organizations. Their framework (theory) incorporated the two main dimensions of program attractiveness and competitive position with a number of imperatives in both dimensions. The imperatives for program attractiveness were "fundability," size of client base, volunteer appeal, and support group appeal. For competitive positions the imperatives were equipment costs and affiliation fees. When plotted on a matrix, these two dimensions produced four strategic types called *enhancers, innovators, refiners,* and *explorers.* In a subsequent study (Thibault et al, 1994), the theory was tested on a sample of 32 national sport organizations. The findings supported the theory and, most importantly, provided a contingency framework for understanding how different sport organizations employ differing strategies to cope with environmental variances.

DEDUCTIVE AND INDUCTIVE REASONING

Deductive and inductive reasoning are two ways of working with theories and knowledge development. They are illustrated in Figure 4-1. **Deductive reasoning** is a process of inquiry in which one works from general principles to specific instances or observations. For example, if a study worked from the principle that involving employees in decisions concerning scheduling of work will lead to lower absenteeism, then the study would be designed or a situation found in which employees are involved in these scheduling decisions. Ways of assessing and measuring if the reality of the employee involvement did in fact fit with the initial theory or principle would be developed. **Inductive reasoning** works the other way. Inquiry from a number of observations and situations leads to a general theory or principle. What principle is captured in the reality of the observations?

USING FOUNDATIONS AND THEORY IN SPORT MANAGEMENT

Good researchers have substantive knowledge in the area they are studying. Moving to more theoretical based research in sport management implies that for the phenomena under study the foundations and frameworks informing the research area will be used. Lambrecht (1991), drawing on Parkhouse's 1987 work, depicted sport management as originating from the two primary disciplines of sport studies and business administration. We can add to this depiction the parent disciplines such as anthropology, economics, sociology, political science, and psychology that inform sport studies and business administration. This is an important message within sport management. To develop substantive knowledge and theory in sport management, exposure to other areas and parent disciplines is necessary. From new insights and knowledges, combined with working knowledge and experience in sport management, greater understanding will be possible.

CONCEPT CHECK

Understanding theory is important in developing new knowledge that will be useful to the practice of sport management. Deductive and inductive reasoning represent ways we work with theory. The two major academic disciplines of sport studies and busi-

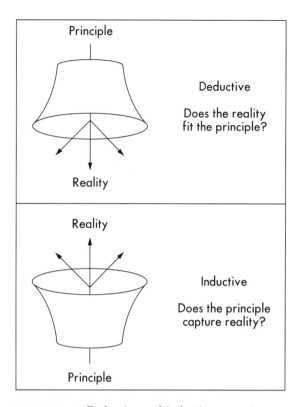

FIGURE 4-1   Deductive and inductive reasoning.

---

ness administration inform sport management. Additional disciplines (psychology and sociology as examples) also inform the field.

VALIDITY AND RELIABILITY

An understanding of the concepts of validity and reliability are important in developing knowledge and theory about sport management. **Validity** addresses the question, "To what degree does this measure or capture what it is intended to measure or capture?" A number of types of validity assist the researcher and reviewer of published work to determine how accurately the measure reflects reality. Researchers working in qualitative and quantitative designs approach validity from distinct perspectives (Lather, 1986). The types of validity defined below help in constructing research designs that validate social knowledge and give confidence to the trustworthiness of the data.

Content validity is the extent to which the items/variables (associated with survey research) represent the subject matter. A "panel of experts" is often used to assess the content validity of items in a questionnaire.

Face validity is the term used to assess if the results seem logical or predictable (Fletcher and Bowers, 1991). In qualitative designs, member-checks (Guba and Lincoln, 1981; Reason and Rowan, 1981) are used. Member-checks involve the participants of the research reviewing the tentative results, with subsequent refinements made in light of these reactions. **Construct validity** is the extent to which a measure reflects a specific psychological trait. Similar to content validity, experts may be used to assess the conceptual appropriateness of measures. Statistical analysis is also used.

Predictive validity suggests that results from one measure can be verified by comparing them with another (Fletcher and Bowers, 1991). For example, if an advertising campaign designed to solicit inquiries about season ticket sales does in fact generate a high number of inquiries, the advertising campaign could be considered to have high predictive validity. **Catalytic validity** as described by Lather (1986) is that in which individuals who have been part of the research develop self-understanding and self-determination through the research process. This is a term specific to qualitative methodology.

Reliability addresses the question, "To what degree will the measure be consistent over time?" Reliability in research can be improved by taking care in developing questions and instructions that will be used in interviews, focus groups, surveys, or experiments. Questions need to be pretested with a small group before the actual research is conducted. Interviewers must be well trained. A common measure of estimating internal consistency reliability used in survey research is on the basis of a coefficient alpha (Nunnally, 1970). Nunnally stresses the importance of assessing reliability and outlines various ways reliability can be assessed. Reliability coefficients of 0.70 or higher for subscale or item measures are considered satisfactory; if, however, decisions are to be made with respect to specific scores, a reliability of 0.90 is considered minimal and 0.95, desirable (Nunnally, 1978).

The analogy of a target to measures of validity and reliability from Babbie (1992) is helpful in understanding these important concepts (Figure 4-2).

In the first square the results are reliable because they hit the target in the same place. The problem is, the results are off the mark and therefore not valid. The second square is valid because the target is being hit closer to the center but lacks consistency. Finally, the ideal situation of validity and reliability—on the mark—as shown in the third square.

A research study by Hums and Chelladurai (1994), which examined fairness around allocation of resources in intercollegiate athletics, was "on the mark" in terms of its reported validity and reliability. The face and construct validity of the instrument, which was developed to assess distributive justice, was based on a panel of experts' feedback on the instrument's relevance, clearness, and conciseness in measuring distributive justice. Additionally, the internal consistency estimates and test, retest reliability estimates were substantial and added empirical support to the instrument.

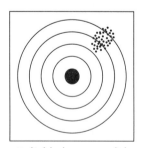
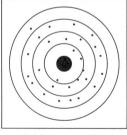
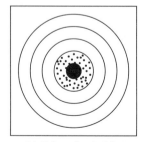

Reliable but not valid   Valid but not reliable   Valid *and* reliable

FIGURE 4-2   Measures of validity and reliability. From Babbie, E. R. (1992). *The practice of social research* (6th ed). Belmont, California: Wadsworth.

QUALITATIVE AND QUANTITATIVE PARADIGMS

In its simplest form our "ways of knowing" of inquiry through research can be thought of as qualitative and quantitative paradigms. The term **paradigm** refers to a way of conceptualizing the theoretical perspective in which we look at the world (Bogden and Knopp Biklen, 1982). Table 4-1 presents selected characteristics of qualitative and quantitative paradigms. Table 4-1 is useful in acquiring an initial understanding of some of the differences underlying the two perspectives. The qualitative-quantitative perspective is a useful way of introducing readers to designs and underlying philosophies.

Qualitative methodologies involve exploration of situations that are lived or observed in everyday life. Interaction with people who are closely connected to the phenomena under study provide rich insights into peoples' conditions, behavior, and perceptions.

Quantitative methodologies involve specifically identified variables that are studied under rigorous test conditions. The scientific method is the standard model followed when conducting empirical research. The steps involved in the scientific method are (1) interest through observation, (2) framing the research question, (3) hypothesis development, (4) experimentation, and (5) analysis and conclusions from research.

QUALITATIVE

Morse (1994) describes qualitative processes as following an analytical scheme that includes *comprehending* what is being observed or talked about, *synthesizing* to make generalized statements about the individuals or things, *theorizing* by offering explanations that connect the data to real world experiences, and *recontextualizing* by thinking about the theory in different settings.

Included in the qualitative paradigm are the research designs of participant observation and direct observation. As outlined by Johns (1992), in **participant observation** the researcher is a functioning member of the group being studied. When the researcher observes, but is not actually involved in the activity, it is called **direct observation.** Mintzberg's classic study of the 1970s, in which he spent a week with each of five male executives assessing what types of activities and

roles the managers were actually involved in, is a good example of direct observation. The results of this direct observational method helped to dispel some of the myths of what managers' activities were thought to be like (Mintzberg, 1975).

A more recent example of direct observation of leaders and work is found in the diary studies of Helgesen (1990) in which, like Mintzberg, she spent time with four top executives. Through this research an exploration of how female leaders make decisions, structure their companies, and work with employees and communities was revealed. Both examples, in their own right, have provided rich information about leaders at work.

Focus groups are another example of qualitative research design for use in sport management (Inglis, 1992). **Focus groups** are moderated discussion groups of 5 to 10 people who are brought together on the basis of some important interest or similarity. Focus groups can be used in a variety of ways. These groups are useful to the research process when developing survey or interview questions (Morgan, 1988), as well as in assisting with the interpretation of survey results. In advertising planning cycles, Fletcher and Bowers (1991) suggest focus group research is important in the stages of the research that ask the questions, "Where could we be?" and "How could we get there?" In-depth input from potential consumers is important.

As the qualitative paradigm seeks to work with people to reach new meanings, social action and change can be a desired outcome. This critical social action seeks to empower the participants. Lather (1986) wrote of "research as praxis," that is, research that is committed to building a more just society by altering maldistribution of power, resources, and services. Within sport management research, aspects of Vail's (1992) work on community delivery systems reflects a social action perspective. In this research, a partnership involving a university researcher and a parks and recreation employee brought representatives of various community sport organizations together to assess the community's sport needs, solutions, roles various partners could play, and structures to facilitate desired change. Background data were collected by means of a survey mailed to 400 individuals and groups in the community. This was followed by focus groups, extensive retreat workshops, and planning sessions, which resulted in a collective

TABLE 4-1   *Selected characteristics of qualitative and quantitative paradigms*

Selected Characteristics	Qualitative	Quantitative	
		Survey Research	Experimental
Goal	Discovering the experience Developing theory	Show relationships Hypothesis testing	Hypothesis testing Prediction
Research site	Participants' locale, close to natural location as possible	Mail	Researchers' locale Laboratory or other experiment set-up
Data			
Collection method	Observation, interviewing	Participant responses	Experiments using scientific method
Using	Interview guides, probes	Surveys	
From	Informants, participants	Respondents	Testing protocol
Sources	Field notes, personal documents, official documents, photographs		Subjects
Variables	Not controlled	Controlled	Controlled
Empiricism	Words as the information		Numbers as the information
Analysis	Content of the experience	Descriptive and/or predictive statistics Bounded by study	
Findings based on	Inference as results emerge from coherent whole, insight, intuition	Survey results	Direct product of observable processes
Theory	Emerges from data to support previous theory or to build new theory	Supported or not supported by data, based on probabilistic model, a priori set alpha level of significance	
Phrases and designs associated with approach	Action research, grounded theory, field work, focus groups, case studies, participant observation, naturalistic	Social survey, descriptive, correlational	Experiment, positivist, statistical

Modified from Bogdan and Knopp Biklen (1982). *Qualitative research for education: an introduction ot theory and methods.* Boston: Allyn and Bacon, Inc. and Morse, J.M. (Ed). (1994). *Critical issues in qualitative research methods.* Thousand Oaks, California: Sage Publications.

vision and structure to more effectively deliver community sport. Change in how sport is delivered and how the sport-related resources are used is occurring in this specific community (Vail, 1992). This research is also a good example of how research designs from qualitative and quantitative paradigms can be effectively used to address research questions. This **triangulation** includes multiple data sources, methods and theoretical schemes (Lather, 1986), and can move the researcher closer to establishing the trustworthiness of the data. Triangulation can be extremely beneficial if the designs are well suited to the questions being raised and the outcomes desired.

SURVEY RESEARCH

Survey research has as its goal the describing and exploring of variables, relationships between variables, and perceptions as offered by individuals through the completion of questionnaires. These goals and other characteristics place survey research primarily within the quantitative paradigm. Survey research is the most extensive research design used in sport management (Olafson, 1990; Paton, 1987). When relationships between variables are studied, we must be careful to note that the correlation that may be found does not imply causation. For example, arena managers may be found to be satisfied with their work and may be found to be in good health. It cannot be suggested from these results that satisfaction causes good health.

Conducting good survey research, like other types of research, requires knowledge of the subject matter and theoretical foundations, as well as knowledge about the design and conduct of the survey, coding of the survey, and analysis. The analysis often requires computers. The type of statistical analysis required will depend on the research question, the design, and response format of the survey. Some research questions involve simple yet meaningful analysis, whereas others involve more complex analysis. Survey research should not be conducted unless the individuals involved have the knowledge, expertise, and time, and the research question has been carefully developed.

EXPERIMENTAL DESIGNS

Experimental designs are placed in the quantitative paradigm. Experimental designs allow for the manipulation of variables under closely controlled laboratory-like settings. In these settings issues of causation and prediction can be addressed. Although experimental research is conducted in many management environments, sport management has not, to any great extent, utilized this research design. Hopefully, this will soon change because there are appropriate areas in which experimental research designs would make a meaningful contribution to the understanding and practice of sport management.

For example, consider a closely controlled laboratory setting in which sport managers are engaged with consumers in simulated decision-making activities involving event ticket pricing, augmented product pricing, and consumer behavior. Similarly, consider the use of a computer program and conditions in which individuals (subjects) are involved in decisions about strategies, expenditures, or organizational crises. These testing conditions would allow the researcher to replicate an organization's environment while controlling for time and access to information factors. Results of these types of experiments would provide valuable information to sport managers and contribute to the theoretical understanding of the concepts under study.

CONCEPT CHECK

The challenge to sport management researchers is to understand qualitative and quantitative research designs. Knowledge derived from qualitative and quantitative inquiry and designs needs to be conveyed in useful ways to practitioners in sport management environments.

EVALUATING PUBLISHED RESEARCH

There are a number of aspects to consider when evaluating published research. Published research takes a variety of forms including the following:

- Books written by one or more authors
- Books edited by one or more individuals, which include chapters written by a variety of contributors (of which this textbook is an example)
- Peer-reviewed journal articles by one or more authors
- Nonpeer-reviewed journal articles by one or more authors

- Abstracts and proceedings of conferences
- Occasional paper series published or circulated by the agencies involved in the production, including government documents and papers from a university
- Popular magazines

There is no definitive order to this list in terms of quality of writing, scholarly rigor, or ability to make a useful contribution to the knowledge base, or to communicate to selected audiences. **Peer-reviewed** journal articles are generally considered to "carry more weight" in terms of scholarly writing and research. A brief description of the process by which an article is published demonstrates the nature of the peer-review process. Manuscripts submitted to the editor of the journal, the *Journal of Sport Management,* for instance, are sent to three reviewers who remain anonymous. These reviewers are from an editorial board, selected for their proven ability in research and writing abilities, to critically yet fairly evaluate the work of their peers. It is not unusual for manuscripts to be rejected for publication (often the acceptance rate is approximately 40% of all manuscripts submitted for review) or to be accepted with major or minor revisions. Once manuscripts are accepted for publication, they appear as articles in the journal. Nonpeer-reviewed writings, such as books, do not go through the same process. The difference between the rigor exposed to manuscripts submitted to peer-reviewed journals and other journals and books should be clear. Even though not anyone can write a book—it is often easier to publish a nonpeer-reviewed abstract, manuscript, or book than a peer-reviewed manuscript.

Some questions to keep in mind when evaluating published research are "What is the source of the information?" "Have the possibilities of where good information may be found been exhausted?", and "Have a variety of sources been used?"

What follows are some guiding questions that need to be answered as published research is reviewed. The published research is classified under research studies, concept pieces, and prescriptive writings.

If the work is the result of a research study: What research question was addressed? What theoretical perspectives inform the work? Who were the subjects/respondents? How was the sample drawn and described? How were the data collected? What methodology(ies) were employed? What type of analysis was included? What key results were reported? How were the results linked to previous studies or theory? Were there recommendations for future research? Were there recommendations for program change or policy development?

If the work is a "concept piece," that is, outlining a concept that is new or derived from another field of study that could be applied to sport management environments: What issue was addressed? What theoretical perspectives informed the work? What links to sport management were made? Was there a clear indication of how the concept is relevant to sport management and how it could be of value to the field?

If the work is prescriptive, that is, suggesting how a particular function or area of sport management should be conducted: What was the topic under discussion? Was there support from other areas for this proposed application or use in sport management environments? Was it communicated clearly?

Questions applicable to all three types of work within inquiry and research in sport management (research studies, conceptual writing, and prescriptive) include: Were assessments and measures of validity and reliability indicated? What is the contribution of this work to the study and understanding of sport management? Does the work make a contribution to your topic of inquiry, your position, or line of thinking?

ETHICS IN INQUIRY AND RESEARCH

Individuals engaged in research have an obligation to conduct the research within ethical guidelines and to report the research accurately. Most institutions have human ethics committees in place that review all research proposals. Application for **human ethics** approval generally involves assurance that the project is well planned, the purpose of the research is clear, and the involvement level of subjects or respondents is detailed. How subjects or respondents are told about their involvement with the research, how they will be treated throughout the duration of their involvement with the research, and how they will be told of their right to withdraw at any time is all part of the proposal for ethics approval. The experience level of the researcher(s) is often included in submissions.

Ethics review committees work to ensure the following:

1. Subjects or respondents enter research projects voluntarily and understand the nature of the risks involved.
2. A plan for obtaining informed consent is in place.
3. If necessary, subjects or respondents will be debriefed at the end of the research project.

Cover letters for surveys and consent forms for participants in focus group research are two common areas within sport management research where good communication between the researcher and respondents or subjects is important. Johns (1992) reminds us that ethical research has a practical side as well. For good research, cooperation between the researcher and subject is necessary. Cooperation is easier to achieve and maintain when people feel ethical questions are being addressed.

The box below shows two examples of how researchers communicate with subjects as respondents in survey research (*1a*) and as key informants in focus group research (*1b*).

The interaction between researcher and respondent is much greater with qualitative methodologies. As such, it is important to ensure that the respondent feels comfortable disengaging at any time during the research and that time is taken to properly debrief after individual sessions and at the completion of the project.

Let us return to our previous example of Vail's work (1992) of the planned partnership between researchers and community sport associations in facilitating desired change. Given the close working relationship between the researcher and community participants, clear communication of the role and expectations of both parties was of extreme importance. Sensitivity on the part of the researchers was necessary to respect the role of the

---

Examples of 1(a) informing subjects in survey research and 1(b) as key informants in focus group research

1(a) Excerpts from cover letters in survey research

You may be assured of complete confidentiality. Your name will not be placed on the survey. Published and reported results will not identify individuals or organizations, and any discussion will be based on group data.

All individual results are confidential and will only be examined by the researchers. Your survey has an identification number for mailing purposes only so your name can be checked off the mailing list when your questionnaire is returned. Your name will not be placed on the survey.

Please do not hesitate to contact us if you have any questions. Thank you for your assistance.

1(b) Excerpt from key informant consent form in focus group research

This session is part of a research project and information will be used to help interpret results of the survey you previously completed. Tape recorders and flip charts will be used. Excerpts from the session will be used for teaching and research presentations and publications. Individual names will **NOT** be directly associated with any statements. We respect that participants have the right to withdraw at any time during the session.

Your feedback on this session, or additional comments you wish to make, are welcome. Please write. Thank you for helping.

Release and agreement by participant

I, _____, have read the above, and I am willing to participate in the session and permit use of the information gathered during the session for the purposes outlined.

Signed: _____ Date: _____

Based on research by Sue Inglis, 1993.

research participants and community members, and to ensure difficulties encountered (for example, differing opinions concerning desired changes) in the process of planning for change were handled professionally.

The close interaction between researcher and participant often requires multiple ways of disengaging from the research process. For example, debriefing sessions involving individual and group members and continued access by the participant to the researcher are commonly used to assist both parties in moving away from the project. These are some of the challenges unique to qualitative methodologies in sport management research.

NEW DIRECTIONS

In developing this section a number of scholars in sport management were contacted.* The purpose was to tap the expertise of others so their ideas on future directions and skills needed could be incorporated in this section. The first question was, "What are some of the areas for research in sport management that should be explored?" The responses offer readers a sense of the scope for future directions. A number of individuals responded, "The field is wide open—there are so many areas and topics to be studied!" Looking at these ideas for future research reinforces the idea that bringing in ideas from other disciplines and experiences opens up tremendous opportunities for study. In doing so, a leadership role is taken in studying sport management in such a way as to link sport in a meaningful way to changing society.

New directions in sport management need to delve into a variety of sport-related environments. Such settings could include sporting good retailers and manufacturers, major corporations that are involved in the sport industry, single and multisport community sport, and amateur and professional sport organizations. Traditionally, sport management research has clustered around intercollegiate athletics. Although intercollegiate athletics play important roles and are of obvious interest to researchers (Paton, 1987), there are important issues in all sport-related environments that could benefit from researchers' attention.

With the call made for sport management to work from theoretical perspectives (Olafson, 1990; Paton, 1987; Slack, 1993), we can look to the areas of business administration, higher education, and public policy as examples of areas that have advanced. These areas, like sport management, are informed by parent disciplines such as sociology, anthropology, economics, political science, and psychology.† Using the framework of organizational behavior and organizational theory and work-related functions introduced earlier in the chapter, a selection of topic areas provided by individuals currently contributing to sport management are as follows:

Organizational behavior

Policy as it affects people

Leadership—transformational, gender, and management

Ethics and values

Decision-making theory

Conflict management

Consumer behavior

Cultural analysis of people and work

Personnel evaluation

Impact of sport on community well-being

Team building

Empowerment

Accountability in sport delivery systems

Organizational theory

Community sport delivery models

Interorganizational links

Economic impact of participation and entertainment sport

Organizational strategy

Design of sport organizations

Policy as it affects structures and products

Comparative studies of sport organizations and other organizations

*Recognition and appreciation are extended to the following sport management scholars who contributed to the ideas expressed in this section: Dr. Bob Boucher, University of Windsor; Dr. Laurence Chalip, Griffith University; Dr. Wendy Frisby, University of British Columbia; Dr. Janet Parks, Bowling Green State University; Dr. Trevor Slack, University of Alberta; Dr. Dave Stotlar, University of Northern Colorado; Dr. Jim Weese, University of Windsor; and Dr. Earle F. Zeigler, Professor Emeritus, University of Western Ontario.
Soucie (1994) provides a current overview of the types of doctoral dissertation topics in administration 1949-1993 as well as the types of articles published in the *Journal of Sport Management* 1987–1993.

Work-related functions/issues
International legal issues
Affects of advertising in sport
International comparative marketing mixes
Increasing attendance at games
Getting more women involved in sport
Increasing job satisfaction

Additional ideas for future research in sport management are found in the Dr. Earle F. Zeigler addresses given at the annual North American Society for Sport Management conference. The importance of scholars in sport management working with the practitioner is a recurring theme. A few ideas from recent lectures are noted here. DeSensi (1994) emphasized and provided a way of understanding and moving from a monocultural to a multicultural organization that would be respectful of full integration of individual and cultural diversity. Understanding and moving toward multicultural organizations involves social action. These she suggests are important directions for sport management. Chelladurai (1992) stressed the importance of considering a broad definition of sport that involves the aspects of providing human services as well as entertainment. This will help in the understanding of the many facets of sport management. Chelladurai also emphasized the need for those in academia and practice to work together so that what is studied makes a contribution to practice. Parks (1992) stressed the importance of bridging the gap between the scholar and the practitioner. Frameworks, she argued, like Boyer's discovery, integration, teaching, and application help us understand the practical.

The second question asked of scholars in the field was "What are the skills and abilities necessary for students (and scholars) to acquire for competence in conducting research in sport management?" It is important to understand previous trails of research and how we would proceed to discover new pathways. The ideas expressed in this section serve as a self-check to see where efforts need to be made to acquire new skills.

Reading, reading, and more reading is basic to conducting good research. Reading of field-related journals as well as journals from other disciplines is essential. Reading about previous research and reading to understand methodologies that will be most appropriate to the research being conducted, and reading from sources outside of North America is important to develop our understandings and knowledge bases from broad perspectives.

Related to reading are problem-solving skills. Integration and imagination are important to extend research agendas beyond the obvious. Our present, obvious way of conducting research in sport management is to use survey design and offer a description of some phenomena. These types of scholarly activity are important, but they are not enough. There is a need to understand what sport managers identify as critical management problems, and there is a need to develop theory based understandings to these problems. Returning for example, to Thibault et al (1993, 1994) we see important insight about how sport organizations develop strategies through the development of the theory and testing of the theory. The conceptual framework will have important implications for sport managers who need to understand why, given particular environmental and organizational characteristics, various types of strategies are employed. The framework is also applicable to other types of sport organizations.

We need to be able to find the links and to access various information sources to learn to make decisions about critical concepts and what is worth knowing. Included in this would be the ability to draw from a variety of literature sources and to take meaningful directions for new research that could make a contribution to sport management as well as to the parent disciplines. The research questions must, where appropriate, have relevance to the practice of management. Learning to formulate realistic research questions is a skill that requires constant refining.

Access to data bases including sport management and data bases from related fields and knowing how to conduct computerized searches is critical. These skills are related to other computer skills that aid the research process tremendously. Both qualitative and quantitative paradigms utilize computers in data entry and analysis.*

---

*For example, the SPSS/PC+ (Statistical Package for the Social Science/Personal Computer enhanced edition) is a commonly used statistical package for quantitative analysis, and the NUD-IST (Nonnumerical, Unstructured Data Indexing, Searching and Theorizing) software is available for qualitative analysis.

Communication skills include good writing as well as the ability to identify and deliver messages in the most effective ways. When the results of our work are communicated, ways that satisfy the academic journal writing as well as other audiences, including classroom situations and practitioners, should be included. Some of the results of our work can lead to policy development and program change.

To summarize, the skills needed to conduct and evaluate good research in sport management that have been introduced in this chapter are understanding theory development and methodologies, the ability to evaluate published research, the ability to read and develop meaningful research questions, computer skills, the ability to conduct the research, and the ability to impart new knowledge to both scholars and sport managers.

CONCEPT CHECK

A variety of sources of published research on sport management are available. Questions to evaluate the written work are helpful in assessing the merits of the work and the meaning to the individual. Individuals conducting sport management research must adhere to ethical guidelines. New directions for research and inquiry in sport management include a variety of areas, and a number of skills are necessary to conduct good research.

SUMMARY

1. A framework that helps us think about the area of sport management includes organizational behavior, organizational theory, and work-related functions such as marketing and legal issues.
2. Inquiry and research in sport management are based on theory development and testing.
3. Deductive and inductive reasoning are used in knowledge development.
4. The foundations of sport management include sport studies and business administration. The foundation is further informed by parent disciplines such as psychology and sociology.
5. Validity and reliability are important concepts in conducting research.
6. Research can be viewed from qualitative and quantitative approaches. Examples of a qualitative approach include focus groups, participant observation, and social action research. Examples of a quantitative approach include survey research, which is the most common design used in sport management research and experimental designs.
7. Of the number of published sources of sport management writing, peer-review journal articles have the most rigorous review process.
8. Ethical considerations are important in conducting research.
9. The topics for future research are endless. The researcher must possess a number of important skills to conduct meaningful research.
10. Where appropriate, the research should be informed by theory.
11. The research conducted in sport management should make a valuable contribution to understanding and improving the practice of sport management.

CASE STUDY

The marketing department of a semiprofessional baseball club approaches a sport management program. The club is interested in having research conducted to answer the following questions:

1. *Who is coming to the games?*
2. *What are the reasons the fans are coming to the games?*
3. *What aspects of the game could be changed to make the game more attractive for the fans?*

The marketing director is interested in other questions that may provide useful information. He or she is also interested in the various designs and research considerations that would be used to address the questions. Before contracting for this research, the baseball club needs a two-page statement by interested individuals or groups. Considering the information contained in this chapter, what would some of the important parts of the statement for the submission to the marketing director be?

REVIEW QUESTIONS AND ISSUES

1. Outline and discuss an example of Kurt Lewin's statement, "There is nothing so prac-

tical as a good theory." The example should
be from a sport management environment.
2. Select an article from the *Journal of Sport
Management*. Decide if the article represents a
research study or a concept piece. Use the
guide questions found on p. 56 to guide discussion of the article.
3. Outline an experiment that could be designed
to test the hypothesis that attention to customer service factors will have an effect on
customer satisfaction.
4. An athletic director at University *X* com-
plains, "Every year I get requests from across
the country to complete surveys. Although I
am sure they are well-meaning studies, I
never see any changes to the problems facing
intercollegiate athletics." Discuss.

REFERENCES

Babbie, E. R. (1992). *The practice of social research* (6th ed.).
Belmont, California: Wadsworth.

Bogdan, R. C. and Knopp Biklen, S. (1982). *Qualitative research for education: an introduction to theory and methods.*
Boston: Allyn and Bacon.

Chelladurai, P. (1992). Sport management: opportunities and
obstacles. *Journal of Sport Management. 6*(3), 215-219.

DeSensi, J. (1994). Multiculturalism as an issue in sport
management. *Journal of Sport Management. 8*(1) 63-74.

Daft, R. C. and Steers, R. M. (1986). *Organizations: a micro/
macro approach.* Glenview, Illinois: Scott, Foresman.

Fletcher, A. D. and Bowers, T. A. (1991). *Fundamentals of
advertising research* (4th ed.). Belmont, California: Wadsworth.

Guba, E. G. (Ed.). (1990). *The paradigm dialog.* Newbury Park:
Sage Publications.

Guba, E. G. and Lincoln, Y. (1981). *Effective evaluation.* San
Francisco: Jossey Bass.

Hamner, W. C. and Organ, D. (1978). *Organizational behavior:
an applied psychological approach.* Dallas: BPI.

Hardy, S. H. and Berryman, J. W. (1983). A historical view of
the governance issue. In J. Frey (Ed.), *The governance of
intercollegiate athletics* (pp. 15-28). New York: Leisure Press.

Hardy, S. (1986). Entrepreneurs, organizations, and the sport
marketplace: subjects in search of historians. *Journal of
Sport History, 13*(1), 14-33.

Harris, H. A. (1967). *Greek athletes and athletics.* Indiana:
Indiana University Press.

Helgesen, S. (1990). *The female advantage: women's ways of
leadership.* New York: Doubleday.

Hums, M. A., and Chelladurai, P. (1994). Distributive justice
in intercollegiate athletics: development of an instrument.
Journal of Sport Management, 8(3), 190-199.

Inglis, S. (1992). Focus groups as a useful qualitative methodology in sport management. *Journal of Sport Management, 6*(3), 173-178.

Johns, G. (1992). *Organizational behavior: understanding life at
work* (3rd ed.). New York: HarperCollins.

Kaplan, A. (1964). The conduct of inquiry. San Francisco:
Chandler.

Lambrecht, K. (1991). Research, theory and practice. In
B. Parkhouse (Ed.), *The management of sport: its foundation
and application* (pp. 28-29). St. Louis: Mosby.

Kyle, D. G. (1987). *Athletics in ancient Athens.* Leiden: E. J. Brill.

Lather, P. (1986). Issues of validity in openly ideological
research: between a rock and a soft place. *Interchange.* Vol.
17 No.4 63-84.

Mintzberg, H. (1975). The manager's job: Folklore and fact,
Harvard Business Review, 53 (4), 49-61.

Morgan, D. L. (1988). *Focus groups as qualitative research.*
Newbury Park, California: Sage Publications.

Morse, J. M. (Ed.). (1994). *Critical issues in qualitative research
methods.* Thousand Oaks, California: Sage Publications.

Nunnally, J. C. (1970). *Introduction to psychological measurement.* New York: McGraw-Hill.

Nunnally, J. C. (1978). *Psychometric theory* (2nd ed). New
York: McGraw-Hill.

Olafson, G. (1990). Research design in sport management:
what's missing, what's needed? *Journal of Sport Management, 4*(2), 102-120.

Paton, G. (1987). Sport management research–what progress
has been made? *Journal of Sport Management, 1*(1), 25-31.

Parkhouse, B. (1987). Sport management curricula: current
status and design implications for future development.
Journal of Sport Management, 1(2), 93-115.

Parks, J. B. (1992). The other "bottom line" in sport management. *Journal of Sport Management, 6*(3), 220-229.

Reason, P., and Rowan, J. (1981). Issues of validity in new
paradigm research. In P. Reason and J. Rowan (Eds.),
Human inquiry: a sourcebook of new paradigm research
(pp. 239-262). New York: John Wiley.

Slack, T. (1993). Morgan and the metaphors: implications for
sport management research. *Journal of Sport Management,
7*(3), 189-193.

Soucie, D. (1994). Management theory and practice. In E. F.
Zeigler (Ed.), *Physical education and kinesiology in North
America professional and scholarly foundations* (279-313).
Champaign, Illinois: Stipes.

Thibault, L., Slack, T., and Hinings, B. (1993). A framework
for the analysis of strategy in nonprofit sport organizations. *Journal of Sport Management, 7*(1), 25-43.

Thibault, L., Slack, T., and Hinings, B. (1994). Strategic planning
for nonprofit sport organizations: empirical verification of a
framework. *Journal of Sport Management, 8*(3), 218-233.

Vail, S. (1992). Toward improving sport delivery: a community perspective. *Journal of Applied Recreation Research,
17*(3), 217-233.

SUGGESTED READINGS

Babbie, E. R. (1992). The practice of social research (6th ed). Belmont, California: Wadsworth.

Slack, T. (1993). Morgan and the metaphors: implications for sport management research. *Journal of Sport Management, 7*(3), 189-193.

Soucie, D. (1994). Management theory and practice. In E. F. Zeigler (Ed.) *Physical education and kinesiology in North America professional and scholarly foundations* (pp. 279-313). Champaign, Illinois: Stipes.

RELATED JOURNALS

Administrative Science Quarterly
European Journal for Sport Management
International Studies of Management and Organization
Journal of Business Communications
Journal of Business Research
Journal of Business Strategy
Journal of Consumer Research
Journal of Management Studies
Journal of Marketing
Journal of Marketing Research
Journal of Organizational Behavior
Journal of Sport Management
Organizational Behavior and Human Decision Processes
Organizational Studies
The Academy of Management Review
Quest

PART II

Human Resource Management

CHAPTER 5

Organizational Theory and the Study of Sport

Trevor Slack and John Amis

In this chapter, you will become familiar with the following terms:

Computer assisted
  manufacturing
Advanced information
  technology
Organizational effectiveness
Organizational structure
Goal attainment approach
Systems resource approach
Internal process approach
Strategic constituents approach
Complexity
Formalization
Centralization
Horizontal differentiation
Vertical differentiation
Spatial differentiation
Configurations
Design-types
Simple structure
Machine bureaucracy
Professional bureaucracy
Divisionalized form
Adhocracy

Operating core
Strategic apex
Middle line
Technostructure
Support staff
Growth strategy
Defensive strategy
Stability strategy
Combination strategy
Diversification
Integration
Turnaround strategy
General environment
Economic environment
Sociocultural environment
Task environment
Domain
Continuous process production
Unit production
Mass production
Routine technology
Craft technology
Engineering technologies

Nonroutine technology
Pooled interdependence
Sequential interdependence
Reciprocal interdependence
Computer integrated
  manufacturing
Organizational size
Decentralization
Legitimate power
Reward power
Coercive power
Referent power
Expert power
Political activity
Programmed decisions
Nonprogrammed decisions
Rational model
Bounded rationality
Rational model of decision
  making
Organizational change

Overview

The sport industry in North America is made up of a wide variety of organizations. There are those such as Reebok and the Atlanta Falcons, whose main purpose is to make a profit for their owners and shareholders. There are others, such as the United States Cycling Federation and Basketball Canada, that are referred to as not-for-profit or voluntary organizations whose purpose is to provide a service to their members. Any money generated is used to further the goals of the organization.

In some cases a sport organization may be part of a larger body such as a state or municipal government. Its actions are, in part, established and controlled by the larger agency. Other sport organizations, such as the International Olympic Committee (IOC) and the National Collegiate Athletic Association (NCAA), operate in a highly autonomous manner. Sport organizations such as Nike, the athletic footwear company, and Brunswick, which is involved in operating bowling alleys and power boat manufacturing, employ thousands of people and operate with detailed policies and procedures. By contrast a local sporting goods store or municipal swimming pool has few employees and operates relatively informally. Some organizations in the sport industry use advanced microelectronic technology such as **computer assisted manufacturing** (CAM) or **advanced information technology** (AIT). Huffy, for example, uses CAM in the manufacture of its bicycles. On the other hand, in organizations that build custom-designed sports equipment, such as handmade skates or specialized bicycles, workers use the skills they have acquired over many years.

The field of organization theory is designed to help us understand why sport organizations such as those just mentioned are structured and operate in different ways. It helps us understand why large sport organizations have different structures than small ones; why sport manufacturing organizations operate in a different way than those in the service sector; and why voluntary sport organizations may pursue different strategies than those designed to make a profit. Organization theory also helps us understand how processes such as change and decision making can be managed. In short, organization theory can make us better managers by providing an understanding of the way sport organizations are structured and operated.

In this chapter we explore some of the central issues in organization theory. We begin by looking at what many sport managers consider the most important issue to address—effectiveness. We look at what constitutes an effective organization and discuss the different models that have been used to explain **organizational effectiveness**. One of the key factors that influences the effectiveness of a sport organization is whether it has an appropriate structure and design. In the next two sections of the chapter we discuss these issues. We examine major concepts used to explain **organizational structure** and look at how these concepts can be used to understand the different designs we see in sport industry organizations.

One main premise of organization theory is that the structure of an organization is influenced by the context in which it operates. To be effective there must be a fit between the structure of sport organization and the pressures that are placed on it by contextual factors such as strategy, size, environment, and technology. Consequently, the impact that each of these factors, or contingencies as they are sometimes called, can have on a sport organization's structure are examined. The role that power and politics, noncontingent factors, can have on the structure of an organization are also explored. In the final part of the chapter we look briefly at two of the more common organizational processes, decision making and change.

EFFECTIVENESS IN SPORT ORGANIZATIONS

All organizations exist to achieve a particular goal or set of goals. It may be pursuing a national championship, making a profit, or developing young athletes. The ultimate goal of most professional sport organizations is to win the major championship in their sport. Yet each season, only one team can achieve this goal. Does this mean that all the other clubs are ineffective? The Colorado Rockies set various attendance records in 1993, the club's expansion year, but were never in contention for the National League playoffs. Was the franchise effective? Effectiveness, quite clearly, is a difficult concept to define and measure. As a result, researchers have come up with various approaches in an attempt to explain this aspect of organizations. Four of these, the **goal attainment, systems resource, internal process,** and

strategic constituents approaches, are briefly outlined below.

Goal attainment approach

The goal attainment approach is based on the identification of primary goals and how well an organization attains or makes progress toward them (Etzioni, 1964). An organization that achieves its goals is seen as more effective than one that does not. It is this approach that has been used most extensively in evaluating the effectiveness of sport organizations (see Frisby, 1986; Chelladurai, 1987). For this approach to be workable there must be a consensus among members of the organization on the goals that are to be pursued. In addition, there must be a small enough number of goals to be manageable.

Despite its simplicity as an easy-to-implement measure of organizational effectiveness, the goal attainment approach is, in a number of ways, problematic. First, in any sport organization, there are often multiple and conflicting goals being pursued. For example, the decision by the Toronto Blue Jays to release highly rated and expensive pitcher David Cone at the end of the 1992 World Series winning season was motivated by the goal of improving financial performance, not by the objective of giving the club the best possible chance of repeating its World Series victory the following season. A second problem concerns the vagueness of some of a sport organization's goals. For example, objectives related to job satisfaction or player development are difficult to quantify and difficult to use in the goal attainment approach. Finally, there is a problem of which goals take precedence within a sport organization, and whether the organization should focus on long- or short-term priorities.

Systems resource approach

Rather than focussing on organizational outputs, as the goal attainment approach does, the **systems resource approach** to organizational effectiveness focuses on the inputs of an organization, specifically its ability to attract scarce or valued resources (Yuchtman and Seashore, 1967). These resources may include members, the fans attending a game, or the income generated from the sales of licensed merchandise. Although securing resources is vital to the survival of a sport organization, and survival is *the* overriding measure of effectiveness, there are several problems with the systems resource approach.

First, care must be taken when using this approach with public sector sport organizations. Because much of the funding distributed to these organizations is often guaranteed, or at least subject to only minor yearly fluctuations, the securing of these types of resources is not an appropriate measure of effectiveness. Second, an organization can be effective even when it does not obtain the most desirable resources. Cameron (1980) cites the example of the Seattle SuperSonics, who in the 1977 and 1978 season were unable to attract any superstars to the team; yet even with a rookie coach and no big stars; they were able to reach the NBA finals in 1978 and win the 1979 championship. Finally, there is difficulty determining the differences between inputs and outputs. For example, a sport club may increase the size of its membership in a particular year, an increase in inputs. However, it might be that one of the club's goals was to increase its membership. In this case the number of members is an output. The systems resource approach is most applicable to understanding sport organizations in situations where outputs cannot be objectively measured, where there is a clear connection between the resources obtained and the final product, and when the supply of resources is not formally guaranteed by another organization.

Internal process approach

As opposed to outputs (goal attainment) or inputs (systems resource), the **internal process approach** focuses on throughputs, the internal activities by which inputs are converted into outputs. Here, indicators of effectiveness can include things such as a supervisor's concern for her or his workers, feelings of group loyalty, good communications, and the personal development of subordinates (Daft, 1992). Some writers propose that the internal process approach should focus on fiscal efficiency (Evan, 1976). Here, measures such as inventory turnover and changes in sales volume are used as criteria for assessing effectiveness.

Although the internal process approach is useful in comparing organizations with different outputs it does have its shortcomings. First, it is often difficult to quantifiably measure criteria such as group loyalty or good communications, which, from this perspective, are indicators of effective performance. Second, this approach takes no account of the notion of equifinality, the means by which two organizations with different internal processes could be equally effective in reaching the same end point. Third, the approach is deficient in that a sport organization can have poor communication and low morale and yet still be considered successful.

Strategic Constituents Approach

The strategic constituents model (Connolly et al., 1980) is a more current means of understanding organizational effectiveness. It provides an integrative approach that takes into account the political nature of organizations. It also acknowledges the fact that organizations consist of a number of constituents, which often have differing goals and priorities. For example, in a professional sport organization, owners frequently have different goals from players. Although both want to win games, owners want to make a profit while players want larger salaries. As a result, the organization's general manager has to work toward a compromise to ensure the future effectiveness of the organization. A major strength of the strategic constituencies approach is that it acknowledges that effectiveness is a complex and multidimensional concept that is affected by pressures internal and external to the organization. As a result, it takes into account the political nature of organizations and the fact that managers have to consider all groups that have an interest in the organization.

The fundamental problem with this approach is the difficulty associated with identifying the relative importance of the different constituents. Individuals and groups within the organization will view various constituents differently. Also, the relative importance of these groups may change over time. However, by offering a more holistic approach than the previously discussed models, and considering an organization as a political system, the strategic constituents approach provides one of the better ways of determining effectiveness.

THE STRUCTURE OF SPORT ORGANIZATIONS

To be effective, a sport organization must be structured to respond to the contextual situation in which it operates. Consequently, an understanding of the different elements of structure is one of the basic tenets of organization theory. The structure of an organization is also important because as Miller (1987) points out, "it influences the flow of information and the context and nature of human interactions. It channels collaboration, specifies modes of coordination, allocates power and responsibility, and prescribes levels of formality and **complexity.**" Although organizational theorists have identified many different dimensions of **organizational structure** (cf. Miller and Droge, 1986; Pugh et al, 1969), the three most commonly found in the literature are **complexity, formalization,** and **centralization.** These three variables have also been shown to be theoretically and empirically applicable to the study of sport organizations (Slack and Hinings, 1987, 1992). Each of these is briefly discussed below.

Complexity

Complexity refers to the extent to which an organization is differentiated, that is, the way in which the organization is divided into different divisions, departments, groups, or individual roles, each with its own tasks and responsibilities. This differentiation may occur either horizontally, vertically, or spatially (geographically).

Horizontal differentiation occurs as a result of the different parts of the organization becoming specialized in different activities. This specialization is carried out in an attempt to increase organization efficiency and can occur in two ways. First, the total work to be performed in the organization may be divided into separate, discrete, and usually narrow tasks. Second, the employment of specialists to perform a range of organizational activities can result in diversely trained individuals bringing different approaches, goals, and terminology to the organization. This can present communication and coordination problems, which can, in turn, increase complexity. For example, in putting together its made-for-television golf "Skins Game," the International Management Group (IMG) must coordinate interactions between players' agents, television producers, event managers, marketing managers, and various lawyers. Despite all of these groups being employed by IMG, each will have different objectives, jargon, and time frames, thus increasing the complexity of the organization.

Vertical differentiation refers to the number of hierarchical levels in a sport organization. The more levels there are, the greater become the problems of communication, coordination, and supervision, hence the more complex becomes the organization. Vertical differentiation often is directly proportional to the size of the organization (Blau and Schoenherr, 1971), and also to the degree of horizontal differentiation. When a job is highly specialized, it is difficult for the worker to relate his or her work to that of others, so control of the work is often passed to a manager. This has the effect of increasing the number of vertical levels in the organization. The number of workers that a manager can viably supervise is referred to as the *span-of-control.*

Spatial differentiation refers to the degree of geographical separation of various divisions of the same organization. Thus an organization entirely based on one site, such as a single-outlet sports shop, has a very low degree of spatial differentiation. On the other hand, a multinational organization such as Nike can be considered highly spatially differentiated because its athletic shoes are designed in Beaverton, Oregon, manufactured in Asia, and distributed through various outlets around the world. This makes Nike's operation much more difficult to coordinate and much more complex than the sports shop.

The more horizontally, vertically, and spatially differentiated a sport organization is, the more complex it becomes. Increased complexity results in an organization in which coordination and communication are more difficult and management more demanding.

Formalization

One of the ways of managing complexity is through the use of formalization. Formalization refers to the extent to which rules, regulations, job descriptions, policies, and procedures govern the operation of an organization. In a highly formalized organization, such as one that uses production-line techniques to manufacture sports equipment, employees will have little discretion over how and when they carry out their tasks. The head coach of a National Basketball Association franchise will, by contrast, find his job far less formalized, with the freedom to set day-to-day activities as he sees fit (provided that his team keeps winning!).

Formalization may vary not just among organizations, but also among departments and hierarchical levels within the same organization. For example, Nike's research and development department will operate under much less formalized conditions than will its manufacturing plants. This is a direct result of the research and development department employing highly trained professionals who require a far greater degree of flexibility in their *modus operandi* than do the less skilled production line workers. Likewise, because of their need to operate quickly and in the best interests of the entire organization, senior managers are usually subject to less formalization than lower level managers.

Formalization allows strict worker control without the necessity for expensive close supervision. It also permits the standardization of outputs, allowing items such as athletic shoes to be designed on one continent, manufactured on another, and sold on a third.

Centralization

Centralization refers to the level of the hierarchy with authority to make decisions. In centralized organizations, decisions tend to be made by the upper levels of management; in more decentralized organizations, similar decisions would be delegated to a lower hierarchical level. As an organization grows larger, it quickly reaches a point whereby it becomes impossible for a single individual to make all decisions necessary for day-to-day operation. In addition to not possessing sufficient expertise in all areas of the operation (e.g., research, manufacturing, marketing, and finance), if one person were to attempt to take responsibility for all decisions, it would take an intolerably long time to make even minor decisions.

Decisions that are regarded as less crucial are delegated to lower levels, allowing senior management to concentrate on strategic decisions affecting the entire organization. In a large university athletic department, for example, there will normally be different individuals or even departments concerned with marketing, publicity, media information, and scheduling. The athletic director (AD), while overseeing all departments, will not be involved with minor details, such as ensuring that every local newspaper has the latest statistics on the men's basketball team, or that the women's soccer team has a balance of home and away fixtures. The AD will likely be more concerned with securing corporate sponsorship agreements, arranging with television companies to broadcast certain home games, and changes to conference regulations. By delegating authority, the AD can maintain control of the athletic department while ensuring that it functions effectively.

Organizations that are highly decentralized are often highly formalized. This allows decisions to be made quickly while maintaining top management control of the organization. This, in fact, brings into question exactly how decentralized such organizations are because even though decisions are made at lower levels, the range of choice in decision making is controlled at the upper levels.

THE DESIGN OF SPORT ORGANIZATIONS

It is something of a truism to say that all sport organizations are different. It has been claimed that there are as many different classes of organizations as there are people who wish to classify them (Carper and Snizek, 1980). Organizations do, however, exhibit various common characteristics. For example, sport organizations may be complex or simple, they may be highly formalized or flexible, they may have centralized or decentralized decision-making mechanisms. When organizations are objectively regarded along dimensions such as these, it becomes possible to classify various combinations of these characteristics to produce **design-types** or **configurations.** A design-type is, quite simply, a particular patterning of structural variables. Various researchers have used different characteristics to classify organizations. In one of the more popular classifications, Mintzberg (1979) uses design parameters such as complexity, formalization, training of members, and centralization, along with contingency factors such as age, size, and environment, to produce five **design-types.** He terms these the **simple structure,** the **machine bureaucracy,** the **professional bureaucracy,** the **divisionalized form,** and the **adhocracy.**

No matter which configuration an organization fits into, it is made up, Mintzberg argues, of five different parts. The **operating core** consists of those employees responsible for the basic work required to produce the final product. At Nike, for example, the operating core consists of those production line workers who physically produce the athletic footwear. The **strategic apex** consists of the senior management of the organization. At Nike, this includes Chief Executive Officer Philip Knight and his staff of top executives. The **middle line** comprises those managers that link the operating core to the strategic apex. At Nike, this would consist of middle management, which links the production facilities, largely located in Asia, to top management in Beaverton, Oregon. The **technostructure** includes the analysts responsible for designing the systems, which standardize operating procedures and outputs. At Nike these include the research and development staff who design new shoes and the production engineers who decide how these shoes will be manufactured. Finally, the **support staff** are the people who provide some kind of support to the rest of the organization. At Nike these include secretarial staff, maintenance engineers, canteen operators, etc.

As well as the five configurations and the five different parts of the organization, Mintzberg proposes five alternative ways in which coordination can be achieved in an organization. Direct supervision is the most basic type and consists of one individual giving instruction to others. An executive director who manages a small national sport organization's head office will generally operate in this manner. All other positions within the office, such as technical director, marketing director, secretary, and receptionist, are supervised by the executive director.

Standardization of work processes occurs when the way work is to be carried out is determined by someone other than the person doing the actual work. Again, returning to Nike, the standardization of work is the role of the design specialists and production engineers; the actual work of making the shoes is done by unskilled production workers. The standardization of outputs occurs when it is the results of the work that are specified, not the way in which these results are to be achieved. For example, the owner of a professional football franchise may instruct the marketing manager to increase average attendance for each of the first five home games by 10% of the previous season's average. However, he or she will leave exactly how this is carried out to the marketing manager.

The fourth way in which coordination can be achieved is through the standardization of skills. Sport medicine personnel and sport lawyers operate with skills that have been standardized through training programs. These skills are further regulated by the professional organizations to which these people must belong. Finally, coordination can be achieved through mutual adjustment whereby processes and procedures are modified through informal communication among parties. An example of this would be a group of people who come together for a limited period and work together to stage a basketball tournament or other similar sporting event.

In each of the configurations described by Mintzberg, one part of the organization and one method of coordination predominates. A small, entrepreneurial business, such as an owner-operated sports store, will be dominated by the owner of the organization, the strategic apex. Because the operation has few employees, coordination is carried out by means of direct supervision. The result of this will be what Mintzberg terms a simple structure.

A sport organization that mass-produces a standard output, such as a baseball bat, will have the technostructure as its dominant part. The stable nature of the production process, whereby thousands of bats are produced to the same specification, is established by designers and engineers. This results in the standardization of work processes being the means of coordination. The operation will be highly formalized with each stage precisely detailed to ensure the constant nature of the end product. The appropriate configuration is therefore the machine bureaucracy.

The rise of professionalism in many industries, sport included, has led to the creation of a configuration known as professional bureaucracy. A professional bureaucracy combines the standardization of the machine bureaucracy with the decentralization, which stems from a professional's need for autonomy. Therefore, although an end product might be narrowly defined, the professional operator has the freedom, within certain guidelines (such as a medical code of ethics), to determine exactly how this end point is reached. In this design-type it is the workers of the operating core that take precedence, with coordination achieved by the standardization of skills. A good example of a professional bureaucracy is a sport medicine clinic.

The fourth of Mintzberg's configurations, the divisionalized form, arises when an organization becomes large and diversifies into other industries, some of which may be outside the area of sport. Brunswick is a good example of a divisionalized form with involvement in power boats, bowling

alleys, and defense products. The creation of divisions, which operate with relative autonomy, results in midline managers as key players in this type of configuration. These are the people who provide the link between the various divisions and the corporate offices.

When environmental uncertainty is high and flexibility is a valued organization characteristic, the appropriate design-type may be an adhocracy. In this configuration, collaboration among various support staff and sometimes operators is favored. Cross-functional groups are created with tasks coordinated by mutual adjustment. The selective *decentralization* that results creates a highly responsive design-type. An example might be an investigative reporting team from a television company assigned to a major sporting event such as soccer's World Cup finals. Consisting of a reporter, a cameraperson, and a producer, this team is put on location to report interest stories as they happen. The team must operate independently as a semiautonomous group and make quick decisions regarding what to cover and how.

It is important to note that the configurations described here are ideal types. It is highly unlikely that organizations that exhibit pure forms of these design-types could be found. Indeed, the examples just cited, although predominantly exhibiting characteristics of the design-type, which they are used to illustrate, all exhibit features of other designs. What these configurations allow, however, is a comparison and contrast of sport organizations along a number of dimensions. As well as providing information regarding what type of sport organization design works best in different situations, these design-types also provide a frame of reference for examining other organizational phenomena. For example, do adhocracies and divisionalized forms formulate strategy in different ways? What about the way in which decision making is carried out, or how conflicts are resolved in different designs? It is this type of insight that increases our theoretical understanding of sport organizations and improves the practical performance of sport managers.

CONCEPT CHECK

There are three primary concepts used to examine the structure of a sport organization: complexity, formalization, and centralization. Organizational design refers to the patterning of structural dimensions.

STRATEGY AND SPORT ORGANIZATIONS

All sport organizations are subject to constant changes in their contextual situation. New competitors enter the marketplace, government legislation that affects business practices is changed, and employment equity programs are stressed. To successfully respond to these and other types of change, sport managers need to formulate a strategy for their organizations. This strategy will require changes in the structure of a sport organization. To be effective, there must be a fit between an organization's strategy and its structure. Strategy is essentially like a coach's game plan. It is designed to help a sport organization achieve its objectives by addressing such issues as what products and/or market segments to compete in; how to best allocate resources; and whether to diversify, expand, or even shut down certain aspects of the organization.

There are four basic types of strategy that a sport organization can follow: a **growth strategy,** a **defensive strategy,** a **stability strategy,** or a **combination strategy.** Growth strategies are pursued through either **diversification** or **integration.** Diversification occurs when a sport organization moves into new products or markets. These may be related or unrelated to the organization's existing business. Reebok's decision in 1986 to buy Rockport, a casual and dress shoe manufacturer, is an example of related diversification. Integration can occur either horizontally or vertically. Horizontal integration involves a sport organization buying another organization, usually a competitor in the same business. Vertical integration occurs when a supplier (backward integration) or a distributor (forward integration) is acquired. In the early 1990s Nike bought out a number of its distribution operations.

Defensive strategies are used if there is a decreased demand for a sport organization's products or services. Defensive strategies may be one of three types. A **turnaround strategy** is used to counter decreasing revenues or rising costs. It may involve cost-cutting measures, layoffs, or a change in the markets in which the company operates. Divestiture involves selling a business or part of a business. Liquidation occurs when a company or part of a company is shut down and its assets are sold to obtain capital.

Stability strategies occur when a sport organization maintains its current level of activity with no intent to grow. The organization strives to retain its market share and/or provide the same level of service as in the past. A combination strategy simply involves a sport organization using the three strategies previously outlined in some combination. The type of strategy a sport organization chooses will influence its structure. Sport organizations, which seek growth in new markets, will require a flexible structure such as a professional bureaucracy or an adhocracy. A sport organization that adopts a more defensive strategy will most likely exhibit a more bureaucratic type of structure.

ENVIRONMENT OF SPORT ORGANIZATIONS

Another factor that influences the structure and operation of a sport organization is the environment in which it operates. Although we can think of the environment as including everything external to the organization, this is of little practical or theoretical use. A more relevant approach is to think of the environment as consisting of two parts, the general (or distal) and the task (proximal).

General Environment

General environment consists of various influences that although not directly affecting the organization, impact on the industry as a whole. These influences can be divided into a number of different sectors (Daft, 1992). Some of the more common are briefly explained as follows.

The economic environment includes elements, which will indirectly affect the sport organization, include the general economic climate, the system of banking that is being used in the country in which the organization exists, and patterns of consumer consumption. For example, in times of economic recession, most people have less disposable income to spend on leisure activities, such as attending sporting events. This may force professional sport franchises to reduce the price of admission, which may adversely affect profit margins.

Sociocultural factors include the class structure of the social system within which the sport organization operates, the culture in which it exists, trends in consumer taste, and the sporting tradition of the locale. For example, the demise of the

World League of American Football was in large part brought about by sociocultural factors, specifically the failure of European fans to take to this traditional North American game.

Legal regulations regarding such things as taxation, unionization, and gender equity can all have a dramatic effect on sport organizations. After a succession of fatalities at English professional soccer matches, notably the 1989 disaster at Hilsborough in Sheffield, England, where 95 people died, tough regulations were introduced regarding obligatory ground safety standards. Because they could not meet these legislated standards, several clubs have in recent years had their applications to join the professional Football League denied.

Ecological issues regarding physical surroundings can play an important role in a sport organization's success. A water-ski school, for example, may find its business disastrously affected by a cold, wet summer.

Technological advancements must be constantly monitored because they may change the nature of the industry in which the sport organization operates. The use of carbon fiber composites in the manufacture of tennis racquets immediately rendered wooden racquets obsolete and hence revolutionized the industry.

Task environment

Task environment is made up of those aspects that directly impinge on the operating procedures of an organization. It is these influences that are characteristically given the most attention by sport organization managers, and these over which they can exert most direct leverage. Typically included would be groups such as suppliers, customers, competitors, members, shareholders, and regulatory agencies. Each sport organization's task environment is unique, with its constituent influences altering over time.

The **domain** of a sport organization denotes the territory in which it chooses to operate and will consequently delineate the organization's *task environment*. Different sport organizations, ostensibly within the same area, may have different *domains* and therefore different *task environments*. Ping (expensive) and Northwestern (cheap), both makers of golf clubs, have identified different *domains*, based on price, in which to operate. As a result, they come into contact with different suppliers, customers, and competitors.

Environmental uncertainty

The degree of uncertainty a sport organization faces determines the extent to which its environment may be deemed dynamic or stable. An organization facing a regular set of demands from an unchanging environment, for example a tennis ball manufacturer such as Wilson, may face stable conditions (Litterer, 1973). By contrast, dynamic environments are characterized by rapid change and much uncertainty. These conditions may be caused by an increased number of competitors, a declining market, legal changes, or the availability of substitute products. Athletic footwear companies, because of the constant battle among competitors to introduce new features and styles, operate in a highly dynamic environment.

All sport organizations endeavor to limit the uncertainties they face. They can attempt to do this either by altering their internal structure, processes, and behaviors; by modifying their external environmental characteristics through such things as long-term contractual agreements with suppliers and customers; or by creating a joint venture with another organization to meet objectives that neither company could attain on its own.

Relationship between environment and organization structure

Environmental uncertainty directly affects organization structure, specifically the attributes of complexity, formalization, and centralization. A sport organization faced with an uncertain environment will have to increase the number of departments and specialist personnel required to buffer the organization from environmental disruption. This is most often achieved by assigning staff to boundary-spanning roles to secure and evaluate relevant environmental information (Child, 1984). For example, the managers of a fitness center may see a societal interest in the relationship between diet and fitness. They may hire a dietician to counsel clients on eating habits and to keep other members of staff who are involved in prescribing fitness programs abreast of subsequent nutritional developments related to fitness. As a result of such a change the complexity of the organization is increased.

Increased levels of complexity require an appropriate means of integrating different individuals and departments. In uncertain environments, flexible rather than highly formalized hierarchical methods of coordination are most effective, resulting in a decrease in *formalization*. This type of arrangement can be seen in a sport law practice. Because of the need to adapt to the requirements of different cases, experts in various aspects of law may be required to work on a particular project. Consequently, the flexibility to move from one case to the next is important. In contrast, in stable environments, sport organizations can capitalize on the economies that result from the use of formalized procedures. Many government agencies involved with the provision of sport services operate in this way. Because of the need to treat all clients equally and the relatively unchanging nature of the services provided, a highly structured organizational design is most appropriate.

The more complex an organization's environment, the greater the amount of information which must be assimilated to make accurate decisions, hence the more decentralized it becomes (Mintzberg, 1979). If the complex environment is perceived as hostile, however, there may be a move to, at least temporarily, centralize the decision-making structure. This ensures that everyone is aware of who is in control and allows important decisions to be made quickly. For example, in September 1984, when Nike found itself having problems because of Reebok's success in aerobics, Philip Knight returned to the presidency of the company, a position he had relinquished only a year earlier (Dodds, 1985).

SPORT ORGANIZATIONS AND TECHNOLOGY

Technology has fundamentally altered the way in which virtually all sport organizations operate. From the use of *computer aided design* (CAD) by large manufacturing companies, to the installation of a personal computer and facsimile machine at a local sports club, technology has become a contingency that has significantly impacted the structure and processes of sport organizations. Although there has been considerable variation in the way researchers have defined technology, it is generally accepted as constituting the materials, knowledge, equipment, and processes required to produce a desired good or service (Perrow, 1967). Although different studies have focused on various facets of technology, in this chapter we concentrate on organizational level technology and the seminal works of Joan Woodward, Charles Perrow, and J. D. Thompson. We also look briefly at the use of microelectronic technologies in sport organizations, and finally we examine the relationship between technology and organization structure.

Research on technology and organizations

During the 1950s, Joan Woodward studied 100 manufacturing organizations operating in the south of England. She grouped the organizations in her study into three major categories: unit, or small batch, production; mass, or large batch production; and **continuous process production.** Organizations involved in **unit production** were seen as exhibiting the least amount of technological complexity. They were less structured than those in the other categories, tended to have a smaller number of hierarchical levels, exhibited lower levels of formalization, and employed a more decentralized decision-making structure. An example of such a sport organization would be a custom bike manufacturer who produces a different bicycle for each customer.

Mass production organizations manufacture large quantities of the same product, often using assembly lines. The process is repetitive and routine with few skilled workers and a high level of formalization. Organizations such as Reebok use this type of mass production to manufacture their athletic footwear.

Organizations that use a continuous process production are highly mechanized so that the production process does not stop. This type of production is associated more with businesses such as oil refineries than sport organizations.

The work of Charles Perrow is more generalizable than that of Woodward, being applicable to both manufacturing and service organizations. During the 1960s, Perrow identified four main technologies, each associated with a different type of organization structure. **Routine technology** is found in bureaucratic types of organizations with control of generally unskilled workers achieved through high levels of formalization and centralized decision making. **Craft technology** requires a more flexible structure and is hence characterized by less formalization and centralization, with coordination achieved through mutual adjustment and the past experience of staff. **Engineering technologies** are analogous to Mintzberg's professional bureaucracies with the professional staff accorded a certain amount of decision-making autonomy to go along with the moderate levels of formalization and centralization. **Nonroutine technology** requires a very flexible structure with low levels of formalization, professionally trained operatives, and decision making made by means of mutual adjustment. Often more than one type of technology will exist in an organization. For example, Reebok will employ routine technology to manufacture its running shoes, but nonroutine technology to design and develop them.

J. D. Thompson's (1967) approach to technology focuses on interdependence among different organization subunits. Different degrees of interdependence require different types of technology. **Pooled interdependence** requires a mediating technology to link together independently operating organizations. For example, each branch of "Club Fit," a Canadian chain of fitness centers, operates independently, yet each contributes to the overall profit or loss of the total organization. As such, the different branches exhibit a pooled interdependence. Complexity is low, with coordination achieved through a highly formalized mechanism detailing appropriate policies and procedures for each branch.

Sequential interdependence is found in a sport organization when the output of subunit A forms the input of subunit B. This is most frequently found in assembly line production, such as in the manufacture of tennis balls, where a standard product is produced repetitively at a standard rate. This type of interdependence requires higher levels of coordination than *pooled interdependence* because of the need to coordinate the various units involved in the production process. Levels of *complexity* and *formalization* are therefore high, with decision making centralized.

Reciprocal interdependence is the highest form of interdependence and is associated with what Thompson terms "intensive technology." The various units involved in this type of interdependent relationship all depend on each other for their inputs. For example, in a voluntary sport organization, volunteer workers, professional staff, administrators, coaches, sponsors, and athletes all need to interact to put on a successful sporting event. Complexity is very high, formalization low, and decision making decentralized. Coordination in such situations is achieved through frequent communication. The people involved are usually highly skilled and hence

able to call on their training and experience to make situations workable.

Microelectronic technologies

Over the last 15 years, many traditional manufacturing and service technologies have been replaced or augmented with microelectronic technologies, most of which are computer related. There are two major facets of microelectronic technology that are impacting on the structure and operations of sport organizations, **computer integrated manufacturing** (CIM) and advanced information technologies. Computer integrated manufacturing refers to the linking together of different parts of the manufacturing process with computers. This includes everything from computer aided design and *computer aided manufacturing* (CAM) to the warehousing, shipping, and servicing of finished products. These techniques are commonly used to design, produce, and distribute a wide variety of sports equipment, from running shoes to tennis racquets.

Advanced information technology involves the linking together of computers through telecommunications systems, thus allowing virtually anyone with a personal computer and modem to send information to, and receive information from, any part of the world. This allows for the prompt identification of key issues and potential problems, as well as a broader participation in decision making.

Relationship between technology and organizational structure

The multidimensional nature of technology and complexity render clear relationships difficult to find. Technologies such as Woodward's mass production, Perrow's routine, and Thompson's sequential are generally associated with bureaucratic types of structures, suggesting high levels of task specialization and vertical differentiation, and hence complexity. However, specialization, as measured by the amount of professional training of the work force, is likely to be low (Hage and Aiken, 1969). When technology is nonroutine (Perrow) or of unit production (Woodward), task specialization and the number of hierarchical levels will be low, but complexity as measured by the amount of the staff's professional training will be high.

There is a clearer relationship between technology and formalization. Generally, the more routine technologies are associated with the greater presence of rules, regulations, and job descriptions (Hage and Aiken, 1969; Gerwin, 1979).

Although there are exceptions (Hinings and Lee, 1971), the majority of studies show at least a slight relationship between the level of technology and the degree to which decision making is decentralized (Child and Mansfield, 1972; Khandwalla, 1974; Hage and Aiken, 1969). Generally speaking, organizations that employ routine technology will be more centralized than those employing nonroutine technology.

SIZE AND SPORT ORGANIZATIONS

Intuitively we all know that large sport organizations operate and are structured differently from small ones. Size is, for many organization theorists, the most important influence on the structure and processes of an organization. In this section, we look at the various ways of assessing **organizational size,** and we also examine the ways in which size impacts on a sport organization's structure.

There are a variety of ways to assess the size of a sport organization: number of employees, market share, number of fans, return on investment, and number of members are all possible measures. In the most detailed examination of the concept of size, Kimberly (1976) suggests that there are four aspects of the concept that can be found within the literature. The first of these is the physical capacity of an organization (e.g., the physical capacity of a professional baseball organization could be measured by the number of fans its stadium can hold). Organizations with stadiums that will hold more fans are seen as being bigger than those with a smaller capacity. A second measure is "the volume of organizational inputs or, occasionally, the volume of its outputs" (Kimberly, 1976). Organizational inputs could refer to the amount of money a voluntary sports club is able to generate. A club with a lot of money would be described as larger than one with less money. In a similar vein, a fitness center with a lot of members (inputs) would be seen as bigger than one with fewer members. If applied to a retail sporting goods store, organizational outputs could be measured by the number of units of an item sold (e.g., athletic shoes). If used to assess the size of a department of sport studies, outputs could be the number of graduates per year.

The third measure of size is the amount of discretionary resources available to an organiza-tion. This could include measures such as the wealth of an organization or the size of its net assets; the bigger the net assets the larger the organization. The final measure that Kimberly suggests can be used to measure size is "the personnel available to an organization," for example, the number of employees or the number of members. This is the most common measure of size, used in more than 80% of studies on this topic (Kimberly, 1976). There is, however, a problem applying this measure to some types of sport organizations. A ski resort would, for instance, have more employees in winter than in summer. There is also a question of how to classify part-time employees. For example, a sporting goods store may hire part-time sales clerks. How are these people recorded when measuring the size of such an organization? Notwithstanding these problems, it is primarily people that have to be managed in any organization and, as such, available personnel is the most widely used and accepted measure of organizational size (Child, 1973).

Within the organization theory literature there has been considerable debate about the impact that size has on the structure of an organization. Despite this debate, the majority of studies acknowledge that size influences the structure of an organization. Most researchers (Khandwalla, 1977; Mintzberg, 1979) have suggested that large organizations are more complex than small ones. This increased complexity arises for several reasons. First, as organizations increase in size it becomes economically feasible to add specialists. For example, a small sporting goods store will not be able to afford its own lawyer and accountant, whereas a large sports equipment manufacturer will have the necessary resources to employ these types of specialists.

Increased size also contributes to complexity in that as sport organizations grow, they tend to diversify. Companies like Nike and Reebok, for instance, although they started off in athletic footwear, have now diversified into apparel and casual footwear. This increase in specialists and/or product diversification requires managing. This is usually accomplished by introducing new levels of management into the organization, which also serves to increase complexity.

With this increase in complexity comes a concomitant need for coordination and control. This can be achieved through direct supervision or the formalization of modes of operation. Because direct supervision is expensive, formalization, through the use of rules, regulations, policies, and procedures, is the most frequently used method of integrating the functions of an organization. It should be noted that the industry in which the sport organization is operating may also affect the size-formalization relationship. In organizations where work is relatively repetitive and unskilled, such as a sport equipment manufacturer, formalization is likely to be high. However, in a professional based structure, a large sport medicine clinic that employs professionally trained staff such as doctors, physiotherapists, and x-ray technicians, formalization is low. The reason for this is that professional training is designed to accomplish the same goals as formalization, that is, "the organization and regularization of the behavior of the members of the organization" (Hall, 1982).

The relationship between size and centralization is some what paradoxical. As Blau and Schoenherr (1971) point out, a large organization places conflicting pressures on its senior managers. This is because size "heightens the importance of managerial decisions, which discourages delegating them and simultaneously expands the volume of managerial responsibilities which exerts pressures to delegate some of them." Despite this paradox, most research has shown that as an organization gets larger decision making is decentralized. There is, however, a caveat in that, as noted earlier, if **decentralization** is accompanied by increasing levels of formalization pertaining to how, when, and by whom decisions should be made, it is questionable if *decentralization* has in fact taken place.

POWER AND POLITICS

In the previous four sections of this chapter we have looked at how an organization's strategy, environment, technology, and size influence its structure. However, despite the explanatory power of these variables in helping to understand organizational structure, there is much that remains unexplained. Some organization theorists have suggested that a focus on the power and politics of organization life can explain much of what the so-called contingency variables leave unexplained. The argument presented by those who subscribe to this viewpoint is that those people who hold power in an organization will adopt the type of structure that will help maintain or increase their power. One way of doing this is to engage in political behavior.

The power to make choices about the way a sport organization should be structured and operated can arise from a number of sources. A sport manager can exhibit **legitimate power** because of his or her position in the organization. For example, the manager of a baseball team can pick any lineup and batting order that he chooses because of the formal position of authority that he holds. He is not required to discuss the decision with his players, although he may wish to do so. Often with legitimate power comes **reward power,** the power to allocate benefits and favors to those who conform to the power holder's demands. The decision of the newly appointed chief executive officer of a ski hill to promote those who have loyally supported his or her rise to the top is a clear example of someone using reward power. **Coercive power** is in some ways the opposite of reward power and can be employed by those who have the power to punish or impose sanctions on others. A coach may use coercive power to "sit out" a player who did not work hard in practice. **Referent power** is the type of power that a person has because people look up to them. College football and basketball coaches may win the respect of alumni and/or players because of the values they espouse. They also may obtain power because of their vast knowledge of the sport: this is termed **expert power.** None of these types of power is discrete and they may even overlap, but either individually or in combination they can be used to influence the structure and operation of a sport organization.

Political behavior is related to power and involves "the ability to use the bases of power effectively" (Mintzberg, 1983). Gandz and Murray (1980) found that the use of political power was a common feature of organization life, particularly at its higher levels. By using political power, sport managers are able to shape the structure of the organizations in which they work. Political power can come through four main activities: building coalitions, using outside experts, building a network of contacts, and controlling information. We will now look briefly at each of these.

Coalitions are built when sport managers spend their time communicating their views to others, building up trust relationships, and building mutual respect with others, both inside and outside the organization. Coalition building occurs in many sport organizations and it is frequently carried on outside the work environment in places like bars, restaurants, and golf courses. Using outside experts or consultants enables sport managers to legitimize their own thoughts about the structure and process of an organization. Frequently, hiring an outside expert is seen as a means of gaining an objective view. However, managers rarely hire individuals whose views are opposite their own.

All managers develop political power by establishing a network of contacts both inside and outside their organizations. We frequently see this type of activity when cities are bidding to host major sports events such as the Olympic Games. Managers from the bidding committee try to build up contacts with the IOC members, politicians, and diplomats who can influence the decision process. Finally, controlling information is a form of **political activity** that can be used to influence the outcome of decision making. Sport managers, by emphasizing facts that support their position and ignoring or deemphasizing other manager's positions, can promote their own ideas about how their organization should be structured and operated. This type of tactic is frequently used by the owners and managers of professional sport teams who are looking for public subsidies for a stadium or arena. Positive facts about the economic benefits of the facility to the community are emphasized, while counter views are suppressed.

CONCEPT CHECK

Strategy, environment, technology, and size are contingency factors that affect the structure of an organization. Sport managers may exercise the power they have and also engage in political activity to influence structure.

DECISION MAKING IN SPORT ORGANIZATIONS

In addition to understanding the structure and design of sport organizations and the contingencies that influence them, sport managers also must develop an understanding of the many processes that take place in sport organizations. Decision making and change are two of the most important of these. Whether it involves deciding on the color of the company letterhead or pursuing a multimillion dollar takeover bid, decision making centers on making a choice between different alternatives (Drucker, 1966). Sport managers must use their judgement to make decisions regarding such things as hiring and firing employees, the addition of new products or programs, and the divestment of divisions that are making a loss.

The decisions that a sport manager has to make can be categorized into two types (Simon, 1960). **Programmed decisions** are repetitive and routine and are based on clearly defined policies, procedures, and/or past experiences. Such decisions may include the number of coaches to hire for a certain number of participants at a children's sport camp, or whether to pass or fail a student in a sport management course. **Nonprogrammed decisions** involve unique situations with few or no established guidelines or procedures to direct the way in which they should be handled. For example, the decision by the IOC to award the 2000 Olympic Games to Sydney, Australia, rather than to Beijing, Berlin, or Manchester, could be considered a nonprogrammed decision.

There are three types of conditions under which decisions can be made. Each is based on the extent to which the outcome of a particular decision alternative can be predicted. A decision is made under conditions of certainty when the costs and benefits of all available alternatives are completely understood. Because of the constantly changing nature of sport organizations, this is an ideal situation, which is rarely, if ever, realized. More common are decisions taken with a degree of risk. Here there is a basic understanding of the available alternatives, but the potential cost and benefits associated with each are not 100% known. Decisions made by the coach of a college basketball team regarding potential sponsorship opportunities may enter into this category. For example, if one shoe company is offering a deal for 5 years at $1,000,000 per year, and the other is offering a 10-year deal at $750,000 per year, which is better? Much will depend on changes in the economy and the future willingness of shoe companies to pay college coaches to have their players endorse products. The decision maker must therefore assign probabilities to possible outcomes and determine the most attractive decision alternative.

Under conditions of uncertainty, the decision alternatives and their potential outcomes are both unknown because there are no data or past experiences on which to base the decision. Decisions such as whether to expand a sport equipment manufacturing company into one of the former Soviet bloc countries, which may offer cheap labor but which has a long history of political instability, would fall into this category.

Although there are various models that attempt to explain the process of decision making, in this chapter we briefly outline the two commonly associated with individual decision making. The **rational model** is an ideal description of how decisions should be made through a linear analysis of the problem and the rational identification of solutions. The implication in this model is that decision making is carried out, as proposed by classical management theorists, to maximize the potential for the attainment of organizational goals. The decision process is seen as a series of linear steps. First, it is determined that a problem exists; the decision criteria are then identified and weighed based on the interests of the organization; all possible alternatives that might solve the problem and meet the criteria are then listed; these alternatives are evaluated against prespecified criteria; finally, the best alternative is chosen (Robbins, 1990). The various assumptions that are made by adherents of this approach are, as Pfeffer and Salancik (1977) note, "so reasonable, so much a part of the ideology of how management is practiced, that most people take them virtually for granted." However, they go on to add, "if we examine them critically . . . we find that some of the assumptions are less than completely persuasive."

Much of the criticism of the rational model that Pfeffer and Salancik (1977) allude to emanates from the work of Herbert Simon (1945) and his concept of **bounded rationality.** Simon suggested that rather then being a completely rational process, organization decision making is bounded by the emotions and limited cognitive ability of managers to process information, by factors such as constraints on the time and money available, and by imperfect information that is available. Because of this managers "satisfice." A limited number of decision alternatives and outcomes are considered, with the manager searching for the first acceptable solution. For example, the owner of a sporting goods store wishing to hire a new employee will hold the position open only until he or she has found a satisfactory applicant. The process will not be extended indefinitely until the ideal candidate has been found. As much as the **rational model of decision making** intuitively appeals to a manager's sense of order, the bounded rationality approach provides a much more realistic account of how decisions are actually made. It also draws attention to the political nature of decision making.

CHANGE IN SPORT ORGANIZATIONS

Sport organizations are in a constant state of transition and so change is another important process that managers need to understand. To survive and grow, a sport organization must be able to adapt to changes in environment, size, strategy, and technology. New people enter the organization, others leave, physical layout is reorganized, and new products and programs are developed. The changes that are being discussed are not the day-to-day fluctuations evident in all organizations but those that are systematically planned and implemented in an attempt to retain or confer a sustainable competitive advantage.

Organizational change can occur in the following four areas: technology, products and services, structure and systems, and personnel (McCann, 1991; Leavitt, 1964). Technological change refers to the changes that occur in production processes, skills and methods used to deliver services, or knowledge base. Tennis racquet manufacturer Dunlop has, for example, undergone profound changes in how it designs, manufactures, and sells tennis racquets as a consequence of technological advances that have seen racquets designed by computers and made from increasingly sophisticated materials such as carbon fiber. A change in products or services may involve the deletion, addition, or modification of the sport organization's various offerings. Structural and systemic changes include modifications to areas such as the sport organization's division of labor, authority structure, or control systems. This is particularly evident when a company such as Mark McCormack's International Management Group (IMG) undergoes rapid expansion. When IMG was a small entrepreneurial company, McCormack took responsibility for virtually all operations. As the company grew, responsibilities had to be delegated, which, in turn, required the implementation of a suitable control system and authority structure. Personnel changes involve altering the ways in which people think, act, and relate to each other.

A sport organization's output, costs, and work force must remain relatively fixed if the organization is to be successful. This complements managerial preferences for stability and predictability. At the same time there is a need to look for new markets, new technologies, and new methods of service delivery. Therefore what is required is an almost paradoxical balancing between change and stability. If incorrectly managed, organization performance can rapidly deteriorate. Productive attention to detail can become an obsession with trivia, rewarding innovation can escalate into superfluous invention, and measured growth can lead to unsuppressed expansion (Miller, 1990).

The impetus for change may arise externally from the environment of the sport organization or from inside the organization itself. There are perspectives that attempt to explain both. For example, contingency theorists (Burns and Stalker, 1961; Lawrence and Lorsch, 1967) and population ecologists (Carroll and Hannan, 1989) focus on exogenous sources of change. On the other hand, resource dependence theorists (Pfeffer and Salancik, 1978), and those who adopt a contextual approach (Pettigrew, 1985; Pettigrew, 1987), stress the interaction of external and internal factors.

The pervasive necessity for change in sport organizations is matched only by the equally ubiquitous resistance to it. This resistance may emanate from the organization itself, or from environmental constituents. Organization members may resist in an attempt to protect their self-interests, particularly if goals relating to power, money, prestige, convenience, job security, or professional competence are threatened as a result of the change (Patti, 1974). Resistance may arise as a direct result of the uncertainty that accompanies change, especially in situations where there is a lack of trust between those initiating the change and those on whom it will impact. Change also may be resisted if different organization stakeholders have differing opinions of the costs and benefits of the proposed change. Finally, change may be resisted because of cost, in terms of time, effort, and money, that it incurs. Different parties may not feel that the benefits of change outweigh the associated costs.

This has become particularly apparent in Canadian national sport organizations with the pressure the government has placed on these organizations to change and adopt a more professional and bureaucratic structure. Despite increases in funding for those organizations that adopted this type of design, the many volunteers who have traditionally controlled them have often refused to accept the loss of power that would result from a move to this type of structural arrangement.

There are various means by which sport organization managers can deal with resistance and implement change. These are not mutually exclusive and often are used in conjunction with one another. Educating organization members about the necessity for change and using communication techniques to keep them informed of how the change is progressing can help reduce resistance. Gaining the participation and involvement of those change-resistant groups through mechanisms such as change teams can ease the planning and implementation process. Providing facilitation and support, through such devices as career counseling, job training, and therapy, to those adversely affected by the change process can address some of the fear, anxiety, and uncertainty that the change process imbues. As a last resort, the process can be somewhat smoothed by techniques of negotiation, manipulation, co-optation, or even coercion, in an attempt to pressure opposition groups into accepting the desired changes.

CONCEPT CHECK

There are many processes that take place in sport organizations. Because of space we have only looked at two of the most important, the process of decision making and the process of change. Others include the process of human resources management, the process of managing organizational culture, and the process of leadership.

SUMMARY

1. For most sport managers the main objective is to develop an effective organization. Effectiveness can be looked at from a number of different perspectives. The strategic constituents approach, which takes into account the

political nature of organizations and the influence this has on effectiveness, is the most useful of these perspectives.

2. To be effective, a sport organization must be structured in order to fit with the demands of the contextual situation within which it operates. The three most common dimensions used to describe the structure of a sport organization are complexity, formalization, and centralization. The way in which the dimensions of organizational structure are patterned is referred to as the design of the organization. There are many different organizational design types that sport organizations may exhibit. Mintzberg (1979) identified five design types or what he terms *configurations:* simple structure, machine bureaucracy, professional bureaucracy, divisionalized form, and adhocracy. Examples of each of these design types can be found in the organizations that make up the sport industry.

3. A sport organization's strategy, environment, technology, and size will all influence the type of structure it exhibits. These variables are called *contingencies* because a sport organization's structure is contingent on them.

4. Structure may also be a product of power and politics. Senior individuals and the members of dominant coalitions within a sport organization will attempt to influence the structure of a sport organization to preserve power and privileged position. The emphasis that some organizational theorists place on power and politics stands in contrast to the rationality of the contingency approach.

5. There are many different processes that occur within a sport organization. We looked briefly at two of these, the process of decision making and that of change. Some people see decision making as a rational process, but many organization theorists challenge this position and suggest that decision makers operate with bounded rationality. That is to say that decision choices are limited by factors such as expertise, organizational politics, and time. Change is also an important process in sport organizations. It is somewhat paradoxical because although sport managers seek stability and predictability, if the organizations they manage are to remain competitive, they must change to meet the demands of their respective markets.

CASE STUDY

In the late 1970s, Paul Fireman was operating his family's fishing and hunting business. While attending a sporting goods trade fair in Chicago, Fireman came across a running shoe that captured his attention. The shoe was called Reebok. *It was manufactured by a small company in northern England. Fireman saw potential in the shoe and, anxious to expand the family business product line, he acquired the rights to sell Reeboks in North America. For the next few years, sales of Reeboks were modest but unspectacular; adidas and Nike were the leaders in the athletic footwear industry.*

In the early 1980s a new fitness craze hit North America; it was called aerobics. Women everywhere joined aerobics classes and as a consequence looked for a functional yet stylish exercise shoe. Fireman saw an opportunity in the aerobics market. Although companies such as Nike dismissed it as "fat ladies dancing to music," and Pentland Industries, a British company with whom Fireman had joined in 1982 to buy the world rights to Reebok, had reservations, he entered the aerobics market. Fireman's strategy was to produce a ballet-type slipper that was soft, stylish, and comfortable. The result was a shoe called the Freestyle. Although initial sales were slow, Fireman and partner Jim Barclay got the idea of promoting the shoe by giving them away to aerobics instructors. Their strategy was a success, and sales of the Freestyle increased so rapidly that Reebok's profits between 1984 and 1985 rose from $6.2 million to $39 million. Reebok shoes were not only used by participants in aerobics classes, but they became a symbol of the fashion conscious.

After Reebok's success, Fireman started to diversify into related markets. In 1987 he acquired Avia, an Oregon-based manufacturer of high-priced athletic shoes. Along with Avia came the rights to Donner Mountain, a manufacturer of hiking boots. Fireman also saw the potential for walking to become the next popular form of exercise, and in 1986 he bought the Rockport Co. of Marlboro, Massachusetts, a maker of casual, dress, and walking shoes.

Since its early years Reebok has grown and changed tremendously. As a result of its acquisitions it is now a much larger company. There has also been a need for it to develop new technologies to stay competitive in the athletic footwear market. The use of PUMP technology is one of the best examples of this change. Also, the company now uses advanced computer technology to manufacture, market, and ship its product. Divisions of Reebok and its related holdings have been created in other countries, and off-shore manufacturing facilities have been established in Southeast Asia.

REVIEW QUESTIONS AND ISSUES

1. Describe the changes in strategy, size, environment, and technology that Reebok has experienced over the last 15 years.
2. What changes do you think have taken place in Reebok's structure since Paul Fireman first acquired the company?
3. What opportunities did Reebok see in its environment as a result of the aerobics craze? How did its response to these opportunities differ from Nike's, and what effect did it have on the respective companies?
4. What type of changes do you think have occurred in the managerial demands that are placed on Paul Fireman since he bought Reebok?

REFERENCES

Blau, P. M., and Schoenherr, R. A. (1971). *The structure of organizations.* New York: Basic Books.

Burns, T., and Stalker, G. M. (1961). *The management of innovation.* London: Tavistock.

Cameron, K. S. (1980). Critical questions in assessing organizational effectiveness. *Organizational Dynamics, 9,* 66-80.

Carper, W. B., and Snizek, W. E. (1980). The nature and types of organizational taxonomies: an overview. *Academy of Management Review, 5,* 65-75.

Carroll, G. R., and Hannan, M. T. (1989). Density dependence in the evolution of populations of newspaper organizations. *American Sociological Review, 54,* 524-541.

Chelladurai, P. (1987). Multidimensionality and multiple perspectives of organizational effectiveness. *Journal of Sport Management, 1,* 37-47.

Child, J. (1973). Parkinson's progress: accounting for the number of specialists in organizations. *Administrative Science Quarterly, 18,* 328-346.

Child, J. (1984). *Organization: a guide to problems and practice* (2nd Ed). London: Paul Chapman Publishing Ltd.

Child, J., and Mansfield, R. (1972). Technology, size, and organization structure. *Sociology, 6,* 369-393.

Connolly, T., Conlon, E. M., and Deutsch, S. J. (1980). Organizational effectiveness: a multiple constituency approach. *Academy of Management Review, 5,* 211-218.

Daft, R. L. (1992). *Organizational theory and design* (4th Ed). St Paul, Minnesota: West.

Dodds, L. (1985, August 21 - September 3). Heading back on the fast track. *Financial World,* 90-91.

Drucker, P. (1966). *The effective executive.* New York: Harper and Row.

Etzioni, A. (1964). *Modern organizations.* Englewood Cliffs, New Jersey: Prentice-Hall.

Evan, W. M. (1976). Organizational theory and organizational effectiveness: an exploratory analysis in S. L. Spray (Ed.), *Organizational effectiveness: theory, research, utilization* 15-28. Kent, Ohio: Kent State University Press.

Frisby, W. (1986). Measuring the organizational effectiveness of national sport governing bodies. *Canadian Journal of Applied Sport Science, 11,* 94-99.

Gandz, J., and Murray, V. V. (1980). The experience of workplace politics. *Academy of Management Journal, 23,* 237-251.

Gerwin, D. (1979). Relationship between structure and technology at the organizational and job levels. *Journal of Management, 16,* 70-79.

Hage, J., and Aiken, M. (1969). Routine technology, social structure, and organizational goals. *Administrative Science Quarterly, 14,* 366-376.

Hall, R. H. (1982). *Organizations: structure and process* (3rd. ed.). Englewood Cliffs, New Jersey: Prentice Hall.

Hinings, C. R. and Lee, G. L. (1971). Dimensions of organization structure and their context: a replication. *Sociology, 5,* 83-93.

Khandwalla, P. N. (1974). Mass output of operations technology and organizational structure. *Administrative Science Quarterly, 19,* 74-97.

Khandwalla, P. N. (1977). *The design of organizations.* New York: Harcourt Brace Jovanovich.

Kimberly, J. R. (1976). Organizational size and the structuralist perspective: a review critique and proposal. *Administrative Science Quarterly, 21,* 571-597.

Lawrence, P. R. and Lorsch, J. (1967). *Organization and environment.* Boston: Harvard Graduate School of Business Administration.

Leavitt, H. J. (1964). Applied organizational change in industry: technical and human approaches. In W. W. Cooper, H. J. Leavitt, and M. W. Shelly (Eds.), *New Perspectives in Organizational Research* (pp. 55-71). New York: John Wiley and Sons.

Litterer, A. J. (1973). *The analysis of organizations* (2nd Ed). New York: Wiley.

McCann, J. E. (1991). Design principles for an innovating company. *Academy of Management Executive, 5,* 76-93.

Miller, D. (1987). Strategy making and structure: analysis and implications for performance. *Academy of Management Journal, 30,* 7-32.

Miller, D. (1990). *The Icarus paradox: how exceptional companies bring about their own downfall.* New York: HarperCollins.

Miller, D., and Droge, C. (1986). Psychological and traditional determinants of structure. *Administrative Science Quarterly, 31,* 539-560.

Mintzberg, H. (1979). *The structuring of organizations.* Englewood Cliffs, New Jersey: Prentice-Hall.

Mintzberg, H. (1983). *Power in and around organizations.* Englewood Cliffs, New Jersey: Prentice-Hall.

Patti, R. J. (1974). Organizational resistance and change: the view from below. *Social Service Review, 48,* 367-383.

Perrow, C. (1967). A framework for the comparative analysis of organizations. *American Sociological Review, 32,* 194-208.

Pettigrew, A. M. (1985). *The awakening giant.* Oxford: Basil Blackwell.

Pettigrew, A. M. (1987). Context and action in the transformation of the firm. *Journal of Management Studies, 24,* 649-670.

Pfeffer, J. and Salancik, G. (1977). Organizational design: the case for a coalition model of organizations. *Organizational Dynamics, 6,* 15-29.

Pfeffer, J., and Salancik, G. (1978). *The external control of organizations: a resource dependence perspective.* New York: HarperCollins.

Pugh, D. S., Hickson, D. J., and Hinings, C. R. (1969). An empirical taxonomy of work organizations. *Administrative Science Quarterly, 14,* 115-126.

Robbins, S. (1990). *Organization theory: structure, design, and applications.* Englewood Cliffs, New Jersey: Prentice-Hall.

Simon, H. A. (1945). *Administrative behavior.* New York: Macmillan.

Simon, H. A. (1960). *The new science of management decision.* Englewood Cliffs, New Jersey: Prentice-Hall.

Slack, T., and Hinings, C. R. (1987). Planning and organizational change: a conceptual framework for the analysis of amateur sport organizations. *Canadian Journal of Sport Sciences, 12,* 185-193.

Slack, T., and Hinings, C. R. (1992). Understanding change in national sport organizations: an integration of theoretical perspectives. *Journal of Sport Management, 6,* 114-132.

Thompson, J. D. (1967). *Organizations in action.* New York: McGraw-Hill.

Yuchtman, E., and Seashore, S. E. (1967). A systems resource approach to organizational effectiveness. *American Sociological Review, 32,* 891-903.

SUGGESTED READINGS

Students who are interested in finding out more about organization theory should probably start by looking at one of the many texts that deal with this area. Stephen Robbins' (1990) book *Organization theory: structure design and applications* is one of the best. Students who want to see how organization theory can be used to understand the structure and processes of sport organizations should see the (1995) text by Slack *Sport organizations: structure, context, and processes.* For those who want to progress further in this area it is suggested that they look at the major journals in the field of organization theory: *Administrative Science Quarterly, Organization Studies, The Academy of Management Review, The Academy of Management Journal,* and the *Journal of Management Studies* are among the best. Also useful and more practically oriented are journals such as the *Harvard Business Review* and *California Management Review.* The *Journal of Sport Management* frequently publishes articles which demonstrate the application of organizational theory to sport organizations.

CHAPTER 6

Group Decision Making and Problem Solving

Laurence Chalip

In this chapter, you will become familiar with the following terms:

Group decision making	Analogies	Delphi panel
Problem solving	Divergent thinking	Facilitator
Decision quality	Convergent thinking	Reinforcing
Subordinate support	Brainstorming	Soliciting
Choices	Nominal group technique	Prompting
Decision failures	Synectics	Probing
Groupthink	Ideawriting	Databases
Group polarization	Crawford slip method	Subproblems
Devil's advocate	Dialectical decision making	Algorithms
Social loafing	Delphi technique	Quantitative models
Status influence	Idea generation	Decision domain
Limited creative flexibility	Judgment	Decision support systems
Plunging in	Idea evaluation	Baseline data
Free rider problem	Stimulus question	Probability estimate
Group process	Role plays	
Mental models	Decision pitfalls	

Overview

Group decision making and problem solving are pivotal tasks for sport managers. This chapter describes occasions when sport managers use group decision making and problem solving.

The chapter describes how to determine whether or not to use a group when solving a problem or making a decision. It goes on to explain the criteria that should be applied to select group members.

Seven techniques that have been prescribed for group decision making and problem solving are reviewed. The techniques are brainstorming, the nominal group technique, synectics, ideawriting, the Crawford slip method, dialectical decision making, and the Delphi technique. It is pointed out that each method may be appropriate under specific circumstances, and it is noted that the methods can be modified or combined to fit specific needs.

Procedures for facilitating group decision making and problem solving sessions are then described. Methods for sequencing the process, assuring balanced participation, and maintaining a task-oriented climate are outlined.

The chapter concludes with a discussion of group decision support systems. It is noted that sports organizations could benefit from greater use of decision support systems.

THE SCOPE OF GROUP DECISION MAKING AND PROBLEM SOLVING

Whether managing a unit, a task force, or an entire organization, managers work with and through groups. During the course of a career, groups may help the manager to create plans, generate ideas, solve problems, make decisions, set agendas, establish policies, and govern. Consider the following examples.

Planning

The Seoul Olympic Organizing Committee wanted to learn about the international impact of the 1988 Summer Olympic Games. New Zealand was chosen as the site for a year-long study of audience response. Since no study of this kind had yet been undertaken, the research team had to plan its methods meticulously. At the early stage of research, five team members met several times per week to discuss the kinds of data required and the necessary tasks for completing the project. As research progressed, team members met weekly to formulate plans for focus groups, interview sampling, media analyses, and data sharing. Throughout the year, each new research phase was planned by the team as a whole. (The research team's findings are reported by Chalip, 1990.)

Generating ideas

Early in 1994, a new company, "Playmakers," was created to provide sport services to organizations in Maryland, Virginia, and Washington, D.C. Playmakers' services were based on ideas generated during day-long creative sessions several months before. At those sessions, four managers with experience in the sports industry met to discuss new services that might be well received by athletes, parents, coaches, and administrators. Problems with existing sports programs were discussed, and successful nonsport businesses were scrutinized for concepts that might be applicable to the sports industry. Resulting ideas for solving problems and borrowing concepts were then aggregated into a comprehensive service plan. That plan established the conceptual foundation for the new sports enterprise.

Problem solving

Problems crop up throughout the normal course of doing business. Solutions to these problems may require input from several departments or experts. For example, in the university's athletic department, concerns about athlete eligibility can precipitate meetings among representatives from the compliance, coaching, and academic support units. Persons from each unit may need to work jointly to adequately diagnose a problem and to formulate a realistic strategy for remedying it.

Decision making

Each year, athletes leaving college sport are drafted onto professional teams. The process requires that decisions be made about who should be drafted and in what order. Those decisions require input from scouts, coaches, and management. These are not individual decisions; they are group decisions (cf., Whittingham, 1992)

Agenda setting

When the Clinton Administration took office in 1993, it made health care reform a leading priority. Since the health benefits of regular exercise are well established, it concerned some sports leaders that sport was not incorporated into the Clinton health agenda. In response, the President's Council on Physical Fitness and Sports called a 2-day "strategic planning forum" in November of 1993. Experts from government, medicine, recreation, sport service organizations, and the sporting goods industry were brought together to discuss ways in which to add sport to the national health agenda.

Policy-making

In 1974, President Ford created the President's Commission on Olympic Sports. That commission formulated the recommendations that served as the basis for the Amateur Sports Act. As part of the Commission's work, it formed groups of experts—one for each Olympic sport. Each group met to discuss the needs for its sport and policies that might address those needs.

Governance

Many sports organizations are responsible to boards or committees elected from the membership or assigned to represent specific constituencies. Local recreational leagues, regional sports associations, and the United States Olympic Committee are governed on the basis of decisions made by groups.

We see that **group decision making** and **problem solving** can become significant elements of the sport manager's work. A substantial body of research has been devoted to understanding the methods and pitfalls of group decision (see Kleindorfer et al, 1993, especially Chapters 6 and 7 of that reference). To be effective, the manager must address three issues: (1) When should a group be used? (2) Who should be included? (3) What methods will optimize the group's activities? Once those matters are addressed, the manager then needs to facilitate the group's efforts and provide appropriate decision support. Each of these tasks is discussed in the next section.

CONCEPT CHECK

Sport managers at all levels of an organization work with and through groups. Groups aid the manager in planning, generating ideas, problem solving, decision making, agenda setting, policy-making, and governance.

WHEN TO USE A GROUP

Groups can be advantageous when solving problems or making decisions (Koopman and Pool, 1991). Consider the following four benefits:

1. More ideas are possible as increasing numbers of persons are included. For example, the four sport managers who met to plan Playmakers were able to identify more existing problems, more potential solutions, and more useful concepts than any one, two or three of them could have generated alone.
2. More information is available. For example, at successive stages of planning for the New Zealand Olympic study, team members were able to share results from portions of the research they had already completed. Consequently, insights from field studies and media studies could be incorporated into focus group outlines and telephone interview schedules.
3. Alternative perspectives become accessible. For example, coaches, compliance officers, and academic support personnel can each contribute different reflections about athlete eligibility and the resources available to address athletes' needs.
4. The fairness of a decision is judged, in part, by who had input. Thus the President's Commission on Olympic Sports sought legitimacy for its recommendations by obtaining testimony from representatives of as many sport organizations as could be invited to Commission hearings (cf., Chalip, 1991).

However, these benefits are not without cost. It is more time-consuming to engage in group decision than to simply make a decision independently. This is particularly true if the matter to be addressed is one over which there is likely to be some conflict (Janis and Mann, 1977). Yet conflict can be beneficial. Although conflict over sensitive decisions can challenge group cohesion, conflict can also aid decision making by prompting the search for information and requiring consideration of alternative views (Putnam, 1986).

These factors suggest the following three criteria for determining whether or not to seek group input into a decision: (1) How important is the quality of the decision? (2) How much do others have to accept or commit to the decision for it to be implemented? (3) How much time is reasonable to make the decision?

Logical analysis suggests that the manager has five alternatives (Vroom and Yetton, 1973): (1) Solve the problem independently, using information available at the time; (2) obtain information from others, but make the decision independently; (3) collect suggestions (as well as information) from others individually, then make the decision independently; (4) collect suggestions and information from others as a group, but make the decision independently; or (5) meet with the group to formulate alternatives, and make the final decision as a group.

Which of these five alternatives the manager should choose depends on the requisite quality, commitment, and time for decision. The first alternative should be chosen in cases when the decision is relatively trivial (i.e., the concern for quality is negligible), particularly if subordinates are likely to accept the decision. It is also chosen when urgency prohibits consultation with others. The second alternative is appropriate when **decision quality** is important, but subordinates are likely to accept the decision. As the need for information and **subordinate support** rises, the manager will move to the third and fourth alternatives. Finally, when deci-

sion quality is important and subordinate support is critical, alternative five is appropriate.

Figure 6-1 illustrates the relationship between situational factors and the choice of decision strategy.

CONCEPT CHECK

The advantages of group problem solving and decision making include more available ideas, more available information, alternative perspectives, and enhanced fairness. Disadvantages of working in a group are time consumption and potential for conflict. However, conflict can also be beneficial if it furthers the group's exploration of ideas. Decision quality, support, and time constraints determine whether or not a manager should seek group input into a decision.

WHOM TO INCLUDE

Groups tend to be most effective when they include from 5 to 12 members (cf., Moore, 1987). The preceding discussion suggests two criteria for selecting group members: (1) persons who have requisite information, and (2) persons affected by the decision or who may have to cooperate in implementing the group's decision. Research into effective group decision making also suggests the value of including persons simply because they add

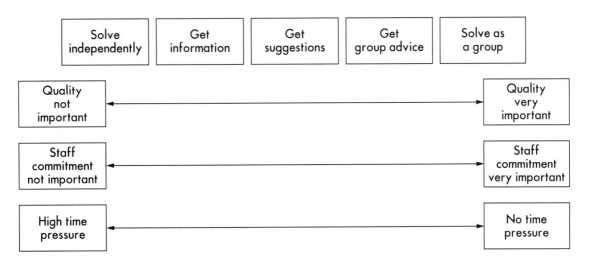

FIGURE 6-1   The relationship between situational factors and choice of decision strategy. (Courtesy Christine Green.)

diverse viewpoints, beliefs, or inclinations (Janis, 1982; Lamm, 1988). This can be particularly important if the decision is relatively risky.

Janis (1982) studied decision processes in four policy failures (the Bay of Pigs invasion, the invasion of North Korea, Pearl Harbor, and the Vietnam War) and two policy successes (the Cuban missile crisis and the Marshall Plan). He concludes that groups whose members readily agree make poorer policy **choices** than do groups whose members dispute options and values. The problem, he argues, is that groups prizing harmony will avoid contentious evaluation of policy alternatives. Consequently, the group will censor input of information or values that are inconsistent with dominant preferences. Since this prevents the group from learning from its **decision failures,** it can cause the group to persist with policies even after they have become overtly detrimental. Janis calls these phenomena **"groupthink."** He describes them this way:

> The more amiability and esprit de corps among the members of a policy-making in-group, the greater is the danger that independent critical thinking will be replaced by groupthink, which is likely to result in irrational and dehumanizing actions directed against outgroups.

The groupthink formulation has generated substantial research. Findings from field studies and laboratory experiments are generally supportive (Manz and Sims, 1982; Schwenk, 1986).

Lamm and Myers (1978) describe a related phenomenon that they call **"group polarization."** Group polarization refers to the tendency of groups to develop positions and attitudes that are more extreme than those held by individual group members before participating in group decision making. Two phenomena account for the polarization. First, group members are reinforced for taking positions that support the direction of group sentiment. This causes members to reinforce gradual shifts in attitude that are more extreme than any individual member's initial sentiment. Second, the group elaborates information and arguments that support its biases. This, in turn, supports the group's continued drift by engendering the impression that evidence is accumulating in support of more extreme positions. The formulation is supported by a substantial volume of research (Lamm, 1988).

Group polarization is a matter of particular concern when a decision involves risk because it can cause groups to choose options that are unnecessarily risky or overly cautious. Groups that begin with a risky bias are likely to become more risky; groups that begin with a conservative bias are likely to become more conservative. For example, when considering the feasibility of a new tournament, a group whose members were all fiscally conservative would be likely to reject the tournament. Conversely, a group whose members favored risky initiatives would be likely to approve the tournament.

Research suggests the following three selection procedures that can reduce a group's vulnerability to groupthink or group polarization (Fox, 1987; Nutt, 1989; Schweiger et al, 1986): (1) New perspectives can be obtained by rotating outside experts onto the group temporarily. (2) Critical evaluators can be incorporated to monitor and review the group's reasoning. (3) One or more group members can be assigned the role of **devil's advocate.**

CONCEPT CHECK

Persons should be selected for a group because they have needed information, will be affected by implementation of the decision, or will bring a distinctive perspective to the group. Groups lacking diversity can succumb to "groupthink" or "group polarization." Critical perspectives, such as a designated devil's advocate, can be incorporated to inject useful conflict and avoid early consensus.

TECHNIQUES FOR GROUP DECISION

Even when the manager is careful to minimize group vulnerability to polarization or groupthink, other pitfalls endanger the efficacy of group decision. Four of these are particularly important: **social loafing, status influence, limited creative flexibility,** and **plunging in.** A number of techniques for group decision making have been reported to aid groups in circumventing these pitfalls. To clarify the circumstances under which each technique becomes advantageous, it is first necessary to describe the four pitfalls.

Since the product of a group's activities is typically a joint product, the rewards to individual group members are rarely contingent on their individual performance in the group. If the decision or problem solution is truly a result of group interaction, it becomes impossible to specify accurately what percentage of the outcome is attributable to each member. In the best group decisions, the products of interaction among group members may be more significant than the discrete bits contributed by individual members. Consequently, it is rarely possible to apportion credit or benefits to each member in proportion to the member's unique contribution. This makes it possible for group members to reduce their individual effort, allowing others to sustain the group's work. This problem of social loafing, sometimes called "the **free rider problem,**" can impede the group's performance (Hardin, 1982).

Social loafing is not the sole cause of differences in individual contributions to the group's activity. Higher status individuals are likely to wield more influence than persons of lower status (Hollander, 1964). Status influence manifests itself both in terms of **group process** and the outcome of the group's work. Higher status individuals are more likely to speak and be spoken to. Their input is likely to be deemed more credible. The group is most likely to choose an alternative preferred by high status members.

The search for alternatives is itself guided by the **mental models** of group members (Cannon-Bowers et al., 1993). Each member of the group understands the problem on which the group is working "by constructing working models of it in their mind" (Johnson-Laird, 1983). A substantial body of work has shown that members will make considerable use of **analogies** to construct their mental models. Collins and Gentner (1987) describe the phenomenon this way:

Analogies are powerful ways to understand how things work in a new domain. We think this is because they enable people to construct a structure mapping that carries across the way the components in a system interact. This allows people to create new mental models that they can run to generate predictions about what should happen in various situations in the real world.

There is, however, a limitation that can become particularly acute as the group works together. Research shows that people often fail to search through an adequate array of analogies when prob-

lem solving (Gick and Holyoak, 1980, 1983). This failure may be exacerbated in the group situation because the group will communicate most effectively if members share a common mental model (Cannon-Bowers et al, 1993). The utility of a common mental model may cause the group to anchor on a single model or a limited subset of analogies. In so doing, the group loses a proportion of its creative flexibility.

Creative flexibility requires a balance of two kinds of thinking: **divergent thinking** and **convergent thinking.** These are separate processes. During divergent thinking, there is an active search for ideas. Ideas are generated, explored, expanded, and recombined. During convergent thinking, on the other hand, ideas are evaluated and compared. Whereas divergent thinking enlarges and elaborates the range of ideas, convergent thinking winnows ideas by evaluating, synthesizing, and selecting. Research on group problem solving shows that groups often plunge into making a decision before they have adequately probed their problem or elaborated a sufficient array of alternatives (Scheidel and Crowell, 1979). In other words, groups too often begin convergent thinking without first having engaged in sufficient divergent thinking.

CONCEPT CHECK

Common pitfalls in group decision making include social loafing, status influence, limited creative flexibility, and plunging in. Creativity can be enhanced by first using divergent thinking to generate and expand ideas, and then using convergent thinking to synthesize ideas and select among alternatives.

An entire consulting industry has grown up to "facilitate" group decisions using techniques originally designed to circumvent one or more of the pitfalls discussed so far. The consulting organization's preferred technique is typically marketed as a magic bullet, capable of enhancing any group process. It is usually offered as a fixed formula whose efficacy depends on precise adherence to sequential steps and specific rules (with which the consulting organization is fully familiar). Alas, no single technique or process is appropriate to all groups or decision situations. However, specialized techniques can prove useful if the manager applies each to circumvent the pitfall it is designed to circumvent. In fact, the methods can often be tailored to specific situations through combination or modification. This point is illustrated in the following description of seven techniques for group decision making and problem solving: **brainstorming,** the **nominal group technique, synectics, ideawriting,** and **Crawford slip method, dialectical decision making,** and the **Delphi technique.**

Brainstorming

The technique of brainstorming was originally developed by the advertising executive Alex Osborn (1948) as a means to elevate the flow of ideas during meetings. It has since enjoyed substantial popularity as a method for assembling a volume of ideas about management problems that can be readily expressed as simple, discussable questions. For example, during the planning phases of Playmakers, brainstorming was used to develop ideas in response to the question, "What activities could a sports camp offer as selling features to parents?" Brainstorming has also been used to collect ideas for questions like, "How can we promote more attendance for this event?" and "How can we reduce our dropout rate?"

The key principle of brainstorming is to separate the phase of divergent thinking from the phase of convergent thinking. The process begins with **idea generation** (i.e., divergent thinking), during which all **judgment** and criticism (i.e., convergent thinking) are disallowed. There are four rules during the idea generation phase:

1. Every idea is welcomed, no matter how wild or silly.
2. No criticism or judgment of any kind is permitted.
3. Produce as many ideas as possible; the goal is quantity, not quality.
4. Combine ideas or piggyback onto an idea wherever possible.

During a brainstorming session, bursts of ideas are often followed by quiet periods. When everyone becomes quiet, it is sometimes assumed that the group has listed its full complement of possibilities, and the idea generation phase is called to an end. However, quiet periods can precede a new flurry of ideas. For this reason, it is usually better to set time boundaries in advance, rather than simply to stop when there seems to be a lull.

The idea generation phase requires a leader who will enforce the rules and encourage participation. It also requires a recorder to keep track of the ideas. Neither the leader nor the recorder should participate in idea generation. However, the leader should be prepared to offer an idea to prompt further thinking if there is a substantial lull during the meeting. For the group to combine ideas, it is preferable to have the recorder write each idea where it can be seen, such as on a blackboard or flip chart.

Once the idea generation phase is completed, the group begins **idea evaluation.** Now judgment and critical appraisal are permitted. Ideas can be eliminated, modified, or further combined.

Group members sometimes become impatient with the rigid separation of divergent thinking from convergent thinking. However, research shows that the technique is effective. Groups using brainstorming produce more ideas and more high-quality ideas than do groups that generate and evaluate ideas simultaneously (Stein, 1975).

Nominal group technique

The nominal group technique (Delbecq et al, 1975) provides a useful variation on brainstorming. It is particularly useful if the time available to meet is too short for a full brainstorming session. Since it begins the group's activities with a period of individual work, it can also reduce the impact of social loafing, status influence, and group polarization. For these reasons, the technique was used extensively during meetings of the New Zealand research team studying the Seoul Olympics.

As with brainstorming, the nominal group technique begins with a **stimulus question.** Like brainstorming, it also requires a leader and a recorder. There are typically four steps for generating a group decision:

1. Each group member silently writes as many responses to the stimulus question as possible. This period of written response could be at the beginning of the meeting, or group members could be required to come to the meeting with written responses already prepared. It is expected

that group members will not have discussed their individual ideas in advance.

2. Each member contributes one idea. The idea is recorded onto a blackboard or flip chart. There is no discussion of ideas. Rather, the leader calls on each member in turn until all ideas are recorded or until the group determines that a sufficient number of ideas have been collected.

3. The group discusses each idea on the list. Each idea is discussed separately. Discussion of each idea continues until members are clear about its meaning.

4. The group ranks the ideas and discusses its rankings. A final choice may be made by majority vote.

Research confirms that in most circumstances the nominal group technique is superior to informal methods of group problem solving (Fox, 1987). It generates a larger number of high-quality ideas and a more even distribution of contributions from members. It is also favorably rated by most participants.

Combining brainstorming with the nominal group technique. When circumstances warrant, key features of brainstorming and the nominal group technique can be profitably combined. For example, during planning for the Olympic studies in New Zealand, the research team was concerned to maximize individual contributions, but members also wanted to synthesize, combine, and piggyback on each other's ideas. So team members were often required to write their ideas before meetings (as in the nominal group technique). These then became the initial input into an all-ideas-welcome collection of new ideas (as in brainstorming). This proved particularly useful for creating research instruments and procedures that were superior to those any individual had envisioned. This experience is consistent with Madsen and Finger's (1978) finding that brainstorming is sometimes facilitated when people develop notes about ideas they intend to propose during the session.

Synectics
There is substantial evidence that people fail to adequately explore the problem domain when problem solving (Bereiter and Scardamalia, 1985).

This impediment can be exacerbated in group situations when there is inadequate development of alternative problem representations. Synectics (Gordon, 1961) is intended to stimulate original group thinking by formalizing the development of analogies.

The technique requires a diverse group of specialists to share information via metaphor and analogy. Once the group is familiar with the problem to be solved, the group leader selects from one of the following four analogy types: personal, direct, symbolic, and fantasy. To understand how each of these works, consider the problem of crowd control at a motorcycle rally (cf., Veno and Veno, 1992). Using a personal analogy, group members might imagine themselves as spectators at the rally. Using a direct analogy, they would explore situations where a comparable function is accomplished, such as a cattle drive. To use a symbolic analogy, the group might compare the role of police officer with that of parent. This analogy would direct the group's attention to such factors as anticipating the needs of spectators and developing a trusting relationship with them. Finally, when using fantasy, anything goes, even magic or science fiction. For example, the group might imagine personal antigravity machines that would allow each spectator to float above the rally.

As each new analogy is introduced, it is the leader's job to steer participants into a detailed analysis. The purpose is to use the analogies to direct participants' minds away from traditional solutions to new insights. To facilitate the process, the group might go beyond discussion to **role plays** or to collecting information about the analogy. For example, in the case of the motorcycle rally, a synectics group might role play the parts of spectator and rally official, or the group might decide to learn more about how cattle are herded.

There is scant experimental evidence showing synectics to be an effective method, although the technique receives substantial favorable comment from users in industry (Stein, 1975). One problem may be that users have trouble applying analogies effectively (cf., Reed et al, 1985; Catrambond and Holyoak, 1987). As the group works with an analogy, it may be necessary for members to seek as many features as possible that are analogous to the group's problem (Holyoak and Koh, 1987). The specification of analogical similarity may further the group's insight.

Combining synectics with other methods. Synectics is intended to help groups extend their thinking by expanding the range of analogies from which they work. This can make it a useful tool in brainstorming or nominal group sessions. For example, it can generate new creative flurries during brainstorming by directing thinking onto new avenues. Similarly, synectics can be combined with the nominal group technique by requiring members to silently prepare a list of analogies for subsequent discussion and exploration.

During the initial meetings to design Playmakers, the four managers made explicit use of analogous situations (e.g., youth tour groups) to facilitate their brainstorming about new sport service opportunities. In some instances the analogous situations were researched in advance of the meeting. Elements of synectics, brainstorming, and the nominal group technique were modified and combined to meet the needs of the planning session.

This example illustrates the key point well—the technique itself is less important than the **decision pitfalls** its methods allow the group to circumvent. The effective manager first determines which pitfalls need to be circumvented, and then uses, modifies, or combines techniques as prescribed by the anticipated pitfall.

Ideawriting

Each of the techniques described so far is designed to circumvent pitfalls during the divergent thinking phase of the group's work. However, it may also be necessary to diminish the impact of those pitfalls during the convergent thinking phase. Ideawriting (Thissen et al, 1980) reduces social loafing, status influence, and group polarization by extending independent work into the phase of idea analysis and evaluation.

The procedures for ideawriting are relatively simple. Each participant responds to the stimulus question by writing his or her ideas on a pad. The pad is then placed in the middle of the group. Each person takes each other person's pad and writes a response, analysis, evaluation, and/or extension. The original writer then reads the responses. Finally, ideas and principles are discussed and summarized.

Although ideawriting does not promote the breadth of creativity fostered by brainstorming or synectics, it enjoys the unique advantage that it can be used with very large groups. Moore (1987) describes an application of ideawriting with 700 participants at an international conference. The participants were divided into small groups of between four and five persons each. Each group worked to identify community needs, such as the need for new sports facilities. Once a list of ideas had been generated, and everyone in the group had responded, the ideas were discussed and the five most promising were selected. Each group then reported its conclusions to the full assembly.

When several small groups present their conclusions, it is common for their reports to be collated and assigned to appropriate committees for further work. Although anecdotal reports (Moore, 1987; Thissen et al, 1980) suggest this procedure to be useful during planning and policy-making, it has not been subjected to empirical evaluation.

Crawford slip method

There are times when ideas collected during the divergent thinking phase are not winnowed. For example, when developing a training manual or listing the full range of an organization's needs, the goal may be to collate as many ideas as possible (cf., Ballard and Trent, 1989). In this instance, the concern is to optimize divergent thinking, but convergent work is primarily a matter of categorizing and organizing, rather than of evaluating and selecting.

The Crawford slip method has proven to be useful for such tasks. Crawford (1983) describes it this way: "Assemble the relevant people; define the target subjects; get everyone to write their ideas—one at a time, in a single sentence, on individual slips of paper; collect and classify all slips; edit the results into final form." Since the method is based entirely on written input, it can be used with groups of any size. Every person who has relevant information or experience should be included. The final collation of results can be performed separately by one or more editors.

Although the Crawford slip method has not been subjected to empirical scrutiny, Ballard and Trent (1989) cite apparently successful applications to preparation of training manuals, design of curricula, diagnosis of an organization's needs, improvement of services, and planning a new product. In sport settings, these applications would seem to be particularly useful for enhancing facility operations, service delivery, or program design.

Dialectical decision making

Some decisions are particularly consequential for the organization. For example, the decision may result in substantial expense, or it may precipitate an irreversible choice among strategic alternatives. In such instances, the evaluation of different ideas may be particularly important. In particular, it might be of interest to determine whether a decision is relatively consistent. In other words, do different groups reach similar conclusions? If they do not, it can be helpful to probe the assumptions from which differences emerge. The best choice may be easier to identify after scrutinizing the assumptions on which different options are based (Kleindorfer et al, 1993).

Dialectical decision making (Mitroff and Emshoff, 1979) is a useful technique in such cases because it requires group members to engage in multiple phases of convergent thinking. This has the added advantage that it can foster synthesis of several different options. Further, since the full group is divided into smaller subgroups, dialectical decision making can also reduce groupthink and group polarization.

The key to dialectical decision making is to develop two or more separate analyses of the decision problem. Each analysis is developed by a group working independently of other groups. At this phase, there are two possibilities: Each group can be instructed to develop its analysis in terms of what it deems the best possible alternatives. On the other hand, if it is important to fully examine a preexisting set of alternatives, each group could be assigned one alternative with the instruction to prepare an analysis that best supports it.

Once each group completes its analysis, group members are recombined to discuss the different analyses and to formulate a new analysis that builds on those of the small groups. At this phase, there are three possibilities: (1) The entire group can be convened to discuss the separate group analyses. (2) One new group can be constructed by assigning a member from each of the original groups. The new group consists of persons who did not work together during the preceding phase. (3) Several new groups can be constructed, each containing one member from each of the original groups.

If more than one new group is constructed, a further round of recombination is possible. In this case, the process of analyzing, recombining, and reanalyzing can be continued for as many iterations as desired. Through successive recombinations and reanalyses, new insights may emerge, or an apparent consensus may develop.

Combining dialectical decision making with other techniques. Dialectical decision making focuses primarily on the analysis of alternatives. As such, it is fundamentally a tool for convergent thinking phases. In contrast, brainstorming, the nominal group technique, synectics, and the Crawford slip method focus primarily on the divergent thinking phase of group decision making. Thus each of these four methods (or a combination) could be used to generate the ideas that will subsequently be analyzed through dialectical decision making. Similarly, when ideawriting sessions have been done in a multigroup fashion, further analysis can be accomplished through group recombinations like those used in dialectical decision making. Again, key components of the various techniques can be adapted or combined as needed for a specific decision task.

Delphi

There are times when the persons required for a decision task cannot meet together. On other occasions, status differences among participating experts threaten the group's impartiality. In such instances, the Delphi technique (Delbecq et al, 1975) can be useful. It is an excellent tool for pooling expert judgment.

The first step of a Delphi process is to establish the **Delphi panel** of experts. Delphi panelists will work anonymously; they are not told who the other panel members are. All correspondence from them goes to a **facilitator** who is not a member of the panel. Panelists remain at their home sites and communicate by mail or electronic mail. Although any number of panelists can be included, execution becomes increasingly labor intensive as panel size grows.

Once the panel is selected, each panelist is sent the Delphi question. Relevant data may also be included. Imagine, for example, that our concern is to determine experts' best judgment about new directions for sport policy. We might send our panel data on recent trends in sport participation, attendance at sports events, and audience ratings for sports on television. The accompanying Delphi question might ask, "What are the keys to enhancing public interest in sport over the next decade?"

Each panelist prepares a written response. The responses are collated and sent to panelists along with any supporting material (articles, statistics, etc.) that one or more individuals want to share. (When necessary, the Delphi facilitator will remove names from material being shared to maintain panelist anonymity.) Each panelist then responds to the new material. The panelist can agree, rebut, clarify, expand, or synthesize. The process of responding, collating, and responding again continues through successive rounds (usually around five) until a group consensus or a clear majority and minority viewpoint have emerged.

Unlike the other methods discussed here, Delphi can take several weeks or months to complete. Even the process of obtaining a panel can prove time-consuming. Nevertheless, the technique continues to be widely used for planning and policy-making (Linstone and Turoff, 1975; Moore, 1987, Chapter 4).

CONCEPT CHECK

Group decision techniques may be divided into those useful in the divergent thinking stage and those useful in the convergent thinking stage. Brainstorming, the nominal group technique, synectics, and the Crawford slip method are used to avoid pitfalls during the divergent thinking phase of a group's work. On the other hand, dialectical decision making focuses primarily on the convergence of ideas. Ideawriting and the Delphi technique bring their methods to bear during divergent thinking and convergent thinking phases. Components of several techniques can be combined as necessary to circumvent decision pitfalls.

FACILITATING GROUP DECISION MAKING AND PROBLEM SOLVING

Formal techniques for decision making do not relieve the manager from the task of facilitating the group's efforts. The adequacy of any decision depends, in part, on the adequacy of the processes by which the group reached its decision (Kleindorfer et al, 1993). Managing a group during decision making and problem solving is a key leadership skill. The requisite components are well studied and readily learned (Maier, 1963; Schwarz, 1994). Three pivotal skills are: sequencing the process, assuring balanced participation, and maintaining a task-oriented climate.

Sequencing the process

Inadequate attention to the sequential elements of team building and problem deliberation is one of the most common sources of poor group performance. Although the necessary procedures and outcomes may seem self-evident to the manager, group members may not share the manager's expectations.

At the outset, the group's goals, purposes, and timetable must be clarified. Group members may arrive at a meeting with varied or fuzzy understandings of what it is the group is going to do. Communication is enhanced and misunderstandings are reduced if fundamental elements of the group's work have been agreed upon. For example, what is the problem to be solved? What choices are to be made? How much time is available for the group's efforts? How will the group's analyses and decisions be reported? To whom? Will implementation of the group's decision be delegated, or will it be the group's responsibility?

Once the group has agreed on its goals, purposes, and timetables, it must establish its methods for operation. The rules for group interaction must be specified, and a basic agenda outlined. Decision rules (e.g., voting, consensus) should be agreed on. If it is likely that the group will need to gather information during its deliberations, an appropriate procedure should be developed. If a formal decision technique (brainstorming, synectics, idea writing, etc.) is to be used, its methods and procedures should be described.

The group is now ready to begin its deliberations. Each of the decision techniques reviewed in this chapter is designed to prevent the group from plunging into choosing an option. When no formal technique is applied, the manager must make certain that the group spends sufficient time exploring members' thoughts about the problem. The group should first be directed to collect requisite information and to share ideas and opinions. Since it is useful to have a variety of proposals and viewpoints on the table, the group should be discouraged from evaluating each alternative as it is presented. Rather, the manager should encourage the group to elaborate and clarify each idea, and to find potential syntheses.

Figure 6-2 illustrates an ideal sequence of tasks when making a group decision. As the discussion progresses, more attention can be paid to evaluating and classifying the various proposals that have been formulated. At this stage, it may be useful to summarize the suggestions and concerns that have been forthcoming and to ask whether any additional matters require discussion. As the evaluation of ideas progresses, the manager can test group consensus by summarizing key points and asking whether these adequately reflect members' appraisal. The process is concluded when a consensus or a clear majority or minority viewpoint emerges.

Assuring balanced participation

The group's work can be compromised by social loafing or status influence. The group leader's task is to encourage contribution and analysis of each member's best thinking. It is the leader's job to make certain that each member remains engaged and that each member's contribution receives adequate attention. To achieve those ends, it is useful to monitor who participates, how often, and with what impact. In this way, the leader seeks to identify persons whose ideas need to be queried or whose contributions require further examination. Four techniques are particularly useful for fostering balanced participation: **reinforcing, soliciting, prompting,** and **probing.**

The way in which points are received can affect members' subsequent willingness to contribute. Members are more willing to contribute when initial contributions have been welcomed. Body language (e.g., nodding, smiling) and verbal acknowledgment (e.g., "interesting point" or "that's something we should explore") encourage further participation. Writing the point on a blackboard or flip chart can also be reinforcing.

When a member has not contributed for some time, the leader can reinvolve them by soliciting a contribution. The solicitation might be as simple as, "Fred, what do you think?" Or it might be useful to solicit a member's contribution in terms of the role he or she plays in the group. For example, the leader might ask, "Sally, how would that idea affect facility operations?"

If one or two members are dominating the discussion, the leader can prompt other views by saying something like, "So far we've spent a lot of time on Chris and Jim's suggestion, let's hear some other possibilities." If a member is preempting other discussion, the leader can point that fact out, "Bill, you've made your point; now we'd like to hear some other views."

Probing can be useful when the group has ignored an idea or has neglected to explore one. If the group seems to be ignoring a contribution, the leader can say something like, "Joe's suggestion seems useful; let's explore it a bit more." If the group has failed to explore a previous idea, the leader can ask, "Jane, can you say a little more about that point you made a few minutes ago?" Sometimes a contribution is ignored because members failed to fully understand it. If that seems to be the case, the leader can ask, "Lee, could you elaborate on that point?"

Maintaining a task-oriented climate

If group members have a stake in the outcome of the group's deliberations, the discussion can become emotional. High emotions can distract the group from a focus on its task. In other instances,

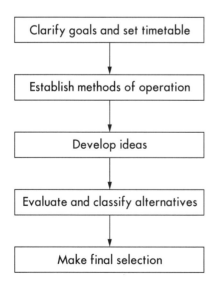

FIGURE 6-2 An ideal task sequence for group decision making. (Courtesy Christine Green).

the group may fail to address relevant hot topics to avoid conflict. In so doing, crucial components of the decision may be neglected. Sometimes a lack of conflict is more detrimental to the group's function than the conflict would be (Tjosvold, 1993). The confrontation of divergent views can clarify requisite needs for information and foster an appreciation of alternative viewpoints.

It is useful for the group leader to state at the outset that diverse views will be important for the group's work. Later, if emotions begin to run high, tension can sometimes be diffused by orienting group members to their common goal. The leader can reaffirm the value of fully exploring diverse views. It may even be appropriate to compliment the group on its frank and open discussions and to restate the group's common goal. If the emotional tone is still high, it may be useful to put the controversial issue aside temporarily and to refocus the group's attention on other aspects of the problem until emotions have cooled.

On some occasions, it may be important to face emotions directly. If a dispute between members is taken personally, the residual resentment can interfere with subsequent deliberations. In such instances, it may be necessary to put the decision task aside, openly discuss the hurt feelings, and reestablish consensus on group goals and processes.

Social norms in most management contexts disallow expressions of anger. This, in turn, can cause the group to avoid potentially controversial elements of a decision. When group deliberations seem to be skirting a delicate issue, an effective instruction might be, "It would seem useful to expand our discussion to include [the delicate issue]." By using leadership authority to steer the group onto a touchy subject, the leader reduces group members' sense of risk. For one thing, members need not fear recrimination for having raised the matter (since they did not). For another, controversial discussion was mandated by the group leader, who thus bears primary responsibility. Peer relations seem less threatened than if the issue had been forced by a group member.

CONCEPT CHECK

Managing group decision making and problem solving is a key leadership skill. A common source of poor group performance is inadequate sequencing of the decision process. Before beginning deliberations, the group should agree on its goals, purposes, timetables, and methods of operation. As the group works, the manager should ensure balanced participation by using such techniques as reinforcing, soliciting, prompting, and probing. Maintaining a task-oriented climate is vital, especially if the discussion has become emotional. The leader is responsible for seeing that controversial discussion and even conflict, when necessary, are not avoided.

SUPPORTING GROUP DECISION MAKING AND PROBLEM SOLVING

A variety of computer-based tools is available to aid group decision making and problem solving. These include **databases** to provide requisite information (Browne, 1993), procedures that break the task into **subproblems** (MacGregor and Lichtenstein, 1991), and **algorithms** (mathematical procedures) to help decision makers develop **quantitative models** of the **decision domain** (Watson and Buede, 1987). Current technologies allow **decision support systems** to be used by the group at the decision site and throughout the group's deliberations (Nunamaker et al, 1991). In the optimal case, each group member has a terminal, and each member's input can be shared visually by projecting it onto a screen that is visible to the entire group. Although sports organizations rarely utilize state-of-the-art decision support technologies, there is some use of databases and formal modeling. Examples include databases of information about players' performances and contracts (Waggoner, 1989) and formal procedures for rating potential draft picks (Whittingham, 1992, Chapter 2).

Since there is substantial room to broaden the scope of group decision support in sport settings, it is helpful to consider some of the reasons that decision support is beneficial. A key value of decision support is that it can provide an empirical check on decision makers' judgments and assumptions. A substantial body of work shows that even experts make consistent (often predictable) errors (Tversky and Kahneman, 1974, 1986). Poor judgments are often persistent because decision makers are typically overconfident about their judgments (Sniezek and Buckley, 1993).

The case of the "hot hand" in basketball provides an instructive illustration. After a player has executed a series of successful shots in close succession, coaches and administrators frequently believe that the player is on a hot streak. However, empirical studies of the phenomenon show it to be a statistical illusion (Gilovich et al, 1985). The probability of success in the player's next shot is in no way predicted by the streak of baskets preceding that shot. Nevertheless, the illusion of the hot hand has continued to condition marketplace estimates of a player's value (Camerer, 1989)—an example of decision error precipitated by fallacious judgment. Decision support systems can help reduce or eliminate biases like these by providing critical **baseline data** and necessary **probability estimates** (Kahneman and Tversky, 1982).

Another way that decision support systems can support the group's efforts is to help structure the task. Decision errors are diminished when decision makers are helped to elaborate their representation of the problem (Jungermann, 1980; Philips, 1983). Facilitation of task sequencing can be particularly useful. Kleindorfer, et al (1993,) describe the following five-step procedure: First, the system prompts the group to develop a single sentence summary of its task. Second, the system displays and stores ideas as the group brainstorms. Third, the system streamlines classification of the ideas. Fourth, the system provides algorithms to help the group rank or rate the ideas. Fifth, the system allows the group to assign tasks for implementing the decision.

A related form of structuring is to elicit from the group the attributes that members agree are important for judging the decision outcome. For example, in choosing a stadium site, city officials might be concerned about such factors as cost of land, impact on local business, impact on local residents, impact on local ecology, adequacy of roads, and accessibility by public transportation. Once the attributes relevant to decision makers are identified, the relative importance decision makers assign to each can be measured. For example, in the case of stadium siting, city officials might rate cost of land much more highly than they rate accessibility by public transportation. Thus cost of land would receive a proportionately higher weighting. After a weight determined for each attribute, alternative choices are assessed by identifying their attributes and applying the appropriate weights (Keeney and Raiffa, 1976). These procedures have been shown to be effective (Politser, 1991) and favorably received by users (John et al, 1983).

The limitations of short-term memory make it difficult for decision makers to absorb and use large quantities of new information (Sanford, 1985, Chapter 5). One useful remedy is to simplify the decision problem by having a model or formula for rating alternatives. For example, eleven NFL teams use the BLESTO ratings of players to help them choose the players they will draft. The BLESTO ratings combine such elements as player height, weight, strength, intelligence, injuries, 40-yard dash speed, position skills, lateral movement, aggression, and quickness into an overall measure of player potential (Whittingham, 1992). Although team management does not rely solely on the BLESTO ratings, the ratings simplify each team's decision making by summarizing an otherwise unwieldy array of information. Research suggests that decisions based on models of this kind are, on average, higher-quality and less prone to error than are decisions based solely on impressions or qualitative judgments (Dawes, 1979).

CONCEPT CHECK

Computer-based group decision support systems provide decision makers with a check on judgments and assumptions. Group decision support systems can also help the group to structure its problem and sequence its deliberations. One particularly useful method of structuring the problem is to identify the relevant attributes of the decision and then rate their relative importance to the decision. Models that aggregate large quantities of information into overall ratings provide another useful tool for simplifying the group's decision task.

SUMMARY

1. In sport management, groups are involved in planning, generating ideas, problem solving, decision making, agenda setting, policymaking, and governance.
2. When compared with individual problem solvers, groups can generate more ideas, locate more information, identify more perspectives, and formulate a decision that seems fairer.
3. When deciding whether to use a group for decision making, the manager should consider requisite decision quality, the amount

of time available to make the decision, and whether implementation of the decision will require subordinates to have helped formulate the decision.

4. Persons who have requisite information or who must cooperate in decision implementation should be included on the decision team.

5. Groupthink and group polarization can be minimized by including outside experts, incorporating critical evaluators, or assigning someone the role of devil's advocate.

6. The group's efforts can be compromised by social loafing, status influence, limited creative flexibility, and plunging in.

7. Brainstorming is a useful technique for collecting a wide array of ideas. Brainstorming separates the phase of divergent thinking from the phase of convergent thinking. During the divergent thinking phase, members are encouraged to contribute as many ideas as they can.

8. The nominal group technique also collects a wide array of ideas by separating the phase of divergent thinking from the phase of convergent thinking. Group members are required to begin by silently writing their ideas. The ideas are then discussed and evaluated.

9. Synectics uses analogies to enhance the group's creativity.

10. Ideawriting requires group members to write their ideas, to read each other's ideas, and to respond in writing. It can be used with small or large groups.

11. The Crawford slip method collects ideas by having participants write each idea on a single piece of paper. The ideas are then categorized and collated. The technique is particularly useful for developing training manuals, designing new services, or diagnosing an organization's needs.

12. Dialectical decision making breaks the group into two or more smaller groups. The analysis and decision of each smaller group is then used as input to formulate a final decision.

13. The Delphi technique obtains an estimate of expert consensus. Members of the Delphi panel work anonymously through several iterations of inquiry.

14. The various decision techniques can be modified or combined as the situation warrants.

15. The three pivotal skills for facilitating the group's work are sequencing the process, ensuring balanced participation, and maintaining a task-oriented climate.

16. Appropriate decision sequencing consists of the following: (a) establishing goals, purposes, and timetables; (b) presenting, elaborating, and clarify ideas; and (c) classifying, summarizing, and evaluating.

17. Methods for ensuring balanced participation include reinforcing, soliciting, prompting, and probing.

18. To maintain a task-oriented climate, the group leader must see to it that the group does not skirt around important yet sensitive issues. When emotions run high, the leader must help the group to refocus on its common objectives.

19. Decision support systems can assist the group by helping to sequence the task, by eliciting key decision attributes and values, by providing baseline data and probability estimates, and by formulating quantitative models for rating alternatives.

CASE STUDY

Court cases have always fascinated the public. The film Twelve Angry Men *takes one beyond the flash of the courtroom and is a classic example of the decision-making process.*

After viewing the film, consider the following questions:

1. *What pitfalls were portrayed, and how did the group work together to circumvent them?*
2. *How might technical decision support have aided the group's work?*
3. *What facilitation techniques would have been useful had the jury foreman known how to use them? When?*
4. *What other techniques might have improved this group's process?*

REVIEW QUESTIONS AND ISSUES

1. What are the relative pros and cons of group vs. individual decision making and problem solving?
2. What criteria should be used to evaluate who should be included in the group?
3. List and describe six pitfalls to be wary of during group decision making and problem solving.

4. Explain the difference between divergent thinking and convergent thinking. Why is it useful for the former to precede the latter?
5. Briefly describe an appropriate task sequence for group decision making and problem solving.
6. Define the four techniques for ensuring balanced participation.
7. How should conflict be managed during group decision making and problem solving?
8. Give an example of a decision problem faced by sport managers that would benefit from technical decision support. What kinds of support would be most helpful? Why?
9. Write a stimulus question about a sport management problem. What kind of organization might seek to obtain an answer to such a question? If you were putting a group together to answer the question for such an organization, whom would you include? Why? What decision techniques would you apply? How? Why?

REFERENCES

Ballard, J. A., and Trent, D. M. (1989). Idea generation and productivity: the promise of CSM. *Public Productivity Review, 12,* 373-386.

Bereiter, C., and Scardamalia, M. (1985). Cognitive coping strategies and the problem of inert knowledge. In S. S. Chipman, J. W. Segal, and R. Glazer (Eds.), *Thinking and learning skills: current research and open questions* (Vol. 2, pp. 65-80). Hillsdale, New Jersey: Lawrence Erlbaum Associates.

Browne, M. (1993). *Organizational decision making and information.* Norwood, New Jersey: Ablex.

Camerer, C. F. (1989). Does the basketball market believe in the "hot hand?" *American Economic Review, 79,* 1257-1260.

Cannon-Bowers, J. A., Salas, E., and Converse, S. (1993). Shared mental models in expert team decision making. In N.J. Castellan, Jr. (Ed.), *Individual and group decision making: current issues* (pp. 221-246). Hillsdale, New Jersey: Lawrence Erlbaum Associates.

Catrambone, R., and Holyoak, K. J. (1987). Transfer of training as a function of procedural variety of training examples. In *Proceedings of the Ninth Annual Conference* (pp. 36-49). Hillsdale, New Jersey: Cognitive Science Society.

Chalip, L. (1990). The politics of Olympic theatre: New Zealand and Korean cross-national relations. In Seoul Olympic Sports Promotion Foundation (Ed.), *Toward one world beyond all barriers* (Vol. 1, pp. 408-433). Seoul: Poong Nam.

Chalip, L. (1991). Sport and the state: the case of the United States of America. In F. Landry, M. Landry, and M. Yerles (Eds.), *Sport: the third millenium* (pp. 243-250). Sainte-Foy, Quebec: Les Presses de l'Universite Laval.

Collins, A., and Gentner, D. (1987). How people construct mental models. In D. Holland and N. Quinn (Eds.), *Cultural models in language and thought* (pp. 243-265). New York: Cambridge University Press.

Crawford, C. C. (1983). How you can gather and organize ideas quickly. *Chemical Engineering,* July 15, 87-90.

Dawes, R. M. (1979). The robust beauty of improper linear models in decision making. *American Psychologist, 34,* 571-582.

Delbecq, A. L., Van de Ven, A. H., and Gustafson, D. H. (1975). *Group techniques for program planning: a guide to nominal group and Delphi processes.* Glenview, Illinois: Scott-Foresman.

Fox, W. M. (1987). *Effective group problem solving.* San Francisco: Jossey-Bass.

Gick, M. L., and Holyoak, K. J. (1980). Analogical problem solving. *Cognitive Psychology, 12,* 306-355.

Gick, M. L., and Holyoak, K. J. (1983). Schema induction and analogical transfer. *Cognitive Psychology, 15,* 1-38.

Gilovich, T., Vallone, R., and Tversky, A. (1985). The hot hand in basketball: on the misperception of random sequences. *Cognitive Psychology, 17,* 295-314.

Gordon, W. J. J. (1961). *Synectics.* New York: Collier.

Hardin, R. (1982). *Collective action.* Baltimore: Johns Hopkins University Press.

Hollander, E. P. (1964). *Leaders, groups and influence.* New York: Oxford University Press.

Holyoak, K. J., and Koh, K. (1987). Surface and structural similarity in analogical transfer. *Memory and Cognition, 15,* 332-340.

Janis, I. L. (1982). *Groupthink* (2nd ed.). Boston: Houghton Mifflin.

Janis, I. L., and Mann, L. (1977). *Decision making: a psychological analysis of conflict, choice, and commitment.* New York: Free Press.

John, R. S., von Winterfeldt, D., and Edwards, W. (1983). The quality and user acceptance of multiattribute utility analysis performed by computer and analyst. In P. Humphreys, O. Svenson, and A. Vari (Eds.), *Analysing and aiding decision processes* (pp. 301-319). Amsterdam: North-Holland.

Johnson-Laird, P. (1983). *Mental models.* Cambridge, Massachusetts: Harvard University Press.

Jungermann, H. (1980). Speculations about decision-theoretic aids for personal decision making. *Acta Psychologica, 45,* 7-34.

Kahneman, D., and Tversky, A. (1982). Intuitive prediction: biases and corrective procedures. In D. Kahneman, P. Slovic and A. Tversky (Eds.), *Judgment under uncertainty: Heuristics and biases* (pp. 414-421). New York: Cambridge University Press.

Kenney, R. O., and Raiffa, H. (1976). *Decisions with multiple objectives: preferences and value tradeoffs.* New York: Wiley.

Kleindorfer, P. R., Kunreuther, H. C., and Schoemaker, P. J. H. (1993). *Decision sciences: an integrative perspective.* New York: Cambridge University Press.

Koopman, P., and Pool, J. (1991). Organizational decision making: models, contingencies, and strategies. In J. Rasmussen, B. Brehmner, and J. Leplat (Eds.), *Distributed decision making: Cognitive models for cooperative work* (pp. 19-46). New York: Wiley.

Lamm, H. (1988). A review of our research on group polarization: eleven experiments on the effects of group discussion on risk acceptance, probability estimation, and negotiation positions. *Psychological Reports, 62,* 807-813.

Lamm, H., and Myers, D. G. (1978). Group-induced polarization of attitudes and behavior. In L. Berkowitz (Ed.), *Advances in experimental social psychology* (Vol. 11, pp. 145-195). San Diego: Academic Press.

Linstone, H. A., and Turoff, M. (Eds.) (1975). *The Delphi method: techniques and applications.* Reading, Massachusetts: Addison-Wesley.

Madsen, D. B., and Finger, J. R. (1978). Comparison of written feedback procedure, group brainstorming, and individual brainstorming. *Journal of Applied Psychology, 63,* 120-123.

MacGregor, D. G., and Lichtenstein, S. (1991). Problem structuring aids for quantitative estimation. *Journal of Behavioral Decision Making, 4,* 101-116.

Maier, N. R. F. (1963). *Problem solving discussions and conferences: leadership methods and skills.* New York: McGraw-Hill.

Manz, C. C., and Sims, H., Jr. (1982). Searching for the 'unleader:' Organizational member views on leading self-managing groups. *Human Relations, 37,* 409-424.

Mitroff, I. I., and Emshoff, J. R. (1979). On strategic assumption making: a dialectical approach to policy and planning. *Academy of Management Review, 4,* 1-12.

Moore, C. M. (1987). *Group techniques for idea building.* Newbury Park, California: Sage.

Nunamaker, J. F., Jr., Dennis, A. R., Valacich, J. S., and Vogel, D. R. (1991). Information technology for negotiating groups: generating options for mutual gain. *Management Science, 37,*(10), 1325-1346.

Nutt, P. (1989). *Making tough decisions.* San Francisco: Jossey-Bass.

Osborn, A. (1948). *Your creative power.* New York: Charles Scribner's Sons.

Philips, L. D. (1983). A theoretical perspective on heuristics and biases in probabilistic thinking. In P. Humphreys, O. Svenson, and A. Vari (Eds.), *Analysing and aiding decision processes* (pp. 525-543). Amsterdam: North-Holland.

Politser, P. E. (1991). Do medical decision analyses' largest gains grow from the smallest trees. *Journal of Behavioral Decision Making, 4,* 121-138.

Putnam, L. L. (1986). Conflict in group decision-making. In R. Y. Hirokawa and M. S. Poole (Eds), *Communication and group decision-making* (pp. 175-196). Newbury Park, California: Sage.

Reed, S. K., Dempster, A., and Ettinger, M. (1985). Usefulness of analogous solutions for solving algebra word problems. *Journal of Experimental Psychology: Learning, Memory and Cognition, 11,* 106-125.

Sanford, A. J. (1985). *Cognition and cognitive psychology.* New York: Basic Books.

Scheidel, T. M., and Crowell, L. (1979). *Discussing and deciding.* New York: Macmillan.

Schwarz, R. M. (1994). *The skilled facilitator: practical wisdom for developing effective groups.* San Francisco: Jossey-Bass.

Schweiger, D. M., Sandberg, W. R., and Ragan, J. W. (1986). Group approaches for improving strategic decision making: a comparative analysis of dialectical inquiry, devil's advocacy, and consensus. *Academy of Management Journal, 29,* 51-71.

Schwenk, C. R. (1986). Information, cognitive biases, and commitment to a course of action. *Academy of Management Review, 11,* 298-310.

Sniezek, J. A., and Buckley, T. (1993). Becoming more or less uncertain. In N. J. Castellan, Jr. (Ed.), *Individual and group decision making: current issues* (pp. 87-108). Hillsdale, New Jersey: Lawrence Erlbaum Associates.

Stein, M. I. (1975). *Stimulating creativity* (Vol. 2). New York: Academic Press.

Thissen, W. A. H., Sage, A. P., and Warfield, J. N. (1980). *A user's guide to public systems methodology.* Charlottesville, Virginia: School of Engineering and Applied Science.

Tjosvold, D. (1993). *Learning to manage conflict.* New York: Lexington Books.

Tversky, A., and Kahneman, D. (1974). Judgments under uncertainty: heuristics and biases. *Science, 185,* 1124-1131.

Tversky, A., and Kahneman, D. (1986). Rational choice and the framing of decisions. *Journal of Business, 59,* 5251-5284.

Veno, A., and Veno, E. (1992). Managing public order at the Australian Motorcycle Grand Prix. In D. Thomas and A. Veno (Eds.), *Psychology and social change* (pp. 74-92). Palmerston North, New Zealand: Dunmore Press.

Vroom, V., and Yetton, P. (1973). *Leadership and decision-making.* Pittsburgh: University of Pittsburgh Press.

Waggoner, G. (1989). It's a whole new ballgame! PCs and baseball. *PC Computing, 2*(6), 61-73.

Watson, S. R., and Buede, D. M. (1987). *Decision synthesis: the principles and practice of decision analysis.* New York: Cambridge University Press.

Whittingham, R. (1992). *The meat market: the inside story of the NFL draft.* New York: MacMillan.

SUGGESTED READING

Crawford, C. C. (1985). Crawford slip method (CSM). *Air Force Journal of Logistics, 9*(2), 28-30.

Eden, C., and Radford, J. (Eds.) (1990). *Tackling strategic problems: the role of group decision support.* London: Sage.

Gordon, W. J. J. (1961). *Synectics.* New York: Collier.

Kleindorfer, P. R., Kunreuther, H. C., and Schoemaker, P. J. H. (1993). *Decision sciences: an integrative perspective.* New York: Cambridge University Press.

Koopman, P., and Pool, J. (1991). Organizational decision making: Models, contingencies, and strategies. In J. Rasmussen, B. Brehmenr, and J. Leplat (Eds.), *Distributed decision making: cognitive models for cooperative work* (pp. 19-46). New York: Wiley.

Mason, R. O., and Mitroff, I. I. (1981). *Challenging strategic planning assumptions.* New York: Wiley-Interscience.

Moore, C. M. (1987). *Group techniques for idea building.* Newbury Park, California: Sage.

Osborn, A. F. (1963). *Applied imagination* (3rd ed.). New York: Charles Scribner's Sons.

Schwarz, R. M. (1994). *The skilled facilitator: practical wisdom for developing effective groups.* San Francisco: Jossey-Bass.

Vroom, V., and Yetton, P. (1973). *Leadership and decision-making.* Pittsburgh: University of Pittsburgh Press.

Watson, S. R., and Buede, D. M. (1987). *Decision synthesis: the principles and practice of decision analysis.* New York: Cambridge University Press.

CHAPTER 7

Human Resource Management in Sport

Wendy Frisby and Lisa Kikulis

In this chapter, you will become familiar with the following terms:

Human resource management (HRM)	Groupthink	Symbols
Personal administration (PA)	External recruitment	Rituals
Competitive advantage	Contracting out	Ideology
Social responsibility	Selection process	Myths
Total quality management (TQM)	Training	Political activity
Traditional paradigm	Development opportunities	Political influence
Internal recruitment	Interpretive paradigm	Critical paradigm
	Organizational culture	Power imbalance

Overview

Human resources are increasingly recognized as the key to strong and effective organizations. As many authors and managers have emphasized, competitive advantage is achieved by investing in an organization's key asset—its people. Even though sport organizations have always relied heavily on human resources such as players, coaches, volunteers, retail staff, facility managers, suppliers, sport marketing directors, owners, chief executive officers, athletic directors, and others, it is surprising to find that very little has been written about human resource management (HRM) within the context of sport. Although sport organizations typically have well-developed strategies in a number of key management areas such as finance, marketing, product development, and program planning, the articulation and investigation of HRM strategies have been mostly overlooked.

Sport organizations face a number of challenges such as increasing competition, diversified and changing markets, declining financial resources, advances in technology, and changes in regulatory environments. To meet these and other challenges, sport managers require a sensitivity to people— their abilities, their values, their differences, their concerns, and their potential. Although well-defined organizational structures, together with financial and marketing strategies, are necessary, they are not sufficient conditions for success. The future success of sport organizations rests on the capacity of sport managers to deal with human resource issues from multiple points of view.

The approach that will be taken in this chapter will be to introduce students to three different ways of analyzing HRM, while drawing on a range of sport related examples. The rationale for adopting this strategy is that each of the three paradigms provide a different "lens" for understanding HRM practices in sport. Thus the reader is presented with a broader perspective than would be possible by relying on any one paradigm. This strategy is in keeping with Morgan's (1988) assertion that managers of the future need multiple mind sets to deal with the realities and complexities of a rapidly changing world. He suggests that the ready-made "recipes for action" and "quick fixes," which are prevalent in the popular management literature and in many HRM textbooks, are often based on partial and simplistic views of organizational life.

Like a photographer who uses different lenses to fully appreciate his or her subject matter, the sport manager can view HRM from a variety of angles. The traditional paradigm (a normal 35-mm lens) enables sport managers to develop an understanding of the observable HRM principles of recruiting, hiring, training, compensating, and evaluating human resources. From this vantage point, sport managers will be concerned with meeting the internal human resource needs of the organization in a cost-effective manner, as well as complying with externally imposed regulations (e.g., human rights legislation).

Some sport managers feel very comfortable with the traditional paradigm because it focuses on the HRM elements that are most visible and easy to control. However, if the traditional view is employed exclusively, managers will have a limited perspective on how human resources operate and contribute to their organizations.

Like the photographer who wants a close-up, sport managers also need to use a "zoom lens" to un-

derstand the aspects of HRM that are not always readily observable and measurable. Anyone who has worked or volunteered for a sport organization will know that politics and conflict are natural and inevitable by-products of human interaction. The interpretive paradigm encourages managers to understand the deeper layers of organizational life from the point of view of athletes, employees, and volunteers. From this angle, it is important to understand how values and beliefs of organizational members shape courses of action and impact on the ability of the organization to achieve its goals and adapt to change. The interpretive paradigm reveals that there is not always consensus and conformity around HRM issues. The cancellation of the 1994-1995 major league baseball season resulting from conflicts between the players' union and the owners over salary caps is an example of this.

The traditional and interpretive paradigms enable sport managers to understand the "hardware" (e.g., the formal policies and procedures used to assess employee potential and performance) and the "software" (e.g., the informal norms, values, beliefs that guide action) of HRM. Yet these two perspectives do not provide a complete picture of HRM in sport. It is not until we use a "wide-angle lens" that we can uncover the "dark side" of HRM. The critical paradigm encourages us to stand back and examine how existing power relationships benefit some groups and get reproduced over time, which, in turn, alienate other individuals and groups. It is only then that issues such as employee exploitation, workplace safety, corruption, and discrimination get raised. A wide-angle lens is needed because many of the issues examined through the critical paradigm are related to broader social, political, economic, and historical conditions that exist outside of the organization.

Together the three "lenses" provide us with a strategy for dealing with HRM in a more holistic way. Still, they are not the only ways of understanding HRM. In recent years, articles have been written about HRM from feminist and postmodern paradigms as well (Hall et al, 1989; Townley, 1993). Although it will not be possible to cover all of these approaches, the reader is encouraged to investigate the additional issues raised by each. The key point to remember is that HRM in sport is complex; consequently, it is not wise to approach the topic from only one fixed and rigid standpoint. Instead, sport managers must be able to analyze human resource situations and choose which lens, or combination of lenses, will deal effectively with the situations encountered.

CONCEPT CHECK

Because human resource management is complex and crucial to organizational success, sport managers need to analyze it from several angles. The traditional paradigm focuses on the readily observable aspects, the interpretive paradigm focuses on the deeper levels of social interaction, and the critical paradigm focuses on the consequences of power relations, which are influenced by broader social, political, economic, and historical conditions.

Before discussing the three approaches to HRM in more depth, it is important to define what HRM is, how it has evolved, and why it is such a prominent part of the sport management process.

HUMAN RESOURCE MANAGEMENT

Human resource management (HRM) has developed over time mainly in response to shifting practical problems facing managers with respect to the recruitment, utilization, and compensation of full-time employees. The area was traditionally called **personnel administration (PA)** and emphasized the tactical ways in which employers could manage employees to increase organizational productivity. This was accomplished through personnel systems whereby prospective employees could be recruited, selected, trained, evaluated, promoted, discharged, and compensated in a cost-effective manner (Friend, 1991). The underlying aim of PA was to control costs for the following reasons:

1. Salaries are often the largest expenditure in most organizations.
2. Productivity is thought to decline when there is low morale and low job satisfaction among workers.
3. There are numerous costs associated with the recruitment, selection, and training of new employees.

4. There are numerous costs associated with grievances and other legal action initiated by employees when they feel that employer actions (or inaction) have been unjust.

The shift in terminology to HRM reflects a more strategic approach whereby people are viewed as the most important resources for accomplishing organizational goals. HRM is essentially a business-oriented philosophy designed to obtain value from employees, which increases competitive advantage in the market place. Instead of seeing employees as cost factors that must be controlled by management, newer approaches to HRM view human resources as assets worthy of investment. In turn, HRM investments are designed to release the creative talents of people to accomplish the strategic plans of the organization.

Although PA often emphasized the need for new employees to fit into specific jobs within existing organizations, progressive HRM strategies focus on hiring people who will be adaptable and willing to change over time. An example of a strategic approach to HRM is the *Sport Discovery Process*, which was developed by the Sport Services Branch of the Ministry of Municipal Affairs, Recreation, and Housing in British Columbia, Canada. Every year, sport executives in provincial sport organizations (e.g., Basketball B.C., B.C. Sport and Fitness Council for the Disabled) are asked to rate the current status of their organizations in a number of areas. The areas that relate to HRM include orientation programs for new volunteers; roles and responsibilities for board members, paid staff, and volunteers; recruiting and hiring practices; professional development opportunities; evaluation and recognition programs; ethical practices; and gender equity initiatives. Sport executives are then asked to indicate what action will be taken in each area in the following year and to justify their decisions. This process helps the sport organizations to set objectives for the following year and is used by the government to make funding decisions (Sport Services Branch, 1993).

CONCEPT CHECK

A strategic approach to HRM in sport would be that instead of viewing human resources as separate from other management activities that involve filling short-term job requirements, human resource practices should have a long-term focus that is closely linked to the achievement of organizational objectives and plans.

WHY HRM IS IMPORTANT IN SPORT

In addition to the cost-control concerns mentioned earlier, there are a number of reasons why managers are starting to view human resources as their most critical resource. The reasons that will be addressed here include the following:

1. Links between HRM and competitive advantage
2. Shift to an information or a knowledge-based society
3. Social responsibility employers have for employees
4. Links between HRM and customer satisfaction
5. Legal considerations

With respect to **competitive advantage,** Pfeffer (1994) concluded from his study of the performance of several U.S. industries from 1972 to 1992 that it was HRM practices that differentiated top performing companies from their competitors. He found that the top performers did not exhibit the characteristics usually associated with success (e.g., being market share leaders, having unique technologies, having access to financial resources, and having little industry competition). The key to competitive success, according to Pfeffer, was to create an organizational culture where human capabilities are maximized. Similar arguments could be made in sport, although studies similar to Pfeffer's have yet to be undertaken in sport. Still, it is the combination of people who create the vision of what needs to be accomplished and who set the strategies in action to carry out these plans that ultimately determines the success of any sport organization.

Another reason why more attention is being directed toward HRM is that society is undergoing a managerial revolution as we shift from a manufacturing-based to an information-based and knowledge-based society. Drucker (1993) contends that the possession of knowledge (rather than the ownership of natural resources, labor, and capital) has become the decisive factor that is affecting pro-

ductivity as we move towards the year 2000. He explains this notion further in the following statement:

In the 1980s and 1990s, during the traumatic restructuring of American business, many thousands of knowledge employees lost their jobs. Their company was acquired, merged, spun off, liquidated, and so on. Yet within a very few months, the great majority found new jobs in which to put their knowledge to work. The transition period was painful, and in about half the cases the new job did not pay quite as much as the old one and may not have been as enjoyable. But laid-off technicians, professionals, and managers found that they had the "capital"—their knowledge; they owned the means of production (Drucker, 1993).

Certainly, if we use the running shoe industry as an example, it is clear that the possession of knowledge in a number of areas, such as technology of running shoe design and trends in the footwear marketplace, are key factors in determining success. In fact, Beck (1992) identified "recreational services," which presumably includes sport, as one of the "high knowledge-intensive industries" that has accounted for 89.5% of new job creation in Canada over the past 7 years.

The growing prominence of HRM is also linked to the notion of **social responsibility** towards employees. In comparison with the past, there is considerable pressure on employers to provide employees with work environments that are safe, that are free from discrimination, that are challenging, and that offer opportunities for advancement. Managers who place a priority on HRM are creating structures and strategies that will instill a sense of commitment to the organization, which in turn allows organizations to retain valued human resources whether they are full-time employees, part-time employees, or volunteers.

Total quality management (TQM) is a concept that has recently been incorporated into the HRM vocabulary. According to Mawson (1993), the three underlying tenets of TQM are a focus on customer satisfaction, seeking continuous improvement, and ensuring full involvement of the entire organization in improving quality. Schneider and Bowen (1993) have found support for the HRM service-quality connection that underlies TQM. That is, their studies show that the way managers treat employees is generally reflected in the way employees treat consumers. Therefore if employee needs are being met, and they work in an environment that promotes and supports quality service, it is more likely that sport consumers such as spectators, retail customers, participants, parents, and others will be satisfied and develop a sense of loyalty to the organization.

On a more practical level, HRM practices are governed by a number of laws, some of which are discussed in other sections of this book. Although it is beyond the scope of this chapter to deal with HRM legislation, sport managers must stay current on laws governing issues such as equal pay, human rights, and labor relations.

CONCEPT CHECK

Competitive advantage can be achieved when human potential is maximized. The transition to an information-based and knowledge-driven society has enhanced the economic value of human resources. This has led to a focus on social responsibility for employees. TQM is one approach used to maximize the involvement of human resources in generating ideas for improved service quality.

HUMAN RESOURCES IN SPORT

The literature on HRM primarily refers to full-time employees in profit-oriented businesses that are large enough to have specialized positions in HRM. Sport managers often face a number of different challenges. They work with a wider range of human resources who may vary considerably in terms of age, education, and experience. Furthermore, sport takes place in a wide variety of settings, some of which are profit oriented (e.g., professional sport, the retail sport industry, tourism-related businesses). Others are nonprofit in orientation (e.g., local sport clubs, schools, charitable organizations, government organizations). The goals and human resource needs of these different kinds of sport organizations are often quite diverse.

Sport employees are not always hired on a full-time basis. Part-time, seasonal, contractual, and volunteer positions are very common in the field of sport and will likely continue to be in an era of declining financial resources. Although larger sport companies and organizations may have specialized HRM positions (e.g., the scout in professional sport, the human resource director for a ski resort), HRM

is often only one of the many functions that a sport manager must perform. Given the diversity of human resource needs in sport (see Table 7–1), it is unlikely that the use of any one paradigm will be effective across all situations.

PARADIGM SHIFTS IN HRM

Several authors lament the fact that HRM lacks a theoretical base to guide research and practice (Ferris and Judge, 1991; Meek, 1992; Steffy and Grimes, 1992). Many of these same authors contend that this is because the assumptions underlying the **traditional paradigm,** which dominates most HRM textbooks and organizational practices, have seldom been challenged. According to Ferris and Judge (1991), the work that has been more theoretical is largely psychological or economic in orientation. A more recent development, as mentioned earlier, is to view HRM from a strategic perspective. However, the limitation of all of these approaches is that they only provide a rational or positivist interpretation of HRM issues. Inspired by scientific management advocated by Taylor in the early 1900s (Brown, 1990), the emphasis is on explaining, controlling, and predicting behavior. Only recently have other paradigms, which have their roots in academic disciplines such as sociology and anthropology, been applied to HRM. The aim of the remainder of this chapter is to illustrate how the application of these paradigms can expand our understanding of the dynamics underlying HRM in sport.

The traditional paradigm

The traditional HRM paradigm, which is closely tied to personnel administration, is concerned with devising systems whereby employees can be recruited, selected, trained, and rewarded to optimize productivity. An emphasis is placed on developing procedures to help managers make objective decisions in each of these areas. Examples of the types of questions that sport managers would have based on this paradigm include the following:

1. How many employees do we need and what kinds of skills and abilities should they possess?
2. Should we go inside or outside our organization to fill vacancies?
3. What types of training will new employees need to fit the requirements of the job?

TABLE 7-1   *Examples of human resources in sport*

Type of organization	Human resources	
University or college athletic department	Athletic director Assistant athletic directors Coaches Facility manager Intramural coordinator	Financial manager Public relations/marketing Director Clerical staff Maintenance staff Student representatives
Retail sport franchise	Franchisor Franchisee Distributors	Part-time and full-time staff Suppliers Manufacturers
Professional sport team	Athletes Coaching staff Concession staff Merchandising staff Financial managers	General managers Marketing directors Medical staff Scouts Facility staff
Municipal sport and recreation department	Assistant director Community developer Director Instructors	Parks and facilities manager Seniors coordinator Special needs coordinator Youth programmer
Event marketing company	Account directors Events managers Marketing representatives	President or chief executive director Vice presidents Player agents
Ski resort	Hill groomers Human resource director Lift operators Instructors	Instructors Marketing director Owner Ski patrollers
Local clubs	Coaches Volunteers Board of directors	Fund raising committee Club members Officials

4. How will we evaluate the performance of our employees and volunteers?
5. How will we reward productive employees in order to retain them in our organization?

The traditional approach usually begins with an inventory of current staff, which involves collecting information on their current positions, skills, and career progression. From here, organizational needs can be assessed to determine if expanding, retraining, or reducing staff is required to meet organizational goals (Culkin and Kirsch, 1986). If new staff or volunteers are required, the next step entails a job analysis where job descriptions are developed. Job descriptions usually have two components: (1) the written statements about what employees are expected to do (e.g., the job specifications) and (2) the types of skills, abilities, education, and experience needed to perform the job (e.g., the job qualifications). Well-written job descriptions can then become the basis for making a number of important decisions about the type of applicants desired, the orientation and training program that will be necessary to assist them in their jobs, and the amount of compensation that they should receive. In addition, decisions to retrain or reduce staff could result in changes to existing job descriptions and reporting relationships between staff and supervisors.

Through the employee recruitment process, sport organizations are simultaneously selling themselves as good places to work as well as attempting to attract the most qualified applicants to vacant positions. Applicants may be recruited from those already working for the organization through job postings and announcements. An advantage of hiring internally is that it is easier to evaluate the knowledge, skills, and abilities of current employees than outsiders. **Internal recruitment** can also become a retention strategy because employees see that there are opportunities for advancement. However, there is a danger that continually hiring from within will create a work force that tends to think and act alike. Some managers think that commonality will create a unified work team, **groupthink.** However, plans that are never seriously questioned or challenged is a limitation of this method (Morgan, 1986).

External recruitment can result in a more diversified work force. Word-of-mouth advertising and the placing of job announcements in professional publications, newspapers, and other outlets are commonly used methods for external recruitment.

In times of economic restraint, **contracting out** is another form of recruitment. Sport organizers might invite specialized marketing firms to bid on one-time, short-term contracts to obtain sponsorship for major events. This strategy allows organizers to draw on the expertise of outsiders without having to assume the salary and benefit expenses of full-time employees.

The **selection process** is very important. This step usually entails a combination of resume analysis, interviews, simulations, and reference checks. Written tests and medical examinations are may also be required. The selection process is different when it comes to choosing volunteers for committee and board of director positions in sport clubs or associations. In this instance, club members usually select volunteers through the election process.

Once employees and volunteers have been recruited and selected, it is important to orient, train, and develop these individuals. Unfortunately, these steps are often overlooked. Sport managers sometimes assume that because new employees or volunteers have the educational qualifications or experience specified in job descriptions, they will automatically be able to perform their jobs well. However, no two jobs are exactly the same because the goals, people, resources, customers, and policies create different work environments.

Orientation sessions are designed to socialize new employees and volunteers into the organization. These sessions provide information about working conditions, reporting relationships, policies, and procedures.

Training, on the other hand, emphasizes the specific knowledge and skills needed to perform the job effectively. For example, athletes are often given play books so that they can learn the offensive and defensive strategies of the particular team. Similarly, someone joining a financial department would need training on the specific accounting system used by that sport organization. The choice of training format will depend on the expected outcomes. On-the-job coaching, apprenticeship training, discussion groups, formal lectures, and role playing are examples of different training formats.

The concept of development has been given more attention in recent years because it is necessary for employees who stay abreast of new ideas, techniques, and strategies. Employee development is also used as a retention strategy because it is recognized that pay increases are not the only factors that motivate people. More and more, employees and volunteers seek opportunities to learn, grow, and keep current. Professional development opportunities (e.g., attending workshops and seminars) and career planning sessions are examples of **development opportunities** that are designed to link the needs of the employee to the needs of the organization.

The duties listed in job descriptions can also form the basis for evaluating the performance of employees. Culkin and Kirsch (1986) provided an example of this. First, all assigned duties on the job description are listed on a performance appraisal form. Then managers rate each employee on their performance for each duty (e.g., 4 = outstanding, 0 = unsatisfactory). Managers are encouraged to write specific examples to support their appraisal ratings which should subsequently be discussed with employees. Rewards such as pay increases, bonuses, and positive feedback can then be allocated. If an employee or volunteer is not performing satisfactorily, performance appraisals can fulfill a corrective function. In the event that unsatisfactory performance continues and an employee's contract must be terminated, the manager has written documentation (e.g., the performance appraisal) to help protect the organization against allegations of wrongful dismissal.

Strengths and weaknesses of the traditional paradigms. Although the traditional paradigm deals directly with a number of important questions that sport managers must address, it is an incomplete way of conceptualizing HRM. One of the problems is that HRM processes are viewed as objective realities that can be observed, measured, and controlled by management. This can result in an over-reliance on the filling out of various assessment forms, many of which have not been adequately tested to determine if they are valid and reliable measures of employee potential, development, and performance. In addition, the emphasis is on controlling behavior to meet specific job requirements, not enticing employees and volunteers to use their creative potential.

Another problem is that the focus is on the individual, not on how groups or coalitions form, conform, or resist HRM practices, which often has considerable impact on the organization. In addition, this approach does not relate human resource practices to the broader social, political, and economic environment in which the organization is situated (e.g., a surplus or lack of available labor, the influx of women into the labor force, and changing regulatory conditions).

There is no doubt that sport managers should be knowledgeable about methods of recruiting, selecting, training, appraising, and compensating their human resources in a way that meets legal requirements. However, a growing number of authors and practitioners have found that the traditional paradigm ignores many of the realities that affect the way in which individuals work in organizations. As is shown in the next sections, there are many other dynamics involved.

The interpretive paradigm

Drawing on insights from anthropologists and sociologists such as Mead, Blumer, and Goffman, the **interpretive paradigm** turns attention away from a top-down approach, aimed at productivity, to un-

derstanding the everyday interactions of people in the organization. The emphasis is on the norms, values, and beliefs that guide actions when there are no explicit procedures to follow, which according to Hard (1992), constitutes the majority of managerial situations. With a "zoom lens," managers are encouraged to examine the ambiguities and meanings that result from social interaction in the workplace, rather than the procedures used to improve managerial decision making. The types of questions that would surface from an analysis of this paradigm include the following:

1. What are the unwritten norms, values, and beliefs that guide actions, and to what degree are they shared by organizational members?
2. Does the organizational culture support traditional ways of conducting business, or does it promote constant improvement, learning, and change?
3. How do employees react to the ways in which managerial authority is (or is not) exercised?
4. What are the politics and conflicts that underlie the HRM process?
5. Will empowering employees by involving them in decision making increase their commitment to organizational success?

Organizational culture, a concept that is receiving considerable attention in the literature, can be analyzed through the "zoom lens." Schein defines organizational culture as:

> A pattern of basic assumptions developed by a given group as it learns to cope with external and internal problems. The basic pattern has worked well enough to be considered valid and is therefore taught to new members as the correct way to perceive, think, and feel in relation to those problems (Schein, 1992).

In sport, a number of different types of organizational cultures are possible. For example, some sport organizations portray themselves as close-knit families, others continually change personnel to maintain a competitive edge, and others have fragmented subcultures, which are in conflict with one another (e.g., player unions and owners, volunteers and paid staff, different departments in a corporation). Although competing values can lead to conflict among organizational subcultures, the interpretive paradigm recognizes that conflict is not always a negative force. Conflict between individuals and groups can lead to the generation of new ideas and solutions, which leads to innovation and creativity.

To understand organizational culture, one must take on the role of an anthropologist by actively observing the functioning of organizations and listening to those who work within them. The most obvious element of organizational culture is known as the *artifacts* (Schein, 1992). Artifacts reflect the way in which organizations publicly present themselves and are revealed in written statements of goals and policies, organizational charts, the way people address one another, promotional materials, and the types of facilities in which work takes place. It is not until deeper elements of organizational culture are probed, however, that we find out how organizations really operate.

To get at the deeper elements, we must understand the symbols, values, ideologies, and myths that shape the ways in which business is conducted. **Symbols** refer to the language and rituals that are used to form the basis of shared meanings, values, and understandings. **Rituals** are the formal behavior that are repeated for specific occasions. Sport is rife with ritual—singing of national anthems, awarding of trophies and medals, the way athletes prepare for games, and the way in which managers run meetings. Dominant language and discourse patterns are symbols that reveal a lot about the underlying values of organizational members and how they justify the actions they take. For example, the language used by sport agents to negotiate salary increases for professional athletes is quite different than the language used by the executive board members of charitable organizations seeking sponsorship for youth sport camps.

Ideology is another element of organizational culture and refers to the set of beliefs that organizational members have about the "correct" way of conducting business. Some sport managers feel that a confrontational and autocratic style is the best way to keep people in line, whereas others believe that listening to employees, customers, and athletes leads to creative decision making and greater commitment to the organization.

Myths are descriptions or stories recounted by organizational members that reveal how organizational members interpret past events and define themselves as unique. When individuals describe their heroes, past successes (or failures) on the playing field, and critical events in their organization's history, underlying belief systems are often exposed.

Organizational culture has been related to HRM primarily in three ways. One strategy has been to uncover the features of successful organizational cultures so that they can be replicated in other organizations. The literature that suggests how North American companies can emulate the Japanese style of management is one example. Another example is Peters' and Waterman's book *In Search of Excellence* (1982), in which the characteristics of successful organizations are identified.

There are a number of problems with the notion of adopting organizational cultures. First, organizational cultures are dynamic, not static. What made an organization successful one year may not make it successful in subsequent years. If managers of retail companies in the sport industry do not react quickly to changes made by their competitors, their performance in the market place can decline dramatically. Second, there is an assumption that organizational cultures can be easily changed by managers. Yet, organizational cultures are very difficult to change, unless there is a catastrophic event such as a merger or takeover that would drastically alter the beliefs, values, and interaction patterns of organizational members (Meek, 1992).

The second way in which organizational culture has been linked to HRM is through the acknowledgment that politics and conflicts underlie the process. Ferris and Judge (1991) depict organizations as being composed of individuals and coalitions with diverse interests who compete for scarce resources (e.g., status, prestige, money). Anyone who has been involved in the organization of a major sport event such as the Olympic Games will have observed many examples of **political activity.** Often the major stakeholders in such events (e.g., organizers, sponsors, politicians, media, athletes, coaches, volunteers, local businesses) have different priorities and want to maximize their positions through such involvements (Simson and Jennings, 1991).

Of particular interest is how **political influence** tactics such as assertiveness, ingratiation, intimidation, and self promotion affect the selection and promotion of individuals in the organization. Ferris and Judge (1991) reported that regardless of the number of objective criteria established to select employees from a pool of applicants, managers, often unconsciously, prefer people who are most like themselves. They argue that this may occur because hiring employees with similar values and characteristics helps the manager to build coalitions, ensure the adoption of corporate cultures, and consolidate his or her own power base. This may be one explanation why there is little diversity in the characteristics of those who occupy senior management positions in sport (Hall et al., 1989).

The Canadian Olympic Association's (COA) recent hiring of Carol Ann Letheren (a long-time volunteer with the COA and the IOC and up until her hiring, the volunteer president of the COA) as the new Chief Executive Officer provides an interesting case study. Christie (1994) reports:

> The COA's Executive Board followed the due process of advertising nationally for applicants, and a search committee drew up a separate head-hunter style list of people it felt were capable of doing the job.... The search committee found no perfect match for the CEO post. Then the executive approached Letheren and asked is she was interested in the job.

Viewing this process from the traditional paradigm, it can be argued that the search committee followed its mandate by searching and seeking an appropriate candidate for the position. Underlying this process, however, are the norms, values, and beliefs that influence how the selection takes place, who is hired, and why (Golden-Biddle and Linduff, 1994). For the COA it was important that they hired someone who knew the organization and who they felt had the skills and experience needed to lead the organization (Christie, 1994). Using the interpretive paradigm, one can see how the COA's values for a cohesive organizational family and reliance on personal networks may have influenced the hiring of their new CEO.

Furthermore, although performance evaluation is depicted as a systematic and rational process which leads to accurate and reliable assessments of performance, Ferris and Judge (1991) have shown that the process is susceptible to political activity. Those being evaluated often use self-serving strategies that inflate their performances, whereas those undertaking evaluations may use subjective assessments of performance based on friendships with employees.

The third way in which organizational culture has been related to HRM is through employee involvement, a process designed to illicit input and commitment from people through a participative decision making process. Employee involvement is closely linked to the term *empowerment*, which contrasts with the emphasis on managerial control which underlies many HRM practices. There are many different strategies of involving employees to give them more decision-making power. Quality circles, self-directed work teams, TQM, representative participation, and employee ownership were some of the alternatives investigated by Cotton (1993). He concluded that not all of these approaches are equally effective.

Cotton (1993) contends that four factors must be present to ensure that employee involvement results in the expected outcomes of greater commitment and creativity. First, managers must be sincerely committed to the concept of employee involvement by understanding how it will contribute to the strategic goals of the organization. Second, the involvement should focus on improving one's everyday work, not on devising policy for the entire organization. Third, employees must have a significant degree of control over the making and implementation of decisions. Finally, the job changes recommended as a result of the employee involvement process should be substantial, not minor or cosmetic.

CONCEPT CHECK

Organizational cultures are difficult to change. Coalitions of interest may influence HRM practices such as hiring to ensure that the values of applicants "fit" the current organizational culture. Participative decision making is a characteristic of an organizational culture that advocates employee involvement and empowerment as a way to enhance organizational creativity and commitment.

Strengths and weaknesses of the interpretive paradigm. The use of the interpretive lens encourages a reanalysis of HRM by focusing on deeper levels of human interaction and how they affect organizational functioning. It soon becomes apparent that the implementation of HRM is rarely a purely rational process. The dynamics of competing values and beliefs, the potential for conflict and political activity, and the need for employment involvement are acknowledged as being crucial dynamics that underlie HRM.

There are, however, limitations to relying solely on this perspective. It is often assumed that managers will be able to identify one unified culture in their organization and mold it to fit their purposes, an approach that is reminiscent of the traditional paradigm. In reality, a unified culture can stifle creativity because of pressure on people to blend into existing ways of doing things. Those with alternative views and values can become marginalized and over time may become alienated from the organization because their voices are not being heard.

Another limitation is that it is very difficult to change the underlying values and beliefs of people which have been reinforced over time (Meek, 1992). A more appropriate strategy would be to create an environment from the bottom up, where diversity in opinions is valued and linked to a desire for constant improvement.

By viewing HRM from a "regular lens" and a "zoom lens," sport managers will have a more complete picture on how human resources influence the success of their organizations. Now we need to switch to the "wide-angle lens" by considering how the critical paradigm can provide an alternative way of analyzing HRM.

The critical paradigm
The **critical paradigm** stems from the work of Marx, Habermas, and other critical theorists and has evolved as a result of dissatisfaction with the traditional and interpretive paradigms. It focuses with the "darker" side of HRM and deals with issues such as domination, corruption, employee exploitation, discrimination, racism, substance abuse, and workplace safety. It is not until these types of issues are explored that changes to current modes of operation can be thoroughly addressed.

The types of questions that sport managers could ask from the critical paradigm include the following:

1. Who benefits and who does not benefit from current HRM practices in sport?
2. How is power exercised and what are the consequences?
3. How can managers change existing HRM systems to accommodate people who may differ in terms of age, race, gender, religion, disability, or sexual orientation?
4. What strategies can managers use to tap the potential that a diverse work force brings to the organization?

5. What role does the manager play in fostering ethical behavior in sport organizations?

The aim of this paradigm is to challenge the status quo and create change in existing systems to eradicate the power imbalances that currently exist. **Power imbalances** in sport, as in other social institutions, have evolved along class, gender, and race lines. In some cases, this has resulted in abuses of power. Parks (1992) provides several examples of this including the use of sacred objects of ethnic groups to promote sport, and the way in which sexual assault crimes by prominent athletes are trivialized in the media. Similarly, Simson and Jennings (1992) uncovered numerous instances of scandals, corruption, and bribery in their investigation of the administration of the Olympic Games. Nepotism, which refers to the preferential hiring of friends and family members, is a further example of an abuse of power.

In other cases, power imbalances result in differential access to decision making positions and participation opportunities in sport. To illustrate this point, research has revealed evidence of "stacking," where whites predominately occupy central positions on sport teams (e.g., quarterbacks), while minority groups are overrepresented in the peripheral, or noncentral, positions (DeSensi, 1991). Furthermore, Parks (1992) contends that "twenty years after the passage of Title IX, women are still grossly underrepresented in coaching and administrative positions in sport." As further evidence of this problem, it has been acknowledged that, in the past, persons with disabilities have rarely been included in the sport policy development process (Active Living Alliance for Canadians with a Disability, 1991).

From this paradigm, HRM practices can also be viewed as instruments of domination, which rely on the labor of athletes, employees, and volunteers to benefit the interests of the few (e.g., owners, sponsors, and politicians). Katz (1993) demonstrated this in the following quote about Nike's use of third-world labor to lower the costs of sport footwear and apparel production:

We're not gouging anybody, Knight [chairman of Nike] says. Our gross profits are around 39 percent, right on the industry standard. We make our profit on the volume. A country like Indonesia is converting from farm labor to semiskilled. . . . There's no question in my mind that we're giving these people hope.

But when Nike points out that it pays a 2,800 rupiah ($1.35 U.S.) daily wage in Indonesia. . . . it is not always satisfying to a public that's reminded daily of the fat endorsement contracts Nike has with scores of athletes (Katz, 1993).

Kjeldsen (1992) discussed the unethical behavior that can result from patterns of domination in college athletics. He contends that because the revenues generated from college football and basketball have become crucial to the prestige and financial viability of many athletic programs and educational institutions, the needs of student athletes have become a secondary concern. What these examples illustrate is that the emphasis placed on winning and profit making in sport has lead to HRM policies and practices that allow exploitation and domination.

When power is exercised in a coercive fashion, athletes and employees may be afraid to complain about poor working conditions for fear of losing their positions and livelihood. Furthermore, sport managers will not always know when athletes are taking illegal performance enhancing substances, when employees are experiencing sexual harassment, or when maintenance workers are being exposed to dangerous chemicals. The critical paradigm encourages sport managers to be proactive with respect to these issues, to encourage open communication, and to take corrective action so that people will to continue to speak out about problems they encounter. In essence, the "wide-angle lens" challenges us to question whether information such as that contained in performance evaluations should be provided to the powerful (e.g. managers, owners, coaches, government officials) about those who are less powerful (e.g. employees, volunteers, athletes), when the less powerful seldom have access to information about the powerful. There is a need, therefore, not only to study the distribution of power and its impact on HRM practices but also to examine how access to information (or a lack thereof) reinforces power imbalances.

There are numerous examples of positive initiatives that have been taken in sport to deal with some of the issues raised by this paradigm. These include the formation of advocacy and support groups, the development of policies and legislation, the reallocation of resources to under-represented groups, and the inclusion of marginalized groups in the decision making process.

However, because the issues are tied to broader social, political, and economic conditions, change has often been slow, small scale, and has not always resulted in the intended outcome. Therefore change must be viewed as an ongoing process, not something that can be accomplished on a short-term, piecemeal basis.

There are a number of reasons why it is important for sport managers to use the critical paradigm more frequently. First, there is strong evidence to suggest that work forces will continue to become more diverse. Thomas (1991) estimated that 85% of new entrants into the U.S. work force are either women, visible minorities, or immigrants. Yet he contends that managers have been given very little information about how to change systems to accommodate differences or how to manage people who are not like themselves. Instead of valuing the different perspectives that these newcomers bring, Thomas (1991) suggested that current administrative systems either discourage their involvement or encourage their assimilation into the mainstream.

Second, more sport corporations are competing in the global marketplace. A diverse work force can help a company make inroads and avoid some of the pitfalls that might occur when new markets are penetrated. At the same time, diversity may result in greater sensivity to the positive and negative impacts that corporations will have on these countries.

Third, if one of the goals of sport is to encourage the adoption of healthy and active life-styles in society at large, it has been suggested that the characteristics of leaders in sport should represent the diversity and needs of the communities they serve (Frisby, in press). It is apparent that although the number of people living below the poverty line is increasing, many sport programs and products are targeted at upper- or middle-income earners who can afford to pay for such services. Unless low-income people, and other groups, are brought into the decision-making process to explore barriers and alternatives, it is unlikely that they will have equal access to the benefits of sport.

Some sport managers would rather avoid the issues raised by this paradigm than deal with them in a direct and proactive fashion. We do not like to talk about power because our institutions, including sport, are built on the value of democracy. When we talk about power, we have to acknowledge the differences between the "ideal" and the "real" and face the fact that there are disparities between the two. In addition, given all the time and financial pressures faced by sport managers, a common response is "We can't afford to look at these issues right now." Perhaps a more appropriate response would be "Can we afford not to look at these issues right now?"

Strengths and weaknesses of the critical approach. The use of a wide-angle lens to investigate the issues raised by the critical paradigm, exposes the dysfunctional or unintended consequences of the traditional paradigm of HRM (Morgan, 1986). Even though discrimination, exploitation, and racism are not the stated goals of any sport organization, traditional HRM practices and policies, such as packaged computer programs to assist in the selection of appropriate job applicants, often reinforce power relationships that reproduce these social problems.

The critical paradigm addresses issues of change to improve the human condition. It encourages us to become aware of the issues, to understand oppressive structures in sport, and to seek alternatives for progressive change.

As Morgan (1986) noted, one of the limitations of the critical paradigm is that it is not clear whether the domination of some groups over others is a conscious conspiracy or not. Regardless of whether power imbalances occur by default or by design, consciousness-raising about the issues tends to create oppositional discourse between groups. Those who have a vested interest in maintaining the status quo will try to diminish or avoid conflict, while others will see it as a necessary precursor for social change. As noted earlier, conflict is not always a negative force, but it creates resistance that will slow change or result in only minor modifications to existing systems.

Another limitation of the critical paradigm is that it is not always clear what the alternatives to current modes of operation are or whether they will result in the desired outcome of balancing power relationships. There must be a conscious effort, therefore, to ensure that existing forms of domination are not simply replaced with new forms of domination. However, to ensure change, it is necessary to move beyond criticism, and envision new possibilities for HRM in sport.

THE NEED FOR MULTIPLE PARADIGMS ON HRM IN SPORT

Best practice today in managing organizational issues is not to choose one model or way of thinking about organizations but to take account of all the models and dimensions of organization which are relevant to a particular situation (Hard, 1992).

Hard (1992) contends that some managers see HRM as a set of mechanical concepts which are susceptible of immutable laws. Other managers become victims of fads, fashions, and quick fixes. Authors such as Hard (1992) and Morgan (1986) have suggested that neither of these approaches will be effective as we move into the next century. Rather, because of the complexities involved in human resource management and rapid changes in the outside world, sport managers will need to carry a number of "lenses" with them. This will enable them to analyze the numerous situations they will encounter from a number of angles and develop more creative solutions than would be possible if only one lens were used.

The "normal lens" is useful when sport managers are dealing with the recruitment, selection, development, and evaluation of athletes, employees, and volunteers. However, if this is the only lens used to view HRM, a number of important concepts and issues will be overlooked. The "zoom lens" enables sport managers to focus on the deeper elements of human interaction to understand how the formation of organizational cultures is linked to the ability of an organization to innovate and adapt. A "wide-angle lens" encourages the sport manager to stand back and critically analyze how broader environmental conditions create serious social problems that are often reinforced, whether intentionally or unintentionally, through HRM. A summary of the main features of the traditional, interpretive, and critical paradigms is presented in Table 7-2.

The use of these lenses provides the sport manager with alternative ways of viewing the "people side" of organizations, which may ultimately be the most crucial factor affecting organizational success.

SUMMARY

1. Human resource management is a business-oriented philosophy designed to obtain value

TABLE 7-2   *Key features of HRM paradigms*

	Traditional paradigm	Interpretive paradigm	Critical paradigm
Aim	To design policies and procedures	To understand the dynamics underlying human interaction	To challenge the status quo and seek social change
Main concepts	Recruitment Selection Training and development Compensation Performance appraisal Productivity	Organizational culture Subcultures Conflict Politics Employee involvement Adaptation and change	Power Domination Discrimination Racism Substance abuse Workplace safety
Main advantages	Provides information to assist decision making and planning Links abilities to the needs of the organization	Focuses on learning and innovation Focuses on the perspectives of employees and volunteers	Examines the consequences of power imbalances Seeks progressive alternatives that are more inclusive
Main limitations	The emphasis is on controlling behavior Ignores many of the dynamics of HRM	Organizational cultures are difficult to change There is seldom one unified organization culture	Domination is not always conscious Alternatives for change are not always clear or effective

from employees. HRM views individual employees as assets or investments and works to release the creative talents of the employee.

2. HRM is important to sport because proper human resource management gives an organization a competitive advantage; provides employees with the information they need to keep productive in their market; will allow an organization to retain and reward valued employees or volunteers; provides an important link between meeting employee needs, which in turn affects customer satisfaction; and ensures that the organization is meeting its legal obligation to its employees.

3. Human resources are all of the individuals involved in establishing and maintaining a sports organization, including university sports programs, retail sport franchises, professional sports teams, municipal sport and recreation departments, event marketing companies, and resorts and clubs.

4. The shift away from the use of the traditional paradigm in HRM is a movement toward examining disciplines that have their roots in sociology and anthropology and looking into the factors that shape the individual and their relationship to the organization.

5. Today's quickly changing society makes it important to use multiple paradigms in human resource management. By no longer being restricted to one "view," HRM can look at a number of new situations and come up with creative solutions to increasingly complex and unusual problems.

CASE STUDY

A state-of-the-art aquatics center is nearing completion, and the City of Leisureville is in the process of hiring a manager for this center. Two internal candidates, who already have positions in the Sport and Recreation Department in the City of Leisureville, have been approached by members of the Selection Committee and encouraged to apply. Lisa Lindquist has several years of work experience, initially as an aquatics supervisor and more recently as a community sports programmer. The second internal candidate, Matt Peterson, has a similar background but fewer years of work experience. As the selection process unfolds, both internal candidates are informed that they have been short-listed along with a third external candidate. During the first set of interviews, Lisa was dismayed by some of the questions posed to her. Most of them dealt with technical matters (e.g., what kinds of chemicals are needed for pool maintenance), rather than with financial, strategic, and human resource issues that an aquatics center manager would have to consider. In addition, she was asked how her family would react to the long hours that she would have to devote to the job. When Lisa discussed her interview with Matt, he revealed that he was asked few questions about technical matters and no questions about his family.

All three candidates subsequently had a second interview for the position and had been waiting over three months for a final decision. Although Lisa and Matt had worked well together in the past, the delay was creating stress and tension between them. Then, Matt received a phone call from a friend at another municipality informing him that Jim Price, the external candidate, had told him during a recent golf game that he had just been hired to manage the new aquatics center in Leisureville. Matt informed Lisa about this conversation and the two of them stormed into the Chair of the Selection Committee's office for an explanation. Both of them were extremely upset and threatened to resign on the spot. The Chair of the committee said she would look into the situation further and would get back to them as soon as possible. She did confirm that Jim Price had been hired for the position.

When other employees heard about how Lisa and Matt were treated, morale in the office dropped considerably, especially amongst the unionized employees who were slated to work in the new aquatics center. Furthermore, Jim Price was about to start his new position in one month and was not aware of the conflict that had transpired as a result of the selection process.

1. Analyze this case from the three paradigms presented in the chapter. In what ways does this case support the contention that sport managers need to analyze human resource management issues from multiple points of view?

2. As the Chair of the Selection committee, (i) what steps would you take to deal with all employees involved in the case, and (ii) what policies would you initiate to ensure that this type of situation does not occur again.

3. Have you or your classmates encountered cases similar to this one? Compare and contrast your experiences and identify how some of these situations could have been handled differently.

REVIEW QUESTIONS AND ISSUES

1. Why is it important to understand HRM in sport organizations?
2. Think of a sport organization with which you are familiar, and list all of the different types of human resources this organization relies on to achieve its goals.
3. Compare personnel administration and human resource management.
4. Why is it important to have multiple ways to understand HRM?
5. What are the limitations of relying only on the traditional paradigm to understand HRM? Given these limitations, discuss the possible reasons why the traditional paradigm is still the dominant way in which sport management in general, and human resource management in sport in particular, are viewed?
6. What elements must we examine if we are to understand organizational culture?
7. Your nonprofit sport organization has just hired a new CEO. This individual was in the running for the position with one other candidate. The individual who got the job had been a former volunteer board member with your sport organization while the second candidate was an experienced business manager with a successful profit-oriented sport organization. Explain how your understanding of this hiring process would differ using the traditional paradigm and the interpretive paradigm.
8. Explain how the critical paradigm can be used as a tool to empower human resources and promote social change.
9. Discuss the paradox of a sport manager who seemingly supports diversity of opinions by

involving employees in decision making but whose employees are not representative of the diversity of the work force in society.

10. Identify some initiatives that have been used to change the power imbalances that currently exist in sport. What are the strengths and limitations of each approach? What additional steps or alternatives could be taken?

11. When we identify strategies on "how to manage human resources" we often support the existing power structure. Yet, when we expose and criticize power structures in sport, those in power often become threatened and oppose change. How can we reconcile these opposing views on HRM?

12. Develop a response to the sport manager who says, "Although the issues raised by the critical paradigm are important, we just cannot afford to deal with them right now."

13. Debate the statement "People are the most important resource in any sport organization."

REFERENCES

Active Living Alliance for Canadians with a Disability (1991). *A blue print for action,* Ottawa: Fitness and Amateur Sport.

Armstrong, M. (Ed.) (1992) *Strategies for human resource management: a total business approach.* London: Kogan.

Beck, N. (1992). The new economy: the rising value of brain power, *The Globe and Mail,* September 2, p. B18.

Brown, R. J. (1990). The management of human resources in the leisure industries. in I. P. Henry (Ed.), *Management and planning in the leisure industries.* London: Macmillan Education.

Christie, J. (1994). Letheren takes on a new position in restructured COA. *The Globe and Mail,* Saturday, September 17, p. A21 & A22.

Cotton, J. L. (1993). *Employee involvement: methods for improving performance and work attitudes,* London: Sage Publications.

Culkin, D. F., and Kirsch, S. L. (1986). *Managing human resources in recreation, parks, and leisure services,* New York: Macmillan.

DeSensi, J. T. (1994). Multiculturalism as an issue in sport management. *Journal of Sport Management,* 8(1), 63-74.

Drucker, P. F. (1993). *Post-capitalist society.* New York: HarperCollins.

Ferris, G. R., and Judge, T. A. (1991). Personnel/human resources management. *Journal of Management,* 17(2), 447-488.

Friend, J. (1991). *Human resources in sport.* Chicago, Illinois: Nelson-Hall Book.

Frisby, W. (in press). Broadening perspectives on leisure service management and research: what does organization theory offer? *Journal of Park and Recreation Administration.*

Golden-Biddle, K. and Linduff, H. P. (1994). Culture and human resource management: selecting leadership in a nonprofit organization. *Nonprofit Management and Leadership,* 3(3), 301-315.

Hall, M. A., Cullen, D., and Slack, T. (1989). Organizational elites recreating themselves: the gender structure of national sport organizations. *Quest,* 41, 28-45.

Hard, K. (1992) Developing the right organization. In M. Armstrong (Ed.), *Strategies for human resource management: a total business approach,* London: Kogan Paige, pp. 45-60.

Katz, D. (1993). Triumph of the Swoosh. *Sports Illustrated,* August, 54-73.

Kjeldsen, E. (1992). The manager's role in the development and maintenance of ethical behavior in the sport organization. *Journal of Sport Management,* 6(2), 99-113.

Mawson, L. M. (1993). Total quality management: perspectives for sport managers, *Journal of Sport Management,* 7(2) 101-106.

Meek, V. L. (1992). Organizational culture: origins and weaknesses. In G. Salaman (Ed.), *Human resource strategies,* London: Sage Publications.

Morgan, G. (1986). *Images of organizations.* London: Sage Publications.

Morgan, G. (1988). *Riding the waves of change.* Toronto: Jossey-Bass.

Parks, J. B. (1992). Scholarship: The other "bottom line" in sport management. *Journal of Sport Management,* 6(3), 220-229.

Peters, T. and Waterman, R. (1982). *In search of excellence.* New York: Harper & Row.

Pfeffer, P. (1994). *Competitive advantage through people.* Boston, Massachusetts: Harvard Business School Press.

Schein, E. H. (1992). Coming to a new awareness of organizational culture. In G. Salaman (Ed.), *Human resource strategies,* London: Sage Publications.

Schneider, B., and Bowen, D. E. (1993). The service organization: human resources management is crucial. *Organizational Dynamics,* 39-51.

Simson, V., and Jennings, A. (1992) *The lords of the rings: power, money and drugs in the modern olympics.* Toronto: Stoddart Publishing.

Steffy, B. D., and Grimes, A. J. (1992). Personnel/organizational psychology: a critique of the discipline. In M. Alvesson and H. Wilmott (Eds.), *Critical Management Studies,* London: Sage Publications. pp.

Sport Services Branch, (1993) *Sport Discovery Report.* Victoria: Ministry of Municipal Affairs, Recreation & Housing.

Thomas, R. R. (1991). *Beyond race and gender: unleashing the power for your total work force by managing diversity,* New York: AMACOM.

Townley, B. (1993). Foucault, Power/Knowledge and its relevance for human resources management. *Academy of Management Review* 18(3), 518-545.

SUGGESTED READINGS

The approach we have taken in this chapter is to understand HRM from multiple points of view. Building on Morgan's

Images of Organizations, Trevor Slack's article in Volume 7, Number 3 of the *Journal of Sport Management* argues for multiple perspectives for understanding sport management. While most of the sport management literature has used the traditional paradigm, there are recent accounts of HRM practices in sport organization that consider both the interpretive and critical paradigms. Janet Parks' article in Volume 6, Number 3 of the *Journal of Sport Management* provides some insightful arguments for uniting theory and practice in ways that contribute to social change in sport.

Students are also encouraged to read Donald Katz's (1994) ethnographic study of Nike entitled *Just Do It.* Katz provides a candid picture of one of America's leading shoe companies. He writes of Nike's cohesive corporate culture and from a more critical perspective, he addresses minority employment practices, boycotts, and the exploitation of workers and athletes. Similarly, Vyv Simson and Andrew Jennings in *The Lord of the Rings* (1992), report on the practices and political activity in one of the world's most powerful sport organizations, the International Olympic Committee. The book is more than a descriptive account of the IOC's organizational culture, it takes a critical perspective of the exploitation of athletes and the gender imbalance on the IOC to mention a few that are HRM concerns.

In the general management literature there are a number of popular press books that provide advice for improving HRM practices. The current focus of much of this literature is on "empowerment." Peter Block's (1987) *The Empowered Manager,* examines the characteristics necessary to create a culture that supports empowerment and autonomy. *Managing the Hidden Organization* (1994) by Terrence Deal and William Jenkins provides real case examples and strategies for empowering those employees who are often unseen and unheard, yet are critical to the organization. This is a reminder to sport managers that the volunteers at the registration booth are just as important as the officials at the starting line and the judges at the finish line.

For a more in-depth examination of the critical paradigm, students are encouraged to read *Critical Management Studies* (1992), which is edited by Mats Alvesson and Hugh Willmott. Not only is a critique of personnel administration provided, but there are chapters in the book which offer a critical perspective on other management concepts including marketing and accounting.

CHAPTER 8

Labor Relations in Professional Sports

Harmon Gallant

In this chapter, you will become familiar with the following terms:

Players' associations	Cartel	Commissioner
Collective bargaining agreements	Free-agency	Negotiation impasse
Standard player contract	National Labor Relations Act	Scope of bargaining
Lockout	(NLRA)	Agency shop
Right of first refusal	Reserve system	Arbitration
Sports agents	Grievance procedures	Final offer salary arbitration
Salary cap	Good faith collective bargaining	Player strike
Revenue sharing	National Labor Relations Board	Collusion
Competitive balance	(NLRB)	

Overview

To understand labor relations in professional team sports, it is necessary to examine the economic structure of the major sports leagues and the legal framework in which they operate. Labor relations between owners and players, and the labor laws, which in large measure regulate their interactions, have become a central focus in the development of American professional sports. Today's professional sports leagues in baseball, football, basketball, and hockey are each evolving major industries. Other

league sports, for example soccer, are not yet a significant factor, though they may become so in the future. Individual performer sports, including tennis, golf, and bowling, generate significant revenues but have organized in ways beyond the scope of this chapter. Similarly, college athletics generate sizeable revenue and fan interest, but this chapter will only consider the question of whether college athletes may be properly considered employees of their respective educational institutions and accordingly compensated. With respect to labor relations, the major development in the professional sports industries in the past quarter century has been the appearance of organized **players' associations.** These associations are presently full-fledged labor unions, and they are recognized as an integral part of the bargaining process with ownership. The unions are well established, but the problems they are attempting to resolve are not easily defined or managed.

Labor law and labor relations are central to understanding the sports industries, but other elements also go into the mix. The sports industries are complex, despite a surface simplicity resulting from their product and the production process. It was not until the 1970s that the major sports had arm's-length bargaining and the **collective bargaining agreements** between players and owners that ensued. After more than a decade of litigation, player strikes and contentious player-owner negotiations, many observers have hoped for a new era of cooperation. Such is not the case. Substantive progress has been made in resolving certain problems, but the true nature of labor-management issues in professional sports is just beginning to be understood and appreciated. By the 1990s, these issues have reached crisis proportions in each of the major team sports, threatening the economic foundations on which the various leagues are based.

ECONOMIC BACKGROUND

The sports industries are different from other sectors of the American economy in several important respects. First, the basic product is the "on-field" game, and is therefore an experience for the consumer rather than a tangible product. It is a particular form of entertainment and is generally considered a segment of the entertainment industry. Second, each sport has individual characteristics that have led to differences in the creation and growth of the leagues in which business is conducted. For example, the various leagues have differences in the number of players per team, the size of the arena or stadium in which the games are played, and the number of games that constitute a championship season.

There are also the following elements to consider for each sport: the injury toll exacted on the players, how well the game is adapted to broadcasting (especially television), and whether or not the sport is able to attract national interest. As a result, the number of viable teams, and their total revenues, varies from league to league. Another factor, making its presence felt in just the last decade, has been a substantial rise in the sale of licensed merchandise, such as trading cards and logo-imprinted apparel. Each of these factors must go into any analysis of the financial value of a professional sports franchise as a business concern (Berry and Wong, 1986).

Considered as an industry, sports is still in its developmental stage. The teams have grown from small businesses with entrepreneurial ownerships (individual or partnerships) into corporate undertakings. Despite media attention given to high player salaries, spiraling franchise sales prices, and local and network television contracts, the overall dollar amount historically generated by the sports industries has been relatively small when compared with revenues of established industries. This is because the product itself, the "game," has a rich history with traditions which are only now beginning to translate into revenues. As a result, a constant upward pressure can be seen on the financial side of sports. Precise figures have been generally unavailable because most professional clubs have been operated as partnerships or closely held corporations, with no obligation to reveal financial information to the public. In any reckoning, however, the professional sports leagues have to be considered a growth industry in the 1990s.

WHERE PROBLEMS OCCUR IN SPORTS LABOR RELATIONS

Each league's basic working agreements between players and owners include the collective bargaining agreement, the **standard player contract,** and league bylaws and rules. Team owners, general managers and players, however, are not always familiar with their contents, and operating procedures often suffer as a result. Modern sports history contains many examples of owner-player conflicts resulting in litigation, when a careful consideration of the business relationship between owner and player might have avoided the need for court intervention. When agents and aggressive player unions are added to the equation, susceptibility to misunderstanding or simple miscalculation of interests during labor negotiations is greatly expanded. Some labor problems may be inherent in the basic structure of professional sports and prove less tractable. Within each sport, however, improvements in team and league administration will perhaps ameliorate many of the labor relations problems common in the professional sports environment (Staudohar, 1989).

CONCEPT CHECK

Because professional sports is not yet a mature industry, its principles of administration are still taking shape as the twentieth century draws to a close. Established industrial models are often inapplicable or improperly adapted to the operations of professional sports leagues.

COMPONENTS OF THE LABOR-MANAGEMENT RELATIONSHIP
Management

The league itself, and its individual clubs, including all nonplayer employees, make up the management component of the labor-management relationship. Players, their agents, and the players' association represent labor's side.

This alignment of interests remains relatively constant, although conflicts often arise within the ranks on each side.

For example, occasionally individual club owners consider an action by the league as contrary to their own interests. In the 1970s and early 1980s, Oakland Raiders owner Al Davis fought National Football League Commissioner Pete Rozelle and the other team owners over the right to relocate the franchise to Los Angeles. The right of an individual team owner to relocate a franchise over the objections of the league was an issue that impacted the operation of the NFL far beyond this particular case. Since it affected the league's ability to govern its member clubs, the entire framework of labor relations within the league structure was also indirectly involved.

A similar case of conflict within management ranks occurred in baseball in 1992, when team owners decided to terminate the employment of Commissioner Fay Vincent and install Milwaukee Brewers owner Alan ("Bud") Selig as "acting Commissioner." Vincent was instrumental in ending the owners' 1990 **lockout** in spring training, and he was consequently perceived by the majority of owners as "pro labor" on the difficult labor

relations issues then plaguing major league baseball. Public criticism of the Vincent firing extended to Congressional threats to repeal baseball's antitrust exemption unless a strong, independent Commissioner was quickly appointed. The owners remained united in their determination to keep the Commissioner's office out of their labor struggles. Their action, however, created a significant degree of player mistrust regarding their intentions in subsequent collective bargaining negotiations.

Labor
The other side of the equation has also been subject to conflict. A current dispute involves Gene Upshaw, director of the NFL Players Association, and a growing faction of the union membership. The National Football League's collective bargaining agreement of 1993 was reached in large part to settle antitrust litigation brought against the league by the NFLPA. As the agreement took effect in 1994, many players voiced resentment over the union's ratification process. A common complaint was that players had inadequate time to consider all aspects of the complicated agreement, resulting in an uninformed and ill-advised player vote ratifying the agreement. Upshaw's tenure as head of the union may be jeopardized as rank-and-file player dissatisfaction grows.

It is most common, however, for disputes to occur between elements on opposite sides of the labor-management equation. One source of conflict arises over the process by which **sports agents** negotiate contracts on behalf of individual players. In 1977, for example, the Boston Red Sox signed several star players, including Fred Lynn and Carlton Fisk, to contracts giving the team a right of first refusal at the end of the contract period. The players' association then filed a grievance because the contract provisions allegedly violated the collective bargaining agreement. The Red Sox subsequently dropped the clauses before arbitration proceedings were held. Currently, league offices in football and basketball closely monitor individual player contracts, and nullify those deemed to violate the restrictions of current **salary cap** provisions. It is evident that in a number of areas, the interests of players, clubs, unions, and agents come into conflict, and not always from the expected direction.

A final concern involves the impact of external sources on the league's administration of operations, especially in labor relations. *Umpires* and *referees* are neither labor nor management elements according to our model, but they have become more active in union organization in recent years and they have a growing influence in their industries. *Television* and *radio broadcasts* have become absolutely vital to the revenue streams accruing to every professional sports team, and they have had a corresponding rise in influence over many administrative issues, including the way games are played and teams are operated. *Stadium* and *arena ownership* often involve municipalities, either in financing or operations or both, so that government becomes a crucial factor in a franchise's economic viability. Each of these external elements bear directly or indirectly on the relationship of labor and management in the classic model of the professional sports industries. One ignores a particular element at his peril (Berry, Gould, and Staudohar, 1986).

CONCEPT CHECK

A professional league, made up of a number of privately owned teams based in various cities, is most often the basic element in the economic analysis of professional sports. The infrastructure of a professional sports league can be described as follows: The league itself and its individual clubs make up the "management" side of the equation; the individual players, their agents and attorneys, and the players' association make up the "labor" side.

THE BASIC ELEMENTS OF MANAGEMENT AND LABOR

Leagues

Organized professional sports leagues in the United States began in 1876, when baseball's National League was formed. Several of its guiding principles have continued throughout the subsequent development of professional sports in this country. Individual clubs began by cooperating with each other regarding the market supply of producers and consumers. The producers were the players, who made the product by playing the games on the field, and the consumers were the fans, whose ticket purchases provided operating expenses and profits.

Each league allocates a territorial market to an individual member team, eliminating intraleague competition for the sports consumer within the territory. At the same time, the league expands to cover the major population centers throughout the country. In this way, a sports league becomes something of a *monopoly* and discourages the formation of rival leagues. The establishment of a viable team in a desirable market greatly decreases the chance a new league can be formed and succeed in that market. Nevertheless, the great expansion and shifts in American population centers in this century have given rise to a number of attempts to establish rival leagues. In basketball, football, and hockey, recent league mergers and expansions resulted from these attempts. In baseball, the American League in 1900 was the last successful attempt to challenge the monopoly enjoyed by an existing league.

To guarantee the league's health as an economic entity, each sport has a method of **revenue sharing.** Contracts with major commercial television networks are divided equally among the member teams in each league. With the great revenue increases in the past decade, the national television contracts have been the primary basis of team financial parity. Hockey has lagged behind the other three major team sports in the acquisition of network television contracts. Clubs contract individually for local broadcast revenue, and great discrepancies in these amounts (between so-called "big market and small market" teams) has been an issue of growing concern among team owners. Additionally, some leagues split gate receipts. The National Football League provides that 40% of regular-season, and 50% of preseason, gate revenues go to the visiting team. In baseball, the visiting team is given 20%, but in basketball and hockey there is no division of gate receipts to the visiting team.

A final allocation of league resources involves those necessary to make the product, which is the pool of player talent. A roughly equal division of these resources is necessary to ensure a competitive product from each team. It has been long established that a lack of **competitive balance** among the league's member teams will drive down fan interest and, ultimately, each team's revenues. For this reason, a number of devices have been created, over time, to control the distribution of player talent to each team. Not every device is used simultaneously by each league, but they have included initial player allocations to new teams, drafts of available professional and amateur players, restrictions on player movement to new clubs, and compensation to old clubs for lost players.

Any restriction on player movement to new clubs has had the, perhaps, unintended effect of suppressing player salaries within a given league. Before the advent of the free-agency era in 1976, only the existence of rival leagues, aggressively competing for player services, has effectively raised the level of player salaries within any professional sports league. Restrictions on mobility have been the primary concern of the players in modern labor negotiations. Players' unions consistently maintain that such restrictions illegally suppress player salaries by eliminating the market for their services (Staudohar, 1986).

CONCEPT CHECK

Sports leagues have the appearance of joint ventures between club owners, but they have in fact operated as **cartels.** *They have as a primary purpose to allocate and control the markets for production and distribution, and have therefore sought to eliminate, within the league, competition over producers (players) and consumers (fans). Any competition in modern sports leagues is avoided as much as possible, within the legal confines of contract, labor, and antitrust laws.*

Member clubs

Individual clubs within a professional sports league are nominally independent legal entities, free to make or lose money depending upon how they operate their businesses. Each team, however, is signatory to a League Agreement, which governs the team's actions as a member of the cartel. In this regard, each team is an equal partner with every other team in the league, subject to league rules and severe disciplinary action for any breach. Therefore each member club must be considered as *both* a private business entity, and a franchise, operated in accordance with league-wide concerns.

In other industries, it is possible for one firm to withdraw to another market. A sports team, however, must have an opposing team to play against to create the game, which is its final product. A professional sports team must stay within its league to stay in business, unless a rival league exists or can be formed. This is a powerful incentive for each member club to comply with its league's bylaws and rules to identify its individual interests with league-wide interests.

Each league has rules providing for disciplinary action, including expulsion, against members. The constitution and bylaws define the disciplinary powers of a Commissioner; in the case of franchise cancellation or forfeiture, the matter is referred to the league's executive committee.

Sanctions have been imposed against league clubs or their owners in a number of situations. For example, league rules were violated by owners trying to improperly lure a player away from another club, so that "tampering" penalties were invoked, on separate occasions, against Atlanta Braves owner Ted Turner, and Oakland A's owner Charles Finley. In 1981, Milwaukee Brewers General Manager Harry Dalton violated a league "gag order" concerning ongoing collective bargaining negotiations, and sanctions were imposed. In 1994, NFL Commissioner Paul Tagliabue threatened to impose a $10,000 fine on any team owner who made public statements deemed unduly critical of the league's new collective bargaining agreement.

Traditionally, each club within a league endeavors to field the best team possible and thereby improve its economic performance. Some teams have sought to become more successful on the field through the acquisition of players in the free-agent player market, and this approach has driven up salaries in each sport. In baseball, the clubs unable or unwilling to compete for these players will, in theory, direct their resources to develop players for their farm systems and future player rosters.

As the player's right to declare himself a free agent has expanded, the pressures on each club to maintain performance levels by acquiring new players (usually other free-agent players) have also grown. But these pressures are balanced by certain economic realities. As a club approaches peak earnings, as determined by attendance and television revenues in its home market, there is a diminished incentive to spend money and improve the product. Spending more on player salaries would result in a reduction in short-term club profits, with no guarantee of improved on-field performance. Each league has a different proportion of owners who believe increased free-agent spending will translate into greater on-field success and consequently greater profitability. Each league has a different free-agent market as a result. What is common to each league at the present time is a belief by owners that an unrestrained free-agent market will destroy their league's viability in the long run (Berry and Wong, 1986).

Players

In each professional team sport, the players are the direct producers of the industry's product, the game; players *are* the product in the estimation of the public (the consumers). It is accurate to say the players are only a part of the game, but in many important respects, they are the most critical part.

With the advent of television, and the commercialization of the sports industries in the last quarter of the twentieth century, professional athletes have attained a cultural status at odds with their legal and economic status as mere employees. Many of the higher paid stars are more aptly considered entrepreneurs or personal corporations. **Free agency** has given rise to a class of athletes properly considered independent contractors from a fan's viewpoint, and possibly in a strict legal sense as well.

From the players' perspective, since fans pay to see them perform, their compensation should be based on the revenues they generate. A player's career is also very short because of injury or the diminished performance of age, and this is another factor, in the players' view, entitling them to high salaries. Most players, therefore, are unified in their opposition to any club or league rules that suppress their salary levels. This is irrespective of any argument offered for their necessity, either the economic viability of certain teams or certain markets, fan loyalty, or competitive balance among clubs. As this chapter will explore more fully in considering the development of players' associations, these forces have had a powerful impact on the course of labor relations in modern professional sports (Berry, Gould, and Staudohar, 1986).

Agents and attorneys

With the advent of a **free-agency** system in each of the major professional team sports, beginning with baseball in the mid-1970s, the marketing of players has been almost completely taken over by sports agents. Some agents are non-attorneys, but with the growing complexity and compensation of contracts, the players' need for the professional services of both attorneys and accountants has increased.

The influence of competent, ethical sports agents has been a positive one, resulting in higher salaries for their clients and the protection of the players' considerable financial resources. Problems and abuses in the player-agent relationship often result from a lack of professional requirements to enter the field. There currently exists a patchwork of individual state licensing provisions regulating sports agents, but in many contexts, agents can enter the contract negotiation process merely by declaring themselves as agents.

If an agent acts in an unethical manner, the result may be any of the following: misappropriation of client funds, recommendation of investments that violate federal securities laws, overcharging of fees for contract negotiation (usually by charging an up-front percentage of an amount the player may never realize), renegotiation of a player's contract without prior authority, or negotiations contrary to a verbal agreement with the client. Agent abuses can be as varied as the imagination of the agent. College athletics, especially football, have had numerous problems in recent years as a result of the involvement of agents. Funds have often been furnished by agents to college athletes during their eligibility to play, in contravention of NCAA rules. Agents have been known to sign college athletes to contracts of representation before the end of their senior-year playing season, also a violation of NCAA rules. Another common prohibited practice is for an agent to loan money to a promising, but still-eligible, college player in order to later represent him in professional contract negotiations. This is an incomplete list of the many devices which sports agents have used to circumvent established rules and ethical practice. The player-agent relationship is an area where regulation by government licensing procedures, or self-governance by agents themselves, seems to be desirable. The role of the sports agent is substantial and can no longer be ignored by management. It impacts the entire structure of professional team sports, and especially the structure of labor relations.

Players' associations

A note on player unions. Professional baseball players have sought to unionize at least five times. In 1885 they formed the National Brotherhood of Professional Ball Players, and through it they attempted to abolish the new reservation system. Three subsequent attempts to organize players failed, and only with the creation of the Major League Baseball Players Association in 1954, and union status in 1966, did players begin to bargain effectively with ownership. The significant development in this change was the passage of the **National Labor Relations Act** in 1935. This federal law created a public policy that granted unions the right to organize and bargain collectively, and it also required management to negotiate in good faith with a union representing a majority of employees. Before this enactment, player associations were merely voluntary associations, which players did not have to join and leagues did not have to recognize or deal with. True labor unions representing player interests then became part of the landscape in professional sports. The NBA Players Association was formed in the early 1950s, the NFL Players Association was formed in 1956, and the NHL Players Association was formally recognized by the league in 1967.

The historical development of the major professional sports leagues has resulted in a two-tier system. Through the collective bargaining process, the players' associations have each established a minimum player salary in their respective leagues. Players have also collectively negotiated several other financial considerations, notably pension payments and rookie salary structures. Individual players, on their own behalf or through agents, negotiate their own contracts. Salary, contract length, guaranteed payments, and bonuses are currently the province of individual negotiations between player and club (Staudohar, 1989).

To fully understand the development of players' associations, and the collective agreements they have negotiated with ownership, we need to examine the reasons why professional athletes have considered it necessary to organize.

By 1966 it was evident that major league baseball's plan for player representation (in its decision-making executive council) did not adequately protect player interests. It was also clear that union membership had provided significant benefits for workers in diverse segments of American industry.

Since player concerns over the **reserve system,** pensions, **grievance procedures,** and minimum salaries had gone unresolved for many years, the benefits of unionization became obvious. The prevailing attitude of players in all major sports was that ownership might not engage in **good faith collective bargaining** unless required to by law; it was, in fact, the establishment of player unions that created the mandate for collective bargaining. This process then transformed the employment relationship in professional team sports.

For many years, there was an active debate over whether player groups were really unions, capable of recognition under the NLRA. Even with official recognition, player unions have had a contentious relationship with management in the collective bargaining process. As a result, the recent history of each major professional sport has seen the players resort to three basic strategies to strengthen their position in the collective bargaining process: (1) antitrust litigation, (2) player strikes, and (3) arbitration of grievances. Antitrust litigation, which forms an essential part of the fabric of labor relations in sports, is considered elsewhere in the text (Jennings, 1990).

CONCEPT CHECK

In each of the four major professional sports, players' associations are fully now recognized as labor unions. As such, they are protected under the provisions of the National Labor Relations Act of 1935. Umpires and referees in these sports have, for the most part, organized in a similar manner.

A model of labor relations in the sports industry

Figure 8-1 shows the interaction of key elements in the sports industry's labor relations. This model has been developed over time to rationally resolve contending claims in the owner-player employment relationship. As in other industries, the principal issues in sports center on the distribution of money and power between players and owners. The government, through statutory enactments and court decisions, regulates the primary relationship, which is between management and labor. This relationship has been formalized under the NLRA-mandated system of union representation and collective bargaining and has in this way

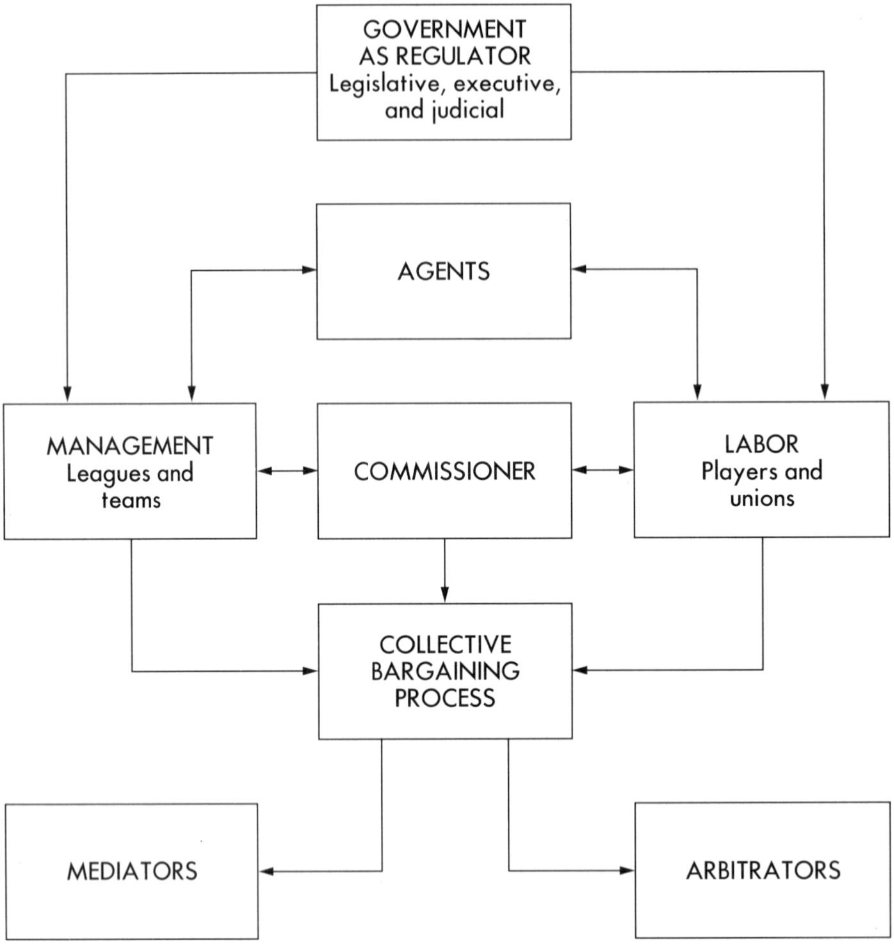

FIGURE 8-1 Interaction of elements in the sports industry's labor relations.
From Staudohar, P.D. (1989). *The Sports Industry and Collective Bargaining* (2nd ed.) Ithaca, New York, ILR Press.

established the basic legal framework through which the sports industry is governed. The **National Labor Relations Board** and the federal courts have interpreted and applied laws pertaining to collective bargaining, the right to strike and antitrust policy in a variety of industries. Therefore each labor dispute in sports is affected by a large body of precedent.

1. *Management* operates through league offices, in conjunction with individual team ownerships. Questions of corporate planning and supervision are decided at this level. Leagues, operating through ownership committees, are responsible for the negotiation of collective bargaining agreements, national television contracts, setting procedures for player drafts, and rule-making to enforce various management prerogatives. Individual team owners have found it necessary to grant this authority to the league of which they are a part, but they retain power in several key areas. Team managements, we have seen, negotiate individual player contracts, but also establish

rules for player movement between teams (subject to the collective bargaining agreement with the players' union), as well as hire their own front-office employees and coaches.

2. *Labor,* as a component of the industry model, is made up of the players and their unions. We have seen how players' associations evolved into unions; as such, their primary aim is to promote effective collective bargaining. The unions engage in five principal functions to further this objective: (1) organizing the membership to support union goals; (2) negotiating contract terms applicable to all players; (3) using pressure tactics, including strikes; (4) enforcing the terms of the collective bargaining agreement through grievance procedures under the NLRA; and (5) conducting meetings, voting on collective agreements and communicating with members, all of which provide internal union organization.

3. The ***Commissioner's*** role, at least in theory, serves both management and labor. The league Commissioner is held forth as a spokesperson on league matters and a guardian of the public interest on questions of the "integrity of the game." In reality, league Commissioners are selected and paid by, and serve at the discretion of, management. In 1992 the owners of major league baseball dismissed Commissioner Fay Vincent and installed one of their members (Milwaukee Brewers owner Bud Selig) as "acting Commissioner." Selig is part of the owners' Executive Council, and collective bargaining on behalf of management is handled through the Council's Player Relations Committee. Critics have suggested that Vincent's intercession to end the 1990 lockout during spring training was responsible for his ouster as Commissioner, illustrating the tenuous nature of the Commissioner's role once labor disputes in a particular sport become heated or reach a **negotiation impasse.** Current threats from Congress to repeal baseball's antitrust exemption often emphasize the absence of an impartial commissioner, and this again points to the interconnected elements of the industrial model. The ultimate resolution of these issues is, at present, completely unsettled.

4. *Agents* are not a formal element of the industry model, since they are involved only in the negotiation of player contracts. One must not underestimate their role in raising player salaries to unprecedented levels, and in marketing players for outside commercial activities. Management-player relations have become more adversarial in recent years as a direct outgrowth of agent participation.

5. *Mediators* and *arbitrators* are neutral parties who may become involved in the collective bargaining process through grievance procedures or impasses in negotiations. Paul Staudohar and other labor economists are of the opinion that the development of labor relations in sports will see mediation and arbitration replace litigation as the preferred method of dispute resolution, as it has in more mature industries (Berry, Gould, and Staudohar, 1986).

CONCEPT CHECK

Players have gained greater economic power and freedom with respect to owners, largely through the efforts of player unions and sports agents. Management, labor, the commissioner, and agents all interact to create a model of labor relations built on collective bargaining procedures. Government regulations oversee the entire process.

Collective bargaining

Workers involved in interstate commerce, which includes athletes in professional team sports, are covered by the National Labor Relations Act of 1935, as amended. Section 7 of the NLRA provides for: (1) the right to self-organization, to form, join, or assist labor organizations; (2) the right to bargain collectively through representatives of their own choosing; and (3) the right to engage in "concerted activities" for employees' mutual aid or protection. This last element includes the right to strike and picket for legitimate ends. The law's provisions are administered by the National Labor Relations Board (NLRB), and enforced by the federal courts.

Unfair labor practices, by either management or labor, are prohibited by the NLRB. The Board also determines which issues are properly within the *scope of collective bargaining.* In professional sports, there are two areas that have been of special concern. One is the allegation that a team or employer has disciplined or discharged a player for participation in union activity. Another involves the allegation that an employer has refused to bargain in "good faith." In this context, the parties to negotiations are required to communicate through a series of back-and-forth proposals, while reasonably attempting to reach an agreement. In certain cases, good faith requires an employer to furnish basic financial information regarding its operation. Traditionally, owners of professional sports teams have been loathe to disclose this data to players' unions. To bolster their demand for a salary cap in major league baseball, the owners did submit financial information to the players union in 1994. Nevertheless, the interpretation and inferences to be drawn from the data are still very much at the center of the conflict.

Individual teams negotiate collectively as a league for the purpose of reaching a contract with that sport's players' union. All active league players are bound by the actions of the bargaining unit, and nearly all players are union members. Since the clubs join together to bargain with the union, the negotiated agreement applies uniformly to each team. It is important to remember that, although certain issues are deemed *mandatory subjects* of collective bargaining by the NLRB, the critical issue of individual player salaries has remained the province of individual club management. Salary caps have now been implemented pursuant to the collective agreements for basketball and football; as a result, individual salaries have come under the increasing scrutiny and intervention of league management. Like so many areas of sports labor relations, the league's power to restrict individual player contracts is an unresolved issue warranting future attention. The established industry model no longer considers individual player salaries solely as a club prerogative. The NBA Players Association is also challenging basketball's college draft and salary cap in court.

Similar player-team-league conflicts can be expected to accompany the implementation of the salary cap scheme in football and basketball.

CONTENTS OF THE COLLECTIVE BARGAINING AGREEMENT

The following areas of concern are typical, but not exclusive, of the matters contained in collective agreements between the players' union and the league (Staudohar, 1989).

1. *Contract length.* It may provide for renegotiation of certain issues during its term, called a *reopener provision.* Most collective agreements in professional sports have been three to five years in length.
2. *Compensation,* including wages, pensions and fringe benefits. Unions in sports only negotiate minimum wage standards, as a rule.
3. *Utilization of labor,* such as work practices, overtime and health and safety concerns. It is here that rules on player *free agency* are made part of the collective agreement.
4. *Individual job rights,* including seniority and discipline. Violence, gambling, and drug abuse by players are regulated in these provisions and are currently matters of significant union and management concern.
5. *Rights of the parties in the bargaining process.* The players' union is usually accorded status as an **agency shop,** so that players electing not to join can be assessed a "service fee" by the union (usually the equivalent of dues).
6. *Methods of administration and enforcement.* Grievance procedures and **arbitration** are usually provided for in this section; if duly negotiated, a no-strike clause would pertain.

CONCEPT CHECK

The NLRA defines the scope of bargaining to include questions of wages (pay, benefits, and bonuses), hours, and working conditions. These areas are deemed "mandatory" subjects of collective bargaining, requiring good faith negotiating between employers and workers. The collective agreements in professional sports vary for each league.

BASEBALL AS A MODEL OF SPORTS LABOR RELATIONS

As America's oldest professional sport, baseball has provided a model of labor relations upon which the other major sports have been patterned. The modern players' union in baseball is the Major League Baseball Players Association (MLBPA). Formed in 1954, the union's early activities were primarily concerned with player pension and insurance issues. In 1966 Marvin Miller was hired as executive director of the MLBPA. Reflecting his background as a labor negotiator in the steel industry, Miller quickly transformed the MLBPA into an effective trade union. In 1968 he negotiated the first collective bargaining agreement between players and owners, resulting in higher minimum salaries, pension increases, and disability and health insurance benefits. To secure a good faith collective bargaining relationship between the parties, the agreement provided for a grievance procedure for the resolution of disputes.

Before 1968, players were permitted to file grievances, but their final disposition was reserved to the commissioner of baseball. The new agreement instituted a system of impartial grievance arbitration, with participants chosen by both sides. In this manner, baseball became the first professional team sport with genuine collective bargaining procedures (Staudohar, 1989).

BASEBALL'S LABOR RELATIONS IN THE COLLECTIVE BARGAINING ERA

The MLBPA's apparent goal during Miller's stewardship was the modification or outright elimination of baseball's *reserve system*. The reserve system was named after the provision in baseball's standard player contract known as the *reserve clause*. The reserve clause stated that if a player failed to sign a contract for the following season, his club could unilaterally renew the contract for one additional season under the identical salary and conditions. A second collective bargaining agreement was ratified in May 1970 for a period of 3 years. The players, however, went on strike for 13 days at the start of the 1972 season. The issue was the amount owners would contribute toward player pensions. Since the strike forced the cancellation of 86 league games, payment for games missed as a result of the strike was another point of contention.

A compromise was reached in the February 1973 collective bargaining agreement, with the owners giving in on pension demands and the players agreeing to forfeit salaries for games not played during the strike. The new agreement broke important new ground, since it provided for **final offer salary arbitration** in cases where negotiations between owners and qualified individual players had reached an impasse. Under this new system, the club submitted the highest figure it was willing to pay, and the player submitted the lowest figure he was willing to accept, with an arbitrator choosing one figure or the other as a binding determination of the player's salary for the following season. The long-established practice of players negotiating salaries individually, with only minimum salary levels collectively bargained by the union, did not change.

Arbitration: the end of the reserve clause in baseball

It should be made clear that unilateral decisions by management on baseball's fundamental labor questions often result in harmful work stoppages. It was through the collective bargaining process that baseball's reservation system was finally toppled. In the 1973 agreement, the individual clubs and the players' union agreed to the use of a grievance-arbitration procedure, with a neutral third-party arbitrator presiding. The collective agreement addressed the reserve system issue in an ambiguous manner. The precise language, contained in Article XV, read as follows:

> Except as adjusted or modified hereby, this Agreement does not deal with the reserve system. The Parties have differing views as to the legality and as to the merits of such system as presently constituted. This Agreement shall in no way prejudice the position or legal rights of the Parties or of any Player regarding the reserve system.
> During the term of this Agreement neither of the Parties will resort to any form of concerted action with respect to the issue of the reserve system, and there shall be no obligation to negotiate with respect to the reserve system.

Despite language that appeared to remove the reserve system from inclusion in the collective bargaining agreement, the agreement also incorporated by reference the Uniform Player's Contract, which still contained the "reserve clause." This latent contradiction went unresolved until Jim "Catfish" Hunter brought a grievance against his Oakland A's club in 1974. Hunter claimed that the team's failure to purchase an annuity under the terms of his player contract was a breach allowing him to become a free agent, eligible to negotiate with any other club. The case went to arbitrator Peter Seitz, who ruled the A's owed Hunter the amount of the annuity plus interest and that Hunter was a free agent. The courts upheld the arbitration ruling, and Hunter signed a 5-year, $3.75 million contract with the New York Yankees. This was the highest salary in baseball history at the time, and it emboldened players to test the reserve clause under the grievance-arbitration procedure.

In 1975 Andy Messersmith of the Los Angeles Dodgers and Dave McNally of the Montreal Expos played without renewing the signed contracts under which they had played the previous season. At the end of the season, each declared himself a free agent eligible to negotiate and sign with any other team in baseball. The players argued, in effect, that the reserve clause in their 1974 contracts only bound them for one additional year, while the owners maintained the reserve clause was perpetual.

In October 1975 the MLBPA filed a grievance on behalf of Messersmith and McNally, asking an arbitrator to declare both players free agents. The owners, citing Article XV of the collective bargaining agreement, contended the grievance was not subject to arbitration, since issues relating to the reserve system were expressly excluded from the contract. The players union answered this argument by declaring that Article XV had been accepted only to pursue the Curt Flood antitrust litigation. The arbitrator, again Peter Seitz, ruled the issue was arbitrable for the reason offered by the union, then went on to side with the players on the question of the reserve clause's applicability for only one year after a signed contract expired (Jennings, 1990).

Seitz' final ruling declared that in the absence of an existing contractual relationship between team and player, the reserve clause had no effect. A signed contract allowed the team to exercise one option of the reserve clause per player for a period of one year. McNally and Messersmith were declared free agents who now could negotiate with any team in either league without restriction. The

arbitration ruling was upheld on appeal in federal court, and the modern era of free agency in professional sports was born.

Baseball: two decades of unrest

Once the existing reserve system had fallen, players and owners still had to negotiate a new reserve system that would fairly balance the needs of both parties. Nearly 20 years later, the issues remain unresolved. In 1976 the MLBPA under Marvin Miller agreed to a new system in which players could become free agents after playing six major league seasons. This gave each major league team, in effect, a 6-year guarantee on a player's services. After this period expired, if the team and player could not agree to a new contract, the player became a free agent.

In 1972 the players had struck briefly at the start of the season over a pension dispute, and 86 games were lost. (The championship race in the American League's Eastern Division was compromised as a result.) In 1976, spring training was shut down for 17 days because of a collective bargaining dispute over the free agency question. The owners had announced they would not open spring training camps without a new collective bargaining agreement, but Commissioner Bowie Kuhn intervened to open the camps on March 17, and the season continued. A new 4-year agreement was signed on July 12, 1976, adopting a 6-year free agency provision with players eligible for salary arbitration after 2 years. A similar lockout occurred during 1990 spring training. Before 1994, however, the only major disruption to a championship baseball season was the 1981 players' strike.

Negotiations between owners and players in 1980 sought to reach a new collective bargaining agreement to take effect in 1981. In the 1976 agreement, the players still had the right to grievance and salary arbitration, but they had finally modified the onerous effects of the reserve clause. Beginning in 1976, players were permitted to become free agents under certain conditions and thereby sell their services to a new team for more money.

By 1980 owners were trying to regain control over player mobility and, consequently, control over player salaries. At issue was the question of whether teams losing players to the free agency market should be compensated by the teams that signed them. The owners' logic was that compensation would dampen the free-agent market and keep player salaries from explosively escalating (Dworkin, 1981).

Baseball's owners and players reached an impasse on the free agency compensation question in 1981. When the owners announced they would unilaterally impose a compensation plan in the absence of an agreement with the players, the union set a strike date of May 29. The union then filed an unfair labor practice charge with the NLRB, claiming the owners had refused to bargain in good faith when they denied the union's request for financial data. The union delayed the strike for 2 weeks while the NLRB sought an injunction in federal court. An injunction would have prevented the owners from implementing the compensation plan and delayed the strike for another year. The court refused to intervene, and the players went on strike on June 12, 1981.

Once collective bargaining negotiations reach an impasse and breakdown, the ultimate weapon of the union is the **player strike.** Each of the major sports has a multiple-employer bargaining structure, so when the players strike, every team is shut down. Corollary businesses, such as network and local television companies and stadium concession stands, are adversely affected. Hotels, restaurants, bars, and airlines also lose revenue when games are cancelled due to a work stoppage. Baseball has endured five such stoppages since 1972, but none as catastrophic as the 1994 strike.

Preparing for the 1981 strike, baseball's owners had purchased $50 million in strike insurance from Lloyd's of London, and they had also created a $15 million strike fund. Players lost salaries as the strike dragged on, but remained unified in their opposition to ownership's demand for a compensation provision. After 713 league games had been cancelled and 50 days had elapsed, the unpalatable prospect of wiping out the remainder of the season brought both sides to a compromise. Free agency rules were tightened, but no compensation was required for players moving to new teams. The players had preserved the right to move to other clubs, and the era of dramatic salary increases continued (Jennings, 1990).

Collusion

In 1985 the free-agent market collapsed when no contract offers for new free agents were forthcoming.

The owners were eventually found by the courts to have engaged in a practice of **collusion,** agreeing among themselves not to bid for free agents and guaranteeing that no offers were made. The courts found that since an existing market had already been established, the owners had acted wrongfully. A $280 million damage award was split up among those players who had found no market for their services as free agents in the years 1985-1987.

The current impasse

By 1993, with the expiration of the current collective bargaining agreement, player salaries under free agency had increased to the point where the average salary was $1.2 million per season. Owners claimed that the continuation of several franchises in the game's current economic condition required revenue sharing between so-called "large-market" and "small-market" teams. The owners tied the plan to the acceptance of a salary cap by the players' union in a new collective agreement. The owners maintained they had to control player salaries to ensure the survival of the game. The players refused to accept a cap system, and when the owners threatened to unilaterally impose a salary cap at the end of the 1994 season, negotiations for a new agreement reached another impasse. On August 12, 1994, the players went on strike rather than complete the season and allow the owners to impose the new system. On September 14, 1994, the owners canceled the remainder of the championship season, as well as all postseason playoffs and the World Series. Despite the owners resolve to "explore all avenues to achieve a meaningful, structural reform of baseball's player compensation system," the collective bargaining mechanism had broken down, and the sport and business of major league baseball ground to a halt.

Months of unproductive negotiations ensued, and in late February 1995 labor negotiations between major league baseball's players and owners broke down. William J. Usery, Secretary of Labor under President Ford and a former director of the Federal Mediation and Conciliation Service, had been appointed in October 1994 by President Clinton to move the parties back to the bargaining table. The player strike had brought a premature end to the baseball season, and direct negotiations between the parties had ended in early September. By the following February, it was clear that Usery had failed to achieve his presidential mandate.

On December 22, 1994, the owners announced they would unilaterally implement a salary cap provision after declaring an impasse in collective bargaining negotiations. The players had long maintained such an action was in violation of federal labor law, and in late January the general counsel of the National Labor Relations Board advised club owners he was about to file a complaint with the NLRB. The purpose was to seek an injunction in Federal court, and force baseball to return to its *status quo ante* prior to the owners' December 22 action. Richard Ravitch, the head of the Player Relations Committee for the owners, left office on December 31, and a committee headed by Boston Red Sox owner John Harrington became directly involved in negotiations for the first time.

The owners took several contradictory steps in early February 1995. On February 3 they promised to restore the pre-salary cap system, but on February 5 they declared that individual clubs could no longer directly sign players to contracts; this function would become the exclusive province of the owners' Central Bargaining Committee. On February 9 the owners announced the end of salary arbitration procedures, long viewed by many of them as an inflationary device in the determination of a player's market value.

As matters deteriorated in early February, Usery emphatically denied he had made any final or formal recommendations to the President for ending the impasse. The two sides seemed more intransigent and irreconcilable than ever. The owners maintained that without a salary cap the economics of baseball were not viable, and the players' union steadfastly held that if a player and his club could not agree on what the player should be paid, the player should be free to seek employment with a new team.

On March 31, 1995, U.S. District Court Judge Sonia Sotomayor in New York granted the injunction sought by the NLRB, preventing the owners from implementing the salary cap system and its attendant provisions. The following week the Second Circuit Court of Appeals, acting through a three-judge panel, denied the owners' request for a stay of the injunction, and ultimately upheld the

District Court's ruling. In response to this judicial action, the players' union announced it would voluntarily end its strike and return to the field to play the 1995 championship season.

After an abbreviated spring training, and the abrupt dismissal of replacement players prepared to proceed with a regular season schedule of games, major league players returned to begin a shortened 144-game schedule. There is still no assurance that a collective bargaining agreement can or will be reached in the foreseeable future, and it is not clear how long the sides will continue to function without one. Fans have shown their displeasure with both sides by curtailing game attendance by about 20%, and the uncertainty hanging over the game in the possibility of another work stoppage continues to erode fan support. Labor relations have remained essentially static during the protracted dispute, with no resolution in sight as of this writing.

Table 8-1 and Figure 8-2 help put the numbers and dollar amounts that led to the most recent conflict into perspective. Figure 8-2 charts the increase in players' salaries since the beginning of free agency, and Table 8-1 tracks the change in baseball's total revenue with the percent of players' payroll.

TABLE 8-1 *The case for and against a baseball salary cap*

Year	Total revenue	Players' total payroll	Percent of total revenues
1985	$720,192,000	$322,557,000	45
1986	798,148,000	355,582,000	45
1987	914,109,000	391,369,000	43
1988	1,007,474,000	443,554,000	44
1989	1,214,833,000	503,373,000	41
1990	1,363,605,000	587,750,000	43
1991	1,539,217,000	736,591,000	48
1992	1,665,106,000	914,014,000	55
1993	1,879,737,000	997,548,000	53

Data from *USA Today.*
For the projected 1994 season, since cancelled, players' salaries were expected to be 58% of baseball's total projected revenues of approximately $1.7 billion.

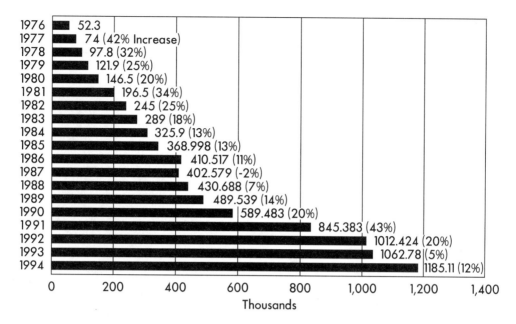

FIGURE 8-2 Average baseball salary since free agency began.
Data from USA Today Research.

The umpires' lockout

In the midst of major league baseball's labor dispute between owners and players, problems arose with the umpires' union. The union had a 4-year collective bargaining agreement which expired on December 31, 1994, and in the absence of a new agreement with the owners they were locked out of spring training camps as of January 1, 1995. Replacement umpires were then hired in contemplation of a 1995 major league season to be played by replacement baseball players.

At issue in the negotiations between the owners and the umpires was the existing salary structure for major league umpires, as well as corollary issues of severance and bonus pay. Richie Phillips, executive director of the Major League Umpires Association, asked for a 53% raise over the current compensation scale, which paid a $60,000 minimum annual salary for rookies up to a maximum $175,000 annual salary for veterans with 25 years of major league service. The umpires also demanded payment of 1994 postseason bonuses,

which had been cancelled because there was no postseason in 1994, and an increase in severance payments from $200,000 to $500,000. The union took the familiar tack of filing an unfair labor practices charge with the NLRB, alleging that American and National League owners had failed to bargain in good faith after the expiration of the old agreement.

The end of the players' strike, occasioned by an injunction prohibiting the owners' unilaterally imposed salary cap, led to a hastily restructured regular season. As regular season games commenced they were staffed by replacement umpires. After several days, in which players expressed growing displeasure with the level of umpiring, the owners unceremoniously dismissed the replacements and reached an accord permitting the regular union umpires to return to work. The new 4-year agreement provides for undisclosed wage-scale increases to be phased in over the course of the contract, and no maximum salary for umpires with more than 25 years of major league service.

CONCEPT CHECK

The concept of a standardized pay schedule, determined by age, position, and seniority, is common in many industrial settings, but has been consistently excluded from labor relations in professional sports. Sports has a two-tier system, and individual player salaries are not subject to collective bargaining. Note, however, that team challenges to salary cap strictures are blurring the traditional division of areas affected by collective bargaining.

RECENT HISTORY: THE FREE-AGENT ERA IN THE OTHER PROFESSIONAL SPORTS
Football

Historically, each of the major professional sports has devised some form of reservation system to hinder a player's freedom to move from one team to another. Compensation systems and other league actions effectively destroyed the player's right to free agency, even with the 1-year reservation system.

Beginning in 1947, football players had to sign a standard player contract, which bound them to their teams for an additional season at not less than 90% of their previous season's salary. In the National Football League, the compensation system was known as the *Rozelle Rule* because Commissioner Pete Rozelle was charged with the task of awarding compensation to those clubs that had lost players to free agency. The practice did have the owners' desired effect of discouraging free agent signings and holding down player salaries. Player dissatisfaction with the NFL's system led to strikes and antitrust litigation, which in turn led to a liberalized free agency system in the 1993 collective bargaining agreement.

In 1974, professional football faced a situation very similar to the current baseball impasse. The 1970 collective bargaining agreement had expired, and the Rozelle Rule governing the movement of players between teams was a sticking point. The rule allowed a player whose contract had expired to sign with a different club, but it also required the signing club to compensate the player's former club. If the two teams could not agree, it was left to the commissioner to award players, draft choices, or cash to the former team. The effect of the rule, which was part of league bylaws, was to destroy the free-agent market for players, since no team wanted to risk losing top players or draft choices at the sole discretion of Rozelle.

The NFL players went on strike during the summer of 1974 to break the deadlock, but after 6 weeks the strike failed, and the players returned. Scabs and rookies had crossed the picket lines to enter training camp, and the 1987 player strike was broken in similar fashion. Nevertheless, the union in each instance had one weapon left in its arsenal—antitrust litigation. This is the one avenue unavailable to baseball players. From 1976 until 1993, NFL players won a series of court victories against the owners, and accomplished what the player strikes never could. The court decisions set the stage for the current free agency system in football.

Professional football survived its free agency crisis largely because of the John Mackey case, filed in a Minnesota federal court in 1975. The trial judge held that the Rozelle Rule was an illegal conspiracy in restraint of trade. As such, it violated antitrust law and denied the players the right to contract freely for their services. It was, in effect, a group boycott or "refusal to deal" by the owners, something the law clearly prohibited. The Federal appeals court upheld the ruling, but warned that a rule governing player movement could be exempt from antitrust law if it was the product of bona fide arm's-length negotiations during collective bargaining. But no such actions had occurred between the owners and the union to save the Rozelle Rule. The court stated:

> It may be that some reasonable restrictions relating to player transfers are necessary to the successful operation of the NFL. . . . We encourage the parties to resolve this question through collective bargaining. The parties are far better situated to agreeably resolve what rules governing player transfers are best suited for their mutual interests out of court (*Mackey v National Football League,* 543 F.2d 606 [8th Cir., 1976]).

It took another generation of court action to get rid of the successor to the Rozelle Rule, "Plan B" free agency. Plan B also undermined the free-agent market and unfairly held down player salaries, but it was successfully challenged by a 1993 antitrust suit (*McNeil v NFL*). This forced the owners back into collective bargaining negotiations with the players' union.

Figure 8-3 charts the change in football players' salary from 1986 to 1994. The average players'

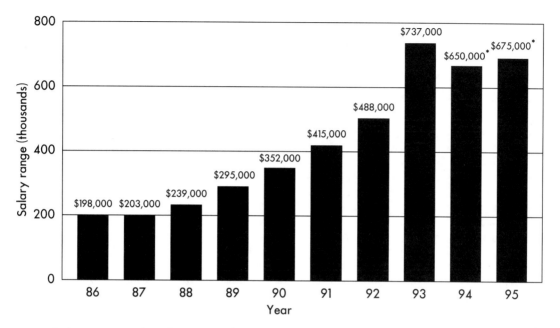

* The average salary for 1994 and 1995 went down due to deferred salary provisions.

FIGURE 8-3   Average football salary, before and including free agency.
Data from USA Today Research and the NFL Players Association.

salary has increased every year in this period with the exception of 1994 because of the salary deferred provisions of players' contracts.

The collective bargaining agreement between NFL owners and the NFLPA took effect in the 1993 season. It will be in effect through 1999, and it provides that players with 5 years' experience can offer their services on the open market once their current contracts expire. A salary cap provision took effect in 1994, setting combined player salaries at 64% of designated gross revenues flowing into the league. The cap falls 1% per year until 1996, then remains stable at 62% until the agreement's final year. A complicated exemption system for free agents was also instituted, allowing each team to designate one "franchise" player, who then must be paid a "top five" equivalent salary for his position to be exempted.

Basketball

In the National Basketball Association, players signing the uniform player contract were originally bound to one team throughout their careers. If the player refused to sign a tendered contract, the team could unilaterally renew his contract for the following season at the same salary rate he was then earning.

In March 1973, a 3-year contract was signed between the NBA and the players' association (NBAPA), the league's first collective bargaining agreement. The NBAPA had filed an antitrust suit against the league in 1970, seeking to halt a merger between the league and the rival American Basketball Association. A month before the NBA's first labor agreement, the U.S. District Court ruled "the player draft, uniform player contract, and reserve clause were analogous to devices which were *per se* violations of the antitrust laws" (*Robertson v NBA*, 389 F.Supp. 867, 1975), and upheld an injunction against the merger. In February 1976 the case was settled out of court when the league agreed to drop the requirement of compensation for free agents, beginning in 1980. Additionally, 1976 would be the last year a standard player contract would contain an option clause. As a result, beginning in 1980, NBA players were allowed to become free agents, subject only to the *right of first refusal* by the team that the player sought to leave. This mechanism allowed the player's old team to resign him by matching any offer tendered to the player by a prospective new team.

In April 1983 the NBA brought professional sports into the salary-cap era. Attempting to solve its financial crisis with a modified free agency system, the league's new collective agreement included a guaranteed revenue-sharing provision. This granted players a minimum of 53% of league gross revenues in total salary payments, and no team could have a roster salary less than 90% of the cap. The original cap amount, in effect for the 1984-1985 season, was $3.8 million per club. With increased revenues, the current figure exceeds $23 million. Nevertheless, NBA players have sought to eliminate the salary cap provision since the collective agreement expired in 1987.

Following the expiration of the league's collective bargaining agreement in 1993, NBA players and owners agreed to a no-strike, no-lockout moratorium through the 1994-1995 regular season and playoffs. The purpose was to avoid a mid-season strike, and continue negotiations toward a new basic agreement.

On July 18, 1994, a Federal court in New York ruled that the league's salary cap, college draft and "right of first refusal" free agency were all legal because they were the product of the collective bargaining process. The NBA Players Association had challenged the validity of the key elements of their basic agreement on antitrust grounds. The Second Circuit Court of Appeals affirmed the ruling, and made it clear the players would not be able to gain, through litigation, the bargaining points which ownership was unwilling to concede in negotiations.

Commissioner David Stern put the ruling in context, stating "the parties have to resolve their differences at the bargaining table and not in court." His counterpart in the process, Charles Grantham, resigned abruptly in mid-April 1995 after serving as executive director of the players' association for seven years. It is unclear whether Grantham was actually forced to resign for failing to make adequate progress in negotiations, but union president Buck Williams of the Portland Trail Blazers said "We weren't overly happy about

the way the office was run." Grantham was immediately replaced by union counsel Simon Gourdine. A former NBA deputy commissioner and chief operating officer, Gourdine is well-acquainted with the issues and personalities involved in the league's labor situation.

As stated, the National Basketball Association conducted its 1994-95 season under a no-strike, no-lockout agreement in the absence of a new collective bargaining agreement between owners and players. A decertification petition on behalf of seven star players, headed by Michael Jordan and Patrick Ewing, was filed with the NLRB on June 21, 1995, the very day on which the union and owners announced an "agreement in principle" on a new six-year collective bargaining agreement. The petition, seeking to remove the NBA Players Association as the authorized bargaining agent for the players, was the beginning of a summer-long campaign by dissident players.

One week after filing its decertification petition, the dissident players claimed they represented more than half the league's players. They proceeded to file a class-action, antitrust lawsuit in the U.S. District Court in Minneapolis, challenging the league's salary cap, rookie draft, and free agent system. The NLRB petition and lawsuit were part of an overall strategy to prevent an impending ownership lockout if the two sides in labor negotiations could not reach an agreement.

On July 1, 1995, the moratorium on work stoppages expired, and the owners promptly instituted a lockout, freezing player contract signings, trades, and any other team preparations in contemplation of the upcoming 1995-96 season. The player representatives, meanwhile, had refused to vote on the proposed labor agreement, insisting that the union leadership return to the bargaining table with owners. A point of special concern for the players was a proposed "luxury tax," to be added to the existing salary cap mechanism, which would have limited the amount free agents could be paid upon resigning with their existing teams.

Once the lockout took effect, the dissident players and the union leadership focused their efforts on the decertification issue. In late July 1995 the NLRB authorized a vote by players on the issue, to be conducted and supervised by NLRB agents at various sites around the country on August 30 and September 7. The quandary facing ownership, as represented in negotiations by Commissioner

David Stern, was to refashion an agreement that would appeal to a majority of players, without retreating on those issues that a majority of owners considered crucial to the league's long-term economic viability. Failure to reach any new agreement, however, appeared likely to destroy the players' union. Ratification of a new agreement, if it could be reached, still depended on a union victory in the approaching decertification election.

On August 8, 1995, the union and owners finally concluded a proposed six-year agreement. The main new feature of the accord was the category of Basketball Related Income, from which the players' share of revenue will be calculated. The players are to receive 48% of "BRI," a figure that for the first time includes income from luxury suites, international television contracts, arena advertising, and licensing fees from NBA Properties. The salary cap remains, but it will be increased from its current $15.9 million to $23 million per team, then move up about $1 million per year during the term of the contract. In place of the luxury tax proposal, each team will be able to sign its own free agent players (if they have been with the club for three years), without regard to the salary cap. If the player has completed a two-year contract with his team, he can sign for a 75% increase or average salary, whichever is greater. A salary cap exception of $1 million per year is granted to each team to sign one or more players, but it can only be exercised in alternate years.

There are two BRI limitations: in the labor agreement's fourth year, the salary cap will be reduced by $500,000 per year if the players' share of BRI exceeds 50.13%; the league can terminate the agreement, or "reopen" in contract parlance, if the players' share of BRI exceeds 51.8% after it has been in effect for three years.

The rookie draft will be reduced from two rounds to just one beginning in June 1998. First-round selections will be limited to three-year guaranteed contracts. After the 1995-96 season, all players can become unrestricted free agents upon expiration of their contracts. The length of player contracts will be restricted to seven years, with designated times for contract extensions to be signed. Also, extensions are limited to 20% salary increases, balloon payments are prohibited, and contract negotiations to reduce a player's salary (to create room for new-player signings under salary cap restrictions) are similarly prohibited.

In the days immediately preceding the decertification vote, the league and union leaders sought to tie the new agreement to a vote against decertification. One player, Mitch Richmond of Sacramento, objected to this tactic by filing an unfair labor practice charge with the NLRB, alleging Commissioner Stern had coerced players to reject all claims by the dissident players.

Faced with the choice of either ratifying the proposed agreement or jeopardizing the upcoming season under the owners' lockout, NBA players voted 226 to 134 to retain the union as its certified bargaining unit. Player representatives from the respective teams then voted to ratify the collective bargaining agreement, 25 to 2, and owners voted in favor by a 24 to 5 margin. The league's enviable record of never losing a game to a work stoppage emerged unscathed from its summer of labor discord, but it is unclear if the players' union will now face rising dissatisfaction among the rank-and-file, just as hockey and football's player unions struggle to maintain a united front in the aftermath of new collective bargaining agreements.

Hockey

The National Hockey League also had a standard player contract that granted the team a right to own a player's services in perpetuity. In every sport the standard player contract is incorporated into the collective bargaining agreement. Hockey players relied on the collective bargaining process to eliminate the "perpetual" player reservation system. In 1975 the *Philadelphia World Hockey Club* case, 351 F.Supp.462, struck down the NHL's reserve system and the owners subsequently recognized the players' right to become free agents after playing out an option season. Hockey retained the compensation award for teams losing free agents, a system referred to as *equalization*. An arbitrator awarded the compensation if the two clubs could not agree, although after 1982 no compensation was required for free agents aged 33 and over.

The National Hockey League's collective bargaining agreement expired on September 15, 1994. On October 1, in the absence of meaningful labor negotiations between the club owners and the players' union, the owners declared a lockout. Two months earlier, Commissioner Gary Bettman had announced major cutbacks in the package offered to the players by the owners. These included pension and medical benefit reductions, as well as reduced arbitration rights and roster sizes. The Commissioner and owners were responding to what they perceived as a refusal to bargain by the players' association. The players, however, claimed that the owners' proposed wage structure was merely a disguised salary cap system, and they did not intend to proceed with negotiations until it was withdrawn.

One week before the lockout, Bettman announced that the 1994-1995 regular season would not begin without a new labor agreement, in order to protect the sport from a mid-season strike similar to the one which had recently damaged baseball. The players responded by promising not to strike during the season and play-offs if the owners would promise in return not to lock them out. The union's counterproposal to the owners featured a complex payroll tax, whereby club salaries beyond a determined amount would be taxed at a specified rate and the revenues derived from the tax would then be transferred to small-market, low-payroll clubs. The payroll tax was rejected by the owners on October 11, and the NHL season was formally postponed.

In mid-November 1994, as games were cancelled and lost revenues were mounting, a group of player agents entered the negotiations by advising league executives the payroll tax was unworkable. In its place, the owners substituted a revised free-agent provision that would allow less player movement between clubs. The owners also empowered the Commissioner to cancel the remainder of the season if no agreement was reached by January 16, 1995; the theory was that a minimum 50-game regular season was needed, and that play-offs had to be completed prior to July 1.

As the January 16 deadline approached, the owners re-submitted the payroll tax plan, and the union solidified in its opposition. On January 4, the union submitted its "final offer," with the payroll tax eliminated, and three days later the NHL Board of Governors responded with its own "final offer," dropping the payroll tax but raising to 32 the age for unrestricted free-agency in the first half of the 6-year agreement. The owners approved the amended proposal by a 19-7 vote, and on January 11, 1995, the players' union leadership, led by Robert Goodenow, accepted it pending ratification by the union membership. After a short training period, the league proceeded to play out a 48-game regular season (pared down from its standard 84-game length), and began the Stanley Cup playoffs just in time to conclude the season by the end of June.

The NHL's new collective bargaining agreement is for a term of six years, but since either side can "reopen" in 1998, it is in effect a three-year operating experiment. A new rookie salary cap is set at $850,000 to $1.075 million, and the provision for salary arbitration allows each owner three "walk-aways" every two years (but not all three in any one year). This means that if an arbitration award is higher than the league-average salary of $550,000, the owner can repudiate the player's contract. There is also a new "Group II" free agency compensation provision, which awards a maximum of five draft picks to a team losing a free agent, if the new team offers in excess of $3.7 million to sign the player.

Finally, the critical "unrestricted free agent" designation is granted to players 32 years of age for the first three years, and that age drops to 31 for the last three years, of the collective bargaining agreement. With no salary cap or payroll tax provision, the agreement is not enthusiastically supported by all owners. Enough of them, however, were willing to adopt it for a 3-year trial, and in this way hockey salvaged its 1994-1995 season. If neither side reopens the agreement, it will run through September 15, 2000.

League salaries
Figure 8-4 charts the average salaries and minimum salaries in the professional baseball, basketball, football , and hockey leagues from 1970-1990.

Salary changes
Figure 8-4, *A*, charts the average salaries in the professional baseball, basketball, football, and hockey leagues from 1970-1990, and Figure 8-4, *B* tracks the change in minimum salary for professional baseball and basketball during the same period.

Table 8-2 compares the terms and conditions of the salary cap in professional basketball and football.

ANTITRUST CONSIDERATIONS
Before the 1970s, players remained subject to the reservation systems imposed by each sport. This was not changed by early unionization attempts or

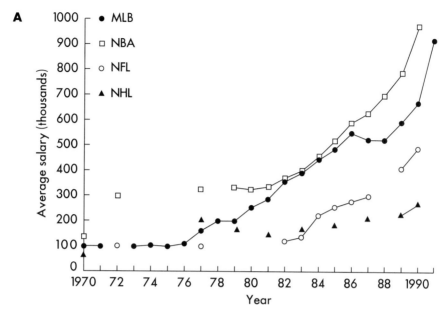

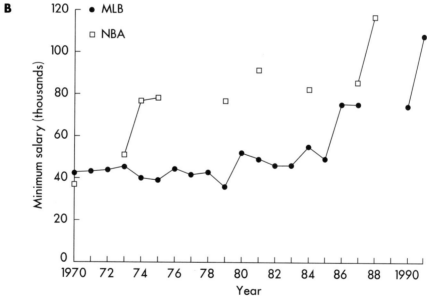

FIGURE 8-4 **A,** Average salaries in pro sports, 1970-1991. **B,** minimum salaries in pro sports, 1970-1991.

From Quirk and Fort, *Pay Dirt: The Business of Professional Team Sports.* Princeton, NJ, Princeton University Press, 1992.

TABLE 8-2   *The salary cap in basketball and football: a comparison*

	National Basketball Association	National Football League
Enacted	1995	1994
Term	6 years	5 years
Teams in league	29	30
Salary cap (per team)	1995-1996: $23 million, with an approximate $1 million increase per season	1995, $37.1 million, plus $4.9 million in benefits
How it works	Players receive 48% of "basketball related income" (domestic broadcast TV and gate receipts, and under the new agreement, income from luxury suites, international television contracts, arena advertising, and licensing fees from NBA Properties); and the sum is divided equally among each team to determine cap figure. Among its loopholes, teams can sign their own players regardless of the salary cap if they have been with the team for 3 years; a player completing a 2-year contract can sign with his team for a 75% increase or average salary (whichever is greater); and each team can exercise a $1 million salary cap extension every other year.	Players receive 64% of defined gross revenues (from TV, gate and some licensing). Teams can't exceed the cap to sign their own free agents, but the cap can be exceeded by pro-rating signing bonuses even if a player receives the payment in a lump sum.

the periodic appearance of rival leagues, which introduced competition for player services. As a result, players sought relief from the reserve clause through antitrust law prosecutions; their argument was that reservation was anticompetitive and a violation of the Sherman Act.

Baseball players were completely unsuccessful in this strategy. A 1922 U.S. Supreme Court decision held that baseball was a sport rather than a business, and as such was not covered by the antitrust laws. Subsequent legal challenges to the reserve clause by baseball players were denied, as the Supreme Court continued to uphold the earlier exemption and suggested Congress should be the one to abolish it.

The other major sports have been more successful in this tactic because the Supreme Court has refused to extend baseball's antitrust exemption to cover any other professional sport. The lack of an antitrust exemption has been the primary cause of eliminating player reservation systems in profes-

sional football, basketball, and hockey. The courts have taken the position that jointly bargained agreements, as contemplated by the National Labor Relations Act, are the proper method of resolving labor questions in professional sports. How well the collective bargaining method actually works to resolve sports labor conflicts is still an issue, but the public policy of encouraging arm's-length bargaining between the parties remains.

COLLECTIVE BARGAINING AND ANTITRUST

The Sherman Act, a 1910 federal law prohibiting agreements which unfairly restrain trade, was clearly instrumental in helping players radically alter existing player reservation systems in football, basketball and hockey. The 1976 *Mackey* case in professional football is the leading precedent. The federal court (Eighth Circuit) ruled that a reservation system was not a per se violation of the Sherman Act, but the NFL's system was deemed improper because it was not a product of bona fide arm's-length bargaining between owners and players.

As stated, the National Labor Relations Act of 1935 granted workers the right to form and join unions, and to engage in collective bargaining with employers. As player associations became certified unions under the provisions of the statute, they acquired the power to use the collective bargaining process in order to negotiate conditions of employment. Through this mechanism, and bolstered by the court's willingness to apply antitrust law to the league's operation, football, basketball, and hockey players achieved a more equal position with the owners. A new era of collective bargaining began in this way.

Baseball owners continue to have the benefit of an antitrust law exemption. There have been periodic Congressional hearings into the matter, and revocation has been often threatened, but as of November 1995 no action had been taken.

COLLEGE ATHLETICS

This final section addresses the question of whether or not college athletes should be considered employees of the university they attend. If so, a model of labor relations will need to be applied to college, as well as to professional sports. Presently, they are treated as "student-athletes" with amateur status, and there are strict rules promulgated and enforced by the National Collegiate Athletic Association (NCAA) governing the source and amount of permissible income.

Since major college sports have become significant revenue producers in football and basketball, a question of fairness is raised if the players are prohibited from sharing in the profits they generate for their schools. Additionally, if a scholarship athlete is injured while performing, his or her right to worker's compensation benefits will hinge on whether he or she is considered an employee in the estimation of the courts.

Some preliminary questions arise when courts address these issues. Does the university have the right to discipline or discharge the athlete? In *Coleman v Western Michigan Univ.*, 336N.W.2d224 (1983), the court defined employment by examining the conditions under which college athletes perform. Before 1973, an athlete who did not withdraw voluntarily from participation in sports, did not engage in serious misconduct, or fail to meet minimum academic standards, could not have his or her 4-year scholarship withdrawn. After 1973 the NCAA gave coaches discretion whether or not to continue an athlete's scholarship from year to year.

The second factor a court considers is whether or not the university had the right to control or dictate the activities of its student-athletes. Since coaches can now make scholarship renewal decisions on the basis of athletic performance, the athletes' activities can jeopardize their scholarship status if at all contrary to the coach's desires.

A third factor is how dependent the athlete is on the benefits of his or her scholarship for the meeting of living expenses. In return for the athlete's services, the athletic scholarship generally provides for room, board, tuition, and books. The court in *Coleman* found this situation met the employment test; it should be noted that additional living expenses in the form of cash, transportation, and equipment have been the most-often violated rules as college players seek to increase the benefits paid them under their scholarships, and athletic programs and "boosters" are often willing to comply.

A related element is the intent that an employment contract exists between university and athlete. In the case of *Rensing v Indiana State Univ.*, 444 N.E.2d 1170 (1983), the Indiana Supreme Court ruled against the compensation claim of an injured football player, holding "there must be a mutual belief that an employer-employee relationship did exist." Since the NCAA rules expressly prohibited athletes from accepting pay for their services, the university could not have considered the athletic scholarship as payment for services rendered.

In deciding the issue of university as employer, the final factor courts have considered in this context is whether the athlete's function was an "integral part" of the university's business. Obviously, the "business" of a university is education, and a student-athlete engages in sports. The proper test, it has been suggested, is whether the athlete's job is just as vital as that of nonacademic personnel, such as security and maintenance workers. It is certainly arguable that major college sports provide an essential public relations function for the school, keeping it in the public eye and encouraging continued identification of alumni with the institution.

As of 1994, proposals to make student-athletes employees of their academic institutions have met varied responses from both the NCAA and legislative bodies. The current system is presently under intensive NCAA review, in an attempt to correct the most serious flaws, but a constant stream of violations and sanctions continue to result. For the foreseeable future, however, no fundamental change in the system should be expected.

In theory, the employment rights of college athletes could be created by a university initiative, but this has never been attempted. Similarly, college athletes could organize into a union and undertake collective bargaining but have not yet done so. For the present, court decisions considering these matters on a case-by-case basis are the only avenues open to college athletes. Legislation and NCAA regulations have been spotlighted by the media, but have offered no tangible results in this area.

SUMMARY

1. Because players were historically denied the right to choose which team to play for, and to switch teams to raise their salary level, the owners were in a much more powerful position. They benefitted from the new revenues radio and television brought into the game, while players' salaries were suppressed far below the level a competitive labor market would have brought them.

2. In response to the reservation system, players in each sport formed players' associations, which evolved into labor unions. This in turn led to the system of collective bargaining between players and owners, which is where labor relations in each sport stand today.

3. The main focus of this chapter has been how employer-employee relationships have developed in America's four major professional team sports—baseball, football, basketball, and hockey.

4. The employer in each situation is the club, or team, and in each sport individual clubs have been organized into professional sports leagues. The employee is the professional athlete who performs on the playing field.

5. Occasionally, competing leagues have come into existence to challenge established operations, and they always have a significant impact on the employment relationships of their rivals.

6. At present, there is only one major league operating in each of the four major sports. While there is competition among the teams in a particular sport for free-agent players, championships and revenues, it is more accurate to view individual teams within a sport as joint venturers with a common interest in the competitive balance and financial soundness of the league as a whole.

7. Players have gained more power in recent years through the organization of player associations into effective labor unions. They have also realized substantial income escalation through the establishment of various free agency mechanisms in each sport, allowing them to change teams under certain conditions and thereby require employers to bid among themselves for player talent.

8. Free agency for players and the existence of rival leagues have been the two driving forces behind rising player salaries in the modern era of professional sports.

9. The labor crisis that each sport faces as the century draws to a close revolves around the question of the proper balance between the rights of team owners and professional athletes.

10. The current situation raises these key questions: What role, if any, should government play in regulating the employment relationship, particularly when labor negotiations between the parties reach an impasse? What rights should players and owners each have in the equation, and what is the public's interest (especially the fans') in the employment relationship?

11. These issues have moved to center stage in the last several years, as players and owners have become more adversarial and less trusting of each other's motives during collective bargaining negotiations.

12. The case of baseball illustrates how destructive the breakdown of labor relations can be. Each sport must answer the critical questions of the employment relationship for itself, but neglecting them jeopardizes their ability to put on the games, which constitute the economic product of professional sports.

13. College athletes have not been recognized as employees by their universities, nor have

they organized into unions. Courts consider their status on a case-by-case basis.

CASE STUDY

On December 7, 1992, the owners of Major League Baseball narrowly voted in favor of reopening the collective bargaining agreement, which was to expire on December 31, 1993, to consider sections on free agency, salary arbitration and minimum salary. The following day, December 8, the owners sent required notices to the Federal Mediation and Conciliation Service and the New York State Mediation Board, advising them that they might lock out players after the 60-day waiting period had elapsed.

On January 13, 1993, the president of the owners' Player Relations Committee, Richard Ravitch, recommended that the owners not use the lockout in 1993. Two weeks later, the two sides met at which time Ravitch made known the owners' view of economic conditions in the game of baseball. On February 17, 1993, the owners voted to tie a revenue-sharing proposal to their demand for a cap on player salaries.

On August 12, 1993, the owners pledged not to lock out players during the 1994 season nor to unilaterally change terms of the collective bargaining agreement through the end of 1994 baseball season. To this point, no revenue-sharing agreement had been reached by the owners. On December 31, 1993, the collective bargaining agreement expired, and three weeks later the owners agreed to a revenue-sharing proposal, contingent on the players' acceptance of a salary cap.

During March 1994 Ravitch made known his position on behalf of the owners in direct talks with the players during spring training. On June 8, with the season now underway, the owners voted to require 75% of clubs' approval for any collective bargaining agreement reached during a players' strike. The following week the owners made their formal salary cap proposal to the players, asking them to split gross revenues 50-50 in exchange for limiting payrolls. The owners also proposed to eliminate salary arbitration but offered to reduce eligibility for free agency to 4 years of service from its present 6 (with the proviso that a player's former club could match any offer until 6 years service had accrued).

On July 18, 1994, the players rejected the salary-cap proposal and asked the owners to lower the requirement for salary arbitration from 3 years to 2, eliminate restrictions on repeat free agency within 5 years, and raise minimum salaries to $200,000 per year. These demands were rejected by the owners, and the MLBPA executive board then voted to set an August 12 strike date. The players did go on strike on August 12, 1994, but both sides agreed to federal mediation. On August 18, mediators announced a representative group of owners would enter direct bargaining negotiations. Secret meetings between Donald Fehr, players union executive director, and Colorado owner Jerry McMorris were held in late August. With no agreement in sight, Acting Commissioner Bud Selig set a September 9, 1994, deadline for cancelling the remainder of the season if no agreement could be reached. The owners provided additional revenue-sharing data to the union during this period, but despite last minute bargaining sessions between owners and the union, no progress was made.

On September 8 the players proposed a 1.5% "tax" on revenues and payrolls of the 16 highest ranking clubs. The money collected would be distributed to the bottom 12 teams in each category; home teams would also share 25% of gate receipts.

This proposal was rejected by the owners on September 9, and on September 14, they voted to cancel the remainder of the 1994 baseball season, including the play-offs and World Series.

In October, 1994, federal mediator William J. Usery called both sides back to the table, and negotiations resumed in mid-November.

CASE SUMMARY QUESTIONS

1. *In reviewing the chronology of events, what could the owners have done differently to save the situation before it reached an impasse?*
2. *What would you have done differently if you had been the players' union negotiator?*
3. *What can other professional sports leagues learn from the experience of baseball in these labor negotiations?*

REVIEW QUESTIONS AND ISSUES

1. What devices can be invoked by each side when an impasse is reached during the collective bargaining process?

2. Is it desirable that players continue to perform when negotiations break down, or is their strike weapon the ultimate guarantee that a collective bargaining agreement will be reached?
3. Should government agencies intervene when collective bargaining negotiations reach an impasse? If so, at what level?
4. What is the proper role, if any, of a league commissioner in labor negotiations between players and owners?
5. Are player salaries too high or too low? What standard of comparison is appropriate?
6. Is a salary cap a viable method of controlling operating costs of professional sports teams? Is it the best method? Should teams be required to reveal their financial information, especially their profitability, to the players' union when a cap on salaries is sought? To the public?
7. If a percentage of ownership revenues is designated for player salaries under a cap system, which revenues should be included? What is a fair percentage?
8. Should the free market alone determine player salaries in professional sports? What about the fans' need to have players stay with one team for a certain period to encourage team loyalties and rooting interest?
9. Has the development of players' unions been a positive influence in the history of professional team sports? Can you think of a better system to protect the interests of the major factions, specifically the players, owners and fans?
10. Is the two-tier system of contract negotiations desirable?
11. What labor issues do you think should be resolved through the collective bargaining process?
12. How can collective bargaining negotiations be encouraged when an impasse occurs between management and players?
13. Assume collective bargaining negotiations reach an impasse. When, if ever, should players call a strike? When, if ever, should owners field replacement players?
14. In the event of a players strike, is a player-owned league a rational economic decision? How would fans respond?
15. In the 1994 baseball strike, were the owners' actions designed to undermine, or "break," the players' union? How can this analysis be made?

GLOSSARY*

Arbitration The process of referring disputes between employers and employees (or between two rival unions) to the decision of impartial adjudicators. Although an arbitrator's decision is legally binding, arbitration differs from judicial processes in two important respects: (1) the disputants have voluntarily agreed to refer the matter to arbitration and have themselves selected the arbitrator, except in rare cases, such as during wartime, when the government may require and appoint arbitrators; (2) the arbitrator holds the hearings, and these are usually much less formal than court proceedings. Also, the arbitrator does not rely solely upon the presentations at these hearings, but if he deems it necessary he may make independent investigations. (See *compulsory arbitration*.)

Bargaining rights Refers to workers' rights to bargain collectively with their employers as established by law and judicial interpretations.

Cartel A group of businesses or nations that agree to influence prices by regulating the production and marketing of a product.

Certification of union An official action or order of the proper government agency (e.g., the National Labor Relations Board) specifying that a union is free from employer domination and includes a majority of the employees in its membership and hence must be recognized by the employer as the collective bargaining agent for all the employees in the collective bargaining unit.

Collective agreement A contract signed by an employer (or his representative) and a union specifying the terms and conditions of employment of those covered by the contract, the status or relation of the union to the employer, and the procedures to be used for settling disputes arising during the term of the contract.

Collective bargaining The process of employer-union negotiation for the purpose of reaching agreement as to the terms and conditions of employment for a specified period.

*From Peterson, Florence. (1945). *American Labor Unions*, U.S. Dept. of Labor, Bureau of Labor Statistics; Harper and Bros., New York, p. 248 et. seq.

Compulsory arbitration The process of settlement of employer-labor disputes by a government agency (or other means provided by the government), which has the power to investigate and make an award that must be accepted by all parties concerned; not to be confused with voluntary agreements between employers and unions to have their disputes submitted for final determination by an impartial agency.

Conciliation An attempt to settle disputes between employers and workers. The term is used interchangeably with *mediation,* although technically mediation is a more passive act of intervention. In the narrow sense, a mediator is a go-between who offers no advice and who may conceivably be able to effect agreement between parties who refuse to face each other. A conciliator, on the other hand, gets the disputants together and takes an active part in the discussions by offering suggestions and advice. Acceptance of the conciliator's recommendations, however, is voluntary.

Labor relations A general term used in connection with any or all matters of mutual concern to employers and employees. Sometimes given a more limited meaning to indicate the kind of recognition in effect between an employer and union. (See *NLRA.*)

Lockout A temporary withholding or shutting down of work by an employer, in protest against employees' actions or to coerce them into accepting his terms.

Mediation An effort by an outside person to bring the employer and worker representatives into agreement. Mediation in its very essence implies voluntarism. Whether performed by a government or a private agency, the parties concerned voluntarily refer the dispute to the mediator with the understanding that her role is to assist them in reaching a settlement rather than make a settlement for them, as in the case of arbitration. (See *arbitration* and *conciliation.*)

Monopoly Control of the production and distribution of a product or service by one or more firms acting together. The effect is lack of competition, higher prices, and nonresponsiveness to consumer needs.

Monopsony Dominance of a market by one buyer or group of buyers acting together.

National Labor Relations Act (Wagner Act) A federal statute passed in 1935 that guarantees to employees in any industry or plant engaged in interstate commerce "the right to self-organization, to form, join, or assist labor organizations, to bargain collectively through representatives of their own choosing, and to engage in concerted activities, for the purpose of collective bargaining or other mutual aid or protection." It established the National Labor Relations Board, whose function is to eliminate on the part of the employer unfair labor practices that impede collective bargaining, to settle controversies with regard to representation of employees, and to certify which union, if any, shall represent the workers in an appropriate bargaining unit.

Strike A temporary stoppage of work by a group of employees in order to express a grievance or to enforce a demand concerning changes in working conditions. Government statistics exclude all strikes lasting less than 1 day or involving fewer than six workers and make no distinction between strikes and lockouts.

REFERENCES

Berry, R., and Wong, G. (1986). *Law and business of the sports industries.* Vol. I Professional Sports Leagues; Dover, Massachusetts: Auburn House.

Berry, R., Gould, W., and Staudohar, P. (1986). *Labor relations in professional sports.* Dover, Massachusetts: Auburn House.

Burk, R. (1994). *Never just a game: players, owners, and American baseball to 1920.* Chapel Hill, North Carolina: The University of North Carolina Press.

Cosell, H., Whitfield, S. (1991). *What's wrong with sports?* New York: Pocket Books.

Dworkin, J. (1981). *Owners versus players: baseball and collective bargaining.* Dover, Massachusetts: Auburn House.

Jennings, K. (1990). *Balls and strikes: the money game in professional baseball.* New York: Praeger.

Johnson, A., and Frey, J. (Eds.) (1985). *Government and sport: the public policy issues.* Totowa, New Jersey: Rowman and Allanheld.

Kochan, T., and Katz, H. (1988). *Collective bargaining and industrial relations.* 2nd ed. Homewood, Illinois: Irwin.

Lowenfish, L. (1990). *The imperfect diamond: a history of baseball's labor wars.* New York: Da Capo Press.

Miller, M. (1991). *A whole different ball game: the sport and business of baseball.* New York: Birch Lane Press.

Noll, R. (Ed.) (1974). *Government and the sports business.* Washington, D.C.: The Brookings Institution.

Quirk, J., and Fort, R. (1992). *Pay dirt: the business of professional team sports.* Princeton, New Jersey: Princeton University Press.

Sands, J., and Gammons, P. (1993). *Coming apart at the seams.* New York: Macmillan.

Scully, G. (1989). *The business of major league baseball.* Chicago: The University of Chicago Press.

Sommers, P. (Ed.) (1992). *Diamonds are forever: the business of baseball.* Washington, D.C.: The Brookings Institution.

Staudohar, P. (1989). *The sports industry and collective bargaining,* 2nd ed., Ithaca, New York: ILR Press.

Staudohar, P., and Mangan, J. (Eds.) (1991). *The business of professional sports.* Urbana, Illinois: University of Illinois Press.

Sullivan, N. (1992). *The diamond revolution: the prospects for baseball after the collapse of its ruling class.* New York: St. Martin's Press.

The Economist, "A Survey of the Sports Business," V.324, n7769, July 25, 1992.

Veeck, B., and Linn, E. (1989). *The hustler's handbook.* New York: Fireside.

Zimbalist, A. (1992). *Baseball and billions.* New York: Basic Books.

SUGGESTED READINGS

Bradley, Bill. (1976). *Life on the run,* Bantam Books, New York. An engaging look at the 1973 NBA championship season by one of the league's star players; provides a rare insight into the game from the player's perspective. (Reissued by Vintage Books, 1995 with a new introduction by the author.)

Cosell, Howard. (1985). *I never played the game,* with Peter Bonventre, Avon Books, New York. A behind-the-scenes analysis of franchise maneuvering and the commissioner's role in baseball and football, during the turbulent 1970s and 1980s. The author's major role in the creation of "Monday Night Football" is also covered.

Cosell, Howard. (1991). *What's wrong with sports,* with Shelby Whitfield, Pocket Books, New York. Cosell's diatribe against gambling, racism and drugs in sports also includes an interesting look at the big business of professional sports and the corruption in college athletics. The legal history of the NFL's battle against free agency is especially useful.

Dryden, Ken. (1984). *The game,* Penguin Books, New York. This book is similar in approach to Bradley's, analyzing the National Hockey League from a star player's viewpoint.

Michener, James A. (1976). *Sports in America,* Random House, New York. A comprehensive sociological anaysis of the burgeoning sports industries in America. This volume may be ponderous

for the beginning student, but it provides helpful insights into several important areas: college sports, the media, government involvement, and stadium financing.

Lowenfish, Lee. (1991). *The imperfect diamond: a history of baseball's labor wars,* (Revised Edition), Da Cappo Press, New York. An excellent history of baseball's troubled labor relations, from the first reserve clause in 1879 to the final basic agreement in 1990.

Miller, Marvin. (1991). *A whole different ball game,* Carol Publishing Group, New York. The definitive book on baseball's modern labor era, by the founding executive director of the Major League Baseball Players Association. Essential to an understanding of the current labor problems in baseball.

Roberts, Randy and James Olson. (1989). *Winning is the only thing: sports in America since 1945,* The Johns Hopkins University Press, Baltimore. The most accessible of the three sociological works included in this reading list. The bibliographical essay is invaluable for the student.

Staudohar, Paul. (1989). *The sports industry and collective bargaining,* 2nd Ed., ILR Press, Ithaca, New York. The standard treatise on the economic and legal underpinnings of labor relations in the four major professional team sports.

Sullivan, Neil J. (1992). *The diamond revolution,* St. Martin's Press, New York. An interesting examination of the business elements in major league baseball.

Veeck, Bill, with Ed Linn. (1965). *The hustler's handbook,* Putnam Books, New York. (Reprint with author's note and epilogue, Fireside Books, New York, 1989). This book should be read as the sequel to Veeck's 1962 autobiography "Veeck—As in Wreck"; together they comprise the most entertaining and illuminating work to date on the ownership of professional sports franchises.

Wilson, John. (1994). *Playing by the rules: sport, society and the state,* Wayne State University Press, Detroit. A comprehensive study of the sociological, legal and economic aspects of college and professional sports in modern American society. This book continues in the tradition of Michener's now-dated *Sports in America.*

PART III

Issues of Policy

CHAPTER 9

Ethics

Scott Branvold

In this chapter, you will become familiar with the following terms:

Absolutism	Moral principles	Deontology
Relativism	Values	Theory of justice
Rationalization	Ethics	Principle of proportionality
Morality	Teleology	Ethical code
Moral norms	Utilitarianism	

Overview

This chapter provides the foundation for a rational application of the principles of ethics to the ethical problems that confront the sport manager. Such principles, some would argue, are not being applied systematically or with any consistency in matters of moral uncertainty. Many would suggest that the present ethical environment is in an abysmal state in all facets of life. Members of society are regularly exposed to accounts of unethical and illegal activities in many basic social institutions,

A debt of gratitude is owed to Dr. R. Scott Kretchmar, whose insightful and substantive comments aided greatly in the preparation of this chapter.

including government, business, and even religion.

There are numerous examples of political corruption at all levels of government. Investigations of ethical misdeeds seem commonplace and often reach the very centers of political power. The cynicism toward government that is so prevalent is fueled by the fact that too often politicians' behavior has not matched the rhetoric that got them elected.

The business world has also been confronted with ethical problems, some of monumental proportions. Several recent polls suggest a very basic distrust of American business and businesspeople (Robin and Reidenbach, 1989). Situations such as the insider trading scheme and the junk bond financing scandal in the late 1980s involving Ivan Boesky and Michael Milken (among others) have done nothing to alter this apprehension. Although the "caveat emptor," or "let the buyer beware" ideology may not be as prevalent or acceptable as it once was, many consumers are still skeptical. The many instances of disregard for consumer safety and the environment that frequently plague business organizations simply add to the perception that business operates in an ethical quagmire.

Even religion, which is the foundation for the moral beliefs of many, has had embarrassing ethical problems. Examples include the indiscretions of prominent television evangelists, which received enormous publicity and damaged the credibility of their respective religious efforts.

The business of sport has not been immune to or isolated from the ethical problems so prevalent elsewhere. The belief that sport is a haven for fair play and justice is largely a romanticized ideal. College athletic programs are being investigated with monotonous regularity, and famous professional athletes routinely appear on magazine covers—for their deeds and exploits *off* the field rather than *on* it. Olympic athletes are banned from competition for drug use, and fitness clubs make outlandish advertising claims while using staffs of high-pressure salespeople with little or no fitness training.

Whether the ethical climate in society and business today is significantly different from other eras or generations is probably subject to debate. In simpler times, conduct was influenced by a more unequivocal set of guidelines. This is a form of ethical **absolutism,** which maintains that there is an eternally true moral code that can be applied with strict impartiality. Increasingly, actions appear to be guided by a sense of **relativism,** a belief that there are no absolutes, and what is right or wrong depends on the situation (Robin and Reidenbach, 1989). Consequences of this relativistic approach include confusion regarding standards and expectations of behavior and a greater latitiude to rationalize one's actions.

Rationalization of actions occurs in a variety of ways. Perhaps the chances of getting caught are slight, or the penalties are minimal. In some circumstances, behavior is justified by saying "Everyone else is doing it!" or "Who's going to be hurt?" Actions may also be rationalized because the stakes are sufficiently high to be worth the risks. For example, the economic incentives of successful college football and basketball programs may be enough to produce recruiting improprieties. This contingent view of what is acceptable may actually create confusion about the nature of ethics. Individuals charged with ethical misconduct frequently defend their actions by saying "I have broken no laws." Rather than viewing the law as the floor for acceptable behavior, many view the law as the standard for ethical conduct. The result is an increasingly regulated society that relies on the law rather than on ethical standards to achieve fairness and justice. Kristol states, "It is a confession of moral bankruptcy to assert that what the law does not explicity prohibit is therefore morally permissible" (Solomon and Hanson, 1983). It seems that rules are now viewed as barriers to get around rather than guidelines by which to live. A monument to this perspective is the voluminous NCAA manual, which undergoes frequent revisions to close the loopholes that are continually sought in order to beat the system. If this represents the standard most people and organizations use to guide their actions, then an ethical crisis does indeed exist.

FUNDAMENTAL CONCEPTS

Developing a foundation for ethical analysis first requires an understanding of the fundamental concepts of *morality* and *ethics*. These terms are often used interchangeably, and although one must not get bogged down in semantics, a brief discussion of distinctions between the two terms is appropriate.

Morality has been defined as the special set of **values** that frame the absolute limitations on behavior. It may include such basic rules as "Don't steal" (**moral norms**), as well as a more general system of duties and obligations (**moral principles**) (Solomon and Hanson, 1983). Rokeach (1973) defines a value as an enduring belief that guides personal behavior and shapes personal goals. He characterizes two types of values; instrumental values (e.g., ambition, courage, honesty), which are viewed as the means to terminal values (e.g., freedom, happiness, security).

De George (1982) and Beauchamp and Bowie (1988) place emphasis on morality's concern with the "good and bad" or "right and wrong" character of actions within the context of social customs and mores of any particular culture. They also stress the idea that morality is based on impartial considerations and that individuals cannot legitimately create their own personal moral codes.

De George (1982) defines **ethics** as a systematic attempt to make sense of our moral experience to determine what rules should govern conduct. This definition suggests that ethics is the study of morality. Beauchamp and Bowie (1988) and Velasquez (1988) seem to support this idea, while stressing that ethics involves the justification and application of moral standards and principles.

CONCEPT CHECK

Although the terms "morality" and "ethics" are used interchangeably, ethicists do note some semantic differences between them. Morality provides the set of values that limit behavior, whereas ethics involves the application of and justification for moral principles.

PERSONAL MORAL DEVELOPMENT

Often morality is viewed as a matter of personal conscience, with everyone entitled to their own moral opinion. However, morality is much more objective than many perceive. Moral development involves the ability to distinguish right from wrong; this ability to make moral judgments and engage in moral behavior increases with maturity (Cavanaugh, 1984).

Lawrence Kohlberg (1976) has developed perhaps the most widely accepted model of individual moral development, which involves three developmental levels with each level subdivided into two stages.

Level I: Preconventional. At this level, a child can respond to rules and social expectations and can apply the labels "good," "bad," "right," and "wrong." These rules, however, are seen as externally imposed (such as by parents) and in terms of pleasant and painful consequences (for example, a spanking for wrongdoing or a piece of candy for desirable behavior). The child does not have the ability to identify with others, so the motivation for action is largely one of self-interest. Stages 1 and 2 within level I reflect largely instrumental orientations. The behavior is not motivated by a moral sensitivity but simply by the consequences of an action—at first avoiding punishment and later receiving rewards and praise.

Level II: Conventional. At this level the expectations of family and peer groups become primary behavioral influences. The individual exhibits loyalty to the group and its norms and begins to identify with the point of view of others. This level is characterized by conformity and a willingness to subordinate individual needs to those of the group. The first stage within this level (stage 3) focuses on a "good boy/nice girl" morality, in which good behavior involves conforming to the expectations of family and friends. Actions are guided by stereotypes of what is normal behavior and are frequently judged by intention. The next stage of this level (stage 4) is termed the *law and order* stage. Right and wrong extends to conforming with societal laws, and there is a recognition of socially prescribed duties, responsibilities, and obligations. De George (1982) contends that most adults live at this conformity stage of development and that many never go beyond it.

Level III: Postconventional or Principled. At level III, there is an attempt to find a self-chosen set of moral principles that can be justified to any rational individual. Proper laws and values are those to which any reasonable people would want to commit, regardless of social position or status. The first stage (stage 5) within this level has a social contract orientation. There is an awareness of conflicting personal views and a sense that the rules should be upheld impartially because they are the social contract. A primary concern in this stage is that laws and duties be based on their overall utility as guided by "the greatest good for the greatest number." Cavanaugh (1984) points out that this stage is the "official" level of moral development of the United States government and the Constitution. The final stage (stage 6) is based on the acceptance of universal ethical principles. At this stage, appropriate action is defined by the conscious choice of universal ethical principles that are comprehensive and consistent and deal with justice, equality, and human dignity. The motivation for adherence to these principles is a basic belief in their encompassing validity and a willingness to commit to them (Cavanaugh, 1984; Kohlberg, 1976; Velasquez, 1988).

CONCEPT CHECK

Kohlberg's model of moral development describes the progression of moral reasoning from the childlike motivations of avoiding a spanking to the mature moral reasoning of taking a principled stand based purely on the "rightness" of the principle. Kohlberg's level III has at its roots the most widely accepted normative ethical theories, which serve as the basis for ethical analysis.

THEORIES OF ETHICS

Normally, references to ethical theories or decision rules take the form of simple ethical maxims, such as the following (Laczniak and Murphy, 1985):

1. *The golden rule:* Act toward others the way you would want them to act toward you.
2. *The utilitarian principle:* Act in a way that results in the greatest good for the greatest number.
3. *Kant's categorical imperative:* Act in such a way that the action taken under the circumstances could be a universal law or rule of behavior.
4. *The professional ethic:* Take only actions that would be viewed as proper by an impartial set of professional colleagues.
5. *The TV test:* Act in such a way that the actions could be defended comfortably in front of a national television audience.

While these maxims may serve as handy rules for ethical conduct, the purpose of this section is to provide a more comprehensive foundation for ethical analysis. Several authors have developed theories for the ethical analysis of actions and decisions. Most of these theories are either teleological, deontological, or some combination of the two.

Theories based on **teleology** (from the Greek meaning "end") assess the morality of actions on the basis of the consequences or results of those actions; the most widely studied of these theories is **utilitarianism.** Jeremy Bentham (1748-1832) and John Stuart Mill (1806-1873) were the most influential developers of utilitarianism, which is predicated on the idea of "creating the greatest good for the greatest number." Actions are evaluated by judging their consequences and weighing the good effects and bad effects. The attempt is to achieve an optimal balance of benefits vs. harms on those affected by the action. Applying utilitarianism to

decision making requires selecting the action that will produce the greatest net social benefit. The good of the group supersedes the good of the individual (Beauchamp and Bowie, 1988; De George, 1982; Robin and Reidenbach, 1989). The major criticisms of the utilitarian approach include (1) the difficulty in measuring utilitarian value, (2) the opportunity for unjust net consequences, and (3) the lack of concern for how results are produced (Beauchamp and Bowie, 1988).

The deontological, or formalistic, approach to ethical analysis was formulated primarily by Immanuel Kant (1734-1804), with more contemporary work done by William D. Ross and John Rawls. **Deontology** (derived from the Greek for *duty*) is based on the idea that what makes an action right is not the consequences but the fact that the action conforms to some absolute rules of moral behavior. Kant's categorical imperative statements serve as guidelines for what would be considered moral behavior. Moral action would (1) be universalizable (that is, it would make sense for everyone in a similar situation to take the same action), (2) demonstrate respect for the individual (that is, others are never treated simply as means), and (3) be acceptable to all rational beings (Tuleja, 1985). Kant's vision was one of universal and consistent application of the rules of morality. His critics maintain that the theory is too vague and imprecise. There are also claims that it does not help resolve the issue of balancing conflicting individual rights and has too little regard for consequences (Velasquez, 1988).

Ross put forth a theory that combined certain aspects of utilitarianism with Kantian theory. He postulated that action is bound by the duties of fidelity, gratitude, justice, beneficence, self-improvement, and noninjury. These are seen as universal moral obligations above and beyond the law, but there is a recognition that some exceptions may exist (Laczniak and Murphy, 1985).

John Rawls has also formulated an influential ethical approach called the **theory of justice.** The major premise behind his proposals is that rules and laws of society should be constructed as if we did not know what roles we were to play in that society (what Rawls terms the "veil of ignorance"). This creates an objectivity and fairness to the ethical principles that guide actions (Cavanaugh, 1984).

CONCEPT CHECK

The most widely accepted ethical theories are either teleological or deontological in nature. Utilitarianism is the most prominent teleological theory, and its focus is on consequences of actions and "creating the greatest good for the greatest number." Deontology has a more absolute orientation, suggesting that what makes an action right is not consequences but adherence to basic moral laws.

MODELS FOR ETHICAL ANALYSIS

The ethical theories in the previous section provide the foundation for numerous models that can aid in evaluating moral dilemmas. An approach suggested by Tuleja (1985) has a utilitarian orientation in which actions are evaluated on the basis of their effect on various constituent groups or stakeholders.

For example, a college athletic administrator has numerous constituents to consider, including school administration, faculty, students, athletes, fans, coaches, alumni, media, and community businesses.

Many of the models use a combination of the basic theories to provide a multidimensional approach to dealing with ethical questions. Goodpaster (1984) summarized three avenues for ethical analysis, one based on utility (maximum benefits), one based on rights, and one based on duty or obligation. Garrett (1966) developed a theory specifically with the business manager in mind that combines concern for outcomes (utilitarianism) and process (deontology) and adds the dimension of motivation. These three components (means, ends, and intentions) are synthesized into what Garrett calls the **principle of proportionality,** which states that undesirable side effects of an action can be accepted if and only if there is some proportionate reason for doing so (Laczniak and Murphy, 1985).

Cavanaugh (1984) has also suggested a tridimensional approach to ethical decision making that includes characteristics of both teleological and deontological theories. He uses utility, rights, and justice as the ethical evaluation criteria. If conflicts arise among the three criteria, further analysis must be done based on the relative importance of the criteria, the freedom with which the action is taken, and the nature of the undesirable

effects. Figure 9-1 provides a flowchart of steps to guide this ethical evaluation process; it is rather simplistic but does provide a system that can be useful in decision making.

CONCEPT CHECK

The models for ethical analysis are built on the foundations of basic ethical theories. They are not designed to provide indisputable answers to every ethical dilemma, but they can provide a systematic methodology for assessing ethical questions and clarifying the alternatives. Cavanaugh's model is but one of many approaches that may be useful in the quest for ethically sound decisions.

PERSONAL ETHICS AND ORGANIZATIONAL RESPONSIBILITY

The foundation for ethical analysis has a personal orientation. The distinction between personal and professional ethics is a difficult matter to address. Ultimately, organizations are collections of individuals and decisions are made and carried out by individuals. This would seem to indicate that the ultimate responsibility for ethical behavior rests with the individual, thereby demonstrating the importance of personal ethics. If this is the case, however, how is it that people who consider themselves to be basically honest and compassionate can act irresponsibly at times? It seems as if a different set of values are applied on the job than are applied outside the workplace. One author cites a former corporate vice-president who says, "What is right in the corporation is not what is right in a man's home or in his church. What is right in the corporation is what the guy above you wants from you" (Jackall, 1988).

Circumstances may arise in which professionally defensible behavior is not always congruent with the guiding principles of ordinary norms. Honesty is a basic virtue; yet, at the personal level the "little white lie" may be a justifiable action for some situations. Are the standards of honesty at the professional level any different?

Advertisers use the "white lie" in many cases; the term *puffery* has even been coined to describe the practice of stretching or bending the truth with inflated claims and exaggerations. Indeed, advertising

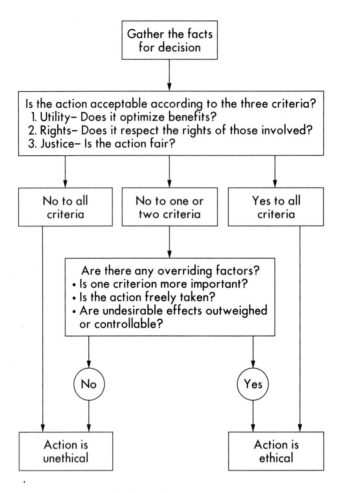

FIGURE 9-1   Flowchart for ethical decision making.
From Cavanaugh, G. (1984). *American values* (2nd Ed).
Englewood Cliffs, New Jersey: Prentice-Hall.

is often considered one of the most ethically suspect aspects of business operations. An example of advertising that is not dishonest but certainly misleading involves food products advertised as "cholesterol free." In many cases these products never had cholesterol, and consumer advocates claim such advertising is misleading because it implies something has been done to remove cholesterol or that other similar products have it. A recent advertisement for a Continental Basketball Association (CBA) franchise encouraged people to purchase tickets to see a team whose roster was purported to

be filled with future National Basketball Association (NBA) stars. Anyone familiar with professional basketball recognizes the extravagance of such a claim, yet many would not question the ethics of such an advertisement.

There are many examples both personally and professionally in which behavior does not adhere to the ideal societal standards of virtue. The frequency of departure from these standards and, perhaps more importantly, the willingness to routinely accept such departures are basic ethical concerns.

Milton Friedman, a prominent American economist, maintains that businesses are amoral entities and the corporate executive's only responsibility is to maximize profit. Yet even this extreme proponent of free market capitalism recognizes that this must be accomplished within the framework of basic societal rules of law and custom. Work values may be developed through conscious organizational effort, or they may evolve without organizational attention. When results are the primary or perhaps only organizational value supported, the consequence may be an "anything goes" ethical climate. Indeed, there are likely to be situations in which unethical behavior will produce greater profits, especially in the short run (Robin and Reidenbach, 1989). Organizations that ignore or even reward unethical behavior are likely to have personnel who behave unethically.

In sport, the scoreboard and the record book have become the final determinants of value and worth for many (Gibson, 1993). Stoll and Beller (1993) contend that this perspective has a tremendous influence on the moral reasoning of sport participants. Their studies indicate that a negative relationship exists between moral development and sport participation and that there is a decrease in moral reasoning the longer the athlete competes in organized sport. This view of athletic success is also likely to influence the decisions of sport administrators as they attempt to make their organizations worthy of the public's attention. Since winning is usually tied to box office success, sport managers are subject to some of the same pressures that athletes encounter.

The role models of an organization will set the tone for the behavior of the entire organization. Kristol states, "Businessmen have come to think that the conduct of business is a purely "economic" activity to be judged only by economic criteria and that moral and religious traditions exist in a world apart, to be visited on Sunday perhaps" (Solomon and Hanson, 1983).

Kjeldsen (1992) identifies three specific subroles that the sport manager has that have important influences on the behaviors within an organization. Managers serve as teachers, administrators, and legislators, each of which are roles that directly influence the ethical climate of the sport organizations they direct.

The leadership of the organization will determine what the dominant perspective is toward ethical behavior. The demands, expectations, and traditions of an organization will be the behavioral guides. The organizational leaders must set clear, unambiguous expectations for the ethical conduct of their employees. When this is done, employees must then be given the authority to act and be held accountable for the ethical quality of their actions. It takes integrity and courage to act on one's values, especially when the stakes are high. An organization and its leaders must work diligently to create a climate in which ethical conduct is a matter of habit rather than one of expedience.

CONCEPT CHECK

The relationship between personal and professional ethics is difficult to determine with great precision. Individuals will bring a personal set of values to the job, but to what extent that set of values will influence job behavior depends on a number of factors, including the strength with which those values are held, the integrity and courage to act upon those values, the ethical environment within the organization, and the role models and leaders that influence the work environment.

ETHICS AND THE PROFESSIONALIZATION OF SPORT MANAGEMENT

Many occupations, including those in sport management, desire recognition as a profession for a variety of reasons. Law and medicine are prime examples of professions that traditionally carry with them prestige, respect, status, and autonomy (De George, 1982). Although the desire for professional status is important and certainly understandable, the purpose of this section is not to debate the merits of sport management as a profession. (For an articulate discussion of the issue of professionalization, see Chapter 13 in *Business Ethics* by Richard De George.)

As sport management strives to move toward a greater professional status, the aspect of autonomy does have particular relevance with regard to ethics. Professions have traditionally been allowed more control to set their own standards and to be self-regulating and self-disciplining. The standards are frequently expressed in the form of an **ethical code,** often developed and enforced by a professional organization. Many businesses and professional business organizations have also developed ethical codes and creeds. The following boxes contain examples of advertising ethics and marketing ethics codes. However, many researchers question the impact some of these codes have had, contending that they lack depth or are filled with platitudes that do little to guide behavior (Robin and Reidenbach, 1989). De George (1982) recommends that a code should (1) be regulative, not simply a statement of ideals, (2) protect public interests and not be self-serving, (3) be specific and relevant to the specialized concerns of the members, and (4) be enforceable and enforced.

Given the differences among organizations, it is unlikely that a generalized code will be widely applicable. This leaves it to each organization to evaluate the ethical implications of its own activities and to develop appropriate guidelines. This process alone will help sensitize the organization to the individual and group responsibilities involved in operating in an ethical manner (Behrman, 1988).

In sport, several coaching organizations have addressed the issue of ethical conduct, including the National High School Athletic Coaches Association in the United States, the Coaching Association of Canada, the American Football Coaches Association, and the National Association of Basketball Coaches. There is little in the literature of sport management that provides any formal treatment of ethics within the field. Zeigler (1989) has expressed the need for those involved in sport management to develop a sound approach to ethics as it relates to their duties and responsibilities and suggests that a comprehensive code of ethics is urgently required.

Developing a code of ethics for sport managers is a problematical undertaking. The breadth of the field makes it very difficult to create a code that has encompassing relevance. In addition, no organization fully accommodates the tremendous variety of practitioners and academicians in the field. The North American Society for Sport Management (NASSM) has approved an ethical creed for sport managers and has a committee to develop an ethical code for the consideration of its members. This process will require cooperation with a wide range of other professional associations in the field, such as the National Association for Sport and Physical Education (NASPE) and closely related occupational and professional groups. The

---

American advertising federation's code of advertising ethics

1. Truth—advertising shall reveal the truth, and shall reveal significant facts, the omission of which would mislead the public.

2. Substantiation—advertising claims shall be substantiated by evidence in possession of the advertiser and the advertising agency prior to making such claims.

3. Comparisons—advertising shall refrain from making false, misleading, or unsubstantiated statements or claims about a competitor or his products or services.

4. Bait advertising—advertising shall not offer products or services for sale unless such offer constitutes a bona fide effort to sell the advertised products or services and is not a device to switch consumers to other goods or services, usually higher priced.

5. Guarantees and warranties—advertising of guarantees and warranties shall be explicit, with sufficient information to apprise consumers of their principal terms and limitations or, when space or time restrictions preclude such disclosures, the advertisement shall clearly reveal where the full text of the guarantee or warranty can be examined before purchase.

6. Price claims—advertising shall avoid price claims that are false or misleading, or savings claims which do not offer provable savings.

7. Testimonials—advertising containing testimonials shall be limited to those of competent witnesses who are reflecting a real and honest opinion or experience.

8. Taste and decency—advertising shall be free of statements, illustrations, or implications which are offensive to good taste or public decency.

Adapted from American Advertising Federation, 1101 Vermont Ave., NW, Suite 500, Washington, D.C. 20005.

---

following box is the ethical creed approved by NASSM at its annual meeting in 1989. This creed is one of the few efforts made in the area of sport management to formally address the issue of professional ethics. Regardless of the status of sport management as a pro-

World marketing contact group marketing creed

1. I hereby acknowledge my accountability to the organization for which I work, and to society as a whole, to improve marketing knowledge and practice and to adhere to the highest professional standards in my work and personal relationships.

2. My concept of marketing includes as its basic principle the sovereignty of all consumers in the marketplace and the necessity for mutual benefit to both buyer and seller in all transactions.

3. I shall personally maintain the highest standards of ethical and professional conduct in all business relationships with customers, suppliers, colleagues, competitors, governmental agencies, and the public.

4. I pledge to protect, support, and promote the principles of consumer choice, competition, and innovative enterprise, consistent with relevant legislative and public policy standards.

5. I shall not knowingly participate in actions, agreements, or marketing policies or practices which may be detrimental to customers, competitors, or established community social or economic policies or standards.

6. I shall strive to insure that products and services are distributed through such channels and by such methods as will tend to optimize the distributive process by offering maximum customer value and service at minimum cost while providing fair and equitable compensation for all parties.

7. I shall support efforts to increase productivity or reduce costs of production or marketing through standardization or other methods, provided these methods do not stifle innovation or creativity.

8. I believe prices should reflect true value in use of the product or service to the customer, including the pricing of goods and services transferred among operating organizations worldwide.

9. I acknowledge that providing the best economic and social product value consistent with cost also includes: A. recognizing the customer's right to expect safe products with clear instructions for their proper use and maintenance; B. providing easily accessible channels for customer complaints; C. investigating any customer dissatisfaction objectively and taking prompt and appropriate remedial action; D. recognizing and supporting proven public policy objectives such as conserving energy and protecting the environment.

10. I pledge my efforts to assure that all marketing research, advertising, sales promotion, and sales presentations of products, services, or concepts are done clearly, truthfully, and in good taste so as not to mislead or offend customers. I further pledge to insure that all these activities are conducted in accordance with the highest standards of each profession and generally accepted principles of fair competition.

11. I pledge to cooperate fully in furthering the efforts of all institutions, media, professional associations, and other organizations to publicize this creed as widely as possible throughout the world.

Draft approved by World Marketing Contact Group in Verona, Italy, September 1976.

fession, this can serve as a foundation for encouraging sport managers to act professionally.

CONCEPT CHECK

One of the characteristics of professionalization is the autonomy that provides opportunity for self-regulation. This often manifests itself in a formalized approach to ethical standards and conduct. Increasing attention is being paid to ethics in many business fields, as reflected by both ethics training and the development of formal codes of ethics. Various sport and recreation organizations have made modest efforts to deal with pertinent ethical concerns, but only very meager beginnings can be reported regarding efforts at formalizing the treatment of ethics in sport management.

IMPLICATIONS FOR SPORT MANAGEMENT PREPARATION AND PRACTICE

As the study of sport management becomes more formalized, one must examine the relationship of ethics and the future of sport management preparation and practice. With the number of academically prepared practitioners in sport management likely to increase substantially, the move toward a greater professional status will probably continue. This trend has implications for the preparation of graduate and undergraduate students in sport management programs. Coursework should contain more material dealing with ethically sensitive issues, and more sport ethics and philosophy courses need to be developed. (The American Assembly of Collegiate Schools of Business [AACSB] accredited business schools are required to include instruction on ethics within their curricula [Laczniak and Murphy, 1985; Robin and Reidenbach, 1989].)

There are ethical issues in virtually every area of sport management coursework. Topics such as honesty in advertising, ticket pricing, ticket scalping, and sensationalism, which focuses on violence and sex, have clear ethical dimensions. Some sport entities express concern over the levels of violence in sport, yet use that violence in many of their promotional efforts. Many other topics such as gender and minority equity issues, athlete exploitation, commercialization, and conflicts of interest can pose situations that have ethical considerations. There are also ethical questions about the social responsibility of sport organizations. This can manifest itself in a variety of ways such as the sale or advertising of alcohol and tobacco, the loyalty an organization should have to a community, the economic impact of sport businesses, and even the responsibility such organizations have as caretakers of the traditions and history of the sport.

Certainly there are numerous ethical issues and predicaments that surround the practice of sport management. One response to these ethical challenges is a more conscientious effort to provide ethical training to both prospective and practicing sport management professionals. Several studies indicate that ethics committees and employee ethics training programs are becoming more prevalent in mainstream business firms (Cavanaugh, 1984; Robin and Reidenbach, 1989). This is likely to occur

NASSM creed

Professional members of the North American Society for Sport Management, living in a free, democratic society, have respect for the worth and dignity of all people in our society. As professionals we honor the preservation and protection of fundamental human rights. We are committed to a high level of professional practice and service, professional conduct that is based on the application of sound management theory developed through a scientific body of knowledge about sport and developmental physical activity's role in the lives of all people. Such professional service shall be made available to clients of all ages and conditions, whether such people are classified as accelerated, normal, or special insofar as their status or condition is concerned.

As NASSM members pursuing our professional service, we will make every effort to protect the welfare of those who seek our assistance. We will use our professional skills only for purposes which are consistent with the values, norms, and laws of our society. Although we, as professional practitioners, demand for ourselves maximum freedom of inquiry and communication consistent with societal values, we fully understand that such freedom requires us to be responsible, competent, and objective in the application of our skills. We should always show concern for the best interests of our clients, our colleagues, and the public at large.

in sport businesses as well, and two particular reasons stand out. With the attention that many sport enterprises receive, unethical actions result in negative publicity that can be very damaging to public support. A very different concern has to do with the increasingly international nature of the sporting business. The international community may have a very different perspective on what actions are ethical and unethical. Reconciling the different cultural mores will require a far more conscientious effort of ethical preparation.

CONCEPT CHECK

There are ethical implications that will affect both academic preparation of sport managers and the practice of sport management as the next century approaches. It is likely that more concerted efforts will be made to emphasize ethical training in both educational and job settings.

There are numerous examples of ethical misconduct in all segments of society, and certainly sport is no exception. The focus of this chapter is to encourage recognition of the ethical dimensions of decision making and to provide a framework for a logical and reasoned approach for dealing with the moral and ethical choices that are certain to confront the sport management professional.

Professional behavior is grounded in personal values, but professional conduct does not always coincide with those personal values or the ideals of societal norms and virtues. To raise the level of professionalism in sport management, it is essential to take a proactive approach to ethical training. Ethical guidelines need to be carefully developed, and prospective sport managers should be schooled in the use of a systematic and analytical approach to the ethical dilemmas that they will undoubtedly encounter.

There is certainly a need for an increased awareness of and concern for the ethical issues of sport management; this is something that can be accomplished in a variety of ways. Incorporating ethical issues into existing academic coursework and developing courses in the ethics of sport are logical beginnings. The development of a code of ethics has begun to assist in providing a framework for ethical analysis. Beyond the classroom, practitioners must provide an environment in which a high standard of ethical conduct is the norm. Strong role models must be available and high expectations clearly outlined, and practitioners must be willing to accept that ethical behavior will not always bring the short-term, immediate benefits so demanded in this culture. The professionalization of sport management will ultimately be a cooperative venture between the academic community and the practitioner in the field. How each partner in this endeavor deals with the issue(s) of ethics will be important in determining the extent to which sport management moves toward a greater professional status.

SUMMARY

1. Numerous examples of ethical misconduct exist in many of the basic social institutions, and sport is certainly no exception.
2. The relativistic approach to ethics creates a more ambiguous behavioral environment, and action is frequently guided by legal standards rather than ethical standards.
3. Ethics and morality are interrelated concepts that provide guidelines for acceptable conduct.
4. Moral development starts with a very self-centered motivation, progresses to conforming with social norms, and ideally reaches the stage in which there is a reasoned belief in and commitment to universal moral principles.
5. Teleology and deontology are the two primary categories of ethical theory.
6. Maxims such as the golden rule are used as "rules of thumb" for ethical conduct, but more extensive frameworks for ethical analysis have been developed.
7. Many useful models have been developed to systematize the task of ethical decision making. Several of these models incorporate characteristics of both deontology and teleology.
8. Personal ethics must serve as the foundation for professional ethics, but the ethical character of the workplace will influence behavior.
9. Organizational and industry standards of conduct are often not congruent with personal standards, and the differences may be difficult to reconcile at times.
10. Development of a code of ethics is a step that established professions have taken but few sport organizations have as yet.
11. The North American Society for Sport Management (NASSM) has developed an ethical creed for sport managers.
12. One implication of sport management progressing toward professional status is an increasing concern for a formal and systematic approach to ethical training and behavior.
13. Ethics training is becoming more prevalent in the academic, as well as the business, setting.

CASE STUDY

You are the athletic director at XYZ State University, a school of 15,000 students that is a member of NCAA Division I-AA. Your athletic program is comprised of 16 sports, but financial constraints have limited your ability to do all you would like with the program. Football has never been a primary revenue source as it is with some major Division I institutions, and attendance has dwindled over the past few years. In fact, football currently produces a larger net loss than any other sport in the program. Nevertheless it holds a very strong traditional place on campus and in the community. The demands of gender equity have also forced resources to be reallocated and have strained the budget to the extent that either new revenue must be found to maintain the program or cuts will need to be made.

One option you are considering is dropping football. Such a proposal would create a furor on campus and in the community, but it has some merit financially and minimizes gender equity problems. Another option presented itself to you recently. The athletic director at MEGA University, a major Division I football power, called to see if you would consider playing them in football at their 90,000 seat stadium for a sizeable guarantee. XYZ and MEGA U. played each other on a regular basis several years ago, with MEGA U. routinely winning by six to eight touchdowns. There is virtually no prospect that the outcome would be much different now. The revenue produced from such a game would certainly ease some of your immediate financial problems, however.

Aside from the purely financial considerations of the scenario presented, there are some important ethical questions that must be addressed. As you weigh the options present, how would you respond to the ethical issues presented in this situation.

1. *Who are the various constituents that will be affected by your decision? How are they likely to react?*
2. *Is it appropriate to place the burden for the department's financial problems on the shoulders of an overmatched football team? What are the possible consequences?*
3. *How might either of these options be rationalized as the best decision?*
4. *What constitutes gender equity? Are there any ethical dimensions to dropping football as a method for achieving gender equity?*

REVIEW QUESTIONS AND ISSUES

1. Cite examples that depict the ethical climate that exists in society and in sport.
2. How are the concepts of ethics and morality related?
3. Discuss the contention that stage four of Kohlberg's model for moral development is the stage from which most adults tend to function ethically.
4. What are the primary characteristics of teleological and deontological theories of ethics?
5. What are the strengths and weaknesses of Cavanaugh's model for ethical decision making?
6. What is the relationship between personal and professional ethics?
7. Explain why personal ethics and ethics in sport management need to be addressed in an academic setting.
8. What is the responsibility of an organization's leadership with regard to the level of ethical conduct exhibited by its employees?
9. What can an organization do to encourage high standards of ethical conduct?
10. Is all legal behavior ethical? Is all ethical behavior legal? Defend your position.
11. What are the strengths and weaknesses of the ethical creed approved by the North American Society for Sport Management (NASSM)?
12. What role does ethics play in the professionalization of sport management?
13. Discuss what barriers you see that impede the ability of the field of sport management to develop an encompassing ethical code.

ETHICAL SITUATIONS FOR DISCUSSION

The situations presented here are but a few examples of the ethical issues that can arise in sport. One or more of the following suggestions may help to make these situations more useful exercises: (1) Evaluate how each situation might be dealt with at stages four, five and six of Kohlberg's model of moral development, (2) Evaluate each situation from both teleological and deontological points of view, (3) Use one or more of the five maxims on p. 152 to assess the appropriate actions in each situation, and (4) Apply Cavanaugh's model for ethical decision making (or some other model of ethical analysis) to the situations in order to arrive at an ethically reasoned response or decision.

1. What are the ethical considerations to be addressed in the decision to use drug testing as a screening tool for prospective employees? What about the use of lie detector tests? Would you submit to such testing? Why or why not? At what point do these tests become an invasion of privacy or a threat to basic constitutional rights?

2. Are the ethical considerations cited above the same for drug testing college and/or professional athletes? If athletes should be randomly tested, should all students? Professors? Administrators? Should drug testing be concerned only with performance-enhancing substances?

3. The hiring of Bill Frieder, former basketball coach at Michigan and current coach at Arizona State University, was a situation that raises some interesting ethical questions for several of the parties involved. Frieder accepted the coaching job at Arizona State just before the start of the NCAA basketball tournament in 1989. At that point he was relieved of his duties at Michigan, and his assistant took over the team (which went on to win the NCAA title). Without being privy to all the details of the situation, it may be difficult to be overly critical of the parties involved. On the other hand, the situation poses some interesting ethical questions. What are the ethical responsibilities of the coach to his team? The University of Michigan? Arizona State University? What ethical standards should Arizona State University be held to in this circumstance? Given that the letter of intent for signing recruits is shortly after the completion of the NCAA tournament, what does Arizona State have to gain and lose by waiting until after the tournament is completed before publicly consummating the deal?

4. It is relatively common practice now for professional baseball teams to offer to pay for the college education of high school draftees as an enticement to get them to sign a professional contract out of high school. Are there any ethical concerns surrounding this practice if baseball administrators are also aware that this is a benefit that players often will not ever use. Is this simply "good business?"

5. Al Davis, the owner of the Los Angeles Raiders, moved the team from Oakland to Los Angeles in the early 1980s, primarily because of the tremendous financial potential of a major market like Los Angeles. Oakland had supported the team well and the team had been very successful playing there, but from a business perspective Los Angeles was deemed to be a more profitable locale. After numerous lawsuits and appeals, the courts affirmed that Mr. Davis indeed had every right to move the franchise wherever he desired. Do professional franchise owners have any ethical obligations to the communities that support them? If so, what are they? Are they different from those of any other business operation?

6. The difference between serving the public well (social obligations) and serving as the social conscience is sometimes difficult to determine. Several examples involving health and fitness clubs may serve to amplify this issue. Should health clubs serve alcoholic beverages in their lounge area? Should they have cigarette machines? Should they provide tanning beds for those who wish to use them? From a business standpoint, each of these may be a profitable service. From a health standpoint, there are various levels of concern about each of these services. What ethical consideration comes into play in making the decision about the provision of such services? By not providing such services, are you playing the role of social conscience and limiting people's freedom to make their own choices?

7. Organizational image is the primary concern of the public relations effort. In many sport organizations the media are important players in the manipulation of that image, and the ethics of this relationship may bear scrutiny on both sides. Is it appropriate to curry the attention of the media through providing free tickets, food, transportation, accommodations, and so on? Should these favors be provided only for favorable coverage? Should the media accept such favors? What are the risks to each party and to the general public with such an arrangement?

8. In many circumstances it may be the actions of others that pose a personal ethical

quandary. In such situations the question of how you tolerate or deal with such behavior becomes the ethical dilemma. Do you report a fellow employee who is skimming small amounts of money from the cash register? Do you accept an outstanding prospective athlete's transcript that you know has been altered? Do you report a supervisor who is providing inside information to a favored supplier about competitors' bids on athletic equipment? What are the circumstances in which you tolerate these situations? Under what circumstances do you take action?

9. Employee and consumer safety are often cited as ethical problems that occur when organizations attempt to balance economic and safety concerns. For example, many considerations go into the decision on what type of playing surface to install. Are there ethical dimensions to this decision? Should artificial turf be used if the incidence of injury or the severity of injuries is higher than on natural surfaces? How much more dangerous would the surface have to be before the risks outweigh the benefits?

10. Personnel matters are often very subjective, and judgments are often influenced by personal philosophies and biases rather than clear-cut personnel policies. The Houston Oilers withheld a starting offensive lineman's pay for a game he missed to be with his wife during the birth of their child. How should such a situation be handled? Does the quality of the player or the importance of the game influence the decision you would make in such a circumstance?

REFERENCES

American Psychological Association. (1977). *Ethical standards of psychologists.* Washington, DC: The Association.

Beauchamp, T., and Bowie, N. (1988). *Ethical theory and business* (3rd Edition). Englewood Cliffs, New Jersey: Prentice Hall.

Behrman, J. (1988). *Essays on ethics in business and the professions.* Englewood Cliffs, New Jersey: Prentice-Hall.

Cavanaugh, G. (1984). *American business values* (2nd Edition). Englewood Cliffs, New Jersey: Prentice Hall.

De George, R. (1982). *Business ethics.* New York: Macmillan.

Garrett, T. (1966). *Business ethics.* Englewood Cliffs, New Jersey: Prentice Hall.

Gibson, J. (1993). *Performance versus results: a critique of values in contemporary sport.* Albany, New York: State University of New York Press.

Goodpaster, K. (1984). *Ethics in management.* Boston: Harvard Business School.

Jackall, R. (1988). *Moral mazes: the world of corporate managers.* New York: Oxford University Press.

Kjeldsen, E. (1992). The manager's role in the development and maintenance of ethical behavior in the sport organization. *Journal of Sport Management, 6* (2), 99-113.

Kohlberg, L. (1976). *Moral development and behavior: theory, research, and social issues.* New York: Holt, Rinehart, & Winston.

Laczniak, G., and Murphy, P. (1985). *Marketing ethics.* Lexington, Massachusetts: Heath.

Rokeach, M. (1973). *The nature of human values.* New York: The Free Press.

Robin, D., and Reidenbach, R. (1989). *Business ethics: where profits meet values systems.* Englewood Cliffs, New Jersey: Prentice Hall.

Solomon, R., and Hanson, K. (1983). *Above the bottom line.* New York: Harcourt Brace Jovanovich.

Stoll, S. and Beller, J. (1993, March). *The effect of a longitudinal teaching methodology and classroom environment on both cognitive and behavioral moral development.* Paper presented at American Alliance for Health, Physical Education, Recreation, and Dance. Washington, D.C.

Tuleja, T. (1985). *Beyond the bottom line.* New York: Facts on File Publications.

Velasquez, M. (1988). *Business ethics: concepts and cases* (2nd Edition). Englewood Cliffs, New Jersey: Prentice Hall.

Zeigler, E. (1989). Proposed creed and code of professional ethics for the North American Society for Sport Management. *Journal of Sport Management, 3,* 2-4.

SUGGESTED READINGS

Bick, P. (1988). *Business ethics and responsibility: an information sourcebook.* Phoenix: Oryx Press.

Braybrooke, D. (1983). *Ethics in the world of business.* Totowa, New Jersey: Rowman & Allanheld.

Desjardins, J., and McCall, J. (1990). *Contemporary issues in business ethics* (2nd Edition). Belmont, California: Wadsworth.

Donaldson, J. (1989). *Key issues in business ethics.* San Diego: Academic Press.

Frankena, W. (1973). *Ethics* (2nd Edition). Englewood Cliffs, New Jersey: Prentice Hall.

Hitt, W. (1990). *Ethics and leadership.* Columbus, Ohio: Battelle Press.

Hodgson, K. (1992). *A rock and a hard place.* New York: AMACOM.

Jones, D. (1992). *Sports ethics in America: a bibliography, 1970-1990.* Westport, Connecticut: Greenwood Press.

Lumpkin, A., Stoll, S., and Beller, J. (1995). *Sports ethics: applications for fair play.* St. Louis: Mosby.

Nash, L. (1981). Ethics without the sermon. *Harvard Business Review, 59,* 79-90.

Nash, L. (1990). *Good intentions aside.* Boston: Harvard Business School Press.

Pastin, M. (1986). *The hard problems of management.* San Francisco: Jossey-Bass.

Rosen, B. (1990). *Ethics companion.* Englewood Cliffs, New Jersey: Prentice-Hall.

Shea, E. (1978). *Ethical decisions in physical education and sport.* Springfield, Illinois: Charles C. Thomas.

Simon, R. (1991). *Fair play: sports, values, and society.* Boulder, Colorado: Westview Press.

Thiroux, J. (1980). *Ethics: theory and practice* (2nd Edition). Encino, California: Glencoe.

Zeigler, E. (1984). *Ethics and morality in sport and physical education.* Champaign, Illinois: Stipes.

JOURNALS

Journal of Business Ethics

Business and Professional Ethics Journal

CHAPTER 10

Tort Liability and Risk Management

Betty van der Smissen

In this chapter, you will become familiar with the following terms:

Tort	Immunity statutes	Waiver
Intentional tort	Gross negligence	Informed consent
Proximate cause	Good Samaritan laws	Comparative fault
Assault and battery	Independent contractor	Reckless disregard
Defamation	Governmental immunity	Negligent hiring
Invasion of privacy	Indemnification	Negligent supervision
Negligence	Reasonable and prudent	Negligent retention
Duty	professional	Avoidance
Unreasonable risk	Foreseeability	Transference
Standard of care	Contributory fault	Retention
Imputed	Primary assumption of risk	Reduction
Doctrine of respondeat superior	Inherent risks	

Overview

This chapter has two major parts. The first discusses basic legal concepts, primarily in the field of tort law. Who is liable in negligence actions is set forth in a section on the doctrine of respondeat superior. The standard of care required of sport managers is described, and then the defenses, which one may use when sued. There are brief sections on intentional torts, such as defamation and assault and battery (player toward player violence) and on products liability (equipment). The last section on legal concepts addresses some legal concerns related to employment torts, particularly physical violence and sexual child abuse by those who work with youth.

The second part applies the legal concepts in focusing on managing "risk exposures" to reduce loss, especially liabilities related to personal injuries of participants and spectators. The four phases in the development of a risk management plan are set forth, with emphasis on the analysis of risks and control approaches (phase 1) and operational procedures to ameliorate risk (phase 3).

Law is pervasive in all of sport management. In a study (Lea and Loughman, 1993) of NCAA schools, it was found that the areas of law for which athletic departments frequently sought advice were:

Area	Percent	Area	Percent
Employment/ personnel	67.29	Insurance	29.91
Execution of contracts	61.68	Television contracts	28.97
Licensing	46.73	Corporate sponsorship	28.97
Title IX	45.79	Merchandising	25.23
Contracts with vendors	45.79	Facility construction	23.36
Radio contracts	32.71	Booster fundraising	22.43
Patent or trademark	31.78	Breach of contract	20.56
Americans with Disabilities Act	29.91	Facility management	20.56

Most of these topics are addressed in various chapters of this book. Advice on aspects of tort liability, the focus of this chapter, was sought by the athletic departments regarding player injury (31.78%), coaches' liability (28.97%), medic's liability (24.30%), and players' liability (20.56%). However, when asked about legal actions brought against them in the past 5 years, they indicated that nearly one third (31.43%) had negligence liability actions and just slightly less than one fifth had NCAA compliance (19.05%) and general administration (17.14%) actions. On the other side, slightly less than one third (29.27%) of the schools had brought (initiated) marketing actions and about one fifth (20.73%) general administration actions against others. This chapter addresses selected basic legal concepts of tort liability and sets forth some risk management guidelines for policies and practices to reduce the risk exposure.

THE FIELD OF TORT LAW

Tort comes from the Latin *torquere*, meaning to twist, tortus. It is a private or civil wrong against a person, an injury to the person, to property, or to one's reputation. The wrongdoer is called a *tortfeasor*. There are two categories of torts, intentional torts and unintentional torts. An **intentional tort** requires an *intent* to harm, that the act done was the **proximate cause** of the injury, and that actual damage occurred. The most common intentional torts in sport and athletics include **assault and battery, defamation,** violence of one player against another player, hazing, and **invasion of privacy.** In contrast, an unintentional tort, or **negligence,** has no intent to injure, but injury does occur.

Negligence

Negligence is an unintentional breach of **duty,** an act of omission or commission that exposes the person with whom one has a special relationship to an **unreasonable risk** of injury, causing damage. There are four elements of negligence, and all four must be proven (occur) for a person to be held liable.

1. *Duty.* A *special relationship* must exist between the injured person and the alleged "wrongdoer," wherein there is a *duty owed* to not expose to or to protect the injured person from unreasonable risk of injury. Usually the relationship is obvious—player and coach, instructor and student, leader and participant, spectator and event sponsor, supervisor and facility/equipment or area user. However, if one who holds a lifesaving certificate is sunning on the beach with a friend, and a swimmer is struggling in the water, there is *no* special relationship requiring the sunbather to rescue the swimmer. There may be a moral responsibility but not a legal duty. However, if the sunbather decides to attempt a rescue, a special relationship is established from this voluntary act, and a duty arises to perform the rescue without negligence. There also may be a special relationship wherein the duty to protect is nondelegable. Such has been held in respect to a school and an athlete (*Wagenblast v Odessa School District,* 1988).

2. *The Act.* Whether or not there is an unreasonable risk and a breach of duty is determined by whether *the act* to protect is in accord with the **standard of care** a professional should give to the person with whom there is the special relationship (see subsequent section on standard of care).
3. *Cause.* The failure to provide the appropriate standard of care is *the cause* of the injury.
4. *Damage. Actual damage* occurred.

CONCEPT CHECK

A tort is a wrong against a person, which injures the person, property, or reputation. The four elements of negligence (unintentional tort) are the duty, the act, proximate cause, and damage.

The doctrine of respondeat superior. In the field of torts, the action is brought by the person injured against the program sponsoring organization or provider of the service and those who represent the organization or provider. Who is liable? A corporate entity is liable for the negligence of its employees, interns, and volunteers; that is, the negligence that injures another is **imputed** to the corporate entity under the **doctrine of respondeat superior,** "let the superior respond." Some refer to this as *vicarious liability.* However, if the employee or volunteer in injuring another acted outside the scope of his or her authority or responsibility, committed an intentional tort (act to harm), or engaged in illegal activity, then the employer is not liable for such injury and does not have vicarious liability. But, the individual "stands alone" and is personally liable for any damages that may be awarded due to the injury.

Inasmuch as both the corporate entity and individuals are sued, it is important to know that in addition to the corporate entity being held liable, the employee or volunteer is individually liable for injury caused by his or her act. In regard to volunteers, about two thirds of the states have **immunity statutes** for volunteers servicing nonprofit organizations, which encompass sport. Nevertheless, the laws in about one half of these states are specific to sport volunteers. Although the volunteer is immune from liability for ordinary negligence, the corporate entity (nonprofit organization) remains liable. However, the volunteer retains personal liability for **gross negligence,** that is, acts which exhibit considerable lack of care, of an aggravated character, as distinguished from a mere failure to exercise due care (ordinary negligence), manifesting an indifference toward and disregard for the duty owed, but falling short of willful conduct to injure.

Do the **Good Samaritan laws** protect employees or volunteers? In all but a couple of states, such laws do not protect them because there is a duty owed to not expose to unreasonable risk. Good Samaritan laws generally apply only to citizens who see an injured person, recognize the need to render aid, and do so "out of the goodness of their heart" and not because they have a duty toward the person in need. They are immune from ordinary negligence but not gross negligence.

And what about game officials or individuals hired for a specific task, such as teaching swimming lessons or conducting an aerobic fitness class? It depends on whether their status is as an employee, for which the corporate entity is liable, or is as an **independent contractor,** which shields the corporate entity from liability (see shifting liability by contract under Transference).

Administrators or supervisors are *not* personally liable for the acts of employees under them. However, they may be liable for acts that enhance the likelihood of injury. For example, such acts may include hiring incompetent personnel (e.g., uncertified lifeguards), failure to have appropriate rules and regulations for the safety of participants, lack of a supervisory plan, and failure to act on maintenance hazards after notice.

Depending on the state, there may be **governmental immunity** for *public* agencies (e.g., schools, municipalities, state institutions) under tort claim statutes. Even in those states that provide for immunity from negligent acts related to the conduct of activity, there usually is liability for dangerous conditions of facilities and areas. However, many tort claims statutes do provide for either authorization of insurance coverage or **indemnification** of employees acting within the scope of their responsibility, that is, the reimbursement for any damages award levied against them.

In some states there is legislation directed toward specific activities, for example, the Ski Responsibility Acts, which retain the liability of managers (corporate entity) for injuries as a result of operations' negligence, such as ski lift malfunction, but places responsibility on skiers for skiing within their ability and knowing how to ski.

CONCEPT CHECK

Under the doctrine or respondent superior, the negligence of the employee or volunteer is imputed to the corporate entity, making the corporate entity liable.

The standard of care. Often one hears about acting like "the reasonable and prudent person." What one must add to that phrase is "for the situation," and the situation in sport is that of a **reasonable and prudent professional.** When one accepts a responsibility, the expectation is that the task will be performed according to accepted standards or practices of the profession. The standard is not determined by the background of the person in charge, such as experience, skill, credentials held, maturity, or knowledge. There is not one standard for beginners and inexperienced persons and another for persons of some years of experience. The participant is owed a duty to be protected from unreasonable risk of harm regardless of who is in charge. The standard is situational and has three determinants. What are the desirable professional practices for (1) the nature of the activity, whether simple or complex; (2) the type of participants, whether exuberant youngsters, physically disabled, persons with mental deficiency (the person in charge must understand the clientele and know how to work with them); and (3) the environmental conditions—is it hot and humid, a class V river; is there lightning, a muddy field, or slippery floors. The leader must be able to "read" the environment and know what to do to protect the participants.

The standard of care is determined by **foreseeability.** Under the circumstances that existed (the situation) could a reasonable and prudent professional have foreseen or expected or anticipated that the participants would be exposed to an unreasonable risk of injury? If so, then there is a responsibility to act to protect the participant. For example, if there is lightning, a reasonable and prudent professional at a golf course or at a swimming pool would foresee potential injury to golfers or swimmers and would act to get golfers off the course and swimmers out of the water. On the other hand, in one case, a group of youth were properly racing in the pool, and a 14-year-old dove into the pool, hitting and injuring one of the racers (*Benoit v Hartford Accident and Indemnity Co., 1964*). The injured swimmer sued, alleging improper supervision. "No," the court said, because the youth watching had always behaved and, thus, it was not foreseeable that this youth would dive into the racers. It must be emphasized, though, that the standard is foreseeability by a professional, not the ordinary person. It behooves every professional to keep up on the best, and latest, practices of the profession.

CONCEPT CHECK

The standard of care required is that of a reasonable and prudent professional. A professional must act to protect the participant or spectator if an unreasonable risk is foreseeable.

Defenses. If one is sued in tort, what are the defenses? Among the various defenses there are three basic types: immunity, contract, and elements of negligence. As indicated in the section on the doctrine of respondeat superior, some individuals and agencies or associations, by statute, may be immune from liability in certain situations and for certain types of acts. Or, as discussed in the later section on risk management, liability may be shifted to another corporate entity or individual by contract. In neither of these two defenses are the circumstances evaluated on their merits as to whether there was negligence.

The defense most commonly used relates to the elements of negligence. An effort is made by the defendants to prove that one or more of the elements was not present and, thus, there would be no liability. Because there seldom is an issue related to whether there was a duty owed or whether the act was the proximate cause of actual damage, most defenses focus on the second element of negligence, the act. In considering "the act," one must look not only at what the defendant(s) (providers of the activity or service) understood or did but also at what the plaintiff (injured) did.

First it should be asked whether an unreasonable risk could be foreseen in the situation by a reasonable and prudent professional, so as to give rise to a duty to perform an affirmative act to protect. If no, then that is a defense. If yes, then the critical question regarding the provider is, was the standard of care given the same as that which is desirable by the profession or standard-setting organization, or did it fall short? Expert witnesses will be brought in to the trial by the defendant to "prove" the care given was, indeed, appropriate, while the plaintiff will have expert witnesses to counter, and the jury will decide "the truth," that is, was the defendant negligent in how the situation was handled? Remember from previous discussion, there are three aspects of a situation that determine the standard of care required. The defendant also will include in its defense something about the consent (assumption of the risk) and conduct (**contributory fault**) of the injured plaintiff.

CONCEPT CHECK

The three basic types of defenses are immunity, contract, and elements of negligence.

PRIMARY ASSUMPTION OF RISK (*Baker v Briarcliff School District*, 1994; *Bush v Parents Without Partners*, 1993; *Ferraro v Town of Huntington*, 1994; *Giovinazzo v Mohawk Valley Community College*, 1994; *Hammond v Board of Education*, 1994; *Laboy v Wallkill Central School District*, 1994; *Schiffman v Spring*, 1994; *Zalkin v American Learning Systems*, 1994.) **Primary assumption of risk,** as a defense, is based on *consent* of the injured party and is a bar to recovery. There are three essential components that go into this consent. First, the participation must be "free and voluntary"; the individual must not be coerced into participating. Second, the individual consents only to those risks that are inherent in the activity, that is, those that are integral to the activity and without which the activity would lose its character. For example, if a person were injured on the pool deck while doing "flip flops," such activity would not be considered inherent in swimming, but extraneous. Also the participant does not assume any risks occasioned by the negligence of the provider, such as defective equipment or improper instruction. The third component for valid consent is knowledge of the activity, understanding in terms of one's own condition and skill and appreciation of potential injuries. If a

participant is experienced and highly skilled, he or she should be fully cognizant of the risks when consenting to participate. On the other hand, if the participant is a beginner, then it is very important that the provider give appropriate instructions and supervision as the participant is learning. In 1994 the consent concept appears to have been extended to include "open and obvious" field conditions, played on voluntarily.

Primary assumption of risk can be either *implied,* knowing the risks encountered, one participates anyway, or *express,* usually a written or oral statement saying specifically that the **inherent risks** are assumed. In some literature and in a few jurisdictions, the term *express assumption of risk* may be used synonymously with waiver. However, as described in a subsequent section, a **waiver** is a contract to not hold the provider liable for ordinary negligence and really has nothing to do with inherent risks. The term **informed consent** also is often used synonymously with primary assumption of risk, for, indeed, the participant must be "informed" before consenting. But informed consent really came from the medical and research fields in that the client, or subject, is informed of the "treatment" to be done and what results can be expected.

SECONDARY ASSUMPTION OF RISK/CONTRIBUTORY FAULT (*Wattenberger v Cincinnati Reds, Inc.*, 1994; See also cases cited under Primary Assumption of Risk.) Secondary assumption of risk is really contributory negligence or fault, in that it is not an acceptance of the inherent risk of the activity but refers to the *conduct* of the participant, that is, it is the participant's behavior that contributes to one's own injury. Such behaviors could include, for example, failure to obey rules, to heed *warnings*, or to follow the sequence of instructions given by the leader. Previously, in the majority of states, any amount (even 1%) of contributory *negligence* or fault by the injured would bar recovery of any award by the injured. But, in the 1990s less than half a dozen states still adhere to this point of view, and most states have merged contributory fault into the concept of **comparative fault** (see next subsection). If the provider (defendant) expects to have available contributory fault as a defense, two practices are essential. First, the provider must set forth appropriate rules, give proper warnings, and instruct as to the desirable sequence. The participant must be informed orally or by written statement as to expected behaviors. Second, there must be a documentation system of just what was "informed" and the practices of the provider in the conduct of activities or services, as well as the behavior or conduct of participants.

CONCEPT CHECK

Primary assumption of risk is when the participant is aware of the inherent risks of the activity and consents to those risks in engaging in the activity. Contributory fault, or secondary assumption of risk, is when the participant engages in conduct that contributes to one's own injury.

CONCEPT OF COMPARATIVE NEGLIGENCE OR FAULT Comparative negligence is not really a defense but a method of computing a damages award—How much does the plaintiff receive? The jury determines the percentage of contributing fault accorded to the plaintiff and the percentage of fault for all defendants aggregated; then the award is made in respect to the ratio of fault. There are two methods provided in the statutes. About a dozen states have what is called the "pure form"; that is, the plaintiff can receive whatever percentage the defendant is at fault. For example, if the plaintiff

was 10% at fault and the defendant, 90%, the plaintiff would receive 90% of the award. Or, if the plaintiff were 80% at fault, only 20% of the award would be received. The other method is the "50/50" approach. Some states say if the plaintiff's fault is "not greater than" the defendant's fault, then the plaintiff may receive the proportionate amount of the award, otherwise no award. Other states, however, will say the plaintiff's fault must be "not as great as" or "less than" the defendant's to receive any pro rata share (plaintiff does not receive an award if fault equal to that of defendants). But, whatever the statutory language, the basic holding is that when the plaintiff contributes more than 50% of the fault toward the injury, then there is no award. Thus the defendant seeks to establish as much contributory fault on the part of the plaintiff as possible, making a documentation system essential. Figure 10-1 depicts comparative negligence percentages and the amount of award.

CONCEPT CHECK

Comparative negligence is a method of awarding damages in ration to the fault (negligence) of the defendants compared with contributory fault of the plaintiff.

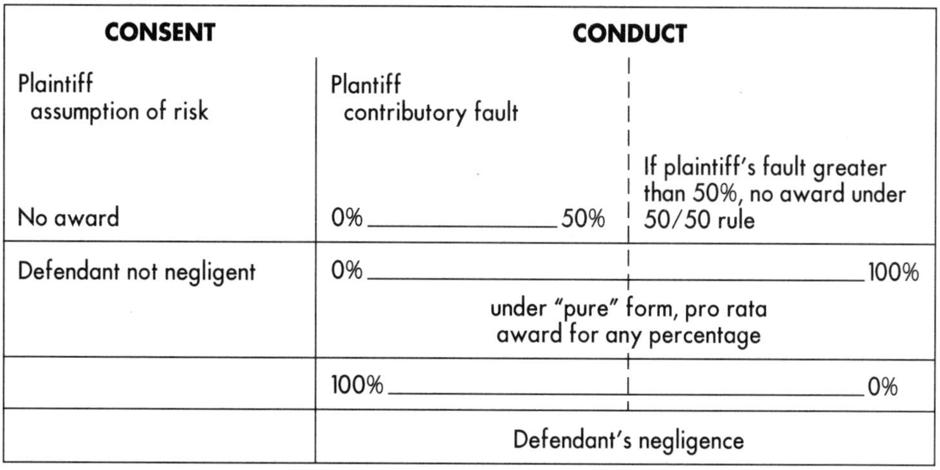

FIGURE 10-1 Comparative Negligence Continuum.
From van der Smissen, *Legal Liability and Risk Management for Public and Private Entities,* Cincinnati: Anderson Publishing, 1990, 1995 supplement.

WARNINGS AND PARTICIPATION FORMS The foregoing defenses are based on the participant having sufficient information to make an informed decision to agree to participate and assume the inherent risks (*consent*) or to engage in the activity in a certain manner, notwithstanding the circumstances (*conduct*). Integral to providing this information are warnings and participation forms.

The essence of warnings is communication to the participant as to how one engages in activity, what is required not to have unreasonable risk of injury, or the condition of the physical environment, including equipment, and the modifications desirable to help prevent injury. For effective communication there are four criteria for a warning: (1) obvious and direct, cannot be subtle; (2) specific to the risk, cannot be generalized but must indicate the risk; (3) comprehendible, in language understandable by the one being warned; and (4) location, at the point of hazard, or at the time when such warning is appropriate. Warnings can come in various forms of communication—oral instruction, video, pictures, posters, literature, signs,—and often it is desirable to use more than one form for emphasis and reenforcement. Warnings are essential in all aspects of programs and services, in skill instruction, use of fitness equipment, swimming on the beach, golfing in inclement weather, slippery dance floors, uneven surfaces or depressions on sport fields, bleacher seat protection, and use of eyeglass guards. Because warnings regarding how to participate to reduce the likelihood of injury are so pervasive, it is understandable that warnings have become one of the most important risk management tools. However, the sport manager to utilize warnings to show contributory fault must keep complete records of the warnings and the behavior (conduct) of the participant related thereto, specifically when the participant ignores or violates the warning.

CONCEPT CHECK

Warnings are efforts to communicate to the participants how to conduct themselves to reduce their exposure to risk or possible injury.

Agreement to participate forms can be used both to provide information regarding the nature of the activity and appreciation of possible injury, which provides a base for assumption of risk defense, and to set forth expectations for the participant, an element in contributory fault. Although such forms are not a contract, and should not be confused with waivers (exculpatory clauses), they do give some documentary evidence of an effort to inform and educate the participant. Even through participants may be minors, they should sign the form, since it is they who are to understand about the activity and the expectations, both as related to activity performance and general behaviors.

Intentional torts

There are several intentional torts of which the sport manager should be aware, and procedures for addressing the potential risks should be incorporated into the risk management plan. Intentional torts often are categorized into (1) disturbance of intangible interests causing emotional and mental stress, such as defamation and invasion of privacy; (2) interference with property, such as trespassing, and (3) interference (physical) with person. Only a few of the selected torts that are most apropos to sport are discussed.

Disturbance of intangible interests. Athletes and coaches, particularly, are public figures and subject to invasion of their privacy and very critical comments, often emotionally distressing. However, such actions must be extreme, going beyond the boundaries of social decency.

Invasion of privacy, the intentional tort, should be distinguished from invasion of privacy, the human right. For the latter, which includes considerations related to drug testing (see Chapter 12). One of the potential risks of invasion of privacy comes from use of photos in promotion. Authorizations should be received from all persons whose pictures appear. Often a photo permission statement will be included in a form for athletic team participation, beginning with youngsters, and on registration or entry forms for tournaments and races.

Defamation is a tort with which all public figures have to deal, but the courts are quite "generous" to fans, commentators, and the public in general in what they can say without defaming [*Stepien v Franklin*, 1988; *Moss v Stockard*, D.C. App. 1990; *Poncin v Arlt*, 1988]. To be held for defamation, a person must communicate, either by written (libel) or spoken (slander) word, to a third person with malice to injure one's reputation, and in fact does so. Truth is a complete defense; however, "fair comment" also is a defense. To be fair comment the statements must involve the activities of the sporting world or whatever professional endeavor in which the public figure is engaged. This must not be malice to injure.

CONCEPT CHECK

Defamation is a statement to a third person with intent to injure one's reputation. Truth is a defense.

Interference (physical) with person. There are several types of torts within physical interference with person, including player against player violence, assault and battery, corporal punishment and physical discipline, and child abuse. One also must recognize the involvement of sport in criminal actions, such as criminal assault and battery. Intoxication and hazing also are concerns.

PLAYER AGAINST PLAYER VIOLENCE One of the concerns in sport has been the aggressiveness in sport with one player injuring another player. There are several legal approaches focusing on intent and consent. Under the first approach, *negligence,* there is no intent to injure, and it is said that a player in engaging in the sport consents to the aggressive play (contact) as permitted by rules or *common usage.* In other words, the player assumes the risks inherent in the sport and aggression is considered in many sports as inherent. However, as to both intent and consent, it is a matter of when the aggressive act that caused injury took place, during the ongoing game play or "after the whistle blew" and play had stopped, with a player usually consenting to the first and not in the latter, which evidences intent to injure since it was after play had officially stopped. Usually the negligence suit is brought against the sponsor of the activity, rather than the individual player, for failure to protect the injured from this "unreasonable risk" encountered, namely, failure to control player behaviors. The second approach is *civil assault and battery,* an intentional tort. However, to prove intent against a player is very difficult when aggressive physical contact is often a part of the game. The defense usually is consent to such conduct by the injured player because it is common practice in play.

In an effort to place responsibility for injury, yet deal with the intent issue, the concept of

reckless disregard has been developed; that is, the player who injures another player acting in disregard for the safety of that other player inferentially *intends* the injury. Situations on which court actions have been brought include a college ice hockey player "butt-ended" with other player's stick, pick-up basketball game, softball player injured ankle in collision at second base, struck by baseball bat thrown by fellow player during gym class, collision in polo match, and racquetball player hit in the face by opponent's racquet. However, in 1993-1994 a modification was evidenced in several law cases in which negligence was construed very broadly and held to be an appropriate standard to govern recreational team contact sports, in that the negligence standard can subsume all factors of sport and can be flexible to permit vigorous competition. It was stated that if a participant creates an unreasonably great risk, then that person is negligent. There is a duty to protect a fellow player from such risk. Regardless of which liability concept is used, it is important that players recognize that they must assume some responsibility for their acts of undue aggression which injures another. As one case involving soccer put it, deliberate, combative, and reciprocal confrontation is intentional misconduct.

Criminal assault and battery is a fourth approach, but not only must malicious intent be shown but also the suit must be brought by the public prosecutor. One cannot consent to criminal acts. Few cases, thus, are brought on criminal assault and battery. Some states (e.g., Iowa and Colorado) have enacted a statutory exception for assaults occurring in sport participation (the players).

HAZING Hazing, not only among college fraternities, but also within sport-related groups (teams, band), has become of such concern that approximately three fourths of the states have passed laws making hazing a crime. A high school football player was injured on the team bus during a hazing incident; the coach failed to prevent the hazing. In a Texas situation, a student was killed from alcohol intoxication during initiation into the lacrosse club. The hazing violated both state law and university regulations. A third case involved hazing at a football camp run by the school board [Reeves by *Jones v Besonen,* 1991, *Haben v Anderson,* 1992, *Tryanowski v Lodi Board of Education,* 1994].

CONCEPT CHECK

A player may be held liable for violence (injury) to another player, but more often, the provider of the activity is sued for negligence for failure to control the player's behavior.

Employment torts

The field of personnel law is extensive and specialized, and several other chapters address different aspects. However, in the 1990s another aspect has become important, employment or workplace torts. Both intentional torts and negligence are involved. The direct act (by the employee) that injured another person, usually a participant, was intentional, but the possible prevention of such act rests in negligence on the part of the corporate entity or employer (administrator, supervisor). The liability for these torts deviates from that usually considered under the doctrine of respondeat superior, which holds that usually a corporate entity is not liable for intentional torts of an employee, since such acts are considered outside the scope of authority and responsibility and not for the benefit of the employer (*Bratton v Calkins*, 1994). The liability is based on a prior act of an administrator or supervisor, who performed his or her responsibilities negligently, and, because of that negligence, the participant was exposed to an unreasonable risk with the potential of injury. And, this negligence is imputed to the employer, as well as retained by the individual. Because civil rights and performance appraisal are addressed in other chapters, only those workplace torts concerned with the employment process are included in this chapter.

Four girls (students), including the 16-year-old manager of the girls' basketball team, were allegedly sexually abused by the basketball coach (*Doe v Coffee County Board of Education*, 1992); action was brought against the school for an alleged sexual molestation of a 13-year-old student by the recreation supervisor (*Doe v Village of St. Joseph*, 1992); a supervisor of a city recreation center (and gymnasium) allegedly sexually molested several girls 6 to 7 years old and a boy 8 or 9 years old and shot one minor's parents (*Williams v Butler*, 1991). Actions in these three cases were brought on **negligent hiring,** a tort recognized at the turn of the decade by a majority of the states, and by the mid-1990s, at least

three fourths of the states had enacted legislation regarding criminal background checks of persons applying for positions, especially for schools, day centers, and private and public sport and recreation programs and services where children are involved.

Negligent hiring refers to employing without an adequate background check a person who has a propensity to inflict harm on others, e.g., participants, especially physical and sexual child abuse, but also violence in general. Such person is considered unfit, in contrast to incompetent. The legal question rests on foreseeability. Did the employer do a "reasonable and adequate" background check so that there was no foreseeability of this type of act occuring, or if more had been done to check would such possible behavior have been foreseeable (Camacho, 1993). The standard for checking is quite high for situations where the employee has direct contact with children.

Although negligent hiring is the most frequent allegation and one that must be protected against, one also must be aware of negligent supervision, negligent training, negligent referral, and negligent retention actions. **Negligent supervision** involves an administrator or supervisor either failing to properly supervise the conduct of an employee or ignoring or being "deliberately indifferent" to an employee's on-the-job conduct, as was alleged in regard to a male elementary school teacher/coach's acts of molestation against three members of the boys' basketball team while engaged in fundraising activities for summer basketball camp (*D.T. by M.T. v Indp. School District*, 1990).

To not discharge when there are indicators of an employee being unfit as related to criminal or psychiatric attributes is **negligent retention.** Negligent retention was the allegation regarding a 55-year-old park employee who worked at the neighborhood playground in general maintenance but who also checked out basketballs, games, and ropes. When a 9-year-old child returned a jump rope to him at the maintenance shed, as she usually did, this time he closed and blocked the door and for more than 2 hours repeatedly raped, assaulted, and sexually abused the child and then threatened to kill her. When finally released, the child ran home to her mother, who took her to the hospital. Knowing of the employee's past criminal record, the city had not complied with its own procedures for placement of such persons, and thus this was considered a breach of duty to an invitee to a public park and negligent retention. Further, it was held that governmental immunity was inapplicable in this situation. $2.5 million dollars were awarded in damages (*Haddock v City of New York*, 1990).

CONCEPT CHECK

Negligent hiring refers to an employee or volunteer being unfit, having a propensity for violence and child abuse, rather than an employee or volunteer being incompetent.

RISK MANAGEMENT

What can be done about tort liabilities related to operations? It is imperative that each agency, organization, business enterprise, or other corporate entity have a risk management plan, up-to-date and implemented. There are many operational policies and practices that can ameliorate the risk exposures. There are two types of risks: the risk of financial loss and the risk of personal injury. Of course, in addition to personal injury causing pain and suffering to an individual, there is often the loss of capability to perform both work-related tasks and personal enjoyment tasks, all of which usually translate into "damages," or financial loss.

A risk management plan is more than safety checklists! It is the systematic analysis of one's operations for potential risks or risk exposures and then setting forth a plan to reduce such exposures. It is an integrating opportunity. It not only is a diagnostic process of preventive actions that forestalls problems but also encourages professional practices and increases employee and volunteer pride, loyalty, productivity, and confidence, as well as promulgates good stewardship of human, financial, and physical resources.

A risk management plan has four phases in its preparation: (1) analyzing risks and determining approaches to control, (2) obtaining statements of policy related to the recommended policies from the policy-making entity, (3) setting forth the desirable operational practices identified and formatting it into a plan, and (4) implementing the plan.

Phase 1: analysis and control approaches

There are three steps in phase 1: (1) identification of risks, (2) estimation of the frequency and severity of each risk, and (3) determining alternative approaches to controlling the risks. This analysis should include all legal aspects of one's corporate entity operations (a legal audit), but this chapter will consider primarily those aspects most related to torts. Initially, this phase should be done very extensively and then reviewed and updated annually as circumstances change, for example change in activities or services, financial circumstances, or personnel.

Assessment. The first two steps can be done together. One identifies all of the actual and potential risks in the operation of activities and services. This can be done more systematically if categorized. See the accompanying box.

Maintenance and program staff should be involved, as well as supervisors and administrators because they are the ones with direct contact with the clientele and have to keep up the facilities, areas, and equipment. Then, as one identifies the risks, the frequency of exposure and potential severity of injury should be assessed. Frequency and degrees of severity can be characterized with descriptive words. The accompanying box provides a guide for this.

The risks, so characterized, can be placed on a matrix to facilitate determining the appropriate control approach, the third step (Figure 10-2).

Alternative control approaches. Now that the risks have been identified and frequency and severity determined, what can be done? There are four basic approaches: **avoidance, transference, retention,** and **reduction.**

AVOIDANCE Avoidance is when one chooses not to offer or to discontinue an activity or service because of the perceived liability. The trampoline is a good example. Some schools, camps, voluntary and private for-profit agencies have chosen to discontinue use, while other will not authorize it. Avoidance is often used when someone does not want to offer an activity or service, "the liability risk is too great." This is an improper use of avoidance. It should be used when one cannot provide the appropriate leadership, facilities, and equipment, and thus the activity has an undesirable risk exposure. It is not the activity that is "hazardous" but the way in which it is conducted that may make it hazardous.

TRANSFERENCE Transference is to transfer or shift the liability to another. This most commonly is done by purchase of insurance. A premium is paid,

---

Categories for risk assessment

1. Property exposures

(Real and personal property, including areas and facilities, buildings, inventories, objects on loan, equipment leased and owned; office, athletic training equipment and supplies; program equipment, e.g., waterfront and water craft)

- Fire damage
- Damage caused by natural elements, e.g., hail, tornado, flood, lightning, wind, rain
- Vandalism and malicious mischief
- Theft and mysterious disappearance
- Damage to property of others

2. Public liability (excluding negligence in program services)

- Malpractice by personnel
- Products liability, e.g., equipment, food
- Contractual liability, including indemnity provisions, e.g., endorsements, "hold harmless" clauses
- Natural hazards
- Advertiser's liability
- Intentional torts, e.g., libel and slander, false arrest or detention, assault and battery, invasion of privacy
- Dram shop and host liquor
- Discrimination or civil liberty violation

3. Public liability, negligence in program services

List types of bodily injuries that might occur in activities or services provided, e.g., swimming, sports league (essentially conducted and supervised programs or services) or on physical facilities/areas, e.g., city park, reservoir lake, parking areas, playgrounds (essentially areas, facilities where the activities are not supervised). Do this in some detail so that one assesses the likelihood and extent of risks one might incur. Then, group by type for an overall view of bodily injury risk potential. Some of the types of bodily injury that might be listed include the following:

- Death
- Quadriplegia or other paralysis
- Brain damage
- Loss of limbs
- Loss of senses (vision, hearing)
- Injury of internal organs
- Strains, sprains, fractures of bones, ligaments, joints
- Cuts, punctures, abrasions

From van der Smissen, *Legal liability and risk management of public and private entities.* Cincinnati: Anderson Publishing Co., 1990, with 1995 supplement.

and the insurance company accepts responsibility for the potential risk which may be incurred. Insurance usually is carried on "risks" of high severity, but low frequency, such as catastrophic injury or loss of a major facility by fire.

Another method to transfer risk is by contract (see Chapter 11). There are several useful ways for the sport manager to use this approach of shifting liability. First, is independent contractor, that is, a person or company is contracted to provide a

Frequency and severity descriptors

Severity degrees from a financial perspective

- Vital

  Losses that would be catastrophic in nature; private enterprise would go bankrupt, tax-based agency would have to increase taxation or bond debt financing, or other special funding would have to be done for the corporation to survive

- Significant

  Losses would require a cut-back in services or financial reallocations

- Insignificant

  Dollar losses can be handled with operating revenues

Severity degrees as seriousness of an injury

- High

  Fatal accident or injury resulting in quadriplegia or severe brain damage

- Medium

  Disabling injury of a lesser severity but of a permanent nature or for an extended time

- Low

  Temporary disability or of minor permanent disablement

Frequency of occurrence, likelihood of an injury or risk to occur, levels

- High or often

  What is high or often will depend on the risk being evaluated; for some risks, often might be yearly, while for certain minor cuts and bruises it might be weekly; thus, in evaluating the frequency, the nature of the risk must be considered

- Medium or infrequent

  Occurs occasionally and probably more often than you would like

- Low or seldom

  Really a rare occurrence

From van der Smissen, *Legal liability and risk management of public and private entities.* Cincinnati: Anderson Publishing Co., 1990, with 1995 supplement.

particular service and assumes the risks incurred in providing the service. Second, when one has a facility or equipment others would like to use, the lease or rental agreement should include a clause of indemnification wherein the user contracts to assume the risks. Also, it is good to specify that the user is responsible for the proper conduct of any activities for which a facility is used, that the user of equipment knows how to use the equipment,

and for both facilities and equipment the behavior of the participants. A third, and very effective, way for adults, is an exculpatory agreement, commonly referred to as a *waiver* or *release.** It is a contract between the provider and the participant not to

---

*Dr. Doyice Cotten, Georgia Southern University, has a series of articles on waivers in *The Journal of Legal Aspects of Sport;* see issues: v 3(2) Fall 1993, v 4(1) Spring 1994, v 4(2) Fall 1994, v 5(2) Fall 1995.

FREQUENCY OF OCCURRENCE

	High or often	Medium or infrequent	Low or seldom
High or vital	A Avoid or transfer	B Transfer	C Transfer
Medium or significant	D Transfer	E Transfer or retain	F Transfer or retain
Low or insignificant	G Retain	H Retain	I Retain

SEVERITY OF INJURY OR FINANCIAL IMPACT

FIGURE 10-2   The Matrix of Severity and Frequency of Potential Losses and Suggested Control Approach.

From van der Smissen, *Legal Liability and Risk Management of Public and Private Entities.* Cincinnati: Anderson Publishing Co., 1990, with 1995 supplement.

hold the provider liable for injuries which may occur due to ordinary negligence. Most states hold waivers valid, if properly written. The criteria for a valid contract must be met (see Chapter 12). Two key principles in writing or for evaluating waivers are (1) clear that it covers all aspects of activity participation and injury from whatever cause, including negligence; and (2) the format provides for conspicuousness of the exculpatory language in a print size that is easily readable.

RETENTION   Retention is the acceptance of the risk within the budget or financial structure of the agency, organization, or business enterprise. This method is used primarily for risks of low severity but high frequency, and could include "losses" or risks such as for physical injuries by providing athletic training room or emergency treatment or for property damage from vandals or theft or for advertising liability.

REDUCTION   These three approaches all relate to potential financial risks, or "losses," and one may use all three for a specific risk, depending on the nature of the risk. The fourth approach, reduction, however, addresses the reduction of exposure through operational management. All risks should be approached from *both* the financial and the operational management perspectives. Other sections of this chapter give some pointers on reducing liability exposure.

CONCEPT CHECK

Risk Management is the assessment of exposure to loss and the attempt to reduce such exposures. Risk control approaches include avoidance, transference, retention, and reduction.

Phase 2: statements of policy

As one reviews alternative approaches to managing risks, there will be certain areas in which the organization's governing body will need to set forth policies, on which then the operating procedures (Phase 3) will be based. For example, What is the policy regarding medical insurance for injuries? Is the family's insurance to be used first? Will the organization cover "minor" expenses of treatment (e.g., ambulance, emergency room, emergency first aid, and athletic training room treatment)? Should only catastrophic insurance be carried by the agency, or should an athlete (or parents) be required to carry such? What is the policy relating to travel—no personal participant cars are to be used, no staff cars to be used, organization insurance to cover staff and volunteer cars, only school vehicles to be used, all transportation is hired as independent contractor? There will not be many, but there are some important policy decisions where there are alternative choices. Usually the sport administrator and/or risk manager will make recommendations for policy.

Phase 3: operational practices and procedures

In this phase, the operational practices and procedures are set forth for the reduction of risk exposure. These must be in detail and specific to all aspects of operations. Of course, each organization will offer its own activities and services and, thus, risk management details will vary from organization to organization. For this reason, a generic outline of tort liability related aspects to be covered in the risk management plan is set forth. Many of the desirable practices will be discussed in other chapters, and there is considerable literature on operation details. Risk management is more than safety checklists. A risk management plan is an integrating opportunity, integrating many operational elements. Although an organization should have a complete legal audit, only operational elements relating to tort liability should be included in the generic outline (see accompanying box).

Phase 4: implementation of risk management plan

A risk management plan encompassing risk analysis, statements of policy, and operational procedures is of little value unless implemented.

Risk manager. Every organization should have a person designated as "the risk manager." This would be a specific position in larger organizations, or an assigned responsibility in smaller organizations. To say all personnel are responsible for risk management is inadequate because everybody's business is nobody's business. There must be a specific person responsible for overseeing risk management. It is this person's responsibility to see that a risk management manual is prepared and regularly updated and that personnel are not only "in-serviced," relating to risk management practices and procedures but also that these are carried out. This person also is in charge of the information and documentation system, which is an integral part of all risk management. There, too, must be monitoring of the plan. Neither the implementation of the plan or its effectiveness assessment just happens. Responsibilities must be assigned and structure set in place to facilitate risk management.

Employee involvement. There should be active interaction between employees and administrators and supervisors. Many organizations establish a special risk management committee, often called the *safety committee,* but risk management is more than safety. This committee is vital not only to implementation of the plan but also to its review and update.

Manual. Guidelines for operationalizing the procedures should be put together into a risk management manual to provide an authoritative guide and immediately available reference for all levels of employees, such as the top administrator or executive, athletic director and coach, the school principal and teacher, youth agency executive and physical director or field staff, program staff, and maintenance supervisor. Not all employees need a full copy of the manual, but it should be available, and pertinent aspects definitely should be given to the employees in accordance with their responsibilities.

Information/documentation system. There must be a system maintained specifically to have available data for risk management. It should include participant forms, health and accident forms, operations information, program data and documents, etc.

Public relations. There should be a public relations program directed toward the concerns of risk management. It is well known that an irritated,

Aspects of operational practices: a generic outline for a risk management plan

I. **General supervisory practices***

A. Supervisory plan: a critical dimension

- Should be written
- Must be communicated to staff
- In-service education program related to responsibilities
- Assignment of personnel in accord with
  - Competence related to the activity or function
  - Suitability to handle clientele (participants)
- Location and number of supervisors
  - Areas of responsibility
  - Pattern of circulation

B. Management of behavior

- Discipline policy and procedures
- Distinguishing horseplay, rowdiness, assault and battery
- Crowd control for large events (plan for control)
- Drug abuse
- Child abuse
- Intoxication
- Antisocial behaviors

C. Rules and regulations

- Establish minimum for safety of participants
- Communicate to participants by various media
- Enforce consistently and fairly

D. Identify dangerous situations and conditions: procedures for remedying

- Physical conditions which are hazardous—inspections (see III Environmental Conditions)
- Activities being engaged in a dangerous manner (see II Conduct of Activities and Services)

E. Security (protection against criminal acts)

- Security plan should be in place for the premises generally, at spectator events
- Safety of person and property—rape, kidnapping, robbery, shootings
  - Concept of foreseeability of felonies

F. Care of the injured and emergency procedures

1. **The emergency procedure plan (in-service the procedures)**

- Rendering the first aid (in-service review of "life-saving" first aid only and those types of injuries most apt to happen)
- Emergency procedures following aid
  - emergency equipment
  - hierarchy of care, e.g., trainers, physician
  - transportation arrangements

---

*The focus of general supervision is supervision of participants and areas and facilities, not other staff. Supervision of staff is a different type of supervision.

Aspects of operational practices: a generic outline for a risk management plan— cont'd.

- know where emergency treatment permissions for minors are
- check vehicles, routes, insurance policies if using participant's
- Disposition and follow-up
- Media contact

2. Accident reporting

- Distinguish accident forms, treatment forms, statistical reporting forms, and insurance forms—know role of each
- Information necessary on an accident form to be useful if get in law suit
  - Inservice how to complete form properly
- Identification of information
- Location of accident (diagram)
- Action of injured
- Sequence of activity
- Preventive measures by injured
- Procedures followed in rendering aid
- Disposition
- Maintaining of records in documentation system
  - Who stores (maintains)
  - Length of time
  - (S/L + 2-3 years, after reaching age of majority)

G. Emergency plans, as appropriate

- Disasters (tornados, fire, flood)
- Runaway children
- External violence, riots, demonstrations

H. Employment torts (selected aspects; most agencies have a separate personnel manual)

- Negligent hiring
- Sexual harassment—the hostile workplace
- Performance and evaluations appraisal

II. Conduct of activities and services

A. Adequacy of instruction and progress

- Skills with progression
- Instruction for safety, courtesies of the game
- Protective devices and equipment
- Rules and regulations

B. Use of warnings and participation forms (see Defenses on p. 167)
C. Maturity and condition of participants

- Age, developmental stage, size
- Physical, emotional, social maturity
- Skill and experience
- Mental and physical capability
- Temporary state of condition, physically and emotionally
- Any permanent disabilities which must be considered as related to the specific activity

Aspects of operational practices: a generic outline for a risk management plan— cont'd.

D. Transportation

- Type of vehicles (leased, chartered, school only)
- Maintenance of vehicles
- Drivers
- Riding to and from events
  - Supervision and permissions
- Routes
- Sharing expenses
- Insurance coverage

III. **Environmental conditions (see also Chapter 13, Managing the Facility)**

A. Equipment

- Appropriate equipment to the activity and participants and adequate protective devices and instructions on how to fit or use
  - Maintenance of equipment is absolutely essential
- Products liability
  - Distinguish inherent hazard in equipment or defect in materials or workmanship from negligence in professional's judgment in use or fit of equipment
  - Do you sell equipment?
  - Standards or approved equipment (not always adequate for activity) a standard is only minimum (CPSC and ASTM standards)
  - Liability chain: manufacturer, retailer, concessionaire, you; number of states have laws limiting the length of time after manufacture and sometimes limits seller's liability
- Rentals
  - On rental agreement, have disclaimer regarding behavior of user and injury to third parties
  - Your responsibility is to have equipment in A-1 shape!
  - Do not assess ability of person renting equipment
  - Beware of donations of used equipment

B. Layout of facility

- Layout and design, especially
  - Rest rooms/shower areas
  - Architectural barriers for the handicapped
  - Layout of activity areas for safety and monitoring
- Vehicular and pedestrian traffic pattern/flow for safety
  - Ease of supervision and control, e.g., entry control
  - Safety, e.g., hidden and/or dark areas
- Law enforcement of the premises

C. Maintenance of areas and facilities
Remember, premise-related injuries are the responsibility of both the owner of the premise and the activity sponsor.

- Inspection records/system (actual vs. constructive notice, liable for both)
  - Surfaces/floors
  - Field maintenance
  - Aquatic facilities

Aspects of operational practices: a generic outline for a risk management plan— cont'd.

- Hazardous materials
- Showers and locker rooms
- Debris, cleanliness, weeds
- Contracting premise repairs
  - Also, parking areas
    - Pedestrian ways and trails
    - Protective barriers (fences, gates, trails)
- Elements of maintenance inspection system
  - Ongoing, part of job description, done daily
  - Formal checklist; detailed, checked, dated, and signed
  - Critical parts inspection; needs a specialist to check condition
  - External, "a pair of eyes" not so familiar with the operation; may be paid consultant or exchange of services with another camp
  - How much time do you get to repair? This depends on the following:
- Density of use
- Likelihood of an injury
- Severity of injury if occurs

D. Health hazards (safe work environment)

- OSHA standards (and State OSHA)
  - Haz/Com and Exposure Control Plan (art materials, maintenance supplies)
  - Blood-borne pathogens (HIV/AIDS) standards
- Sanitation of food service areas, aquatic areas, bathhouse
- Care of poisons and inflammables
  Environmental audits (contaminants)
  In one case the users of the park (members of soccer club, children playing), township park employees, and neighbors sued, claiming exposure to toxins from 40 years of dumping waste into a landfill, which became a park (*Redlands Soccer Club v U.S. Dept of Army*, 1992).

unsatisfied customer or participant is prone to bring legal action much quicker than a person toward whom care, concern, and taking care of "minor" expenses, are exhibited.

Monitoring the plan. Risk management is an ongoing process; not only must it be integrated into the very fiber of an organization, but also its effectiveness and cost-efficiency of risk management practices must be systematically evaluated and adjustments made, as appropriate.

SUMMARY

1. Unintentional tort or negligence was discussed in relation to who is liable, the stan-

dard of care required, and the defenses that may be used when one is sued for negligence.
2. The concepts of primary and secondary assumption of risk and comparative fault were set forth in terms of both defenses and operational practices.
3. Intentional tort, particularly violence of players against players and defamation, was described.
4. Employment torts, especially negligent hiring, was introduced as a relatively new concept in youth sport.
5. The four phases of the process of risk management were discussed. They are as follows: (1) analysis, (2) statements of policy, (3) operational practices, and (4) implementation.

6. A generic outline of operational practices and procedures for management (reduction) of risk exposures, focusing on supervisory practices, the conduct of activities and services, and the environmental milieu was presented.

7. Implementation of risk management plan through identifying a risk manager, involving employees, establishing an information/documentation system, and monitoring the efficiency and effectiveness of the plan was set forth.

CASE STUDY

Use this case study as a review of the concepts of negligence and issues in sport management liability. The scenario is adapted from the case cited. You should review the actual case, a catcher-base runner collision in informal softball game [Crown v Campo, 643 A.2d 600 (N.J. 1994)].

A group of individuals regularly participated in informal softball each week. The composition of the teams varied week to week, but with a core group and friends or bystanders filling in to make a complete team. There were no independent officials, although the game was played under the general rules of softball. The plaintiffs were generally agreed that there was a no-slide rule, since whenever a player did slide, the other team seemed to invoke the rule. However, there was some difference among the plaintiffs as to the scope. That is, was the rule a general no-sliding or one that merely prohibited runners from purposely running into infielders in order to break up a tag or double play. They did all agree that the purpose was to prevent injuries. On the other hand, the defendants insisted that no rule governed sliding at all.

On this day, a runner (defendant) was on first base. A ball was hit to the shortstop, who flipped it to the second baseman for a force-out. However, the runner slid into second base, taking the legs out from beneath the second baseman. After that play, the plaintiff witnesses stated that the other players reminded the defendant runner that sliding was prohibited; the runner acknowledged the rule and indicated his willingness to abide by it. Defendant runner, however, testified that his slide into second base did not result in any warning about sliding.

With the runner now on second base (he was safe!), the next batter hit a ball to right field. As the outfielder relayed the ball to the first baseman, the defendant runner rounded third and headed for home. The plaintiff catcher testified that he was standing on the first-base side of home plate, left foot touching the right side of the plate, body turned toward first ready to receive the relay throw from the first baseman. As defendant runner approached the plate, he lowered his body and barrelled into catcher's left side, reeling catcher backwards, and with runner ending up on top of catcher's lower leg. The catcher maintains that the runner had plenty of room to run past him and touch home plate, since catcher was on first base side. The plaintiff catcher alleges that defendant runner deliberately ran into him to dislodge the ball from his glove to avoid the out. The defendant testified that when he approached home plate, the catcher was straddling the plate with a foot on either side, so the only way to reach home plate and avoid a tag was to slide. He slid feet first into the catcher's left leg, resulting in a torn knee ligament, which required surgery.

REVIEW QUESTIONS AND ISSUES

1. Was the conduct of the defendant base runner negligence, reckless, or intentional? Under which conduct, if any, was defendant liable to plaintiff? What is the standard of care that should be adhered to in this type of informal softball game? Does it differ from a league competition game? If so, how? If this had been an "instructional" game, such as Little League or a physical education class, what difference, if any, would it make in bringing the law suit?

2. Should informal recreational activities, such as this softball game, serving a societal interest to many people, in the interests of public policy, be accorded partial immunity for simple negligent conduct and have liability only for the more egregious (notably bad) or wilful and wanton behaviors? What about the immunity statutes for volunteer athletic coaches in some states? What type of liability protection do such statutes give?

3. Did the plaintiff catcher, in playing this informal softball game under usual rules of the game, assume inherent risks of the game of softball? What are the inherent risks? Was this action an inherent risk? If the catcher did assume the risk, should defendant be liable?

Is this type of injury foreseeable in an informal game like this one? Foreseeable by whom? If so, or if not, what difference would it make in liability?

4. What effect does a rule, like a no-sliding rule, have on the liability of the players? If this had been a sponsored game, would it be any different if a rule were violated? If there, indeed, was a warning to defendant when he slid in to the second baseman, what difference, if any, would that make on his liability to the plaintiff?

5. What if this had been a league game under sponsorship and the adults playing had signed a "waiver"? Who would be liable and for what? What would the waiver have "waived"?

6. If protective equipment had been involved, such as catcher's equipment, either not having it on or not in good condition so that it did not adequately protect, what would the issues of liability be? [*Baker v Briarcliff School District*, 1994, a field hockey situation.]

7. If a muddy field had been involved and the baserunner slipped and seriously injured himself, or slid into the catcher ostensibly unintentionally, or if the catcher in taking position slipped into the pathway of the runner, what would the issues of liability have been? [See *Schiffman v Spring*, 1994, a soccer situation.]

8. If you were the owner of the ball diamond being used, what risk management strategies might you use to reduce your risk exposures related to the environmental conditions of the field? First, identify what risk exposures you would have (include both financial strategies and reduction).

9. You are the sponsor of a softball league and in charge of the management of the teams, the concessions and spectators, the officials, et al. What risk exposures would you have in the areas of supervision and conduct of activity? What risk reduction strategies (operational practices and procedures) would you use to reduce your risks?

REFERENCES

Baker v Briarcliff School District, 613 NYS 2d 660 (1994).
Benoit v Hartford Accident and Indemnity Co., 169 So. 2d 925 (1964).
Bratton v Calkins, 870 P. 2d 981 (Wash. App. 1994).
Bush v Parents Without Partners, 21 Cal. Rptr. 178 (1993).
Camacho, R. (1993). How to avoid negligent hiring litigation, 14 *Whittier Law Review* 787–807.
County Board of Education, 852 S.W.2d 899 (Tenn. App. 1992).
D. T. by M. T. v Indp. School District No. 16, 894 F.2d 1176 (10th Cir. 1990).
Doe v Village of St. Joseph, 415 S.E. 2d 56 (1992).
Ferraro v Town of Huntington, 609 NYS 2d 36 (1994).
Giovinazzo v Mohawk Valley Community College, 617 NYS 2d 90 (1994).
Haddock v City of New York, 554 NYS 2d 439 (1990).
Hammond v Board of Education, Carroll County, 639 A.2d 223 (1994).
Laboy v Wallkill Central School District, 607 NYS 2d 746 (1994).
Lea, M., and Loughman, E. (1993). Crew, compliance, touchdowns & torts. The Entertainment and Sports Lawyer, Vol. II, No. 3, Fall, 1993, pp. 14–25. Schools in NCAA Divisions I–A, I–AA, I–AAA, and II were included in the study.
Moss v Stockard, 580 A. 2d 1011 (D.C. App. 1990).
Poncin v Arlt, 428 N.W. 483 (Minn. App. (1988)).
Stepien v Franklin, 528 N.E. 2d 1324 (1988).
Redlands Soccer Club v U.S. Dept of Army, 801 F. Supp. 1432 (M.D. Pa. 1992).
Schiffman v Spring, 609 NYS 2d 482 (1994).
Wagenblast v Odessa School District, 758 P.2d 968 (1988); see also *Seal v Carlsbad Indp. School District.*, 860 P.2d 743 (N.M. 1993).
Wattenberger v Cincinnati Reds, Inc., 33 Cal. Rptr 2d 732 (1994).
Williams v Butler, 577 So. 2d 1113 (La. App. 1991).
Zalkin v American Learning Systems, 639 So.2d 1020 (Fla. App. 1994).

SUGGESTED READINGS

References on various topics have been cited throughout the chapter. It would be helpful if students looked up these cases and articles to obtain further insights.

The law is a dynamic field and ever relevant to what is happening in society; therefore, it is essential that sport managers endeavor to "keep up with the times." How? Rather than give some specific articles to read, resources are indicated.

Books

(SSLASPA has an extensive resource list of books on both amateur and professional sports, including risk management.)

Daugherty, Neil, David Auxter, Alan Goldberger, and Gregg Heinzmann. (1993). *Sport, physical activity, and the law.* Champaign, Illinois: Human Kinetics Publishers.

van der Smissen, Betty. *Legal liability and risk management for public and private entities.* Cincinnati: Anderson Publishing Company, 1990 with 1995 supplement, three-volume, approx. 1500 pp., a softcover edition available which excludes Part B.

Wong, Glenn M. (1994). *Essentials of amateur sports law.* Westport, Connecticut: Praeger 2nd edition.

Newsletters and magazines

Athletic Business each issue has two "departments"—*Sports Law Report,* edited by Glenn M. Wong *Liability Sports,* edited by Rick Berg

From Gym to the Jury
The Center for Sports Law and Risk Management
6917 Wildglen Drive
Dallas, TX 75230
12 pp. newsletter, 6 issues per year

Sports Law Monthly
10460 Roosevelt Blvd, Box #163
St. Petersburg, FL 33716-3818
12 pp. newsletter, issued monthly

Associations

The Sports Lawyers Association (focus on professional sports)
2017 Lathrop Ave.
Racine, WI 53405
The Sports Lawyer
12 pp. newsletter published bimonthly

The Sports Lawyers Journal
annual journal for articles by students edited by Tulane Law School's Sports Law Society

Society for the Study of Legal Aspects of Sport and Physical Activity (SSLASPA)
Dr. Andy Pittman
Dept. of HPER, Baylor University
Waco, TX 76798-7313
Legal Aspects of Sport & Physical Activity
newsletter published 3 times a year, pp. varies
Journal of Legal Aspects of Sport
published twice a year

Current issues

Almost daily in the newspapers are items of legal import. Students should watch for these articles. They need not be on sport, but they may be legal issues or concepts being addressed in class, such as equal opportunity, sexual harassment, tort reform, products liability, sport injuries, antitrust and player unions. The instructor should use these current happenings in the legal field to keep students up-to-date. The local papers will have articles, but of special value are *USA Today, The New York Times,* and the *Wall Street Journal.*

Contract Law and Sport Applications

Linda A. Sharp

In this chapter, you will become familiar with the following terms:

Worst-case scenario	Restoration	Covenant not to compete
Form contracts	Mitigation	Rollover clause
Integrated whole	Actual authority	Guarantee
Offer	Apparent authority	Liquidated damages
Acceptance	Perquisites	Cap on price increases
Consideration	Liquidated damages	Promissory estoppel
Legality	Buyout	Disparity in bargaining power
Capacity	Penalty clause	Indemnification
Statute of Frauds	Termination for cause	Certificate of insurance
Monetary damages	Reassignment clause	Additional insured
Specific performance	Constructive discharge	
Rescission and restitution	Restrictive covenant	

Overview

The purpose of this chapter is not to provide one with the skills necessary to draft contracts nor to solve challenging issues of contract interpretation. However, after studying the material herein, the student should (1) appreciate the extent to which numerous issues in sport management are related to contract law, (2) become familiar with some basic tenets of contractual interpretation and contract law, (3) become conversant with various contractual transactions in sport settings (e.g., an employment contract with a coach, a game contract, a sales contract, an athletic grant-in-aid, a facility lease, a contract with a game official, or a contract with a team physician) and the important aspects of each transaction from an administrative perspective, (4) understand the role of legal counsel in helping one draft and interpret a contract and acquire a preventive mentality, and (5) realize that a document's strength is dependent upon each party's respective power in negotiating the transaction.

It would be ludicrous to suggest that anyone, absent legal training, should draft contracts for an organization. However, it is important to be informed about contract law, to be able to choose legal counsel wisely and be able to converse with him or her in a knowledgeable manner. Contracts simply represent a determination of how parties wish to structure a particular undertaking. Therefore, the more legal counsel knows about one's business and about the particular transaction in question, the better the document should be. Do not assume counsel knows what you want to accomplish; your role is to educate counsel about the transaction in the context of a particular sport setting.

As discussed earlier, risk management is a very important concept for your business. The principles of risk management extend well beyond the realm of personal injury and one should adopt a preventive mentality in conjunction with all contractual dealings. Normally, for a transaction of any magnitude, extensive negotiation takes place. Therefore, you have the luxury of time to allow you and your legal counsel to structure a transaction so that it best protects your interests.

In conjunction with the preventive mentality, it is important to understand that attorneys draft a document envisioning the **worst-case scenario.** Any contract, drafted poorly or well, will work for the parties when their relationship is amicable because the parties do not question their obligations or look for ways to get out of the relationship.

However, with contracts, just as in life, parties may not maintain an amicable relationship throughout the entire term of the contract. It is when a relationship sours that the parties need the guidance of a contract. Therefore, even though it may seem perverse to envision the termination of a transaction when the parties are happily engaged in entering into a contract, it must be done to protect the client. If the relationship goes awry and the parties need to seek judicial relief, the contract must be explicit in its terms and provisions for termination.

There are, of course, drafting and negotiation advantages to being the party that drafts the document. However, there is a tenet of contractual interpretation that may come into play. Any ambiguity in a document will be resolved by a court against the party that drafted the document. In view of this interpretive canon, the drafting party must take extra precautions to draft a document that is clear and incapable of multiple interpretations.

FORM CONTRACTS

Every business has a number of repetitive transactions for which **form contracts** may be used. These documents are drafted by legal counsel to fulfill a particular need. Therefore, it is ill-advised to make alterations to such a document without the advice of counsel. Although the temptation may be great to alter a clause or strike a word or phrase, this tampering can cause unintended interpretive problems for a court.

In interpreting a contract, courts try to adhere to the parties' intentions as evidenced in the document. However, in doing so, the court is reading the document as an **integrated whole;** every part of the contract should be consistent with every other part. When people make piecemeal changes to a document, they unwittingly may alter other parts of the document because they may not understand the way that various parts of the document fit together. Therefore tinkering with a form contract may result in a great deal of harm.

Alternative form contracts or clauses should be prepared by counsel so that these acceptable deviations from the standard form may be used by administrators. Also, periodic review of form contracts is advisable to make sure that they are still in concert with the transaction. Businesses sometimes change the way that they do something but do not change the underlying contract. When this happens, numerous problems may result.

INTRODUCTORY CONTRACT PRINCIPLES

"A contract is a promise, or set of promises, for breach of which the law gives a remedy, or the performance of which the law in some way recognizes a duty" (Restatement, Second, Contracts, 1981, Sec. 1).

The major legal concepts involved in the formation of a contract are offer, acceptance, consideration, legality, and capacity.

1. An **offer** is a conditional promise made by the offeror to the offeree. An offer usually includes the following essential terms: (1) the parties involved, (2) the subject matter, (3) the time (and place) for the subject matter to be performed, and (4) the price to be paid.
2. An **acceptance** can be made only by the party to whom the offer was made.
3. **Consideration** involves an exchange of value wherein one party agrees through a bargaining process to give up or do something in return for another party's doing the same. Consideration is often viewed as the essential term needed in a contract to make it legally enforceable. Without consideration, there may be a promise to do an act, but it may not be legally enforceable as a contract.
4. **Legality** means that the underlying bargain of the contract must be legal for the contract to be considered valid by the courts. The courts will not enforce illegal contracts, such as gambling contracts, contracts with unlicensed professionals, contracts with loan sharks, and so forth.
5. **Capacity** is defined as the ability to understand the nature and effects of one's acts. In regard to contracts, the general rule is that anyone who has reached the age of majority (18 in most states) has the capacity to enter into a contract. An exception to this rule is an intoxicated individual, with whom a contract is deemed void.

STATUTE OF FRAUDS

In general, oral contracts are enforceable, assuming the parties have evidence to show on what terms they are in agreement. However, the **Statute of Frauds** provides that there are certain types of agreements that must be written to be enforceable. Among these agreements, which may be applicable to a sport setting, are (1) agreements for the sale of land or an interest in land, (2) agreements for the sale of goods in excess of $500, and (3) contracts not to be performed within one year from the date of the agreement (Calamari and Perillo, 1987). For two sport cases dealing with the third aspect, see *Dickens v Quincy College*, 615 N.E. 2d 381 (Ill. App. Ct. 1993) and *Sports/Media Sales Co. v Rasmussen*, 691 F. Supp. 156 (N.D. Ill. 1988).

REMEDIES

The purpose of damages in contract law is "to place the aggrieved party in the same economic position he would have had if the contract had been performed" (Calamari and Perillo, 1987, Sec. 14-4). Thus, the purpose is compensatory not punitive, and punitive damages may not be recovered in a contract action, except in rare circumstances, such as fraud.

The court will not award damages based on mere speculation. Damages must be proven with reasonable certainty (Restatement, Second, Contracts, 1981, Sec. 352). Generally, damages may be recovered for those items that arise naturally from the breach as well as damages that are in the contemplation of the parties at the time the contract is entered into (Calamari and Perillo, 1987, Sec. 14-5).

The usual type of award in a contract action is **monetary damages.** For example, in a contract for the sale of goods, the usual measure of damages is an amount equal to the difference between the contract price and the market price. School A contracts with Store B to buy a certain brand and model of football at $50 per unit. Store B, however, breaches the contract and refuses to sell School A the footballs promised. School A, therefore, gets bids from other stores in the area for the same brand and model football. The best price that School A can get is $60 per ball. Therefore, the damages incurred by School A are $10 times the number of balls to be purchased.

Another remedy, available only in cases where monetary damages will not adequately compensate the injured party, is **specific performance.** This remedy provides that the breaching party must perform the act as promised in the contract. The remedy is limited to cases in which a sales contract for a unique item is breached. For example, if you contract to purchase the original jersey worn by Babe Ruth on August 18, 1921, and the seller refuses to convey that item to you (breach), the appropriate remedy may be specific performance. Monetary damages cannot cure the breach because you cannot purchase that specific Ruth jersey anywhere else for any amount of money.

However, specific performance may *not* be used in a personal-service contract (e.g., an employment contract). For example, if Shaquille O'Neal decided to breach his employment contract with the Orlando Magic, the Magic could not compel him to perform as specified in his contract. This restriction on the availability of specific performance exists for two basic reasons: (1) to make someone do something against his or her will is not looked favorably upon by the law because it resembles involuntary servitude, and (2) there are severe enforcement problems in this type of situation. In regard to the latter point, one can see the inherent difficulty in ensuring that Shaq was playing to the best of his abilities if the court forced him to perform. How would a court enforce whether he got enough rebounds or blocked enough shots? Therefore in an employment situation, the court will not order a person to complete a personal-services contract for his or her current employer.

Another type of remedy is **rescission and restitution,** which is an action to cancel a contract and to restore the parties to the status occupied prior to the contract. This remedy may be available in cases involving fraud, duress, or mistake.

A final remedy is **restoration,** in which the court allows the parties to rewrite a contract to conform to their true intentions. This remedy is appropriate in cases of mutual mistake or where, through oversight, all of the contract terms were not specified.

Last, there is the principle of **mitigation,** wherein the nonbreaching party must make reasonable efforts to lessen the consequences of the breach. For example, in the sale of the footballs mentioned above, School A had an obligation to obtain the footballs for the lowest price available from the vendors to which School A had reasonable access. Therefore, if one store offered the footballs at $75 per ball and another store offered the same footballs at $60 per unit, School A, under the principle of mitigation, should accept the $60 bid so that the contract damages sustained are $10 per ball, not $25 per ball.

AUTHORITY TO CONTRACT

In order for business to be conducted, employees within an organization are given the ability to contract with outside parties in certain limited areas up to a specified monetary limit. This limit, conveyed to the employee, is known as the person's **actual authority.** What happens if the employee exceeds actual authority when contracting

with a third party? Can your organization be held accountable for that particular transaction?

For example, assume that the business manager in an athletic department has actual authority to contract up to $5,000. However, the manager signed a contract with equipment Vendor X for $7,500. What argument will Vendor X use to enforce the contract against the university regardless of the fact that the business manager exceeded actual authority? Vendor X will use the principle of **apparent authority** to try to bind the organization. "Apparent authority arises when the principal's behavior, as reasonably interpreted by a third party, causes that party to believe that the agent is authorized to perform an act or make a contract" (Metzger et al, 1986). Therefore, the vendor will argue that it had no actual knowledge of the real limit of authority possessed by the business manager; and absent that information, it was reasonable business practice to rely upon the business manager's ostensible authority to engage in a transaction of this nature. There are two key points to remember: (1) the vendor does *not* know the actual limit of authority, and (2) the transaction must be a reasonable exercise of authority in view of the transaction in question, based on trade custom and established business practices. Therefore, while it may be reasonable for a vendor to believe that a business manager may have actual authority of $7,500, it would be ludicrous to suggest that a business manager would be able to contract for the renovation of a facility worth $500,000. Because a vendor cannot use the concept of apparent authority to its advantage if it has actual knowledge of an employee's limit of authority, you may wish to construct documents so that it is clear to a third party (e.g., by a line for a countersignature) that any transaction in excess of X dollars may not be entered into by only one employee.

EMPLOYMENT CONTRACT

For the purposes of this discussion, you are the athletic director at Books and Balls University (BBU), a Division I institution that values both academic and athletic achievements. You are overjoyed that you have reached a preliminary understanding with I. M. A. Scholar, a highly regarded coach, to head your football program. University legal counsel will be meeting with you in approximately 1 hour to discuss the particulars of the Scholar contract. What are the major points that you will address?

Termination clauses

Although you are euphoric at the prospect of securing Scholar for BBU, your euphoria must give way to the harsh reality that coaching contracts are frequently breached. It is not uncommon for a university to terminate a coaching contract without cause before the term of the contract expires—a breach of contract by the university. Likewise, a coach may decide to leave a school for another coaching opportunity prior to the end of the contract term—a breach by the coach. Therefore you must give great attention to the termination clauses because they may have severe economic ramifications for the parties. Draft these clauses with the worst-case scenario in mind—that a party to the contract may wish to breach.

Breach by the university

The basic principle of contract law to keep in mind is that the breaching party is responsible for all damage that reasonably flows from the breach and for damage that is in the contemplation of the parties at the time the contract is made. Therefore it is beyond dispute that the coach would be entitled, upon breach by the university, to his salary and the normal benefits of university employment (e.g., health insurance and pension benefits). However, the matter of dispute often becomes the coach's entitlement upon breach to **perquisites** (i.e., those benefits that the coach received because he was in the position of head football coach). The seminal case for this issue is *Rodgers v Georgia Tech Athletic Association,* 303 S.E.2d 467 (Ga. Ct. App. 1983). In this case, Pepper Rodgers, the former football coach at Georgia Tech, was fired from his position with 2 years remaining on his contract. Although Georgia Tech, the breaching party, paid his salary for those 2 years, Rodgers sued for the value of the benefits and perquisites that were received from the Georgia Tech Athletic Association and from other sources by virtue of his coaching position. These perquisites included such items as (1) profits from radio and television shows, (2) profits from his summer football camp, (3) the use of an automobile and payment of auto expenses including gas, maintenance, repairs, and

insurance, (4) memberships in a number of country and tennis clubs, and (5) housing in Atlanta for Rodgers and his family. These extensive perks numbering 29 items, greatly exceeded the value of Rodgers' salary.

The Georgia Court of Appeals found a legal basis on which Rodgers could recover in regard to some of the alleged perquisites because the rather nebulous language in the contract did not make it clear exactly what the defendant athletic association was responsible for in the event of breach. Further, using contract principles related to damages, the court decided that even though some of the perquisites were not provided by the Georgia Tech Athletic Association, some of the items could have been contemplated as a probable result of the breach and were, therefore, recoverable.

In view of this precedent, it is important that the university try to limit the items for which it could be responsible in the event BBU breaches its contract with Scholar. Therefore, the contract should state explicitly what items the university intends to provide as compensation. From BBU's viewpoint, it must be clear that the university provides no other compensation and is not responsible for any other compensation. The purpose of this clause is to limit the amount recoverable by Scholar should the university terminate Scholar's contract without cause.

Obviously, when Scholar and his attorney negotiate the contract with you and BBU's counsel, Scholar will take the position that the university should be responsible, upon breach by the university, for all perquisites, regardless of the source. BBU will take the position that it is responsible only for the compensation it provides (i.e., salary and pension and health benefits). Usually, the parties will arrive at some mutually satisfactory amount that will be paid upon breach. This amount, which is known as **liquidated damages** or **buyout,** is compensation that is reasonably related to the amount of damages that will actually be sustained in the event of breach. The parties cannot quantify the exact amount of damages in advance; they can, however, stipulate a reasonable estimate of the probable loss (Restatement, Second, Contracts, 1981, Sec. 356(1)). This type of clause is recommended, but the parties should be sure to draft it as discussed above and not to draft it as a **penalty clause.** Penalty clauses are written into a contract in order to sanction the breaching party, and the monetary sanctions do not actually bear a relationship to the amount of damage to be incurred. Courts will not uphold penalty clauses.

Breach by the coach

It is not only the university that may breach an employment contract; coaches often breach their agreements. This possibility should be addressed in the employment contract. It is legally permissible to include a clause that provides that Scholar would be liable to the institution for liquidated damages (buyout) if Scholar breaches the agreement. For example, Jim Valvano chose to remain at North Carolina State in 1988 instead of taking a position at UCLA because his contract contained a buyout provision of approximately $575,000.

Although the possibility exists to include such a contract clause, BBU may wish to consider the operational ramifications of doing so. If BBU gets the reputation of being inflexible in drafting such provisions, it may deter some coaches from taking a position with BBU. This is an issue in which the legal aspects need to be balanced against administrative realities. The legal provisions that may be used to protect BBU are only one facet to consider.

Termination by the university for cause, and coach's responsibilities

In the previous discussion, the breaching party could be held liable for damages. However, if the university terminates the contract for a justifiable reason—for cause—it is not in breach and does not owe damages to the coach. In fact, BBU's ability to **terminate for cause** is based on the fact that Scholar would have failed in some way to meet his obligations under the contract and is in breach.

Therefore it is important to specify Scholar's responsibilities so that, if necessary, BBU may allege that Scholar failed to meet one or more of these responsibilities. There are numerous programmatic responsibilities Scholar must take on— including budgeting, scheduling, recruiting, evaluation of coaching staff, and public relations that should be addressed. Further, the contract should explicitly address Scholar's obligation to abide by all NCAA, conference, and university rules and regulations. BBU also should incorporate specific language that directs Scholar to make every effort to ensure that the academic requirements of all student-athletes are met.

In stating Scholar's responsibilities, BBU also may wish to consider the inclusion of a **reassignment clause** stating that, although the intent is to hire Scholar as football coach, BBU reserves the right at any time during the term of the contract to reassign Scholar to other duties, usually administrative, that are in line with Scholar's abilities. This clause is used by BBU to retain flexibility and to permit it to reassign Scholar without a claim by Scholar that he was hired *only* to coach football and that a reassignment would serve as a **constructive discharge** (i.e., a breach of the contract by the university).

Restrictive convenant

In addition to the buyout clause, discussed above, there are two other methods that BBU may consider to induce Scholar to stay for the entire term of his contract. First, if BBU has the resources, it may be possible to offer Scholar an extra monetary incentive to honor the entire contract period. This bonus could be in the form of cash, a base salary increase, or the forgiveness of mortgage payments. For example, Barry Alvarez, the current football coach at the University of Wisconsin-Madison, will receive a bonus of $1 million if he continues to coach at that university until the expiration of the contract in the year 2009.

A second mechanism for keeping a coach from breaching a contract is the **restrictive covenant** or **covenant not to compete.** This clause basically provides that if a coach breaches the employment contract, he or she is prevented from or limited in taking other employment opportunities that are in competition with the university position just vacated. These clauses are disfavored in law because they place restrictions upon the right to pursue one's livelihood, so they must be narrowly drafted in terms of time period, scope, and geographic area. The enforceability of these clauses varies widely and is controlled by state law (Covenants not to compete, 1991).

Term of employment

The term of employment may be for a stated number of years, or a **rollover clause** may be used. Note that universities in some states are forbidden by law from entering into an agreement that exceeds 1 year.

BBU should negotiate for a term with a fixed number of years, perhaps with an option to renew, but BBU does not want a rollover clause in the contract. The rollover clause provides that a coach always has a commitment from the university for a specific number of years. At the end of each year, the contract's term is automatically renewed for another year unless one party notifies the other of the intention not to roll over. For example, if BBU entered into a 3-year term with Scholar using the rollover clause, Scholar would continue to have a 3-year term at the end of each year in which BBU let the term roll over.

Rollover clauses are often poorly drafted and result in an ambiguous understanding of what the term actually is. It also puts the university in the position of having to give years of notice of its intention to let the contract expire, which is poor personnel relations (Stoner and Nogay, 1989).

Disclosure of outside income

The NCAA requires annual disclosure by an employee to the university president of all athletics-related income earned from outside sources. This mandate should be incorporated into the coaching contract. The income may include consultation fees from shoe or equipment manufacturers, fees from sports camps, housing benefits, complimentary ticket sales, or income from radio and television programs.

CONCEPT CHECK

The negotiation and drafting of a coaching contract should be approached in a comprehensive fashion. Parts of the contract fit together and cannot be altered without affecting other aspects of the agreement. Termination provisions must be drafted in conjunction with both the duties and responsibilities section, and the compensation section of the employment contract. If the university breaches the agreement (terminates without cause), it wants to limit the amount of compensation it owes the coach to salary and health and pension benefits, whereas the coach wants to receive compensation for all the perquisites received by virtue of the coaching position. Usually a liquidated damages or buyout clause will be drafted to deal with this. A buyout clause also may be drafted to protect the university if the coach breaches. Further,

the drafting of the document must take into consideration applicable state law, NCAA regulations, and university regulations and policies

---

GAME CONTRACT

The athletic director at BBU is negotiating with Sports "R" Us University (SRUU) to play a nonconference football game at SRUU in the fall of 1996. Both BBU and SRUU are football powerhouses, and this game will certainly sell out SRUU's 90,000-seat stadium. What are the essential elements in the game contract that will be drafted for this contest?

Location, date and, time

Football schedules for Division I institutions are determined many years in advance, and it is imperative that no scheduling conflicts arise. Make sure that the date and time listed in the contract are in accord with the preliminary negotiations. If a neutral site is chosen for a particular contest, one team should be designated as the home team.

Game officials

Because this is a nonconference game, the contract should indicate how the officials will be chosen. There may be provision for a split crew or for a neutral crew of officials.

Guarantees

It is important that the remuneration that BBU will receive for participating in this game is set forth precisely. The remuneration (**guarantee**) may be a fixed amount or a percentage of the net revenue for the game. BBU may receive—in addition to the above or in lieu of all or a portion of the above—hotel, travel, and/or meal expenses. If BBU is to receive a percentage of the net game revenue, the term *net revenue* should be defined. Also, a date should be set on which BBU will receive its compensation. For example, if BBU plays SRUU in early September but the contract provides for payment at the end of the season, SRUU would have use of that money for several months. If the guarantee is a large sum of money, this could result in substantial gain for SRUU. Therefore, BBU wants the money as soon as possible after the contest. To avoid any disputes pertaining to the calculation of the guarantee, there should be a provision for auditing the pertinent documentation.

Complimentary tickets

The number of complimentary tickets allocated to each team must be negotiated, and issues pertaining to bench and sideline passes, and admission of the band and cheerleaders must be addressed.

Broadcast rights

Radio rights generally belong to the home team. Television rights also belong to the home team unless there are conference agreements that take precedence.

Termination provisions

Although it may be unethical to do so, the reality is that sometimes a party may breach its game contract, often because of the prospect of greater financial gain by playing another school. This eventuality must be considered and provided for by incorporating a **liquidated-damages** clause. Liquidated damages is a method that makes a reasonable estimate of the damages to be sustained in the event of breach. In this situation, if SRUU breached this contract and BBU had negotiated for a percentage of net revenue, the liquidated-damages provision would approximate this amount. Penalty clauses may not be used. For example, it would not be appropriate to provide that if SRUU breached the agreement it would pay BBU $1.5 million as a penalty for breaching the agreement. If, however, the damage to be sustained would actually approximate $1.5 million, that figure would be upheld as a reasonable estimate of the damage to be sustained. Also, schools may wish to consider a clause that allows for the cancellation of a contract for cause should one school be subject to NCAA penalties that may prevent the team from being seen on television. If the contest was scheduled to be televised, considerable income may be lost, and a school should have the option of cancelling a contract if a large amount of money from broadcast rights would be lost.

Because of the recent spate of teams leaving previous conference affiliations, many conferences have notice provisions to which their teams must adhere in order to leave a conference without breach. The Northeast Conference requires members to post $250,000 to protect the conference against a school violating the notice provision (Wong and Carton, 1992).

CONCEPT CHECK

Game contracts must set forth the particulars of a transaction and make sure that all economic provisions are properly defined. Guarantees are an important consideration for revenue-producing contests. Termination clauses should be drafted with the concept of liquidated damages in mind.

SALES CONTRACTS

The business manager for athletics at BBU is negotiating with a national hotel chain for the provision of pregame meals for its men's basketball team at various locations during the upcoming season. What are important aspects of contracts for the sale of goods or services? What points should the athletic manager be especially cognizant of for this type of transaction?

Use of the vendor's contract

In many situations, a sales transactions drafted by the vendor will be used. One must remember that the document was drafted by the vendor's legal counsel to protect that company's best interests. Therefore the athletic manager should be prepared to seek amendments to language which is unfavorable to BBU. The vendor might approach the document as if it were carved in stone and incapable of alteration. However, if the vendor wants to retain business, the document, even though it is a standard form, *can* be altered.

Quantity and quality of goods and services

A contract should clearly indicate the quantity of goods ordered and describe the goods and services with particularity. For a team meal contract, the athletic manager should be aware of the notification provisions regarding the number in the athletic-team party. There will be a clause providing that BBU must give a certain amount of notice to the hotel regarding the exact number of meals to be prepared. Failure to attend to such a provision may result in paying for more meals than are actually needed or not having enough meals ordered to satisfy the size of the party.

Price of goods and services

What is the price of the goods and services? When is payment due? Are there provisions for the establishment of credit? Is there a discount for early payment? In the team meal contract, there is sure to be a provision in the hotel contract in which any increase in the meal's cost from the date the contract was signed to the date of actual service will be passed on to BBU. This type of clause is unacceptable; and if the athletic business manager has the necessary negotiating power, the contract should read that the price agreed to on the date of the contract is fixed, regardless of increases in food prices, cost of labor, etc. One way to structure this is to agree on a **cap on price increases**—an agreement to increases of X%, but anything beyond that will be assumed by the hotel. The use of a cap on price increases is important in any sales transaction in which the contract is signed well in advance of the actual date of performance.

Guarantees

Although the law implies warranties concerning goods, these apply only relative to the fitness of the items for their purposes. BBU, as the buyer, may not find the goods to be satisfactory, but this may not be a breach of warranty. BBU wants some guarantee that if the goods are unsatisfactory it will receive monetary compensation or alternative goods that are satisfactory. In the team meal contract in question, BBU should make sure the vendor does not have a clause allowing "reasonable substitutions" in the meal. The hotel's view of what is a reasonable substitution may be greatly at odds with a coach's or trainer's view of what is a reasonable substitution. In this situation, the business manager should negotiate for *no* substitutions by the hotel unless the substitutions have been approved by the team trainer or other appropriate team representative.

Cancellation provisions

The timing of cancellation should be set. In addition, the method by which a party may cancel should be delineated (e.g., notice by registered mail at least X days prior to the transaction). If no specific method of cancellation is set, it is important to cancel in such a way that documents the cancellation.

Options for renewal

Often a party may negotiate a favorable contract that may be renewed at the same favorable terms by giving notice to the other party in a time frame specified in the contract. A buyer should make sure there is a system to keep track of such dates so there is no chance of failure to renew a favorable contract.

CONCEPT CHECK

Some important aspects of sales contracts are (1) quantity and quality of goods and services, (2) the price of goods and services and method of payment, (3) guarantees regarding the satisfaction of the buyer, (4) cancellation provisions, and (5) options for renewal. As a buyer, a cap for price increases should be set and "reasonable substitutions" should be defined and allowed only with the approval of the buyer.

ATHLETIC GRANT-IN-AID

The athletic director at BBU will meet soon with Jerry Jock, a former football player whose grant-in-aid was not renewed for his senior year. Jerry had received an athletic scholarship for 3 years, but the football coach decided not to award Jerry a scholarship for his senior year on the basis that Jerry was not contributing enough to a winning effort. The notice of nonrenewal was given as required by NCAA regulations. Further, the form used by BBU to award athletic financial aid clearly states that "the maximum length of any grant-in-aid to a student-athlete is for a period of one academic year." According to the contract language, no reason was needed by the coach to refuse to renew Jock's grant-in-aid. Is there any basis on which Jock and his lawyer can attempt to make a case that BBU should renew Jock's grant-in-aid? What if Jock was given verbal assurances by an assistant coach when he was recruited that he would be given aid for all his years at BBU, provided he retained academic eligibility? What if Jock relied on that assurance in choosing to attend BBU? Does it help Jock's case that BBU's practice is to grant automatic renewal of aid from year to year and that this was an expectation held by all BBU athletes?

In the case of *Taylor v Wake Forest University,* 191 S.E.2d 379 (N.C. Ct. App. 1972), the court analyzed the athletic scholarship as a contract between the student-athlete and the university. The university extends an offer for a scholarship, which is accepted by the athlete who chooses to attend that school. The consideration by the university is the grant-in-aid, and the athlete's consideration is participation in the sport. The grant-in-aid document evidences this agreement, which is limited to a year's aid by the NCAA.

In the case of Jerry Jock, his attorney would not make an argument based on the language of the contract itself. Rather, the relief sought—renewal of the scholarship for his senior year—is predicated on an argument based on another doctrinal principle: **promissory estoppel,** the elements of which are (1) a *promise* is made that should reasonably be expected to induce reliance, (2) there is *reliance* upon the promise, and (3) *injustice* to the promisee results from the reliance. In an action based on promissory estoppel, detrimental reliance is being used as a substitute for the contractual element of consideration (Restatement, Second, Contracts, 1981, Sec. 90).

In this type of case, the courts are trying to remedy an injustice that resulted because one party relied on a promise made by another party. In this case, the assistant coach made a promise to Jock that he would have aid for his years at BBU. Jock relied upon this promise as evidenced by his choice to attend BBU. The injustice would be the economic loss Jock would suffer with the loss of his scholarship in his senior year. The court would also look at the relationship between the parties and find the reliance factor to be heightened because a representative of the football program of a powerful institution made this representation to a relatively naive 18- or 19-year-old person. This **disparity in bargaining power** would make a stronger case for Jock.

The representations made by coaches as to "full rides" for 4 years are in conflict with the written grant-in-aid, which is restricted to a 1-year term. This may subject schools to possible liability based upon promissory estoppel in a case such as the one described above. This poses a difficult administrative response because coaches may argue that if forced to divulge the reality of the 1-year scholarship, they may be at a recruiting disadvantage with schools that offer the prospect a complete 4-year package. This issue has both legal and ethical ramifications.

CONCEPT CHECK

Although the grant-in-aid document may state that the scholarship period is only 1 year, coaches often recruit

athletes based on contrary representations. If the athlete relies upon such representations to his or her detriment, the remedy of promissory estoppel may apply.

FACILITY LEASE*

The general manager of the Grand Central Arena (GCA), a multipurpose facility that houses a variety of sporting events, concerts, and the circus—is in charge of preparing leases for upcoming events. Hoosier University (HU), a well-known basketball powerhouse, wants to lease the facility next year for a game with its rival University of Horseland (UH). What are some critical elements of this lease transaction that protect the interests of GCA, the lessor, in this transaction?

Rental

From the lessor's perspective, it is important to derive a profit on the transaction regardless of the economic success or failure of an event. Therefore a base rental amount normally is designated, with provision that the lessee will pay this amount *or* a percentage of the gross receipts derived from ticket sales, whichever is the greater amount. In this way the lessor is guaranteed a certain amount; but if the event proves profitable, lessor will derive benefit from that occurrence. The term *gross receipts* must be defined precisely to avoid disputes.

Restrictions on the use of facilities

It must be clear for what purpose the lessee is using the facility and should be restricted to that purpose only. In this case, the use would be restricted to a basketball game between HU and UH. Further, the lessee (HU) agrees to be bound by all applicable federal, state, county, or municipal ordinances and by the operating rules and regulations of the facility. Limitations on the use of advertising

---

* There are documents of this nature that are titled *license* instead of *lease*. It is beyond the scope of this chapter to discuss the technicalities of this legal distinction, which has important ramifications. The traditional distinction, however, is "that a lease is a conveyance of exclusive possession of specific property, for a term less than that of the grantor, usually in consideration of the payment of rent, which vests an estate in the grantee.... A licensee, on the other hand, merely makes permissible acts on the land of another that would otherwise lack permission" (Friedman, 1990).

in the facility and restrictions on alterations of any part of the facility are set.

Concessions

Lessor may reserve and retain the rights and revenues relating to the facility's concessions. A comprehensive list of what this encompasses should be included. If GCA agrees to allow HU to sell concessions, a percentage of those receipts shall be taken by GCA. Any restrictions relating to the sale of alcoholic beverages must be noted.

Liability and insurance issues

The lessor wants to structure the lease so that any occurrence that transpires during the term of the lease will have monetary ramifications for the lessee and not for the lessor. For example, if this point was excluded in the lease, what would GCA's liability be if during the pregame warmup a GCA employee, in the scope of his or her duties, acted negligently, resulting in injury to a spectator? Under usual tort principles, GCA could be held liable under respondeat superior because its employee acted negligently while in the scope of employment. Obviously, this outcome is not favorable to GCA; and as lessor, GCA wants to incorporate language into the lease that may alter this outcome.

Therefore, GCA will put an **indemnification** provision into the lease that states that HU "will indemnify and hold harmless GCA against any and all claims for loss, injury, or damage to persons or property, including claims of employees of lessee or any contractor or subcontractor, arising out of the activities conducted by lessee, its agents, members, or guests." Basically, indemnification is a method to protect an entity from financial loss in the event of a judgment against it. The indemnification agreement comes into play after an award has been made. Lessee (HU) would reimburse GCA for the amount of recovery.

Note that this provision is written very broadly to protect the interests of GCA. It is written so that it includes any occurrence related to the use of the facility, even if a GCA employee is at fault. Even though it may seem suspect to have a provision whereby the lessee basically assumes the financial ramifications of something it may not have caused, this type of provision is an accepted part of commercial transactions, and will be enforced by the courts, assuming that it is drafted properly.

Of course, an agreement to reimburse a party after a judgment rendered against it is a useless provision if the indemnifying party has no assets. That is why the insurance provisions are critical. GCA will mandate that HU provide insurance as specified in the lease by GCA. As evidence of this, HU will provide GCA with a **certificate of insurance** from HU's insurance carrier that attests to the coverage mandated by GCA. Also, GCA wants to have direct access to the insurance proceeds should something occur. This can be accomplished by having HU name GCA as **additional insured.** Doing this means that for the purposes of insurance coverage which is applicable to this lease, if an occurrence arises for which insurance is applicable, GCA is named on the policy as an insured party as is HU.

Relationship of the parties

GCA does not want to be considered a partner or joint venturer with HU. This is essential because a partner is responsible for obligations incurred by any other partner. GCA wants it made clear that there is no partnership between the parties; rather, the only relationship that exists is one of lessor-lessee. A statement to the effect that HU's employees are not agents or employees of GCA should be included to avoid any implications of respondeat superior for the actions of these persons.

CONCEPT CHECK

The facility lease signifies that the lessor allows the lessee to use the facility for a particular time period, for a designated purpose, and for a specified amount of compensation. The rental amount is often a minimum fixed amount which may increase if the percentage of gross receipts reaches a certain level. The lessor wants to protect itself from any economic ramifications of possible occurrences resulting in liability or loss during the term of the lease. It does so by incorporating indemnification provisions and mandating that the lessee obtain a certificate of insurance and place the lessor as additional insured on the applicable policies.

CONTRACTS WITH GAME OFFICIALS

The courts generally have held that game officials are considered independent contractors and not employees of a school district or university. On this point, see *Farrar v D. W. Daniel High School*, 424 S.E.2d 543 (S.C. Ct. App. 1992). However, to protect the contracting organization from a worker's compensation claim, should the referee be injured during the event, the contract should clearly reinforce the referee's independent-contractor status. This will protect the organization against liability under respondeat superior should the referee act negligently.

CONTRACTS WITH TEAM PHYSICIANS

Usually a university does not wish to be considered the employer of a team physician. Therefore the document developed to reflect the agreement between the parties should state that the physician is rendering services as a consultant for which she or he will be paid a lump sum. It is important to reinforce the fact that the physician is an independent contractor and is not acting as the agent, employee, or servant of the university.

SUMMARY

1. Adopt a preventive mentality in your contractual dealings, and work with legal counsel to draft documents that best protect your interests.
2. To protect your interests, contracts should be drafted by envisioning the worst-case scenario.
3. Form contracts are helpful to use in repetitive business transactions and should not be altered without consulting legal counsel.
4. The major legal concepts involved in the formation of a contract are offer, acceptance, consideration, legality, and capacity.
5. The Statute of Frauds provides that certain transactions must be in written form to be enforced by a court. These transactions include (1) contracts for the sale of goods in excess of $500, (2) contracts for the sale of land or an interest in land, and (3) contracts that cannot be performed within 1 year from the date the contract is entered into.
6. The usual type of award in a contract action is monetary damages that attempt to compensate the aggrieved party for the loss of his or her bargain.
7. Specific performance is available only in

those cases in which monetary damages will not suffice (e.g., a sales contract for a unique item). Specific performance is not applicable to personal-service contracts.
8. A third party may be able to enforce a contract against an organization even if an employee exceeded his or her actual authority in doing so, if the third party can show that it was reasonable to believe in the employee's apparent authority to engage in that transaction.
9. Termination clauses are important aspects of employment contracts with coaches. If the university breaches the contract, it wants to limit the damages recoverable to the coach's salary and related health and pension benefits. The coach, however, wants compensation for all the perquisites that he or she lost upon contract termination.
10. Liquidated damages, or buyout, are agreed-upon compensation to be paid by a breaching party when a contract is terminated without cause. This cannot be a penalty but rather must be compensation reasonably related to the amount of damages to be sustained upon breach.
11. If a university wishes to terminate a coach's employment contract for cause, the responsibilities of the coach need to be specifically stated in the contract.
12. A restrictive covenant provides that if a coach breaches an employment contract, he or she is prevented from or limited in taking other employment opportunities that are in competition with the university position just vacated.
13. Game contracts need to set forth the particulars of the event. Guarantees are an important consideration and must be defined carefully. Termination provisions should incorporate liquidated-damages clauses.
14. Sales contracts must address (a) quantity and quality of goods and services, (b) the price of goods and services and method of payment, (c) guarantees regarding the satisfaction of the buyer, (d) cancellation provisions, and (e) options for renewal.
15. The university athletic grant-in-aid is limited to a 1-year term by NCAA regulation. If

coaches make representations to the contrary, upon which an athlete relies to his or her detriment, promissory estoppel may apply.

16. The facility lease signifies that the lessor allows the lessee to use the facility for a particular time period, designated purpose, and specified amount of money. The lessor wants to protect itself from the economic ramifications of any possible occurrence resulting in liability or loss during the term of the lease. It does so by incorporating indemnification provisions and mandating that the lessee obtain a certificate of insurance and place lessor as additional insured on the applicable policies.

17. Contracts should be structured so that game officials and team physicians are considered independent contractors.

CASE STUDY

You are the legal counsel for J. J. Starbucks, men's basketball coach at Wheatland University (WU), a Division I university. Starbucks has come to you for advice regarding his employment contract with WU. Although the term of his contract does not expire for another 2 years, Starbucks is concerned that the university may try to terminate his contract before next season because the basketball team just finished with its worst record in 20 years. Several prominent boosters are putting pressure on WU's board of trustees to fire Starbucks immediately.

Apart from the poor performance of his team, Starbucks has been a model coach. He carefully abides by all NCAA, conference, and university rules and regulations. Starbucks closely monitors the academic performance of his team, and the graduation rate of his players exceeds the university's rate for nonathletes. In addition, he is active in the community and volunteers his time to a number of projects.

Starbucks has told you he has heard rumors that the university may try to reassign him to other duties—namely, as facility manager. He strongly opposes this reassignment, even if the university continues to honor his current contract.

Starbucks' base salary is $100,000 per year. He receives a number of perquisites, including payment for radio and television shows, profits from his summer basketball camp, and income from a shoe contract with a major manufacturer. The value of the perquisites equals $150,000 per year, bringing Starbucks' total annual income to $250,000.

You have reviewed Starbucks' employment contract and have established that there is no reassignment clause nor any buyout provisions in it. Further, the language in the contract is rather nebulous, making it unclear exactly what WU is legally responsible for in the event of their breach of the contract.

1. *What arguments will you raise on behalf of Starbucks if WU wants to reassign him to an administrative position?*
2. *How will you respond if WU alleges that it can terminate Starbucks for cause?*
3. *If WU terminates Starbucks' contract without cause, what damages should your client recover? Respond to WU's contention that WU is not responsible for the perquisites that Starbucks received as part of his compensation. Use the Rodgers case to strengthen your argument.*

REVIEW QUESTIONS AND ISSUES

1. How can you apply a preventive mentality to your contractual dealings? Explain the worst-case scenario in drafting contracts.
2. Explain the use of form contracts. Why is it ill-advised to make changes to such a document without the assistance of legal counsel?
3. Explain the concepts of offer, acceptance, consideration, legality, and capacity.
4. Explain the Statute of Frauds. Give two examples of how it could pertain to transactions in sport settings.
4. What are the types of remedies available in breach-of-contract actions? What is the purpose of monetary damages? When is specific performance applicable? Can it be used to compel someone to perform an employment contract? Why or why not?
5. Explain the principle of mitigation.
6. Contrast the concept of actual authority with apparent authority. Give an example of when a third party might argue that apparent authority could bind an organization to a contract.
7. What are some major points to address in an employment contract between a coach and a

university? Discuss the role of the termination clause in the event the university breaches and the concepts of perquisites and liquidated damages/buyout. Contrast liquidated damages with a penalty clause.

8. If a coach breaches an employment contract with a university, is the principle of liquidated damages/buyout legally applicable? Aside from the legal issues, why might an athletic director hesitate to incorporate such a provision into an employment contract?

9. For what purpose might a university put a reassignment clause in a coach's contract?

10. What two methods, besides the buyout clause, might a university incorporate into an employment contract to induce a coach not to breach his or her employment contract? What are the limitations of the restrictive covenant?

11. What is a rollover clause? What are its disadvantages for a university?

12. Explain the guarantee provisions in a game contract. What related provisions should be incorporated to protect an institution's interests if it will be the recipient of the guarantee?

13. What are the important elements in any sales contract? If you were dealing with a hotel contract to serve team meals, what additional provisions should you be cognizant of?

14. What are the elements of promissory estoppel? How could it apply in an athletic grant-in-aid scenario?

15. From a lessor's viewpoint, what are some critical provisions to incorporate in a lease? Explain the concept of indemnification and its relationship to requiring a certificate of insurance and being named as an additional insured on lessee's policy.

16. Why structure a relationship with game officials and team physicians so that they are considered independent contractors?

REFERENCES

American Bar Association, Section of Labor and Employment Law. (1991). *Covenants not to compete.* Washington, DC, BNA Books.

American Law Institute. (1981). *Restatement (second) of the law of contracts.* St. Paul, Minnesota: American Law Institute.

Calamari, J. and Perillo, J. (1987). *The law of contracts* (3d Edition). St. Paul, Minnesota: West Publishing Co.

Dickens v Quincy College, 615 N.E.2d 381 (Ill. App. Ct. 1993).

Farrar v D. W. Daniel High School, 424 S.E.2d 543 (S.C. Ct. App. 1992).

Friedman, M. (1990). *Friedman on leases* (3rd Edition). New York: PLI.

Greenberg, M. (1992). Representation of college coaches on contract negotiations. *Marquette Sports Law Journal* 3:101-109.

Metzger, M. et al (1986). *Business law and the regulatory environment,* (6th Edition). Homewood, Illinois: Richard D. Irwin.

Rodgers v Georgia Tech Athletic Association, 303 S.E.2d 467 (Ga. Ct. App. 1983).

Sharp, L. (1990). *Sport law.* Topeka, Kansas: NOLPE.

Sports/Media Sales Co. v Rasmussen, 691 F. Supp. 156 (N.D. Ill. 1988).

Stoner, E. and Nogay, A. (1989). The model university coaching contract (MCC): a better starting point for your next negotiation, *Journal of College and University Law,* 16, 43-92.

Taylor v Wake Forest University, 191 S.E.2d 379 (N.C. Ct. App. 1972).

Wong, G. and Carton, P. (August, 1992). Footloose schools pay the price. *Athletic Business,* 16.

SUGGESTED READINGS

Berry, R. and Wong, G. (1993). *Law and business of the sports industries, vol. II* (2d Edition). Westport, Connecticut: Praeger Publishers.

Murphy, J. (March, 1991). Signed, sealed and delivered. *CAM Magazine,* 41-42.

Sharp, L. (April-May, 1991). Coaching contracts, *Strategies,* 17-19.

CHAPTER 12

Constitutional and Statutory Law

Annie Clement

In this chapter, you will become familiar with the following terms:

First Amendment	Equitable hiring process	Sherman Act (1890)
Freedom of religion	Affirmative action	Antitrust
Freedom of speech	Evaluation	Clayton Act (1914)
Freedom of the press	Equal-protection clause	Norris-LaGuardia Act (1932)
Invasion of privacy	Title IX	National Labor Relations Act
Searches and seizures	Disparate impact	Collective bargaining
Fourth Amendment	Equity by enrollment	Interstate commerce
Drug testing	Civil Rights Act Restoration	Reserve clause
Fourteenth Amendment	(1987)	Rozelle Rule
Procedural due process	Civil Rights Act (1991)	

Overview

The United States Constitution is the primary law of the nation. In addition, each state has its own constitution or primary law. Federal and state statutes, executive orders, and city ordinances are laws enacted by legislative bodies to ensure efficient management at all levels of government. Statutes often contain descriptions of administrative and enforcement authority. Federal-government powers are limited to the U.S. Constitution; the remaining powers are within the individual states' jurisdictions. State courts are bound by the U.S. Constitution and respective state constitutions. Constitutional and statutory laws may be litigated in state and federal civil courts; statutory laws may be enforced by agencies designed to carry out the particular laws.

The First, Fourth, and Fourteenth Amendments to and Article 1 of the U.S. Constitution play an important role in the interaction between sport management professionals and their clients. Historically, the First and the Fourth Amendments applied only to actions of federal agencies; today, as a result of the incorporation of the Fourteenth Amendment in a cause of action, state agencies (such as recreation commissions and schools) are covered.

This chapter contains discussion of the freedoms of religion, speech, and press of the First Amendment and the search and seizure, drug testing, and privacy elements of the Fourth Amendment. Fourteenth Amendment due process in the context of employment, equal protection, and relevant statutes will be discussed. Article 1 of the Constitution provides the foundation for antitrust and labor law analysis.

FIRST AMENDMENT

The **First Amendment** states, "Congress shall make no law respecting an establishment of religion, or prohibiting the free exercise thereof; or abridging the freedom of speech, or of the press; or the right of the people peaceably to assemble, and to petition the Government for a redress of grievances" (U.S. Constitution, First Amendment). First Amendment rights are the freedoms of religion, speech (including symbolic protest), and press. In making a decision about the freedoms of religion, speech, and press, the courts balance the needs of the public against the rights of the individual.

Freedom of religion

Under the First Amendment's **freedom of religion clause,** the government may not enact laws that aid a particular church or religion. Also, the First Amendment guarantees the right of religious belief and the freedom to practice that belief. The amendment separates church and state, and protects people in their religious beliefs. The establishment clause of the First Amendment allows, for example, free bus transportation and textbooks to parochial schools and prohibits salary supplements to nonpublic school teachers and tuition reimbursement to lower-income families.

Two First Amendment areas of litigation important to sport managers are prayer at public sport events and the leasing of public facilities to religious groups.

Prayer in public sport events. In *Lee v Weisman* (1992), the U.S. Supreme Court found that conducting a religious exercise at a high school graduation was in violation of the First Amendment to the U.S.

Constitution. The court held that "the Constitution forbids the state to exact religious conformity from a student as the price of attending her own high school graduation."

Doe v Duncanville Independent School District (1993) considered the prayer issue in relation to athletic events. Jane Doe, as a member of Duncanville's Reed Junior High School basketball team, was subjected to prayer (usually the Lord's Prayer) in the locker room after each game, during practice, at pep rallies, and at the year-end award ceremony. Students in the Duncanville schools routinely received Gideon Bibles. On one occasion, a history teacher called Jane Doe a "little atheist." Although Doe refused to participate in the prayers, she did not file a complaint about the prayers for a number of years. Finally, she felt she could no longer continue to function normally in the prayer-intense environment. Her motion to the court was for a temporary restraining order and a preliminary injunction. The purpose of the motion was to stop prayer in her school. Doe's motion was granted; the defendant school appealed. The U.S. Court of Appeals for the Fifth Circuit agreed with the lower court and with Jane Doe. However, the court of appeals did have one exception: to maintain the *Mergens* decision, which allowed student-initiated prayer (*Board of Education of Westside Community Schools v Mergens*, 1990). Thus, student-initiated prayer was allowed in the Duncanville Independent School District, while administrator-, coach-, or teacher-initiated prayer was prohibited.

Leasing of public property to religious organizations. In *Fairfax Covenant Church v Fairfax County School Board* (1994), the church filed suit against the school district when the school district's property leasing-fee schedule was found to charge churches more money than other groups to lease facilities. The district court ruled for the plaintiffs (church); the court of appeals affirmed the district court's decision.

Lamb's Chapel (1993), a U.S. Supreme Court decision involving leasing or other use of a public facility, is considered under religious freedom and freedom of speech. The State of New York authorized local school boards to use school property, not in use for school purposes, for a number of purposes; religious purposes were not included. The church, through its minister, made two formal requests to use a school facility for the showing of a religious film series on family values and child rearing. The church's request was denied. The district court granted Lamb's Chapel summary judgment, holding that the denial of the church's access to the school premises to exhibit the film violated the church's freedom of speech. Although both of these cases involved public school properties, similar decisions could be expected in public recreation environments.

Freedom of speech

Freedom of speech is the freedom to speak, to remain silent, to discuss with others, and to advocate and communicate ideas. Ideas can be conveyed, but language that is obscene, libelous, or slanderous is not protected. Verbal or expressive speech in public is not to be suppressed unless it interferes with the normal mainstream of society or causes harm to others. The courts will examine the following points to determine whether speech should be protected:

1. What: subject of speech
2. To whom speech is directed
3. Where: location of the speech
4. How: manner of delivery

Speech may be symbolic protest or merely speaking out. For example, the wearing of black armbands—first by high school students protesting the United States' involvement in the Vietnam War (*Tinker v Des Moines School District* 1969), then by football players protesting the scheduling of a game (*Williams v Eaton*, 1970) and protesting the system for selecting a homecoming queen (*Boyd v Board of Directors of McGehee School District*, 1985)—has served as a model of symbolic protest.

In *Tinker*, junior and senior high school students in Des Moines, Iowa, violated school policy by wearing black armbands to protest the U.S. government's military involvement in Vietnam. They were suspended from school and told they could return when the armbands were removed. The U.S. District Court "upheld the constitutionality of the school authorities' action on the grounds that it was reasonable in order to prevent disturbance of school discipline." The U.S. Court of Appeals for the Eighth Circuit, in reversing and remanding the lower court's decision, made a number of points:

1. The meaning of armbands in the circumstances of this case was entirely divorced

from actually or potentially disruptive conduct by those participating. It was closely akin to "pure speech," which we have repeatedly held, is entitled to comprehensive protection under the First Amendment.
2. It can hardly be argued that either students or teachers shed their constitutional rights to freedom of speech or expression at the school house gate.
3. The prohibition of expression of one particular opinion, at least without evidence that it is necessary to avoid material and substantial interference with school work or discipline, is not constitutionally permissible.

The court went on to state that the Constitution did not permit state officials to deny a form of expression that "neither interrupted school activities nor sought to intrude in the school affairs or the lives of others."

University of Wyoming football players (*Williams v Eaton*, 1970) began wearing black armbands to protest the university's scheduled game with Brigham Young University, a Mormon institution. They opposed the Mormon's claimed religious beliefs about African Americans. Athletes were dismissed from the team for engaging in a protest; however, they retained most of their playing privileges. The athletes' complaint—filed in the U.S. District Court of Wyoming against the coach, athletic director, members of the board of trustees, and the president of the university—stated that their dismissal from the team "constituted a deprivation of the plaintiffs' right to peaceably demonstrate under the Constitution of the United States and that the plaintiffs were suspended and dismissed from the University of Wyoming football team without cause and for the sole reason that they wore armbands in peaceable and symbolic demonstration, thus exercise their rights protected by the First, Ninth, and Fourteenth Amendments. The U.S. Court of Appeals, Tenth Circuit, held "that the athletes' First Amendment rights to freedom of speech could not be considered more important than the right of Brigham Young University to practice its religion."

African American football players refused to play the homecoming game after discovering what they perceived to be an illegal process for selecting the homecoming queen (*Boyd v McGehee School District*, 1985). They were suspended. The court found that the football players had grounds for their belief that the contest had been manipulated.

Numerous other sport groups, including Olympic athletes, have used actions to symbolize their feelings. In general, the courts have permitted such gestures and have denied them only when the actions were thought to be disruptive of the peace of the setting or to threaten the safety of members of society.

Dambrot v Central Michigan University (1993) was a First Amendment challenge to Central Michigan University's "discriminatory harassment policy" and the university's decision to not renew the basketball coach's yearly contract. The issue was the coach's use of the word *nigger* in a locker room pep talk. The coach, Mr. Dambrot, was white; most of the players were African American. Plaintiff coach claimed the word was used in a "positive and reinforcing" manner. When the use of the word became known outside the locker room, the coach asked the athletic director to interview members of the team. The athletic director found that the African American players were not offended.

A player who had left the team complained of the incident to the university's Affirmative Action Office, which found that Mr. Dambrot had violated the university's discriminatory harassment policy and suspended him for 5 days. The coach, in an effort to provide his side of the incident, gave an interview to the student newspaper, which led to a student demonstration. The coach's contract was not renewed, with the basis for nonrenewal the university's perception that the events and campus disruption would render him unsuccessful as a coach. One week later, Mr. Dambrot brought suit against Central Michigan University (CMU) for violation of his due-process rights, violation of the Elliot-Larson Civil Rights Act, and for defamation, a violation of his First Amendment right to free speech. A number of the basketball players joined him in the suit.

Dambrot was successful in his challenge of the constitutionality of CMU's discriminatory harassment policy, and the court permanently enjoined the university from further enforcement of the policy. CMU was successful in its termination of the coach, and both parties agreed to dismiss, without prejudice, the defamation count. CMU's discriminatory harassment policy was found to be vague and a suppression of speech described as both illegal and remarkable. No direct relationship was found on most of the issues for the team members who had joined their coach in the suit.

Plaintiff Dambrot relied on a theory that when CMU's policy was found to be unconstitutional under the First Amendment's suppression of speech, his sanction and termination would be a violation of his First Amendment rights. The court's response was that even though CMU's policy was found unconstitutional, Dambrot's statements had not been analyzed under the freedom-of-speech analysis used by the court in public-employee termination. The public employee "is required to show (1) that his speech was on a matter of public concern, (2) that if it was, then it was entitled to protection (after a balancing test is applied), and (3) that any First Amendment violation was a substantial factor in termination (Connick, 1983)." The court found Dambrot's statements not a matter of public concern and therefore not protected by the First Amendment.

Freedom of speech permits speech that does not interfere with the normal functioning of society or cause harm to others. This analysis takes on specificity when the person speaking is a public employee speaking out while on the job.

Freedom of the press

Freedom of the press is freedom to write and draw, which is similar to freedom of speech. Absolute freedom of thought and belief is guaranteed. In *Marcum v Dahl* (1981), female basketball players at the University of Oklahoma filed a complaint after being notified that scholarships for the coming year would not be renewed. The incident started when plaintiffs commented to the press that if the current coach was hired for the following year they would not play. Plaintiffs contend that the refusal of the defendants to renew their scholarships was motivated by the plaintiffs' statement to the press, that the comments to the press were constitutionally protected by the First Amendment, and that the failure to renew the scholarships was in derogation of their First Amendment Rights. The court concluded "that the plaintiffs' First Amendment rights were not violated by the defendants' refusal to renew the plaintiffs' athletic scholarships."

Freedoms of speech and press depend upon the circumstances under which they are used; certain language is not protected. Courts use a test that considers the clear and present danger of the speech or press and balances the interests to be protected.

Invasion of privacy

Invasion of privacy, closely related to the Fourth Amendment's search and seizure clause, is often found in drug testing and the reporting of a suspicion of drugs. This right has been challenged among amateur and professional athletes. The state's interest with reference to drug testing is the health of athletes, particularly that of minors, and the establishment and maintenance of the natural competitive qualities of the performers. The athletes interest is privacy. Details of invasion of privacy will be discussed under the Fourth Amendment.

CONCEPT CHECK

The First Amendment to the U.S. Constitution provides for freedom of religion, speech, and press. Freedom of religion guarantees all persons the right of belief and the freedom to practice their beliefs. The First Amendment separates church and state, prevents the establishment by the state or federal government of religion, and protects people in their religious beliefs. Two areas of First Amendment concern to sport managers are prayer in public sport events and the leasing of public property by religious organizations.

FOURTH AMENDMENT

"The right of the people to be secure in their persons, houses, papers, and effects, against unreasonable **searches and seizures,** shall not be violated, and no warrants shall issue, but upon probable cause, supported by oath or affirmation, and particularly describing the place to be searched, and the persons or things to be seized" (U.S. Constitution, **Fourth Amendment**). The system for analyzing facts under the Fourth Amendment is the same as that used in a First Amendment analysis: balancing the needs of the state against the needs of the individual.

Searches of lockers (*In the Interest of Isiah B.,* 1993) and testing for drugs at the college (*University of Colorado v Derdeyn,* 1993; *Hill v National Collegiate Athletic Association,* 1994) and professional (*Reynolds v The Athletic Congress of the U.S.A,* 1992) levels have been the primary subjects of litigation in sport management.

School locker searches

A Wisconsin case (*In the Interest of Isiah B.,* 1993), in which a random search of students' lockers was conducted following the school's identification of guns on school property, was found to be a violation of the students' Fourth Amendment rights. The state argued that each student had received a written policy establishing the school's right to ownership and control of the lockers.

This decision and the drug-testing decisions that follow place a responsibility on professionals to make and enforce policies and penalties and to make these policies and penalties known to students and their parents, when appropriate, and to participants, when necessary. Proof, by signature, of participants' knowledge of rules and penalties, is also recommended. When drug testing is to occur at strategic times, such as the finals of an event, athletes are to be made aware of the time, place, and conditions under which they will be tested.

Athletes have challenged a number of the systems for obtaining drug samples as an invasion of privacy; therefore, state statutes and results of state court decisions should be checked before making policy.

Drug testing

Leaders in athletics believe that **drug testing** is necessary for the safety and health of the athletes and to maintain fair competition. They believe that athletes are far more inclined than the average student to consider the use of banned substances as a means of improving strength (e.g., steroids) and increasing concentration. Research is insufficient to support or refute the position; however, research is adequate to alarm society about the consequences of the use of banned substances. Maintaining fair competition is important because athletes should not be pitted against "robots" or forced to engage in competition where skill and commitment to training is overshadowed by the use of banned substances.

"Analysis of drug testing programs in industry shows that when the test was a part of the pre-employment examination of all employees, the courts tended to uphold the test; but when the test was given to persons employed for many years, it was not upheld.

In order for the test to be upheld among veteran employees, there has to be reason to believe that the employee is on drugs" (Clement, 1988).

The following examples are taken from intercollegiate and Olympic athletics. Challenges are to league rules, university policies, and standards employed in the drug-testing industry. *University of Colorado v Derdeyn* (1991, 1993, 1994) involves the constitutionality of the drug-testing program for intercollegiate athletics at the University of Colorado-Boulder. The university's drug-testing policy was instituted to prepare athletes for the mandatory NCAA drug-testing policies to which the university had agreed. The tests "ranged from random testing of athletes' urine samples obtained under direct visual observation to a system that depended on "reasonable suspicion" based, in part, on random rapid-eye-movement examinations.

A bench trial determined that the program violated the students' Fourth Amendment rights and their rights under the Colorado Constitution. Also, the consent given by the students for the conduct of the tests was found to be coerced. This decision was affirmed by the Colorado Supreme Court. The court stressed that when student consent was not voluntary, it could not be used to validate an unconstitutional search. The University of Colorado's petition to the U.S. Supreme Court for a writ of certiorari was denied May 4, 1994, and their petition to the same court for rehearing was denied June 20, 1994.

In January 1994, the Supreme Court of California ruled in *Hill v National Collegiate Athletic Association (NCAA)* (1994) that the NCAA drug-testing program did not violate the plaintiff's California constitutional right to privacy. Individual student privacy was balanced against the NCAA's need to maintain an equitable form of competition and a safe playing environment. In contrast to the presentation by Colorado in the previous case, NCAA presented a history of problems in athletics that suggested a need for supervision of drug use among participants.

Hill v NCAA was the result of a long struggle in which Hill and the parties to the case, prior to Hill, were successful in the trial court and the court of appeals. The trial and appeals courts examined the invasion-of-privacy issue with NCAA, under an analysis used with federal agencies that required NCAA to prove a compelling state interest and the absence of alternative methods for accomplishing its goal.

In the Supreme Court of California (1994), NCAA was treated as a private actor and asked to adhere to a far lower standard of privacy that noted that private actors did not have the power of the government but had a right of association. The court stated that persons choosing to be elite athletes agree to a whole series of intrusions, including the reporting of medical information to trainers and coaches, dressing in same-sex locker rooms, and frequent physical examinations. Further, the court noted that the "NCAA's rules contain elements designed to accomplish the purpose, including (1) advance notice to athletes of testing procedures and written consent to testing, (2) random selection of athletes actually engaged in competition, (3) monitored collection of a sample of a selected athlete's urine in order to avoid substitution or contamination, and (4) chain of custody, limited disclosure, and other procedures designed to safeguard the confidentiality of the testing process and its outcome."

Reynolds v International Amateur Athletic Federation (IAAF) (1991) was a case that challenged the management and accuracy of drug tests. Reynolds, a world class runner, was randomly tested in August 1990 by the IAAF following a meet in Monte Carlo and found to have the anabolic steroid nandrolone in his system. He was suspended from competition for 2 years and was ineligible for the 1992 Olympics. Reynolds appealed his suspension, but he was unable to obtain the information he needed to prepare for the internal hearing scheduled for January 1991. As a result of his inability to prepare for the hearing, he filed a lawsuit enjoining The Athletic Congress (TAC) and the IAAF from conducting the hearing. Reynolds based his case on evidence that his positive test was an error and that a similar test, taken 7 days later, showed no trace of the banned substance.

In March 1991, the Court held that Reynolds failed to exhaust his administrative remedies and stayed the action. In June 1991, the Sixth Circuit Court of Appeals vacated the judgment and ordered the case dismissed. The decision resulted from Reynolds' refusal to use TAC's administrative procedures.

Reynolds then used the recommended administrative procedures by participating in an arbitration session governed by the Amateur Sports Act and the U.S. Olympic Committee's constitution. The arbitration decision exonerated Reynolds, finding strong evidence that the urine sample tested did not belong to Reynolds. IAAF refused to accept the arbitrator's decision or to lift Reynolds's 2-year suspension because the arbitration had not been conducted under IAAF or international rules. Reynolds appealed the IAAF refusal to accept the arbitrator's decision to TAC, a procedure required by IAAF rules. TAC made the same positive decision that the arbitrator had made, finding strong evidence that Reynolds's drug test results were in error. Again, IAAF refused to accept the decision and decided to conduct its own arbitration in London, England, in May 1992. IAAF found the drug test to be valid and upheld the 2-year suspension.

Reynolds then filed an action against IAAF in the Southern District of Ohio alleging breach of contract, breach of contractual due process, defamation, and tortious interference with business relations. He requested a temporary restraining order that would allow him to compete in the Olympics and money damages. IAAF refused to appear in the case, stating that the district court did not have jurisdiction over the IAAF. The district court issued a temporary restraining order that prevented the IAAF from interfering with Reynolds as he prepared to try out for the 1992 U.S. Olympic team.

In June 1992, the district court, following a hearing in which TAC now opposed Reynolds, issued a preliminary injunction permitting Reynolds to participate in the Olympic trials. Its findings were that the court had personal jurisdiction over the IAAF and that Reynolds would be likely to succeed in a court of law on the merits of his claim. Note that TAC, which had supported Reynolds in the earlier hearings, now opposed him.

On the afternoon of the above decision, TAC filed a motion asking for a "stay" of the court's decision. The stay was granted, and it stopped Reynolds from entering the Olympic trials. The next morning, Reynolds filed an emergency motion with the U.S. Supreme Court, Justice Stevens, asking that the district court "stay" be vacated (removed). Reynolds's request was granted; he could compete in the 1992 Olympic trials.

IAAF announced that athletes who competed with Reynolds at the U.S. Olympic trials would be barred from competing in the Barcelona Olympics. TAC filed an application to the Supreme Court to bar Reynolds from competing, but the court refused to hear the request. Reynolds was allowed to compete in the trials and made the team as an alternate for the 400-meter relay. IAAF refused to let Reynolds compete in the 1992 Olympics, and TAC removed him from the team roster.

In September 1992, Reynolds filed a supplemental complaint to the district court. IAAF did not respond; TAC did not appear in the proceedings. The district court awarded Reynolds $27,356,008, including treble punitive damages. In February 1993, Reynolds began garnishment proceedings against four corporations with connections to the IAAF to obtain his damage award and brought suit against the federation. This time, the Sixth Circuit Court of Appeals decided that it did not have jurisdiction (authority) over the IAAF, an international agency. As a result of the court of appeals decision, the judgment of the district court (for Reynolds, with money damage) was reversed and remanded to the district court, where, according to the ruling, the district court would probably also dismiss the case for lack of personal jurisdiction over IAAF.

Reynolds not only identifies problems associated with drug testing but the complexity of national and international court rules when a decision to suspend an athlete is challenged.

CONCEPT CHECK

The Fourth Amendment provides a right for persons to be secure against unreasonable searches. Locker searches and drug testing are Fourth Amendment areas of interest to sport managers. Lockers belong to the agency that owns the lockers and can be searched without probable cause. Persons using lockers should be made aware of their rights.

Drug testing is important to athletics to ensure the safety and health of athletes and to maintain equitable competition. Results of court decisions show that random drug testing has been prohibited in universities when permission for the tests was found to be coerced but accepted when the NCAA took the leadership in obtaining permission.

FOURTEENTH AMENDMENT

The **Fourteenth Amendment** states, in part, "No State shall make or enforce any law which shall abridge the privileges or immunities of citizens of the United States; nor shall any State deprive any person of life, liberty, or property, without due process of law; nor deny to any person within its jurisdiction the equal protection of the laws" (U.S. Constitution, Fourteenth Amendment). All state actions are covered under the Fourteenth Amendment to the Constitution; private actions are not covered. Private actions can become covered as a result of explicit statements in the many statutes used in conjunction with the U.S. Constitution. Analysis under these laws is the balancing of the interests of the state against the rights of the individual. Procedural due process and equal protection are the areas of greatest significance to the professional sport manager.

Procedural due process

Procedural due process is a system that enables members of society to be assured of fair treatment. This fair treatment will be explained in the context of employment, a subject of vital interest to the sport manager. Procedural due process is the provision of an opportunity for an individual to be heard, to defend personal actions, and be assured of fair treatment before a right or privilege is taken away. Due process systems are used so often that professionals will need to tailor a system to meet their needs from time to time. Because many factors enter into the formulation of a due process system, consultants in law and the area to be covered should participate in the design of the system. The following are basic concepts to consider in creating a system:

1. Knowledge of charge and complaint
2. A right to a hearing in which one may choose to use an attorney or other counsel
3. Opportunity to respond to charges with adequate time to prepare the response
4. Opportunity to present witnesses and to question witnesses presented by others

Employers and administrators have a number of well-defined responsibilities to their employees. Procedural due process becomes a constitutional issue in the hiring process and the evaluation system.

Equitable hiring process. Hiring systems differ among businesses. For years, the most popular employer-employee relationship was known as "at

will." The employer had a task to be done, sought out a person believed capable of carrying out the task, and offered the job and a wage, and both mutually agreed to the arrangement with a handshake. When the employer no longer wanted or needed the employee, the employee was asked to leave. If the employee no longer enjoyed the work environment or had a better offer, he/she was free to leave. "Two-weeks' notice" has grown to be a popular termination period in this type of work relationship. Another characteristic of at-will employment is that the reason for termination is seldom public knowledge and often is unclear to one of the parties involved in the agreement. Many people continue to be employed in this manner today. In addition, most part-time employment is at will.

Labor unions have made drastic changes in the at-will employment pattern in the past 50-75 years. Labor unions are private associations formed to represent groups of workers with common needs and a common desire to obtain the best wages possible for the entire group. They also negotiate contracts with individual businesses.

Employment contracts are another form of employer-employee work relationship. They are written agreements that identify tasks to be accomplished, the period of employment, and salary. Such contracts are specific agreements between one employee and a particular business.

Contract, labor union, and at-will relationships are the employer-employee relationships most often used in business and industry in the United States.

Today's employment environment is subject to federal laws created in an effort to remedy discrimination based on race, color, sex, age, religion, national origin, and handicaps. The Equal Pay Act (1963) and a number of Executive Orders of the 1950s and 1960s paved the way for discrimination legislation in employment. Title VII of the Civil Rights Act (1964), the Age Discrimination in Employment Act (1967), the Rehabilitation Act (1973), and the Americans with Disabilities Act have fashioned the framework for most civil rights legislation. Title VII of the Civil Rights Act (1964) prohibits discrimination in the work environment due to race, color, sex, religion, or national origin. Affirmative action and equal-opportunity employment are the results of Title VII. The Age Discrimination Act established a protected group for persons 40-65 years old; the rehabilitative acts accomplished the same goal for the handicapped. Although the acts mentioned above refer to government contractors only, the Supreme Court has extended the requirements concerning race discrimination to private employers.

The Equal Employment Opportunity Commission (EEOC) is the federal government agency responsible for administering most of the discrimination legislation and regulations. Under equal opportunity, when a job vacancy occurs, provision is made for all qualified individuals to be made aware of the existence of the vacancy, to submit papers for review, and to obtain the position if best qualified.

Affirmative action is a special program designed to remedy past discriminatory practices in hiring minority groups. It is used when discrimination has been found. The program provides an opportunity for the protected group to receive special attention in employment until such time as its number is proportional to the percentage of employees in the nonprotected group. For example, if 60% of the population available for a certain job is African American, an affirmative-action program will continue until a particular work force has a 60% African American membership. Affirmative-action programs are influenced by the availability of skill and talent and a past record of discrimination. Employers may volunteer to an affirmative-action program or be required by the court or an administrative agency to establish one in response to a finding of discrimination.

Employment systems are designed to rapidly locate the best talent pool available for a particular job. Skilled talent is a high priority for any business, and most employers are equally interested in being equitable in their hiring practices. The following system was devised with guidance from the decisions in *Griggs v Duke Power Company* (1971), *Equal Employment Opportunity Commission v Atlas Paper Box Company* (1989), and *Ward Cove Packing Company v Atonio* (1989). The system is designed to guide the administrator in hiring personnel.

Preparation

1. Visit with members of the personnel office to learn of the standards and expectations of the employer.
2. Become conversant with labor union and other contract agreements that affect the job.
3. Determine the status of the agency's or corporation's affirmative-action program. If such a program exists, is it voluntary or mandated? (Note requirements specifically related to job advertising.)

Job description

1. Create an accurate, comprehensive job description with a cross section of the job's significant tasks.
2. Recommend qualifications that will be essential to the successful candidate's capacity to carry out the tasks mentioned in the job description. Avoid listing degrees or special work experiences that are unrelated to the job.
3. Keep qualifications in line with job requirements. Evidence documenting why any candidates were not suitable should be maintained. Such information will be essential if a challenge is made to the selection process.
4. Advertise the job in publications read by potential candidates. Provide adequate time for parties interested in the position to apply. All persons, including minorities, who are qualified for the job are to know of the job and have had adequate time to make their intentions known.

Pool of candidates

1. Advertise so as to obtain the best pool of candidates for the position. Advertisements should permit professionals to nominate persons for the job.
2. Make application information easy to understand. Request all information that will be essential to preliminary screening in the public announcement.
3. Enforce published deadlines.

Screening of candidates

1. Conduct preliminary screening specifically related to objective published criteria. The nature of this type of screening may allow for a few rather than a large number of people to be involved in the process. A small group can make decisions using objective criteria. As the process becomes more subjective, the size of the screening committee increases.
2. Use check sheets, with job criteria, to evaluate applications.

3. Second- and third-level screenings, required for a large number of candidates, follow in sequence. Each level of screening involves the use of a new, more detailed check sheet. Check sheets need not require forced choices. When narrative is employed, agreement on the meaning of terms should be reached prior to the use of the screening tool.
4. Continue screening until the interview pool is determined.
5. Determine screening instruments, use of recommendations in decision making, and the number of candidates that will constitute the interview pool prior to the initiation of screening.

Interviewing and selecting candidates
1. Candidates selected to be interviewed may be rank-ordered or merely listed. Make the decision to rank or list prior to screening.
2. Employ interview procedures that provide an in-depth assessment while allowing for a sufficiently civil process so that the candidates retain an interest in the position.
3. When necessary, provide in-service training to interviewers to guard against the possibility that an interviewer might ask a discriminatory question. Questions about a candidate's age or marital status, the likelihood that his/her spouse will move to the city, and provisions for child care are prohibited.
4. All finalists should understand the employment relationship under which the job will be classified: at will, union, contract, or other. When the relationship is a contract, the candidate should understand the nature of the contract and the items that the contract will contain.
5. Interviewers must submit evaluations for each candidate. Candidates may be listed or rank-ordered.
6. Make the final selection.

Documentation
1. Outline all the steps within the hiring process prior to instituting the search.
2. Review this process to ensure that the needs of the job have been clearly defined and that equity exists.

3. Date and sign all screening and interviewing check sheets and reports.
4. Inform applicants of their status at certain stages in the process. Those eliminated in the initial review should be informed at once. Some search committees choose to inform applicants eliminated prior to the interviews. The only requirement is that eliminated candidates be informed at the completion of the search.
5. Make sufficient documentation so that—in the event of a claim that calls either the search and screening process or the content of the job description into question—evidence exists to enable the persons directly involved to explain their actions.

In sum, you should establish a coherent plan, follow the plan, and document each step of the process.

Evaluation
Employees must receive a fair and equitable **evaluation** based on the elements in the job description and the day-to-day tasks of the job. *Griggs v Duke Power Company* (1971) is the court decision that has played the most important role in establishing the need for job requirements that are directly related to job performance for both hiring and evaluation. If certain specifications—such as a college degree or a specific in-service training—are given a high priority in evaluation, then evidence must exist to show that the requirement is essential to successful job performance.

The results of evaluations should be discussed with and available to employees. Where serious deficits in work habits are identified, a due process system must exist to permit employees to present their side of the situation. Opportunity must also exist for rehabilitation of deficits and for the monitoring of the success or failure of the rehabilitation program.

Policies on termination must be established—if possible, in writing. A system of warnings preceding termination, including a rehabilitation program, should be in place. These policies must be related to job responsibilities and executed in such a way that the rights of the employee are paramount.

Evaluation of personnel should be directly related to the position description and the day-to-day responsibilities of the job. Even though a specific system of evaluation is employed by an industry, it is expected to evaluate performance in line with the elements identified in *Griggs v Duke Power Company* (1971), *Brunet v City of Columbus* (1986), *Ward Cove Packing Co. v Atonio* (1989), and the procedural due process system of the Fourteenth Amendment to the U.S. Constitution. Under *Griggs, Brunet,* and *Ward Cove*, procedural due process is the basis for employee evaluation and initial employment in state and federal agencies. Only those skills and knowledge directly related to the job and the day-to-day tasks of the work environment may be included. (Private agencies may or may not adhere to this system.)

A fair evaluation system is based on the description of and tasks demanded by a job. It should include the opportunity for the employee and employer to assess the execution of those tasks. When disagreement about the successful execution of the tasks occurs, a process must be available to resolve the dispute.

A procedural due process system should be available for use at any time. Its availability is essential when an employee receives a negative evaluation or is to be suspended or terminated. The procedural due process system should be included in the employee handbook or in related documents. Procedural due process is an appeal process that contains but is not limited to the following steps:

1. Written notice of all charges against the employee, including dates, times, and details of the specific charges that, if proven, would justify a penalty.
2. Establishment of a time and date for a hearing. Adequate time should be provided to enable the employee to prepare for the hearing.
3. Representation, including legal representation, may or may not be permitted in the hearing. This decision is made at the time of the establishment of guidelines, not shortly before a specific hearing. Also, the decision to use legal counsel and the technique of cross examination is made at the time the system is created.
4. The hearing provides the opportunity for all sides to present their case. All versions of the problem are presented.
5. An impartial panel shall hear the presentation. The status and authority of the panel and its leader must be known to all parties.

6. Effort should be made, if possible, to negotiate a viable settlement.
7. A decision is made. The decision should be accompanied by a written report of the rationale for the decision.
8. The proceedings should be recorded and made available to the employee.
9. In most employment environments, it is assumed that the next level of appeal will be to a court of law. When the problem concerns discrimination, the appeal may be to an administrative agency.

Tarkanian v NCAA (1987), *NCAA v Tarkanian* (1988, 1993) and *University of Nevada v Tarkanian* (1994) involved a number of legal theories, including due process. The NCAA began investigating the University of Nevada-Las Vegas (UNLV) shortly after Jerry Tarkanian became head basketball coach in 1973. In 1976, after a 2½- year investigation, the NCAA Committee on Infractions confronted UNLV with a report of 72 violations that they alleged occurred between 1970 and 1976. Six additional violations were added at a later date. The Nevada State Attorney General's Office investigated the allegations by interviewing the persons accused. UNLV submitted responses—including a large number of affidavits, sworn statements, and documentary evidence—to support denial of specific rule violations.

NCAA held a hearing and found 38 violations of NCAA rules, naming Tarkanian in 10 of them. Further, they "directed UNLV to show cause why additional penalties should not be imposed against it if it did not suspend Tarkanian from involvement with the university's intercollegiate Athletic Program for two years" (*Tarkanian v NCAA*, 1987).

In September 1977, UNLV, after conducting a hearing on the matter, suspended Tarkanian. Tarkanian brought suit against UNLV and obtained an injunction, which is a court order that directs a party to stop doing or to do some specific act. In this case, the court directed UNLV to stop the suspension of Tarkanian, or to let him return to his coaching position. The court then reversed the injunction for Tarkanian's failure to be willing to include the NCAA in the law suit (*University of Nevada v Tarkanian*, 1979). In essence, the court said that Tarkanian had to sue the NCAA in addition to UNLV.

In July 1979, Tarkanian sued again, this time naming both UNLV and NCAA, and received another injunction stopping his suspension. Tarkanian argued that he was without a formal procedural due process, but NCAA rulings do not include procedural due process for persons accused of violations.

In August 1987, the Supreme Court of Nevada held that NCAA, as an actor in a state agency, was required to use a procedural due process and that Tarkanian had a right to due process. NCAA petitioned the U.S. Supreme Court (*NCAA v Tarkanian*, 1988). It reversed the Nevada court's decision, stating that NCAA actions were not state actions and therefore the NCAA did not have to provide Tarkanian with an opportunity for procedural due process. This decision held (contrary to an earlier decision regarding television contracts) that the NCAA was a private organization that UNLV had the freedom to join or not join. The U.S. Supreme Court remanded the case back to the Nevada Supreme Court, stating that UNLV was in charge of disciplining faculty members and that UNLV, as a state agency, was required to adhere to procedural due process.

Tarkanian then moved for an order imposing costs, including attorney fees, against UNLV. His motion was granted in June 1992, and UNLV appealed. Tarkanian was awarded attorney fees. He was not able to obtain a financial settlement from NCAA, but he did receive a settlement from UNLV.

The results of the Tarkanian Supreme Court decision place the responsibility for evaluating, reprimanding, and terminating state employees in the hands of the state agency and prohibit state agencies from carrying out third-party orders. This case prohibited UNLV from carrying out the NCAA's request to suspend Jerry Tarkanian without a procedural due process opportunity.

CONCEPT CHECK

Successful employee-employer relationships are created in the employment process. To affect positive relationships, attention must be paid to the preparation of a comprehensive job description, obtaining qualified candidates, and careful screening, interviewing, and selection of candidates.

These successful relationships are maintained when the employer provides an equitable evaluation system. Should an employee not be making satisfac-

tory progress on the job, a carefully constructed procedural due process system should be used, first to counsel the employee toward success and then, if that is not possible, to provide the employee with full legal rights in the termination process.

EQUAL PROTECTION

The Fourteenth Amendment's **equal-protection clause** states, "No State shall make or enforce any law which shall . . . deny to any person within its jurisdiction the equal protection of the laws." An equal-protection challenge must show that groups of people are being treated differently, without justification, than is the total population. A regulation that arbitrarily or unreasonably subjects an identified group of people to a regulation violates the *equal-protection* clause.

An equal-protection challenge in scholastic or collegiate sport might be a complaint by a group of people (women) that they are being treated different from others (men) in athletics and that no justification exists to warrant the difference in treatment. One woman or a group of women (class action) might retain an attorney and bring a legal action against a public school or a college for sex discrimination under the Fourteenth Amendment to the U.S. Constitution.

The first use of the Fourteenth Amendment in sport discrimination suits is believed to be Jerry Hunter's 1956 defense to a charge of the crime of participating in a wrestling competition (*State v Hunter*, 1956). The court denied her constitutional claim, stating "that there should be at least one island on the sea of life reserved for men that would be impregnable to the assault of women."

Among the cases that prompted the creation of **Title IX** of the Educational Amendments of 1972 and influenced their operating guidelines were *Brenden v Independent School District* (1973), *Hollander v Connecticut Interscholastic Athletic Conference, Inc.* (1971), *Reed v Nebraska* (1972), *Haas v South Bend Community School Corporation* (1972, 1973), *Bucha v Illinois High School Association* (1972), and *Rittacco v Norwin School District* (1973).

Brenden, Hollander, Reed, and *Haas* were complaints in which high school women requested the opportunity to participate on men's teams when no team was available to women. In most cases, the high school league had established the rule; the school district was merely enforcing the rule. Hollander's challenge to run on the cross-country team was denied. Reed's request to play on the golf team was granted, as was Brenden's request to play tennis. Haas was granted an opportunity to play on all men's teams in which no team existed for women. Note should be made that the requests were granted in Nebraska, Minnesota, and Indiana and denied in Connecticut.

Two class action suits, denied by the courts, were *Bucha* (1972) and *Rittacco* (1973). Bucha challenged the events selected for women swimmers. At that time, females were not permitted to perform in long-distance events. Rittacco challenged a Pennsylvania law that prohibited mixed teams and competition. This was one time in which the courts ruled for separate-but-equal opportunities; separate-but-equal opportunities were always denied in litigation involving race.

Title IX of the education amendments (1972)

Title IX states that "No person in the United States shall, on the basis of sex, be excluded from participation in, be denied the benefit of, or be subject to discrimination under any education program or activity receiving Federal financial assistance" (Title IX of the Education Amendments of 1972). Title IX, a federal statute, extended the principles articulated under the Fourteenth Amendment to all schools, public and private, that rely upon federal and state funds. Title IX is enforced by the Department of Education, which can withhold federal funds for violation of the statute. *Cannon v University of Chicago* (1979) extended Title IX to private or individual causes of action; *North Haven v Bell* (1982) extended the law to employment.

Title IX was envisioned by its creators as a way of convincing young women to participate in mathematics and science programs and to aspire to careers similar to those selected by men. The originators of Title IX did not view it primarily as a means of creating equity in athletics. Shortly after Title IX was implemented, athletics, a visible component of most school programs, became a public focus.

Many of the complaints in the early days of Title IX were resolved within the school districts, by other agencies, or by the Office of Civil Rights. Among the few complaints that went to court were *Yellow Springs Exempted Village School District v Ohio High School Athletic Association* (1981), *Gomes v*

Rhode Island Interscholastic League (1979), and *Petrie v. Illinois High School Association* (1979).

In *Yellow Springs,* a school district, not a student, brought action against the state high school league that the rule on contact sports was unconstitutional and in violation of Title IX. Middle-school girls had tried out and made the men's basketball team. The school district was forced by the Ohio High School Athletic Association to eliminate the qualified girls or withdraw from the league. The U.S. District Court, Southern District of Ohio, ruled for the female student athletes; the court of appeals reversed. The court was asked to rule on Title IX in general but refused to do so.

In an effort to divert attention from athletics, three cases—two in athletics, *Othen v Ann Arbor School District* (1981, 1982) and *Bennett v West Texas State University* (1986), and one general university case, *Grove City v Bell* (1984)—successfully petitioned the courts to make Title IX "program specific." *Grove City* is the case usually mentioned in this context and the one that has been favored by the popular press. *Program-specific* meant that only those programs receiving direct federal funding were subject to Title IX. Sports, seldom financed from federal dollars, were freed from the Title IX jurisdiction. The *Othen, Bennett,* and *Grove City* rulings brought the Title IX investigative system of the Office of Education to a halt. Title IX was no longer important to athletics.

It should be noted that the Fourteenth Amendment to the U.S. Constitution and various state civil rights laws continue to be used effectively in the quest for equal opportunity for women in sport. The results of decisions using the U.S. Constitution and state laws has led to the new civil rights legislation.

Equity for women in athletics has been influenced by (1) the Fourteenth Amendment equal-protection clause, particularly disparate-impact theory referred to as "equity by enrollment," (2) Title IX, (3) decisions in *Haffer* (1987), *Ridgeway* (1988), *Blair* (1989), *Franklin* (1992), and *Roberts,* and (4) the Civil Rights Acts (1988, 1991). These major elements in the quest for gender equity are presented, in chronological order, in the following pages.

DISPARATE IMPACT

The legal theory that has had the greatest impact on today's cases is **disparate impact,** a theory that evolved in employment discrimination litigation and that involves practices that appear to be neutral in their treatment of different groups but fall more harshly on one group than another (*Teamsters v. United States,* 1977). *Hazelwood* provided a method of analysis for use in identifying patterns and practices of discrimination under disparate impact that includes history, statistics, procedures, and specific instances. Disparate-impact theory in sport is "participation by enrollment."

To achieve equity in athletics under the theory of disparate impact, an institution of higher education or secondary school must show that the percentage of females and males given the opportunity to play in sport is the same as the percentage of females and males attending the institution. An institution with a student body of 30,000—16,000 females and 14,000 males—with 600 berths in competitive athletics, 300 under scholarship, is summarized in Table 12-1.

Under the disparate-impact theory, the quality of all opportunities must be equal. Budgets do not have to be equal, but resources must enable the field hockey team, for example, to reach the same level of competence as the opportunities provided for the football team. Assistant coaches, trainers, and others must be adequately prepared to enable males and females to achieve an equal level of recognition in their sports.

The equal-protection clause of the Fourteenth Amendment, Title IX of the Education Amendments (1972), and various state equal-rights statutes provide protection against and avenues of redress for discrimination, and they have been used most often in athletics. Generally, female high school athletes have employed the Fourteenth Amendment to gain entry to sports; college athletes have used Title IX for the same purpose. When available, both collegiate and scholastic female athletes have used state equal-rights statutes. (See Heckman [1992] and Clement [1987] for detailed discussions of these cases.)

It appears that gender integration will shape athletics in the 1990s in the same way racial integration changed the schools in the 1960s. Athletics has become the vehicle for change!

LEADING CASES

Ridgeway, Haffer, and *Blair* are cases that have charted the course in discrimination and that will assist the professional in analyzing programs for equity.

TABLE 12-1   *Equity by enrollment*

	Enrollment	Participation (%)	Berths	Scholarships
Male	14,000	47	282	141
Female	16,000	53	318	159
Totals	30,000	100	600	300

Ridgeway v Montana High School Association (1988), the most comprehensive decision in athletics at the secondary level, was a class action suit brought on behalf of all Montana high school girls against the High School Athletic Association alleging violation of Title IX, the Fourteenth Amendment to the U.S. Constitution, and the Montana Constitution. The plaintiffs claimed discrimination existed in the number of sports, the seasons of play, the length of seasons, practice and game schedules, and access to facilities, equipment, coaching, trainers, transportation, the school band, uniforms, publicity, and general support. The parties accepted an agreement that provided for equal opportunity and placed a court-appointed facilitator in charge.

Haffer v Temple University (1987) concerned Temple University women currently participating in athletics and those who had been deterred from participating because of sex discrimination. Their claims focused on three basic areas: the extent to which Temple University afforded women students fewer "opportunities to compete" in intercollegiate athletics, the alleged disparity in resources allocated to the men's and women's intercollegiate athletic programs, and the alleged disparity in the allocation of financial aid to male and female students. The complaint alleged discrimination in opportunities to compete, expenditures, recruiting, coaching, travel and per diem allowances, uniforms, equipment, supplies, training facilities and services, housing and dining facilities, academic tutoring, and publicity. These actions were in violation of the Fourteenth Amendment and the Pennsylvania Equal Rights Amendment. The court ruled for the plaintiff in all areas except meals, tutoring, facilities, and scheduling.

Blair v Washington State University (1987) was similar to the foregoing decisions, except that the trial court chose to exclude football in the equity calculation. The plaintiff appealed the football decision, and the Washington Supreme Court reversed the decision, requiring that football be included in all calculations for finance and participation. Although this decision is precedent for the State of Washington, it serves as an example in other states.

Civil Rights Restoration Act (1987)

The **Civil Rights Restoration Act (1987)** restored Title IX to its original strength and removed the program-specific status. Title IX was once again applied to an entire institution and to all of the institution's programs.

Civil Rights Act (1991)

The **Civil Rights Act (1991)** strengthened disparate-impact theory by placing the burden of proof on those who practice discrimination, not on those who suffer discrimination. For example, when discrimination is alleged in a university athletic department, the athletic department and the university have the burden of proof: They must show evidence of equitable participation in intercollegiate athletics and in intramural and club sports and must demonstrate that no discrimination occurred or currently exists.

Further, the 1991 Civil Rights Act provided the victims of intentional discrimination with the right to recover damages, including compensatory and punitive damages. Punitive damages are based on reckless indifference. Incidentally, the U.S. Senate, in its deliberations, suggested that this legislation would be effective in encouraging voluntary settlements.

Although most schools and colleges openly admit inequities in their athletic programs, many claim that they do not intend to discriminate and that the courts will find it extremely difficult to prove they are intentionally discriminating. Given the fact that in January 1992 the U.S. Office of Education circulated a memo to college and university presidents warning them to be careful of sex discrimination laws when they make decisions about eliminating sport teams, it does not seem that it will be difficult to prove that a college president who ignores the memo has intentionally discriminated (Lederman, 1992).

Franklin v Gwinnett County Public Schools

Franklin, a sexual-harassment complaint, enables victims of discrimination to be compensated under Title IX. In February 1992, the U.S. Supreme Court granted money damages under Title IX (*Franklin v Gwinnett,* 1992). Judges White, Blackmun, Stevens, O'Connor, Kennedy, and Souter "held that a money damage

remedy is available for an action brought to enforce Title IX." Prior to this case, civil rights complaints in athletics have requested that the number of sports or the opportunities for participation in sports be added and schools be prohibited from dropping women's sports. Now plaintiffs may request monetary compensation for lost opportunities.

Recent cases

Among the institutions of higher education filing equity complaints in 1992 and 1993 were the University of New Mexico, Bowdoin College, Rutgers, Auburn University, College of William and Mary, Indiana University of Pennsylvania, the University of Texas, five institutions in California, Colorado State University, Brown University, and Colgate University. At the same time, coaches began filing suits and receiving damage awards.

Sanya Tyler, women's basketball coach at Howard University, received a verdict of $1.1 million in her equal-pay claim (Wong and Barr, 1993). And Oklahoma State University's women's golf coach has sued under the Equal Pay Act.

As Marianne Stanley began to negotiate a new contract as head women's basketball coach at the University of Southern California (USC), she decided—based on her outstanding coaching record—to request a multiyear contract for a salary similar to that paid to the men's basketball coach. She also asked for increases in the salaries of her assistant coaches. USC refused her request and told her that they would find another coach because she was no longer under contract. She was forced to accept a salary in the range in which she had been paid previously or lose her job. Stanley brought suit against USC for $8 million, alleging sex discrimination and retaliation, wrongful discharge, breach of implied contract, and conspiracy (*Stanley v University of Southern California,* 1994). Although she lost an injunction that would have enabled her to retain her position, she continues in her action against the university.

Many of the higher-education cases occur in response to budget cuts that affect both men's and women's sports. The courts are ruling that women's sports can not be cut until equity by enrollment, or proportionality, is achieved.

Roberts v Colorado State Board of Agriculture saw current students and former members of the women's varsity fast-pitch softball team bring suit challenging elimination of Colorado State University's softball and baseball teams in June 1992 in response to budget cuts. The district court and the U.S. Court of Appeals, 10th Circuit, have required the university to hire a coach and put softball back into its program.

In *Cohen v Brown University* (1992), women gymnastics and volleyball team members brought a class action suit against Brown University, a private college, following the demotion of their teams from varsity to club status. The U.S. District Court for the District of Rhode Island issued a preliminary injunction restoring the teams to varsity status. The U.S. Court of Appeals, First Circuit, affirmed.

Cook v Colgate University (1993) saw former members of the women's ice hockey team bring suit to elevate their sport from club to varsity status. Colgate University was ordered by the district court and the court of appeals to make ice hockey a varsity sport, and the university appealed. The case became moot when the last student involved graduated; a new complaint has been brought by current students.

CONCEPT CHECK

Equal protection and Title IX are the leading legal theories in sex integration in athletics. They have been strengthened in recent years by the Civil Rights Acts of 1987 and 1991. The Civil Rights Act of 1987 brings Title IX to full strength after the court decision Grove City *ruled that Title IX was program-specific and no longer covered athletics. The Civil Rights Act of 1991 gave money damages, compensatory and punitive, in Title IX decisions.*

Disparate impact is the legal theory functioning when an athletic department is examined for conformity with Title IX.

ARTICLE ONE OF THE U.S. CONSTITUTION

Article 1, Section 8, Number 3 states that Congress shall have the power "to regulate commerce with foreign nations, and among the several States, and with the Indian tribes"; Number 18 gives Congress the power "to make all laws which shall be necessary and proper for carrying into execution the foregoing powers, and all other powers vested by this Constitution in the Government of the United states, or in any department or officer thereof." This congressional authority has been further ex-

panded by the Sherman Act (1890), the Clayton Act (1914), the Norris-LaGuardia Act (1932), and the National Labor Relations Act, a result of amendments to the Wagner Act (1935) and the Taft-Hartley Act (1948). Antitrust and labor relations theories in these laws influence the rights of players and team owners in professional sports.

Labor laws

Sherman Act (1890). The **Sherman Act (1890)** set the stage for the evolution of **antitrust** law. Its purpose was to promote competition in the business sector through regulations designed to control private economic power. Professional sport, a private business operated to make a profit, comes under the labor laws. Section 1 of the Sherman Act states, "every contract, combination in the form of trust or otherwise, or conspiracy, in restraint of trade or commerce among the several States, or with foreign nations, is declared to be illegal. Every person who shall make any contract or engage in any combination or conspiracy hereby declared to be illegal shall be deemed guilty of a felony."

Section 2 states that "every person who shall monopolize, or attempt to monopolize, or combine or conspire with any other person or persons, to monopolize any part of the trade or commerce among the several States, or with foreign nations, shall be deemed guilty of a felony."

The Sherman Act regulates interstate commerce, including goods, land, and services. Price fixing, for example, is outlawed. Violations of the act are examined by the courts using a rule-of-reason test that balances the illegal practice against the anticompetitive effect. Procompetitive and anticompetitive goals are examined in an effort to find the least restrictive means to reach a legitimate procompetitive goal. For example, is the restraint of a professional player's movement from one team to another the least restrictive method of maintaining equity in competition? Is the restraint of a professional player to a 1-year contract commitment to a particular team a viable method of maintaining equity in competition?

Clayton Act (1914). Sections 4 and 6 of the **Clayton Act (1914)** are significant to professional athletes as they negotiate individual contract components and collective-bargaining agreements. Section 4 states that "any person who shall be injured in his business or property by reason of anything forbidden in the antitrust laws may sue therefore in any district court of the United States in the district in which the defendant resides or is found or has an agent, without respect to the amount in controversy, and shall recover threefold the damages by him sustained, and the cost of the suit including a reasonable attorney's fee. The court may award under this section . . . simple interest in actual damages for the period beginning on the date of service of such person's pleading."

Section 6 states that "the labor of a human being is not a commodity or article of commerce. Nothing contained in the antitrust laws shall be construed to forbid the existence and operation of labor, agricultural or horticultural organizations, instituted for the purpose of mutual help, . . . or to forbid or restrain individual members of such organizations from lawfully carrying out the legitimate objects thereof; nor shall such organizations, or the members thereof, be held or construed to be illegal combinations or conspiracies in restraint of trade under the antitrust laws." The Clayton Act strengthens and defines the Sherman Act. The act gives direction to athletes seeking redress for violations of antitrust and labor laws. Unfortunately, baseball's exemption from antitrust laws, discussed later, has denied baseball professionals a means of redress.

Norris-LaGuardia Act (1932). The following is taken from the interpretation of Section 102, Public Policy of the United States in the Act: "Whereas under prevailing economic conditions developed with the aid of governmental authority for owners of property to organize in the corporate and other forms of ownership association, the individual unorganized worker is commonly helpless to exercise actual liberty of contract and to protect his freedom of labor, and thereby to obtain acceptable terms and conditions of employment, wherefore, though he should be free to decline to associate with his fellows, it is necessary that he have full freedom of association, self-organization, and designation of representatives of his own choosing, to negotiate the terms and conditions of his employment, and that he shall be free from the interference, restraint, or coercion of employers of labor, or their agents, in the designation of such representatives or in the self-organization or in other concerted activities for the purpose of collective bargaining or other mu-

tual aid or protection; therefore, the following definitions of and limitations upon the jurisdiction and authority of the courts of the United States are enacted."

The Norris-LaGuardia Act defines, and in some authors' opinions, restricts the incidents in which federal courts can grant an injunction in labor disputes. In the 1945 *Bradley* case, the U.S. Supreme Court pointed out that corporations that engaged in price control of products, created monopolies, or violated other aspects of antitrust would lose their labor union antitrust exemption.

The **Norris-LaGuardia Act (1932),** and the sections of the Clayton Act that it reinforces, protects union activity from antitrust scrutiny. Union-management agreements that are a product of "good-faith" negotiations receive protection from antitrust law. The exemption or protection applies where restraint on trade primarily affects only the parties to the collective-bargaining agreement. This restraint is a mandatory subject of bargaining, and the exemption is a product of arm's-length negotiation. This reasoning is used in nearly all antitrust actions in professional sport.

National Labor Relations Act. Under 29 U.S.C. 157, the **National Labor Relations Act,** "Employees shall have the right to self-organization, to form, join, or assist labor organizations, to bargain collectively through representatives of their own choosing, and to engage in other concerted activities for the purpose of collective bargaining or other mutual aid or protection, and shall also have the right to refrain from any or all of such activities except to the extent that such right may be affected by an agreement requiring membership in a labor organization as a condition of employment."

It is an unfair labor practice for either an employer or a labor organization to restrain or coerce an employee in the exercise of his or her rights. It is also an unfair labor practice for a labor organization to refuse to bargain collectively with an employer that is the official representative of its employees. The National Labor Relations Board (NLRB) is authorized by the act to hear and render decisions on unfair labor practices. It also has the power to petition the U.S. district court for appropriate temporary relief or a restraining order. The National Labor Relations Act guides businesses and members of unions, including athletic-player unions, in negotiations and in implementing collective-bargaining agreements in sport.

Antitrust cases

Through the years, sport has presented some unique issues to the courts for antitrust examination. The sport industry differs from other businesses in many ways. A consumer who is unhappy with the goods or services of a typical business can seek out another source of supply, while in sport there is no real substitute for the college and professional sports market. Gary Roberts (1991) notes that a legal problem in antitrust claims in sport is defining "the relevant market that the plaintiff claims has been monopolized. The market definition must include both a product and a geographic dimension—for example, professional football entertainment in the United States."

Another unique characteristic of sport is that its product (or service) is the competition between teams. Equity (a level playing field!) must be maintained to enable live spectators and television audiences to observe close, exciting, and competitive encounters. League owners are forced to work together to secure the league while at the same time engaging in fierce competition with the other members of the league.

Only in sport does a player join a **collective-bargaining** unit and then negotiate individually for additional resources. In business and industry, the employee is either a member of a union, accepting the results of a collective-bargaining agreement, or an independent worker, negotiating an individual employment contract. Athletes, upon employment, automatically become members of a players' union, which negotiates basic elements of the work, economic, and fringe package. All athletes accept the results of this agreement, and outstanding athletes then bargain, usually through their agents, for additional economic and work-related privileges.

Unique among sports are the three U.S. Supreme Court decisions that have exempted baseball from all antitrust laws. In *Federal Baseball Club of Baltimore v National League of Baseball* (1922), the Supreme Court held that baseball was exempt from the Sherman Act because it did not meet the definition of **"interstate commerce."** Justice Holmes stated that professional baseball "business is giving exhibitions of baseball, which are purely state affairs."

The suit, for treble damages, had been brought by members of the Federal League against the National and American Leagues, challenging restraints on player movement in professional sports. The **reserve clause,** a part of all players' contracts, bound a player to a team until the team released him or contracted him to another team. Further, the reserve clause prohibited other teams from making offers to signed players. Once a player signed the initial contract, all control of his future was placed in the owner's hands. The system was justified to maintain competitive balance by preventing one team from hiring all the good players.

In 1953, the Supreme Court had a chance in *Toolson v New York Yankees* to reverse its earlier decision and deny baseball the antitrust exemption awarded in 1922. The issue was that the reserve clause was an alleged violation of the Sherman and Clayton Acts. The plaintiffs focused their complaint on television in an effort to demonstrate interstate commerce. The court reaffirmed *Federal Baseball*, saying that the business of baseball had operated successfully for 30 years and the antitrust exemption should stand. The two dissenting justices, Burton and Reed, argued that during those 30 years baseball had become big business, with significant impact on interstate commerce, and should be subject to the antitrust laws.

Flood v Kuhn (1972) involved the professional player Curt Flood, who was traded to another club without his knowledge. The Supreme Court, in maintaining baseball's antitrust exemption, noted that professional baseball's long-standing exemption from antitrust law was an established aberration not held by other sports but that it should be allowed to stand.

As a result of these decisions, state courts have issued similar holdings in response to antitrust claims in baseball.

Players filing antitrust complaints. Although other sports profit from minor antitrust exemptions, baseball's exemption has not been extended to all sports. Television network pools, blackouts of nonlocal telecasts when the home team is playing at home, and blackouts of home team games when it is playing in home territory constitute antitrust exemptions. These exemptions exist in a number of sports, but football appears to profit most from them.

In 1974, football players decided to challenge the Rozelle Rule under antitrust law (*Mackey v National Football League*, 1976). The **Rozelle Rule** was a practice started in the 1960s that required a team signing a veteran free agent to compensate the team that lost the player. Compensation was usually a player or draft-choice trade. Although different from baseball's reserve clause, a system football players had previously worked under, the new Rozelle Rule was viewed as equally offensive. Even more difficult for football players to understand was the fact that football was subject to antitrust law, which should have given them greater freedom.

The district court found that the Rozelle Rule violated the Sherman Act. The Eighth Circuit Court of Appeals affirmed the district court. Following the *Mackey* decision, a right-of-first-refusal compensation was developed through the collective-bargaining system. Under this rule, owners were permitted to match outside players' offers and by so doing retain a player's service. The right of first refusal was not popular with players; they believed that it gave too much control to the owners. In light of the fact that the first-refusal system of compensation was negotiated by the players' union and that unions usually have limited antitrust exemptions, the players had a difficult challenge in their many trips to court to attempt to change the first-refusal system (*Power v National Football League*, (1991). Finally, in *McNeil*, Judge David Doty played a major role in crafting contract provisions that have become the current standard. Teams now have exclusive rights over players for their first 3 years in the league; in years 4 and 5, players remain under a limited right of first refusal; and at the end of year 5, players become unrestricted free agents. Salary cap implementation is accompanied by free agency in the 4th year. A number of categories, such as "franchise player" and "designated transition player," have been established to accommodate the needs of outstanding talent. These arrangements are the subject of current debate in newspaper sports pages.

Owners filing antitrust complaints. Two cases, *Piazza v Major League Baseball* (1994) and *Sullivan v National Football League (NFL)* (1994), discuss professional team owner antitrust problems. *Piazza* was a suit filed by a partnership that attempted to buy the San Francisco Giants and move them to Tampa/St.

Petersburg. The partnership was outbid by a purchaser who promised to keep the Giants in San Francisco but paid $15 million less than the amount offered by Piazza. Among the many legal theories in the complaint were antitrust issues. The court denied Major League's motion to dismiss based upon the antitrust exemption, holding that the exemption was limited only to the reserve clause and that the reserve clause was not an issue in this case.

In *Sullivan* (1994), the plaintiff, founder of the New England Patriots, received a jury award of $38 million, trebled to $114 million, from the National Football League for violating antitrust laws by restricting him from selling stock in the club to the public. The damage award was reduced to $17 million in December 1993. In September 1994, the First Circuit Court of Appeals set aside the entire award and ordered a new trial, which has not yet been conducted.

Antitrust in sport can best be described as a theory in process. Through the years, labor law has been applied by the courts differently, in various sports and in various owner-player situations. Congress is currently studying the relationship between antitrust law and sports. Bills have been introduced in both the Senate and the House that could overturn baseball's antitrust exemption.

CONCEPT CHECK

Article One of the Constitution and the Sherman, Clayton, Norris-LaGuardia, and National Labor Relations Acts establish the antitrust and labor relation theories and laws that influence the rights of players and team owners in professional sports. The Sherman and Clayton Acts promote competition and prohibit monopolies; the Norris-LaGuardia Act addresses the needs of the individual; and the National Labor Relations Act provides a road map for collective bargaining.

Professional athletes have used the courts to gain freedom from contract restraints imposed by team owners. While considerable progress has been made, the fight continues.

SUMMARY

1. The U.S. Constitution is the primary law of the country, and each state has a constitution or primary set of laws. In addition, federal

and state statutes have been enacted by legislative bodies to ensure efficient management of the federal and state governments.

2. The First Amendment to the U.S. Constitution includes the rights of religion, speech, and press.

3. The Fourth Amendment to the U.S. Constitution involves privacy rights.

4. Under the First and Fourth Amendments, the courts balance the needs of the state against the needs of the individual.

5. Primary elements of the Fourteenth Amendment are due process and equal protection.

6. Procedural due process enables an individual to be heard, to defend his or her actions, and to be assured of fair treatment before a right or privilege is taken away.

7. Hiring-system agreements include at-will, labor unions, and employment contracts.

8. The primary federal laws affecting employment are the Equal Pay Act (1963), Title VII of the Civil Rights Act (1964), the Age Discrimination in Employment Act (1967), the Rehabilitation Act (1973), and the Americans with Disabilities Act.

9. Affirmative action is a program designed to remedy past discriminating practices in hiring minority groups.

10. An effective system for hiring personnel includes preparation, identification of job responsibilities and requirements, obtaining an applicant pool, screening applications, interviewing, selecting, and documenting the entire process.

11. Employee evaluations are tailored with due process in mind.

12. An equal-protection challenge must show that groups of people are being treated differently, without justification, than the general population.

13. Title IX states that "No person in the United States shall, on the basis of sex, be excluded from participation in, be denied the benefit of, or be subject to discrimination under any education program or activity receiving Federal financial assistance."

14. Disparate impact involves practices that appear neutral in their treatment of different groups but fall more harshly on one group than another.

15. The Civil Rights Act (1987) restored Title IX to its original strength. Title IX was eroded between 1972 and 1987 by a number of court cases that narrowed the scope of Title IX.

16. The Civil Rights Act (1991) strengthened disparate-impact theory by placing the burden of proof on those who practice discrimination and provided for both punitive and compensatory-damage recovery.

17. Article 1 of the U.S. Constitution and the Sherman, Clayton, Norris-LaGuardia, and National Labor Relations Acts identify the rights of players and team owners in professional sports.

18. The Sherman and Clayton Acts promote competition and prohibit monopolies.

19. Violations of the Sherman Act are examined by the courts using a rule-of-reason test that balances the illegal practice against the anticompetitive effect.

20. The National Labor Relations Act serves as a guide for collective bargaining.

21. Sports differ from business and industry in market, product definition, and employment agreements.

22. Three U.S. Supreme Court decisions, *Federal Baseball*, *Toolson*, and *Flood*, have maintained baseball's antitrust exemption.

23. The Rozelle Rule was a practice that required a team signing a veteran free agent to compensate the team that lost the player.

24. Under the right-of-first-refusal compensation, owners were permitted to match outside players' offers and by so doing retain a player's service.

25. Owner litigation is threatening baseball's antitrust exemption. Only time will tell whether the exemption is the reserve clause or all of baseball.

CASE STUDY I

The equal-protection clause of the U.S. Constitution and Title IX assist the athletic administrator in determining equity in sport. A high school district has a student population that is 55% female and 45% male and sports budgets of $85,000 for boys and $65,000 for girls. One hundred and forty boys participate in sports, while female participation is 100.

Analyze equity in this setting using the equal-protection clause and Title IX.

CASE STUDY II

Professional baseball players are automatically members of a players' union and reap the benefits of union membership. In addition, many players employ an agent to negotiate additional wages and benefits. Owners have reserved various rights in arriving at player agreements. Among them are the reserve clause, trading players to other teams, and the Rozelle Rule.

How do athletes' agreements, including owners' rights, differ from employment agreements in business and industry?

REVIEW QUESTIONS AND ISSUES

1. Using the results of court decisions, explain the U.S. Constitution's First Amendment freedoms of religion, speech, and press.
2. Can a school locker be searched under the Fourth Amendment?
3. Explain the balancing system used by the courts in First and Fourth Amendment decisions.
4. Trace the court decisions in the *Reynolds* case in an effort to understand the rights of the Olympic Committee.
5. Explain procedural due process, identifying when and how it is used.
6. How do the results of the *Tarkanian* court decision fit into the due process system?
7. Explain the relationship between the Fourteenth Amendment's equal-protection clause and Title IX of the Education Amendments (1972) in athletics.
8. Explain disparate-impact theory.
9. Chart a local athletic department participation rate to see if it would meet the current court ratio of equity within 5%.
10. How do labor laws define antitrust relationships?
11. Explain the rule-of-reason test.
12. How does the National Labor Relations Act serve as a guide to collective bargaining?
13. Identify and explain the unique characteristics of sport as a business.
14. Contrast baseball's antitrust exemption with the treatment of other sports under antitrust law.
15. Explain the Rozelle Rule, which was challenged in the *Mackey* case.
16. Explain the results of the *McNeil* decision and its impact on collective bargaining.
17. What are the antitrust violations in *Piazza* and *Sullivan*?

REFERENCES

Bennett v West Texas State, 799 F 2d 155 (5th Cir Ct 1986).

Blair v Washington State University, 740 P 2d 1379 (Wash 1989).

Board of Education of Westside Community Schools v Mergens, 496 US 226, 110 S Ct 2356 (1990).

Boyd v Board of Directors of McGehee School District No. 17, 612 F Supp 86 (1985).

Brenden v Independent School District, 342 F Supp 1224 (1972), affirmed 477 F 2d 1292 (1973).

Brunet v City of Columbus, 642 F Supp 11214 (1986); appeal dismissed, 826 F 2d 1062 (1987); cert denied, 108 S Ct 1593 (1988).

Bucha v Illinois High School Association, 351 F Supp 69 (1972).

Cannon v University of Chicago, 441 US 677 (1979).

Civil Rights Restoration Act (1987), Public Law 100-259, 102 (1987).

Civil Rights Act (1991), Public Law 102-166 (1991).

Clayton Act (1914), 15 USC 15, 4 and 6 (1914).

Clement, A. Legal theory and sex discrimination in sport. In Adrian M, ed (1987): *Sports women*, Basel, Switzerland, Karger Press.

Clement, A. (1988), *Law in sport and physical activity*, Dubuque, Iowa, Brown & Benchmark.

Cohen v Brown University, 991 F 2d 888 (1993); 809 F Supp 978 (DRI 1992).

Connick v Myers, 461 US 138, 103 S Ct 1684 (1983).

Cook v Colgate University, 992 F 2d 17 (2d Cir 1993); 802 F Supp 737 (NDNY 1992).

Dambrot v Central Michigan University, 839 F Supp 477 (1993).

Doe v Duncanville Independent School District, 994 F 2d 160 (1993).

Equal Employment Opportunity Commission v Atlas Paper Company, 868 F. 2d 1489 (1989).

Fairfax Covenant Church v the Fairfax County School Board, 17 F 3d 703 (1994).

Federal Baseball Club v National League of Baseball Clubs, 259 US 200 (1922).

Flood v Kuhn, 407 US 258 (1972).

Franklin v Gwinnet County Public Schools, 112 St Ct 1028; 117 L Ed 2d 208; 60 USLW 4267 (1992).

Gomes v Rhode Island Interscholastic League, 441 US 958; 99 S Ct 2401 (1979); 469 F Supp 659 (1979) vacated as moot, 604 F 2d 733 (1979).

Griggs v Duke Power Company, 401 US 424, 91 St Ct 849 (1971).

Grove City College v Bell, 465 US 555, 79 L Ed 516, 104 S Ct 1211 (1984); 687 F 2d 684 (3d Cir, 1982), pet for cert. granted, 103 S Ct 1181 (1983).

Haas v South Bend Community School Corporation, 289 NE 2d 495 (1972).

Haffer v Temple University, 524 F Supp 531 (ED Pa 1981), affirmed 688 F 2d 14 (3d Cir 1982).

Haffer v Temple University, 678 F Supp 517 (ED Pa 1987).

Haffer v Temple University, 115 FRD 506 (ED Pa 1987).

Hazelwood School District v United States, 97 S Ct 2736 (1977).

Heckman, D. (1992). Women and athletics: a twenty year retrospective on Title IX, University of Miami Entertainment and *Sport Law Review* 9(1):1-64.

Hill v NCAA, 865 P 2d 633 (1994).

Hollander v Connecticut Interscholastic Athletic Association, Inc., Civil No. 12-49-27 (Super Ct, New Haven, Conn, March 1971); appeal dismissed 295 A 2d 671 (1972).

In the interest of Isiah B., 176 Wis 2d 639; 500 NW 2d 637 (1993).

Lamb's Chapel v Center Moriches Union Free School District, 113 S Ct 2141; 124 L Ed 2d 352 (1993).

Lederman, D. US Draft memo on sex equity in college sports, *Chronicle of Higher Education* 38(22):1, 1992.

Lee v Weisman, 12 S Ct 2649 (1992).

Mackey v National Football League, 543 F 2d 606 (1976).

Marcum v Dahl, 658 F 731 (1981).

McNeil v National Football League, 790 F Supp 871 (1992).

National Labor Relations Act, 29 USC § 157.

NCAA v Tarkanian, 102 L Ed 469 (1988); 795 F Supp 1476 (1992); 10 F 3d 633 (1993).

Norris-LaGuardia Act (1932), 29 USC §102 (1932).

North Haven v Bell 102 S Ct 1912, 72 L Ed 299 (1982).

Othen v Ann Arbor School District, 507 F Supp 1376 (ED Mich. (1981); affirmed on grounds not involving Title IX, 699 F 2d 309 (1982).

Petrie v Illinois High School Association, 75 Ill App 980, 394 NE 2d 855 (1979).

Piazza v Major League Baseball, Civil Action No. 92-7173 (ED Pa 1994); 836 F Supp 269 (1993); 831 F Supp 420 (ED Pa 1993).

Powell v National Football League, 764 F Supp 1351 (1991); 930 F 2d 1293 (1989); 690 F Supp 812 (1988); 678 F Supp 777 (1988).

Reed v Nebraska Athletic Association, 341 F Supp 258 (D Neb 1972).

Reynolds v The Athletic Congress of the U.S.A. Inc., 23 F 3d 1110 (1994); 841 F Supp 1444 (1992).

Ridgeway v Montana High School Association, 858 F 2d 579 (9th Cir 1988); 633 F Supp 1564 (1986); 638 F Supp 326 (1986).

Rittacco v Norwin School District, 361 F Supp 930 (1973).

Roberts, G.R. Professional sports and the antitrust laws. In Staudohar, P.D. and Mangan, J.A. (1991) The business of professional sport, Chicago, 1991, University of Illinois Press.

Roberts v Colorado State, 814 Supp 1507 (D Colo) (Roberts I), affirmed.

Roberts v Colorado State Board of Agriculture, 998 F 2d 824 (10th Cir, 1993) (Roberts II); cert denied, 114 St Ct 580 (1993).

Sherman Act (1890), 15 USC 1 and 2 (1890).

State v Hunter, 300 P 2d 455, 208 Ore 282 (1956).

Stanley v University of Southern California, 13 F 3d 1313 (1994).

Sullivan v National Football League, 34 F 3d 1091 (1994); 839 F Supp 6 (1993); 785 F Supp 1076 (1992).

Tarkanian v NCAA, 741 P 2d 1345 (1987); 810 P 2d 343 (1989); 114 S Ct 1543 (1994); petition to US Supreme Court for writ of certiorari denied.

Teamsters v United States, 431 US 324 (1977).

Tinker v Des Moines, 393 US 503 (1969).

Title IX of the Education Amendments (1972), 20 USC 1681 (1976).

Toolson v New York Yankees, 346 US 356 (1953).

United States Constitution.

University of Colorado v Derdeyn, 863 P 2d 929 (Colo 1993); 832 P 2d 1031 (1991); 114 S Ct 1646 (1994); petition for writ of certiorari denied; 62 USLW 3843 (June 20, 1994); petition to US Supreme Court for rehearing denied.

University of Nevada v Tarkanian, Supreme Court of Nevada, No. 23494 (July 7, 1994); 594 P 2d 1159 (1979).

Ward Cove Packing Co. v Atonio, 104 L Ed 2d 733 (1989).

Williams v Eaton, 310 F Supp 1342 (1970).

Wong, G.M. and Barr, C.A. (1993). Equal Paybacks, Athletic Business, September.

Yellow Springs Exempted Village School District v Ohio High School Athletic Association, 647 F 2d 651 (1981).

SUGGESTED READINGS

Clement, A. (1988). *Law in sport and physical activity,* Dubuque, Iowa, Brown & Benchmark.

Butterman, A.H. (1994). Baseball's antitrust exemption and an owner-imposed salary cap: can they coexist? *Entertainment and Sports Lawyer* 12(3): 3.

Champion, W.T. (1991). *Fundamentals of sports law,* Rochester, New York, Lawyers Cooperative Publishers.

Heckman, D. (1992). Women and athletics: a twenty year retrospective on Title IX, *University of Miami Entertainment and Sports Law Review* 9(1):1-64.

Vargyas, E.J. (1994). *Breaking down barriers: a legal guide to Title IX,* Washington, D.C., National Women's Law Center.

Weiler, P.C. and Roberts, G.R. (1993). *Sport and the law,* St. Paul, West.

Wong, G.M. (1988). *Torts and sports,* Dover, Massachusetts, Auburn House.

PART IV

Facilities

CHAPTER 13

Managing the Facility

Aaron Mulrooney and Peter Farmer

In this chapter, you will become familiar with the following terms:

In-house	Housekeeping	Bootleggers
Request for proposals (RFP)	Setup and breakdown	Budget cycle
Mission statement	Walk-up sales	Generally accepted accounting
Booking	Will-call location	procedures (GAAP)
Tentative-hold reservation	House scale	Event settlement
Contracted reservation	Performance scale	House expenses
Boilerplate contract	Point of sale	Internal auditing process
Promoter	Stocking	External audit
Earned media	Convenience foods	Standard operating procedures
Respondeat superior	Vendors	(SOPs)
Event coordinator	Hawkers	

Overview

Professional management can influence the supply of sports events and well-organized services, and provide the patron with an enjoyable time. Management philosophy will determine the number and type of staff, as well as the extent of services provided in-house as opposed to those that are contracted out. The quality of management for major sport facilities can determine the ability of the facility to attract and retain tenants. Income and profitability for the facility owner, staffing requirements, building condition, and service levels (fan comfort) also are affected by management. This chapter will investigate the various types of facility management and the major components of the management team.

TYPES OF MANAGEMENT

There are a number of management alternatives: those operated by their owners, by the primary or anchor tenants, by not-for-profit entities, or by private management companies.

Owner

This management organization may be public or private (Laventhol and Horwath, 1989). If owned or operated by a government agency, operational efficiency is constrained or reduced by the regulations and procedures that are often associated with governmental bureaucracy. Such items as purchasing procedures; contract approval processes (often by the legislative body); hiring, promotion, and dismissal of personnel; and other government policies (including just plain politics, such as patronage) are just a few of the operational performance areas of the building that are affected by bureaucracy. To alleviate this situation, many publicly owned facilities have moved toward independent authorities, such as not-for-profit operations and private management companies (Laventhol and Horwath, 1989).

The main problems facing privately owned and managed facilities are enormous costs and human resources. Because of these burdens, many privately owned facilities have opted to move toward not-for-profit operations and private management companies.

Not-for-profit operations

These entities generally involve a commission or a board of directors, appointed by a governmental body to act as an agent of the local government (Laventhol and Horwath, 1989). This board is exempted from numerous government regulations and procedures in order to run an efficient facility. Over time, however, the quality of the board may deteriorate as political patronage and reputation become standard operating procedure.

Private management: the future alternative

Although sport facilities have traditionally been owned and governed by public authorities, the situation appears to be changing. Sport facilities were originally designed as a community economic-impact entity, but many facilities have become a drain on community resources. In difficult economic times, this burden on the taxpayer can be significant.

If a facility has significant problems or is unable to realize its managers' expectations, alternative management organizations, other than an **in-house** group, should be considered. One of these alternatives is private management. This type of management enables the governmental or institutional entity to maintain control over the facility, but with the opportunity to:

- Reduce or eliminate an operating deficit
- Offer patrons improved service
- Increase the quantity and quality of the events booked
- Become part of a larger facility network, which would facilitate greater opportunities
- Provide greater operational flexibility concerning policies and overall operational structure

These advantages have enabled this facility management alternative to experience dramatic growth over the past decade. It is interesting to note that a number of different types of management groups—ranging from hotels, to food service groups, to specialty facility management groups—have entered this competitive arena. Each of these management groups evaluates a facility's needs based on its current financial picture, staffing requirements, marketing needs, event scheduling, and the political situation.

PRIVATE-MANAGEMENT SELECTION PROCESS

After resolving any obvious internal problems and disagreements, the facility's governing body will initiate the private-management selection process. The first step is the issuance of a **request for proposals (RFP)** (IAAM, 1990). This formal process begins with the issuance of statements outlining what is expected from a contracted management organization. Materials should be attached to provide the responding management organization, with an overall picture of the facility's present situation. Such items as long- and short-term plans and projections, actual and projected budget and income, annual and usage reports, and existing contracts should be included.

The second step is dispatching the RFP document to all major management groups, as well as prominently displaying it in all appropriate trade and professional publications. The RFP bid response period varies from 30 to 90 days, depending upon conditions. The RFP also should indicate whether the bid will be a public process, open to the press, and whether bid proposals will be available to competitors (IAAM, 1990).

Third, all interested participants/bidders will be provided with a facility tour and an in-depth examination of the RFP. Addenda will be prepared as a result of the meeting between bidders and the facility governing body.

Fourth, all proposals that are received before the deadline are reviewed by a designated body and finalists are determined. All bidders will be notified as to their success or failure in the bidding process. The finalists are provided with an opportunity to give a personal presentation to the review body. At this stage, the bidders have the right to know about their competition and the stage of the decision process. It is important that flexibility be part of the process because bidders sometimes need to change their proposals as new information becomes available.

Fifth, following the personal presentations, one bidder should be selected to proceed into the negotiation stage, which involves representatives from both groups as well as legal assistance. Negotiations are initiated through a written document based on the RFP and the proposal. An agreement is apparent when there is resolution of the differences between these two documents.

The final (approval) stage comes at the end of the negotiation phase, when the final authority (e.g., the commission or state legislature) approves the contract (IAAM, 1990).

CONCEPT CHECK

Although many facilities are managed by their owners or by not-for-profit governmental agencies, the current trend is toward contracting with private management companies. These companies should be required to submit competitive bids through the request-for-proposals (RFP) process.

OPERATIONS

Operations are the most complex and comprehensive function in all of sport facility management. Facility operations managers have a wide variety of departmental responsibilities, including event coordinating, engineering, security, maintenance, and housekeeping. They must possess an adequate knowledge of budgeting, cost control, methodology, and negotiation skills to effectively complete their job responsibilities.

Operations of a sport facility vary significantly from the operations management of most businesses, although the underlying principles are similar. Operations management in a major sport facility focuses on how services are produced, rather than the production of those services, which is the traditional definition of operations management.

Management teams

A sport facility is operated by a management team. This team, depending upon the facility's size and function, is headed by an individual titled general manager, CEO, or executive director. Other members of this team oversee marketing, public relations, advertising, and operations. This section focuses on management functions, especially those associated with the general manager's office. These functions include philosophy, mission, policies and procedures, organizational elements, booking and scheduling, contracts, the management manual, and evaluation procedures.

Policies

A policy is a definitive course of action selected from various alternatives, in light of given conditions, to guide and determine present and future decisions. Policies are developed from the **mission statement**, which should be the basis for establishing all aspects of the operational procedures (Thompson, 1990). A policy is the reason—the why—behind management's decision to function in a particular manner.

Procedures

Procedures are the "how" of accomplishing policies. They are the established, traditional way of doing something, and they include a series of steps to be followed by facility staff members to accomplish their assigned duties. From the outset, the manager will encounter numerous problems, from change orders to equipment purchases to overseeing the entire project to ensure that the final product is what was intended. Prior to the facility's opening, the building manager should establish a philosophy and tone, as well as appropriate building policies and operational procedures. These general policies and procedures should then be effectively communicated to staff, tenants, and the general public in a manner that clearly reflects the parameters under which the facility is to be used.

Philosophy

The philosophy of the facility manager should provide a basis for establishing guidelines and a proper orientation to operations. This philosophy may be based on the attitude that the facility should either serve the community without concern for profit and proper management control or exhibit fiscal responsibility through the control of appropriations and revenues, with the goal of breaking even or earning profit. A combination of the two approaches might be preferable to the either/or philosophy, but local circumstances might dictate the final choice.

Mission statement and goals and objectives
The operation of all facilities is guided by a mission statement or an operational direction. While many facility organizations, especially those tied to government agencies or large corporations, have formal mission statements, others operate with general and wide-ranging guidelines. It is these mission guidelines that provide the parameters for developing an organization's budget.

Goals and objectives that support and justify the facility's mission, or statement of purpose, need to be developed. They should be developed by competent management and compiled from input from all operational personnel (Hitt, 1985).

Goals are the achievable statements of purpose, or expectations, provided by management personnel. If fulfilled, they justify the fiscal resources requested in the budget document. Generally, sport facility goals are not as formalized as in other industries (e.g., increase sales by 18% and open new markets in the South).

Objectives are the supporting qualifications of the specified goals, not the goals themselves. All objectives should be measurable, quantifiable, and subjective. Most facilities, depending on their size, are departmentalized, but management should involve all personnel, regardless of their duties. This participative-management approach (a bottom-up rather than top-down approach) is vital if all personnel are expected to support the mission, goals, and objectives of the facility.

CONCEPT CHECK

To be successful as an entertainment complex, a sport facility must define its mission, philosophy, procedures, and policies, as well as establish specific goals and objectives.

ORGANIZATIONAL AREAS
Within a facility, there are important operational areas that need to be considered in order for the facility to operate smoothly and effectively, including:

- Booking and scheduling
- Marketing, public relations, and advertising
- Security
- Safety and medical services
- Housekeeping and maintenance
- Box office
- Concessions and novelties
- Traffic and parking
- Financial management
- Risk management

BOOKING AND SCHEDULING
Event booking and scheduling is one of the most important areas of concern in maintaining a facility. A facility without events has little purpose because events are the primary source of revenue, the lifeblood of any facility. In addition, booking and scheduling and public relations are the departments most responsible for molding the facility's image by direct association with the sponsor and by their ability to coordinate the facility's schedule.

To comprehend the different approaches to scheduling, a facility's mandate must be understood. Facilities differ not only in their public/private management approach but also in their mission. A public facility is obligated to provide for the scheduling of community events, whereas a private facility, depending upon its formation agreement, may limit charitable and nonprofit activities.

A privately operated facility has the ability to promote its own events, although many do not because of legal ramifications. A privately managed facility can actively court business and aggressively seek to attract events by bidding or presenting comprehensive proposals to promoters.

Whatever the facility's purpose and mission in attracting and promoting events, the general approach to booking is reserving a specific space, within a specific facility, for a specific date, at a specific time, for an agreed-upon amount of money. **Booking** is the act of engaging and contracting an event or attraction.

Attracting an event
The first step in securing an event is the development of a positive public image. One key to developing a positive image is the production of a facility brochure, detailing the specifications of the

building, staff, types of events, and event suitability. A well-planned and -produced informational brochure should be directed to all individuals who might be interested in securing the facility for a planned event. Events that are successful should be featured prominently in future facility publications, which should be revised annually.

Other elements in attracting events are maintaining visibility with local and national promoters, visiting appropriate trade fairs and conventions, and networking with other facilities. Success in booking an event is much more likely to result not from walk-in trade but whom you know.

Scheduling

Scheduling is the reservation process and coordination of all events to fit the facility's available time. This reservation process involves scheduling a series of like events (e.g., football games or symphony concerts) and providing the best possible event mix to fit the facility's usage. Event dates must be properly spaced (not overlap). Individuals responsible for scheduling must have an in-depth knowledge of operational functions and be able to secure the appropriate number of events for the facility, while not overtaxing the staff, overworking the building, overspending the budget, or saturating the marketplace.

For the scheduling process to maintain its cohesiveness, it is imperative that the record of scheduled events be solely under the control of a single individual who writes and erases information from the scheduling book. Changes in arrangements and notification of event alterations are this designated individual's unique responsibility.

Reservation process

There are two categories of reservations for space in a public facility, tentative and confirmed.

Tentative-hold reservations are made when an organization requests a specific date and time on the facility calendar but no actual contract has been prepared. If another organization desires the same date and time and can provide the necessary earnest money, the facility scheduler will contact the original tentatively scheduled organization and inquire about its intention to book the facility. It is not uncommon to have a succession of first, second, and third tentative holds on a given date or set of dates because they are often requested a year or more in advance.

After notification, confirmation will be requested and a contract readied. Customarily, the facility notifies the scheduled organization of its placement and any resultant changes in the schedule.

A confirmed reservation, or **contracted reservation**, refers to an organization that has placed a deposit for the agreed-upon date and time and contract negotiations have commenced. A facility should establish guidelines concerning the length of time a tentative hold may remain on record. At the same time, the facility should be as flexible as possible about the confirmation period. Different types of events require different confirmation and condition deadlines, depending on circumstances and the promoter's reputation. Any facility that hopes to maintain its integrity must adopt a reservation system that is fair and reasonable.

Contracting

After an organization confirms a tentative hold, the next step is to negotiate the contract. A contract consists of an offer, an acceptance, and a consideration. The concluded agreement creates obligations for all parties involved. After negotiations are finished, there are five requirements to complete a contract:

1. Consideration: legal value (money) and mutual obligation of both parties
2. A valid offer and a valid acceptance
3. The substance of the contract must be legal
4. A specific duration (time) for the contract
5. A written and/or verbal contract

It is necessary that qualified individuals design, prepare, and understand the contents of the contract, which should consist of mutually agreed upon terms. This will ensure that the facility is not bound to terms in an agreement that it cannot meet.

Most facilities do not retain a full-time attorney to create a contract for each new facility event. Instead, a boilerplate contract containing a standard form is used. The **boilerplate contract** is similar to an apartment lease, with language in a standard form and with appropriate "fill-in-the-blanks" to address specifically agreed-upon terms.

Boilerplate contracts provide consistency and generally reflect a situation favorable to all parties. Variations in language concerning events provide a more streamlined contractual device. Addenda may be used to create a more customized form, enable modification or elimination of contract clauses, or clarify changes that have been agreed upon by both parties.

Contracts should be kept as simple as possible to avoid confusion and expedite the contractual process. Large facilities that host a variety of events use three basic boilerplate contract forms, each addressing different event types:

- Ticketed events, open to the public, require language addressing ticket sales, gate proceeds, ushers, and ticket takers. Addenda usually refer to elements concerned with insurance, special financial arrangements, and promotions. Public events require more precise contractual procedures because the facility endeavors to preserve the security of patrons and maintain building control.
- A nonticketed or closed event, such as a convention or trade show, deals with display booths and banquets but not invitations or ticketing. Contracts for these events are less complex because the event is not open to the public, thus reducing liabilities.
- A small event held in a facility's meeting room, such as a prom or a seminar, eliminates the need for the manpower of a large event that uses the arena. The contract in this case is simple and straightforward.

In contract negotiations, the main objective is to maintain control and direction for the facility. The facility maintains control over the building during an event by providing security, ushers, ticket takers, first aid, and special insurance arrangements. Such control reduces the facility's liabilities.

CONCEPT CHECK

The booking and scheduling process is an important aspect of achieving success in a facility. Events must be properly scheduled and contracted so that all parties know their rights and responsibilities. Formal policies and procedures will make this phase of facility management operate more smoothly.

MARKETING AND PROMOTIONAL-STRATEGY DEVELOPMENT

During the negotiation stage, the **promoter(s)** and facility marketing organization should be in contact to determine the type and extent of facility involvement with the proposed event. The level of facility involvement will hinge on the event type and the promoter's approach to marketing its event.

In some cases, the client(s) will undertake the entire marketing operation, from contact with the local media (radio, television, and newspapers) to promotions being run in the facility on the day of the event. This type of control will depend upon the experience and expertise of the promoters in the development of their events. Client-controlled promotion will limit the cost of the event to the facility but also lower the amount of revenue due to the facility at the time of settlement.

In most cases, promoters will not have developed ties with the local community and media. If this is true, they will often want the event's entire marketing campaign to be organized by the facility marketing organization. This marketing responsibility requires the development of a marketing plan.

Initial marketing efforts

After the establishment of the initial marketing assumptions (based on research) and the marketing plan and budget, the real work begins. The first phase, depending upon the event and the results of market research initiatives, begins with the establishment of contact with the local media. This initial contact includes discussion of the purchase of media time or space, and sets up some form of trade/promotion with these media. It is imperative that this media advertising be targeted at the appropriate audience (O'Shaughnessy, 1988).

At the same time, the group sales department attempts to contact corporations and service groups in an attempt to book groups for the upcoming event. Such promotional activities as press conferences and star athletes visiting key "publics"—commonly known as **earned media,**—should be planned and carried out. According to Will Peneguy of the New Orleans Super Dome, these public-awareness activities should be scheduled in close proximity to the actual event, while the initial media contact could be as much as a year in advance.

Awareness and information are the keys to a successful marketing campaign. Once these are achieved, the job of attracting people to a facility becomes an easier task.

SECURITY

Security functions usually fall under the jurisdiction of the operations department in most facilities. In large facilities a full-time, in-house security staff is employed. This compounds the responsibilities of the operations manager because in-house security officers are employees of the facility and it assumes liability for any negligent actions on their part under the legal doctrine of **respondeat superior**.

Therefore it is vitally important that proper rules and procedures be established, written, and made accessible to all members of the security department (Jewel, 1992). These rules and procedures should provide security personnel with a clearly delineated picture of restrictions and limitations, and what specific behaviors are expected of the staff within the scope of their employment. This area is a constant source of legal headaches for a facility.

It is vital that all employees, from administration to ticket-takers, understand facility policies and required responses. Any problem that arises must be resolved quickly, with limited public knowledge of the incident. A facility that has stringent policies and procedures that are developed for the protection of patrons will help reduce liability.

Alcohol

The majority of patron problems involve the excessive consumption of alcohol. However, most of today's facilities have minimized this problem by adopting strict policy guidelines pertaining to alcohol distribution during events. The essence of this policy is that there are specified times within a game, concert, or other event when alcohol will not be available for sale. To ensure that this policy is adhered to strictly, beverage sellers should be educated to recognize signs of unacceptable intoxication or purchases attempted by underage patrons. Even with strict policies concerning alcohol consumption, problems are inevitable.

SAFETY AND MEDICAL SERVICES

An emergency is any incident or situation that has resulted in, or could cause, the injury of employees, patrons, or visitors. Examples of potential emergency situations are bad weather, fire, bomb threat, medical emergency, airplane crash, utility loss, and hazardous material. These situations can occur in a facility at any time, but how prepared are facilities to handle them when the situation arises?

Authority

It is important that a definitive chain of command be established to maximize coordination and direction in emergency situations and to quickly deal with such emergencies. During any event in a public facility, a staff member should be empowered with the authority to take charge and make decisions when a problem arises. This staff member is usually the **event coordinator** or the operations manager, whose responsibility is to ensure that every facet of the event goes according to schedule and that problems are resolved in a professional and timely manner.

Emergency response training

Response to an emergency situation by the facility staff must be prompt and professional. The difference between a well-trained response and an erratic, poorly trained response could be the difference between life and death. An emergency response plan should be devised for all perceivable emergency situations. It is vital to thoroughly train all personnel who will most likely be involved in these response procedures.

Emergency response procedures

Each facility is unique—different from all other facilities—so, it is necessary for each facility to develop its own emergency response procedures. A detailed plan covers facility staffing, physical attributes, event type and classification, and type and numbers of appropriate emergency medical personnel per event. Constant communication with emergency medical staff, strategically positioned with the necessary response equipment and supplies, is required for immediate and appropriate reaction.

Emergency procedures are vital in large-scale situations, such as a bomb threat, a fire, or a mechanical

Date _____

Time _____

Keep caller talking. Give excuses (can't hear, bad connection, etc.)

Caller's message (exact) _____
_____
_____

Where is the bomb? _____

What time will it go off? _____

What does it look like? _____

What kind of bomb is it? _____

Why are you doing this? _____

Who are you? _____

Details of caller

Man/ Woman/ Child   Old/ Young

Voice: loud – soft – raspy – high pitch – pleasant – deep – intoxicated

Manner: calm – angry – rational – irrational – coherent – incoherent – emotional
          righteous – laughing

Speech: fast – slow – distinct – distorted – stutter – nasal – slurred – lisp

Background noises: Factory – trains – planes – bedlam – animals – music – quiet –
          office machines – voices – street – party – kids

Language: excellent – good – fair – poor – foul

Accent: local – foreign – race

DO NOT DISCUSS THE CALL WITH ANYONE ELSE!

FIGURE 13-1   Bomb threat procedure.

failure (Figure 13-1 provides a bomb threat procedure). In each instance, a specific procedure should be followed to ensure maximum safety. An evacuation plan must be understood and implemented correctly by the entire facility staff. Safe evacuation of patrons, in a professional and orderly manner, will minimize panic and resultant injuries. In most large facilities, ramps and other nonmechanical exit devices are employed in emergency situations; elevators or escalators should not be used under any circumstances. When an unusual situation develops, where no specific plan has been established, management must select the most appropriate and efficient response choice.

_____

CONCEPT CHECK

Establishing security and emergency procedures is of the utmost importance when managing a facility.

Improper security procedures can result in the injury of patrons and lawsuits against the facility. Providing emergency services also has legal ramifications, but the facility is ethically bound to provide a safe and enjoyable environment.

HOUSEKEEPING AND MAINTENANCE

Housekeeping and maintenance are functions designed to keep a facility clean and prepared for patrons. The task of cleaning a facility is one that cannot be underestimated.

Housekeeping in a facility is not like cleaning a house because the areas to be cleaned and maintained are vast and varying: bleacher seats, portable seats, large restrooms, loges, carpets, tile and concrete floors, and numerous stairwells, elevators, and upholstered seats, to name just a few.

Maintenance and housekeeping duties consist of many different functions and responsibilities. Maintenance components include structural maintenance, equipment maintenance, **setup** and **breakdown** of events, and custodial functions (Jewel, 1992). Maintenance management also requires awareness of and adherence to federal and state regulations, as well as the ability to implement preventive maintenance and safety plans within the facility. Housekeeping is the physical cleaning and arrangement of the facility and its furnishings. (Figure 13-2 can be used as a guide for a maintenance schedule.)

Once the general mission statement has been developed, a plan for housekeeping and maintenance should be established. Management should consider the facility type, location, relationship to other facilities in the community, traffic access, usage level, types of groups using the facility, available labor, sources of revenues, and financial bottom-line responsiveness. This plan should establish guidelines concerning purpose, operation, storage, staffing, inventory, repair, and safety:

- Purpose: A facility should provide clean, well-organized, and safe spaces and equipment for events, lessees, and audiences.
- Operation: To operate effectively, a facility should have space and equipment set according to event requirements before the lessee's move-in time. It should operate the event efficiently by answering all late requests in a timely manner and maintaining

an acceptable level of cleanliness in all areas during the event. Every attempt should be made to prevent safety violations. At the close of any event, all equipment should be secured, all refuse should be disposed of, spaces and equipment should be cleaned and returned to their original status, and all deficiencies should be reported and corrected in a timely manner.
- Storage: The storage of equipment should allow for quick identification and inventory; maximum space utilization; convenience to using area; protection against tearing, bending, scarring, water or dust accumulation, broken parts, and/or damage of any other kind; proper spacing; and safe handling.
- Operations staff: The operations staff should be organized into two or three departments, such as housekeeping/arrangements, engineering, or technical. These areas may be further subdivided. The housekeeping/arrangements section could be subdivided into such groups as (1) set-up crew(s), providing for set-up and striking events, and (2) deep-cleaning crew, which would be scheduled to complete major cleaning tasks, such as carpet shampooing, tile stripping and waxing, and glass washing.
- Housekeeping/arrangements: All set-up crews should be comprised of a foreman, one or more leadmen, and part-time workers as required. These crews will operate 8 hours per shift, 3 shifts per day, 7 days per week.

CONCEPT CHECK

A clean and well-maintained environment does much to improve the mood of the patrons. Housekeeping and maintenance should have high priority when managing a facility.

BOX OFFICE

The box office is probably one of the most important areas involved in sport facilities today. The box office, although not a complicated operation, is the public's initial contact with the facility and the entity that financially drives the operation, collecting the majority of revenue for all events.

Concourse Restroom Maintenance

Condition of restrooms at the start of shift

MEN EAST_____   WOMEN EAST_____
MEN NORTH_____   WOMEN NORTH (2)_____
MEN WEST_____   WOMEN WEST_____
MEN S.E. _____   WOMEN S. (2) _____
MEN S.W. _____   WOMEN S.W. _____

Record of maintenance during shift

Restrooms	Time (maintained and/ or checked)					
MEN EAST						
WOMEN EAST						
MEN NORTH						
WOMEN NORTH (2)						
MEN WEST						
WOMEN WEST						
MEN S.E.						
WOMEN S. (2)						
MEN S.W.						
WOMEN S.W.						

Maintenance needed or repairs to be made: _____
_____
_____

Attendants on duty: _____ Date:_____

FIGURE 13-2   A sample maintenance schedule.

Too often the box office area is the least-thought-about area in facility planning. It is assumed that people will tolerate confusion and discomfort to buy a ticket for a desirable event. This may be true, but to make patrons feel good about spending their money, the box office should be organized and easily accessible to the customer.

The size of the box office area should accommodate the sale and distribution of tickets. An adequate number of windows should be available to handle an unexpected number of **walk-up sales**. It is suggested that sales windows be located on all sides of the facility rather than just at the main entrance to the facility (Jewel, 1992).

To adequately serve the public, it is suggested that each sales window be capable of selling the entire price range of tickets and generate sales of 400-700 tickets during the night. (This figure will vary depending on the type of ticket-selling machines that are being used and the speed of the machines' operator. Therefore it is safe to assume that if you have an 18,000-seat facility it should have 18-24 windows available for ticket sales. Although this is an optimum number of windows, most sport facilities will not have enough space for this many windows. The above ratio of windows to projected sales is a useful rule of thumb, and with good record keeping and the use of historical data, one can gauge the number of ticket windows needed for a particular event. Nothing will turn a patron off faster than having to wait in line for a ticket and miss part of an event because of poor planning by the facility.

The main entrance to the facility should contain about 40% of the ticket-selling windows, with the other 60% distributed among the other entry areas of the arena. Box office lobbies should be of sufficient size to allow patrons to line up in front of the windows. (Remember, few people stand in line alone; the entire family or groups of friends stand in line together.)

Under normal circumstances, a covered area 30-50 feet deep should be provided in front of the selling windows. If possible, some ticket windows should be located on the outside of the building. This will allow for ticket sales in several locations and prevent lines from backing up against the turnstiles, which are generally adjacent to the ticket-selling windows. An outside ticket-selling window is also a good idea for the sale of tickets for future events, which would permit the sales without the need to open the building.

All box office windows should be located outside the turnstiles in an area that is easily accessible to the public. Specific windows should be designated for will-call and reservations, preferably in a separate area away from the main entrance. These windows tend to cater to the repeat business patron, and a separate window and entrance seem to promote future sales.

Box office personnel

Depending upon the size and mission of a facility, personnel number and designation vary considerably. As an important operational part of a facility, the box office requires a minimum number of full-time staff. Normally, the box office manager and two or three assistants are the only full-time staff members, with the remaining employees hired as part-time personnel.

The box office manager has the sole responsibility for the box office operation and supervision of all personnel. This individual is responsible for ordering, selling, and distributing event tickets, as well as for the final box office statement. Policy development, personnel selection and placement, safety, and discipline of box office personnel are additional responsibilities. The box office manager and his/her assistants work closely with promoters and all facility operations personnel.

Box office policies

Box office policies are relatively uncomplicated, with the ultimate goal to provide an efficient and secure service-oriented operation. Employees should be instructed in appropriate dress and attitude. Areas of policy should include

- Courtesy toward patrons
- Familiarity with event seating
- Efficient ticket processing

Working conditions

The box office generally operates from 8:30 A.M. to 4:30 P.M. on nonevent days and until intermission on event days, depending on ticket demand.

Public relations

All personnel should be instructed about the appropriate techniques for meeting and greeting the ticket-purchasing public and about proper dress and etiquette.

Equipment operations

Equipment operations include ticket counters (tickets divided into numerical sequence, by price breaks, or by rows and sections according to the seating plan); cash drawers for cash placement and stub count at the end of the day; computer terminals and printers for printing computerized tickets; cash registers; and telephones and answering machines to provide messages and record ticket orders.

Sales policies

When tickets are sold, all transactions involving the sale are final for the specific event. When an event has concluded, it is vital that all ticket sales, after accounting for unsold and complimentary tickets, equal the revenue generated. In other words, capacity minus total tickets sold equals unsold tickets plus appropriate evidence for all transactions.

Refunds and exchanges

The general rule is that *no* refunds or exchanges should take place. All sales are final. This rule results from the fact that the facility and its personnel are agents for the promoter and do not make the rules. Any refund or exchange policy must be approved in writing by the facility contractor or promoter.

Telephone orders

Procuring tickets by telephone is usually acceptable as long as certain restrictions are in place:

- A ticket for a seat should be held for only 3 days.
- Telephone ticket orders should be accepted only if the promoter and facility management agree that this would be an appropriate sales method to be employed for a specific event. Telephone sales should be event-specific.
- All telephone orders should be recorded as cash transactions.

Mail orders

For convenience, patrons should be permitted to order tickets through the mail. This not only creates another avenue to sell tickets for that specific event, but permits the facility to provide information concerning future events when the tickets are returned to the patron.

Will call

Every facility should establish a **will-call location**. It is imperative that when a patron arrives for ticket pick-up, proper identification is produced before the tickets are provided to the patron.

Lost tickets

Refunds and exchanges are subject to the agreement of the promoter (see above). However, in the case of a ticket lost prior to the event, the ticket manager should have the discretion to issue a duplicate ticket and void the original ticket. If the ticket manager decides that the patron should purchase a new ticket, then the original ticket can be returned to the box office for a full refund prior to the performance. This lost-ticket policy impacts on the facility's image, and every effort to resolve the situation should be encouraged without exceeding the limitations of prescribed authority.

Ticket purchases

The numbers of tickets purchased by a patron is up to the discretion of the box office manager and subject to the agreement of the promoter. There is usually no set limit to the number of tickets purchased.

Scalping

Scalping can be a serious problem; and although the facility and box office can do little to combat scalping, there are usually local laws that address the problem. In fact, most authorities arrest and fine scalpers.

Ticketing variables

There are a number of elements concerned with ticket sales and operations, such as the following:

- Capacity: The box office should strive to maximize revenue by selling every seat in the facility. It should be remembered that the configuration and capacity of each event is different, depending on the event type and requirements.
- Seating: There are two types of seating arrangement in a facility, regardless of configuration: (1) reserved, where a specific seat is designated for each patron. This type of seating arrangement is prevalent at events such as athletic contests and concerts. This arrangement provides the patron with "first come, best seat" when buying tickets. (2) General admission is a seating arrangement used primarily at lower quality, egalitarian productions. This arrangement implies that all patrons purchasing tickets will receive the same quality seating opportunity as those who purchase tickets in advance. Although both methods appear to have inherent inequities, a compromise arrangement is to provide tiered seating prices (e.g., ground floor: $30; 2d floor: $15; etc.), which all professional sport facilities use.
- Ticket type: The ticket is a contract (agreement) between the management/promoter and the purchaser of the seat. The box office manager should deal only with a reputable, bonded ticket company when ordering ticket stock. All tickets should be ordered well in advance of an event, to minimize the

chance of error. This policy should be in place regardless of the ticket type (i.e., ticket roll or computerized tickets). Computerized tickets, although much more expensive than the traditional ticket stock, have certain advantages, such as event information printed on them: name of sponsoring organization, ticket price, program name, performance date and time, facility name and seat location. Also, appropriate advertising can be included on ticket stock.

Ticket sales strategy

Although ticket sales strategy and policy will be codirected by the marketing department, it falls under the purview of the box office. Elements of this strategy are

- Pricing: The box office, the marketing department, and the promoter jointly develop a ticket sales strategy. A decision needs to be made regarding whether tickets will be sold on a **house scale** (i.e., pricing established by the box office) or by a **performance scale** (i.e., pricing established by the event promoter).
- Incentives: There are many traditional types of sales incentives that have been used, including discounted tickets or tickets that make use of unusual seating areas (e.g., standing room) or special circumstances. These are determined by the promoter and/or the box office. Group sales are made to groups for a price reduction, which is beneficial when an event has a lower ticket demand or corporate involvement is required. Season tickets predominate at athletic or theatrical events presented on a seasonal basis.

Daily reporting

A daily transaction or report form—which provides the facility with a record of daily transactions that have occurred, should be completed for all ticket sales, mail orders, and anything else deemed important by management.

Event summary

Although the event summary is prepared by the business office, the box office must initiate the process by providing event information at the conclusion of each event. The information should cover ticket prices; ticket categories, including complimentary or other special ticket classifications; and the number of tickets sold and unsold.

Computer ticket management

As facilities investigate various options to minimize personnel costs, eliminate cumbersome operational procedures, and become "auditor-friendly," a computerized ticket system is an ideal solution. This computer-operated system is dependent on software options. It provides the box office with patron information at the **point of sale**, organized either alphabetically, by postal code, or by subscriber number; a computerized mailing list, updated daily, which can be used for notification of upcoming events or to solicit patron response for a specified performance; and the ability to monitor ticket sales versus marketing efforts. If money is spent on advertising or direct-mail solicitations, these promotional efforts need to be compared to ticket sales.

Alternative revenue sources

Although some alternative revenue sources have been mentioned previously, they are important in ensuring profitability.

CONCEPT CHECK

The box office of a facility has enormous responsibilities. It must make sure that patrons can purchase tickets and enter the facility in a timely fashion. And because large quantities of cash are handled by the box office, reliable staffing is a must. Finally, the staff must be courteous because the box office is the first contact the patron will have with the facility's personnel.

CONCESSIONS AND NOVELTIES

A facility's food service is the business operation that prepares, delivers, and sells food and beverages to customers. There are three forms of food service operations: concessions, catering, and novelties (which includes programs). In this presentation, catering will be included in the area of concessions.

Concessions

Concessions play a vital role in the success of a facility. A well-operated concessions department is frequently a major determining factor in the financial success of any sport facility. It is an accepted fact that food and drink go hand in hand with sports and recreation.

For example, during 1989-1990, the Superdome in New Orleans reported that concessions revenue amounted to $7.5 million, or 60% of its operating revenue. At a smaller sport facility, Fogelman Basketball Arena at Tulane University, a 72% net profit was reported on concessions operations in the facility in 1990.

In order for a concessions operation in a facility to survive, much more than serving good food at a reasonable price is required. It demands that management has a knowledge of marketing, financial management, business planning, purchasing, inventory management, business law, insurance, advertising, and personnel.

Stocking

Stocking is an important component of the concessions operation. The manager must initially decide which products to purchase based upon quality, price, service, and customer acceptance. The staff of a facility often taste-tests items to determine the best products. Today, the most popular foods appear to be hot dogs, nachos, popcorn, peanuts, soft drinks, and beer.

When deciding on the quality of products, one should scrutinize past records carefully. Nonperishable items (e.g., cups, napkins, and other paper goods) should be purchased in large quantities for the whole season. Perishable or time-sensitive items (e.g., hot dogs and buns) must be ordered fresh for every event. In large facilities, restocking takes about 1 week, while in smaller facilities it takes approximately 5 hours. Some interesting facts about concessions are:

- Beer and alcohol account for a high percentage of concession profits.
- Popcorn is probably the largest revenue producer in terms of margin. The cost of a box of popcorn is about 5 cents, while patrons pay $2.00-$2.50 a serving.
- Concessions sales are constant 1 hour before a game; and 80% of sales take place at halftime, while only about 20% of sales take place after halftime.

Convenience foods

All the foods in concession stands are called convenience foods. There are three types of **convenience foods** that facilities stock: frozen, powdered, and dehydrated. Frozen foods include a large selection of fruit juices and meat, in a variety of sizes from individual servings to amounts sufficient for volume feeding. Dehydrated and powdered foods are appropriate for facilities because they can be stored for long periods of time without spoilage and are often packaged in bulk. They require only water or a short period of cooking for reconstitution. Some of the dehydrated and powdered foods on the market today are seasonings, soups of many varieties, milk, pastry mixes, sauces, gravies, and beverages.

The wide variety of convenience foods available enables concession stands to present a varied menu to the public and permits employees with limited knowledge and little training to prepare appetizing "fail-proof" dishes. Convenience foods enable operators to save money, time and labor, especially in the areas of cleaning, trimming, packaging, storing, cooking and serving.

The development of convenience foods and disposable packaging, containers, and utensils has enabled food service operations to become efficient and practical. Disposable products in common use are semirigid foil pans, plastic pouches, foil and plastic packets, foam containers, cardboard containers, and other disposable items, such as plates, cups, eating utensils, doilies, aprons, and uniforms. Boil-in-a-pouch and chemically generated foods have been developed to reduce both cooking time and cost.

Other developments involve foil and plastic packets that encase individual servings of condiments (e.g., tomato sauces, mayonnaise, salt, pepper, etc.) and foam or cardboard containers preshaped for specific carryout items. These disposable products enable minimally trained labor, with minimal equipment, to serve a variety of well-prepared convenience foods and other products that are easy to stock and dispense. These products also reduce sanitation problems.

The concessions operation should not only stock good food but also have adequate storage space and an appropriate location(s) for the spectators. In large facilities, service elevators are located near the various storage areas and near all seats. There should be enough concession stands to serve the total number of seats, and any patron should be able to reach the nearest food stand in about 40-60 seconds.

Concessions advertising

Concessions operations should be bright, colorful, well lit and decorated with attractive pictures of the food and beverages being served. Menu boards should be installed to clearly indicate products and prices. Signage should be in neon that is not the same color as the building. At large facilities, pictures of food should be displayed on the menu board. Pictures of brand name products, easily recognized by customers, eliminate questions about the quality of the merchandise. Further, to keep lines moving, most menus should list all prices in increments of 25 cents. Simple combinations should be listed on the menu in large, readable print to provide direction for the customer and to eliminate complex orders that can result in lost sales or patrons missing a portion of the event while waiting in line for food.

Concessions should be well organized, with clear indications of where patrons should line up for service. Equipment, food, and cash registers should be conveniently located so that customers can be quickly served by a single person in each selling section. It is important that employees be trained to manage large crowds and keep lines moving. At the same time, they should be encouraged to increase sales through suggestive selling techniques. They should attempt to convince the customer that all items are reasonably priced and that buying a larger size actually results in saving money.

Alcoholic beverages

In a facility operation, alcoholic beverages are the most profitable segment of the concessions operation. In fact, alcohol and beer manufacturers sponsor facilities and events to promote their products. There is a downside to this situation, of course, especially when there is community opposition to the sale of alcohol in the facility, particularly to the underaged and individuals who may drive an automobile after the event has concluded.

Another element that needs to be considered is the liability that the facility can incur if an accident occurs involving a patron who indulged in alcohol while attending a facility event. There have been lawsuits won by patrons where the facility, event, and concessionaire all have been held liable for fights or injuries due to the consumption of alcohol.

Concession maintenance

Employees should keep themselves well groomed and their workplace clean because customers may have a negative reaction to employees or concession stands that appear to be unclean. Large facilities usually employ a supervisor for every concession stand, and no employee is allowed to leave until the stands are spotless. At some large facilities (e.g., the Superdome, with 10,000-12,000 employees working concessions annually), most of the employees belong to nonprofit groups, such as softball leagues, Girl Scouts, Boy Scouts, or church groups, who volunteer their labor, with each group receiving a percentage of sales. To ensure cleanliness and compliance with health guidelines, floor drains and adequate ventilation and exhaust systems must be installed in stand and kitchen areas.

At the end of an event, employees must cope with a significant volume of refuse from disposable products. This debris should be removed through incineration, which requires a minimal amount of space because the paper items and some plastics are reduced to ash. A second method is to use a shredding machine that converts plastics and paper into a pulp by removing excess water and shredding the fiber. A third method, compression, packs refuse under pressure to reduce its size for ease of removal.

Hawkers/vendors

Another highly profitable aspect of the concessions operation is **vendors**, or **hawkers**, who take food or beverages to the patrons in their seats. Hawkers generate substantial sales because many patrons want food and beverage service but do not want to miss any of the event.

Trends

Recent trends in concessions operations now provide name brand products (e.g., Popeye's Chicken and Domino's Pizza), for which the facility receives a percentage of sales. In the near future, many of the items served at concession stands will be more healthful foods, such as soup and salads. There will probably also be specialty operations, such as a sweet shop with a large assortment of candies or a hot dog shop with several combinations (e.g., cheese dog, chili dog, onion dog, or turkey dog). In the beverage area, there is often a demand during rush periods at sporting events for fast bar service. To satisfy this demand, computers have been used to control the mixing and pouring of any one of 1000 beverages in 4 seconds, with the liquor content in each being uniform.

Another recent innovation is to place frozen foods in an oven drawer and set a timer. After the correct time has elapsed, the oven automatically turns off and the door opens. The advantages of this innovative cooking equipment are that it saves time and requires much less space than conventional equipment.

Along with the recent trends of serving brand name products, more healthful foods, specialty shops, and new equipment for bartending and cooking, new packaging has been developed. For example, the package of the future may be a rigid aluminum foil dish and cover with a pull tab, containing a hamburger, french fries, condiments, and wipe-and-dry towels. Pulling the tab before opening the cover will break a heat capsule that after 30 seconds will bring the contents to eating temperature. The ultimate development would be self-destruction of the container when its cover is replaced.

Food safety and sanitation practices

To control food contamination and the spread of disease, every employee must have knowledge of basic food safety and sanitation practices. Food services attract all types of bacteria, insects, and animal pests because they provide them with the three basic ingredients necessary to sustain life: food, water, and warmth.

To eliminate contamination, food service management needs to inspect delivery vehicles to ensure that they are properly refrigerated and sanitary. All products should be accredited and inspected by the appropriate government agencies. Upon delivery, crates or boxes should never be stored outside when unloading because insects can infest them and be introduced into the concessions operation. In addition, all spills should be cleaned up as soon as they occur, and food should be refrigerated until needed and cooked as soon as possible.

Another important way to inhibit food contamination is personal hygiene. Every employee must be aware that hands are a primary source of contamination. Every time employees scratch their head or sneeze, they are exposing their hands to bacteria that will spread to anything they touch. All employees should practice basic hygiene methods. For example, they should have short or controlled hair, clean hands and short nails, a daily shower or bath, clean clothes, and no unnecessary jewelry; be clean shaven; and not smoke in the proximity of the food and beverages. In addition, ill employees should not attend work, because they can expose the food preparation and service areas to bacterial contamination.

In most communities, there are regulations that affect food service operations. In fact, most employees are mandated to pass some form of medical examination (e.g., tuberculosis test) and complete a written examination concerning the handling of food.

Novelties

The success of novelty sales depends upon applying the appropriate formula to each situation. The following are four different novelty formulas that have been traditionally used:

- Flat fee: This negotiated fee is paid directly to the facility, usually for a nonticketed event (e.g., meetings, school graduations, or religious services). This fee should be collected in advance or be part of the deposit.
- Percentage of vendor sales: This is a common fee arrangement wherein the vendor pays the facility a percentage of the sales, ranging from 5% to 20%, depending upon the parties involved, facility, and event.
- Percentage of facility sales: In this arrangement, the facility, which is responsible for inventory and all sales, receives a percentage of total sales. This is a profitable method for the facility operation and is preferred because the facility knows the amount of inventory on hand and controls its flow. At the close of an event, with the final inventory completed, the vendor will receive a percentage of sales,

ranging between 55% and 75%. The facility will then pay the sellers out of the facility's percentage of sales, which could range from 5% to 20%.

■ Fee per person: This method is profitable for the facility and the easiest to handle by all parties. The vendor agrees to pay the facility a set amount per person in attendance, including complimentary tickets. The fee will vary from event to event, depending upon the attraction and vendor items and may range from 1 cent to 25 cents per person. This fee should be collected in advance or by the first intermission, based on anticipated attendance or house capacity.

Sales personnel

Training can make a difference in the simple areas, such as appearance, uniforms, and the attitude of the vendors. However, training how to sell is extremely important if the operation is to generate profit. Another factor is the employment of experienced novelty-sales personnel. Although anyone can sell T-shirts or novelties, it takes a special ability, developed by experience, to generate the type of sales desired in a novelty operation.

Shoplifting is not limited to retail outlets. Novelty personnel should be trained to control their stock so that the only items that leave the stands are those that are sold. This is extremely important at such events as concerts, where a large number of people will want to purchase T-shirts and other items.

Splits and deals

If an event threatens to bypass the market and facility because of a better novelty deal in another facility, reworking the deal and split should be considered. There is no accepted standard formula to follow, because competition between facilities will dictate the requirements and generate the business.

Bootlegging

It is common practice for most major events, where novelties are sold, to obtain a federal injunction regarding copyright law infringement. This provides police with the authority to confiscate unauthorized merchandise and/or arrest its vendors. Local ordinances that govern the sale of items on the street can be most beneficial in eliminating **bootleggers**.

CONCEPT CHECK

Most patrons know that they will be paying more for food and other items within a facility. It is important that the sales staff and the products must be of the highest quality. Patrons are becoming more and more demanding of concessions, and the facility must rise to meet these expectations.

TRAFFIC AND PARKING

Traffic flow is an extremely important part of a patron's visit to a major facility. There are two main components of traffic flow: the flow on the public streets to the facility and the flow within the parking lot if there is on-site parking. Figure 13-3 is a sample organizational roster that can be used to ensure that personnel are properly assigned to assist the flow of traffic in a facility's parking lot.

Although public streets are controlled by either the local police or the state highway patrol, the facility should make every effort to coordinate traffic flow in its lots with that of the public streets. One of the most common complaints at events that draw very large audiences is the time it takes to get into and leave the facility's parking lots. A trend in some of the newer facilities being built in urban areas is to take advantage of public transportation (trains and buses).

There are three common revenue-generating methods appropriate for a facility: a direct collection on a per-car basis; a dollar charge per ticket issued; and a flat rate for specific events. Additional sources of parking revenue can be generated from selling preferred, personalized parking spaces; per-event, all-event, season, or annual parking passes; valet parking for VIP parking at a standard fee per automobile; and marketing parking lots for new or antique cars, motor homes, ski or boat shows, carnivals, food festivals, grand prix races, driver safety school, and swap meets.

FINANCIAL MANAGEMENT

Every sport facility operation should have a business operations unit. In small facility operations,

Parking Personnel Posting Sheet

Event:_____   Date: _____

Supervisors: _____   Supervisors:_____

_____   _____

Cashiers:

West: (1) _____

         (2) _____ _____

         (3) _____ Leader

Center: (4) _____

         (5) _____ _____

         (6) _____ Leader

East#1 (7) _____

         (8) _____ _____

East#2 (9) _____ Leader

       (10) _____ _____

       (11) _____ Leader

North (12) _____

       (13) _____

       (14) _____ _____

       (15) _____ Leader

Time out:

East#1 : (1) _____(2)_____(3)_____

East#2 : (1) _____(2)_____(3)_____

West# : (1) _____(2)_____(3)_____

North#: (1) _____(2)_____(3)_____

Center : (1) _____(2)_____(3)_____

Misc Info:_____

_____

_____

Attendants:

East#1: (1) _____ (5)_____

       (2) _____ (6)_____

       (3) _____ (7)_____

       (4) _____ (8)_____

East#2: (1) _____ (5)_____

       (2) _____ (6)_____

       (3) _____ (7)_____

       (4) _____ (8)_____

West: (1) _____ (5)_____

       (2) _____ (6)_____

       (3) _____ (7)_____

       (4) _____ (8)_____

North: (1) _____ (5)_____

       (2) _____ (6)_____

       (3) _____ (7)_____

       (4) _____ (8)_____

Center (1) _____ (5)_____

Lot: (2) _____ (6)_____

       (3) _____ (7)_____

North (4) _____ (8)_____

Reserve: (1) _____ (2)_____

Loge: (1) _____ (2)_____

Point: (1) _____ (2)_____

FIGURE 13-3   Parking personnel posting sheet.

much of this function is delegated to one individual and the remainder, especially the tedious, time-consuming tasks, is contracted to an outside organization.

General accounting and finance concepts, for the most part, will be left to other courses that deal in depth with these functions. Discussion in this chapter will focus on the essential elements of the facility business operation: type and process, white papers, event settlement, auditing, payroll, risk management, and bad debts.

Budget

Although a sports facility operates on a day-to-day basis, the most important element of business operations is the development of the budget document. A budget is simply an estimate of receipts and payments for a period of time, usually 1 or 2 years. It is also important as a predictive tool, for it can anticipate the flow of revenues and expenditures and be used as a tool of control. A budget is a guide to the financial expectations of a facility and an expression of management's plans (Garrison, 1982).

Political: government budget process

Most sport facilities today are involved in one way or another with government. It is critical for a general manager to have some knowledge of the political process and methodology pertaining to the public budgeting process.

Most state and local governments operate on periods longer than 1 year—in many cases, a biennium (2 years). Therefore, budget requests for public sport facilities may have to be submitted 1 ½ years prior to actual budget appropriation. By necessity, this projected budget is limited in scope and detail and is often inaccurate. Frequently, expenses are inflated and income deflated because of the numerous hearings, volatile economies, and the political nature of the budget process. Even though the final approved budget may seem to be "carved in stone," if the desired bottom line is not reached, political advocates can lobby for an adjustment to the budget.

Operational budget process

The submission of a budget request to a government agency does not hinder internal budget operations. Operational budget submissions are usually prepared up to 60 days before actual implementation. This time limitation provides limited flexibility when compared to the governmental product.

Budget cycle

There are four phases in the **budget cycle**: preparation, presentation and adoption, execution and postexecution, and audit.

The preparation of the budget begins with the establishment of the facility's mission, goals, and objectives. The overall objective of the entire process of preparing the budget is to end up with a budget which is coordinated into a well-balanced program. The program impact is the heart of any budget justification that allows the facility to achieve the stated mission if . . . given the requested resources (IAAM, 1990).

The next step is the actual preparation of financial data, which requires a review of past budget items. After review, the new financial data and their justifications are submitted as a draft that, hopefully, is acceptable to management. These materials provide information concerning the levels of personnel services, wages, benefits, materials, supplies, utilities, and services for the facility operation.

The presentation of a draft or revised budget document is a political process, particularly in large facilities. Initially, the budget document is circulated among proactive supporters for their input and approval. This document should be clear and precise and include any supporting documentation (e.g., letters, charts, comparison statistics, etc.) that may provide the reader with insight and understanding. After the supporters review the document and suggest changes, the revised document is circulated to the entire audience. At this time, the budget preparers must be ready to defend the document in an open forum. As soon as the document is approved and adopted by the assemblage, it is ready for interpretation and execution.

Once the budget is adopted, senior management (especially the general manager,) is charged with its dissemination among the various facility departments. All budgeted groups, such as operations or engineering and maintenance, are obligated to maintain control over spending, using techniques such as monthly statements to maintain control of expenditures. Monthly meetings are recommended to ascertain whether budget goals and objectives are on target or need adjustment. It is important to remember that while certain budget limits are carved in stone, the budget document is flexible enough for some accommodation. Any substantial shift in facility goals and objectives will require a budget review and revision. The budget document and resulting implementation then must be altered accordingly. However, the prime directive, regardless of potential alterations, is to achieve the mission, goals, and objectives established at the outset of the process.

Simply put, this procedure evaluates whether or not all the budget assumptions were achieved and the mission fulfilled. In any budgeting situation, it is critical that fiscal budget limitations be adhered to. Overspending in any budget situation, private or public, is unacceptable. The evaluation process determines the level of success and is employed in the development of the next budget document.

Facility accounting

Accounting within a sport facility is similar to that of any other business operation. The only exception is that the operations involved with government demands are simpler and need not be responsive to stockholders, unlike a private facility operation.

However, accounting procedures generally involve three fundamental accounting disclosures:

1. Managerial (internal) accounting is based on projections resulting from income and financial data. This information will be used to guide management's decision making efforts.
2. Financial (external) account reports primarily involve an income statement, a balance sheet, and a cash flow statement. These reports are subject to auditing and must conform to the **generally accepted accounting procedures (GAAP)** that are used by accountants in preparing such reports (Walgenbach, Dittrich, and Hansen, 1980). External reports are not tax reports.
3. Tax accounting reports that are compiled in accordance with the guidelines of the taxation authority (i.e., the Internal Revenue Service).

All external communications are subject to an annual audit by an independent auditing firm, to report the financial status of the organization. It is important that these audits be objective and unbiased because the confidence of the public, as well as the stockholders or bondholders, is important to the future financial health of the facility management organization.

Event settlement

The **event settlement** process uses procedures normally involved in cost accounting or managerial accounting. This procedure is used to compute the operational costs of producing an event. Evaluation of this data guides management decisions, which in turn affect future events.

There are two costing systems employed in this event settlement procedure. The first is process costing, which is primarily used in industry and costs the entire operational process. The second is job order costing, where costs or expenses, such as labor and overhead, are identified by the job. The job order costing method is better suited to the special-order production needs of a sport facility (Davidson and others, 1988).

Sport facilities should analyze cost data both before and after an event settlement because they will (1) provide an operational measure in terms of dollars generated, (2) assist management in economic and negotiating decisions, (3) justify the need for greater funding, resources, and reimbursement, and (4) provide accountability. If an item is overlooked in the development of a settlement estimate at the end of an event, the facility or management group will have to suffer the loss, because recuperation will be impossible.

Any services associated with the production of an event are channeled into the costing of that event. These sources known as **house expenses**, include such things as a plumber retained to unstop toilets and prevent a potential flood; stagehands and light operators; a specific facility setup configuration, such as a basketball floor; and the security guard assigned to the box office to protect the facility's deposits against theft. These services cannot be charged to the event promoter because they are the responsibility of the facility and are not recoverable cost items.

A cost accounting system enables the facility business office to itemize detailed contractual elements of the event/promotion and those that define the responsibilities of the facility's management (Garrison, 1982). Expenses must be collated and recorded; otherwise, facility management will absorb these expenses rather than pass them on to the promoter. The event settlement process, especially at a concert, usually begins about midway through the performance and may conclude before the end of the show. The only real concern after settlement is completed is that the show does not run over the projected time allotment; in that case, additional costs accrue to the facility management.

If the event settlement process has not been completed before the event has ended and the promoter has left, the likelihood of recapturing one's investment is probably "slim to none." Groups that have a good reputation and have been dealt with successfully over the years build up a level of trust and are considered stable operations. Their events are usually resolved within 10 days of the event closure. With all other events, a facility would normally require a hefty deposit. In fact, it would be expected that in the majority of cases the rent would be paid 30 days in advance, rather than after the event.

Policies covering event settlement procedures are event-specific and part of the facility management philosophy. The bottom line is that every penny the facility spends for an event that is caused by the event must be accounted for and, hopefully, fully recovered by the facility.

Auditing

Regardless of business classification or location, safeguarding management's operating and financial controls are the objective of the audit process. There are two segments of the auditing process: the internal audit and external audit (Walgenbach, Dittrich, and Hansen, 1980).

Internal audit. The internal audit is a management tool that ensures that the company's assets are used properly and safeguarded at all levels. It is vital that all employees adhere to company policy and follow established procedures. There are two crucial elements within this **internal auditing process**: asset security and personnel compliance. Asset security involves the internal accounting control procedures. Substantial losses sometimes occur due to the theft of products or funds or the misuse of funds or equipment. It is important to realize that every employee is a *potential* thief. Personnel compliance attempts to provide personnel with operational guidelines to protect both the employee and the organization from potential future litigation. Appropriate supervision of employees should include random visitations to a facility—at night, on the weekend, or at unusual times. Management should attempt to vary its visits and not be predictable.

It is prudent to establish a paper trail, which is a collection of documents that can be used in an audit to substantiate any transactions involving the exchange of goods. Cash register tapes, purchase orders, requisitions, checks, contracts, ticket sale reports, and concession reports are often part of this paper trail. This information should be retained in the event of litigation arising out of employee dishonesty.

External audit. An **external audit** examines the organizational accounting records and financial statements to make certain that they are appropriately prepared and not misleading. The external auditor, usually a certified public accountant (CPA), tests and checks the accounting system underlying the financial statements, using the accepted American Institute of Certified Public Accountants (AICPA) auditing standards. This exter-

nal audit is known as the *attest function*, which provides independent assurance as to whether appropriate procedures have been used.

Problem resolution

The internal auditing process should be an ongoing practice by management throughout the year, while the required external audit can be quarterly, although it is usually annual. Both these audit processes are necessary to maintain the financial health and credibility of an organization. If an individual or group that is trusted and holds security clearance is involved in a facility problem, the penalty should be quick and should fit the crime. It is important that an example be set for all personnel. Management must have extremely tight control because its credibility is on the line. If there is any infraction or other problem, swift action must be initiated to resolve the situation, keeping in mind any potential fallout.

Payroll

Payroll in a facility denotes, as in any other business, the compensation paid to employees on a regular basis. In a sport facility operation, the majority of employees are seasonal and part-time (employed no more than 37 hours per week). These employees are usually paid on a weekly basis at an hourly rate. Full-time employees (employed at least 40 hours a week) are paid biweekly or monthly. Overtime pay begins when an employee works more than 40 hours a week. The rate of pay for this overtime is 1 ½ times the regular rate. Unionized employees are sometimes reimbursed at higher rates. Full-time employment is classified as either staff or management. The staff (line) classification usually includes hourly employees, while management is paid a salary, regardless of the time spent on the job.

The employee remuneration package consists of both wages/salary and deductions. Examples of some of these deductions are Social Security, federal income taxes withheld, state and local income taxes, state disability insurance, unemployment compensation, and any voluntary employee deductions. The employee's net (take-home) pay is calculated by taking the employee's gross pay (wages earned) and subtracting all the appropriate taxes and other deductions. At the end of the financial year, every employee, regardless of employment status, will receive a W-4 form prepared by the accounting division of the operation.

Payroll represents the largest portion of the total cost of any operation. All records pertaining to payroll must be maintained by the employer to prepare annual tax calculations and support the audit process. To satisfy government, union, and employee expectations, it is important to use a payroll method that is facility-specific and that satisfies all the conditions established. Instead of using a manual payroll operation, a facility can use one of several computer software applications available for calculating payrolls. These can be customized for a facility's special needs.

CONCEPT CHECK

Financial management is an extremely important aspect of facility management. Budget payroll and event settlement are probably the main features of financial management. To successfully manage this area, the facility manager must know something about accounting terminology and procedures.

RISK MANAGEMENT

Risk is defined as a hazard or the possibility of danger or harm. Risk management focuses on limiting exposure to harm to the facility (Berlonghi, 1990). The most common danger that a sport facility manager attempts to minimize is injuries to patrons at the facility, which create the potential for lawsuits. These lawsuits, can cause substantial monetary losses to the sport facility. The obvious goal of minimizing injuries and avoiding lawsuits and monetary losses may sound easy, but in fact it is a very complicated and difficult task to do correctly.

In order to be efficient at this task, the risk manager should identify the possible risks, assess their likelihood, calculate how to respond to the risks, and create standards and procedures (a strategic plan) for decreasing the risks.

Identification stage

In the risk identification stage, the facility manager must discover the various risks that may cause losses during any given event. There are primary and secondary factors that must be addressed in order to reduce the likelihood of losses to the sport facility. Primary factors are the base of operations at every sport facility, and each sport facility manager must consider them when trying to reduce risk. These factors are within almost complete control of the sport facility manager. It should be noted that while a well-trained staff is the risk manager's best tool for identifying risks, staff members can also be risks themselves.

Risk assessment

The assessment of risks should be systematic, using amount and frequency of loss as the two criteria. A matrix can be created that allows a consistent approach to the assessing process. Figure 13-4 gives the sport facility manager 25 categories in which to classify any identified risk.

Risk treatment

The next stage, risk treatment, can also be accomplished with the use of a matrix. As you can see from Figure 13-5, the matrix is now filled with various treatments for risks based on the five frequencies of occurrence and the five amounts of loss.

Avoidance

Clearly, one should avoid risks that cause a great amount of loss or occur frequently. For example, a sport facility should never hold an event that has caused great damage to sport facilities elsewhere or that has equipment that is inherently dangerous, such as diving boards in swimming pools. Holding an event that has caused extensive property damage at other facilities and/or led to lawsuits would not be prudent. This type of event should be avoided altogether. The sport facility manager is an effective risk manager if he or she does not allow such an event to take place in the interest of eliminating all potential losses that might occur.

Transferring risks

This treatment of identified and assessed risks focuses on the sport facility manager's knowledge that certain losses will occur but it is difficult to determine the approximate losses involved and the frequency of occurrence. The matrix has identified these risks more or less as middle of the road risks. Looking at the matrix, however, does reveal that some very high losses are included. We do not

	Very frequent	Frequent	Moderate	Infrequent	Very infrequent
Very high loss					
High loss					
Moderate loss					
Low loss					
Very low loss					

FIGURE 13-4   Risk assessment matrix

	Very frequent	Frequent	Moderate	Infrequent	Very infrequent
Very high loss	Avoid	Avoid	Shift	Shift	Shift
High loss	Avoid	Avoid	Shift	Shift	Shift
Moderate loss	Shift	Shift	Shift	Shift	Keep & Decrease
Low loss	Keep & Decrease	Keep & Decrease	Keep & Decrease	Keep & Decrease	Keep & Decrease
Very low loss	Keep & Decrease	Keep & Decrease	Keep & Decrease	Keep & Decrease	Keep & Decrease

FIGURE 13-5   Risk assessment matrix with treatment for risks and five frequencies of occurrence.

wish to avoid these risks because the frequency of their occurrence is moderate or below. Also, the risks that occur very frequently are moderate and therefore should not be avoided.

Keeping and decreasing risks

The final option for treating risks is to keep the risk and attempt to decrease the amount of loss the risk can cause. We can see in the matrix that risks that are to be kept and decreased are those that have low or very low potential for loss. A sport facility can accept these risks because there is very little chance of suffering substantial losses. Of course, this assumes that once the sport facility manager decides to keep the risk, proper precautions are taken to decrease the occurrence of and the monetary loss associated with

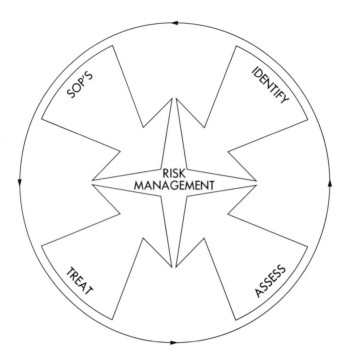

FIGURE 13-6   The risk management process.

the risk. This is accomplished by developing standard operating procedures, which is the final step in the risk management process.

Standard operating procedures

Under **standard operating procedures (SOPs)**, the sport facility manager develops a strategic plan that will provide the most efficient and effective way to decrease the occurrence of risks. The strategic plan is basically a step-by-step set of instructions that give detailed directions for the appropriate courses of action, given the event and the risks associated with it. SOPs should be developed for both risks that are transferred and risks that are kept and decreased. (See Figure 13-6 for an illustration of the risk management process.)

CONCEPT CHECK

It is extremely important to realize that risk management is a dynamic process that must continually be analyzed and modified. By following the risk management process, the facility manager can make the

facility safer for patrons while reducing potential liability situations.

SUMMARY

1. The trend in facility management is toward private management companies rather than in-house operations. Private management companies are solicited through the request-for-proposals (RFP) process.
2. In order to effectively manage a facility, a mission statement—along with policies, procedures, goals, and objectives—must be established.
3. Booking and scheduling deals with obtaining events and contracting with the promoters of the events. It is important to have a good fit between the facility and the event in order for operations to be effective.
4. Marketing and promotions attempt to publicize events and attract patrons to them. Exposure is the key element in the success of the marketing campaign.
5. Proper security and emergency procedures must be developed in order to minimize law-

suits and provide a safe environment for patrons to enjoy the events.

6. The box office is in charge of ticket sales and admissions. It is an extremely important aspect of the facility because it handles a great deal of money and it is the first part of the facility that patrons deal with.

7. Concessions and novelties have become an increasingly important aspect of facility management. Expectations of patrons have increased to the point where concessions need to provide a higher level of food products and other items to meet these expectations.

8. Financial management deals with budgeting, event settlement, and auditing. These aspects of facility management require knowledge of the practices and principles of accounting and finance. Because many crucial decisions are based upon budget, event settlement, and auditing documents, it is extremely important that all of them be professionally prepared.

9. Risk management's purpose is to provide a structure to alleviate liability problems that could lead to significant financial losses. Also, the process of developing standard operating procedures for a facility provides a safe environment for the patrons.

CASE STUDY I

You have just been hired as the facility manager for the Coliseum. The president of the Coliseum wants you to create an operations manual that will help the building run more efficiently while making your job easier to perform. The following is a list of priorities given to you by the president of the Coliseum:

1. *Operations management: Describe and diagram the optimal organizational structure. This structure should include position descriptions and projected salaries.*

2. *Risk management: Describe the overall function of risk management within your arena. Give five potential risk management scenarios and explain in detail their resolution using risk management principles.*

3. *Marketing: Develop a marketing plan for your facility, including projected costs and benefits and two advertising campaigns for your facility.*

4. *Event management: Describe this process in your facility, including a chain of command for personnel (parking, security, ticket takers, ushers, etc.).*

Choose a special event that could be held at your facility, and describe what special-event management needs this event might create.

5. *Concessions/food service: Describe the function of concessions in your facility. Give reasons why you would or would not own the concessions, have an agreement to get a percentage of concessions, or simply lease the space for concessions.*

CASE STUDY II

Assume that you are the facility manager at the Coliseum. Develop a standard operating procedure (SOP) for spills (something you forgot to do in your operations manual.) In this procedure, you need to describe what role, if any, the various departments would play in reporting, monitoring, and/or cleaning up spills.

After you have written your SOP, discuss the following problem. (Assume that the SOP has been put into effect and that it is reasonable in terms of implementation.)

A spill has just taken place, and the following events occur: (1) Three ticket takers see the spill and do nothing, (2) two security guards see the spill, but they are called to a fight and do not report the spill until 15 minutes after they spotted it, (3) an usher immediately reports the spill but does not keep patrons from walking in the area, (4) the cleaning crew cleans the spill 40 minutes after it was notified of it (45 minutes after it occurred), and (5) a patron slipped and fell because of the spill, broke an ankle, and is suing the Coliseum for $45,000.

REVIEW QUESTIONS AND ISSUES

1. Describe the advantages of contracting with private management companies.
2. What is RFP? Describe this selection process.
3. Define booking and scheduling.
4. Describe the reservation process. Comment on the statement that this process is not fair.
5. How does the mission of the facility influence its reservations and priorities?
6. How would you resolve a problem of two sport promoters desiring the same date and time?
7. Identify the four components of operations management.
8. List the operations manager's responsibilities.
9. When coordinating an event, what are the elements considered important from an operational perspective?
10. List the important elements concerned with the development of an emergency manual.

11. What measures need to be taken to ensure prompt and professional emergency response training for facility staff?

12. Define the terms *housekeeping, maintenance, engineering,* and *structural and equipment maintenance.*

13. List the elements of a maintenance and housekeeping plan.

14. Explain the following terms: *in-house food service management, concessions, stocking, convenience foods,* and *hawkers.*

15. Under what circumstances would you let an in-house food service management operation contract?

16. Explain the following terms: *novelties, bootlegging,* and *merchandising deals* with sport teams and athletes.

17. Why is the box office an important segment of the facility operation?

18. Identify the important components of box office operations.

19. What is a budget?

20. How does the political/government budget process differ from the private/operational budget?

21. Identify and comment on the phases of the budget cycle.

22. Describe the various budget types that can be involved in a facility budget.

23. Identify and describe the phases of a white paper. How does this apply to a sport facility?

24. Describe how event settlement works in a sport facility.

25. List internal auditing procedures that could be used in the various segments of the facility operation.

26. Why is it important to develop collections procedures?

27. Identify traditional revenue sources and operational segments in a facility.

28. List additional revenue sources.

29. Identify the essential elements of the risk management process, and describe the function of each.

REFERENCES

Berlonghi, A. (1990). *The special event risk management manual,* Dana Point, California, author.

Davidson, S. et al. (1988). *Managerial accounting: an introduction to concepts, methods and uses,* Chicago, Dryden Press.

Garrison, R. (1982). *Managerial accounting,* Plano, Texas, Business Publications.

Hitt, W. (1985). *Management in action,* Columbus, Ohio, Battelle Press.

International Association of Auditorium Managers. (1990). unpublished proceedings, Ogelbay, Virginia, School for Public Assembly Facility Management.

Jewel, D. (1992). *Public assembly facilities,* Malabar, Florida, Krieger Publishing.

Laventhol and Horwath. (1989). *Convention centers, stadiums, and arenas.* Washington, D.C., Urban Land Institutes.

O'Shaughnessy, J. (1988). *Competitive marketing: a strategic approach,* Boston, Unwin Hyman.

Thompson, A. and Strickland, A. (1990). *Strategic management, concepts and cases,* Homewood, Illinois, BPI Irwin.

Walgenbach, P., Dittrich, N., and Hansen, E. (1980). *Principles of accounting,* New York, Harcourt Brace Jovanovich.

SUGGEST READINGS

Appenzeller, H. and Lewis, G. (1985). *Successful sport management,* Charlottesville, Virginia, Michie Co.

Boyden, E. and Burton, R. (1957). *Staging successful tournaments,* New York, Associated Press, pp 42-52.

Griffen, J.H. (1967). *The new athletic director's handbook,* Danville, Illinois, School Aid Co, pp 30-55.

Harris, A.J. (1988). *Disaster plan: a part of the game plan?,* Athletic Training, 23: 59, Spring.

Jewel, D. (1992). *Public assembly facilities,* Malabar, Florida, Krieger Publishing.

Jury, J. Event check list, University of Wisconsin-Stevens Point.

Lake, L. (1979). *The planning process,* Business Processes.

Sutton, W. and Griner, D. (1988). *Physical education 881: facilities management.*

Thomason, P. and Perdue, R. (1987). *Festivals and special events,* JOPHERD, pp. 54-57, April.

Torkildsen, G. (1983). *Leisure and recreation management,* New York, EF Spon.

Walter, S. (1985). *National sports festival planning manual: a guide to conducting multi-sport events,* 2 vols, Colorado Springs.

Wilson, J. and Udall, L. (1982). *Folk festivals: a handbook for organization and management,* Knoxville, Tennessee.

PART V

Marketing

CHAPTER 14

Sport Marketing: A Strategic Approach

Dianna P. Gray

In this chapter, you will become familiar with the following terms:

Intangibility	Market segmentation	Trading out
Product extensions	Niche	Positioning
Strategic market management	Product	Promotion
Strategic planning	Services	Advertising
Distribution	Attributes	Sales promotion
Demographics	Benefits	Personal selling
Product usage	Marketing support system	Public relations
Psychographic analysis	Core product	Marketing plan
Lifestyle	Product growth curve	
Target market	Bartering	

Overview

A thorough understanding of sport marketing theory and its application is a requirement for success in the sports industry. Whether employed in upper-level management or in an entry-level position, the sport professional realizes that marketing is integral to the successful operation of an organization. The purpose of

this chapter is to present concepts relevant to sport marketing and discuss the application of these concepts as practiced by sport organizations. This will be achieved by defining sport marketing and illustrating sports' unique characteristics, explaining the marketing management process, identifying and analyzing consumers, introducing the concept of marketing communication and the marketing mix, and developing a strategic marketing plan. The student who is cognizant of the

Acknowledgment is given to Bill Sutton for his contributions in revising this chapter.

strategic marketing management process will more fully understand the role of marketing in the sport organization.

WHAT IS SPORT MARKETING?

A definition of sport marketing must be preceded by a definition and examination of marketing. McCarthy (1975) defines *marketing* as the performance of activities that direct the flow of goods and services from producer to user to satisfy the customer and accomplish the organization's objectives. Kotler (1976) defines marketing as the human activity directed at satisfying needs and wants through exchange processes. These activities or processes require a communication network established on the basis of inquiry, needs, and fulfillment of needs through product development, delivery, and exchange.

More closely related to sport is a concept defined as lifestyle marketing. Hanan (1980) defines *lifestyle marketing* as a strategy for seizing the concept of a market according to its most meaningful, recurrent patterns of attitudes and activities and then tailoring products and their promotional strategies to fit these patterns. Sport attendance and participation studies (Miller Lite Report, 1983; Sports Poll '86, 1986; ESPN/Chilton Sports Poll, 1995) document not only the patterns of sport-related attitudes and activities but also their frequencies and intensities. The essential question is whether sport as a product differs significantly from other goods and services. Mullin (1983, 1985, 1993) maintains that sport has certain characteristics in its core, extensions, and presentation that make the sport product unique, requiring an approach that may, at times, lay beyond the concerns and approaches of "mainstream" business marketing. The following is a brief examination of those unique sport qualities that alter traditional marketing approaches and dictate the "locus of control" of the sport marketer.

Intangibility and subjectivity

Simply put, the consumer takes nothing away from attending a sport event but impressions and memories. The wide variety of possible impressions and interpretations of the event pose a challenge for the sports marketer—namely, to achieve a probability of consumer satisfaction. For example,

consider a group of five people attending a professional baseball game. One member of the group might remember that parking was difficult and expensive; another might have been disappointed with the outcome of the game; a third may have been impressed by the quality of the pitching matchups; the fourth member of the group may have been disappointed in the lack of scoring; and the fifth person may remember enjoying the event because of the social interaction with the other members of the group. Each member of the group had an opinion that—although not necessarily related to the core, or game itself—will influence future purchasing decisions regarding that product. In describing baseball, Veeck illustrates the **intangibility** of the sport product by stating, "The customer comes out to the park with nothing except the illusion that he is going to have a good time. He leaves with nothing except a memory" (Veeck and Linn, 1965).

Inconsistency and unpredictability

One of the great attractions of sport, for participants or spectators, is the belief that on any given day any team or individual, regardless of past performance, can win. Many factors can affect the outcome of a game or contest. Such factors include injuries to players, player trades, momentum, motivation, and environmental conditions, such as weather and time of year. These factors and the "lack of script" interact to guarantee that each game, event, or contest will be unique and the outcome will not be guaranteed.

Product perishability

The original sport product can be sold no later than the day of the event. In reality, it should be sold well before the date of the contest to help ensure franchise stability, consumer interest, and product credibility. There is no consumer market for yesterday's boxing match or basketball game. In professional sport, as well as basketball and football at the majority of NCAA member schools, tickets should be presold to guarantee stable revenue and to generate profits. If tickets are not presold, attendance and, subsequently, gate receipts will depend on performance; and if performance is poor or not up to expectations, revenue will suffer.

Emotional attachment and identification

Numerous studies have been conducted to measure the attitudes and behavior patterns of Americans regarding sport participation and attendance, as well as the effect of sport on the lives of Americans. The Miller Lite study of 1983 and the ESPN/Chilton Sports Poll of 1995, revealed, among other findings, the tremendous effect sport has on the daily lives of Americans. The *Sports Illustrated* study Sports Poll '86 established the most popular sports activities in terms of participation and the types of activities in which Americans were participating. Each of these studies also surveyed the attitudes of Americans toward sport, the results of which indicate that approximately 95% of American society is affected by sport (reading, discussing, listening, watching, or participating) each day.

Evidence of the prevalence of sport can also be seen by examining the growth of the sports industry. In 1987, sport was a $47.2-billion-a-year enterprise (Sandomir, 1987); by 1989, that figure had risen to $63 billion (Compte and Stogel, 1990). In 1990, the gross national sport product (GNSP) was calculated at $180 billion, making sport one of the 25 largest industries in the United States (Associated Press, 1991). Sport is not simply another big business; it is one of the fastest-growing industries in the United States, and it is intertwined with practically every aspect of the economy—from advertising and apparel, computer technology and virtual-reality games, to travel and tourism.

The development of merchandising departments in all professional and major college athletic programs has given interested fans an opportunity to identify with a particular sports team (or individual) by purchasing uniform replicas or related team apparel. The sale of licensed products accounted for $6.2 billion in 1990 (Associated Press, 1991). Table 14-1 identifies the top three teams from the NFL, MLB, NBA, and NHL, in terms of the popularity of logo clothing.

Focus and locus of control

In mainstream business marketing, marketers play a critical role in determining the composition of their organizations' marketing mix (how the four P's will be blended and used) and positioning. In sport marketing, the marketer's input is inappropriate and thus is not actively sought. Players are acquired, traded, platooned, and used with no input from the sport marketer, whose responsibility is to market the tickets for the game. Although the trade or acquisition of a particular player may help or hurt attendance, these decisions are not the functions of a sport marketer. Scheduling and/or determining the opposition is another factor that is outside the scope of a sport marketer, yet it has a significant effect on attendance in team sports (Rudman and Sutton, 1989). Similarly, in participant sports, crucial factors such as weather or road construction are outside the locus of control of sport marketers but have significant effects on demand at golf, tennis, and ski facilities. Thus, the focus of the marketer is on **product extensions** that are within (the locus of) his or her control. Table 14-2 further presents the unique characteristics of sport, examining the market as well as the four P's of the marketing mix.

With these characteristics in mind, *sport marketing*, for the purpose of discussion in this chapter, will

TABLE 14-1 *ESPN Chilton sports poll**

Licensed sportswear: most popular teams regarding logo clothing			
NFL	MLB	NBA	NHL
1. Cowboys	Braves	Bulls	Sharks
2. Raiders	Yankees	Hornets	Penguins
3. 49ers	White Sox	Lakers	Kings
			Rangers (tie)

*The poll surveyed 11,839 U.S. residents who consider themselves "at least somewhat of a sports fan" over the course of one year (January 4, 1994-January 2, 1995).

TABLE 14-2 *Unique sport characteristics*

Market	Sport organizations compete and cooperate simultaneously
	Sport consumers consider themselves experts
	Wide fluctuation in consumer demand (seasonal, weekly, and daily demand differences)
Product	Intangible
	Subjective
	Produced and consumed on same site
	Inconsistent
	Perishable/no shelf life (must presell)
	Publicly consumed; affected by social facilitation
	Sport marketer has no control over core product
Price	Difficult to price using conventional methods
	Small percentage of total money spent by consumer goes to sport organization
	More money obtained from product extensions, TV, etc. (indirect revenues)
	Only recently required to operate as a for-profit organization
Promotion	Tremendous media exposure
	Businesses want association with sport
Place/distribution	Produced and consumed in same place
	Atmosphere contributes to enjoyment
	Sport marketer should focus efforts here
	TV and media; tickets

---

be defined as "the identification of organizational and product-related characteristics and the incorporation of these characteristics in the development, presentation, positioning, and delivery of the sports product through promotional and media strategies to the selected consumer target market(s)."

CONCEPT CHECK

Sport marketing has unique characteristics and considerations not found in most areas of product marketing. Intangibility, subjectivity, inconsistency, unpredictability, perishability, emotional attachment and identification, social facilitation, public consumption, and focus and locus of control are factors that interact to form a series of challenges for the sport marketer.

STRATEGIC MARKET MANAGEMENT
Strategic market management is a system designed to help management make better marketing decisions. A strategic decision is the creation, change, or retention of a strategy (Aaker, 1988). Philip Kotler (1987) defines the strategic market planning process as the managerial process of developing and maintaining a strategic fit between the organization's goals and resources and its changing market opportunities. The tangible result of this planning process is a marketing plan. Later in the chapter, the development of a marketing plan will be covered in detail.

Strategic planning
A key component of the **strategic planning** process is conducting an environmental analysis (Kotler, 1987; Aaker, 1988). An environmental analysis is an assessment of the "climate," including internal and external factors, that may or may not affect marketing efforts. For example, in intercollegiate athletics the environment would include the university itself, the athletic department, the local community, alumni, state government, media, boosters, corporate sponsors, and, in this particular case, the

Overview of strategic market management

External analysis	Self-analysis/internal analysis

• Customer analysis
   Segments, motivations, unmet needs
• Competitive analysis
   Identity, strategic groups, performance, objectives, strategies, culture, cost structure, strengths, weaknesses
• Industry analysis
   Size, projected growth, industry structure, entry barriers, cost structure, distribution system, trends, key success factors
• Environmental analysis
   Technological, governmental, economic, cultural, demographic, scenarios, information need areas
	• Performance analysis
	   Return on assets, market share, product value and performance, relative cost, new product activity, manager development and performance, employee attitude and performance, product portfolio analysis
	• Determinants of strategic options
	   Past and current strategy, strategic problems, organizational capabilities and constraints, financial resources and constraints, flexibility, strengths, weaknesses

↓	↓
Opportunities, threats, and strategic questions	Strategic strengths, weaknesses, problems, constraints, and questions

STRATEGY IDENTIFICATION AND SELECTION

• Specify the mission
• Identify strategic alternatives
  • Investment strategies by product market
        Withdraw, milk, hold or enter/grow
  • Strategies to gain sustainable competitive advantage
        Functional area strategies
        Assets and skills
• Select strategy
  • Consider strategic questions
  • Evaluate strategic alternatives
• Implementation—the operating plan
• Review of strategies

From Aaker, D. (1988) (2nd Ed). *Developing business strategies,* New York, John Wiley.

federal government. How can the federal government affect the operations of an intercollegiate athletic program? It can enact legislation altering the tax-exempt status of gifts to the college athletic program, particularly contributions made to ensure priority seating, a product requiring a donation for the right to purchase tickets. Such legislation affects not only the importance of marketing

efforts but also the scope and direction of those efforts. The box above presents an overview of strategic market management and the planning process.

It is important that the marketer conduct an environmental analysis of the historical market, as well as the present market climate and future market assumptions. In considering a city as a possible expansion site for a professional sports team, the league office would wish to understand the sports attendance history of that city, as well as sports and entertainment competition for the entertainment dollars of that city's populace. For example, if the city of Pittsburgh were being considered for a possible NBA expansion franchise, an environmental analysis would provide the following information:

Past professional basketball franchises
- Pittsburgh Rens (ABL)
- Pittsburgh Pipers (ABA)
- Pittsburgh Condors (ABA)

It would also reveal that the Philadelphia 76ers played a limited schedule in Pittsburgh in the late 1960s.

Current sports competition
- Pittsburgh Steelers (NFL): some seasonal overlap
- Pittsburgh Pirates (MLB): some seasonal overlap
- Pittsburgh Penguins (NHL): direct competition; arena managed by hockey ownership
- University of Pittsburgh: Division I college basketball
- Duquesne University: Division I college basketball
- Robert Morris College: Division I college basketball

In addition to these competitors, there are college basketball programs at the Division III, NAIA, and junior college levels and high school sports programs in basketball, hockey, and wrestling.

This type of research during the planning process provides a realistic assessment of the market and should also reveal past practices that were successful or failed. This process is one part of a situational analysis, which assesses strengths, weaknesses, opportunities, and threats (SWOT analysis).

The sport marketer also uses strategic market management to identify potential customers and then classify market segments. Once the segments are identified, the sport marketer targets the appropriate market segment(s) and develops the core marketing strategy. This includes the selection of target market(s), the choice of a competitive position, and the development of an effective market-ing mix to reach and serve the chosen consumers (Kotler, 1987).

The strategic market planning process justifies resource allocation, personnel decisions, media use, and ultimately organizational direction by defining organizational objectives. The strategic market planning process then enables the marketer to consider strategies that may or may not be used in the organizational marketing efforts to achieve those objectives. Such strategies may be related to price, promotions, distribution, packaging and positioning.

CONSUMER BEHAVIOR

The focus of marketing begins and ends with the customer/consumer. Kotler (1972) states that a customer orientation, backed by an integrated marketing approach aimed at generating customer satisfaction, is the key to achieving the organization's goals. Knowledge of the consumer is so important for effective marketing that a variety of disciplines have studied it.

Marketing starts with an analysis of the consumer. Think of consumers as people who are trying to solve a problem. The consumers' problem could be described as the perceived difference between the *way things are* and the *way they wished them to be*. Thus, in an effort to satisfy needs, wants, and desires, consumers purchase goods and services. In other words, consumers purchase goods as one way of solving the problem of the *current situation* versus the *desired situation*. A young man feels he doesn't have a sufficiently masculine physique, so he joins a health and fitness club and begins a weight-lifting regime. An elderly woman concerned about decreased mobility and her resulting loss of independence enrolls in an adult fitness class. A recent MBA graduate who wishes to impress his colleagues and friends purchases a season ticket for the Chicago Bulls, an NBA franchise. As you can readily see, consumers must deal with a number of "problems" in their daily lives. A better understanding of why consumers behave as they do provides sport marketers with the needed information to effectively develop programs that solve consumers' problems and to then communicate that to respective target audiences.

When one considers the diversity of sport and recreation participants, spectators, and the various sport and entertainment options available today, it is not difficult to hypothesize that each consumer may be seeking different attributes and realizing different benefits and satisfaction, from the same sport or activity. Whereas one fan enjoys the tension of a no-hitter, another is bored by the lack of offensive production.

The sport marketer seeks to maximize consumer satisfaction so that the spectator or participant will demonstrate repeat behavior. The sport marketer has various choices available to try to increase consumer satisfaction (i.e., increase the benefits and/or reduce the costs). However, a knowledge of what motivates or deters the consumer from attending an event or participating in an activity is imperative before such attempts are made. On the surface, it may seem obvious why individuals "consume" or participate in sports. Nevertheless, the reasons for choosing one form of sport entertainment or other activity over another are not self-evident. It should be apparent that the study of how and why consumers decide to attend sports events or engage in a particular sport activity is an important, yet complex, facet of sport marketing.

What then, are the factors that motivate consumption of various sport and leisure products and services? What are the factors that prevent or deter consumption of or participation in sport?

One method marketers use to understand consumers is based on the work of social psychologists, who posit that beliefs and attitudes, as well as one's environment, greatly influence behavior (Bandura, 1977; Ajzen and Fishbein, 1980; Zajonc and Marjus, 1982; Engel, Blackwell, and Miniard, 1986; Ajzen, 1991; Ajzen and Driver, 1991).

There are at least three factors researchers have identified that appear to influence consumers' behavior relative to participation in or consumption of sports. Environmental, social, and cultural variables, collectively referred to as *sociocultural factors,* are known to influence behavior (Ajzen and Fishbein, 1980; Ajzen, 1985; Engel, Blackwell, and Miniard, 1986; Ajzen and Driver, 1991). The people with whom one associates—family, friends, and colleagues—have a potential influence on sport, entertainment, and activity decisions. One reason sport marketers collect demographic data on consumer markets is to develop marketing strategies based on the effects of sociocultural factors; people from the same environment tend to have similar interests and act similarly (Engel, Blackwell, and Miniard, 1986; Cialdini, 1993; Brooks, 1994).

Another important area that experts agree has some influence is one's personal or psychological state. Here is where sport marketers, in their effort to provide for consumers' wants, seek to better understand what is going on in the mind of the consumer. This factor includes one's attitudes, beliefs, and motivation. Attitudes and beliefs play a role in the consumer's psychological state because attitudes are a learned behavior and an expression of one's values and opinions. People have attitudes—positive, negative, or neutral—toward all objects. For our purposes, an attitude is an *index* of the degree to which a person likes or dislikes a sport or activity. How a customer feels about a particular sport or activity is based on information from previous experiences and is stored in the mind as an attitude (Settle and Alreck, 1986). In an effort to build favorable attitudes toward a sport or activity *before* the customer even decides to try the sport, sport marketers emphasize the sport's various characteristics and benefits through promotional messages. This tactic is also used *after* customers attend a sports event or engage in an activity, in another effort to reinforce any positive attitudes held by the consumer.

Another aspect of one's personal/psychological state is motivation. Although motivation is a complex area and is difficult, if not impossible, for the sport marketer to quantify, it is an important aspect of understanding consumer behavior. *Motivation* can be defined as a theoretical construct involving an internal need state that gives impetus to behavior and a directional component that gives general direction to a variety of responses serving the same general function for the organism (Runyon, 1982). Keep in mind that motivation is a theoretical construct, which cannot be observed directly; only behavior can be observed. It is only after observing behavior that sport marketers can infer motives and then design appropriate marketing communications and promotions. Mullin, Hardy, and Sutton (1993) have identified achievement, affiliation, health and fitness, and fun and entertainment as the four most frequent motives in the literature on motivation and sport consumption. Determining customers' wants and needs is a basic axiom of marketing. However, accomplishing this is not as easy as it might appear.

Identifying and targeting sport consumers

To be successful in the highly competitive sport and entertainment business, the sport marketer must know something about the people who will be the ultimate consumers. This learning process consists of examining the characteristics and needs of the target market, including the consumer's lifestyle and purchase decisions, so that product, distribution (place), promotion, and pricing decisions are made accordingly. By knowing as much as possible about the consumer, the sport marketer can satisfy the target markets, keep consumer dissatisfaction to a minimum, and remain competitive by maintaining or increasing market share.

Before beginning to plan ways of marketing a sport product or service, the sport marketer should answer some general questions about the consumer. First, who is the consumer of the product or service? Here the marketer is trying to obtain information about the **final consumer**, the person who actually decides to purchase the product or service. Where does the consumer live? How does the consumer learn about the available sport and entertainment opportunities? To what forms of media is the consumer exposed? How far in advance of the event does the consumer decide to attend or participate? When does the consumer purchase the ticket to the event? What does the consumer do before the game (pre-event) and after the game (postevent)?

After getting general information about the sport consumer, the marketer seeks answers to more specific questions. At this stage, the marketer begins to compose a profile of the sport consumer by examining demographic information. Consumer **demographics** are the statistical descriptions of the attributes (characteristics) of the population. By looking at demographic information, both individual characteristics and overall descriptions, the sport marketer can develop consumer profiles that may pinpoint both attractive and declining market opportunities. Figure 14-1 illustrates some of the common factors that are used to determine a demographic profile.

One of the best ways to obtain demographic information is to conduct primary research, usually by means of a survey. This is not always feasible because of financial or time limits; however, there are several secondary sources of information. These sources provide the sport marketer with information about the general population, as well as specific information about sport consumers. The *Census of Population* is a publication of the federal government that provides a wealth of demographic data. Census data are gathered only once every 10 years, so current data may be lacking. However, population statistics from other sources—such as chambers of commerce, public utility companies, and marketing firms—can supplement the census data. Sport-specific demographic data can be obtained from individual sport franchises, the national offices of the major sport leagues, sport marketing firms, institutions and private corporations that have commissioned studies, or university libraries.

The Simmons Market Research Bureau, Mediamark Research, and other marketing research companies annually conduct personal interviews with

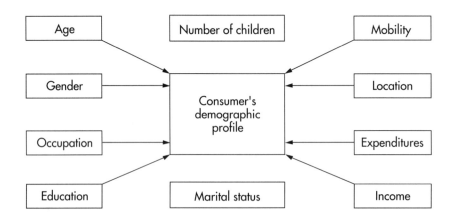

FIGURE 14-1   Factors that determine a demographic profile.

TABLE 14-3 *Secondary information sources: print*

Print sources	Description
American Sports Analysis	Includes participation data for sports and other physical activities
Sporting Goods Industry Financial Performance	Published by the Sporting Goods Manufacturers Association (SGMA)
National Sporting Goods Association Reports	Consumer demographics for sport-related products
Mediamark Research, Inc.	Participation, sports attendance, spectating, and media habits reported
The Lifestyle Market Analysis	Demographic and lifestyle information on sport spectators and participants
The Almanac of Consumer Markets	Demographics, lifestyles, and segmentation techniques
Statistical Abstract of the United States	Summary statistics on social, political, and economic organizations in U.S.; breakdown of dollars spent on sporting events, goods, etc.
Findex	Worldwide directory of market research reports, studies, and surveys; sporting goods/equipment.
The Sports/Fitness/Leisure Markets	Fairchild publication containing participation, spectating, and purchasing information
Simmons Market Research Bureau	Participation, sports attendance, spectating, and media habits reported

subjects on many consumer issues, including sport participation and live and televised sport viewing. Most university libraries have the results of these studies, a volume of which is usually devoted entirely to sport and leisure.

There are also a variety of serial publications and electronic databases (CD-ROMs) that offer the marketer demographic information. *American Demographics* is a monthly magazine that specializes in demographic data on specific sports. Other secondary sources of demographic information include the Women's Sport Foundation, *The Sports Business Daily, Athletic Business, Club Business* (publication of the International Racket Sports Association), *USA Today, The Wall Street Journal,* and local newspapers. Tables 14-3, 14-4, and 14-5 list additional print and electronic sources.

Zeroing in on your customer base: demographics, psychographics, and lifestyles

Although the information gathered from secondary sources can help the sport marketer identify potential consumers, it is at best general information. Specific information about current consumers should be collected directly, if possible. The tools

TABLE 14-4 *Secondary information sources: periodicals*

Periodical sources	Description
Team Marketing Report	Monthly sport marketing and sponsorship newsletter
American Demographics	Demographic trends; statistics on impact of demographics and psychographics
Sporting Goods Dealer	Focuses on sports equipment
Amusement Business	Stadium/arena statistics; entertainment marketing
Brandweek	Licensed merchandise figures for sport teams

TABLE 14-5 *Secondary information sources: electronic*

Electronic/CD-ROM sources	Description
Nexis/Lexis (CD-ROM online)	Includes full texts of newspapers, magazines, wire services, and broadcast transcripts. Relevant libraries and files: MARKET and TRENDS; MARKET and MKTRPT; SPORT; MARKET; and RPOLL (Roper Poll)
ABI/INFORM Global Edition (CD-ROM online)	Abstracts and indexing to articles from over 1,000 academic, management, marketing, and business journals

available for this purpose—the survey, the exit poll, and the focus group—have proven to be effective. However, the most feasible way of gathering information on current consumers is to conduct an in-arena or club members survey.

In-arena survey. When preparing to survey current consumers or members, the sport marketer, with the organization's management, should determine the objectives for the survey. What information does the organization need? How is this information to be gathered? How much will it cost? How will the information be used after it has been collected? These and other questions must be answered before actually starting the data collection phase of the project. Although the following steps are not offered as a comprehensive guide to conducting survey research, they have been used successfully by many sport marketers to obtain primary data on sport consumers.

1. Preparation: Determine the objectives of the research project in cooperation with management.

2. Questionnaire development: Prepare a questionnaire that integrates the objectives of the project and that will elicit answers to questions about the sport consumer.

The following box identifies the three most common bases of segmentation and lists typical variables that may be used to generate questions for the questionnaire.

After developing the questionnaire, give a draft copy to the athletic director or general manager and other colleagues for their feedback. Figure 14-2 is an example of a questionnaire used by Indiana

---

Bases of segmentation

Segments can be based on personal and geographic demographics and lifestyles.

Personal demographic segmentation measurements

Gender: Male or female
Age: Child, teenager, adult, senior
Education: High school, college, beyond college
Income: Low, middle, or high
Marital status: Single, married, divorced, or widowed

Geographic/demographic segmentation measurements

Population: location, size, and density
Climate: Warm or cold
Media present: Local, regional, and/or national
Commerce: Tourist, local worker, resident

Lifestyle segmentation

This segment includes, among other measurements, **product usage**, a key dimension for sport marketers. Other examples of lifestyle measurements include the following:

Social class: Lower-lower to upper-upper
Family life cycle: Bachelor to solitary survivor
Brand loyalty: None, some, complete
Beliefs and involvements: Causes people are concerned about
Attitudes: Neutral, positive, negative
Leisure interests: How people spend their non-work hours

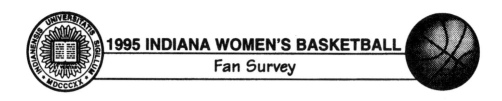

1995 INDIANA WOMEN'S BASKETBALL
Fan Survey

We'd like your help. In a continuing effort to better serve you and provide you with the best in college sports entertainment, we'd like your opinion. Please take a few minutes to complete and return this survey.

1. How many IU women's basketball games did you attend <u>last</u> season (1993/94)?

☐none   ☐one   ☐two   ☐three   ☐four
☐ five   ☐six   ☐seven   ☐ eight or more

2. Counting this game how many IU women's basketball games have you attended <u>this</u> season? (1994/95)?_____

3. How many years (including this year) have you been attending Hoosier women's basketball games?

☐one   ☐two   ☐3 to 5   ☐6 to 10   ☐11 or more

4. Which time do you prefer regarding attending IU women's basketball games?

☐Friday night
☐Sunday afternoon
☐No preference
☐Not a factor in my decision to attend

5. How did you find out about <u>today's/tonight's</u> game? (check all that apply)

☐Team schedule card or poster
☐IU Credit Union
☐Newspaper
☐Radio
☐Television
☐Word of mouth

FIGURE 14-2   The first page of a questionnaire used by Indiana University to gather information about its fans.

University's athletic department to gather demographic and product usage information about its fans.

3. Distribution: Obtain a copy of the arena or stadium floor plan to help determine how the questionnaire will be distributed to the seats. It is also important to plan how to allocate the completed questionnaires. The following strategy has consistently resulted in a return rate of 85% to 90%:

   a. Assign each section of the stadium or arena a number. Using a table of random numbers (or a computer program that generates random numbers), select the sections that will be targeted, as well as the seat numbers from each row in the identified sections.

   b. After the customers are comfortably seated, give them a copy of the questionnaire and a pencil. Giving fans a questionnaire when they enter the arena through turnstiles will *not* result in a good return rate. Many of the questionnaires distributed this way end up on the arena floor or in the trash receptacles.

   c. Announce periodically that a survey is being distributed, and encourage the attendees to cooperate. One of the most successful tactics to get consumers to fill out the questionnaire completely is to offer an **incentive**. This may take many forms, including a bumper sticker, a key chain, or the chance to be in a lottery for an attractive prize. The incentive should be discussed with management during the preparation phase.

   d. Ushers or other facility personnel should collect the questionnaire before the contest begins. Fans are at the event because they are interested in the game, not because they want to fill out a questionnaire. Having ushers* or other

personnel collect the questionnaires shortly after the fans have completed them is preferable to asking the fans to drop the questionnaire into a collection box as they exit the arena or stadium.

4. Analysis: After the questionnaires are collected, the data must be coded and analyzed. This can be done by a marketing research firm or the computer systems department at a nearby university.

After analyzing the questionnaires and examining each of the variables individually, the sport marketer develops profiles of the consumer groups. Figure 14-3 summarizes the demographic characteristics of "all game attendees" for the Indiana Pacers (NBA).

Although demographics are valuable in giving the marketer an understanding of large-scale similarities and trends about the consumer and the market segments, the data do not reflect the cultural or social factors that influence consumers. The sport marketer also needs to identify consumer's concerns. What are the customer's preferences in music, television, and other entertainment? What are the consumer's political, religious, or environmental concerns? One solution to this dilemma is to understand the market segment's psychographics (values and attitudes) and lifestyles.

The technique marketers use to measure values and attitudes is **psychographic analysis**. Consumers' activities, interests, and opinions (AIOs) are inventoried by asking respondents various questions about their work, sport activities, family, social life, education, and political preferences. Psychographic analysis is important to sport marketers because it presents a more detailed and accurate picture of the consumer and helps sport marketers refine their demographic screening. Table 14-6 lists some of the variables explored in the activities, interests, and opinions categories.

Lifestyle marketing

Lifestyle marketing provides a platform for the delivery of products and services. Used strategically, it can cut through the clutter of the marketplace and communicate your message directly to your target audience. By knowing the consumer's **lifestyle**, the marketer can develop a relationship with the consumer and create the best match between the consumer and the sport product or

*It is the author's opinion that it is best to have personnel other than the ushers collect the completed questionnaires. The ushers, although usually cooperative, must attend to crowd control, and their primary responsibility is the seating of stadium or coliseum guests. Students from nearby institutions, preferably from sport management programs, can assist by collecting the questionnaires.

The Pacers **SCORE BIG POINTS**
with educated, executive sports fans.

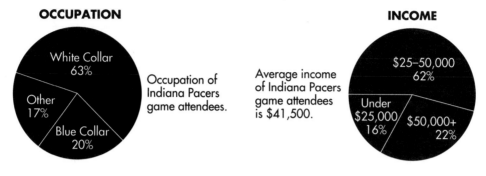

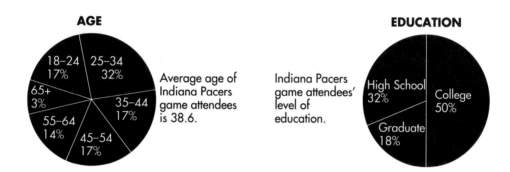

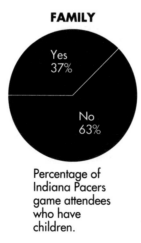

Percentage of
Indiana Pacers
game attendees
who have
children.

FIGURE 14-3   Demographics of all game attendees.

TABLE 14-6 *Typical psychographic variables*		
Activities	**Interests**	**Opinions**
Work	Family	Themselves
Hobbies	Home	Social issues
Social events	Job	Politics
Vacation	Community	Business
Entertainment	Recreation	Economics
Club membership	Fashion	Education
Community	Food	Products
Shopping	Media	Future
Sports	Achievements	Culture

From Plumber, J. (1974). The concept and application of lifestyle segmentation, *Journal of Marketing* 38(1): 33-37.

TABLE 14-7 *Consumption rate groupings*	
Usage segment	**Identification pattern**
Heavy user	Season ticket holders Club members and/or contract-time holders
Medium user	Miniseason plan users Heavy single-game/event ticket purchasers
Light user	Infrequent single-game/event ticket purchasers
Defector*	Individuals who have used the sport product in the last 12 months but who have not made a repeat purchase since that time
Media consumer	Individuals who do not go to the stadium or coliseum but rather "follow" the team or sport via the media
Unaware consumer	Individuals who are unaware of the sport product and its benefits
Uninterested consumer	Individuals who are aware of the sport product but choose not to try it

From Mullin, B. (1983). *Sport marketing, promotion and public relations,* Amherst, Massachusetts, National Sport Management.
*Levin defines *defectors* as people who have attended an organization's event at least once but have not returned within the last 12 months. In many cases, disenchanted heavy users become defectors; in other cases, defectors are individuals who did not gain sufficient satisfaction on the initial purchase or trial.

service. Lifestyle segmentation includes, among other factors, products usage, a key dimension for sport marketers. Product usage is traditionally divided into light, medium, and heavy users. As shown in Table 14-7, Mullin (1983) identifies four more sport-specific, product usage categories.

College, professional, and private sport and leisure organizations pay the most attention to the heavy user—that is, the season ticketholder or the club participant who has a yearly rather than a 3-month membership. The percentage of consumers who are heavy users varies from sport to sport, franchise to franchise, and club to club. Some baseball organizations rely heavily on the light user, the person who purchases a ticket 1 hour before a game. Other baseball organizations rely more on season ticket sales. Some football organizations sell out stadiums every week and have long waiting lists of loyal fans who want to purchase season tickets, whereas others have difficulty selling out one game. In a similar fashion, fitness and health clubs put a great deal of effort into the renewal of annual memberships, usually at the end of the "indoor" season, because the late spring and summer months are low-usage months, even among heavy users, at most clubs.

Sport marketers should realize the importance of classifying consumer markets by product usage rate. The differing needs of light, medium, and heavy consumers must be satisfied as much as possible. Furthermore, the marketer should consider the light consumer's needs as much as the heavy user's because today's light consumer could be tomorrow's medium or heavy consumer. An overdependence on the heavy or medium consumer at the expense of the light user could be shortsighted. For example, in the mid-1980s, the men's basketball program of Cleveland State University enjoyed great success. The team played in a small gymnasium to capacity crowds. Students, faculty, and the community alike had to stand in line for the opportunity to purchase single tickets the day of the game. Had they wanted, the Cleveland State athletic department could have presold the entire season. However, the administration did not want to alienate the light and medium users, knowing that in the next 5 years a new and much larger home arena would be built. If these consumers had been denied the opportunity to watch the team play occasionally, they might have lost interest in the team in the future. Knowing that selling out the new arena would be more difficult and the future financial success would depend on some of the light and medium consumers becoming season ticketholders (heavy users), the marketing staff maintained opportunities for all three consumer levels. Near-sellout crowds when the new, larger arena opened, verified this strategy.

CONCEPT CHECK

Strategic market management is a systematic process by which managers evaluate the sport organization's strengths and weaknesses, measure the competition and external environment, and then develop a marketing strategy that matches the team's goals with the opportunities in the marketplace. Developing a profile of current consumers, including demographic and psychographic information, is an important component of the strategic plan.

DEVELOPING A TARGET MARKET STRATEGY

Once a clear, quantified picture has been determined of who the customers are, the sport marketer is ready to segment and select the target market(s) to which an appeal will be made. Theodore Levitt, in his book *Marketing Imagination* (1986), said that if marketers were not thinking about market segmentation, then they were not thinking. The strategy of target marketing is based on the concept that it is more profitable to zero in on a specific and often narrow market using a focused approach than it is to use the shotgun approach of attempting to appeal to every consumer.

Defining the target market

Market targeting consists of the decision processes and activities conducted to find a market to serve (Luck and Ferrill, 1985). Market research should identify unsatisfied or partially satisfied needs. However, because there is an almost infinite number of differences in the population and because not all needs are universal, it is highly unlikely that a marketer will be able to satisfy all needs. The marketer needs a method to divide, or segment, the population in some manner and then to target the respective segments. Market segmentation is an attempt to identify and then classify potential consumers into a homogeneous group (similar age, sex, education, preferences, and so on). Once the target market is identified, the marketer can then plan the strategy to reach the targeted segment (a selected portion of the entire available market) and initiate the exchange process.

There are three proven methods of defining and satisfying a target market: (1) mass marketing (undifferentiated), (2) marketing segmentation (concentrated), and (3) multiple segmentation (differentiated).

In mass marketing, a single, undifferentiated marketing strategy is used to appeal to a broad range of consumers. In market segmentation, the marketing plan is designed to appeal to one well-defined market segment, or group of consumers. In multiple segmentation, a marketing plan is designed to appeal to two or more market segments, with specialized approaches developed for each well-defined consumer group. Table 14-8 compares the three methods for defining a target market.

Mass marketing. In the past, millions of dollars were spent marketing a product to some "typical" or "average" consumer. However, no company or organization can survive in today's competitive marketplace by selling to a mythical average customer. The mass-marketing (undifferentiated) approach does not recognize different lifestyles or market segments; the focus of this marketing strategy is on the common needs of consumers, rather than on their differences. Within a mass-marketing approach, different consumer groups are not identified or sought.

Although a mass-marketing approach is not the sport marketer's principal method of reaching consumers, it does have a place in the marketing of

TABLE 14-8   *Methods for developing a target market*

Marketing approach	Mass marketing	Market segmentation	Multiple segmentation
Target market	Broad range of consumers	One well-defined consumer group	Two or more well-defined consumer groups
Product	Limited number of products under one brand for many types of consumers	One brand tailored to one consumer group	Distinct brand for each consumer group
Price	One "popular" price range	One price range tailored to the consumer group	Distinct price range for each consumer group
Distribution	All possible outlets	All suitable outlets	All suitable outlets—differs by segment
Promotion	Mass media	All suitable media	All suitable media—differs by segment
Strategy emphasis	Appeal to many types of consumers through a uniform, broad-based marketing program	Appeal to one specific consumer group through a highly specialized, but uniform, marketing program	Appeal to two or more distinct market segments through different marketing plans catering to each segment

From Evans, J. and Berman, B. (1988). *Principles of marketing,* New York, Macmillan.

the sport product. Brad Berry, director of marketing for the Indianapolis Ice of the International Hockey League (IHL) uses mass mailings as a low-cost way of getting ticket and game information to Indianapolis area residents. The Ice, working with local banks and the Marsh grocery store chain uses statement stuffers* and schedule cards as its primary mass-marketing approaches. Any entity that mails retail bills or statements—such as banks, utility companies, department stores, or stores that will allow the display of pocket schedules—can be approached for these cooperative ventures.

Market segmentation. Nearly all businesses and organizations serve a multitude of market segments, and future market share will be won by the sport organizations that do a better job of identifying and targeting different market segments. A market segmentation, or concentrated, approach identifies and approaches a specific consumer market through a tailored marketing strategy that caters to the specific needs of the chosen segment. Market segmentation is an efficient way to achieve a strong following in a particular market segment.

One caution should be noted, however: After identifying two or more potential market seg-

---

*Statement stuffers are coupons or advertisements that are sent to consumers with a bill or invoice. The company sending the bill absorbs the mailing costs, which usually does not entail cost beyond what was already involved in mailing the bill or invoice. The sport organization assumes the cost of developing and printing the coupon or advertisement. In addition to the obvious publicity for the sport organization, the company sending the bill or invoice engages in positive public relations, as well as association with a sport franchise.

ments, the segment with the greatest opportunity should be selected as the target market, not necessarily the segment with the most consumers. The largest segment may not provide the greatest opportunity because of heavy competition or high consumer satisfaction with a competitor. Finding a niche* is a key to successful market segmentation.

Multiple segmentation. A multiple segmentation approach combines the best aspects of the mass-marketing and segmented-marketing approaches. It is similar to the segmented-marketing approach except that the sport organization markets to two or more distinct segments of the market, with a specialized plan for each segment. Sometimes a sport organization will market to consumers through a mass-marketing strategy to reach a very broad audience and also use a segmented approach geared to specific segments. The more unique segments there are, the better a multiple-segmentation approach will be.

For example, the Youngstown Pride (formerly a team in the World Basketball League), used an approach segmented by age groups. Youngsters between the ages of 6 and 15 were targeted and invited to join the Pizza Hut Fan Club, a benefit of which was a free season ticket. Students aged 16 to 22 were targeted for a student season ticket, available for $75, which was $125 less than the regular season ticket price. Finally, consumers aged 24 and above were targeted with an offer of a regular season ticket, costing $200, because a reduced price was not necessary to attract these people to games. Brochures describing the appropriate offer were sent to these segments, followed by individual telephone calls.

Steps in planning a segmentation strategy

Figure 14-4 depicts the six steps in developing a segmentation strategy. First, the sport marketer should determine the characteristics of consumers and their need for the product or service. In this step, geographic, demographic, and lifestyle information is collected. Next, the consumers' similarities and differences are analyzed; and third, a

---

*Sport marketers attempt to find a unique position in the marketplace by distinguishing their sport product from competing products. This unique position is called a *niche*.

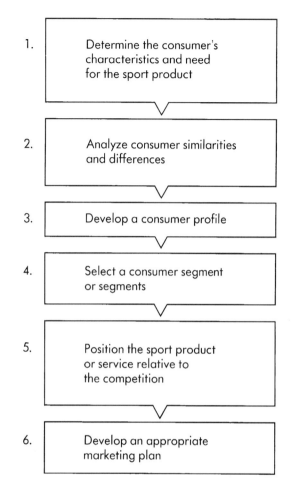

1. Determine the consumer's characteristics and need for the sport product

2. Analyze consumer similarities and differences

3. Develop a consumer profile

4. Select a consumer segment or segments

5. Position the sport product or service relative to the competition

6. Develop an appropriate marketing plan

FIGURE 14-4 Six steps in planning a segmentation strategy.

consumer market profile is developed. These profiles help to define the market segments by combining consumers with similar characteristics and wants into distinct groups.

At this point, the sport marketer must make some decisions. The segment(s) that offer(s) the greatest opportunity must be selected. The marketer decide how many market segments to pursue. The sport organization's financial and human-resources must be evaluated and compared with the cost of developing this segment. The timing of the marketing efforts must be decided.

Fifth, once a market segment has been selected, the organization must look at its competitors and, considering this competition, select a niche. Finally, a marketing mix is developed for each target market.

CONCEPT CHECK

For the best results, a sport marketer should develop a campaign that is highly focused and directed to a specific group of people. This practice is called target marketing. The three methods of reaching the target market(s) are mass marketing, market segmentation, and multiple segmentation. The sport marketer must identify and target different market segments to succeed in today's changing marketplace.

FACTORS INVOLVED IN THE MARKETING OF SPORT: THE FOUR Ps PLUS

As has previously been explained, marketing is a complex process, and its success (to culminate in an exchange) requires the formulation of a strategy to attract and reach potential consumers. That formula is composed of the traditional elements of the marketing mix—product, price, promotion, and place (distribution)—*plus* some other distinct, yet interdependent, facets that vary with the nature of the product or service and with the target market. An examination of these facets will aid in understanding the complexities of developing the *marketing mix* (Figure 14-5).

THE SPORT PRODUCT
Product v service

A **product** is any item that can be offered for sale or barter to satisfy the needs of customers. **Services,** which are also marketed by sport and fitness organizations, are activities or benefits that are offered for sale or barter to consumers. Product benefits are the aspects of the product that satisfy the consumers' needs. According to Luck and Ferrell (1985), a product is a bundle of tangible attributes and intangible benefits that buyers perceive they will obtain if they enter into a transaction. The bundle includes everything, favorable and unfavorable, that a buyer receives in the exchange. Lazer and Culley (1983) interpret a product as containing three dimensions: **attributes, benefits,** and a **marketing support system** (Figure 14-6). Attributes are associated with the **core product** itself and include such elements as ingredients,

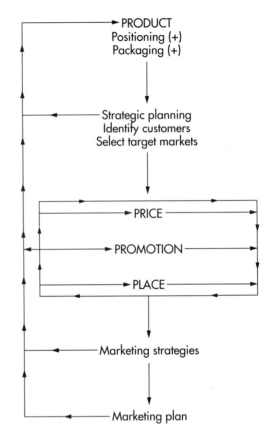

FIGURE 14-5 The four Ps plus of the marketing mix.

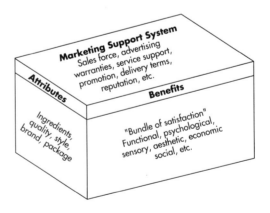

FIGURE 14-6 Basic product dimensions. (From Lazer, W. and Culley, J. (1983). *Marketing management,* Boston, 1983, Houghton Mifflin Co.)

TABLE 14-9   *Dimensions and elements of the sports product*

Attributes	Benefits	Marketing support system
Team (Ohio State, Celtics, 49ers)	Thrill of winning	Rain-out guarantee
Seat location	Expected enjoyment	Ticket services
Athletes	Uncertain outcome	Customer satisfaction guarantee
Presence of superstars (Michael Jordan, Martina Navratilova, Ken Griffey, Jr.)	Social interaction	Media advertisements
Coach (Bob Knight, Tara Vanderveer, Pat Riley)	Identification with the team	
Quality of the opponent	Fun and enjoyment	
The contest (U.S. Open, Wimbledon, Super Bowl, Final Four)		
Presence of promotional event or giveaway		

quality, style, brand, color, packaging, and manufacturing style and preparation. Attributes are the tangible product features and are observable, concrete, measurable, and intrinsic to the core product. Product benefits are defined as what the consumer perceives as meeting his or her needs, such as comfort, increased self-esteem based on status, warmth, safety, pleasure, and so on. Don't confuse features and benefits; features are elements of the product that *deliver* a benefit. The third element, called the marketing support system, includes any (if any) and all services provided in addition to the core product. Table 14-9 lists some of the various elements of the three product dimensions.

Attributes can change because of injuries, trades, weather, and so on. Benefits can change because of the outcome of the contest, other activities that occur with large crowds at sporting events, traffic congestion, parking, and crowd behavior. This is both a blessing and a curse for the sport marketer. The very characteristics of sport that endear it to the pubic—including player personalities, pomp and pageantry, ritual, uncertain outcome, emotion, public consumption, and opportunity for socializing—also make it difficult to market.

Marketing support systems are recent refinements in the sport product. Certain teams have fan satisfaction guarantee programs (Cleveland Indians); most now have family-seating and alcohol-free sections; and most also have sales departments specializing in types of ticket sales (such as group, season, or corporate). A product is generally seen as having a growth curve (Figure 14-7). A **product growth curve** is the story of the product's sales. The four stages of the growth curve—introduction, growth, maturity, and decline—are accompanied by the formulation and implementation of strategies and procedures designed to ensure profitability and growth and minimize profit loss and product decline.

An excellent example of a sport-related product growth curve is the case of the Air Jordan basketball shoe. During its introductory stage, the Air Jordan basketball shoe was accompanied by an expensive advertising campaign and aided by an NBA ruling that the shoes, initially available in only black with red-and-white trim, solid red, or white with black-and-red trim, could not be worn in official NBA games. Michael Jordan's on-court performance also aided the product's introduction and helped the product gain momentum through the growth stage. The growth stage was characterized by heavy demand and increased production and distribution outlets. As the sales of the shoe skyrocketed, market imitators began producing shoes

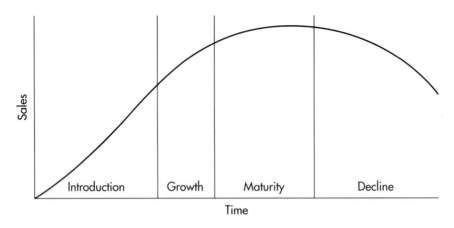

FIGURE 14-7   Product growth curve.

of similar style, color, and quality, as well as shoes of lesser quality and similar appearance. During the maturity stage, the price of the shoe declined to meet market challenges and counteract declining growth.

As sales began to decline, Nike launched a new market offensive by introducing basic white and team-colors Air Jordan shoes, thus opening a new market by offering a product that high school and collegiate teams would wear because the colors no longer were limited. Later strategies included use of exotic leather, further technological modifications, the introduction of a clothing line, and the offering of the product for youths, toddlers, and babies.

CONCEPT CHECK

The sport product is difficult for the sport marketer to control because it is intangible, unpredictable, perishable, and consumed as a social event. For these reasons, the product benefits and product extensions must be marketed. All products have a growth curve, which includes the introduction, growth, maturity, and decline stages.

PRICE

Price is very visible and intrinsically related to the other major elements of the marketing mix—product, promotion, and place (distribution). And because of discounts, rebates, coupons, and promotional incentives, it is considered controllable and flexible. Price involves the determination of goods and services and the calculation of value of the exchange that can be used by all parties involved in the transaction (Luck and Ferrell, 1985). In mainstream marketing, price tends to be a key strategic consideration and, in some cases, the most important component of the marketing mix. Sport—in particular, spectator sport—does not give price the same strategic importance as does mainstream business. In a 1989 study of 3009 fan responses in two selected National Basketball Association cities, Rudman and Sutton (1989) found that the cost of tickets ranked fourth in importance in one city and fifth in another city, behind such considerations as opponent, team record, presence of superstars, and effect of the game on league standings.

Consumers equate price with value. A product that is deeply discounted or even free may be perceived as having little or no value. Bill Veeck would never give away tickets, no matter how poorly his team was performing. According to Veeck, "Tickets are the one thing I have sell. To give them away is to cheapen the product I am selling" (Veeck and Linn, 1962). Similarly, when new sports leagues launch franchises in cities with existing professional sports teams, the new product usually is priced nearly the same as the existing product. Offering the new sports ticket at a lower price would tell the public that, in one way or another, the new product must be inferior to the existing product (Mullin, 1983).

Pricing strategies

Early in the planning process, the sport marketer will have to choose a pricing strategy. Price is most commonly considered as an amount of money; however, it can be more broadly defined as anything of value that is exchanged. **Bartering** (also known as **trading out**), a common practice in sport marketing, consists of an exchange that does not involve money. Tickets, program ads, scoreboard space, and arena signage are valuable commodities to some companies. Sport organizations should use these commodities to trade for goods and services that are needed to execute the campaign (Hardekopf, 1989).

Indiana University's director of marketing and sponsorship, David Brown, uses this strategy to trade women's volleyball and basketball tickets for radio advertising. The university gives 1000 tickets to selected local radio stations in exchange for advertising equal to the face value of the tickets. For example, if the face value of the ticket is $5, the amount of advertising traded would be $5000. The radio station gives away pairs of tickets over the air, resulting in a minimum of 500 "mentions." An additional feature of this **trade-out** agreement is that three additional mentions per giveaway are required, resulting in a total of 15,000 advertising spots over the course of the season.

The University of Kansas attempted to stimulate attendance at its 1989 football games by offering season tickets at two prices. Seats between the 10-yard lines were the higher priced, at $90 each. The 7000 seats located outside the 10-yard lines were priced at $65. This area was called the Hawk's Nest; and because it had been sparsely populated in the past, all revenue would be "new" revenue. According to Doug Vance of the University of Kansas athletic department, "The reduced rate is intended to make it more affordable for fans to become season ticket buyers" (Jayhawks . . . , 1989).

The key to a successful pricing strategy is to react to market demand and the elasticity or inelasticity (how price changes affect or do not affect the consumer and thus the demand for the product) of that consumer demand. In other words, does a price increase or decrease affect demand? In most cases, pricing strategies do not stand alone. Promotional

strategies and product positioning may alter perceived value and in some cases, actual price (for a time). Such strategies combined with pricing usually increase consumer demand for the product.

CONCEPT CHECK

Price is a very visible element of the marketing mix. Although it is most often thought of as a dollar amount, it can include anything of value that is exchanged. Exchanging tickets for services, especially advertising, is a form of bartering, or trading-out, and it is a common practice in sport marketing. Discounting tickets for an event is another useful strategy for the sport marketer.

POSITIONING

Before we discuss promotion and advertising, it is important to understand the concept of **positioning**. One of the classics in the marketing literature is the book *Positioning: The Battle for Your Mind* (1986) by A. Ries and J. Trout. According to the authors, positioning "starts with a product, a piece of merchandise, a service, an institution, a company, or even a person. But positioning is not what you do to a product. Positioning is what you do to the mind of the prospect. That is, you position the product in the mind of the prospect."

With so many sport products and services available today, each accompanied by countless advertisements, consumers have become immune to the plethora of traditional marketing communications. They do this in self-defense; there just isn't enough room in their heads to store every piece of information about every product. The result is that either consumers put products into neat little categories or they ignore them.

The concept underlying positioning is relatively simple: Find a hole (or niche) and fill it. People generally pick one or two product attributes to associate with a product, then file the information. When they need said attributes, the product associated with them comes to mind.

7-Up found a niche in the soft drink industry and out-positioned Coke. Even though Coke's marketing budget was many times larger, 7-Up was able to turn Coke's bigness (and their caramel coloring) against them. How? By positioning themselves as the "Un-Cola." 7-Up represented an alternative beverage for those consumers who wanted a non-cola soft drink.

Positioning can use such factors as price, age, distribution, use, benefits, size, time, and technology to communicate a product's message (Ries and Trout, 1986). A classic example of the use of a positioning strategy in sport involved the Stowe, Vermont, ski resort area. A column in *Harper's Bazaar* by travel writer Abby Rand listed what she perceived to be the top ski resorts in the world: Stowe, Vermont; Aspen, Colorado; Courcheval, France; Jackson Hole, Wyoming; Kitzbünel, Austria; Portillo, Chile; St. Christopher, Austria; St. Moritz, Switzerland; Sun Valley, Idaho; and Vail, Colorado. Seizing the opportunity to position itself as simultaneously elite and accessible, Stowe developed advertisements that showed the shoulder patches of the top-10 ski resorts, with the caption "Of the world's top ten ski resorts, only one is in the East. You don't have to go to the Alps or the Andes or even the Rockies to experience the ski vacation of a lifetime. You need only head for the Ski Capital of the East: Stowe, Vermont" (Ries and Trout, 1986). By mentioning the top-10 ski resorts in the world, the advertisement created an elite list in the consumer's mind, forming the basis for comparison of all resorts not on the list. Professional sports have been positioned as having the most talented athletes in the world, and this positioning has been the downfall of new sport leagues as they have attempted to compete with the established leagues.

Another popular form of positioning, this time used in spectator sports, is to position a sporting event as more than the activity itself. This is done primarily through such promotions as "fireworks night," appearance by the Famous Chicken (formerly known as the San Diego Chicken), and so on. The positioning is that you are receiving something more for your money, a bonus. Family nights are a promotion and a pricing strategy that help position the sporting event as a family affair, something wholesome and traditional that gives the family an opportunity to share an event. As mentioned previously, time of day is a positioning factor, and time of day has been used effectively to market a sport event as a business person's special—a game (usually baseball) scheduled for

early to midafternoon on a weekday. It is positioned as a way for a business person to entertain clients, reward employees, and so on. Taking this positioning a step further, professional basketball and hockey teams have created a ticket package aimed at the business person who may work late, have clients to entertain, and so on. The business person's special package usually contains all weeknight games and is positioned as being tax deductible (as an entertainment expense) and an effective way to impress clients and sponsors. The package may also be developed to combine private-club accommodations (if available), giving the business person another reason to purchase the product.

Yet another interesting sport marketing example of positioning is seen in the competition for teams and vacationers between Florida's Grapefruit League and Arizona's Cactus League. (Note: The Grapefruit League and Cactus League are nicknames for the exhibition leagues composed of Major League Baseball teams using Florida and Arizona, respectively, for spring training.) The Cactus League has attempted to position itself as the leader in certain factors that are weaknesses of the Grapefruit League. For example, the Cactus League emphasizes as its strengths dry heat for player conditioning, the number of playing dates available without inclement weather, the short travel distance between cities, and the proximity to the hometown. This positioning capitalizes on the Grapefruit League's weaknesses of high humidity, frequent rain, and longer travel distances between locations (Governor's Special Task Force on Cactus League Baseball, 1988). The key to this positioning is that very little can be done to reposition the Florida league regarding the first two factors, which are natural conditions. Thus the Cactus League enjoys a natural geographic advantage and can concentrate other positioning efforts on facilities, community and corporate support, governmental involvement, and even attracting Japanese professional baseball teams.

Marketing research—in particular, consumer feedback and reactions—is the key to successful positioning. Marketing research is the key because your marketing solution is not inside the product or even inside your own mind, but instead inside the mind of the prospective consumer (Ries and Trout, 1986). The following box shows how

---

Positioning of K-Swiss tennis shoes

Product: tennis shoes

Target market: upper-middle-class occasional athletes

Competition: Nike, Reebok, Converse, Prince, Diadora

Product's benefits: wearer will look and feel better in the classic K-Swiss design

How differentiated from competition: K-Swiss uses a 25-year-old, classic, all-white design; focus is on performance, not frills and gimmicks. Competition uses celebrity endorsers, bright colors, new-age designs with pumps and air-cushioned soles, and other "gimmicks."

K-Swiss, a small athletic footwear company, positioned its shoe versus Nike and other footwear manufacturers.

PROMOTION

Promotion, another of the *P*s in the marketing mix, is a process in which various techniques are used to communicate with consumers. Sport promotions are most successful when the message the marketer wants to convey is directed toward one or more target markets.

Communication process

The communication process in sport marketing is no different from that used by marketers of other products. A knowledge of the communication process is useful in understanding how a message travels from its origin, the sport marketer, to its intended receiver, the fan or consumer. Figure 14-8 shows a communication model and its implications for sport marketers.

Let's examine more closely how the communication process works in sport marketing:

1. The *source* of the message is the sport marketer of the sport organization. Keeping the sport organization's philosophy and mission in mind, the sport marketer must decide what message will be sent about the product or service (team, club, event, lesson) and to whom (target market) the message will be directed.
2. The sport marketer *encodes* the message by choosing the words, sounds, symbols, or pictures to be used to communicate the intended message. In actuality, the encoding is almost always done by an advertising agency hired by the sport organization.
3. The *channel* is the vehicle the agency uses to get the message to the receiver. This could take any number of forms, from a personal invitation to an ad placed in a newspaper or a commercial on network radio or television.
4. The *receiver* is the target market that the sport marketer wants to receive the message.
5. The way the message is understood by the receiver or target market is the *decoding* aspect of the communication process.
6. The *response* is how the target market reacts to the message. Are consumers motivated to purchase the product or service, or do they merely acknowledge hearing or seeing the message?

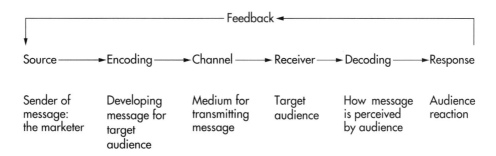

FIGURE 14-8   The communications model.

7. *Feedback,* or evaluation, is a measure of the success in getting the intended message to the target market. Marketing research, ticket sales, and attendance indicators give the sport marketer feedback on how well the message was communicated.

At any or all points of the communication mechanism, there is a possibility that noise* will distort the message. Therefore, it is important to learn how clearly the intended message is being received.

Promotional mix

The communications model (Figure 14-8) can be useful in planning marketing communications via the promotional mix, which includes advertising, personal selling, publicity, and sales promotions. Before implementing any promotion, however, the sport marketer should map out the goals of the campaign. A key to the effective use of promotional strategies and activities is determining what you wish to accomplish and designing a specific promotional activity to reach this identified outcome (Successful Promotion, 1985). The following steps can serve as a general outline for planning a **promotion:**

1. *Define your target market.*
2. *Set measurable objectives.* How will you motivate the target market(s) to take the desired action?
3. *Determine the strategy.* How will you motivate the target market(s) to take the desired action?
4. *Research various promotional ideas.* Talk to other sport marketers, at both the professional and institutional (high school and college) levels for ideas. Visit health and fitness clubs in your locale. Other sources for ideas include the library (for books that catalog promotions), marketing organizations, and local businesses.
5. *Select the promotional approach.* Choose one that is the most likely to be successful with the target market(s).
6. *Develop a theme for the promotion.* Devise a short, catchy slogan to attract the attention of the target market.

7. *Create support materials.* These materials should be in the form of advertising, sales promotions, and publicity.

Using spectator sport as an example and having a goal of increasing attendance, the marketer would need to know who attends and who does not attend, what promotional efforts have been used in the past, and how successful the promotions were. Similarly, the marketer needs to identify variables that attract fans or affect a fan's decision about whether to attend a game. Marcum and Greenstein (1985), in a season-long analysis of selected professional baseball teams, identified day of the week, opponent, and type of promotion as factors affecting attendance. Hansen and Gauthier (1989), through a small cross-section of marketing personnel from a variety of professional sports, found that team quality, price, entertainment, competition, and convenience were factors affecting attendance. Table 14-10 ranks 11 attendance factors identified by Rudman and Sutton in a 1989 study of 3009 fans who attended professional (NBA) basketball games in two cities.

Keep in mind that the promotional mix used for one product, event, or service may not be appropriate for another. Sometimes the emphasis will be on personal selling; at other times, advertising will be the primary need.

Advertising. Because of the tremendous role of media in sport, advertising is probably the most crucial element in the promotional mix. **Advertising—** that is, presenting a paid message about the sport organization's product or service—is possibly the most readily identifiable form of communication in this country. Billions of dollars are spent annually on advertising, involving the following traditional and sport-specific media:

Newspapers	Outfield fences
Direct mail	Radio
Scoreboards	Painted transit advertisements
Magazines	Pocket schedule cards
Posters	Athlete endorsements
In-arena signage	Ticket backs
Television	Game programs
Outdoor advertising	

One of the most popular forms of advertising used in sport marketing is endorsements. Endorse-

---

*Noise is any interference that distorts the message or prevents the receiver from receiving or understanding the message.

TABLE 14-10   *NBA attendance factors**

Factor	Cleveland		Indiana	
	Average score	*Rank*	*Rank*	*Average score*
Opponent	3.28	1	1	3.51
Superstar	3.10	2	2	3.45
Standings	3.08	3	5	2.54
Record	2.99	4	6	2.46
Price/cost	2.73	5	4	2.63
Game day	2.56	6	3	2.75
Weather	2.50	7	7	2.28
Arena access	2.30	8	9	2.09
Game time	2.27	9	8	2.24
Television	2.26	10	10	1.96
Event/promotion	1.83	11	11	1.82

*Survey results are composed of the responses of 3009 people. Means reflect Likert scale, ranging from 1 (never) to 5 (always).

ments feature a well-known or noteworthy athlete who endorses the benefits of a particular product or service. Miller Brewing Company used former athletes to endorse the qualities of its Miller Lite beer, namely taste and low calories. Nike has used athletes to introduce and endorse two of its "flagship" products, the Air Jordan basketball shoe and the Cross Training Shoe, made famous by two-sport star Bo Jackson. Endorsement contracts sometimes contain performance and morality clauses to protect the sponsor from damages resulting from association with a "tainted" athlete. Such contracts may require drug testing, restrict the athlete's lifestyle, or require that the athlete use the product.

Advertising usually follows the AIDA (Attention, Interest, Desire, Action) formula, which attempts to persuade the receivers of the message (target audience) to change their behavior (responding to the ad by purchasing a ticket). The AIDA formula shows the stages a prospect undergoes in deciding to purchase a product or service. The sport marketer wants the consumer to experience all of the AIDA stages in response to advertising communications.

Selecting the advertising medium is the first step. The key element in selecting the medium to carry the advertising message is determining which medium will best reach the target market.

All of the media—including newspapers, radio and television stations, and magazines—have conducted their own studies to describe the audience they reach. The sport marketer should match the demographics of the sport audience with those of the advertising medium.

Another factor to be considered in selecting the medium is the cost. It is much more expensive to advertise on a national network affiliate than on a local cable network. Advertising via television may be the best way to reach the target market, but a limited budget may mean that other outlets, such as radio or outdoor advertising, have to be used. The sport marketer should also consider other creative advertising outlets, such as shopping cart placards, grocery bags, bus posters, banners on streetlight poles, or electronic messages (e.g., on marquees) in an attempt to convey a message to prospective consumers. Figure 14-9 shows a number of advertising strategies that are successful in increasing consumer interest in a product or service, as well as revenue.

Creating an advertising plan to ensure continuity in the marketing communications effort is necessary. The following steps can serve as a guide for developing such a plan:

1. *Set objectives for advertising.* What does one want to accomplish? Create an awareness of a

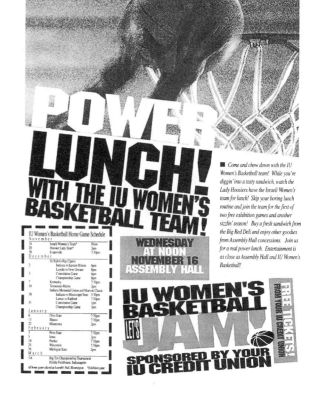

FIGURE 14-9   **A** and **B,** Selling corporate advertising in the form of signage is a popular source of revenue used in most arenas and stadiums.
C, Scheduling special events such as this exhibition lunch is another way to increase fan turnout.

D

If You're Over 55, This Could Be The Fountain Of Youth.

A lot of good things happen when you exercise regularly.

You're stronger. More independent. Less stressed. Have a better self-attitude.

You feel stronger. You're healthier. Which often leads to lower health costs.

Which are several very good reasons to join LifeCenter Plus. The health and fitness center is designed especially for the special requirements of the over-55 adult.

LifeCenter Plus features a fitness center, aerobic rooms, walking track, swimming pool, sauna and whirlpool. Not to mention companionship, camaraderie, and a place where everybody knows and welcomes you.

If you're over 55, join LifeCenter Plus today.

Because it's not how old you are — it's HOW you are old.

Present this coupon when signing up for club membership and receive $50 OFF initial membership fee. This coupon is not valid with any other offer.

SAVE $50

Expires 7/8/89.

LifeCenter *plus*
5133 Darrow Road
Hudson, Ohio 44236 (216)655-2377

FIGURE 14-9, cont'd.   D, This newspaper ad makes excellent use of target marketing, aiming at people aged 55 and older.

product or service? Rouse consumers to action—that is, to purchase a ticket? Maintain current consumers' support? Improve an existing image?

2. *Develop an advertising budget.* Research the costs of advertising in each of the media.
3. *Create an advertising theme.* Develop a catchy slogan relating to the team, event, or club.
4. *Select the media outlet.* Choose the outlet that provides the "biggest bang for the buck."
5. *Create the advertisement.* This can be done in-house or by a local advertising agency.
6. *Develop a media schedule.* When will each advertisement be run? Will the advertising be spread over the entire season or focus on the preseason?
7. *Evaluate the differences of the marketing message.* Use marketing research to evaluate the effectiveness of the advertising strategy. Precampaign and postcampaign testing, recall tests, and postcampaign purchase monitoring are common techniques used to measure advertising effectiveness.

Sales promotion. **Sales promotion**, another part of the promotional mix, is any activity that cannot be called advertising, personal selling, or publicity. However, like the other aspects of the promotional mix, the goal of sales promotions is to induce the consumer to purchase the sport product or service. Sales promotions include many strategies, such as the following:

Coupons	Gifts or premiums
Free samples	Point-of-purchase displays
Contests	Cash refunds
Giveaways	Sweepstakes

In sport marketing, most promotional strategies are in the form of a sales promotion. For example, Northwestern State University of Louisiana was experiencing low student attendance at home football games during the 1982 and 1983 seasons. The football team had a losing record during both seasons, and research showed that most students went home on weekends, including football weekends. The goal (focus) of the promotional campaign for the 1984 season, then, was to persuade students to remain on campus and attend football games. Promotional efforts before and during the 1984 season included pep rallies, special intramural contests, miscellaneous activities in the student union on Thursdays and Fridays, gifts, food, and "tailgate parties." The result of these well-targeted promotional strategies was an average increase in attendance of 3000 per game, and two attendance records were set (Successful Promotion, 1985).

Using a theme as part of a promotional strategy can also be very effective. The University of Iowa used as a promotional theme an attempt to set an NCAA attendance record, and it drew a NCAA-record crowd of 22,157 to a 1985 women's basketball game (White, 1985). A theme, sometimes called a *creative component,* can be used throughout a season. The theme, which should be present in all functions of the marketing effort, will cause the greatest interaction with potential audiences and the media.

The marketing theme should enable the intended audience to form a mental image, impression, or association with the product (Sutton and Duff, 1987). Such was the case with the very successful 1981 promotion of the Oakland A's (now Athletics) titled Year of the Uniform. This promotion was targeted at youth up to 14 years old and was designed to "guarantee" that the youth attended multiple games, because an individual needed to attend at least six games to receive the entire clothing set and an additional two games for giveaways, such as balls and mugs. Attendance at Year of the Uniform games, which were strategically scheduled against quality opponents to maximize attendance and related non-gate revenues, was 40% to 60% higher than on other, nonpromotion days.

Personal selling. Personal selling is another form of promotion that can be very successful if the marketer capitalizes on its unique strengths and uses it in the right situations. **Personal selling** is direct interpersonal communication to inform and persuade. The advantage of personal selling in persuading and informing is that it allows the salesperson to interact with the prospect by explaining, questioning, and refuting objections. A common form of sport-related personal selling takes place in the health and fitness club industry. The personal selling usually takes place after the prospect samples the product through a free visit. At the conclusion of the visit, the prospect is briefed about the benefits of membership and *may* be offered a financial incentive to join the club immediately. If the prospect has objections or reservations, the salesperson has a list of responses to refute the objections and break down resistance. Although the methodology of personal selling does not include coercion, in some cases it is used in the hope of closing a sale.

Personal selling can take place face to face or through **telemarketing**, a form of personal selling using the telephone to inform and persuade and to offer the consumer an opportunity to purchase goods or services. Telemarketing has been a very effective sales tool for spectator sports. Telemarketing companies that specialize in the management of telemarketing campaigns and that train salespeople often contract to sell season tickets, group tickets, game plans, or selected individual tickets for professional teams, as well as for colleges and universities that face difficult marketing tasks or limited resources. The team or organization usually contracts to pay the telemarketing company's expenses and a percentage of income generated. The contract may or may not include a minimum payment regardless of the success of the campaign sales.

The selling plan of personal selling, like many of the other techniques of sport marketing, entails a routine that will help the marketer organize the sales process (Evans and Berman, 1988; Seglin, 1990). The following outlines the typical steps in a selling plan:

1. *Determining sales objectives.* How much of the product is one attempting to sell?
2. *Preparing.* Know as much about the product or service as possible. Salespersons should try to put themselves in the consumer's shoes and think of questions the customer may want answered. Learn about the competition and the marketplace in which the team or organization is competing.
3. *Prospecting.* Develop a list of prospective consumers for the product. Avoid blindly calling potential consumers because the odds of success are low. The success rate improves markedly when prospects are referred by current customers.
4. *Approaching.* Learn as much as possible about the prospect and decide how to solicit this consumer's business.
5. *Making the sales presentation.* Use the AIDA formula to get the consumer's attention,

maintain interest in the product or service, and arouse a desire for the product or service.

6. *Closing the sale.* Persuade the consumer to act and purchase the product or service.

7. *Conducting followup, or postsale, communication.* To ensure that the consumer is satisfied with the product or service, maintain contact with him or her. This builds a rapport with the consumer and encourages future purchases and consumer referrals.

Publicity and public relations. Publicity differs from advertising in that it is *nonpaid*, nonpersonal communication about a product or organization. Usually the sponsor is not identified, and the message reaches the public because of its newsworthiness. Nonprofit agencies involved in recreation, such as the YMCA, YWCA, and YMHA, or national governing bodies (NGBs), such as those for U.S. swimming or gymnastics, usually depend on publicity as a primary tool to communicate with the public. A great deal of publicity comes through news releases. A news release tells about an event or activity that is newsworthy and that merits publicity through the appropriate media (usually print media). A news release should tell the who, what, where, when, why, and how in concise and timely format and should be given to the appropriate media personnel by the agency or organization. Most nonprofit agencies and organizations depend on publicity as the prime way of generating awareness of their missions and programs. To assist local YMCAs, the National YMCA office issues press kits for specific programs. For example, a press kit for youth soccer may provide a release containing information about soccer participation in the United States and quotes from physicians or soccer players about the benefits of play and competition. Often the local program director merely inserts the information about registration, place, and time for the local program.

A unique form of publicity in professional sport has been undertaken by the United Way and the National Football League. Television messages, paid for by the NFL, promote and publicize various United Way agencies and services within the home cities of each NFL franchise. These publicity spots are unique in that they also serve as advertisements for the National Football League by promoting the activities of its players and the charitable activities and functions of the league.

Public relations is a sport organization's overall effort to create a positive image for itself with its target market(s) and the community in which it operates. Public relations is the overall plan for conveying this positive message, but publicity is the tool that communicates the message (Seglin, 1990). The following box lists some of the avenues that publicity can take.

CONCEPT CHECK

Promotion is the process of communicating with the consumer about the sport product. The sport marketer must be aware that interference or noise in the communication process may prevent the consumer from receiving or understanding the intended message. This knowledge is useful in planning and implementing the promotional mix. Elements of the promotional mix are advertising, sales promotions, publicity/public relations, and personal selling. The marketer develops promotional strategies to get the consumer's attention, arouse interest in the product, create a desire, and ultimately motivate the consumer to purchase.

PLACE

Place in the marketing mix is the geographic location of the target market, the location of the product (such as the stadium, arena, or club), and the point of origin for distribution of the product or service. Distribution is the transfer of products, goods, and services from the producer to the consumer. Products move from the producer to the consumer through channels of distribution—any series of firms or people who participate in the flow of the product or service to the consumer (McCarthy and Perreault, 1990). The length of the distribution channel varies; it may be direct or may require wholesalers, retailers, and assorted other middlemen. Probably the most unique aspect of this distribution process in the case of spectator sports is that the product does not move from the production site to a consumer outlet. The production and consumption occur at the same site—the stadium, club, or arena. Thus the consumption site in sport is perceived to be more critical than the distribution channels of traditional marketing. This same perception accounts for the emphasis on color and product extensions, such as juice bars, lounges, and child care facilities, in the construction of new,

---

Publicizing your event

News Media

Radio
Television
Newspapers

Publications

Professional journals
Magazines
Periodicals
Tabloids
Newsletters

Printed materials

Posters
Brochures
Fliers

Special promotions

Phonathons
Shopping malls
Lobby displays
Bus posters
Billboards
Marquees
Bulletin boards

Direct mail

Personal letters
Brochures
Invitations

Personal contacts and presentations

Service clubs
Professional organizations
Chamber of commerce
YMCA/YWCA
Institutional organizations
Public-affairs programs
Conferences
Festivals
Classes
Word of mouth
Other institutions

Advertising

News media
Publications
Ticket outlets
Miscellaneous

---

comprehensive health and fitness clubs. Several factors associated with the location may affect the success of the enterprise. Among these factors are accessibility, attractiveness, and the actual location.

Accessibility has been described as a variable that affects fan attendance at professional sporting events (Marcum and Greenstein, 1985). Accessibility—or the relationship between the location of the product presentation and the location of the target market or consumer—is a key aspect of sport marketing. Accessibility is a convenience factor, and the consumer's perception of convenience may significantly affect the success of the enterprise. Such access factors as highways, public transportation, transportation costs, route (direct or indirect), and length of time required to reach the facility can significantly affect consumer traffic and success in reaching the target market.

Another function of the place concept is attractiveness. Is the place (arena, facility, and so on) attractive (both inside and outside)? How does the attractiveness factor function in drawing potential consumers? Do all of the qualities of the place combine to form a pleasing attraction, or do some elements conflict with other aspects, weakening the total attractiveness? For example, consider Candlestick Park, home to both the San Francisco 49ers (football) and the San Francisco Giants (baseball). A location at the mouth of the bay sounds very attractive; but when the location brings fog, wind, and cold (weather in October and November is often better than during the summer), the picturesque location is overcome by these combined meteorological effects to make the place unattractive (Nelson, 1989). The construction of a new facility, especially in a unique facility—such as the

Toronto Sky Dome or Camden Yards—can serve as an attraction and can become a marketing tool in itself. After the opening of the Sky Dome in June 1989, the Toronto Blue Jays enjoyed 15 consecutive sellouts; and as of August 26, 15 of the final 22 games were also listed as sellouts (Waddell, 1989).

Although the technological innovations of the Sky Dome (such as the retractable roof) are greatly appreciated and ensure fan comfort, the new trend in facility design, especially in baseball, is to "take the nostalgia and intimacy of old ball parks and marry it to modern amenities. . . . [It produces] a stadium that becomes a permanent marketing tool which helps bring people into the ballpark" (Murphy, 1988). The success and attractiveness of Camden Yards in Baltimore (home of the Baltimore Orioles) and Jacobs Field (home of the Cleveland Indians) supports this type of facility design and construction.

The issue of location is also complicated by the location's appropriateness for the activity. The prestige of the facility or the public's opinion of the facility also affect its success. At Ohio State University, field hockey, soccer, and lacrosse are played in Ohio Stadium, a facility that seats about 90,000 spectators. Although the matches in these sports rarely attract more than a few hundred spectators, the prestige of playing in the stadium helps recruit athletes and also implies that the sport is more important than it would be if it were played on a field in another part of the campus.

Establishing the distribution network

Given the effects of the media on sport and the fact that most sport products cannot be physically delivered to the consumer, sport marketers use the media to develop their market. Marketing one's event through a wide-broadcast network not only generates widespread interest in and awareness of the product, but can also have a direct effect on sales by creating "media consumers" who could become light users at a later date (Mullin, 1985). The scope of this chapter does not permit a full treatment of this aspect of sport marketing. More information on setting up a broadcast network can be found in the Mullin, Hardy, and Sutton (1994) and Mason and Paul (1988) books listed in the References section at the end of the chapter.

Another way of distributing a product to consumers is by telephone. The University of Kentucky uses a 900 number and an extensive radio network to get information about the Wildcats basketball team to its alumni and fans. Interested parties throughout the United States can call a 900 number for information about upcoming games, comments from the coaching staff, game statistics, and player profiles. In addition to the 900 system, any restaurant or similar establishment that has closed-circuit radio can arrange to broadcast Kentucky games live. Wildcat fans around the country can enjoy Kentucky basketball games that they otherwise could not hear.

Ticket distribution

The physical distribution of event tickets is an important part of the place aspect of the marketing mix. The goal of the ticket distribution system is to encourage consumer purchases by making the system as convenient and accessible as possible. Strategies used by sport organizations include the following three tactics: First, the selling of tickets is franchised to third-party companies such as Ticketron or Ticketmaster. The advantage of such a contract for the sport marketer is the connection with a well-established, highly visible network of ticket outlets. A consumer can go to any of their ticket outlets and, thanks to the computerized ticket system, buy the desired seat(s) from the pool of available seats for a particular event. After the consumer selects the seat(s), the computer prints the event ticket. This system enables the consumer to choose seats from all the unsold seats rather than having to select from a limited allotment of tickets. However, a disadvantage of this system is the sport marketer's loss of control over the operation and a loss of the ability to monitor consumer satisfaction. Franchised ticket outlets sell tickets for many organizations and do not promote any particular game or event. They also charge consumers a service fee, often as much as $3 per ticket sold.

Second, establishing ticket outlets in local banks and large department or grocery stores is a popular strategy. This system is especially effective in areas where there are no third-party ticket outlets. The Houston Astros have a creative approach to ticket distribution with their Astros van. Mike Levy, the Astros' director of season ticket services, says that to sell more tickets one must "go to the people rather than expecting them to come to you." In an agreement with a local automobile dealer and a cellular telephone company, the Astros are given the use of a van that transports ticket office personnel into the community to sell tickets to upcoming games.

The front office has set an ambitious schedule in which the van goes out every day during the season. On weekdays, the van travels to stores of the Astros' supermarket sponsor; and on weekends, it tours shopping malls and major department stores. The van's schedule is announced at all home games over the radio and in the local print and electronic media. When the team is playing on the road, Orbit, the Astros' mascot, travels with the van.

So popular is this system that people wait at the announced sites, camera in hand, to take pictures of the mascot and to purchase tickets for games. This distribution system and promotional strategy have realized positive results for the Houston team and have brought increased ticket sales, both those tickets bought on impulse and those that are renewals.

Finally, having customer-oriented in-house ticket operations is a necessary tactic. This includes expanding the hours of operation so that consumers can come to the ticket office before or after work and during their lunch hour. The ticket office should be open late at least one evening a week. Telephone numbers, including 800 numbers, should be available for the convenience of consumers who wish to charge their tickets to credit cards. Tickets should also be available for pickup by consumers just before the game at the will-call window.

CONCEPT CHECK

The element of place in the marketing mix is both the physical sport facility and the physical distribution of the product by means of tickets. The transfer of the product to the consumer is made through channels— that is, ticket outlets. Other ways of distributing the sport product include telemarketing, 800 or 900 numbers, and through the media.

PACKAGING

Packaging, or product presentation, is also a key factor in successful sport marketing. The importance of packaging in traditional marketing is un-

derscored by the following quote, "Packaging is a medium of persuasion in an island of neglect" (Heller, 1989). In other words, too much is assumed about the consumer's point-of-purchase decision. Heller states that the package should function as an advertisement and should make its promise loud and clear. Obviously, this philosophy has a great deal of merit for traditional products, but what does it mean for the sport product? Is there an effective packaging methodology for the sport product? With sporting goods and related sports products, the package can explain the product's benefits, such as Nike's "air system" or Asic's "gel system." Packaging also can explain the benefits of a larger sweet spot on a tennis racket or the strength and control of graphite skis. Is there a similar package concept for spectator sport?

The factors that make packaging spectator sport different are the same factors that make spectator sport different from more traditional products. That is, the intangibility of the spectator sport product requires the packaging to be composed mainly of expectations. Second, the packaging, because of the nature of the spectator sport product, is not used at the point of purchase but must be informational and is used *before* the actual event. Brochures, pamphlets, and image-related advertising are the essential packaging forms used for spectator sports. Highlight films, depicting the high points of the past season, are also integral to the packaging function, in that they illustrate the "ingredients" contained in the product.

Some examples of packaging techniques used in professional sports are selling groups of tickets for games held on weekends; "Super Saturday," a variation of the weekend package containing only Saturdays; or miniplans, a group of games from the entire season, combining strong and weak attractions. Other offers include promotional events, weekend and weekday games, and limited game packages, such as the Six Pack or Baker's Dozen, whereby the fan or the organization selects specific games. The benefits of such packages are the low initial cost of tickets for a limited number of games, the fact that seats are guaranteed, and usually a "free," or bonus, game (e.g., 13 games for the price of 12).

Another form of packaging is the flex book: a series of coupons that may be redeemed at the box office for games of the customer's choice. The flex book is attractive because it enables the consumer to choose any games with no date restriction, and it usually offers the benefit of one "free," or bonus, game. The limitation of the flex book from the consumer's perspective is that the seats are limited by availability, and consumers are cautioned to redeem their coupons as soon as possible to guarantee a seat for the games of their choice. In most cases, flex coupons are not redeemable at the gate on game day, forcing some advanced planning by the consumer. On the other hand, the consumer may use all coupons for one game or elect to attend a variety of games, giving the consumer a degree of discretion. The flex book is usually used in cases where ticket demand is less than the supply. In cases where demand exceeds supply, packing is limited and often is confined to season tickets and "mini season" tickets.

Another packaging technique is to combine the primary product with product extensions. An excellent example was devised by the Peoria Chiefs, a baseball club of the Class A Midwest League. The Chiefs designed packages for groups that included game tickets and concession or souvenir items for a discounted price. For example, a $5.50 group ticket (available to groups of 20 or more) included a general-admission ticket, popcorn or peanuts, a 22-ounce soda in a souvenir plastic cup, and a team yearbook (purchased separately, the items would cost $6.50). According to Mark Vonachen, the Chiefs' director of group sales, "The packages have been effective in luring groups to the park for the first time because it makes it easy for people who haven't been here before" (New Packages . . . , 1989). Figure 14-10 further illustrates the possible scope of product extensions.

FIGURE 14-10   Product extensions—such as mascots, contests, half-time shows, and special events—add to the "sport package" by providing entertainment in addition to the core, or the game itself.

CONCEPT CHECK

The four Ps (product, promotion, price, and place) PLUS (positioning and packaging) provide a formula to help the sports marketer reach potential consumers. These facets may be manipulated, emphasized, combined, and integrated to help achieve the correct strategy for the chosen target market(s).

MARKETING PLAN

The tangible result of the strategic planning process and development of the marketing mix (four Ps plus) is the **marketing plan**, a document that provides the framework for the marketing process of the sport organization. The sport marketer's research becomes most effective when it is incorporated into a systematic, formal marketing plan.

Successful marketing is like a successful team: Both the coach and the team members need to have and follow a game plan. A marketing plan is a game plan for the sport marketer. It enables a sport organization to establish objectives, priorities, schedules, budgets, strategies, and checkpoints to measure performance. This section introduces the components of a marketing plan and outlines its most important elements. See the following box for a list of important questions that should be considered in putting together any marketing plan.

Marketing plan outline

I. Background and environmental analysis
   A. Analyze relevant past and current marketing data. Developing a marketing plan

---

*Your marketing plan should provide
answers to the following questions:*

1. What is your product, and how does it benefit your customers?
2. Who, exactly, are your customers?
3. What business are you in, and what is your position relative to your competitors?
4. What barriers exist to keep competitors from taking your customers?
5. Who is/are your target market(s)?
6. How will you communicate with your customers? What is your positioning and advertising strategy? Do you have a creative theme?
7. What are the various promotional techniques and media channels you will use to reach your audience?
8. How much will it cost to market your product or service?
9. What month will you implement the various promotional techniques and media messages?

---

gins with a clear understanding of "where you are."

B. Determine the history of the organization, previous target markets, and the sport organization's philosophies (written or unwritten) that may have an impact on marketing programs.

C. Analyze the external environment by reviewing the economic indicators that may affect your product or service. Governmental agencies, trade associations, libraries, and business publications are excellent sources of data on the economic conditions that affect sport.
   1. Use this information to determine market potential and trends in market behavior.
   2. Assess the political and social trends that affect sport.

D. Analyze the internal organization and construct an organizational chart for it.

E. Perform an analysis of competitors. Knowledge of competitors is critical in designing effective marketing strategies. It is impor-

tant to understand what the competition is doing even if one believes it is wrong.
   1. Most necessary information about competitors can be found in the following sources:
      a. Newspaper articles.
      b. Annual reports.
      c. Company or department literature.
      d. Trade journal articles.
   2. Evaluate the strengths and weaknesses of all components of the competition's marketing mix.

II. Consumer analysis and target market(s) identification.
   A. Perform consumer analysis.
      1. List consumers who are served.
      2. Include consumer demographics.
      3. If available, include psychographics, such as purchase frequency, brand or team loyalty, where tickets are purchased or service is enjoyed, and so on.
   B. Determine target market(s).
      1. Select market segments that are the most likely consumers for the product or service.
      2. Develop a profile of target market segments.

III. Specify objectives. The sport organization should set marketing objectives that help the organization achieve its goals.
   A. What is one setting out to do in the plan? Set goals and objectives as specific quantities to be achieved by specific deadlines. Objectives must be stated in measurable terms.
   B. Marketing objectives generally are stated as a percentage of market share for a particular product or service, penetration of certain market segments, and sales growth for all or selected product lines or tickets.

IV. Determine marketing strategies. How does one plan to achieve his or her objectives?
   A. Strategies are built using a mixture of the *four Ps*—product, price, promotion (advertising), and place (distribution)—plus positioning and packaging.
   B. Use the following steps to develop marketing strategies:
      1. Describe the product and the strategy

that will be used to accomplish the stated objectives (as determined in section III).

2. Set prices for each product line or service. Pricing objectives must match objectives for product lines. Describe the pricing objective for each product line or service.
3. Describe the distribution objectives for each product line or service. Using new distribution channels may offer opportunities to gain a competitive edge. Alternate distribution channels include direct mail, door-to-door sales, electronic shopping, and site flexibility.

V. Specify the advertising and sales promotion program. Before setting an advertising budget, determine the goals of the advertising.
   A. The creative component is the essential core of the approach—what sets one apart. Develop a slogan for the campaign.
   B. Increasing sales, gaining market share, and accomplishing marketing objectives all require sales promotions. Promotions include couponing, public relations, trade shows, and specialty advertising. Determine the sales promotion's objectives and strategies for each product line or service.
   C. Identify the advertising strategies and media (print, radio, television, specialty, direct mail, point of purchase, or other), including the approximate cost and frequency of the advertisement.

VI. Set the marketing budget. The budget should reflect the projected costs of the proposed marketing plan.

VII. Set the marketing activities timetable. Prepare a schedule, calendar, or chart showing the events, ads, and so on that will be used, the person responsible for completing each task, and the month in which the activity should be completed.

SUMMARY

1. Sport marketing has its roots in traditional marketing but is also distinct in a variety of ways.
2. Sports are consumed for a variety of reasons, some of which may have little or no relation to the intent of the producer of the product. The sport marketer must be aware of these motivations for consumption of the product.
3. The marketing of the sport product should be strategically and systematically planned. The strategic plan gives a framework to the entire marketing process.
4. Because of the unpredictability of the sport product, the sport marketer must market both the core product and the product extensions.
5. The focus of sport marketing is on identifying and selecting the target market(s) and then developing a marketing mix that will appeal to the selected target(s). To learn the needs of sport consumers, the marketer must conduct demographic and lifestyle analyses.
6. Sport-marketing concepts act as a formula (the four Ps PLUS) and function in an interrelated manner to produce the effect that the marketer planned to achieve. Each of these factors can be manipulated to reach a target market, create awareness, provide information, or force a reaction.
7. Product usage information is crucial to sport marketing. Because product usage varies, the marketer must develop strategies that address the needs of light, medium, and heavy users. Overemphasizing strategies targeted to the heavy users, particularly if it means neglecting light and medium users, could cost a sport organization in the future.
8. Positioning a product is necessary today because of the overwhelming volume of advertising. The concept of positioning is to differentiate—position in the mind of the consumer—your product from your competitor's product.
9. The sport marketer must select a pricing strategy early in the marketing planning process. Price is the most visible and flexible component of the marketing mix, and it contributes to the consumer's perception of the value of the sport product.
10. Knowledge of the communication process is essential for the sport marketer and can be useful in planning the promotional mix, including advertising, sales promotion, publicity, and personal selling. Before launching

any promotion, the sport marketer should set the goals of the promotional campaign.

11. Advertising, because of its vast reach and high cost, and sales promotions, because of their flexibility, are important aspects of the promotional mix.

12. The marketing plan is a written document, resulting from the strategic planning process, that guides the sport marketer throughout the season.

CASE STUDY
STRATEGIC SPORT MARKETING: THE MIDDLE SIZE UNIVERSITY FOOTBALL PROGRAM *

Marketing plans are produced from the interaction of management objectives, management strategies, strategic plans, and marketing strategies. Two important products of this interactive process are the marketing objectives and the target markets. A key element in this process is the use of marketing research. The case of Middle Size University's football program demonstrates how this interactive process works.

Middle-Size University (MSU) is a community, inner-city campus with an enrollment of 20,000 students. Fewer than 1000 students live in university dormitories. The university is located in a city of about 325,000 people; the metropolitan area has slightly more than 900,000 residents. Management objectives were set by an executive committee of the athletic council made up of local business people (all of whom were men), university administrators, and athletic department administrators. The principal management objective was to increase revenues produced by the football program. More specifically, the executive committee wanted to improve the football program from an average loss of $185,000 a year to an average profit of $250,000 a year. The move was to be completed over 5 years. Management strategy targeted the following revenue producing areas: television and radio, donations, and ticket sales. Management and marketing personnel developed separate strategic plans for each of the three revenue-producing areas. The three separate plans then were combined into an overall marketing strategy with the principal theme of promotion of football—that is, marketing the extensions as well as the core product. The following analysis deals only with ticket sales and emphasizes the relationship between marketing objectives and the target market.

To determine marketing objectives and target markets, the marketing department used a series of four market research studies. The first study analyzed the product (football team's won/loss record, number of star players, and general drawing power) and the local competition for entertainment dollars. The study made the following points:

1. *Even though the football program won 60% of its games over the preceding 5 years and had star players each year, paid attendance averaged only 15,000 for the 5 years. The stadium capacity was 31,500.*
2. *Season ticketholders accounted for only 12% of total ticket sales.*
3. *The university football team competed for spectators with 34 local high school football teams. An average of 20 games were played each Friday by local teams. Local teams were spread across three divisions; the top division offered high-quality high school football.*
4. *The university played its football games on Saturday afternoon or evening. Both of these times competed directly with thoroughbred horse racing, which was a popular spectator sport throughout the state.*
5. *The university football team competed for attendees with three other Division I football teams within the state. The other schools were within driving distance of MSU and had substantial followings within the metropolitan area.*
6. *The university football program competed directly with local cultural events. In one instance, a festival designed to highlight local ethnic culture was held on the same day the university football team played at home.*

The second market research study gathered demographic data about the metropolitan area and local businesses from the local chamber of commerce. The key points of this report included:

1. *Per capita income varied by specific locations within the city and the metropolitan area. These*

---

*Information for the case study was gathered by Professors Lawrence Fielding and Brenda Pitts over 3 years. Research on all cases is still being conducted. Solutions to problems are available on request. Send requests to Dr. Brenda Pitts and Dr. Lawrence Fielding, University of Louisville, Sport Administration Program, HPER Department, Louisville, KY 40292.

figures were compared with property and housing costs. The result was a grid of the metropolitan area that correlated ZIP codes with personal-income ranks.

2. Local businesses were ranked based on five factors: location of corporate headquarters, location of regional headquarters, business type, business size, and business financial strength.

The final two market studies were related. One study surveyed spectators at football games, and the other surveyed spectators at basketball games.* The surveys gathered information on demographics, reasons for attendance, frequency of attendance, and whether spectators were season ticketholders or walk-in trade. Result of the two surveys were then compared. This comparison of the two spectator groups resulted in three important discoveries:

1. Basketball and football season ticketholders tended to be in the middle- or upper-income bracket.
2. Nearly one third of all basketball season tickets were sold to local corporations and businesses, compared to only 5% for football.
3. More than 60% of basketball fans expressed an interest in football to the extent that they watched two or three football games each week during football season.

Based on the market studies and directed by management's objective to increase revenue, the following marketing plan was proposed:

1. Link the purchase of the good, better, and best basketball seats with high donations and the purchase of football tickets. The seats sections in the football stadium and the basketball arena were graded into best-seat sections. To obtain the best seats for basketball games, basketball season ticketholders were required to donate a specific amount of money to MSU's athletic fund and to purchase football season tickets in addition to basketball season tickets. The target market for this strategy was the business community. Special box seats were set aside for businesses that purchased at least 12 season tickets; purchasers of 6-12 season tickets were grouped in special sections;

special services were offered with these special group season ticket purchases.† Business donors were also listed in the program. Football and basketball were marketed as events that could attract clients or consumers and promote company name recognition and good will.

2. Link lower donations with basketball tickets and football tickets. This approach copied the previous approach, except that the size of the required donation was substantially lower and the seats were farther from the action (better graded). The target market for this strategy was smaller businesses and higher-income people. Smaller businesses were courted in the same manner as the larger businesses. Higher-income individuals were approached through direct mail, based on the income grid developed in the second marketing research study. Again, the objective was to sell group season tickets.

3. Link basketball season tickets with football season tickets by offering special seats and special prices. The idea was to set aside a third level of good seats at basketball and football games for those who purchased season tickets for both football and basketball. As an added inducement, a 20% discount on both football and basketball season tickets was offered to purchasers willing to buy both. The target market for this option was middle- and upper-income individuals. The "special offer" was marketed through direct mailings that were restricted to the middle- and upper-income sections of the metropolitan area.

4. Establish bargain seat packages to sell to lower-income groups. Family plans for football games and special one-game offers were developed to attract spectators. These plans were advertised on radio and through the newspaper and frequently were linked with the purchase of products at local businesses.

1. What groups at Middle-Size University were involved in developing the marketing plan for football?
2. What part does marketing research play in developing marketing plans?
3. What effect did the management objective—to increase revenues—have on the development of the marketing plan?

---

*Basketball spectators were surveyed because the basketball program at Middle-Size University was extremely successful. Market researchers wanted to know whether basketball fans were significantly different from football fans and whether basketball spectators had any interest in football.

†For example, the company box package included free parking, free programs, television monitors, and a cash bar.

4. *Who are the direct and the indirect competitors of the MSU football program?*
5. *Why did the marketing plan link basketball season tickets with football season tickets?*
6. *What criterion was used to segment the consumer market?*
7. *What are the differences between the marketing approaches for the market segments?*
8. *Even though team quality is an important factor in marketing, the marketing plan developed does not consider this factor. Is this an oversight? Why would team quality not be considered?*
9. *What other activities would you suggest MSU use to promote its football program?*
10. *Will the marketing plan developed increase revenues? Why or why not?*

REVIEW QUESTIONS AND ISSUES

1. What are the unique characteristics of sport, and how do these differences affect the marketing of sport?
2. Using the Target Group Index or Mediamark marketing reports (or similar marketing research data base), identify the demographic and, if available, lifestyle profile of a sport's participant and spectating audience (e.g., NBA, NFL, World Cup Soccer, etc.)
3. What does the term *market segmentation* mean? What are the types of segmentation that are commonly used, and how does segmentation help the sport marketer identify the target market?
4. Discuss the steps in identifying a target market when marketing "official" clothing of a professional sports team (you might select one of the popular teams from the list in the chapter). How might this target differ from that of a target market for official clothing of a college or university?
5. What does the term *product* mean? Describe the attributes and benefits of a sport product or service.
6. What are the differences between core product and product extensions? Which of these concepts is more important to the sport marketer? Why?
7. What does the term *positioning* mean? How would you attempt to position a three-on-three basketball tournament (to be held for

the first time on your campus) to students? To alumni? To the community?
8. What techniques and strategies would you use to promote your three-on-three campus basketball tournament? Justify your choices.

REFERENCES

Aaker, D. (1988). *Developing business strategies,* ed 2, New York. Wiley.

Ajzen, I. (1991). Benefits of leisure: a social psychological perspective. In *Benefits of Leisure.* State College, Ventura, Pennsylvania.

Ajzen, I. (1985). *Attitudes, Personality, and Behavior.* Chicago, Illinois, Dorsey Press.

Ajzen, I., and Driver, B.L. (1991). Prediction of leisure participation form behavioral, normative, and control beliefs: an application of the theory of planned behavior. *Leisure Science, 13*(4), 185-204.

Ajzen, I., and Fishbein, M. (1980). *Understanding attitudes and predicting social behavior.* Englewood Cliffs, New Jersey, Prentice-Hall.

Associated Press, (1991). *Sports industry slowing in 90s,* Associated Press, August 24.

Bandura, A. (1977). *Social learning theory.* Englewood Cliffs, New Jersey, Prentice-Hall.

Brooks, C. (1994). *Sports marketing: competitive business strategies for sports,* Englewood Cliffs, New Jersey, Prentice-Hall.

Broyles, J. and Hay, R. (1979). *Administration of athletic programs: a managerial approach,* Englewood Cliffs, New Jersey, Prentice-Hall.

Cialdini, R. (1993). *Influence: science and practice,* ed 3, New York, HarperCollins.

Compte, E. and Stogel, C. (1990). Sports: a $63.1 billion industry, *The Sporting News,* pp 60-61, January 1.

Engel, J., Blackwell, R., and Miniard, P. (1986). *Consumer Behavior.* Chicago, Illinois, Dryden Press.

ESPN/Chilton Sports Poll '95.

Evans, J., and Berman, R., (1990). *Marketing,* ed 4, New York, Macmillan.

Evans, J., and Berman, R., (1988). *Principles of marketing,* New York, Macmillan.

Governor's Special Task Force on Cactus League Baseball, (1988).

Govoni, N., Eng, R., and Galper, M. (1986). *Promotional management,* Englewood Cliffs, New Jersey, Prentice-Hall.

Hanan, M. (1980, 1990). *Life-styles marketing: how to position products for premium profits,* New York, AMACOM Book Division.

Hansen, H. and Gauthier, R. (1989). Factors affecting attendance at professional sport events, *Journal of Sport Management, 3*(1):15-32.

Hardekopf, B. (1989). *Creating a winning marketing campaign,* College Athletic Management, pp 35-36, January.

Heller, R. (1989). The supermarketers, New York, EP Dutton.

Jayhawks hope pricing change will attract fans, *Team Marketing Report* 1(9): 8, (1989).

Johnson, W., and Packer, A. (1987). *Workforce 2000: work and workers for the 21st century,* Indianapolis, Hudson Institute.

Kotler, P., (1976). *Marketing management: analysis, planning and control,* ed 3, Englewood Cliffs, New Jersey, Prentice-Hall.

Kotler, P. (1987). *Strategic marketing for non-profit organizations,* Englewood Cliffs, New Jersey, Prentice-Hall.

Lazer, W., and Culley, J. (1983). *Marketing management,* Boston, Houghton Mifflin.

Levinson, J., and Godin, S. (1994). *The guerilla marketing handbook,* New York, Houghton Mifflin.

Levitt, T. (1986). *Marketing imagination,* New York, The Free Press.

Levitt, T. (1960). Marketing myopia, *Harvard Business Review,* pp 45-86, July-August.

Luck, D., and Ferrell, O. (1985). *Marketing strategy and plans,* Englewood Cliffs, New Jersey, Prentice Hall.

Marcum, J., and Greenstein, T. (1985). Factors affecting attendance at major league baseball, part II: a within-season analysis, *Sociology of Sport Journal* 2:314-322.

Mason, J., and Paul, J. (1988). *Modern sports administration,* Englewood Cliffs, New Jersey, Prentice Hall.

McCarthy, E. (1975). *Basic marketing,* ed 5, Homewood, Illinois, Richard D. Irwin.

McCarthy, E., and Perreault, W. Jr., (1990). *Basic marketing,* ed 10, Homewood, Illinois, Richard D Irwin.

Miller Lite report on American attitudes toward sports, New York, (1983). Research and Forecasts.

Moore, M. (1988). The Pittsburgh Pirates Baseball Club: market research report, fan surveys (unpublished).

Mullin, B. (1985). *Characteristics of sport marketing.* In Lewis, G. and Appenzeller, H. eds, Successful sport management, Charlottesville, Virginia, The Michie Co.

Mullin, B. (1983). Sport marketing, promotion and public relations, Amherst, Massachusetts, *National Sport Management.*

Mullin, B., Hardy, S., and Sutton, W. (1993). *Sport marketing,* Champaign, Illinois, Human Kinetics Publishers.

Murphy, B. (1988). Stadiums: back to the future, *Sports Marketing News* 3:13.

Nelson, K. (1989). San Francisco, *Sport Magazine* 80:10.

New packages boost Chiefs' group sales. (1989). *Team Marketing Report* 1(8):4.

Plumber, J. (1974). *The concept and application of lifestyle segmentation,* Journal of Marketing 38(1): 33-37.

Ries, A., and Trout, J. (1986). *Marketing warfare,* New York, McGraw-Hill.

Ries, A., and Trout, J. (1986). *Positioning: the battle for your mind,* New York, McGraw-Hill.

Rudman, W., and Sutton, W. (1989). *The selling of the NBA: market characteristics and sport consumption.* Presentation at the National Basketball Association's Annual meeting, Palm Springs, California, September.

Runyon, K. (1982). *The practice of marketing,* Columbus, Ohio, Charles E. Merrill.

Sandomir, R. (1987). *The gross national sports product,* Sports Inc 1(1): 14-18.

Schlossberg, D. (1980). The baseball catalog, New York, Jonathan David Publisher.

Schreiber, A. (1994). *Lifestyle and event marketing: building the new customer partnership,* New York, McGraw-Hill.

Schreiber, A. (1994). *Sports marketing: competitive business strategies for sports,* Englewood Cliffs, New Jersey, Prentice-Hall.

Settle, R., and Alreck, P. (1986). *Why they buy: American consumers inside and out.* New York: John Wiley.

Sports Illustrated. (1986). *Sports poll '86,* New York, Lieberman Research.

Stotlar, D. (1994). *Sports marketing and sponsorship,* Dubuque, Iowa, Wm C Brown.

Successful promotion: identify the problem before trying to solve it, *Athletic Business,* pp 22-23, March (1985).

Sutton, W. (1987). *Developing an initial marketing plan for intercollegiate athletic programs,* Journal of Sport Management 1(2): 146-158.

Sutton, W., and Duff, R. (1987). *Creating themes to market your athletic programs,* Athletic Administration 22(5):17-18.

Sutton, W., and Migliore, R. (1988). Strategic long range planning for intercollegiate athletic programs, *Journal of Applied Research in Coaching and Athletics* 3(4):233-261.

University of Pittsburgh, Department of Economics, (1977). *An economic impact study of the Pittsburgh Pirates Baseball Club on the city of Pittsburgh,* Pittsburgh, University of Pittsburgh.

Veeck, W., and Linn, E. (1965). *The hustler's handbook,* New York, Putnam Publishing Group.

Waddell, R. (1989). Attendance ups and downs for major league baseball teams, *Amusement Business* 101(34): 18, 31.

White, J. (1985). Presentation at the NCAA marketing and promotions seminar, Cincinnati.

Zajonc, R., and Markus, H. (1982). Affective and cognitive factors in preferences. *Journal of Consumer Research,* 9(10), 123-131.

SUGGESTED READINGS

Brooks, C. (1994). *Sports marketing: competitive business strategies for sports,* Englewood Cliffs, New Jersey, Prentice-Hall.

Cialdini, R. (1993). *Influence: science and practice,* ed 3, New York, HarperCollins College Publishers.

Levinson, J., and Godin, S. (1994). *The guerilla marketing handbook,* New York, Houghton Mifflin.

Levitt, T. (1960). Marketing myopia, *Harvard Business Review,* pp 45-86, July-August.

Mullin, B., Hardy, S., and Sutton, W. (1993). *Sport marketing,* Champaign, Illinois, Human Kinetics Publishers.

Ries, A., and Trout, J. (1986). *Positioning: the battle for your mind,* New York, McGraw-Hill.

Stotlar, D. (1994). *Sport marketing and sponsorship,* Dubuque, Iowa, Wm C Brown.

CHAPTER 15

Sponsorship

Dave Stotlar

In this chapter, you will become familiar with the following terms:

Sponsorship	Leveraging	Pricing
Exchange theory	Target markets	Cost-plus method
Philanthropy	Demographics	Competitive-market strategy
Advertising	Product sampling	Relative-value method
Return on investment	Merchandising	Valuation
Market research	Sponsor agreement	Ambush marketing
Media exposure	Legal counsel	Cross-promotion

Overview

On a worldwide basis, sport organizations and corporations have entered into partnerships wherein each agrees to assist the other in forwarding their own objectives. One such partnership is sport **sponsorship.** For sports organizations, it's an effort to obtain funds from sponsors to operate their sports events and programs. For corporations, it's a chance to get their products in the minds of consumers. This relationship originated decades ago, but it has increased in popularity and sophistication over the last 15 years (Wilkinson, 1986; Ensor, 1987; Asimakopoulos, 1993; Graham, 1993; Irwin, 1993). It has been estimated that more than 4000 U.S. companies involved in sports marketing and sponsorship spent $4.25 billion on their sponsorship programs in 1994. Worldwide spending was $9.6 billion for 1993, with a growth rate anticipated at 15% (IEG, 1993a).

PHILOSOPHICAL BASIS FOR SPONSORSHIP

Initially, sports professionals must develop an understanding of sponsorship from a philosophical view. Sport sponsorships are based on the **exchange theory:** "If you give me something, I'll give you something." Therefore the definition of a sport sponsorship is a situation wherein a sport organization grants the right of association to another company or organization. As we will see, the right of association can take many forms.

A determination must be made early in discussions between the parties involved regarding whether the exchange can be equal—can be equal as opposed to will be equal. Some sponsorship arrangements cannot provide equal value to both parties—for instance, the junior high school sports program that is asking for money to print its sports program. Any corporation that provides these funds is actually doing it for **philanthropy** rather than for financial reasons. However, a company that pays a fee to put its corporate logo on the side of a race car in the Indianapolis 500 may be able to generate an advertising value that substantially exceeds the amount paid. Irwin (1993) noted that "in years past, corporations provided financial assistance to sporting events and athletic programs for philanthropic purposes, [but] today's corporate interests are strictly promotionally motivated."

CONCEPT CHECK

Those who desire to obtain a sport sponsorship must make an initial determination with respect to their ability to deliver commensurate economic value in the exchange. If this criterion cannot be met, a philanthropic approach is mandated.

A key step in making a sponsorship proposal appealing to a sponsor is to provide a comparison of the requested amount to competitive **advertising** costs and value. Each potential sponsor is engaged in other marketing activities, each of which has a price and a value. You must study and prepare data that show the benefit of sport sponsorship in terms that the corporation can evaluate. Remember, the person who agrees to give you the sponsorship must be able to defend her or his decision to the corporate management or stockholders.

A key component in the sponsorship process is the measurement of **return on investment** (ROI). Is there an equivalent increase in sales attributable to the sponsorship? Conventional data relating to the advertising and promotions conducted by corporations show that only about 16% of the promotions produced sales that were greater than the costs of the promotion (Abraham and Lodish, 1990). These authors also believe that if a promotion is not effective in increasing sales within a 6-month period, it will never produce sales. With this in mind, it becomes essential for those entering a sport sponsorship to accurately and quickly measure the impact and success of the partnership. Recent data on VISA International's Olympic sponsorship produced data that measured a 3% increase in customer preference from before the Olympic games to after their completion. Although that may not seem like a large increase, 3% of a multibillion dollar industry is a considerable amount of money.

Sport managers must be fully cognizant of the data with which to demonstrate the accomplishment of specified corporate objectives. This should be provided by the sport organization or event owner, but it is occasionally collected by the sponsor. Motorola conducted its own market research to investigate the effectiveness of its motorcycle team sponsorship in Europe and found that it received a 6-to-1 return (IEG, 1993b).

CONCEPT CHECK

Sport organizations that use sponsorship as a marketing tool must be prepared to evaluate sponsorship in the same manner as other marketing efforts.

According to research data, "sponsorship may send a more convincing message than traditional advertising" (Performance Research, 1991). The study found that 70% of golf enthusiasts could recall the sponsors of events, whereas only 40% could remember the television commercials aired during the events. However, one should not underestimate the power of broadcasting commercial advertising during sports programs. Only about 8% of television viewers can recall commercials aired during nonsports programs.

One can also have professional **market research** firms collect data for you. One such company is Performance Research, which conducts research in the area of sponsor exposure for companies involved in the trade. It conducts field-based research in such areas as aided and unaided recall, advertising awareness, responses to promotions, product usage, and brand loyalty.

During the Olympic games, Performance Research studied the recognition by consumers of Olympics sponsors (1992, 1994a, 1994b). Before the games, they found, 34% of consumers were still unaware that 1994 was an Olympics year and 43% could not name any Olympics sponsors. Of those who could name a sponsor, Coke was the leader, with an awareness of 22%. Studies conducted during the Olympics showed that 50% to 75% of those surveyed recognized Coke (Performance Research, 1994b; Stotlar, 1992).

Sports organizations have a variety of objectives, but two of the most prominent are finance and media exposure. Interestingly, these are the same objectives that sponsoring corporations seek.

CONCEPT CHECK

Establishing a base for a sponsorship relationship is paramount to its success. The sport organization and the sponsor must work together in all facets of the relationship. According to Wilkinson (1988), "in an ideal relationship between the organization and the sponsor, each helps the other meet its objectives."

Because sponsorship is "playing a more central role in corporate thinking, it becomes more important to understand consumer reaction to sponsorship efforts and to research the influence of sponsorship on attitudes" (Sandler and Shani, 1993). In general, only 3% of the public feel that sport sponsorship is a "bad thing" (IEG, 1993a). At the same time, however, some consumers think that sports are becoming too commercialized.

With regard to the Olympic games, 53% of the consumers surveyed felt that the games were overcommercialized, yet "64% said they would be likely to buy a product which sponsors or financially supports the Olympics over one that doesn't" (Turner, 1992). More recent data show that about 20% of consumers selected products because the company was an Olympic sponsor (Sandler and Shani, 1993; Performance Research, 1994b). In addition, 28% indicated that Olympic sponsorship impacted their daily purchasing habits (Performance Research, 1994b). In another study, "Olympic sponsors were perceived as both 'friendly' and 'global'" by consumers (Performance Research,

1992). Probably the most revealing data indicated that 69% of consumers felt that "the fact that a company is an official sponsor has no impact on my purchase habits" (Sandler and Shani, 1993). Although the research data are mixed in their summary of consumer reaction to sponsorship, you could argue that if the companies didn't think that it was a good investment, the billions of dollars now committed to sport sponsorship would disappear.

According to Irwin (1993), "without the support of corporations, the world of sport, as we know it, would collapse." This may seem dramatic, but the world of sport has become increasingly dependent on corporate sponsorships for operating revenues. For example, 40% of the U.S. Olympic Committee's 1992-1996 budget came from sponsorship and licensing revenue. In addition, 90% of the top NCAA universities have corporate sponsorship programs in place (Irwin, 1993). Thus the relationship between sport organizations and sponsors must include advantages to all parties involved.

RESEARCHING SPONSORSHIP PROSPECTS

Many sports marketers fail to adequately prepare themselves to enter the sponsorship business. The key to success is the ability to research prospective companies. Probably the best place to start is to obtain a thorough understanding of the corporate sponsorship environment. The International Events Group (IEG) in Chicago has organized a corporation around the sponsorship industry, and its publication, *IEG Sponsorship Report*, is an important tool in researching prospective sponsors. The *Report* listed the brand name products that most frequently sponsored events: Coca-Cola, Pepsi, Budweiser, Miller, AT&T, American Airlines, Coors, Kodak, Gatorade, and Ford. Its research also provides the categories and their responses to future plans for sponsorship. For example, in the airline category, 28% of the carriers were planning to increase their sponsorship activities, whereas 72% were going to decrease their involvement. In the health care sector, 88% were anticipating an increase, and only 12% were contemplating a decrease (IEG, 1993b).

Sponsorship proposals are considerably more effective if they tie sponsorship elements specifically to objectives of the sponsoring corporation (Irwin, 1993). One of the more effective steps in investigating corporations' objectives and goals is gaining access to their corporate literature, such as the annual report. This document will tell you a lot about the inner workings of a company. There are, however, many things that a company doesn't want its shareholders to know that you need to know. From this perspective, you can read clippings from area papers or talk to people who do business with the company. Just knowing who holds what office is not enough; you have to know who the power brokers are in the organization.

One good example is the Coca-Cola Company. The best point of access for a sponsorship with Coke is the local bottler. More than 90% of the proposals funded by Coke come through to corporate headquarters with support from the local bottling company. The corporate belief is that if the local bottlers are in favor of an event and believe that it will have a positive impact on sales, then it's worth doing. However, the local distributor for other corporations may not have the money, the interest, or the authority to enter into this type of arrangement.

Additional research must be done on a corporation's prior sponsorship experiences. If it has had good experiences, your chances will be better; if it has had one or more bad experiences, you will have a difficult time demonstrating that your results will differ.

EXAMINING SPONSORSHIP OBJECTIVES

Irwin (1993) identified **media exposure** as one of the three most highly rated factors by sponsors in judging sponsorship proposals. *Telling* sponsors that they will get media attention is valuable, but *measuring* it provides data for legitimizing the corporation's involvement in sports marketing. In short, it helps them to help you. In a service-related business, it's your responsibility to provide them with these data.

Another consideration is **leveraging** media coverage through sponsorship. You are going to be spending money on advertising anyway, so why not seek a media sponsor and arrange for a 3-to-1 arrangement (for $3 worth of media space or air time, you give them $1 credit toward sponsorship). This will give you more advertising for your dollar, your sponsors more media benefit, and the media source special-event associations (Cone, 1991).

Irrespective of the validity of calculating the value of camera/action shots on an equal basis

with actual ads, it gives the sponsors (or marketing managers) data with which to defend their decisions to use sport as a marketing vehicle. In an analysis of the CART/PPG Indy Car World Series, Sponsors Report (1991) indicated that each of the top 10 series and event sponsors averaged $3.6 million in exposure for the series. Each of the top 10 car teams' sponsors averaged $6.2 million in exposure value over the season.

In another example of media exposure, the promoters of Vail 99 (referring to Vail, Colorado's bid to host the 1999 World Cup ski finals) sent First Lady Hillary Rodham Clinton and her daughter, Chelsea, Vail 99 ski coats to wear during their trip to the 1994 Olympic Winter Games in Lillehammer, Norway. When interviewed on global television, Mrs. Clinton was asked about the Vail 99, and she said that she and the President support Vail's bid for the world championships. Individual merchants in Vail also donated $1000 each to Vail's bid in hopes that consumer traffic during the event would increase their sales (Carrier, 1994).

The ability of sponsors to receive positive visibility and increase sales with favorable publicity has been shown to be an attractive mechanism for sponsors. Yet "keeping a sponsor happy and running a responsible event can be a fine line to walk. We will not do anything to sacrifice the . . . quality of the event. Event organizers that put their sponsor's needs first and the event's needs second are . . . heading for trouble" (Weilgus, 1989).

Another argument that has been forwarded as a rationale for sponsorship is that by selling corporate advertising in community recreation facilities, participants could be offered the same level of programming without an increase in user fees. In Canada, approximately 50% of the public recreation centers have sold facility sponsorships (Schmidt, 1993).

Before undertaking a sponsorship, most corporations develop a seat of criteria for evaluating possible opportunities. This process has been discussed extensively (Wilkinson, 1986; Ensor, 1987; Irwin and Asimakopoulos, 1992; Irwin, 1993). Typical factors to be considered beyond the media aspects previously discussed include the following:

Target markets

There has to be a careful match between the **demographics** of the sponsor's consumers and the audience/participants of the sports event. In discussing their sponsorship of a golf tournament, one Acura (automobile) executive said the golfing market was its most desirable demographic target. Irwin (1993) stressed the importance of this when he said, "the audience profile, which is rapidly becoming the most important element of a sponsorship proposal, needs to go beyond simply reporting attendance figures and must comprehensively describe who attends the events." The sport organization has several avenues through which this information can be provided. The organization can collect its own data, or it can use secondary data collected by a commercial firm.

At the University of Northern Colorado, turnstile operators use Universal Product Code (UPC) scanners to record students' ID cards when they enter the stadium. With this information, the university can identify exactly who came to the game. Although only 50% of colleges collect this type of information, it is essential for sponsors. Consumer research firms such as Simmons Market Research Bureau also collect similar data on a nationwide basis. Their data can be used to relate to sponsors the "typical audience" for specific sports events. Their study of media and markets also provides data on television viewership of sports events. These will provide a rough idea of the audience profile for sports events.

The geographical reach of the sponsorship is also important. According to Brewer (1992), "if you're targeting an audience in the Southeast, you may want to get involved with stock-car racing. It's the same with any marketing strategy; know your audience." Research commissioned by NASCAR indicated that its fans had the following characteristics: 78% male, 73% married, an average of 42 years old, 81% home owners, with 3.4 cars per household, and 87% earning $35,000 to $50,000 per year (Performance Research, 1994c). These data are imperative when attempting to select sponsors who have these people as their primary consumers. You simply cannot make a good match without good data.

Product sampling opportunities

"Qualitative research shows that sampling is the single best way to convert people" (International Events Group, 1993d). To calculate the benefit for the sponsor, one can compare the cost of the sampling to the anticipated return. Sampling can convert about 10% of product users to the company's product. Assume that the typical consumer purchases $20 of the company's product per year, with a profit of $15. If the company spent $100,000 ($50,000 each for the sponsorship and for the cost of labor and products) for the sampling, there would need to be almost 7000 conversions, which could only be realized if the event drew a crowd of about 70,000. Events can be both cheaper and more effective than other avenues of sampling. For example, the Los Angeles Marathon assembles "goodie bags" for participants, with product samples supplied by sponsors (International Events Group, 1993d). For many years, U.S. Swimming also used this technique to provide a sponsor's sunscreen products for its members. In another example, Kodak uses its Olympic sponsorship to get its product into the hands of thousands of professional photographers who spend considerably more (or more often recommend corporate film purchases) than normal consumers.

It is your responsibility to control sampling. Sponsors generally do not want consumers to take multiple samples, which would detract from product sales. Depending on the type of product, the timing of distribution is critical. You would certainly want to hand out the above-mentioned sunscreen to people on their way into the event on a sunny day. However, you may not want to provide cookie samples to incoming consumers because it could hurt your concession sales. For large or perishable products, it may also be wise to distribute them as people exit the venue. If you do any postevent research, it is also a good idea to ask about the samples provided.

OTHER CONSIDERATIONS
Client entertainment

People will pay incredibly large sums of money for the opportunity to play in a "pro-am" golf event with a top golfer. Although the power to invite business associates to a skybox still carries substantial weight in some sponsorship decisions, these affinity factors are declining. The Minnesota Timberwolves of the NBA have made extra seats on their team plane available to their sponsor, Miller Brewing Company (International Events Group, 1993d). VIP parking and seating, hospitality suites (or tents), and specially designed event apparel are other perquisites that accompany sport sponsorships. In some corporations, sport sponsorships are considered "an ego buy used by CEOs to impress their partners" (McManus, 1989).

Some research has indicated that these elements are not primary factors in the decision to sponsor an event. Kuzma, Shanklin, and McCally (1993) found that client entertainment ranked significantly lower than other marketing elements. However, it should be noted that the events included in the study were amateur sports. Research regarding this factor for professional or world class events (e.g., America's Cup, Olympics) may yield different results.

The management of an event is also a consideration for sponsors. In a 1988 brochure for the Olympics, the agency noted that "a company is judged by the company it keeps." The past history of the organizing committee and the professional reputation of the staff are critically important because the image of the corporate sponsor is being placed in the hands of the sport organization.

The image of the products and services offered must also result in a good match. Because sport is associated with a healthy lifestyle, many sponsors may seek to relate their products to that image. Campbell's is one example; it has sponsored fitness programs for kids and Olympic athletes preparing for competition. Research has shown this to be very effective. According to consumers, "Olympic sponsors were perceived as 'healthy' " (Performance Research, 1992).

Merchandising

Merchandising is an area in sport that has experienced incredible growth during the 1990s. The merchandising and licensing business has, according to industry data (Lesly, 1992; Irwin and Stotlar, 1993), annual sales that exceed $11.1 billion per year. While the major professional leagues own and sell the rights to teams' names, the auto-racing licensing programs are often run by the sponsors. In 1994, Miller Beer had 200,000 requests for its NASCAR Racing team merchandise before the racing season even began. Most people would agree that having 200,000 people willing to pay money to wear your logo would be a positive sponsorship outcome.

Sponsorship options

Brooks (1994) suggests that sponsorship provides a variety of "athletic platforms" that can serve as the basis for sponsorship: individual athletes, facilities, or an event. Each of these must be selected in reference to corporate goals and objectives. A single platform will be a good fit for all companies. Individual athletes can give a corporation a personal touch. Texaco effectively used race driver Mario Andretti to give motivational speeches to their top executives on what it takes to be a winner. However, "the effectiveness of any individual spokesperson is limited by consumer perception of their credibility" (Performance Research, 1991). In recent years, problems have often developed around individual athletes as representatives of a company. Sports celebrity endorsers have been involved in drinking-and-driving incidents, legal charges surrounding their behavior, and other public indiscretions. This type of publicity does the sponsor more harm than good.

One effect of celebrity bad behavior has been that sponsors have increasingly turned to events. Events don't do drugs or molest children. Someone will win, and the sponsor can associate with the winner. It should be noted, however, that events are not risk free either. In the late 1980s, the PGA became embroiled in the controversy surrounding the racial membership policies of golf courses where tournaments were being played.

Each component in the platform that is made available for sponsors has its strengths and weaknesses. The task for sport managers is to find an appropriate fit between the company and the sport organization.

Sponsorship models

Conceptual models for managing sport sponsorships have been derived from field-based applications. The model presented (Irwin and Asimakopoulos, 1992; Figure 15-1) has been derived from existing sponsorship proposals and agreements. By examining this model, administrators can gain the skills necessary to effectively work with sponsorship partners. Specific examples and procedures are presented for you to use as models in building sponsorships for your sport organization.

One aspect of sport sponsorships that has been difficult to foresee for many managers is that corporations often would rather deal with large projects than be burdened by a multitude of small ones. One of Volvo's specific recommendations for sport sponsorship is that high-cost deals are more profitable

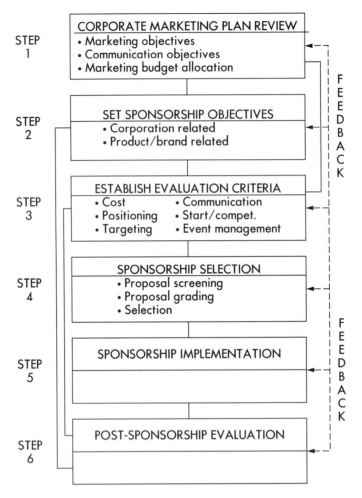

FIGURE 15-1 Six-step approach to sponsorship management. (From Irwin, R. L. and Asimakopoulos, M. (1992). An approach to the evaluation and selection of sport sponsorship proposals, *Sport Marketing Quarterly,* pp 43-51, December.)

and less work than numerous small ventures (Volvo and Sport Sponsorship, 1990). Therefore, it is important to offer the company several options in its sponsorship agreement, ranging from exclusive ownership of all events and opportunities to smaller and less expensive options, such as in-kind donations or program advertising.

The framework for this, like any business relationship, is established through the **sponsorship agreement.**

SPONSORSHIP AGREEMENT

Reed (1990) indicated that the laws pertaining to sports sponsorship are not well defined. She recommends that the contracts between the sponsor and the event/property holder be carefully constructed. Remember, consult your **legal counsel** so that all matters are included in the contract in clear language with mutual understanding. The most critical points to be addressed in the contract include the following.

Terms like *title sponsor* and *official supplier* have no standard meaning in the industry. Therefore, you must clarify the rights the sponsor is getting and the rights the promoter is retaining. You also need to preserve the value of the sponsor's exclusivity. This factor was rated as the most important, above television exposure, by Canadian firms (International Events Group, 1992). Avoiding competitors is only part of the problem. Developing an appropriate sponsor mix is also a consideration. You should carefully match each sponsor with other sponsors, products, and corporate image. For instance, based on the 1994 Olympic Winter Games, the U.S. Figure Skating Association may not want to offer the category "official legal counsel." Pizza Hut may not want an "official antacid" for an event if it were a title sponsor. McDonald's would not want to have Pepsi as the official soft drink because of its ties with Coca-Cola. If a soft drink company is secured, be sure to give attention to the contracts at the venue and any conflicts that might arise.

Each partner should strive to protect each other's trademarks and logos. Cooperation is always intended, but abuse can occur if the issue is not addressed. Typically, any use of an event logo or corporate trademark requires the owners' approval unless it is specially covered in the contract. Both parties need to be protected from liability through insurance. A sponsor does not want to be sued by an injured spectator or participant. Most events arrange for special coverage for all parties involved in an event. You might even have "insurance coverage" as a sponsorable category.

The agreement must include details on the use of the sponsors and event logos, including facilities and uniforms. Most sport organizations—including the IOC, USOC, NCAA, NFL, MLB, and NBA—have rules regarding the size of corporate logos that can be displayed on team uniforms. The primary catalyst in the logo issue was ski racers who, at the end of a race, immediately raised their skis in the air, logo toward the TV camera. Olympic gold medalist (1994) Diann Roffe-Steinrotter not only sported her Rossignol skis but lifted her Carrera goggles to reveal her Vail 99 headband promoting Vail's bid to host the 1999 World Cup ski finals (Carrier, 1994).

NASCAR strikes deals with sponsors and requires all drivers to place NASCAR's sponsors' logos on its cars for each race. Specific rules exist for the placement of the logos on the race cars (Figure 15-2). The winning drivers of NASCAR races engage in a furious practice in victory lane: They constantly change hats sporting various sponsor logos. Not only does this give each sponsor its moment in the sun (and camera lens), but it's in the contract. Even the sequence is prescribed.

In 1990, the NCAA published guidelines for all corporations involved in sponsoring its championships. In this document, the NCAA maintains absolute control over the sponsors' signs, advertisements, and even their specific wording. The NCAA document requires that "all advertising copy and promotional activities by NCAA national corporate partners utilizing the NCAA's name or registered marks must have prior approval of the NCAA" (National Collegiate Athletic Association, 1991).

One also needs to protect an event from being stolen. Many contracts contain a clause that prohibits the sponsor from staging a similar event for a specified number of years. However, problems can arise because of the difficulty of protecting the idea of an event or sponsorship. A situation such as this occurred with a national biathlon competition in the early 1990s. An agency representing the biathlon competition had proposed sponsorship to Adolph Coors Brewing Company. The event was conducted in 1988 and 1989 as the Coors Light Silver Bullet Biathlon Series, but when it came time for renewal in 1990, Coors delivered a form letter that stated "While COORS will evaluate your proposal for possible use in the future, it cannot make any commitments until the programs have been reviewed. . . . Please be advised that COORS may be developing similar or related projects, independent of any promotional ideas or proposals . . . submitted" (International Events Group, 1990). A few weeks after the event, the organizer received notice that Coors would not be renewing its contract and had, in fact, hired one of the agency's subcontractors to stage future events for Coors (International Events Group, 1990).

Protection against unfulfilled promises should also be addressed in the contract. If an event promises to deliver a designated number of spectators or TV audience share, it should be written into the contract and possibly backed financially through a letter of credit (Reed, 1990). The penalties (or bonuses) should be preset in writing so that all parties clearly understand the stipulations.

THE ULTIMATE
FLEET VEHICLE

The sheet metal on stock cars is intently watched by millions of fans, so it is prime advertising space. The 33 advertisements on this car follow elaborate rules. Here's how it works.

1 Vehicles in NASCAR races are divided into sections, with each section reserved for different kinds of sponsors. The primary sponsor of this car, Coca-Cola, paid more than $1 million for the right to put Mello Yello's logo on the hood and side panel.

2 Contingency sponsors like Sears DieHard pay $100,000 to $200,000 for the right to put small decals on the front side panel. DieHard paid a larger fee to NASCAR and obtained the right to put its sticker above the center of the front wheel. Right Guard deodorant paid less money and sent its check directly to the car owner, so it has to stay below the hub.

3 Associate sponsors pay between $150,000 and $450,000 for the rights to the rear side panel. Donzi and Uniden placed their logos as close as possible to the center of the car to increase the number of times a camera will focus on them. Behind-the-tire logos don't get nearly as much media exposure.

4 The post behind the front side window usually carries the carmaker's name. The rear side window post sometimes carries the owner's name, but here it has been sold. The space between the windshield and front window can also be sold, but on this car, it's not for sale. Added together, the commercials on this car are worth several million dollars a season for the car owner and NASCAR.

Source: Gossage-McFarland Sports Marketing. Harrisburg. North Caroli.

FIGURE 15-2 The ultimate fleet vehicle.
(From American Demographics, 14 (11), November 1992, a publication of Dow Jones & Co., Inc. Artwork courtesy of Gossage-McFarland Sports Marketing, Harrisburg, North Carolina.)

298

Additional aspects of the agreement have been addressed by Brooks (1990). The types of event signage that will be available and the number, location, and responsibility for making and hanging them are all important matters to be covered in a contract. The actual production, installation labor, and postevent procedures are also essential points. Most sponsors do not want to risk their corporate image with the presentation of their logos on banners and signs. Therefore, most sponsors will oversee the production of an event's signage. However, organizers should be careful and supervise the installation. In one situation, at the (now defunct) Denver Grand Prix, Marlboro put up more than its allotted signs and erected them in places that had not been agreed to by event organizers. Only on the morning of the race did the organizers notice the problem, and it was too late to correct the situation. It's debatable whether it was an error or a strategic move by Marlboro to gain more exposure.

Most agreements control a sponsor's signs, advertisements, and even their specific wording. The difference between using the terms "official sponsor" and "official supplier" may mean thousands of dollars from a company, and one would not want to allow a minor sponsor to detract from the value sold to a major contributor.

Sometimes the selection and control of signage precludes existing signage in a local facility or secured by participating teams. Is your agreement enforceable regardless of the venue's or the team's previous sponsorship commitments? The signage issue has been addressed by the NCAA in its contract for championship events, which states that "permanent, previously existing contracted advertising displays that were accepted by the NCAA at the time the NCAA event site was determined . . . shall not be illuminated. All advertising must be covered at all championship sites unless protected by prior contract" (National Collegiate Athletic Association).

An organization's mailing lists and the use of individual athletes are often key factors in sponsorship. Many sponsors would like to use both for their benefit. You have probably kept records from advance ticket orders, season ticket holders, or association members. Corporations can use these to strengthen ties to consumers. Direct-mail campaigns are more effective if they come through an organization with which the consumer already has an association. Some sponsors like to use participants in their promotions. Be careful if you promise to provide them because they may not allow you to make agreements for their appearance with sponsors. If you have a participation contract with the athletes, this stipulation should be part of the contract. All participant agreements should also contain a clause that allows for photographs to be taken at the event that may contain an athlete's likeness and provide a release for that photograph's use by the event and sponsors.

There is a concern about the length of sponsorship agreements. There has been a steady increase in contract coverage over the past few years. Data have shown that long-term agreements (a minimum of 3 years) provide better results for both partners. Industry data indicated that in 1993 the average length of a sponsorship agreement was 5 years (International Events Group, 1993b). Therefore, the right of first refusal is always an element of interest. Sponsors generally like to have the right to future options for an event. They have placed their reputation on the line with you and should be accorded this consideration. Remember, this is partnership that can benefit all of the participants.

Corporations occasionally enlist an agency to assist them with securing sport sponsorships. In North America, 68% of sponsorship deals are initiated by the sponsoree and only 14% are handled by an agency. The remaining 18% are selected when sponsors review proposals received in response to a request for proposals (RFP) distributed to interested parties. Although data are not available on a worldwide basis, the situation in Europe was found to be nearly identical to that in the United States and Canada (International Events Group, 1993c).

According to Gearson (1994), if you want to use an agency to secure a sponsorship for your company, there are several factors to consider. Although many agencies create advertising campaigns and sponsorship proposals, some have little or no knowledge of the corporation's marketing plan. Sponsorship activities must be directly tied to the company's marketing plan, with significant measurement of resulting sales and revenue. Only as a partnership, where the company and the agency work together, can the end product be successful.

PRICING SPONSORSHIPS

The prices for sport sponsorship can range from a few hundred dollars to the $250 million paid by Coca-Cola for the 1994-1998 NBA agreement. Brooks (1994) details three different approaches to sponsorship **pricing.** The **cost-plus method** involves calculating the actual expenses incurred in providing the sponsorship package with an inclusion for profit for the organization. Expenses include all items included in the package, such as tickets, parking, dinners, souvenirs, and signage. A reasonable profit margin can be added, and the package ensures that the sponsorship will generate a profit.

The second method described by Brooks is the **competitive-market strategy.** The competitive market has changed since the 1980s. Early in the development of sport sponsorships, leverage was on the side of the event holder. Major events like the Indianapolis 500 would have many companies that wanted to sign sponsorship deals, and sometimes a bidding war erupted between potential sponsors. However, as more sport organizations and events entered the field, leverage shifted to the companies, which could then choose their options from a broad field of opportunities. As with any product pricing strategy, one must be competitive with alternative sponsorship options. The problem is trying to discover their price. With retail products, you can go to a store, pick up a company's product, and see how much is being asked. In the sponsorship business, it is difficult to know the pricing structure of competitors' packages.

In amateur sport, most organizations are not-for-profit organizations and must make public reports on their financial operation. These could also be used for information. Newspapers and trade journals appear to be the best source of information. Stories about skiers' head bands during the 1994 Olympic Winter Games reported that sponsorship prices ranged between $15,000 and $25,000. The sponsor would obtain a quick return on investment from television exposure if that skier won an Olympic medal or a World Cup event.

Probably the most widely used method of sponsorship pricing is the **relative-value method.** Brooks (1994) reported that this strategy is based on the market value of each sponsorship component. For example, program ads could be compared to ads in the newspaper, scoreboard signage to billboards, and public-address announcements to radio advertising. The issue here is whether the comparison is legitimate. Is the same impact achieved? Is one message more powerful than another? The International Events Group (1992) reported that media impressions from event coverage are considerably less effective than a direct advertising message. If the event places the sponsor's logo in its media purchases, the value is about 10% of the media cost; however, if the event is given real advertising spots and space from a media sponsor, the value would be equal to the full rate offered to other advertisers.

Valuation is the most critical aspect of pricing. What is the *real* value of anything? You can offer a rental car company seats in the VIP section for the event as part of its package, but how much are those tickets worth: $50, $100, or what? Those seats will not be sold anyway. They will all be distributed to sponsors, so just print $100 on the ticket (the ink doesn't cost anything!). It's perfectly legitimate because the rental car company is going to calculate its provision of cars at $75 per day, even though it could never get that on the open market. One should also accept in *trade-out* only those items that one would have had to purchase. During the 1990 Goodwill Games, a wine company donated thousands of bottles of wine as part of its sponsorship agreement. The organizers couldn't sell it, and there were only so many parties where it could be given away. The arrangement did not reduce costs for the organizers and did not yield the positive results anticipated by the sponsor.

In the early 1990s, an additional factor was introduced by the Internal Revenue Service (IRS) to complicate this approach. The IRS uses something called an *unrelated business income tax* (UBIT) to collect monies on profits received by not-for-profit organizations. Its ruling (which has been extensively modified by Congress) said that in fact a sponsorship that included advertising, signage, PA announcements, and other tangible assets was in fact income for the organization and taxable at 30%. Corporate "donations" to not-for-profit organizations were not taxable. This led to a situation where the closed-door negotiations between the sponsor and the event would center around these concepts, but they would never be put in writing or in a contract.

The type of value exchanged is an important element in price negotiations. Industry data indicate that 47% of the sponsorships are cash payments from the sponsor to the event owner (sport organization). Twenty-eight percent of the deals are in-kind (product donations), with another 25% of the arrangements combining the two forms of exchange (International Events Groups, 1993b). In all of these negotiations, one shouldn't forget to include the associated labor costs for producing the sponsor's services.

IMPLEMENTATION

The execution of each detail prescribed in the sponsorship agreement is the implementation goal. Most sports administrators have developed highly successful planning and implementation strategies. Some of those used in the business world are also beneficial. Systems such as the Harvard project review, critical-path method (CPM), and project evaluation and review technique (PERT) provide a viable framework for sponsorship management.

The task of implementation does not fall only on the shoulders of the sport organization. A sponsor must clearly understand that purchasing a sponsorship is only part of its commitment. It must leverage its association across all of its marketing elements. A generally accepted ratio suggests that a sponsor must spend at least as much money promoting its association with the event (or sportsperson) as it paid for the rights. One expert said, "for every $600,000 you spend to sponsor an event, be prepared to spend another $600,000 aggressively supporting and promoting that sponsorship through consumer tie-ins, advertising, and public relations" (Brewer, 1992).

CONTROVERSIES

Ambush marketing is a company's unauthorized association with your event, team, or organization (Turner, 1992). One of the more notable examples involves American Express credit cards. It is not an official sponsor for the Olympic Games. However, advertising during the games allowed the company to successfully convince some consumers otherwise. Research studies conducted during the last two Olympiads indicate that this technique is effective. In 1992, data showed that while 55% of consumers accurately identified VISA as the official Olympic credit card sponsor, 30% thought American Express was the sponsor (Turner, 1992; Sandler and Shani, 1993). The data for the 1994

Winter Olympics seemed to support the official sponsor. These data showed that the percentage of consumers recognizing VISA had climbed to 66%, while those selecting American Express had declined (Performance Research, 1994b). This would also seem to support the idea that long-term sponsorship deals tend to solidify the association in the mind of the consumer.

IOC officials "attacked American Express as . . . the 'most flagrant' practitioner of ambush marketing." The chief executive officer for the 1996 Atlanta Olympics has said that it is incorrect to assume the only way to measure the value of a sponsorship is how you were perceived during the 16 days of the Games. Nevertheless, from the sponsor's perspective, one executive said, "if the IOC can't stop ambush marketing, it might have trouble convincing its patrons to renew their sponsorship" (Turner, 1992).

Ambush marketing surrounding the 1984 Olympics prompted the IOC to develop The Olympic Programme (TOP) for the 1988 Olympics to diminish the possibility of successful ambushing. Although it has not totally prevented ambush, the program has provided one-stop shopping for many of the world's largest companies and has made Olympic sponsorship less complicated. In the TOP program, sponsors obtain exclusive rights to the Olympic marks (five rings) and are also able to sponsor all of the individual National Olympic Committees (NOCs) throughout the world.

Similarly, the Atlanta Committee for the Olympic Games (ACOG) and the USOC entered into an agreement to try to curtail ambush marketing for the 1996 Olympics. Together they formed the Atlanta Centennial Olympic Properties (ACOP) to jointly market the 1996 games. The packages offered at $40 million were designed to be "ambush-proof." Sponsors would purchase the rights to sponsor the Atlanta games and receive USOC status for the same price. The problem was that individual sports organizations within the Olympic movement could continue to sell their own sponsorship packages. For example, United Sates Track and Field could still sell a sponsorship package to Nike while the USOC was selling one to Reebok. ACOP offered up-front monies to the NGBs to help protect their sponsors; but because the most recognizable NGBs could secure more money from sponsors than ACOP was offering, only the less popular NGBs signed up. Even ACOG and the USOC could not come to agreement on the "official airlines." Delta had supported Atlanta's bid for the games, and United had been a long-time supporter of the USOC, so two official airlines were allowed.

From the consumer's perspective, the most important data indicated that while 21.5% felt "angry at companies that try to associate themselves with the Olympic games without being an Official Sponsor," 42.4% disagreed (Sandler and Shani, 1993). In addition, 75% of the consumers researched by Sandler and Shani during the 1992 Summer Olympics were not concerned about differentiating between official sponsors and nonsponsors.

The IOC is so concerned about ambush marketing that it has produced a brochure about the subject (International Olympic Committee, 1993). The brochure even developed a new term for the practice: *parasite marketing*. In fact, the leading Olympic sponsor research company reinforced the problem by saying, "Unless the IOC, USOC, NGBs, sponsors, and networks figure out a way to stop this from happening in the future, their $40 million rights fee contracts won't be worth the paper they're printed on" (Performance Research, 1994b).

Probably the most heated debate in sport sponsorships is over the use of tobacco and beer companies in sporting-event sponsorships. This debate extends to the ownership level of major league sports teams. Labatt Brewery (Toronto) owns the Toronto Blue Jays of the American League, and Anheuser-Busch not only owns the St. Louis Cardinals but has sponsored just about every sport known to humankind. In addition, Miller Brewing Company has made substantial donations to the U.S. Olympic Training Center. An examination of the major spenders in the sponsorship arena shows a multitude of tobacco and alcohol companies. Many people feel that blending alcohol and tobacco with the healthful benefits of sports is hypocritical.

The association between sport and tobacco accelerated in the early 1970s, when tobacco ads were banned from television. At that time, Phillip Morris began its association with sport through the Virginia Slims Tennis series; NASCAR started the Winston Cup racing series; the Marlboro Cup in horse racing was initiated; and yachting's Salem

Pro Sail began. Tobacco had found a productive medium in sport. However, litigation in the early 1990s, *Federal Trade Commission v Pinkerton Tobacco Company* attempted to address some of the problems. The *Pinkerton* ruling resulted from Pinkerton Tobacco's use of sporting events to advertise its Red Man smokeless tobacco. The court's findings contained a cease-and-desist order outlining several methods used by Pinkerton that were in violation of FTC and FCC television and advertising regulations.

While Phillip Morris ($75 million) and RJR Nabisco ($40 million) have ranked among the top corporations in sponsorship spending, several moves have been made on the part of regulating bodies to restrict tobacco advertising in sports. The NCAA forbids both alcohol and tobacco advertising at championship events. The U.S. Congress has also considered legislation that would prohibit tobacco sponsorships of sports. In Canada, however, a 1991 ruling in Quebec Superior Court overturned Canada's ban on tobacco advertising on freedom of speech issues.

Controversies exist in other areas of sponsorship. Since the middle 1980s, many of the most prominent sports events have sold *title sponsorship* of the event. This means that the sponsor's name has become part of the event name. Many in the media have fought this trend and have tried to negate the value sought by the sponsor. A *Chicago Tribune* managing editor said, "I'd never use sponsor names if I could get away with it" (International Events Group, 1994). However, the general policy with newspapers and electronic media is to use the sponsor's name in conjunction with the first mention. Regarding another aspect of this issue, the ABC, CBS, and NBC networks "refused to use a title sponsor's name for college bowl games unless the sponsor also bought commercials within the broadcast" (Walley, 1989). As you can see, this controversy is still alive and well, with little being proposed for resolution.

A considerable debate has also developed over the supplements to coaches' salaries paid by many shoe companies. Do conflicts of interest occur? Does payment to a college or a coach mean that the college is endorsing one shoe over another? If it is a publicly funded institution, does the shoe contract have to go out for bids? The situation also infiltrated the 1992 Summer Olympics in Barcelona. The coach of the U.S. track team had been on the Nike payroll for many years. No problem, but when he removed one runner from the 4 × 400 m relay team and replaced him with a Nike runner who had not run in the qualifier, heads began to turn (DeFord, 1992). Nike was also embroiled in the uniform dispute. Many members of the U.S. Olympic basketball team had contracts with Nike for shoes and apparel. However, Reebok was the official supplier of award uniforms for the USOC. When the U.S. team won the gold medal, some players refused to wear the Reebok uniforms on the awards stand. In a compromise, the USOC allowed them to open the collar of the uniform to cover the Reebok logo. In reference to the "Dream Team," a USOC executive said "they may be your Dream Team, but they're my worst nightmare" (DeFord, 1992).

CONCEPT CHECK

Sport marketers should be aware that not all members of the community will embrace their involvement with all corporate sponsors. Many will see the association with alcohol and tobacco companies as counterproductive to the interests of sport.

TRENDS

Internationally, sport sponsorship is also growing rapidly. An interesting point was made about the terminology used to describe this situation. Woods (1993) suggested that the word *foreign* be dropped from all discussion of marketing and sponsorship. Rather, he said the word *international* was more appropriate. This parallels the business world's change in terminology from *foreign* companies to *multinationals*. As noted by the Sports Marketing Council of Canada, data indicated that sponsorship of sporting events was increasing. It estimated the 1988 market at $100 million and growth at 15% per year. In Greece, the trend resembles that of the United States in the 1980s. From 1988 to 1991, the amount of money committed to sport sponsorship in Greece increased over 300% (Asimakopoulos, 1993). In France, 1993 expenditures reached $600 million (Fr 3.5 billion, with 12 of the largest sponsors being banks.) Changes in the Eastern European community have also presented opportuni-

ties for sponsorship. With the breakup of the Soviet Union, sponsorships are now abundant in Russia. Its hockey rinks are adorned with corporate signage, and team merchandise sales are booming. Reebok has entered a multiyear agreement as the sponsor of the Russian Olympic Committee and has opened 10 retail outlets nationwide (Graham, 1993).

Another trend involves teamwork between sponsors. Because of the substantial investments that sponsors make in sports events, they want to gain the maximum advantage. In an activity called **cross-promotion,** sponsors work with each other to extend their recognition. A natural match could occur with a food sponsor and a drink sponsor combining to provide a "hospitality event." When Michael Jordan had sponsorship from Wheaties breakfast cereal and Wilson basketballs, they agreed to jointly promote a coupon offer on Wheaties boxes that could be sent in for a discount on a basketball. Wilson also offered Wheaties discount coupons with the purchase of a basketball. In another case, the sponsors of a bike race used the portable showers provided by Teledyne and another sponsor agreed to stock them with its shampoo and soap products. In this way, both sponsors benefited.

This type of cooperation can penetrate the entire sponsorship. For example, in the 1994 World Cup agreement between advertisers and TV they agreed to superimpose sponsor logos at the bottom of the TV screen with the game clock so as not to disrupt the games. "All of the sponsors wanted soccer to be covered properly. This type of advertisement will be a reinforcement of who the real sponsors of the television broadcast are" (World Cup, 1993).

Little things mean a lot

Attention to little details can have a major effect on one's success. In this section, a few experiences, both positive and negative, are offered for review. During one event, where one of the major sponsors was a brewing company, a reception for sponsors was scheduled in a hotel executive suite. The person who planned the reception thought all of the details for the reception had been covered. The invitations had been sent out, the room decorations were assembled, name tags had been made, and the bar and bartender had been arranged with the hotel. However, when the bar was set up by the hotel, the sponsoring brewing company's beer was not available; only their competitor's product had been stocked by the hotel. Although the sponsor understood the problem, event organizers were monumentally embarrassed.

When the managers of a series of surfing events were searching for sponsors, they kept their staff busy switching the Cokes and Pepsis in the corporate board room's refrigerator during negotiations between their two most promising sponsor candidates. Although it may seem trivial, one doesn't want to be pushing hard to secure Coca-Cola as a million dollar partner and pull a Pepsi out of the refrigerator!

In another case, the event organizers were working hard to get all of their sponsorable categories filled. They were extremely happy when they secured Budget as their car rental company. The problem was that General Motors had been the primary title sponsor for several months. As they soon found out, Budget's rental fleet consisted primarily of Fords.

Often the presentation of ideas is just as important as the concept itself. For the 1994 Goodwill Games, organizers used computer-generated graphics to show the actual stadiums with sponsor signs in place. Although one may not be able to commission state-of-the-art computer graphics, sample program ads, banners, and gift items adorned with the sponsor candidate's logo can certainly be provided. This will not only show the sponsor what its money will buy, but show that you care about how the corporation is represented.

SUMMARY

1. With industry leaders projecting a future growth rate in sports sponsorships of 15% per year, it is apparent that sport sponsorships will continue into the next century (Special Events Report, 1990). It is essential for the sport manager to fully comprehend this marketing element.
2. The relationship between a sport organization and event owners involved with sponsorship must include advantages to both parties. A well-developed sponsorship can provide market value and increased profits for corporations, scarce operating revenues for sport organizations and events, and a full spectrum of sports events for participants and spectators.
3. Through a properly structured sponsorship agreement, one can ensure that benefits for both the sport organization and the sponsor(s) are achieved.
4. With models derived from existing sponsorship proposals and agreements, one can develop the skills necessary to succeed in the exciting world of sport sponsorships.

CASE STUDY

As the organizer of an event, you entered into a television agreement with a national cable network to televise the finals of your national swimming championship to ensure that your sponsors would have a platform for their message. In the agreement, you guaranteed the television appearance of Olympic 100 m freestyle gold medalist Chris Nathan. In your negotiations with Chris, you agreed to pay an appearance fee and all expenses to the meet, and Chris signed the contract. However, when the event began, it was clear that Chris was out of shape and was not swimming well. Chris did not qualify for the finals in the 100 m freestyle or any other event. On the morning of the finals, a network executive came to you with questions about your contract guaranteeing the television appearance of Chris. The network is demanding that unless Chris appears in a race, no broadcast rights fees will be paid and the event will not be aired. The major sponsors begin calling because they have heard that the event may be canceled from television. In the sponsorship contract, you guaranteed that the event would be televised nationally and that the sponsors' venue signs would have on-camera air time. How would you work to resolve this situation?

REVIEW QUESTIONS AND ISSUES

1. What are the essential elements for a well-written sponsorship contract?
2. What issues would need to be addressed if you were offered a considerable amount of sponsorship money by a local brewing company for your college?
3. Discuss the pros and cons of selecting an individual athlete as a representative for a company's products. In a group, select a product and athlete spokesperson.

REFERENCES

Abraham, M. M. and Lodish, L. M. (1990). Getting the most out of advertising and promotion, *Harvard Business Review,* pp 50-60, May-June.

Asimakopoulos, M. K. (1993). Sport marketing and sponsoring: the experience of Greece, *Sport Marketing Quarterly,* 2(3): 44-48, September.

Brewer, G. (1990). New spins on sports, *Incentive,* p 42, December 1992.

Brooks, C. (1990). Sponsorship by design, *Athletic Business,* pp 58-62, December.

Brooks, C. M. (1994). *Sports marketing,* Englewood Cliffs, New Jersey, Prentice-Hall.

Carrier, J. (1994). Sponsors dig Olympic gold, *Denver Post,* pp 1A, 20A, March 18.

Cone, W. W. (1991). How to leverage ad promotion budgets through media sponsorships, *Special Events Reports,* pp 4-5, April 8.

DeFord, F. (1992). The money games, *Newsweek,* pp 18-19, August 10.

Ensor, R. J. (1987). The corporate view of sports sponsorships, *Athletic Business,* pp 40-43, September.

Federal Trade Commission v Pinkerton Tobacco Company, U.S. Federal Trade Commission file 9023006, October 28. (1991).

Gearson, R. F. (1994). What to expect from your ad agency, *Fitness Management,* pp 22-23, January.

Graham, P. J. (1993). Obstacles and opportunities for the marketing and sponsoring of sport in Russia, *Sport Marketing Quarterly,* 2(2): 9-11, June.

International Events Group. (1990). Coors proposal format, *Special Events Report,* p 5, June 25.

International Events Group. (1992). Survey reveals what sponsors want, *Sponsorship Report,* pp 6-7, September 7.

International Events Group. (1993). 1994 sponsorship spending will exceed $4 billion, *Sponsorship Report,* pp 1-2, December 20.

International Events Group. (1993). 1994 quantifying sponsorship, *Sponsorship Report,* pp 4-6, November 15.

International Events Group: Sponsorship report, assertions, *Sponsorship Report,* pp 45, February 14.(1993).

International Events Group. (1994). Crediting sponsors, *Sponsorship Report,* pp 4-5, March 14.

International Olympic Committee, (1993). Ambush marketing, Lausanne, Switzerland, International Olympic Committee.

Irwin, R. L. (1993). In search of sponsors, *Athletic management,* pp 11-16, May.

Irwin, R. L. and Asimakopoulos, M. (1992). An approach to the evaluation and selection of sport sponsorship proposals, *Sport Marketing Quarterly,* pp 43-51, December.

Irwin, R. L. and Stotlar, D. K. (1993). Operational protocol analysis of sport and collegiate licensing programs, *Sport Marketing Quarterly,* 2(5): 7-16.

Kuzma, J. R., Shanklin, W. L., and McCally, J. F. (1993). Number one principle for sporting events seeking corporate sponsors: meet benefactor's objectives, *Sport Marketing Quarterly,* 2(3): 27-32, September.

Lesly, E. (1992). What's next, Raiders' deodorant?, *Business Week,* p 65, November 30.

National Collegiate Athletic Association. (1991). *Guidelines for corporate participation in NCAA championships,* Document 7368, Mission, Kansas, July.

Performance Research. (1991). *Economic slump,* Newport, Rhode Island, May 14, Performance Research.

Performance Research. (1992). *Olympic marketing study: can't beat the feeling,* Newport, Rhode Island, February 28, Performance Research.

Performance Research. (1994). *Olympic sponsorship study: what Olympics?,* Newport, Rhode Island, February 8, Performance Research.

Performance Research. (1994). *Olympic sponsorship study: and you thought Nancy and Tonya were bad,* Newport, Rhode Island, March 4, Performance Research.

Performance Research. (1994). *Will the real NASCAR please stand up?,* Newport, Rhode Island, January 31, Performance Research.

Reed, M. H. (1990). Legal aspects of promoting and sponsoring events, *Special Events Report,* pp 4-5, March 26.

Sandler, D. M. and Shani, D. (1993). Sponsorship and the Olympic games: the consumer perspective, *Sport Marketing Quarterly,* 2(3): 38-43, September.

Schmidt, S. (1993). Alternative revenue, *Athletic Business,* p 20, November.

Sponsors Report. (1991). CART/PPG Indy car world series, Ann Arbor, Joyce Julius and Associates, pp 9-14.

Stotlar, D. K. (1993). Sponsorship and the Olympic winter games, *Sport Marketing Quarterly,* 2(1): 35-46.

Turner, M. (1992). Circle the rings, "ambush" ads hit, *Atlanta Journal,* p A6, March 3.

Walley, W. (1989). Sports and sponsors, *Advertising Age,* pp 3, 75, June 12.

Weilgus, C. (1989). Little things make a difference, *Athletic Business,* p 16, March.

Wilkinson, D. G. *Event management and marketing institute,* Willowdale, Ontario. (1988). Sport Marketing Institute.

Wilkinson, D. G. (1986). *Sport marketing institute,* Willowdale, Ontario, Sport Marketing Institute.

Woods. (1993). Attracting foreign sponsorship for American events: the myth, *Sport Marketing Quarterly,* 2(2): 9-11, June.

World Cup. (1993). *Between the lines,* Ernst and Young, p 11.

SUGGESTED READINGS

International Events Group (IEG): *Legal guide to sponsorship,* Chicago, International Events Group.

Irwin, R. L. and Asimakopoulos, M. (1992). An approach to the evaluation and selection of sport sponsorship proposals, *Sport Marketing Quarterly,* pp 43-51, December.

Stotlar, D. K. (1993). *Successful sport marketing plans,* Madison, Wisconsin, Brown and Benchmark.

CHAPTER 16

Sport Licensing

Dick Irwin

In this chapter, you will become familiar with the following terms:

License	Royalty audit	Exclusive agreement
Licensor	Royalty exemption	Nonexclusive agreement
Licensee	Trademark	Joint-use agreement
Royalty	License agreement	Promotional Licenses

Overview

Trademark licensing, a topic too frequently omitted from sport management and marketing texts, has become a primary responsibility of both amateur and professional-sport administrators. The earliest form of sport-related licensing may have been when Roman athletes were paid for the use of their images on products sold at the Circus Maximus. Today, sport organizations and personalities grant, or **license,** second parties the right to produce merchandise bearing associated designs or individual likenesses.

The National Football League (NFL), under the direction of commissioner Pete Rozelle, was the first American sport organization to formally establish a licensing program in 1963, under the direction of NFL Properties (Rosenblatt, 1988). Following the NFL's pioneering efforts, the remaining major professional-sport leagues, many national sport governing bodies, and major sporting events, from the Olympics to college bowl games, have become **licensors** of their associated logos, symbols, or designs. Furthermore, over 100 colleges and universities have followed suit and established licensing programs, frequently designating the department of intercollegiate athletics as the financial beneficiary as well as the home of program operations (Irwin and Stotlar, 1993). Much like their Roman-era predecessors, today's sport personalities have also granted manufacturers the right to use their likeness on various products. Therefore it is imperative that today's sport managers be well versed in the field of licensing.

According to *Team Licensing Business,* the sales of sport-licensed merchandise is projected to exceed $10 billion by 1995, an increase of almost 20% since 1990 (Figure 16-1). As revealed in the figure, significant increases in domestic sales of sport-licensed products have been realized by all professional-sport leagues, as well as by the collective collegiate licensing industry.

Battle, Bailey, and Siegal (1990) cited the following four factors as the primary contributors to the phenomenal growth in sales of college-licensed products that are applicable to the surge in sport licensed products:

1. The increasing popularity of American sports and resulting media coverage
2. Significant developments in imprinting technology
3. The maturation of licensing as an industry
4. The financial challenges facing sport managers

The prolific demand for these products has provided sport organizations and product manufacturers and retailers with a healthy revenue source. Manufacturers, or **licensees,** and retailers realize their profits from basic supply-and-demand principles, and licensing has provided an effective tool in expanding the marketplace for sport-logoed products. No longer must adoring fans attend an event or visit the campus bookstore to purchase merchandise bearing the logo of their favorite team. Now these items may be obtained at the local mall or ordered through the mail. This has led to the creation of "officially licensed outlets" that have tallied more than $600 million annually (McLaughlin, 1998).

The sport licensor derives its earnings in the form of a **royalty** fee, generally 6%–10% of the manufacturer's wholesale price and typically passed on to the consumer through an increase in product price. The fee appears quite modest considering that the unlabeled product has little or no market value until the sport logo is affixed. Even so, major professional-sport franchises and a number of major colleges have realized annual royalties in excess of $1 million (Fichtenbaum, 1988; Rosenblatt,

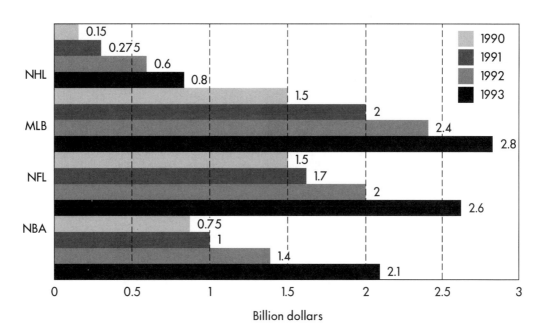

FIGURE 16-1   Domestic sales of sport-licensed merchandise.
Data compiled from *Team Licensing Business,* May 1994.

1988; Sandomir, 1988; Grassmuck, 1990). A list of the most popular teams, in terms of 1993 gross retail sales, is found in Table 16-1.

A properly administered licensing program provides more than just financial dividends. The benefits of licensing, enjoyed by the licensor as well as licensee, should include protection against unauthorized, counterfeit, or improper logo usage; promotion through the increase in popularity of both the sport property and the manufacturer; and, ultimately, the ability to profit from merchandise sales.

Protection and control of logo usage has been identified as the fundamental benefit of establishing a licensing program (Sykes, 1985). As the demand for logoed products has expanded, so have the abuses of logo usage. In addition to using the logo—a legally protectable property of the sport organization—without authorization, merchandise of poor quality bearing inappropriate statements or images began to appear in the marketplace. Therefore it became necessary for the logo "owners" to regulate who was producing merchandise bearing the logo and how it was being displayed.

The logos used by professional-sport franchises, college athletic programs, or sporting events are recognized as trademarks of those respective organizations. A **trademark** is defined as "any word, name, symbol, or device or combination thereof adopted and used by a manufacturer or merchant to identify and distinguish his goods" (15 U.S.C. 1127).

The classification of team logos as trademarks permits sport organizations, including university athletic programs, to capitalize on powerful trademark law aimed at restraining unauthorized production and distribution of merchandise bearing these marks. As the industry of trademark licensing has realized its greatest degree of growth, the laws that govern such activity have experienced considerable modification, providing the licensor with powerful ammunition in the fight against commercial counterfeiters. Therefore the sport licensing program administrator should become familiar with the laws that govern this activity in order to exploit them to their full potential.

Although not required for legal protection, consideration should be given to the actual registration of logos as trademarks. Federal trademark law, derived from the Lanham Act, renders the highest degree of legal protection and provides for both civil and criminal penalties to be levied against unauthorized product vendors (Bikoff, 1989).

CONCEPT CHECK

The logos used by professional sport franchises, college athletic programs, or sporting events are recognized as trademarks of those organizations, thereby qualifying for federal trademark law protection against unauthorized users.

A survey of licensing program administrators from the NBA, NFL, NHL, Major League Baseball, NCAA, and the U.S. Olympic Committee revealed that a majority of marks claimed by each program has been registered with the federal trademark commission (Irwin, Stotlar, and Mulrooney, 1993). In fact, several respondents indicated that hundreds of logos had been federally registered as trademarks. Federal registration is denoted by the placement of a ® adjacent to the logo (Figure 16-2). This level of protection does not come without a cost. The fee for federal trademark registration of a logo is several hundred dollars per mark per product category (Shinner, 1989).

TABLE 16-1   *Top-selling team licensors, 1993*

NHL	MLB	NFL	NBA	Colleges
Anaheim	Colorado	Dallas	Chicago	Michigan
Florida	White Sox	Raiders	Charlotte	Florida State
Chicago	Atlanta	San Francisco	Orlando	Georgetown
Pittsburgh	Florida	Miami	Phoenix	North Carolina
San Jose	Yankees	Washington	Knicks	Alabama

Data compiled from *Team Licensing Business*, May 1994.

FIGURE 16-2   Trademarks of **A,** Georgetown University, **B,** University of Michigan, and **C,** University of Kentucky.

In order to secure federal protection of organizational trademarks, registration has not been mandatory. Unregistered trademarks have been protected under unfair-competition principles (Ala, 1989). Reliance on unfair-competition principles, or common trademark law, has inherent disadvantages and will require the licensor to demonstrate that the manufacturer's use of the mark was likely to create confusion in the mind of the consuming public about the authenticity of the goods (Wong, 1986). In an effort to demonstrate such consumer confusion about the authenticity of unauthorized logo usage, the NFL successfully used consumer surveys as evidence in a case involving unregistered trademarks (*N.F.L. v Wichita Falls*, 1982). Frequently, licensors will request that a trademark symbol (™) be placed adjacent to unregistered logos as a means of demonstrating a claim of ownership.

In some instances, state registration, which is a more expedient and less expensive process, may be warranted when use of the organizational logos is limited to intrastate commerce. Such is the case with most school-oriented, regional sporting events and minor league programs. However, other than demonstrating that the logo in question has actually been registered, state registration offers no greater protection than common trademark law (Shinner, 1989). It is strongly recommended that the licensing program administrator consult with a legal specialist prior to making decisions about the registration of organizational logos—the common practice among professional-sport licensing programs (Irwin, Stotlar, and Mulrooney, 1993).

The sport licensing program administrator must determine which logos are going to be licensed. An inventory of all names, symbols, designs, slogans, and images should be conducted in an effort to determine which items will be made available for commercial usage. Popular slogans such as the "Fab Five," referring to the five starting freshmen on the University of Michigan basketball team, and the "Bad Boys," referring to the Detroit Pistons championship team's tough style of play, had significant market demand and subsequent commercial value.

The licensing administrator should also consider capitalizing on a provision within the Trademark Revision Act (1988) that has enabled licensors to claim or register a mark prior to its actual use (Ala, 1989). This is of particular interest when creating a team slogan or planning a season's advertising campaign. Early registration should guard against "accidental" reproduction, which can lead to cluttering or devaluing the organization's message. In turn, the organization has the opportunity to maximize speculative commercial value of the proposed slogan.

Under the 1988 Trademark Revision Act, new franchises have capitalized on market demand for logoed merchandise well in advance of the team playing a game. As can be seen in Table 16-1, new franchises led the way in 1993 gross sales for the NHL and Major League Baseball. It would appear likely that the addition of the Carolina Panthers and the Jacksonville Jaguars to the NFL and new NBA franchises in Toronto and Vancouver is sure to stimulate significant sales. No better example of the benefits provided by speculative preregistration may have occurred than when Pat Riley, the coach of the New York Knicks, registered the word *threepeat* in reference to the Chicago Bulls' 3-year reign as NBA champions. It is assumed that Riley's speculation paid enormous dividends following the Bulls' 1993 championship.

In an effort to fully employ the legal rights provided by trademark law, the licensing administrator must design and enforce written operational policies and procedures. In order to standardize program operations, a policy manual containing all operational policies and procedures should be drafted and stored in a readily accessible location, with additional copies available upon request (Irwin, 1991). Informational brochures that reflect the licensing-program operational protocol should be prepared

for circulation to prospective licensees and other interested parties. Suggested licensing-program operational protocols, derived from an analysis of licensing procedures for the NBA, NFL, NHL, NCAA, U.S. Olympic Committee, Major League Baseball, and 100 colleges (Irwin, Stotlar, and Mulrooney, 1993), will be addressed in the following sections.

LICENSEE RECRUITMENT

Active recruitment of licensees is essential for any licensing program to flourish. The most common recruitment tactics employed by sport licensors have been personal contact, direct mail, and trade show networking (Irwin and Stotlar, 1993). Prospective licensees should be provided with operational policy material and details of licensor support programs aimed at generating awareness at the retailer and consumer level as well as protecting against unlicensed counterfeit competitors.

LICENSE APPLICATION PROCESS

Manufacturers interested in obtaining a license should be required to make a formal application, including information regarding its financial reliability, production capabilities, anticipated marketing and distribution channels, logo usage intent, and current or past licensing references (Appendix 16-A). Approval criteria, such as royalty production standards, should be established for the review process prior to the issuance of any license (see Appendix 16-B for a copy of the NCAA license agreement).

PRODUCT REVIEW PROCEDURES

As a quality control measure, a thorough review should be conducted of each product under consideration for license, including the packaging, wrapping, and advertising literature (Gareau, 1988), as well as an inspection of the production facilities (Stone, 1986). Lack of proper product screening may result in product liability litigation being brought against the licensor because consumers perceive a licensed product to be of higher quality (Kennedy and Geist, 1990). Therefore, it is imperative that a detailed evaluation be completed of all prospective licensees and their products.

LICENSE EXECUTION

When a licensee has met the established standards, a **license agreement,** or contract, should be executed. The antecedent to effective program enforcement has been the licensing agreement because this covenant sets the legal parameters for the licensor–licensee relationship (Appendix B).

Types of agreements

Several types of licenses exist: exclusive, nonexclusive, joint-use, and promotional. An **exclusive agreement,** typically issued on a per-product-category or geographical basis, is more prevalent among professional-sport licensing programs, as demonstrated by the NBA's "less is more" philosophy (Nichols, 1994a). License exclusivity enables the licensor to limit the number of licensees producing goods in a particular product category or geographical region, thereby facilitating stronger "partnerships" with the licensor. Limiting the number of licensees allows for easier detection of unlicensed, counterfeit merchandise and expedites communication between the licensor and licensee. The licensee benefits from the "exclusive" classification as well as the limited competition. A number of the dominant licensed merchandise manufacturers have indicated a preference for more exclusivity among sport licensing programs (Klemm, 1991).

On the other hand, the execution of a **nonexclusive agreement** fosters competition among licenses within the same product category and allows "cottage" vendors to participate in the licensing industry. Unfortunately, claims have been made that the use of nonexclusive license agreements is leading to an oversaturation of the licensed product marketplace adversely affecting the overall quality of goods (Klemm, 1991).

Two or more licensors may wish to execute a **joint-use license** agreement allowing their respective logos to appear together on merchandise. Cartoon characters and opposing teams make ideal joint licensors—for example, the NHL's incorporation of the Muppet characters within all 26 team logos on children's merchandise (Nichols, 1994b) and the NCAA's incorporation of participating team logos on national championship merchandise (Krupa, 1988). Typically, the royalties generated from joint-use agreements are split evenly between the licensors.

Promotional licenses simply allow a licensee to use licensed marks in a short-term promotional campaign, such as a premium product giveaway by a local fast-food restaurant (Battle, Bailey, and Siegal, 1990). Typically, the licensee is interested in capitalizing on the goodwill of the licensor, while both parties benefit from the awareness generated.

Generally, all licenses, with the exception of the promotional license, are executed on an annual or biannual basis. Any breach of the agreement should result in automatic revocation, and renewal should be based on the licensee's sales activity and adherence to predetermined quality standards.

CONCEPT CHECK

Sport organizations and personalities license, or grant, second parties the right to produce merchandise bearing associated designs or individual likenesses.

COUNTERFEIT DETECTION AND REDUCTION

It is incumbent upon all licensing administrators to establish counterfeit detection and reduction procedures. The implementation of a systematic market surveillance program requiring staff members to regularly "police" or "shop" the local marketplace, including game day vendors, is vital to the overall success of licensing program operations. Unfortunately, a survey of collegiate licensing program administrators revealed that less than two thirds had implemented such a program (Irwin and Stotlar, 1993). Therefore licensees, who have essentially paid for protection against unfair competition, should query the support provided by the licensor for the removal of counterfeit goods from the marketplace and only license with those actively protecting against pirating activities.

When "shopping," each staff member should be equipped with an up-to-date list of authorized licensees and copies of the licensing program policy manual. As a means of facilitating the recognition of licensed products by program "police agents," as well as the consuming public, each of the major sport programs has employed some type of identification label (Figure 16-3). Professional-sport licensing programs employ the services of the Coalition to Advance the Protection of Sports Logos (CAPS) to assist with the counterfeit detection and reduction process (Bullington, 1994). Some of the organizations, such as the NBA, have their own internal intellectual property enforcement operations.

Upon detection of counterfeit merchandise, staff members have the legal right to confiscate all

A

B

C
D

FIGURE 16-3   **A,** Official licensed product logo for the NHL. **B,** National Football League shield. **C,** Major League Baseball logo. **D,** License product logo for the NBA.
A, copyright, the National Hockey League. Artwork provided by and used with permission from NHL Enterprises Inc., New York. **B,** registered trademark of the NFL. Artwork provided by and used with permission from NFL Properties, New York. **C,** the Major League Baseball trademarks depicted herein were reproduced with permission from Major League Baseball Properties, Inc., New York. **D,** Used with permission of the National Basketball Assocation. Copyright 1995 NBA Properties, Inc., New York, 10022.

products bearing organizational logos and should issue the vendor **and** the manufacturer a cease-and-desist notice. When faced with the difficulty of obtaining the names of counterfeit vendors and the fact that they will likely disappear after being served with papers, numerous college licensing programs have obtained "John Doe" temporary restraining and seizure orders against game day vendors selling unlicensed logoed merchandise (Battle, Bailey, and Siegal, 1990). On behalf of their clients, between 1993 and 1994, CAPS seized $22 million in counterfeit products and printing equipment, according to Trademark Management of Lacanda, California. Counterfeit detection should be followed by personal contact, preferably from the licensing program's legal specialist, reminding the offending party of the licensor's rights and its intent to enforce these rights. If necessary, additional recourse may include litigation.

Each of the respective major professional leagues has at one time initiated litigation against manufacturers and/or vendors of unlicensed merchandise (Irwin and Stotlar, 1993). However, limited proceedings are available because most cases have been settled out of court. Although it has been reported that the NFL annually investigates more than 300 cases involving trademark infringe-

ment or unauthorized logo usage (Jones, 1984), the successful litigious record of licensors appears to have persuaded the pirates to cease production and/or distribution after receiving notification. A list of suggested case readings involving sport licensors has been provided at the conclusion of this chapter.

CONCEPT CHECK

*Upon detection of counterfeit merchandise, staff members have the legal right to confiscate all products bearing organizational logos and should issue the vendor **and** the manufacturer a cease-and-desist notice.*

ROYALTY AUDITS

As a means of verifying the accuracy of royalty reports—which accompany royalty payments and are typically provided by the licensee on a quarterly basis—the licensor may randomly conduct audits of licensees. These audits frequently reveal underpayments, commonly as a result of honest accounting errors. The licensor may choose to have these audits performed by a designated representative of the organization or use the services of an auditing specialist.

ROYALTY EXEMPTIONS

At the discretion of the licensor, exemptions from royalty payments may be granted. An exemption may be granted at either the producer or consumer level. Although sport organizations commonly employ a compulsory, nonexempt policy, college licensing programs generally exempt university departments (consumer level) from paying a royalty on items purchased from licensed suppliers that are only for internal consumption and are not available for resale, such as office supplies (e.g., letterhead stationery) and athletic equipment (Irwin and Stotlar, 1993). From a record-keeping perspective, the compulsory, nonexempt policy would appear to be more advantageous to both the licensor and licensee. Otherwise, it is the licensee who is held responsible and to whom purchasers are not required to pay a royalty.

LICENSING PROGRAM PUBLIC RELATIONS

Licensors should consider facilitating networking opportunities among current licensees and the retail community. This may be accomplished by distributing to retailers a licensed-product catalog containing a list of all licensees and their representatives or through mini–trade shows that allow licensees to display and take orders for the current year's licensed product line. Most important, it is recommended that licensors attempt to recognize manufacturers and retailers of licensed products with certificates of appreciation or point-of-purchase displays acknowledging the valuable relationship between the parties. Major League Baseball Properties has made a strong commitment to visit and service retailers of MLB-licensed products (Klemm, 1994).

CONCEPT CHECK

It is recommended that licensors attempt to recognize manufacturers and retailers of licensed products with certificates of appreciation or point-of-purchase displays acknowledging the valuable relationship between the parties.

LICENSING PROGRAM PRODUCT PROMOTIONS

It would behoove the sport licensing program administrator to employ an integrated promotional mix in an effort to enhance general awareness of licensed products to the consuming public. The most popular promotional media employed among sport licensing programs are event programs, broadcast media, and trade publications (Irwin and Stotlar, 1993). In some cases, the licensor has contained costs by mandating in the license agreement that licensees must produce advertising materials that display the licensor's products (Irwin and Stotlar, 1993). A co-op advertising approach among licensor and retailer is employed by the professional sport licensing programs (Klemm, 1994).

CONCEPT CHECK

The sport licensor derives its earnings in the form of a royalty fee, normally 6% to 10% of the manufacturer's wholesale price, which has enabled major professional-sport franchises and a number of major colleges to generate in excess of $1 million annually.

PROGRAM ADMINISTRATIVE ASSISTANCE

Although professional-sport licensing programs are administered exclusively with internal resources, administrative support can be obtained from a number of professional licensing agencies. Most college licensing programs have chosen to secure this type of administrative support and contracted with a licensing agency. A licensing agency, which typically represents several licensors as well as a bank of licensees, has the capability to provide services for legal consultation and representation, auditing, and promotions. Battle, Bailey, and Siegal (1990) have identified the following advantages of contracting with a licensing agency:

1. The size and diversification of staff and services
2. The strength provided by the number of licensors and licensees
3. Operational consistency and continuity
4. Leveragability of new programs
5. Licensor's ability to retain program control

6. The compensation system, typically a percentage of royalties generated

It would appear that the greatest strength of a licensing agency is its sensitivity to the practices of the industry. However, it should be noted that operational consistency has not yet been achieved among college programs contracting with a licensing agency (Irwin and Stotlar, 1993). Therefore if program administrative assistance is sought, a thorough investigation of the licensing agency is highly recommended. Licensing program administrators should query the staff's background, seeking assistance from agencies employing individuals who have gained experience working as licensors and licensees; request a list of current *and* former clients; request a copy of the agency's protection enforcement procedures; and request the submission of a promotional plan specific to the licensor's program.

It is difficult to imagine that the demand for sport-logoed products will continue to grow at the pace experienced over the past decade. However, sport-licensing administrators have already begun to develop programs that will maintain, if not stimulate, the sales volume of licensed products into the twenty-first century. The following sections highlight emerging trends within the field of trademark licensing.

DEVELOPING NEW PRODUCTS AND PENETRATING NEW MARKETS

In order to increase interest in and the popularity of hockey among new markets of fans, specifically those in warmer climates, the NHL is actively supporting the games of roller hockey and street hockey (Nichols, 1994b). Participants in these activities will of course need a jersey, a helmet, knee and elbow pads—and why not buy one emblazoned with a NHL logo? Therefore, in the spring of 1995, National Hockey League Enterprises launched a street hockey apparel line (Nichols, 1994b). Furthermore, in an effort to explore nontraditional product categories, MLB Properties and NBA Properties are both looking into the possibility of licensing household products and gift lines (Klemm, 1994; Nichols, 1994a). Staying abreast of consumer trends is essential for continued growth of licensed products.

INTERNATIONAL DISTRIBUTION

As the popularity of American sports has increased internationally, so have the sales of American sport-logoed products (Figure 16-4). Although distribution in Canada and Mexico has occurred for some time (Irwin, 1990), the administrators of American sport and collegiate licensing programs are now taking a vested interest in the international

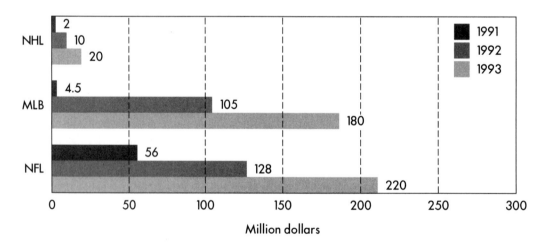

FIGURE 16-4   International sales of sport-licensed merchandise.
Data compiled from *Team Licensing Business*, May 1994.

marketplace initiating efforts to ensure product distribution globally. Awarding franchises internationally, such as the NBA's newest additions of Toronto and Vancouver, virtually assures a stronger international following and subsequent merchandising opportunities. When considering international business, it is imperative that the licensing administrator explore the trademark laws in the anticipated countries of distribution and investigate the feasibility of consulting with a licensing agency familiar with international issues (Revoyr, 1988).

LICENSEE EXCLUSIVITY

Following the NBA's less-is-more philosophy, other sport licensors are downsizing the number of their licensees (Nichols, 1994b). This has been advocated for collegiate licensing in an effort to facilitate industry standardization (Irwin, Stotlar, and Mulrooney, 1994) because several licensees have expressed a desire to terminate collegiate licensing activities (Klemm, 1991).

INTERNALIZATION OF PROGRAM OPERATIONS

Although at one time a majority of the sport and 87% of the collegiate licensing programs were assisted by licensing agencies, none of the sport programs and only 60% of the college programs remain (Irwin and Stotlar, 1993). It is projected that this internalization of licensing programs will continue as more administrators of sport and collegiate licensing programs become familiar with the operational complexities.

SUMMARY

1. The benefits of licensing include **protection, promotion,** and **profit.**
2. Several types of licenses can be granted: exclusive, nonexclusive, joint-use, and promotional.
3. A systematic market surveillance program requiring staff members to regularly "police" the local marketplace, including game day vendors, is vital to the overall success of a licensing program.
4. The sport licensing program administrator should employ an integrated promotional mix in an effort to promote the availability of products to prospective licensees, retailers, and the general public.

CASE STUDY

You have recently been hired as the assistant commissioner for marketing of the newly formed Continental Hockey League, comprising 10 teams, located in Denver, Memphis, St. Louis, Cincinnati, Cleveland, Salt Lake City, Minneapolis, Milwaukee, New Orleans, and Indianapolis. One of your responsibilities is to establish a league-wide licensing program that is managed from your office in Minneapolis. Next week, the league is holding a press conference to announce its inaugural season, to begin next year.

The commissioner has asked that you provide a marketing plan, including a delineation of the revenue enhancement strategies that will be employed to ensure that the league generates income from the licensing program. Prior to the press conference, the commissioner has also requested that you share with the owners how licensing will be used to promote the league in the respective franchise markets.

REVIEW QUESTIONS AND ISSUES

1. What are the fundamental benefits of establishing a trademark licensing program?
2. Explain the differences between federal, state, and common trademark law.
3. Explain the inherent advantages and disadvantages of contracting with a licensing agency.
4. What effect does licensing have on the marketplace?
5. What emerging trends do you see that will have an impact on the sales of sport-licensed products?

REFERENCES

Ala, J.V. (1989). The new trademark law, Case and Comment, 94(5):3–7

Battle, W.R., Bailey, B.B., and Siegal, B.B.: *Collegiate trademark licensing.*

Bikoff, J.L. (1990). *The impact of product liability law on collegiate licensing programs,* paper presented at the ACLA Fourth Annual Meeting, Santa Cruz, California.

Bullington, T. (1994). Counterfeiting: screen printers pay high price for breaking licensing regulations, *Imprintables Today,* pp 30–32, February 14.

Fichtenbaum, P. (1988). Hockey comes out of the ice age, *Sports, Inc,* p 26, December 5.

Gareau, R.N. (1988). Corporate licensing—the world's fastest growing marketing discipline, *Trademark World* 14: 22–26.

Grassmuck, K. (1990). Colleges fight bootleggers as sales boom for goods that bear logos and emblems, *The Chronicle of Higher Education,* pp A32–33, 36, February 21.

Irwin, R.L. (1990). *Development of a collegiate licensing paradigm,* unpublished dissertation, University of Northern Colorado, Greeley.

Irwin, R.L. (1991). A license to profit, *College Athletic Management 3* (1):18–23.

Irwin, R.L., and Stotlar, D.K. (1993). Operational protocol analysis of sport and collegiate licensing programs, *Sport Marketing Quarterly* 2 (10):7–16.

Irwin, R.L., Stotlar, D.K., and Mulrooney, A.L. (1993). A critical analysis of collegiate licensing policies and procedures, *The Journal of College and University Law* 20(2):97–109.

Jones, C.B. (1984). Champions of confusion in trademark law: Champion Products v University of Pittsburgh, *Journal of Law and Commerce* 4:493–516.

Kennedy, E., and Geist, R. (1990). *ACLA Licensee Handbook,* East Association of Collegiate Licensing Administrators, Lansing, Michigan.

Klemm, A. (1991). Maturation or saturation; has collegiate licensing gone overboard? *Team Licensing Business* 3(5):16–17.

Klemm, A. (1994) Young superstars twinkle in the 125th year of our national pastime, *Team Licensing Business* 6(6):36–39.

Krupa, G. (1988). Big bucks on campus, *Sports, Inc,* pp 24–25, December 5.

Macnow, G. (1988). Takin' it to the bank, *Sports, Inc,* pp 22–23, December 5.

Nichols, M.A. (1994). NBA Properties: building on the strength of the brand, *Team Licensing Business* 6(6):26–29.

Nichols, M.A. (1994). NHL Enterprises: the next frontier, *Team Licensing Business* 6(6):31–35.

Rosenblatt, R. (1988). The profit motive, *Sports, Inc,* pp 18–21, December 5.

Sandomir, R. (1988). Baseball comes from behind, *Sports, Inc,* pp 16–17.

Shinner, M. (1989). Establishing a collegiate trademark licensing program: to what extent does an institution have an exclusive right to its name?, *Journal of College and University Law* 15(4):405–429.

Stone, M.J. (1984). How to administer a licensing program, *The Merchandising Reporter* 5(6):3–4.

Sykes, W.D. (1985). *The three ps of licensing,* The Canadian Bookseller, pp. 8–11, March.

Wong, G.M. (1986). Recent trademark law cases involving professional and intercollegiate sports, *Detroit College of Law Review,* pp 87–119.

SUGGESTED READINGS

Association of Collegiate Licensing Administrators (ACLA): Resource Book, East Lansing, Michigan, ACLA.

Boston Professional Hockey Association, Inc v Dallas Cap and Emblem Manufacturing, Inc, 510 F 2d 1004 (1975).

Licensing book, New York, Adventure Publishing.

National Football League Properties, Inc v Wichita Falls Sportswear, Inc, 532 F Supp 651 (1982).

Team licensing business, Scottsdale, Ariz, Virgo Publishing.

University of Georgia Athletic Association v Laite, F 2d 1535 (1985).

University of Pittsburgh v Champion Products, Inc, 566 F Supp 711 (WD Pa 1983).

Appendix 16-A: NCAA Licensing Data Application

Reprinted by permission of the National Collegiate Athletic Association, Mission, Kansas, 66201.

NCAA
LICENSING
DATA

P.O. Box 1906 • Mission, Kansas, 66201 • 913/384-3220

A. Company Name: _____

Address: _____

Telephone: _____

Principal Contact: _____

B. Full description of each product you are requesting to have licensed:

C. Description of Company:

1. _____ Corporation; in what state? _____

_____ Partnership; please list partners: _____

_____

_____ Proprietorship _____

2. Manufacturer:

a. Raw Material _____ Source: Internal _____ External _____

b. Fabrication _____ Source: Internal _____ External _____

If more than 50 percent of the finished product described utilizes product material imported into the United States, please check here _____ .

D. Products currently manufactured and/or distributed:

1. _____

2. _____

3. _____

4. _____

5. _____

6. _____

Appendix 16-A: NCAA Licensing Data Application–cont'd

Reprinted by permission of the National Collegiate Athletic Association, Mission, Kansas, 66201.

E. Please indicate below which of these products have been licensed by other concerns, and which licenses you have been approved to use:

Product: Licensed by:

1. _____

2. _____

3. _____

4. _____

5. _____

6. _____

F. Pricing:

1. Suggested retail (per unit) _____

2. Suggested wholesale (per unit) _____

3. To licensor (per unit) _____

G. Areas of Distribution:

1. National _____

2. Regional (list regions) _____

   _____

3. Local (list areas) _____

   _____

H. Sales Distribution of Products:

Check method used and provide information requested.

1. ☐ Direct sales force _____

   Number in sales force _____

2. ☐ Outside sales representatives_____

   Number of representatives _____

Appendix 16-A: NCAA Licensing Data Application–cont'd
Reprinted by permission of the National Collegiate Athletic Association, Mission, Kansas, 66201.

3. ☐ Jobbers _____

    Number of jobbers _____

4. ☐ Mail order _____

5. ☐ Shows/Fairs _____

6. ☐ Exhibitions _____

7. ☐ Trade markets _____

I. Products sold through what type of outlets:

1. Mass merchandisers (list by name): _____

2. College bookstores: _____

3. Sporting goods stores: _____

4. Specialty stores _____

5. Discount stores _____

6. Other (describe): _____

J. Marketing and Advertising:

Please check those used and, if regional or local, indicate areas.

Media Type	National	Regional	Local
Television	☐	☐ _____	☐ _____
Radio	☐	☐ _____	☐ _____
Print	☐	☐ _____	☐ _____
Point-of-purchase	☐	☐ _____	☐ _____
Outdoor	☐	☐ _____	☐ _____
Transportation	☐	☐ _____	☐ _____
Other	☐	☐ _____	☐ _____

Appendix 16-A: NCAA Licensing Data Application–cont'd

Reprinted by permission of the National Collegiate Athletic Association, Mission, Kansas, 66201.

1. Date organized or incorporated: _____

2. Please list owners, partners or officers: _____

Name: Title:

a. _____   _____

b. _____   _____

c. _____   _____

d. _____   _____

L. Bank References:

Bank   Address/Phone

a. _____

b. _____

c. _____

Submitted by: _____

Title: _____

Date: _____

Reprinted by permission of the National Collegiate Athletic Association, Mission, Kansas, 66201.

LICENSE AGREEMENT

AGREEMENT effective _____ , 19 _____ , and executed on the _____ day of _____ , 19 _____ , between the NATIONAL COLLEGIATE ATHLETIC ASSOCIATION, 6299 Nall Avenue, P.O. Box 1906, Mission, Kansas 66201 (hereinafter called the NCAA), and _____ (hereinafter called "LICENSEE").

WHEREAS, the NCAA is a voluntary unincorporated association of colleges and universities located throughout the United States; and

WHEREAS, the NCAA has its name, the phrases "National Collegiate Championship," "NCAAction," "National Collegiate Championships," "College World Series" and "The Final Four," and the letters "NCAA" registered before the United States Patent Office as well as its seal and logo (hereinafter collectively referred to as "the NCAA name"); and

WHEREAS, the NCAA has obtained from some of its member institutions the non-exclusive right to sublicense the use of their names and marks (hereinafter collectively referred to as "Member names"); and

WHEREAS, LICENSEE is a corporation organized under the laws of _____ and engaged in the business of manufacturing, promoting, selling and distributing _____ ; and

WHEREAS, LICENSEE desires to use the NCAA name in connection with the manufacturing and marketing of _____ ; and

WHEREAS, LICENSEE desires to use Member names jointly with the NCAA name in connection with the manufacture and marketing of some of said products.

NOW, THEREFORE, for and in consideration of the mutual promises, covenants and payments hereinafter set forth, the parties hereby agree as follows:

1. **Grant of License.** The NCAA hereby grants to LICENSEE the right to use the NCAA name and the Member names set forth in Exhibit "A" attached hereto, which exhibit the NCAA may from time to time modify by additions or deletions. All uses of the marks licensed under this Agreement shall inure to the sole and exclusive benefit of the owners of the said marks.

2. **Term.** The first "Contract Year" shall be the period of time beginning on _____ , 19 _____ , and ending _____ , 19 _____ . The second "Contract Year" shall be the period of time beginning on _____ , 19 _____ , and ending _____ , 19 _____ , and the third "Contract Year" shall be the period of time beginning on _____ , 19 _____ , and ending _____ , 19 _____ .

3. **Prominent Display of Marks.** If a Member named is displayed on a product licensed hereunder, the NCAA name must also be displayed on said product.

4. **Minimum Royalties.** LICENSEE agrees to pay to the NCAA minimum royalties of $ _____ for the first three Contract Years, subject to the termination of this Agreement in accordance with Paragraph 24, payable in installments of $ _____ on the signing of this Agreement, $ _____ on or before _____ , 19 _____ and $ _____ on or before _____ , 19 _____ .

5. **New Logos.** LICENSEE may, from time to time, develop new logos or insignia bearing the NCAA name for use on approved products to be manufactured and sold by LICENSEE. Any such logos or insignia shall at all times be the property of the NCAA and shall remain subject to the terms and provisions of this Agreement, including approval by the NCAA before any such use of same.

6. **Marketing and Prior Approval.** LICENSEE agrees that it will use the NCAA name and Member names only in connection with the marketing of products listed hereinabove, all of which shall be manufactured by LICENSEE, or under LICENSEE's direction and control, the specific type, kind, design, style and quality of which shall have been approved in advance in writing by the NCAA. In rendering its approval, the NCAA will be governed by reasonable standards of style and quality. If any products marketed hereunder shall be of lesser quality than the samples submitted to the NCAA for approval, LICENSEE shall, upon reasonable notice from the NCAA, withdraw said products from the market and replace them with conforming products without charge or setoff to the NCAA, and shall indemnify the NCAA against any charge, suit or claim brought by reason of the lesser quality of said products. Marketing by LICENSEE will be done in such a way as to preserve the integrity, character and dignity of the NCAA and advance its purpose of fostering higher education.

LICENSEE shall provide the NCAA in advance with samples of all licensed products and related literature, labels, artwork, displays, and advertising and promotional materials, and none shall be used or thereafter changed without the advance written approval of the NCAA.

7. **Geographical Limitation.** LICENSEE agrees that products using or bearing the NCAA name shall be marketed, sold and distributed only in the United States of America, its territories and possessions, and that LICENSEE will not export any such products, or sell same for export, outside of said areas.

8. **Advance Written Approval.** LICENSEE agrees that in order to protect and preserve the character and purposes of the NCAA, it will not use or market any product using or bearing the NCAA name without the advance written approval of the NCAA. The NCAA agrees to provide LICENSEE with its written approval or rejection within twenty (20) days following receipt of each written request for approval submitted by LICENSEE for the use of the NCAA name. The NCAA agrees to provide LICENSEE with its written approval or rejection within ninety (90) days following receipt of each written request for approval submitted by LICENSEE for the use of the Member name.

9. **Non-Exclusive Grant.** LICENSEE understands that its rights hereunder shall not be exclusive and that the NCAA and its member institutions may, during the time this Agreement is in effect, authorize any other person, firm or corporation to use the NCAA name or Member names in the marketing in the United States, its territories and possessions, of products listed hereinabove.

10. **Heat Transfer Methods.** LICENSEE agrees it will not utilize heat transfer methods to apply the NCAA name or Member names to licensed products.

11. **Label or Hang-Tag.** LICENSEE shall affix a label, hang-tag or other denotation to every product sold hereunder, in a form approved by the NCAA, stating that the product is officially licensed by the NCAA.

12. **Marketing Standards.** LICENSEE acknowledges familiarity with the purposes and high standards of conduct adopted by the NCAA as set forth in its constitution, and agrees to observe same at all times in the promoting and selling of articles of merchandise bearing the NCAA name or Member names. In order to maintain the NCAA's identity and its member institutions' respective identities with intercollegiate athletics, LICENSEE agrees that all literature, labels, artwork, displays, advertising and promotional materials, and activities pertaining to articles of merchandise bearing the NCAA name or Member names shall be separate and distinct from any similar materials used or activities engaged in by LICENSEE relating to professional athletics.

13. **Percentage Royalties.** In further consideration of the rights herein granted to LICENSEE, LICENSEE agrees to pay the NCAA royalties equal to six and one-half percent (6½%) of net sales (gross sales less returns, discounts, postage, documented uncollectibles, freight, insurance and any import duties) of its products listed hereinabove that bear the NCAA name. When said products also bear a Member name, the applicable percentage shall be eight percent (8%).

14. **Marketing Effort.** LICENSEE agrees to advertise, promote and develop each product approved for marketing hereunder in a manner customary in the trade for the marketing of new products. LICENSEE agrees to expend not less than three percent (3%) of gross sales during each Contract Year for such purposes. At the close of each Contract Year, LICENSEE shall render an accounting to the NCAA of all sums expended by it for advertising, promotion and development of products sold hereunder. LICENSEE's failure to advertise, promote and develop, as herein provided, any product approved for marketing hereunder, or LICENSEE's failure to make royalty payments when due during any Contract Year, shall entitle the NCAA to terminate this Agreement upon thirty (30) days' written notice.

15. **Royalties Statement.** The percentage royalties herein provided shall be payable to the NCAA, except to the extent offset each year by minimum royalties, on a calendar quarterly basis. Within thirty (30) days after the end of each calendar quarter, LICENSEE will calculate and present to the NCAA a statement setting forth the net sales of each approved product for the preceding period, the aggregate amounts expended for advertising, promotion and development, and the net amount of royalties due to the NCAA. Each such statement shall be signed by an officer of LICENSEE, and there shall be contemporaneous payment to the NCAA of the amount owing.

16. **Financial Reports.** Financial reports provided by LICENSEE to the NCAA shall list separately information about sales and receipts pursuant to this Agreement, and shall include an itemization of revenues from sales of each product bearing each Member name.

17. **Indemnification by the NCAA.** The NCAA represents and warrants that it has and will have, throughout the

Appendix 16-B: NCAA License Agreement–cont'd

Reprinted by permission of the National Collegiate Athletic Association, Mission, Kansas, 66201.

initial term of this Agreement and any extension or renewal thereof, the right to use the NCAA name and Member names at least to the full extent of the rights granted under this Agreement to LICENSEE, and that the making of this Agreement by NCAA does not violate any agreements, rights or obligations existing between it and others.

18. **Indemnification by Licensee.** LICENSEE agrees to indemnify fully and save harmless the NCAA, its officers, agents, employees, and each and all of its member institutions of and from any and all claims, demands and causes of action, costs and expenses, including attorneys' fees, arising out of anything done or purported to have been done by LICENSEE, or any of its agents, under this Agreement. In the event that any such claims arise during the term of this Agreement, the NCAA shall endeavor to cooperate with LICENSEE in protecting LICENSEE's rights granted herein.

19. **Resale and Distribution to Public.** LICENSEE shall sell the licensed products to jobbers, wholesalers or distributors for resale and distribution to the public through direct mail, and to retail stores and merchants for resale and distribution directly to the public. In the event the LICENSEE sells or distributes the licensed product at a special price directly or indirectly to itself, including, without limitation by specification, any subsidiary related in any manner to LICENSEE, or any officers, employees, directors or major stockholders of LICENSEE or any subsidiary, it shall pay royalties with respect to such sales or distribution based upon the price generally charged the trade by LICENSEE.

20. **Licensee's Representations.** Without limitation upon other provisions of this Agreement, LICENSEE agrees that during the term of this Agreement:
    (a) It will not attack the title of the NCAA in and to the NCAA name or any trademark or service mark pertaining thereto, nor will it attack the validity of the license granted hereunder.
    (b) It will not knowingly harm, misuse or bring into disrepute the NCAA name.
    (c) It will manufacture, sell, advertise, promote and distribute the licensed product in an ethical manner, and in accordance with the terms and intent of this Agreement.
    (d) It will not create any expenses chargeable to the NCAA without prior written approval of the NCAA.
    (e) It will not, without the NCAA's prior written consent, enter into any sublicense or agency agreement for the sale or distribution of the licensed product, but consent is not required for LICENSEE's suppliers, distributors or dealers who make any part of or distribute or sell the licensed products.

21. **No Assignment.** This Agreement may not be assigned or transferred in whole or in part without the written consent of the NCAA, except that LICENSEE may assign the contract to any wholly owned subsidiary of LICENSEE and, in conjunction with an NCAA championship, may assign rights to an on-site silkscreen printer in accordance with the terms of the Notification heretofore provided to LICENSEE, which Notification is attached hereto as Exhibit "B" and incorporated herein by reference.

22. **Disposition of Inventory.** Upon termination hereof, all rights of LICENSEE to use the NCAA name and Member names shall forthwith terminate except as to approved uses thereof on merchandise then on hand as inventory, which may continue to be sold under the terms of this Agreement for a period of six (6) months thereafter, subject to the percentage royalty payments provided herein.

23. **Records.** LICENSEE shall keep complete and accurate records of all sales upon which royalties hereunder may accrue; and the books, records and accounts of LICENSEE pertaining to its business relating to this Agreement may be inspected and audited by the NCAA or its agents at any time during normal business hours upon giving reasonable notice to LICENSEE.

24. **Termination upon Breach.** Without limitation upon the terms of Paragraph 14 hereof, if either the NCAA or LICENSEE shall fail to perform any of the terms or conditions of this Agreement, and such failure or breach shall not be cured within thirty (30) days after giving written notice thereof, the other party shall have the right to terminate this Agreement without prejudice to the right of compensation for losses and damage thereby sustained, or to any other remedies provided by law.

25. **Controlling Law.** This Agreement shall be considered to have been entered into in the State of Kansas, and shall be interpreted in accordance with the laws of that state.

26. **Insurance.** LICENSEE will obtain and maintain, throughout the term of this Agreement, product liability insurance in the amount of $1,000,000 per occurrence for bodily injury and property damage. Said insurance will protect the named insureds against any claims, demands, or causes of action or damages, including costs and attorneys' fees, arising out of any alleged defects in the licensed products, or the use thereof. Said insurance

Appendix 16-B: NCAA License Agreement–cont'd

Reprinted by permission of the National Collegiate Athletic Association, Mission, Kansas, 66201.

will name the NCAA, Collegiate Concepts, Inc. (CCI), International Collegiate Enterprises, Inc. (ICE), and the member institutions listed on Exhibit "A" as said exhibit may from time to time be modified, as additional insureds. Said insurance will not be cancellable until at least thirty (30) days after written notice of cancellation is given to the NCAA. LICENSEE shall furnish to the NCAA a certificate of such insurance demonstrating that the above-stated coverage is in effect.

27. **Accrual of Rights and Benefits.** The rights and benefits accruing to the NCAA under this Agreement shall also accrue to the benefit of NCAA member institutions and CCI/ICE to the extend of their participation herein.

28. **Notices.** Notices by a party under this Agreement shall be deemed given when the same shall have been mailed, provided the same is mailed registered or certified, return receipt requested, and the postage is prepaid, addressed to the other party at the address listed above, or to such other address as the party may have subsequently furnished in writing to the other for this purpose.

29. **Entire Agreement.** This document constitutes the entire agreement between the parties hereto. There are no warranties or representations save as are expressly set out herein.

30. **Non-Waiver.** The acquiescence by either party to the late or incomplete performance of any duty or obligation to be performed hereinunder by the other party is not a waiver of the requirement of timely and complete performance of any and all duties or obligations arising subsequent thereto.

31. **Copies to CEOs.** Upon request by the chief executive officer of any active member institution that is directly affected hereby, the NCAA may provide a copy of this Agreement to such person.

32. **Final Execution.** This Agreement shall not be binding upon the NCAA unless and until it is duly executed by the Executive Director of the NCAA or his designee.

IN WITNESS WHEREOF, the parties hereto have caused this instrument to be executed by their duly authorized officers on the day and year first above written.

THE NATIONAL COLLEGIATE ATHLETIC ASSOCIATION

By _____

Title _____

_____

By _____

Attest: _____   Title _____

PART VI

Economics and Finance

CHAPTER 17

Economics and Sport Management

Tim Berrett

In this chapter, you will become familiar with the following terms:

Economics	Complement	Black market
Gross national product	Substitute	Externalities
Gross domestic product	Supply schedule	Public goods
Gross national sports product	Supply curve	Social demand curve
Microeconomics	Equilibrium price	Economic-impact study
Macroeconomics	Excess demand and supply	Cost-benefit analysis
Demand schedule	Laws of supply and demand	Multiplier effect
Demand curve	Price ceilings	

Overview

Managers of sports organizations are confronted with a variety of issues: how many staff to hire and at what salary; what levels to set membership user fees; whether to operate a concession booth and how to distribute the profits from such a venture; how to react to competition from other fitness clubs; how to allocate the space available in your facility among competing potential uses; whether to invest in new equipment; and how to predict the likely effect on your business of a change in consumer tastes or income levels. Although the number of problems may appear daunting, one area of

study that can offer solutions to many of the dilemmas that sport managers face is economics.

Economics has been defined as "the study of the use of scarce resources to satisfy unlimited human wants" (Lipsey, Purvis, and Steiner, 1988). At first glance, this rather general description of the subject might not appear to have a direct link with the management of sport. However, a second definition of economics as "the social study of the production, distribution, and consumption of wealth" (Greenwald and Associates, 1983) provides some insight into the association between sport management and economics. This is particularly so when one considers that sport managers are involved in the production and consumption of a variety of sports goods and services and that they are also responsible for distributing sport products. Whether they realize it or not, sport managers are as susceptible to the laws of economics as are any other managers in business, government, or not-for-profit organizations.

THE LINK BETWEEN SPORT MANAGEMENT AND ECONOMICS

In many instances, substantial amounts of money (or *scarce resources*) have been devoted to sport. These are resources that could have been spent (or *allocated*) elsewhere in order to satisfy a variety of human wants and needs, such as food, shelter, clothing, education, or other forms of entertainment. The study of economics assists our understanding of how decisions regarding the allocation of scarce resources are made at a number of different levels of analysis, ranging from the societal level, through the industry and firm levels, to the level of the individual consumer. Economic analysis can aid our understanding of why different levels of government provide public money for the financing of sport programs and facilities, whether it be overtly and directly (as in the case of the former Soviet Union and German Democratic Republic) or less openly (as in the case of the public subsidization of professional sport franchises via the construction and financing of stadiums). At the industry level, economics can provide a basis for investigating the factors that make some industries more profitable than others.

Economic theory can be used to analyze the issue of expansion in professional sports leagues. Competition among different firms in the athletic-equipment industry can be analyzed using economic principles, as can the use of revenues from some college sports (notably football and men's basketball) to finance sports that are unable to sustain themselves financially. The theories propounded by labor economists can shed light on the question of salaries and rewards of professional athletes. At the individual level, economists have developed theories that explain how decisions about the use of leisure time are made by people in order to maximize their enjoyment from life, given that they face certain budgetary constraints.

Another way in which the study of economics and sport management are juxtaposed is in the analysis of the bearing that the sport industry has on overall economic activity. There can be little argument that professional sport has some degree of economic impact, particularly when one considers spiraling professional salaries, television contracts, and sponsorship revenues. The same is becoming increasingly true in amateur athletics. Under the leadership of Juan Antonio Samaranch, the International Olympic Committee (IOC) has begun to tap the huge potential for generating private funding for its operations in the form of television revenues and commercial sponsorship (Simson and Jennings, 1992). At the elite international level, the agents representing some track and field athletes threatened to boycott the 1993 world championships of the ironically named International *Amateur* Athletics Federation (IAAF; emphasis added) unless prize money was paid (Hollobaugh, 1992). Intercollegiate athletics involve the administration of scholarships to individual athletes and the setting of admission prices for spectators. Furthermore, the television contracts that the National Collegiate Athletic Association (NCAA) can secure for an event such as the Final Four basketball tournament, together with the amount of money that circulates around the annual football bowl games, illustrate that college level sports are as susceptible to the laws of economics as are their professional counterparts.

Even part-time athletes are not immune from the impact of economics on sport. Recreational joggers pay up to $200 for a pair of running shoes; aerobics instructors are provided with free shoes by the major manufacturers to act as living advertisements for their products; private fitness clubs must determine how much they will charge customers in order to generate maximum profits; and intramural athletics at schools and colleges often involve the assessment of user fees.

Purists might long for the halcyon days in which sports were less commercialized. Even some people who now make their living from managing sport have been known to bemoan the attention that sports receive on the business pages. Indeed Paul Beeston, the president of the 1992 and 1993 world champion Toronto Blue Jays, made a plea in a keynote speech at the 1993 North American

Society for Sport Management conference that baseball get off the business pages of our newspapers and back onto the sports pages. However, it is becoming ever more apparent that sport and business are now inextricably linked.

It is beyond the scope of this chapter to provide the reader with a thorough grounding in the discipline of economics. While adhering to the adage that "a little knowledge is a dangerous thing," the intent of the chapter is to provide readers with an understanding of some basic economic principles and how they can be applied by sport managers. Having read and understood the contents of this chapter, the reader should be able to critically evaluate and comment on some of the economic issues surrounding sport management.

CONCEPT CHECK

Economics is concerned with the allocation of a limited amount of resources to individuals and other economic agents with unlimited wants. Almost every aspect of sport, ranging from professional sport to recreational hobbies, is susceptible to economic analysis. Economic theory can be used to analyze a number of questions and problems that sport managers face on a daily basis.

CONTRIBUTION OF SPORT TO ECONOMIC ACTIVITY

The most comprehensive measure of a nation's total output of goods and services used by economists is the **gross national product** (GNP). The GNP can be calculated in two ways, by examining either expenditures or income. If there are no errors in calculation, each method should give the same overall result. The first approach is to add all expenditures on goods and services produced. Such expenditures includes consumption spending of individuals and not-for-profit organizations; business spending on investment in equipment, inventories, and new construction; government (federal, state/province, and local) spending on the purchase of goods and services; and the net sale of goods and services abroad. The income approach involves the summation of all earnings collected in the production of goods and services and includes

wages, interest, and gross profits. A related measure of national output is the **gross domestic product** (GDP), which differs slightly from GNP. The measurement of GDP ignores income resulting from net foreign investment, while GNP includes such income.

The contribution of the sport and leisure industry to the GNP of a number of Western countries is becoming increasingly important. In the United Kingdom, the Henley Centre for Forecasting (1986) reported that the sports business in that country amounted to £4.4 billion in the fiscal year 1984-1985, equivalent to about 1.4% of GDP. The economic impact of sport in the United Kingdom had increased to £8.3 billion in 1990, equivalent to about 1.7% of GDP (Sports Council, 1992). In 1989, Canadians spent approximately $4.5 billion (Canadian) on sporting goods, in addition to $3.7 billion to use such facilities as golf courses, fitness clubs, bowling alleys, ice rinks, and fitness clubs (Fennell and Jenish, 1990). In the United States, the impact of sport on the nation's economy also has been noteworthy. A joint study conducted by Wharton Economic Forecasting Associates and *The Sporting News* estimated that the sports and leisure industry in the United States in 1988 amounted to some $63.1 billion (Comte and Stogel, 1990). This figure represented an increase of 7.5% over the previous year's $58.7 billion.

The **gross national sports product** (GNSP) is derived in a fashion similar to the GNP: either by totaling the expenditures within the economy on sport and leisure goods and services or by summing the total incomes accruing from the production of sport and leisure goods and services. In 1988, the GNSP accounted for 1.3% of the total GNP of the United States. Although this may not appear to be a significant contribution to overall industrial activity in the economy, when one considers that the sport and leisure industry ranked 22 overall, ahead of both automobile manufacturing and petroleum, it is apparent that the industry is an important contributor to wealth, employment, and output in the United States. Of the $63.1 billion total expenditure, in 1988, $22.8 billion was spent on leisure and recreational sports (an increase of 5.5% from 1987) and a further $19 billion on sporting goods (up 5.2% from the previous year) (Comte and Stogel, 1990).

MACROECONOMICS AND MICROECONOMICS

In any economic system (whether it be a primarily socially planned one such as China or the former Soviet Union or a predominately market-driven one such as the United States), most problems studied by economists can be classified into four basic issues:

1. What is produced, and how is it produced?
2. What is consumed, and by whom is it consumed?
3. What are the overall levels of inflation and unemployment?
4. What is the extent of growth of economic output in the overall economy?

The first two questions are dealt with in the study of **microeconomics,** which is concerned with data in individual rather than aggregate form. This branch of economics deals with the allocation of resources to individual producers and the distribution of a nation's output to its population. Thus, microeconomics is concerned with the pricing of individual goods and services and with the income and employment of an individual firm. Investigations of the price of running shoes, the level of salaries of professional athletes, the cost of season tickets to see the New York Rangers, and the sponsorship of the soccer's World Cup by Master-Card are all instances where microeconomic analysis can be used to inform sport managers.

The second set of issues investigated by economists (i.e., inflation, unemployment, and growth) are treated in the study of **macroeconomics.** This branch of economics is more concerned with aggregate data and the overall health of an economy, rather than the functioning of individual consumers, firms, or markets. Thus, macroeconomics is concerned with the general price level in an economy, national output, total levels of employment, and the rate of economic growth. Sport may be considered a macroeconomic issue in the case of an injection of public expenditure on construction projects (some of which may be sport and recreation facilities). In this situation, expenditures on sport and recreation will have an impact on overall employment levels and perhaps also on the overall price level and inflation in the economy (depending on how the investment program is financed).

However, given that the sport industry (even in the United States) is only a small proportion of the overall economic output, the remainder of this chapter will deal primarily with microeconomic issues rather than macroeconomic ones. This is not meant to imply that macroeconomic policies have no effect on the sport industry, but merely that the scarcity of space allotted to this subject matter dictates that these pages be employed in the most parsimonious manner. In the majority of cases, the application of economic principles to the study of sport management will involve micro- rather than macroeconomic principles. Furthermore, given the recent demise of most centrally planned economies in the world, the remainder of the chapter focusses on how the first two questions posed above are answered via the decentralized decisions of buyers and sellers in markets.

CONCEPT CHECK

Microeconomics is concerned with the allocation of resources to individuals and firms. It deals with data in individual form. Macroeconomic analysis utilizes aggregate data to investigate the overall state of an economic system. The sport industry is measured by the gross national sports product (GNSP) which is the sum of all expenditures on sport and leisure goods and services. It forms a growing proportion of the total economic output of many countries. The total economic output of a country is measured by adding all incomes (including net foreign investment income) accruing to residents of that country and is referred to as gross national product (GNP).

SUPPLY AND DEMAND: THE NUTS AND BOLTS OF ECONOMICS

Although there is much more to the study of economics than the "law" of supply and demand, it is useful for understanding how the market system operates. In order to understand the concept of a market price, first it is necessary to appreciate what determines the demand and supply of a particular good or service, such as athletic shoes.

Demand

The *quantity demanded* of athletic footwear is the total number of pairs that all individual households are willing to buy of such shoes in a certain time period. (The quantity demanded by all households is, of course, the sum of purchases of each individual household). The demand for any commodity depends on a number of variables, including its price, income, prices of other commodities, and consumer tastes. In order to assess the influence of each of these variables on the demand for athletic shoes, it is useful to consider them individually by holding all but one of them constant. When isolating the effect of one variable and holding others constant, the Latin phrase *ceteris paribus* is used by economists.

A basic economic principle applying to the price of any commodity is that the lower the price, the higher the quantity of product will be demanded. In the case of athletic footwear, if everything else is held constant and the price of shoes falls, then consumers will be more able to afford athletic shoes than other commodities in order to satisfy their desires. Because the relative price of athletic shoes is now lower than all other goods, it is reasonable to assume that the total number of shoes demanded will increase. The relationship between quantity demanded and price is shown by a **demand schedule.** Table 17-1 illustrates a hypothetical demand schedule for athletic shoes.

Table 17-1 shows the quantity of shoes that would be demanded, *ceteris paribus*, for six different possible prices. For example, if the price of athletic shoes were $120 per pair, the demand schedule tells us that 50 million pairs of shoes will be demanded. If the price increases to $150 per

pair, then the quantity demanded falls to 40 million pairs. There are, of course, a wide variety of other possible prices (such as $125 per pair) that are not shown in Table 17-1. In order to see such possible combinations of price and quantity, it is possible to draw a **demand curve** (Figure 17-1).

In Figure 17-1, the price of shoes is plotted on the vertical axis and quantity demanded on the horizontal axis. The demand curve shows the quantity of shoes that consumers wish to purchase at each price, such that each point on the demand curve shows a particular price-quantity combination. A movement along the demand curve is referred to as a *change in quantity demanded*. For example, if the price of athletic shoes decreases from $120 to $90 per pair, there will be a increase (rise) in quantity demanded.

Table 17-1 and Figure 17-1 illustrate the possible demand schedule and demand curve for athletic shoes on the assumption that variables other than price remain constant. However, a change in any of the other variables will cause the demand curve to shift to a new position. If the demand curve shifts to the right, more athletic shoes will be demanded at each and every price; if the demand curve shifts to the left, fewer shoes will be demanded at each price. The effect of a change in selected variables is outlined below.

Income and population. If the average household income increases and price remains constant, it would be expected that consumers will purchase more of most commodities. On aggregate, a rise in household income will shift the demand curve for most goods to the right, so that more of those goods will be demanded at each price.* If a constant total of GNP is redistributed among the population, the demand for athletic shoes may change. If, for example, the government introduces tax breaks for the elderly and compensates for the loss of revenue by increasing tax on younger members of the population, there is likely to be a reduction in demand for athletic footwear. This is

---

TABLE 17-1 *Hypothetical relationship between price and quantity demanded of athletic footwear*

Quantity demanded per year (million pairs)	Price per pair ($)
30	180
40	150
50	120
60	90
70	60
80	30

*There are exceptions to this generalization. If a rise in income results in a lower demand for a particular commodity, that commodity is said to be an *inferior good.* Inferior goods are usually consumed in large quantities by the poor, who are unable to afford alternatives.

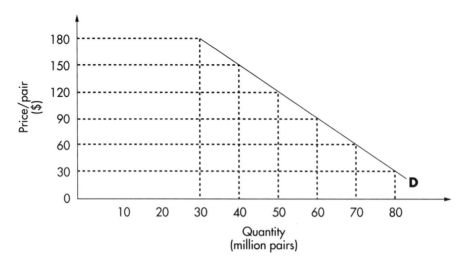

FIGURE 17-1   Hypothetical demand curve for athletic shoes.

because most athletic footwear is purchased for use by consumers under the age of 45. As a result of having a lower level of after-tax income, younger consumers are likely to reduce their purchases of most goods (including athletic footwear), as explained above. This reduction in quantity demanded by people under 45 is unlikely to be made up for by the elderly.

Although an increase in population by itself will not increase demand, an increased number of employed consumers is likely to increase the GNP. When this occurs, the new consumers will demand additional products. Therefore, an increase in population will usually result in a rightward shift of the demand curve for commodities.

Price of other goods. The price of other goods also affects the demand for athletic shoes. If the price of a **complement** to athletic shoes, such as fitness club membership, increases, one would expect that the number of people wishing to purchase athletic shoes in order to attend such facilities will decrease. Although some people will find other forms of fitness activity (such as jogging), others will no longer require the use of athletic shoes. Thus, the quantity of athletic shoes demanded at each price will fall. If there were an increase in the price of admission to swimming pools (a **substitute** product for athletic footwear),

one might expect more people to take up non-aquatic sports and therefore wish to purchase athletic footwear. The result of this will be to increase the demand for athletic shoes at each price. Conversely, if the price of swimming were to fall, then some people would switch their fitness activity to swimming and the demand of athletic shoes would decrease.

Tastes. A change in consumer tastes will also affect the demand curve for athletic shoes. In the 1980s, the degree to which jogging was fashionable increased dramatically. As a result, the demand for athletic shoes also increased. If, however, doctors were to warn of an increased risk of suffering from arthritis as a result of participating in high-impact exercise, then some people would switch their fitness activity to a nonimpact workout, such as swimming. As a result of such a negative change in tastes, the demand curve for athletic footwear will shift to the left.

CONCEPT CHECK

Where each of the variables other than a commodity's price are held constant and the price changes, there will be a change in quantity demanded, as depicted by a movement along the demand curve. Where one or more of the above variables changes, there will be a shift in the entire demand curve, or a change in demand. An increase in demand means that the entire demand curve shifts to the right; a decrease in demand means that the entire demand curve shifts to the left.

Supply

In order to determine the actual number of athletic shoes that will be produced and sold, one must look at how firms determine what they will supply to the market. The *quantity supplied* of athletic shoes is the total number that firms wish to sell per unit of time. Market supply is the sum of the individual supply of all firms producing a particular commodity. The quantity supplied of any product is determined by four key variables: its price, the price of inputs used in its production, the goals of firms, and the availability of technology. In order to determine the influence of each of the four variables, the others must be held constant.

First, one is interested in determining the influence of price on the supply of athletic shoes to the market, *ceteris paribus*. A basic economic principle is that the higher the price of a commodity, the greater the quantity of that product will be supplied. In the case of athletic footwear, if everything else is held constant and the price of shoes increases, then producers will wish to supply

TABLE 17-2 *Hypothetical relationship between price and quantity supplied of athletic footwear*

Quantity supplied per year (million pairs)	Price per pair ($)
70	180
60	150
50	120
40	90
30	60
20	30

more shoes. This is because profits earned from supplying athletic shoes are likely to increase if the costs of producing them are held constant. The relationship between quantity supplied and price is shown by a **supply schedule.** Table 17-2 illustrates a hypothetical supply schedule for athletic shoes.

The supply schedule shows the quantity that producers wish to sell at given prices. As with the demand schedule, there are other price/quantity combinations that are possible, and these can be illustrated on a **supply curve** (Figure 17-2). The supply curve shows the relationship between quantity supplied and price, *ceteris paribus*. A

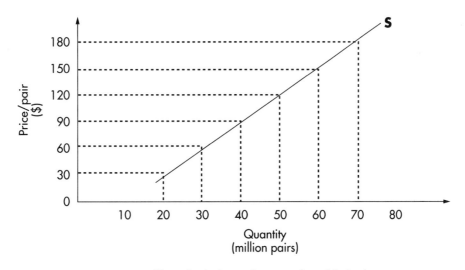

FIGURE 17-2   Hypothetical supply curve for athletic shoes.

change in the quantity supplied is shown by a movement along the supply curve. As in the case with the demand curve, a change in any of the variables, other than price, that influence supply will result in a shift of the supply curve.

Price of inputs. If there is a change in the price of inputs that athletic-shoe manufacturers use, then the supply curve will shift. If, for example, Nike's labor costs increase, then there would be less profit for Nike at each price. Therefore, Nike would offer fewer pairs of shoes for sale at each price and the supply curve would shift upwards and to the left. However, if Nike were able to find a new source of cheap labor that reduced its overall costs of production, then the supply curve of its product would shift downward and to the right. The same argument holds for other inputs, such as machinery and materials.

Goals of firms. It is usually assumed that firms pursue a goal of maximum profits. This might not always be the case, however. For example, the managers of Reebok might be concerned that its market share is lower than that of Nike and might aim to overtake its rival, even if this means that its profits suffer. This would have the effect of shifting the supply curve down and to the right (i.e., Reebok would sell more shoes at a given price). Conversely (!), LA Gear might worry about its image in society and avoid using cheap Asian labor to manufacture its shoes. The effects of this would be to increase costs (and possibly reduce profits) and shift the supply curve upward and to the left.

Technology. A technological change that results in decreased production costs will increase the profits of supplying a particular commodity. For example, computerization of the design phase of running shoes would speed up the process and thus increase profitability (provided that the productivity gain outweighed the cost of computerization). As with any other technological advance that reduces the cost of production, the result of this would cause a rightward shift in the supply curve.

CONCEPT CHECK

Where each of the variables—such as technology, price of inputs, and firm objectives—are held con-

stant and the price changes, there will be a change in quantity supplied, as depicted by a movement along the supply curve. Where one or more of the variables, other than price, that affect supply changes, there will be a shift in the entire supply curve, or a change in supply. An increase in supply means that the entire supply curve shifts to the right; a decrease in supply means that the entire supply curve shifts to the left.

Price Determination

Thus far, demand and supply have been considered separately. In order to determine the actual price at which consumers wish to purchase the same number of athletic shoes that producers are willing to supply, it is necessary to combine the supply and demand schedules. It can be seen from Table 17-3 that there is only one price at which the supply of athletic shoes is equal to demand. This price is $120.

At a price of $90, there will be an *excess demand* of 20 million pairs of shoes. This is because consumers will wish to purchase 60 million pairs of shoes, while producers will only want to supply 40 million pairs. Meanwhile, at a price of $150, there will be an *excess supply* of 20 million pairs. At that price, producers are willing to supply 60 million pairs, but consumers are only willing to purchase 40 million. **Equilibrium price** occurs where the quantity demanded equals the quantity supplied and there is no **excess demand or supply**. At an equilibrium price of $120 per pair, the value of the total market for athletic shoes in our example would be $6 billion (i.e., 50 million pairs × $120 = $6 billion).

These conditions are also illustrated in Figure 17-3. The size of a shortage (excess in demand) or surplus (excess in supply) can be read from the horizontal distance between the two curves at each price. There is only one price at which there is neither a shortage nor a surplus: the equilibrium price. At any price above the equilibrium price, a surplus will exist (i.e., producers wish to produce more shoes than consumers are willing to purchase). At prices below the equilibrium price, a shortage will exist.

LAWS OF SUPPLY AND DEMAND

Having first outlined how an equilibrium price is obtained, the laws of supply and demand can now be explained. As described in the preceding sections, there are four possible shifts that can occur

TABLE 17-3 *Hypothetical demand and supply schedules for athletic shoes*

Price per pair ($)	Quantity demanded	Quantity supplied per year (million pairs)	Excess demand (+) Excess supply (−)
180	30	70	−40
150	40	60	−20
120	50	50	0
90	60	40	+20
60	70	30	+40
30	80	20	+60

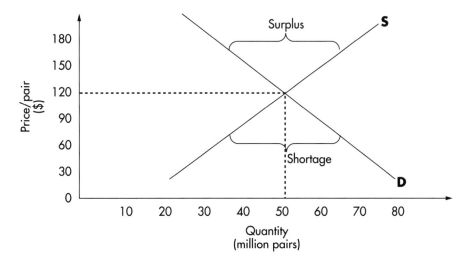

FIGURE 17-3   Price determination in the market for athletic shoes.

in the supply and demand curves: Demand can rise (the demand curve shifts to the right), demand can fall (the demand curve shifts to the left), supply can rise (the supply curve shifts to the right), and supply can fall (the supply curve shifts to the left).

The laws of supply and demand are:

Assuming that there is no change in supply,

1. A rise in demand causes both the equilibrium price and quantity to increase.
2. A fall in demand causes the equilibrium price and quantity to decrease.

Assuming that there is no change in demand,

3. A rise in supply causes an increase in equilibrium quantity and a decrease in equilibrium price.

4. A fall in supply causes a decrease in equilibrium quantity and an increase in equilibrium price.

CONCEPT CHECK

There is only one market equilibrium price of a commodity, and it is determined by the interaction of the forces of supply and demand. If the price exceeds the equilibrium, there will be a surplus; if the price is lower than the equilibrium, a shortage arises. The laws of supply and demand predict the likely effects of shifts in the supply and demand curves on equilibrium price and quantity.

While the laws of supply and demand may appear abstract in nature, they are a very useful tool for sport managers to understand. With a few minor modifications, the number of applications of these relatively simple laws is almost limitless. In some cases, the interaction of the forces of supply and demand is a direct one between buyers and sellers. Such a situation is described in Case Study 2 (a commodity exchange in sports cards), at the end of this chapter.

The interaction between buyers and sellers of a commodity is not always as direct as in Case Study 2. However, the principles by which a market price is determined are equally applicable to other market situations. For example, if a producer of soccer balls sets its price at too high a level, it will find that it is left with unsold inventory (i.e., there is excess supply). In order to reduce inventory, the producer will either have to reduce the price or attempt to change consumer behavior in order to shift demand to the right. The theory of supply and demand can also enable sport managers to predict the likely effects of market intervention. For example, the likely effects of NCAA-imposed limits on scholarships available to intercollegiate athletes can be anticipated. The motivations for such **price ceilings** include the facilitating of fair competition among teams with differing access to funding (e.g., as a result of small media markets) and the prevention of excessive pressure on student-athletes to perform in the athletic arena. In this case, the supply curve represents the supply of eligible skilled athletes, and the demand curve represents the aggregate demand for the services of the athletes.* If the price (in this case, the value of the scholarship) were set above the existing market clearing price, the legislation would have no effect. If the scholarship level were set below the market equilibrium level, then a shortage of athletes would arise because demand would exceed supply. If the scholarship cap were effective, some other means of allocating the available supply of skilled athletes would develop. One method would be to allow coaches who first approach

athletes to have the power to sign them for their services at the capped rate. A more likely scenario, though, is one in which a **black market** arises (wherein commodities are sold illegally in violation of the restrictions imposed). Although it might be possible to restrict colleges from officially making payments in excess of the capped rate, it is very difficult to keep tabs on the individual incomes of each athlete. In order to attract the best athletes to their team, some coaches might be tempted to offer other forms of inducement (such as no-show jobs, guaranteed grades, etc.) The effect of such actions would be to ensure that the equilibrium scholarship paid combined with the value of other inducements would rise to the precapped level.

The motivation of firms to engage in sponsorship of sports can also be analyzed using supply and demand theory. For many sport managers (whether they be managing a professional major league franchise, college athletic program, or amateur-sport national governing body), the funding provided by corporate sponsorship is often seen as the financial lifeline for their organization's continued ability to function. It is therefore important for managers of sport organizations to realize the economic rationale for corporations to become involved in such a relationship. One means of increasing demand for a particular product is through increased advertising. The intention of such expenditure on the part of producers is to create a change in tastes among consumers. Although sponsorship can achieve a number of corporate objectives simultaneously, one of the more frequently cited is to increase awareness of the sponsoring corporation or its product (Abratt, Clayton, and Pitt, 1987; Meenaghan, 1991).

PUBLIC FUNDING OF SPORT

Thus far, the chapter has dealt with the provision of sport and recreation goods and services by individuals and corporations that are motivated by the potential to realize a profit. However, sport managers can also be employed by various government agencies involved in the provision of sports. For example, in former Eastern European communist states, government intervention in sport extended to substantial direct assistance for elite amateur athletes and teams. Such state funding of sport has been emulated to a lesser extent in some Western countries, such as Canada and Australia.

---

*In actual fact, the demand for any factor of production (of which labor is one example) is related to the contribution of that factor to the output of the employer. It is beyond the scope of this chapter to offer a detailed account of how such a *derived demand* is determined.

Even in the United States, where there has been a strong commitment to the notion that the private sector should provide finances required for sport facilities and programs, it has been suggested that the market model is both inefficient and inequitable (Wilson, 1988). The role of government in the funding of sport in the United States is now wideranging. For example, public money is directed toward the provision of parks and swimming pools for public use, toward hosting certain sports events, and toward direct financial aid for the construction of sports facilities for professional sports franchises. In addition, the nonprofit status of national sport governing bodies exempts them from paying certain taxes.

The economic rationale for public-sector involvement in the provision of sport and leisure goods and services revolves around the notion of **externalities.** In the discussion of the market for athletic footwear, it was assumed that these goods were private in that they only provided benefit to the user. In the production or consumption of some goods, however, there are spillover effects, or externalities, that affect nonusers. Consumption externalities arise where the activity results in a cost or benefit for others who are not a direct party to the activity and who do not pay for its production. An example of a positive externality is where young people may be encouraged to participate in sports and, as a result, there is likely to be a reduction in delinquency and urban violence (Wilson, 1988). Another example is where people derive a benefit merely from having the opportunity to use a facility (such as a park or trail system) that they do not necessarily exercise. In a free market, the owner of such a facility would not get any payment for the option benefit that he or she is providing (Gratton and Taylor, 1985). A negative externality may arise where the noise generated by a power boat race pollutes the atmosphere for other lake users, who are not compensated for their loss of enjoyment. The existence of externalities provides a strong argument for government intervention in the private economy in order to ensure that a socially optimal level of goods and services is produced.

The rationale for public intervention in the production of sport goods and services is further enlightened by the distinction between public and private goods. While private goods provide benefits only to the person who uses them, **public goods** display two characteristics that result in problems when they are allocated by the market mechanism. The first of these distinguishing features is that of *nonexcludability.* Once a public good has been produced, it is not possible to prevent any individual from enjoying the benefit associated with its production. For example, when Brazil won soccer's World Cup in 1994, it was not possible to prevent a supporter of that team from feeling a certain amount of pride and jubilation, despite the fact that most of the fans had not contributed in any way to the success. The health benefits that society derives from mass participation in sport are also nonexcludable in that a generally healthier population is a benefit to everyone because of greater industrial productivity and reduced health care costs. It is not possible to exclude any individual from such benefits, even if they do not themselves participate in sporting activities.

The second distinguishing feature of a public good is that it is *nonrival* in consumption. This means that the fact that the good is enjoyed by one individual does not preclude another individual from benefitting from it. For example, it is likely that a certain amount of prestige will be associated with attending a university, the football or basketball team of which has won a national title. The fact that one student can benefit from this prestige status (such as in a case where a potential employer consequently holds the university in higher esteem) does not prevent other students from enjoying exactly the same advantages.

The quantity of a public good displaying positive externalities produced in the free market will be less than the optimal amount. This is because producers and purchasers will not consider the spillover benefits to nonpurchasers of the commodity that is produced. In such a situation, a **social demand curve** exists that is to the right of the market demand curve. This is because at any given market price, consumers do not consider externalities and are willing to purchase less of a commodity than is optimal for society as a whole. In order for the socially optimal level of output of the public good to be produced, there must be some incentive for the private sector (e.g., a subsidy), or government production of the commodity.

Figure 17-4 illustrates the situation in which a positive externality exists. Under free-market

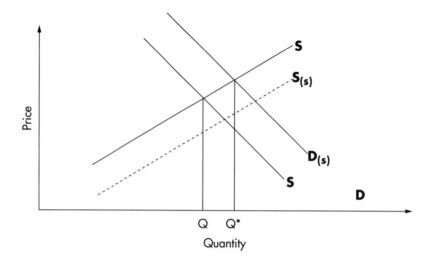

FIGURE 17-4 Social demand curve and the market demand curve.

conditions, the equilibrium quantity of the good that will be produced is depicted by Q, the level of output at which the private supply (S) and demand (D) curves intersect. However, the socially optimal level of output is Q^*, the level of output at which the private supply (S) and social demand ($D_{(s)}$) curves intersect. In order to increase the level of output from Q to Q^* while being willing to accept the lower market price depicted by the market demand curve (D), producers could be offered a subsidy so that their supply curve shifts to the right ($S_{(s)}$). The supply curve shifts because producers will be willing to provide more at a given market price. The amount of the per-unit subsidy is the vertical difference between S and $S_{(s)}$.

In situations where there is a negative externality, the social demand curve will be to the left of the market demand curve, and the socially optimal level of output will be lower than that produced in the free market. In order to reduce production of such a commodity, a tax might be imposed on it, thus shifting the market supply curve to the left, or government regulations or production quotas might be imposed.

CONCEPT CHECK

There are a number of reasons why governments are involved in the provision of a variety of sport and recreation goods and services. One rationale for government intervention in sport is that a market failure occurs as a result of externalities. Public goods that display the features of nonexcludability and nonrivalness are generally underprovided in the free-market system because the social demand curve lies to the right of the market demand curve.

ECONOMIC IMPACT STUDIES

Public funding of sport has become not only an economic issue but also a political one. Decision makers in government are often required to weigh the costs and benefits of supporting a particular sporting event in their jurisdiction or of providing government support for a professional sports franchise. One way in which this is done is through the commissioning of **economic-impact studies.** The purpose of such studies is to inform decision makers as to the likely fiscal effects on the local economy of hosting an event or team. Such economic-impact studies tend only to investigate the positive benefits that hosting a team or event might provide for the local community. A more comprehensive approach (and one that is rarely employed) is a full **cost-benefit analysis** of a particular project that, as its name suggests, investigates both the merits and the demerits of various policy options.

The aim of an economic-impact study is to estimate the direct and indirect influences of an event or project on a regional economy. Such studies are employed by state and municipal governments in order to assist in their decision making about whether they should offer to be a host community for a project, such as a multisport games event or a national championship. It is important to realize that many decisions must be made with incomplete information because the cost of gathering such data is prohibitive. This is true in economic-impact studies, and any evaluation of the findings of such a study should be cognizant of its limitations.

For a typical event, there are three major components of economic impact that should be considered: pre-event impact; during-event impact; and post-event impact. Pre-event economic impacts include those incremental activities that are carried out in preparation for the event. These include capital expenditures on facilities that are constructed solely for the event; incremental capital expenditure by the private sector to service the event; and incremental expenditures by both public and private sector on materials, products, and services for the event. During the event, there will be expenditures by participants, spectators, media, and volunteers assisting with its organization. Post-event impacts include expenditures on facilities (for maintenance), expenditures on materials and goods and services, and tourism expenditure generated by the exposure of the host community during the event.

In each of the major components of economic impact, it is important that only those expenditures that are associated with the event be considered. For example, if a community has already committed to building a new gymnasium when it is awarded the basketball tournament at a multisport event, only those additional expenditures on the gymnasium that are required by the organizing committee to bring the venue up to standard and that would not otherwise have been spent should be considered to be a capital expenditure impact. Similarly, only expenditures by visitors to a host city who are attracted by the event should be considered. For those other tourists who would have visited the region even without the event, only those additional expenditures that they incur as a direct consequence of their attending the event should be considered.

One element of economic-impact studies that is often misunderstood—and consequently misused—is

the **multiplier effect.** The multiplier is a tool used by economists to estimate the magnified impact that changes in investment spending have on total income. The notion of the multiplier was initially employed by Kahn and is an element of Keynesian economics, in which it is argued that one way of reducing unemployment (under certain conditions) is to stimulate demand by public investment. The basic idea of the multiplier is that money spent on a project (whether it be a capital project, such as the construction of a new sports stadium, or a one-off event, such as a city's hosting of a national championship) sets off a chain reaction of other, related spending. The initial spending increases the incomes of workers who are directly engaged in the project. These workers then increase the incomes of merchants with whom they do business. The merchants then increase the incomes of their suppliers, and so on. However, because people do not spend all of any new income they receive on local goods and services (they might save a certain proportion and spend some money on imports), there is a finite effect of the initial injection of spending. The final effect of the multiplier can be calculated by dividing 1 by the proportion of new income not spent locally.* For example, if people save 15% of any additional income and spend 25% on goods and services not produced locally, then the value of the local multiplier is $1/0.4 = 2.5$. Thus, if a project injects \$1 million into the economy initially and 40% of all new income is either saved or spent on goods and services produced outside the region, the ultimate effect on local income would be \$2.5 million. If the proportion of new investment spent locally is only 25%, the value of the multiplier would be $1/0.75 = 1.33$. Thus the greater the amount of new investment that is spent locally, the higher will be the multiplier effect.

CONCEPT CHECK

Economic-impact studies are used to investigate the likely effects of an event on local economic activity.

---

*This formula is derived from adding the cumulative effects of an initial injection of spending on a local economy. If \$1 million is spent initially and 40% is directed to savings or outside the local economy, then \$600,000, (i.e., 60% of \$1 million) is subsequently spent locally by the recipients of the initial injection of \$1 million. Of the \$600,000, 40% (i.e., \$240,000) is directed outside the local economy and 60% (i.e., \$360,000) is spent locally. In the subsequent rounds of spending, \$216,000, \$129,600, \$77,760, \$46,656, \$27,994, \$16,796, \$10,078, etc. is spent locally. The sum of local spending is \$2,500,000.

These studies consider both the direct and indirect effects of spending related to an event. The indirect economic effects are often calculated using the multiplier, which estimates the amount of the new spending that recirculates within the local economy.

SUMMARY

1. The study of economics is a useful tool for the student of sport management. This chapter does not aim or claim to be a primer in economics, but it is hoped that the student will now understand some of the issues facing sport managers from an economic perspective.
2. Although the sport industry makes up a fairly small proportion of overall GNP, this does not mean that there is no place for economic analysis in the management of sports. The sums involved are significant when one considers that the industry accounts for over $60 billion in output per year.
3. The sport industry is no different from any other in terms of the applicability of economic analysis. The allocation of limited resources to the production of sporting goods and services is subject to the same laws as the allocation of these resources to education, food, shelter, and other forms of entertainment.
4. The analysis and laws of supply and demand provide a starting point for the understanding of how these scarce resources are allocated. These laws are applicable to a number of problems facing managers of sport organizations.
5. Sport is considered in many cases to display public-good characteristics because some of its

benefits are nonexcludable and nonrival. Public goods are generally underprovided in the free-market system because social benefits are not accounted for in market demand analysis.
6. Economic-impact studies are used in order to determine whether a particular project or event is likely to provide economic benefits for a community. Such studies illustrate that some facets of macroeconomics are applicable to the study of sport. This is because they consider the effects of an event on such things as overall economic production and employment levels.

CASE STUDY I
ATHLETIC-SHOE MARKET

It has been estimated that the world market for sports shoes is worth in excess of $11 billion (wholesale prices). The four largest players in this market are Nike (21%), Reebok (16%), Adidas (10%), and LA Gear (5%). In the United States alone, the market for athletic shoes is valued at approximately $6 billion (Hugh-Jones, 1992). The 1980s and 1990s have witnessed the growth of three leading manufacturers of athletic footwear in the United States. In 1990, Nike led the industry with $2.2 billion in sales; Reebok sold just over $2.1 billion; and LA Gear established itself as third in the industry with $900 million in sales. Table 17-4 illustrates the growth of sales of these three companies from 1986 to 1990.

What factors might have caused the increase in sales of athletic footwear in the late 1980s? What are the likely effects of an aging population on the market for athletic shoes? How would the imposition of heavy taxes on the import of shoes

TABLE 17-4   *The athletic-footwear market leaders in the United States*

Year	Nike	Reebok	LA Gear	Total
		Sales ($ million)		
1986	1,069	919	36	2,024
1987	887	1,389	71	2,347
1988	1,203	1,786	223	3,212
1989	1,711	1,822	617	4,150
1990	2,235	2,159	902	5,296

Source: Data from annual financial reports.

affect their supply? Why do shoe manufacturers spend so much money promoting their products via advertising and sponsorship? What factors would you consider in introducing a new shoe to the market? Answers to these questions and many others in the field of sport management can be found by applying the economic principles of supply and demand.

CASE STUDY II
TRADING CARDS: A MARKET EXAMPLE

Information Networks, Inc., based in Norwalk, Connecticut, operates SportsNet, an electronic sports card dealing service that links some 3500 sports card stores and individual dealers across North America. The price of sports cards is determined on the network through the interaction of the forces of supply and demand. SportsNet operates in a fashion similar to any stock or commodity exchange, such as the New York Stock Exchange. A dealer places an offer to buy a card on the computer-linked network. Other dealers who are linked to the network scan the orders placed. If a dealer can fill the order from his or her inventory, he or she replies with an offer price. The two dealers (buyer and seller) negotiate on price and the deal is finalized when the seller sends his or her acceptance via SportsNet. Over 35,000 buy or sell messages come across the SportsNet screens weekly, with up to $5 million worth of trades being completed (Roush, 1994).

The trading card and accessories industry in the United States in 1988 was worth a total of $408 million, a 16.7% increase from the previous year (Comte and Stogel, 1990). It has been suggested that the sports card industry is now worth approximately $2 billion a year (Roush, 1994). The interaction of the forces of supply and demand influences the price that a sports card can command in the market. The supply of original cards is generally restricted by the manufacturers, such as Upper Deck, Topps, Sky Deck, and Score Board. The price of a product in which supply is severely restricted is influenced by shifts in the demand curve.

At the end of 1993, a card depicting Michael Jordan at batting practice in a Chicago White Sox uniform was selling for about $12 per card. When Jordan quit basketball and attempted to make a career change to baseball, the price of the card more than doubled, to $25, in April 1994 (Roush, 1994).

The reason for the increase in price was that there were more people willing to buy the card at $12 than there were cards available. In effect, there was a rise in demand for the card because of a change in tastes. With a fixed supply of cards (vertical supply curve), the equilibrium price had to increase. If Jordan's baseball career turned out to be less than auspicious, as initially appeared to be the case, it is likely that fewer traders would wish to buy the card. The effect of this would be to shift the demand curve to the left and thus decrease the market clearing price of the card.

REVIEW QUESTIONS AND ISSUES

1. What are the approaches used to measure the size of an economy and the impact of sport on it? What are the likely economic effects of an aging population on the size and makeup of the sports industry?
2. Using supply and demand analysis, outline the possible effects of the inclusion of women's hockey in the Olympic games. Among other things, consider the effects on hockey equipment manufacturers, ice arenas, coaching programs for hockey, and the administrators of competing sports, such as ringette, speed skating, or indoor soccer.
3. Use the concept of a public good to provide a rationale for a local government to subsidize the construction and operation of a sports stadium.
4. Outline the steps that you would take to conduct an economic-impact study for a proposed Olympic sports festival in your city.

REFERENCES

Abratt, R., Clayton, B., and Pitt, L. (1987). Corporate objectives in sports sponsorship; *International Journal of Advertising* 6:299-311.

Cairnes, J., Jennett, N., and Sloane, P. J. (1986). The economics of professional team sports: a survey of theory and evidence, *Journal of Economic Studies* 1: 1-80.

Comte, E. and Stogel, C. (1990). Sports: a $63.1 billion industry, *The Sporting News*, pp 60-61, January 1.

Fennell, T. and Jenish, D. (1990). The riches of sport, *Maclean's*, pp 42-45, April 9.

Gratton, C. and Taylor, P. (1985). *Sport and recreation: an economic analysis*; London, England, E and F N Spon.

Greenwald, D. and Associates. (1983). *The McGraw-Hill dictionary of modern economics: a handbook of terms and organizations*, 3, New York, McGraw-Hill.

Henley Centre for Forecasting. (1986). *The economic impact and importance of sport in the UK,* Study 30, London, England, Sports Council.

Hollobaugh, J. (1992). A piece of the pie, *Track and Field News,* pp 22-23, November.

Hugh-Jones, S. (1992). Survey of the sports business, *The Economist,* July 25.

Johnson, A. (1993). *Minor league baseball and local economic development,* Urbana, Illinois, University of Illinois Press.

Lipsey, R., Purvis, D., and Steiner, P. (1988). *Macroeconomics,* ed 6, New York, Harper and Row.

Meenaghan, J. (1991). The role of sponsorship in the marketing communications mix, *International Journal of Advertising,* 10:35-47.

Noll, R. (1974). *Government and the sports business,* Washington, DC, Brookings Institute.

Noll, R. (1988). *Economics of sports leagues.* In Uberstine, G. ed, *Law of professional and amateur sports,* New York, Clark Boardman Co.

Quirk, J. and Fort, R. (1992). *Pay dirt: the business of professional team sports,* Princeton, Princeton University Press. Week, p 58, April 11.

Scully, G. (1989). *The business of Major League Baseball,* Chicago, University of Chicago Press.

Simson, V. and Jennings, A. (1992). *Lords of the rings,* Toronto, Ontario, Stoddart.

Sports Council. (1992). *Economic impact of sport in the UK in 1990,* London, England, Sports Council.

Wilson, J. (1988). *Politics and leisure,* Boston, Unwin Hyman.

SUGGESTED READINGS

For a more detailed theoretical analysis of the economics of sport and recreation, students are encouraged to read Gratton and Taylor (1985) and Noll (1974). A brief overview of the economic impact of the sports business worldwide is provided by Hugh-Jones (1992). A study of the local impact of baseball on an economy is offered by Johnson (1993). Discussions of the economics of professional team sport are provided by Cairnes, Jennett, and Sloane (1986) and by Noll (1988), while a less theoretically oriented approach is taken by Quirk and Fort (1992) and Scully (1989). (The full citations of all these titles are listed above, in the References section.)

CHAPTER 18

Accounting and Budgeting

Elizabeth Barber

In this chapter, you will become familiar with the following terms:

Accounting	Income statement	Liquidity ratios
Cash accounting	Sales	Leverage ratios
Accrual accounting	Gross sales	Activity ratios
Balance sheet	Net sales	Profitability ratios
Assets	Cost of goods sold	Budget
Current assets	Gross profit	Object classification budget
Long-term investments	Gross margin	Line item budget
Fixed assets	Operating expenses	Increment-decrement budget
Book value	Net income	Program budget
Cost value	Net profit	Performance budget
Depreciation	Net loss	Planning programming budget
Market value	Percentage column	system
Liabilities	Cash flow analysis	Zero-based budgeting
Current liabilities	Journals	Capital budget
Long-term liabilities	Sales journal	Enterprise fund system
Equity	Disbursement journal	Fund accounting

Note: Otho G. Bendit, formerly of the University of Notre Dame, and Linda S. Koehler, University of the Pacific, contributed to this chapter.

Overview

The management of the annual budget or financial accounting statements will be the responsibility of all managers in the field of sport. The depth and breadth of their knowledge, of course, will be situation-specific, but all managers must be able to read and interpret financial statements and prepare and control an annual budget. The intention of this chapter is not to make the reader an accountant, but rather to help the future sport manager become accounting- and finance-literate. Most business operations will always retain the services of a professional accountant, in addition to the on-site manager, but this is no reason for the sport manager not to be familiar with financial management.

Whether the enterprise is public (owned by the municipality or other government), nonprofit (college, university, YMCA, youth sport club, and the like), or private (in legal terms, the three forms of business ownership are sole proprietorship, partnership, or corporation, with examples being professional sport teams, health clubs, and retail stores), financial knowledge is imperative to the success of business operations. Managers that don't use proactive methods of financial control will soon find themselves unemployed.

This chapter will cover two major topics. The first part of the chapter will discuss principles of accounting; financial statements, including balance sheet, income statement, and cash flow analysis; and computing and interpreting ratios that are applicable for profit-oriented enterprises. The second part of the chapter will discuss principles of accounting, along with different types of budgeting, for nonprofit organizations, municipalities, and government-owned operations.

DEFINITION AND ROLE OF ACCOUNTING

Accounting can be defined as the collection of financial data about an organization (Bendit and Koehler, 1991). The process includes gathering, recording, classifying, summarizing, and interpreting data. Accounting examines an enterprise's profit or loss, determines how it occurred, and determines assets and liabilities, all in relationship to the form of business ownership. These entities can be related to one another to provide information about the financial status of the business. This information helps the sport manager in the planning process and in making crucial financial decisions.

Cash vs. accrual accounting

A manager that uses **cash-accounting** methods records revenues and expenses *only* when cash is actually received. For example, charge sales are not reported until the charge is paid or when the charge account has a zero balance. The same is true of charged purchases. When a business receives merchandise and the bill is not payable for 30 days, then the reporting of the expense only occurs when the bill is paid.

Accrual-accounting methods record revenues and expenditures as they occur—that is, a charged sale or a charged purchase is recorded on the same day it takes place under the accrual method.

Professionally speaking, the accrual method is the most often used because it is believed to show the most accurate picture of the revenue and expenditures of the business.

FINANCIAL STATEMENTS

A manager's primary task in financial management involves ensuring a profit for the enterprise, having current information on the financial condition of the business, and knowing the cash flow of the operation to prevent shortages. With this in mind, the following financial statements become the working tools of the sport manager. These financial statements are normally used by private (for-profit) business enterprises, but in some cases of public/nonprofit ownership, a manager could be expected to use them. This is especially true of the balance sheet.

Balance sheet

The **balance sheet** is considered one of the most important financial statements. The four main uses of the balance sheet are that it (1) shows changes in the business over a period of time, (2) shows growth or decline in various phases of the business, (3) shows the business's ability to pay debts, and (4) through ratios, shows financial position.

Assets. The balance sheet is exactly what the name implies. It shows a balance in a business's assets as compared to the liabilities and owner's equity. On the left side of the balance sheet, one will find a listing of the assets (see Table 18-1). **Assets** are considered to be what a business owns. The listing of assets is considered individual accounts. For example, the value that coincides with

TABLE 18-1 *Balance sheet: ABC Sporting Goods yearly report*

Assets		Liabilities	
Current assets		**Current liabilities**	
Cash	$ 20,000	Accounts payable	$ 7,200
Accounts receivable	8,000	Short-term loans	0
Inventory	50,000	Interest payable	6,000
Short-term investments	5,000	Current portion of	
Prepaid expenses	3,720	long-term loan	12,000
Total current assets	86,720		
Long-term investment	0	**Taxes payable**	
		Accrued payroll	2,300
Fixed assets		Total current	
Land	0	Long-term liabilities	27,500
Building: $48,000 cost		Long-term liabilities	
accumulated (50 yr.)		Loans payable	72,000
depreciation of		Total liabilities	$ 99,500
$1920, book value	46,080	Equity	
Fixtures: $35,000 cost	28,000	Montague's investment	20,000
accumulated (10 yr.)		Hicklin's investment	20,000
depreciation of $7,000, book		Plus net income	81,000
value		Less total partner	
Furniture: $10,000 costs	8,000	withdrawal	41,000
accumulated (10 yr.)		Total partner equity	$80,000
depreciation of $2,000,		Total liabilities and equity	$179,500
book value			
Automobiles: $15,000 cost	10,700		
accumulated (7 yr.)			
depreciation of $4,300,			
book value			
Total fixed assets			
	85,100		
Total assets	$179,500		

the asset called inventory would be backed up with an inventory account record. Assets can be divided into (1) current assets, (2) long-term investments, and (3) fixed assets.

Current assets are considered cash on hand and any asset that can be converted to cash within 12 months from the date on the balance sheet. Examples of current assets include accounts receivable (charges owed by customers), inventory (wholesale cost), temporary investments (e.g., interest-bearing bank accounts, certificates of deposits (CDs), stock in another business that will be converted within one year, and prepaid expenses (e.g., rent, insurance).

Long-term investments are any investment made by the business that has a maturity date beyond one year. One example would be a CD purchased with a 5-year payoff date. **Fixed assets** are the items a business owns that cannot be sold without changing the business operations. Examples of fixed assets are real estate (land and buildings), furniture, equipment, and automobiles. The value listed on the balance sheet is called the **book value** (BV). The book value is the **cost value** (CV) minus the depreciated value (D)(CV − D = BV).

This should not be confused with the market value, which is the amount of money an item could be sold for.

Depreciation is a legal term used by businesses to lower the value of an asset as it gets older. After an asset is purchased and begins to be used in daily operations, the value of that item diminishes. The straight-line method of depreciation estimates the "life" of an asset, the amount of time one would expect this asset to last. For example, what is the life expectancy of a car? If it's estimated to be 7 years and the original cost of the car was $14,000, then every year $2000 would be deducted from the book value of the car listed on the balance sheet. This is not to say that in 7 years the car does not have any **market value,** but rather, for the purpose of calculating the assets of this business, the car has been totally depreciated for income tax purposes because depreciation is tax-deductible (Table 18-1).

The total amount of assets will be found at the bottom of the asset side of the balance sheet. It is computed by adding together the total current assets, long-term assets, and fixed assets.

Liabilities. **Liabilities** are considered a business's debt, how much money the business owes to other parties. Liabilities are found in the right-hand column of the balance sheet and are divided into current liabilities and long-term liabilities.

Similar to current assets, **current liabilities** are those debts that must be repaid within 1 year. Examples of current liability accounts include accounts payable (goods and services purchased on credit, usually payable within 30 days), short-term notes (amount of principal owed to a lender, totally payable within 1 year), the current portion of long-term notes (current principal amount due), interest payable (interest due on either short-term or long-term notes), taxes payable (only applicable to a corporation that owes corporate taxes), and accrued payroll (salaries or wages due).

Long-term liabilities include all the loans a business may have that are not currently payable. These are usually larger loans that were acquired to purchase large items (fixed assets), such as real estate, automobiles, and fixtures needed to open a business for operations.

All the current liabilities and long-term liabilities are added together to come up with the total for liabilities owed.

Equity. Owner's **equity** is the amount of money invested by owners. In a sole-proprietorship, the business begins with the amount of money the owner invested from personal funds. In a partnership, it is the amount of money each partner invested individually. Earned income is added to the owner's investment. Subtracted from this amount are any withdrawals made by the owner. This amount would now be considered the total owner's equity. Equity is found underneath liabilities on the balance sheet (see the following box). This should be defined individually for each owner.

Equity equation

Owner's investment
+ Income earned
− Withdrawals made
Owner's equity

In a corporation, the equity would include all the stockholders' purchased shares of stock.

Once the total liabilities and the total equity are calculated, these two figures are added together. The combined values should equal (be balanced with) the total assets found in the column on the left.

Income statement

Another extremely important financial document is the income statement. The income statement and the balance sheet are often used by bankers or interested investors when it comes to making decisions about lending to or investing in a business. The importance of these two documents can not be overstated.

The purpose of the **income statement** is to analyze the success of a business. The profit (or loss) of a business is found in the income statement. This allows a manager to compare the cost of running a business with the sales generated. The purchases and distributions made to the owners rely on the income statement. An income statement is read from the top down. The top line is the gross proceeds, with the bottom line reflecting the net income (see Table 18-2). The exact items found on the income statement will depend on the nature of business. The following information discusses typical items listed on many business's income statements.

TABLE 18-2   *Income statement: ABC Sporting Goods, yearly report*

	Amount ($)	% of net sales
Revenue		
Gross sales	273,200	101
Less sales returns and allowances	3,200	1
Net sales	270,000	100
Cost of sales		
Beginning inventory	50,000	18.5
Plus purchases	135,000	50
Total goods available	185,000	69
Less ending inventory	50,000	18.5
Total cost of goods sold	135,000	50
Gross profit	135,000	50
Operating Expenses		
Salaries and wages	22,000	8
Commissions	2,300	1
Advertising	1,500	0.5
Insurance	2,500	1
Depreciation	9,300	3
Interest	6,000	2
Office supplies	800	0.02
Utilities	2,200	1
Miscellaneous	7,400	2.7
Total operating expenses	54,000	20
Total operating income	81,000	30
Pretax income	81,000	30
Tax on income (corporation only)	0	
Net income (net profit)	81,000	30

Sales. **Sales** figures always appear first on an income statement. **Gross sales** are the total amount of revenue (excluding sales tax) that is generated. Revenue that is obtained through ticket sales, merchandise purchased, food service, memberships, etc., is considered gross sales. If a business has a return policy—where money is given back to dissatisfied customers—this amount should be subtracted from the gross sales figure. Other values that should be subtracted are called *allowances* (e.g.,

discounted sale price, cost of stolen or shoplifted merchandise, losses incurred from damages, and prompt-payment discounts). The resultant figure is called **net sales.**

The **cost of goods sold** (sales) must be calculated (see the equation in the following box). The beginning inventory's value is based on the wholesale cost of the merchandise. The value should be calculated on the first date of the income statement, usually the beginning of the year. The addition of the purchased inventory should include all purchases throughout the entire period (usually 1 year). From the total amount of merchandise, the ending inventory is subtracted. Ending inventory is the cost of the "remaining in inventory" on the last day of the year.

Cost of goods sold

$$\frac{\begin{array}{r}\text{Beginning inventory} \\ + \text{ Purchases}\end{array}}{\text{Total goods}}$$

$$\frac{\begin{array}{r}\text{Total goods} \\ - \text{ Ending inventory}\end{array}}{\text{Total cost of goods sold}}$$

When the cost of goods sold is subtracted from net sales, the resulting value is called the **gross profit** or **gross margin.**

Operating expenses. **Operating expenses** include all other expenses a business accrues during day-to-day operations. Examples of operating expenses include salaries, insurance, rent or loan payments, advertising, and utilities. The income statement is used by most business owners to complete income tax forms. For that purpose, you will find such deductions as depreciation, even though it is not considered actual cash paid out by the business. Depreciation is used to replace fixed assets that have been used during normal business operations; in other words, it is considered the cost of doing business (Ellis and Norton, 1988).

Earnings before taxes and taxes due. A business owned as a sole proprietorship or a partnership is not responsible for paying federal income taxes.

The owners of the business are required to declare the percentage of the business profit that is attributable to their specific percentage of ownership on their individual income tax. Only the corporation is required to pay corporate income tax on the business's profits. State or local municipalities may have separate laws that govern a specific location. The business owner should be aware of this; but if this isn't the case, this section of the income statement can be omitted.

Net income or net profit. **Net income** is the amount of money remaining after all expenses (liabilities) have been paid. This amount can be used for retained earnings for the business, divided among partners, or used to pay dividends to stockholders in the corporation. If the business accrues a **net loss** over the year, the amount of the loss will be shown in parenthesis—e.g., (4800) represents a $4800 loss.

Percentage column. The **percentage column** is a very useful management tool. It can show a manager what percentage of the net sales is being spent in specific areas of the business. If a particular percentage appears to be too high (higher than last year's income statement or higher than the standards set in this type of business operation), the manager will know that the expense should be lowered. For example, if the cost of goods sold in a retail operation is 75% of the net sales, most managers would consider this percentage too high. To remedy this situation, one could either raise the retail price so that net sales would increase or search for other wholesale vendors that would sell merchandise to the business at a lower cost, which would decrease the cost of goods sold.

Cash flow analysis

Cash flow financial statements serve a third purpose for the sport manager. The information found in the cash flow document is a detailed accounting of receipts (revenue) and disbursements (expenses). Cash flow does *not* tell the manager the business's financial condition (balance sheet), nor does it show the profit or loss (income statement) of the business. It only shows the manager "cash in" and "cash out." Cash flow is normally documented monthly. This gives the manager the abil-

ity to analyze the financial situation over a period of time. Also, after several years of business operations, the manager is able to see patterns of cash flow that might indicate the need for a short-term loan or, just the opposite, periods of time when cash is abundant and should be invested for maximum profit opportunities. Table 18-3 shows an example of a cash flow analysis.

TABLE 18-3 *Cash flow analysis: ABC Sporting Goods, 1st quarter 19XX*

	January	February	March
Sales			
Inventory			
Clothing	2,300	2,700	3,400
Equipment	10,540	1,500	9,900
Layaway paid	1,320	1,000	4,000
Total sales	14,160	5,200	17,300
Less cost of sales	7,300	7,000	7,200
Gross margin	6,860	(1,800)	10,100
Less expenses			
Salaries	1,200	1,200	1,200
Commission	800	300	0
Advertising	100	300	100
Insurance	0	1,250	0
Loan payment	700	700	700
Office Supplies	150	70	50
Utilities	250	250	200
Miscellaneous	300	200	540
Total	3,500	4,270	2,250
Cash Flow			
A − B = C Surplus (or deficit)	3,360	(6,070)	8,850
Cash balance			
Cash at start	0	3,360	290
Cash flow	3,360	(6,070)	8,850
Bank loan (L) or rent (R)		3,000L	3,000R

Journals

Journals (sometimes referred to as *ledgers*) are the financial documents that the sport manager uses for recording all financial transactions during day-to-day operations. Most businesses use two basic record books: sales journals and disbursement journals (Pickle and Abrahamson, 1986).

Sales journals. **Sales journals** record cash sales and receipts of daily income. The journal headings are based on the exact specifications for the business. For example, a stadium operation might define its journal headings as ticket sales, concession sales, group sales, and Skybox sales. See Table 18-4 for an example of a sales journal from a golf club.

A more detailed look at the sales receipts is warranted if the manager wants more specific information. In the case of the golf course's greens fees and pro shop sales, it might be appropriate to divide sales into cash and charge categories. Or membership dues could be divided into new memberships and renewals. The options are virtually unlimited, the point being that every business should design its sales journal in the manner deemed appropriate.

The sales journal can also be used to verify the amount of cash that is deposited in the bank daily. By adding the columns, it is easy for a manager to see if discrepancies exist. The totals are also used for the income statement and cash flow analysis.

All the financial statements should be used to cross-check one another.

Disbursement journal. The **disbursement journal** is similar to the sales journal in its format. The column headers are changed to reflect expenditures specifically defined by the individual business. Examples of disbursement category headings are payroll, all types of vendor purchases (e.g., merchandise, food, beverages), advertising, and insurance. The income statement and cash flow analysis documents should use the same terminology (Table 18-5).

The columns of the disbursement journal are usually totaled at the end of the month, although some businesses choose to do it more often. The uses of this information are numerous. For example, the columns that coincide to the items on the income statement can be used to formulate that financial document, and the total amount for checks written can help the manager check bank statements.

A more detailed explanation of how to set up journals can be found in many small-business management courses and textbooks.

RATIOS

Ratios are computed by comparing items found on the three financial statements. Ratios are used to evaluate specific aspects of the financial well-being

---

TABLE 18-4   *Sales journal*

Date	Account or description	Greens fees ($)	Pro shop ($)	Food and beverages ($)	Lessons or tournaments ($)	Member fees ($)
June 1	Daily sales	366	127.43	100.20	55	1,500
June 2	Daily sales	824	447.60	275.75	110	9,000
June 3	Daily sales	455	235.75	155.45	0	500
June 4	Daily sales	875	455.00	325.40	330	2,500
June 5	Daily sales	1,225	347.25	466.65	220	0
June 6	Daily sales	665	348.50	207.65	55	0
June 7	Daily sales	235	473.90	768.45	2,300	0
Week total		4,645	2,435.43	2,299.55	3,070	13,500

TABLE 18-5 *Disbursement journal*

Date	Payee or account	Check no.	Amount of check ($)	Vendor Inventory ($)	Advertising ($)	Payroll ($)	Food and beverages ($)
June 1	T. Jones, Mgr.	1010	987.43	0	0	987.43	0
June 1	A. Stone, Mgr.	1011	632.76	0	0	632.76	0
June 1	Philadelphia Beverage	1012	98.10	0	0	0	148.10
June 2	Spalding Golf Distribution	1013	887.66	887.66	0	0	0
June 2	WMMR Radio	1014	350.00	0	350.00	0	0
June 4	MaxFli Golf Supplies	1015	544.78	544.78	0	0	0
June 5	Pennsylvania Liquor Authority	1016	99.75	0	0	0	249.75
	Total distribution	—	3,603.48	1,432.44	350.00	1620.19	397.85

of a sport business. Good managers will use a variety of ratios because they help identify trouble spots. The use of ratios does not show the cause of or solution to financial problems, but it is extremely useful for clarification. Ratios can be used to track overtime and project the future.

There are industry-wide standards that can be used for comparisons, and they can be found in the publications of Dun and Bradstreet, Accounting Corporation of America, and Robert Morris Associates, as well as in trade magazines and other publications issued by trade associations. One useful source of information on ratios is the *Almanac of Business and Industrial Financial Ratios* (Pickle and Abrahamson, 1986).

This section does not include an exhaustive discussion of ratios. Dozens of ratios could be produced for each business, but usually only a few key ratios are helpful (Siropolis, 1994). The most pertinent and useful ratios for the sport manager are discussed below.

Liquidity ratios

Liquidity ratios measure a business's ability to pay its current debt. Liquidity is another term used to show whether a manager is controlling the short-term costs while covering ongoing expenses (Ellis and Norton, 1988). Following are two examples of liquidity ratios.

Current ratio. The current ratio measures a business's ability to pay its current debts with current assets.

$$\text{Current ratio} = \frac{\text{Current assets}}{\text{Current liabilities}}$$

A current ratio of 2:1 is considered acceptable. This means the business has twice as many current assets as it does current debt.

Acid-test ratio. The acid-test, or quick-test, ratio looks for a 1:1 ratio of current assets to current debt. When calculating the current assets, however, the inventory and prepaid expenses are subtracted because they can not be referred to as cash.

$$\text{Acid test} = \frac{\text{Current assets} - \text{Inventory} - \text{Prepaid expenses}}{\text{Current Liabilities}}$$

Leverage ratios

Leverage ratios (also referred to as *debt ratios*) show three characteristics of a business: (1) debt related to equity, (2) the ability to borrow money, and (3) the ability to pay debt when it is due (Ellis and Norton, 1988). Stockholders and bankers are very interested in this information. Following are two examples of leverage ratios.

Debt-to-equity ratio. The debt-to-equity ratio shows the percentage of the business that is owned by the stockholders (partners or sole proprietor) as compared to the amount of the business that is owed to creditors.

$$\text{Debt-to-equity ratio} = \frac{\text{Total liabilities}}{\text{Owners' equity}}$$

A ratio of 1.0 shows that equal amounts of the business are attributed to owners and creditors. If the ratio is greater than 1.0, creditors are due more than owners own; and a ratio less than 1.0 shows that the owners have more invested then the creditors have financed. A debt ratio less than 1.0 is preferable to bankers. This ratio is important to keep the business from becoming overextended in terms of debt. The sport manager should make financial decisions that improve this ratio over time so that more of the business is owned by the stockholders (partners or sole proprietor).

Debt-to-assets ratio. This ratio is often used by bankers when making loan decisions. The debt-to-assets ratio shows what percentage of total business funds are actually debt. The bank looks for the lowest possible percentage. If the business has a high ratio of debt to assets, the bank may still lend it money, but at a higher interest rate. The business is considered a higher risk for defaulting (not being able to make payments) on a loan.

$$\text{Debt-to-assets ratio} = \frac{\text{Total liabilities}}{\text{Total assets}}$$

Activity ratios

The third group of ratios are called **activity** (or efficiency) **ratios,** which show how effectively a business is using its assets in relationship to sales (Crossley and Jamieson, 1994).

Inventory turnover ratio. This ratio tells a business how long it takes to sell out inventory. The total number of times a year and the exact number of days it takes to deplete the inventory is the information obtained with this ratio. With this knowledge, a manager can decide if too much or too little inventory has been purchased.

$$\text{Inventory turnover} = \frac{\text{Cost of goods sold}}{\text{Average inventory}}$$

$$\text{Average inventory} = \frac{\begin{array}{c}\text{Beginning} \\ \text{inventory}\end{array} + \begin{array}{c}\text{Ending} \\ \text{inventory}\end{array}}{2}$$

$$\text{Inventory turnover in days} = \frac{365 \text{ days}}{\text{Inventory turnover}}$$

The average inventory should be calculated. This is especially true for a seasonal business, such as a sporting goods store that specializes in ski equipment. If 365 days divided by the inventory turnover tells the manager that the inventory is sold too slowly, the manager knows not to order so much inventory in the future. Having too much inventory is a poor way to manage finances.

Assets-to-sales ratio. The assets-to-sales ratio is sometimes referred to as the assets turnover ratio. Net sales compared to total assets show how actively and effectively business assets are being used to generate income (Crossley and Jamieson, 1994).

$$\text{Assets-to-sales ratio} = \frac{\text{Net sales}}{\text{Total assets}}$$

If a business has a large amount of income tied up in accounts receivable, another good ratio to use is the accounts receivable turnover, which allows a business to know how many days it takes to turn inventory into cash. Because we live in an era of bank credit cards, this ratio isn't as important to know for this type of charge is instantly cash for the business when it is deposited into the bank.

Profitability ratios

The final ratios deal with the financial profit of a business. The income statement and the balance sheet are used to calculate **profitability ratios.** By using these ratios, the manager should improve performance in controlling expenses that will in turn reflect an increase in earnings (return on investment).

Net profit margin. This ratio shows a business's ability to generate a profit on sales. The ratio shows how well a manager manages the day-to-day operation of a business by showing how much of each dollar earned is considered profit.

$$\text{Net profit margin} = \frac{\text{Net income}}{\text{Sales}}$$

A business could choose to compute this ratio using net income before tax or net income after tax, depending on the ratio desired. The advantage of computing the net profit margin before taxes is because taxes increase as a business earns more money. Taxes can have a drastic effect on profit, so computing the net profit margin before taxes gives a more accurate picture if similar businesses want to compare profit ratios.

To figure the business's rate, the same ratio can be used by changing the denominator (the numerator, net income, remains the same). Substitute for the sales figure equity, and find out the business's return on equity; substitute (long-term liabilities + equity) and find out the return on total investment; or substitute assets to learn the return on assets.

SUMMARY OF ACCOUNTING

Accounting practices vary with the form of business ownership, but the three most commonly used financial statements are the balance sheet, the income statement, and the cash flow analysis. All three financial statements serve a different purpose and should be used together. Journals are used to record all sales and disbursements, whether either cash or accrual accounting methods are used.

Ratios are extremely useful management tools. The information from the financial statements is calculated in various ratios to determine many financial aspects of the operations. Major financial management decisions should be made from using ratios.

The intention of the previous section was to prepare the sport management student with a working knowledge of accounting practices. More in-depth knowledge can be obtained in a small-business management or accounting and finance course.

CONCEPT CHECK

The three financial statements used to manage the financial aspects of a business are the balance sheet, income statement, and the cash flow analysis. The balance sheet shows the financial condition of the business; the income statement shows profit or loss in the business operations; and cash flow analysis shows cash sales and disbursements records.

ACCOUNTING FOR PUBLIC/NONPROFIT ORGANIZATIONS

Most organizations that operate as a nonprofit enterprise (e.g., private universities or nonprofit clubs that are supported by voluntary contributions and other sources) or that are organized as a part of a governmental agency (municipalities and state-owned universities that are tax supported) receive allocations from the general fund of the overall unit. These entities are established under specific regulations and restrictions, by law, to operate on a nonprofit basis. Therefore, they are not subject to income tax laws. In sport management, examples of these types of operations are school athletic programs, community youth sport programs, club sport programs, and municipal golf courses.

Each year, a public/nonprofit organization submits a budget request to its superior body (e.g., city council budget review committee, university financial officer, board of directors). A sport manager will be competing for funds with many other groups within the organization (unless it is an athletic department that is expected to be self-sufficient). The way in which the budget is presented, the selection process for the items included on the budget, and the related justifications are three extremely important tasks required of a management team. Remember that a sport or athletic program is only one part of a large picture, and the preparation and administration of an effective budget is probably one of the best public relations tools a manager can use, internally and externally. On the other hand, the mishandling of funds, when other constituencies are vying for a "share of the same pot," can be professional suicide.

Types of budgets

By definition, a **budget** is a statement of financial position based on estimates of expenditures and suggested proposals for financing them—in other words, a management plan for revenue and expenses of an organization for a period of time (usually 1 year). Some of the criteria to consider when establishing a budget are past revenues generated, changes in prices or fees, marketing research predictions, the current promotion and advertising strategies, and the economic environment of the general public and the institution (Bendit and Koehler, 1991). The following list includes practical advantages of budgeting:

1. It substitutes a plan for "chance" in fiscal operations; foresees expenditure needs; and organizes staff, along with the work that needs to be accomplished.

2. It requires review of the entire operation (all divisions and subdivisions) in terms of funds available and revenue needs; it prevents over-budgeting (padding).
3. It promotes standardization and simplification of operation by establishing priorities and objectives, and it eliminates inefficient operations.
4. It provides guidelines for a staff to follow.
5. It provides the governing body with factual data for evaluating the efficiency of the operation.
6. It helps the taxpaying public (contributors) see where revenues are coming from and what expenditures are for.
7. It acts as an instrument for fiscal control.

Object classification budget. The **object classification budget** is one of the most traditional types of budgets and one of the easiest to understand. To conceptualize an object classification budget, one must understand the basic premise of structure that the budget uses: It is established using an object classification that defines the areas of expense in a uniform grouping of categories. The following is a typical classification system:

1000 Services: Personnel
    1100 Salaries, regular
    1200 Salaries, temporary
    1300 Wages, regular
    1400 Wages, temporary
    1500 Other compensations
2000 Services: Contractual
    2100 Communication and transportation
    2200 Subsistence, care, and support
    2300 Printing, binding, and advertising
    2400 Utilities
    2500 Repairs
    2600 Janitorial
3000 Commodities
    3100 Supplies
    3200 Materials
4000 Current charges
    4100 Rents
    4200 Insurance
    4300 Refunds, awards, and indemnities
    4400 Registrations and memberships
5000 Current obligations
    5100 Interest
    5200 Pensions and retirement
    5300 Grants and subsidies
    5400 Taxes
6000 Properties
    6100 Equipment
    6200 Buildings and improvements
    6300 Land
7000 Debt obligations

The advantage this budget's classification is the uniformity of the numbering system and the ease in setting up the budget. The clarity among similar organizations can be very helpful to the sport manager for the purpose of making comparisons.

Line item budget. The **line item budget** is very similar to the object classification budget, and these two budgeting systems are the most often used in the public sector. The term *line* refers to the listing of each item on a line in the budget; the items are not defined by a numbering system, they are simply listed by name. This allows for more flexibility than the object classification budget. See Table 18-6 for more details on setting up a line item budget.

In the early 1900s, line item budgets listed every single cost item—for example, each employee's name was listed under the salary/wage category. The complexity of this method is obvious. Now a budget includes expenditure categories in an effort to simplify the system (Deppe, 1983).

Increment-decrement budget. This type of budget is considered an extension of the object classification and line item budgets. The increment budget consists of adding or deleting a certain percentage to the current budget. The increases or decreases can be attributed to specific line items or object classifications or the overall budget will reflect equal adjustments based on the percentage. The purpose of the **increment-decrement budget** is to provide a predictable growth or decline over a period of time, which allows for planning, especially long-range planning (Kelsey and Gray, 1986).

Program budget. The **program budget,** unlike the three previous budgets, separates an organization by unique units. A program budget could easily be adopted by an athletic department. Each sport would develop a separate budget, with a narrative description of the sport's goals and those features of its program that are deemed to be the most important. This allows the athletic director to compare the various budget requests and make

TABLE 18-6 Line item budget for XYZ Swim Pool and Club

	Current budget	Proposed budget
Personnel		
Manager	$ 4,000	$ 4,500
Guards	6,300	6,700
Instructors	2,800	3,000
Coaches	1,200	1,500
Maintenance	1,000	1,200
	15,300	16,900
Supplies		
Office supplies	350	450
Operating supplies	4,600	5,000
Repair and maintenance supplies	3,500	3,900
Miscellaneous	500	600
	8,950	9,950
Operations		
Utilities	4,200	4,500
Telephone	400	500
Insurance	1,300	1,400
Printing and advertising	600	700
Security	500	650
	7,000	7,750
Capital expenditure		
Equipment	3,500	4,000
	3,500	4,000
	$ 34,750	$ 38,600

decisions based on a fuller understanding of their needs instead of simply looking at lines and numbers. The three components of a program budget are (1) agency goals, (2) program goals, and (3) unique features of the program. This process is then followed by a line item or object classification budget.

Performance budget. The difference between a program budget and a performance budget is minute. The purpose of a **performance budget** is to explain what services are being provided by the institution rather than just how much money is being spent. The budget is broken into categories or service activities. Each category is defined by the amount of time that is involved to perform the activity. Then a cost can be attributed to each activity. The manager has a great deal of financial control and can be precise when using this type of budget (Kelsey and Gray, 1986).

Planning programming budget system (PPBS). The focus of this type of budget is on the end product of the service provided rather than the actual cost. One of the purposes of the PPBS is to provide a rationale for each of the competing budget units within an agency or department. The budget provides a narrative picture of the expenditures rather than simply listing the amount of money spent. When resources are scarce, this budget type can be a useful management tool (Kelsey and Gray, 1986).

Zero-based budget. A **zero-based budget** is based on the premise that an organization begins each year with no money. From that point, a budget is prepared by justifying each expenditure as if it were a new expense. The purpose of this type of budget is to control overbudgeting and waste. The manager has to scrutinize the reasonableness of every budget request in relationship to the whole department.

This method is a radical departure from traditional methods that look at past costs, add an increment for projected expenses, and continue to operate in the same manner year after year (Deppe, 1983).

Capital budget. A **capital budget** describes capital expenses that include long-range budget items. A capital budget usually covers a number of years—as many as 10 years. It includes major purchases, such as new buildings and equipment, that are not found in operating budgets that only cover 1 year. Capital budgets, like program budgets, require a narrative explanation or justification for each expense.

Enterprise funds

A newer method of financial management that is being implemented in many public/nonprofit organizations is called the **enterprise fund system.** The premise that this system works on is that every individual program of operation is viewed as a separate enterprise. The revenue generated by the enterprise is then used to finance the enterprise's operation. Originally, the enterprise fund system expected the operation to break even, which meant that the enterprise needed to generate at least as much income as was budgeted for expenses. But it is more common today to expect a profit. In a municipal setting, this could mean that the profit generated by a financially successful enterprise, such as the community golf course, could be used to fund another program, such as the "latch-key program" for underprivileged youth, which is known to lose money.

Fund accounting

Fund accounting is a standard method of accounting used by many government operations (Rossman, 1984). A fund is defined as a fiscal and accounting entity with a self-balancing set of accounts recording cash and financial resources, with liabilities and equity. The format of the financial document is very similar to the balance sheet. The accounts are separate operations (programs or activities) within the organization, and they include funds that aren't necessarily reflected in day-to-day operations, such as capital funds, benefits funds, or retirement funds. The segregation of the fund accounts usually has been specified by external sources, such as the board of directors (Rossman, 1984).

Annual reviews of the accounts will be used to evaluate the activities that took place within the segregated fund. Decisions will be made on the fund account's future, based on the growth or decline in the financial picture of the account.

SUMMARY OF ACCOUNTING FOR PUBLIC/NONPROFIT ORGANIZATIONS

Separate budgets can be written for expenditures and revenues or the projected revenue should be included in the expense budget. Most departments or programs have some method for generating income. Projected revenues should be estimated in the same way expected expenses are. Whether it be in ticket sales, user fees, or memberships, the amount of income required to operate the programs should be projected. This can be very useful in getting approval of the budget from the financial director, because it shows potential. The type of budget chosen will be decided upon by the institution or the department, so the sport manager should become familiar with a variety of methods.

The sport manager will have two important functions when it comes to dealing with the financial affairs of the department. The first is to oversee disbursements made by each unit, making sure that budgets are not overspent. The second is to develop a budget that will make it possible for the institution to realize the highest possible return on its investment (Lewis and Appenzeller, 1985).

Enterprise funds and fund accounting are two terms the sport manager should be familiar with because of their implications for public/nonprofit financial accounting.

CONCEPT CHECK

The two most important tasks a sport manager will have to master when it comes to budgets is to (1) prepare and justify the annual budget and (2) control the expenses and disbursements once the budget has been approved.

PROBLEMS AND SOLUTIONS

The following problems and solutions will help illustrate the financial statements and accounts that a sport and fitness enterprise might use. The first problem and solution concern the balance sheet and profit and loss statement (income and expense statement) for a professional team. This problem demonstrates that, although the accounts a professional sport team uses may vary from those used in other sport and fitness settings, the accounting procedures remain the same. Refer to both this chapter and Chapter 4 in solving the problems.

PROBLEM 1: BALANCE SHEET AND INCOME AND EXPENSE STATEMENT

The ABC professional football team's fiscal year ended March 31, 1995. The accountant's trial balance showed the following accounts and amounts as of that date. Prepare a balance sheet and statement of income and expense for ABC, placing these accounts in the correct categories. When the statements are completed correctly, the asset category and the liability category on the balance sheet each will total $1,365,000. The net profit on the income and expense statement will be $570,000.

Notes payable	$ 35,000	Mortgage payable	$ 75,000
Equipment repairs	35,000	Fixed assets—building	1,220,000
Security	56,000	Salaries and wages	2,160,000
Prepaid advertising	10,000	Cash in banks	100,000
Entertainment	120,000	Accrued salaries	22,000
Game income	3,200,000	Administrative travel	82,000
Advertising	68,000	Depreciation expense	32,000
Accrued taxes	16,000	Shareholders' equity	1,198,000
Supplies	52,000	Prepaid insurance	36,000
Taxes	140,000	Team travel	1,361,000
Reserve for equipment depreciation	20,000	Television income	1,400,000
Accounts receivable	32,000	Reserve for building depreciation	116,000
Medical insurance	160,000	Accounts payable	19,000
Radio income	260,000	Program income	36,000
Cash on hand	5,000	Fixed assets—equipment	80,000
Parking income	120,000	Liability insurance	180,000
Inventories	18,000		

SOLUTION TO PROBLEM 1: BALANCE SHEET AND INOME AND EXPENSE STATEMENT

To produce the balance sheet and income and expense statement for ABC, the preceding accounts must be placed on the proper statement as an asset, liability, income item, or expense item. The following shows the accounts in the proper statements:

Balance Sheet

Assets (Debits)		Liabilities (Credits)	
Prepaid advertising	$ 10,000	Notes payable	$ 35,000
Accounts receivable	32,000	Accrued taxes	16,000
Cash on hand	5,000	Reserve for equipment depreciation	20,000
Inventories	18,000	Mortgage payable	75,000
Building	1,220,000	Accrued salaries	22,000
Cash in banks	100,000	Shareholders' equity	1,198,000
Prepaid insurance	36,000	Reserve for building depreciation	116,000
Equipment	80,000	Accounts payable	19,000
	$1,501,000		$1,501,000

Income (Credits)		Expense (Debits)	
Games	$3,200,000	Equipment repairs	$ 35,000
Radio	260,000	Security	56,000
Parking	120,000	Entertainment	120,000
Television	1,400,000	Advertising	68,000
Programs	36,000	Supplies	52,000
	$5,016,000	Taxes	140,000
		Medical insurance	160,000
		Salaries and wages	2,160,000
Less: Expenses	4,446,000	Administrative travel	82,000
Net profit	$ 570,000	Depreciation	32,000
		Team travel	1,361,000
		Liability insurance	180,000
			$4,446,000

At this point, the assets and liabilities do not equal the $1,365,000 as shown in the problem presentation. This is because the building and equipment depreciation reserves should be reclassified to the asset side of the balance sheet as a reduction of the building and equipment fixed assets, thus showing the net book values of these assets. The following reconciles the assets and liabilities to the $1,365,000 figure, which also will be on the completed balance sheet.

Income Statement

	Assets	Liabilities
Total before depreciation reclassification	$1,501,000	$1,501,000
Less: Building depreciation	(116,000)	(116,000)
Less: Equipment depreciation	(20,000)	(20,000)
	$1,365,000	$1,365,000

In reviewing the completed balance sheet, note that the asset and liability accounts are listed and placed on the statement according to the customs of a standard balance sheet. That is, the cash items are listed first in the assets, and fixed assets are listed last. Likewise, accounts payable is the first item in the liabilities, and shareholders' equity is listed last.

On the income and expense statement, the expense accounts typically are listed in alphabetical order, as can be seen on the completed statement.

ABC professional football team
Balance sheet March 31, 1995

Assets			Liabilities	
Cash on hand		$ 5,000	Accounts payable	$ 19,000
Cash in banks		100,000	Notes payable	35,000
Accounts receivable		32,000	Mortgage payable	75,000
Inventories		18,000	Accrued salaries	22,000
Prepaid insurance		36,000	Accrued taxes	16,000
Prepaid advertising		10,000	Shareholder equity	1,198,000
Fixed assets—equipment	$ 80,000			
Less: Reserve for equipment depreciation	20,000	60,000		
Fixed assets—building	1,220,000			
Less: Reserve for building depreciation	116,000	1,104,000		
Total Assets		$1,365,000	*Total Liabilities*	$ 1,365,000

ABC professional football team
Statement of income and expense
For the fiscal year ended March 31, 1995

Income

Games		$3,200,000
Television		1,400,000
Radio		260,000
Parking		120,000
Programs		36,000
Total Income		$5,016,000

Expenses

Administrative travel	$ 82,000	
Advertising	68,000	
Entertainment	120,000	
Equipment repairs	35,000	
Depreciation	32,000	
Liability insurance	180,000	
Medical insurance	160,000	
Salaries and wages	2,160,000	
Security	56,000	
Supplies	52,000	
Taxes	140,000	
Team travel	1,361,000	
Total Expenses		4,446,000
Net Profit		$ 570,000

PROBLEM 2: BUDGET FORECASTING

The following represents the financial operations for August for the fitness center in the Hotel Deluxe. August is a very strong month for revenues. However, in September, revenue from some sources declines. Last year's records show that in September local membership revenue dropped 30% from August, guest passes dropped 35%, and revenue from massage and miscellaneous income remained relatively constant. As the accountant, you know that some expense items will not change in September. However, the advertising, printing, and group insurance expenses will all increase by 10%, and guest supplies and employee bonuses will be reduced to $200 each. Based on this information, what is the projected net profit (loss) for the month of September?

Hotel Deluxe
Fitness center
August 1995

	Description	August amount	Percentage
Sales			
	Local memberships	$8,000	74.8
	Guest income	1,500	14.0
	Massage income	1,000	9.3
	Miscellaneous income	200	1.9
	Total sales	$10,700	100.0%
Expenses			
	Payroll		
	Salaries/wages	$5,000	62.2
	Payroll taxes	600	7.4
	Worker's compensation	650	8.1
	Employee bonuses	250	3.1
	Group insurance	500	6.2
	Total payroll	$7,000	87.0%
	Other Expenses		
	Linen(staff uniforms, towels)	$200	2.4
	Guest supplies	250	3.1
	Advertising	150	1.9
	Printing	200	2.4
	Office supplies	70	0.9
	Telephone	50	0.6
	Equipment (maintenance/repair)	90	1.1
	Miscellaneous expenses	50	0.6
	Total other expenses	$1,060	13.0%
	Total expense	$8,060	100.0%
	Department profit (loss)	$2,640	

SOLUTION TO PROBLEM 2: BUDGET FORECASTING

The September forecast is determined according to the figures from August of the current year and the trends from September of the previous year. Projected sales are obtained by calculating the percentage of change in September of last year compared to August and applying this percentage to August figures for this year. For example, local memberships for September would be 30% less than those in August ($8000 − $2400 = $5600).

Forecasting expenses for the month of September requires adjustments in the figures for five categories. The August costs for advertising, printing, and group insurance each must be increased by 10% (that is, advertising expenses will increase to $165 from $150 for the month of September). The employee bonuses and guest supplies line items each should be recorded as $200.

In this particular example, the manager of the fitness center in the Hotel Deluxe would anticipate a net loss of about $270.

Hotel Deluxe
Fitness center
Forecast: September 1995

Description	August amount	Percentage	Percentage of increase (decrease) over 1993	September amount	Percentage
Sales					
Local memberships	$8,000	74.8	(30)%	$5,600	72.0%
Guest income	1,500	14.0	(35)	975	12.5
Massage income	1,000	9.3	—	1,000	12.9
Miscellaneous income	200	1.9	—	200	2.6
Total sales	$10,700	100.0%		$7,775	100.0%
Expenses					
Payroll					
Salaries/wages	$5,000	62.2	—	$5,000	62.2%
Payroll taxes	600	7.4	—	600	7.5
Worker's compensation	650	8.1	—	650	8.1
Employee bonuses	250	3.1	(20)%	200	2.5
Group insurance	500	6.2	10	550	6.8
Total payroll	$7,000	87.0%		$7,000	87.1%
Other Expenses					
Linen (staff uniforms, towels)	$200	2.4		$200	2.5%
Guest supplies	250	3.1	(20)%	$200	2.5
Advertising	150	1.9	10	165	2.0
Printing	200	2.4	10	220	2.7
Office supplies	70	0.9	—	70	0.9
Telephone	50	0.6	—	70	0.6
Equipment (maintenance/repair)	50	0.6	—	50	0.6
Miscellaneous expenses	90	1.1	—	90	1.1
Total other expenses	$1,060	13.0%		$1,045	12.9%
Total expense	$8,060	100.0%		$8,045	100.0%
Department profit (loss)	$2,640			($270)	

CASE STUDY I: PREPARING THE INCOME AND EXPENSE STATEMENT

The statement of income and expense (profit and loss statement) covering the past fiscal year for the athletic department must be submitted to the university accounting office in 1 month. As the director of athletics, you are responsible for several programs. One is varsity sports, which include football, women's basketball, men's basketball, women's volleyball, and men's baseball as revenue-producing sports. Non-revenue-producing sports in your program are track, wrestling, swimming, tennis, and field hockey. In addition, there are several club sports under your direction. These are soccer, rugby, lacrosse, water polo, and crew. Finally, your department oversees a fitness program offered to faculty, their partners, retirees, and students.

1. *What are some typical accounts you would use for each program?*
2. *What special income and expense accounts are you likely to encounter for each program?*
3. *Into what major categories would the income and expense statement be divided?*
4. *What types of indirect overhead would you have for each program?*
5. *How would indirect overhead expenses affect your figures?*

CASE STUDY II: PREPARING THE BUDGET

As manager of a corporate fitness program, it is your responsibility to submit a budget for the next fiscal year to the director of human resources and development. The fitness program, which employs two fitness specialists and you, has operated for 3 years and has consistently lost money. The director of human resources and development has agreed to subsidize the program with an additional $2000, with the understanding that a portion of the funds will be allocated to a marketing and advertising campaign.

1. *What steps would you take in planning and preparing your budget?*
2. *From whom would you solicit information?*
3. *What options do you have when allocating funds?*
4. *What changes in the budget would you propose?*
5. *Would the process of forecasting be helpful to you? If so, how?*
6. *How might asking "what if" questions be useful?*

REVIEW QUESTIONS AND ISSUES

1. What is accounting, and what is the difference between cash accounting and accrual accounting?
2. What are the three financial statements most often used in business, and what is the major purpose of each?
3. What are assets, liabilities, and equity in reference to a business? How is each used on a balance sheet? What is depreciation?
4. What is the difference between gross sales, net sales, gross profit, and net profit?
5. How does one calculate the cost of goods sold?
6. What are some examples of operating expenses?
7. What are sales and disbursement journals, and how are they used?
8. How does accounting differ in a private business operation versus a public/nonprofit organization? Give examples of each type of business operation.
9. What are the most commonly used types of budget? Describe how each type is set up.
10. What are enterprise funds, and how are they being used in public operations?
11. What is fund accounting, and who would be most likely to use it?

REFERENCES

Bendit, O.G. and Koehler, L.S. (1991). Accounting and budgeting. In Parkhouse, B.L. *The management of sport: its foundation and application,* St Louis, Mosby Year Book.

Crossley, J.C. and Jamieson, L.M. (1993). *Introduction to commercial and entrepreneurial recreation,* Champaign, Illinois, Sagamore.

Deppe, T.R. (1993). *Management strategies in financing parks and recreation,* New York, John Wiley and Sons.

Ellis, T. and Norton, R.L. (1988). *Commercial recreation,* St. Louis, Times Mirror/Mosby.

Howard, D.R. and Crompton, J.L. (1980) *Financing, managing, and marketing recreation and park resources,* Dubuque, Iowa, Wm C Brown.

Kelsey, C. and Gray, H. (1986). *The budget process in parks and recreation,* Reston, Virginia, AAHPERD.

Lewis, G. and Appenzeller, H. (1985). *Successful sport management,* Charlottesville, Virginia, Michie Co.

Pickle, H.B. and Abrahamson, R.L. (1986). *Small business management,* New York, John Wiley and Sons.

Rossman, J.R. (1984). *Fund accounting: a management accounting strategy.* In Bannon, J.J., eds, Administrative practice of park, recreation and leisure services, Champaign, Illinois, Management Learning Laboratories.

Siropolis, N. (1984). *Small business management: a guide to entrepreneurship,* Boston, Houghton Mifflin Co.

SUGGESTED READINGS

Crimmins, J.C. and Keil, M. (1983). Enterprise in the non-profit sector, Washinton, DC, Partners for Livable Places.

Current issues in leisure services: looking ahead in a time of transition, Washington, DC, 1987, International City Management Association.

Keiser, J.R. (1989). *Principles and practices of management in the hospitality industry,* New York, Van Nostrand Reinhold.

Kirsch, S. and Cryder, R. (1990). *Revenue policy manual: 10 steps in developing a public policy,* Wheeling, West Virginia, Revenue Sources Management School.

Lee, R.D., Jr. and Johnson, R.W. (1989). *Public budgeting systems,* Rockville, Maryland, Aspen Publishers.

Mason, J.G. and Paul, J. (1988). *Modern sports administration,* Englewood Cliffs, New Jersey, Prentice-Hall.

Parks, J.B. and Zanger, B.R.K. (1990). *Sport and fitness management: career strategies and professional content,* Champaign, Illinois, Human Kinetics.

Patton, R.W. and others. (1989). *Developing and managing health/fitness facilities,* Champaign, Illinois, Human Kinetics.

Tracy, J.A. (1983). *How to read a financial report,* New York, John Wiley and Sons.

CHAPTER 19

Financing Sport

Tom H. Regan

In this chapter, you will become familiar with the following terms:

Financing sport	Revenue bonds	Financing activities
Cash flow	Certificates of participation	Operating activities
Exemption	Tax increment financing (TIF)	Cash inflows
Municipal securities (munis)	Revenue streams	Cash outflows
General-obligation bonds (GO)	Investing activities	

Overview

Professional, college, and interscholastic organizations require financing options and opportunities to compete in the business of sport. Leagues, teams, and communities are challenged to maintain and support adequate facilities and teams for sport organizations.

Financing sport-related facilities often requires public, private, and joint public/private financing. The financial arrangements surrounding sport may be the most creative area of business outside the playing field. Financing sport business is a simple enough concept: You must have adequate funds to enable the landlord, tenant, and team owner to start, expand, and continue operations.

The purpose of this chapter on **financing sport** is to explain a few of the various types of financing needed for different sport organizations and establish the need for cash flow management. The fact that funds are needed is the simple part. Where they come from is another matter. We will identify the sources of different financing options. **Cash flow** is essential to a successful sports enterprise. Sport is seasonal in nature, and teams play specific schedules during assigned times. The management of cash flow requires knowledge of finance, accounting, and basic business principles such as the *time value of money* and *discounted cash flow*. The list is by no means exhaustive, but it is a strong foundation for the sport business manager.

THE PUBLIC NEED

It is important for government leaders to attract professional teams to their region or city. In the

United States, cities compete to attract and retain professional sports franchises. Federal, state, and local governments subsidize the financing of sports facilities. Financing arrangements are a key element to attract teams and investors. A key element of the funding plans is the **exemption** from federal and most state and local income taxes on the interest earned on qualified **municipal securities (munis)** that could be issued to finance these stadiums. The borrower can then sell bonds at a lower interest rate than if the interest were taxed.

Government authorities are usually proponents of stadiums. They claim that without the necessary local support, teams might choose to relocate and the cities would lose employment, tax revenues, and other indirect benefits. Government opponents claim that benefits are probably overstated and likely future costs are understated, making probable the need for even more public support in the future.

Sport facility financing

"If you build it, they will come," is the familiar passage from the hit movie *Field of Dreams*. Professional, college, interscholastic, and touring sports require adequate facilities to practice and play the game, in addition to attracting fans. The United States has great athletic facilities throughout the country. Often stadiums become a source of regional community pride—for example, Oriole Park at Camden Yards in Baltimore, Maryland, and The Ballpark, in Arlington, Texas.

The majority of professional and university sport facilities have traditionally been financed by municipal debt, with annual debt service funded from the municipality's general fund or from one of several other revenue sources. In recent years, the recession, an increase in construction costs, and municipality budget constraints have resulted in the financial participation of various private-sector organizations. Private-sector participation in financing facilities is primarily due to the increase in available revenues generated by the facility. These public, private, and joint public/private financing arrangements are necessary for sport facility construction today.

Public-facility financing

Sport arenas, stadiums, and multipurpose facilities are large capital projects for municipalities. Several

mechanisms are used in structuring public-sector participation in sports facility development, expansion, and renovation. Among the most common public-financing instruments are bond issues backed by general obligations and/or dedicated revenues, lease appropriations bonds (certificates of participation), and tax increment bond financing. For a breakdown of public-financing instruments, see the following box.

Public-facility financing options

- General-obligation bonds
- Revenue bonds
- Certificates of participation
- Tax increment bonds

State and local governments issue bonds in the capital market to finance their capital spending programs: construction of arenas, stadiums, parking lots, and infrastructure upgrades. Infrastructure improvements include roads and water, sewers, and other utilities. Investors call these bond issues *municipals* because they are issued by municipalities; they are also called *tax-exempts* because the interest investors receive is exempt from federal taxation. Most states also exempt income tax on the interest earned from their bonds, although there are differences among the states. For example, South Carolina citizens do not pay state income tax on bonds issued by a state municipality, while bond interest earned from out-of-state bonds is subject to state income tax.

General-obligation bonds. **General-obligation (GO) bonds,** backed by the full faith and credit of the issuing body (state, local, or regional government), usually require the use of *ad valorem* (property) taxes—taxes levied according to the value of one's property. The more valuable the property, the higher the tax. General-obligation bonds typically result in a lower cost of issuance and a higher credit rating, and the bond size is often reduced because a debt reserve fund is not always required. In some cases, the bonding capacity of the municipal unit for other capital needs can be reduced.

Revenue bonds are special obligations in public financing that are payable solely from a particular source of funds, which may include tax/surcharge revenues from hotels and motels, restaurants, sales, liquor and beer, cigarettes, rental cars, and other sources. For a list of public-facility funding sources, see the following box.

Public-facility funding sources

- Hotel tax
- Meal tax
- Liquor tax
- Sales tax
  - Auto rental tax
  - Property tax
  - TIFF Districts
  - Business license tax
- Utility tax
- Road tax
- Public and private grants
- State appropriations
- Taxi tax
- Team tax

No pledge of state, regional, or local ad valorem tax revenues is required; however, the typical revenue bond does carry a higher interest rate and require a higher debt service coverage ratio and debt service reserve.

Certificates of participation (COPs). This public-financing mechanism involves a governmental entity creating a corporation to buy or build a public facility, such as an arena or convention and visitors' center. The corporation then issues certificates of participation (COPs) to raise money to buy/build the public facility. The government leases back the building, and the lease payments pay back the bonds. All this happens without a public vote.

Although COPs seem to be traditional bonds, they are *not* backed by the full faith and credit of the government entity that issues the bonds. In a recession-hammered environment, when real estate values and property tax collections decline, COPs and lease appropriation financing become popular with local governments looking to fund projects. But because these securities are not backed by the full faith and credit of a municipality, they are a greater risk than a general-obligation bond and are rated a full step lower.

Tax increment financing (TIF)

Tax increment financing transactions are based on the incremental property tax value of the ancillary economic development projects that are triggered by a major new facility. The tax base of a defined area identified as the tax increment financial (TIF) district surrounding the capital project is frozen, and any increases in the tax base are used to repay tax increment financing bonds. The area surrounding the facility may be one or more counties/parishes.

The economics of any tax increment financing district are highly dependent on the development potential of a chosen site and its surrounding land. It is essential to anticipate future revenues on increases in ad valorem taxes or funding sources, which are listed in the box at left.

Other public-sector contributions

The general public indirectly subsidizes sport organizations in other ways. There are a number of ways facilities have obtained additional public funding or the government has directly reduced interest costs or borrowing requirements. A few of these mechanisms include the purchase or donation of land; funding of site improvements, parking garages, or surrounding infrastructure; and direct equity investments or construction of related facilities, either directly or through an independent authority, and lending the government's credit by guaranteeing payment on new debt. Public-sector financing is extensive in professional sport franchises. Cities, states, and regional communities have financed the construction of major arenas, stadiums, and convention centers for the benefit of the economic community. A recent trend is a joint financial arrangement, described in the next section.

CONCEPT CHECK

Facility construction often requires public-financing instruments. General-obligation bonds, revenue bonds, certificates of participation, and tax increment bonds are the primary financial mechanisms used by municipalities to develop, expand, and renovate facilities. Each public-financing instrument has advantages and disadvantages, depending on the financial situation of the community and the issuer.

Private and joint public/private financing

The recent trend seems to be toward joint public/private partnerships. Public/private partnerships have been used for the financing of major public-assembly projects, particularly sports facilities. Typically, the public sector uses its authority to implement project funding mechanisms, with the private sector contributing project-related or other venue sources. The expanded revenues generated by the facilities and their tenants have resulted in increases in the level of private participation in facility financing. Several of the private-sector revenue streams that have been used in structuring facility financing include the items in the following box.

Private-sector revenue streams

- Premium seating
- Building rent
- Corporate sponsorship
- Lease payments
- Vendor/contractor equity
- Parking fees
- Merchandise revenue
- Advertising rights
- Concessions revenue
- Naming rights
- Food and beverage serving rights

Recent examples of joint public/private participation are illustrated in Table 19-1. It is clear that there has been extensive state and local government interest in the development of sports and other public-assembly facilities in recent years, and there are a variety of means with which to structure the financing for those facilities. Expanding building-operations and tenant revenue streams has encouraged a public/private partnership whereby public-sector financing vehicles (various bonding techniques) are supplemented with private-sector revenue streams. Creative financial arrangements allow communities to benefit economically and create a lifestyle conducive to public opinion. Table 19-1 provides examples of how communities created a financial vehicle to build sport and entertainment facilities.

Examples of financing new stadiums include the following: the Alamodome in San Antonio, Texas, is a 77,000 seat domed arena. The Alamodome was completely funded by an additional 0.5% sales tax on all retail sales. The $170 million project was completed in 1993 and is now debt free. Therefore the facility now only has to cover operational expenses, not bond premium and interest expenses.

Another example is Coors Stadium, which was built for the Colorado Rockies, the newest member of baseball's National League. The Rockies attracted more than 4,600,000 fans during the 1993 season. Coors Stadium was completed for the 1995 season opener in Denver, at a cost of $179,803,016. Financing the stadium required a vote by the public to collect 0.1% sales tax upon all taxable retail sales within the jurisdiction of a special tax district that includes the Colorado counties of Adams, Arapahoe, Denver, Jefferson, Boulder, and Douglas. Colorado state legislators allowed the special tax district to be created in H.B. 90-1172, thereby creating a financial mechanism to provide a sales tax revenue stream to finance the $158 million in revenue bonds necessary to build Coors Stadium.

A key element in financing sport-related facilities is the relationship between government and entrepreneurial sport owners. A public/private partnership exists between the parties to create an entertainment and economic opportunity to improve the regional economy. Without this relationship, few professional or collegiate programs could financially exist. Financing facilities and the revenue streams shared between the tenant and the municipality are essential for attracting and retaining sport franchises, special events, and fans.

The proper financial team needs to be assembled in order to design, organize, and finance a public, private, or public/private facility. Components of a successful team should include the following members:

- Issuer/owner
- Facility management
- Feasibility consultant
- Examination accountant
- Business plan consultant
- Financial advisor
- Architect
- Cost estimator
- Design builder
- Construction manager
- Senior underwriter
- Co-underwriter
- Bond council
- Issuer's council

The financing team must work together to achieve the goals and objectives of the community or owner. Each facility scenario is different and requires careful analysis. Successful facility financing is a partnership between the regional community, the owner/tenant, government, and the financial institutions (Figure 19-1).

CASH FLOW IN SPORT

All good business requires the proper utilization of cash. Sport is a seasonal business that requires careful cash management. In professional sport, it costs hundreds of millions of dollars to purchase an existing team and tens of millions to acquire an

TABLE 19-1   *Financing participation for public/private facilities*

Arena	Public participation	Private participation
Alamodome	City revenue bond backed by 0-5% sales tax	Arena revenues
America West Arena	City revenue bonds backed by excise taxes	Naming rights Arena revenues
Bradley Center Arena	Land donation purchased with general bond issue	Local family donation
Charlotte Stadium (proposed)	Land donation	Naming rights Arena revenue Premium seating deposits Luxury suite revenue
Coors Stadium	Special tax district revenue bond secured by sales tax increase of 0.1%	Naming rights Arena revenues
Delta Center Arena	City tax increment financing bonds	Private loan secured by building revenue Naming rights
Cleveland Cavaliers Arena	County general-obligation bonds Luxury tax allocation	Private donations and foundation contributions Premium seat deposits and revenue
Target Center Arena	Tax increment financing bonds	Loan secured by arena and health club revenues Naming rights
Ballpark in Arlington	City revenue bond secured by sales tax increase Infrastructure improvements	Luxury suite revenues Ticket surcharge Seat options Concessionaire payment

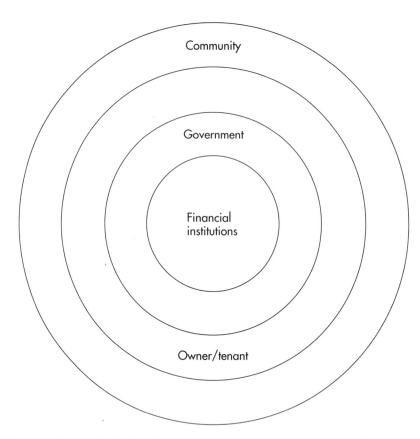

FIGURE 19-1   Successful facility financing is dependent on relationships between the community, owner/tenant, government, and sponsoring financial institutions.

expansion franchise. For example, the Baltimore Orioles were recently purchased for an estimated $173 million, and the Philadelphia Eagles are expected to receive approximately $185 million. Major League Baseball expansion teams in 1993 were required to pay $95 million for the privilege of joining the league; National Football League owners required a franchise fee of $140 million; and the National Hockey League expansion franchise fee was $50 million.

Major collegiate athletic departments often have budgets in excess of $20 million. The athletic director must be a fund-raiser, budget director, and professional manager. The college athletic department requires proper use of cash flow to help finance and schedule stadium maintenance, sport expansion, and any postseason play.

CONCEPT CHECK

A trend toward public/private partnerships for the financing of major sport facilities is becoming more common. The private sector realizes the potential benefits of programming the facility for additional revenue streams. Public/private partnerships are decreasing municipalities' involvement in operating stadiums.

Revenue streams

Sports create revenue streams and produce cash very quickly. The major revenue producers are ticket sales, concessions, advertising, broadcasting (local radio and television and national media), parking, preferred seating, licensing agreements, and miscellaneous revenue. Professional sport organizations negotiate a contract with the municipalities. For example, the Colorado Rockies' lease includes the following terms with the Special Tax District and the city and county of Denver. Table 19-2 identifies the sharing of revenue in a publicly financed stadium.

The Colorado Rockies' stadium agreement is beneficial to the team, as Table 19-2 indicates. The public officials must consider the overall business relationship between the owners, other Major League Baseball owners, and the subsidizing public. Each must feel the new franchise in Colorado has a reasonable opportunity to be economically successful.

Leagues, teams, cities, and businesses need cash flow to successfully operate. Cash flow is defined as reported net income plus amounts charged off for depreciation, depletion, amortization, and extraordinary charges to reserves that are bookkeeping deductions and not paid out in actual dollars. The primary purpose of a cash flow statement is to provide relevant information about cash receipts and disbursements of an enterprise during a particular period. This will aid investors (partners), creditors, and others to:

1. Assess the team's ability to generate a positive future net cash flow
2. Assess the sport enterprise's ability to meet its obligations
3. Assess the difference between net income and cash receipts and disbursements
4. Assess the effects of both cash and noncash investing and financing during a period

The term *cash* in FASB 95 refers to cash in the bank and all short-term liquid investments that can be readily converted to cash. Examples of items considered to be cash equivalents are marketable securities with less than 3 months maturity, treasury bills, commercial paper, and money market funds.

Cash receipts and disbursements are classified as operating, investing, or financing activities. In sport organizations, it is often difficult to compare teams, and the statement of cash flows provides an opportunity to compare similar enterprises. **Investing activities** include the purchase or sale of secu-

TABLE 19-2   *Colorado Rockies Stadium agreement summary*

Date of agreement	March 14, 1991
Term	17 years, with option to renew for 5-year term
Sharing of revenue	
Admissions	Starting in the year 2000, team pays 2 ½% of net taxable income, provided partners of team have received distributions equal to 5% of contributions
Concessions	Team keeps all revenue
Parking	Team keeps all revenue
Advertising	Team keeps all revenue
Other events	Team keeps all revenue
Television revenue	Team keeps all revenue
Stadium Club	Team keeps all revenue
Set fees	—
Reimbursements	Starting in 1995, team pays city up to $150,000 a year for operating costs if city's costs exceed revenues
Miscellaneous	—
Sharing of gosts	
Field maintenance	Team
Stadium maintenance	Team
Game day	
Ushers, etc.	Team
Security	Team
Cleaning	Team
Utilities	Team
Field equipment	Team
Concession equipment	Team

Data from Hurt, Richardson, Garner, Todd and Cadenhead: Stadium lease arrangements. In International City Managers Association, Sports and Special Events Conference, San Antonio, Texas, 1993.

rities or other entities, sale or purchase of fixed assets, and loans made or payments on loans received. **Financing activities** include issuing securities, borrowing, paying of dividends, buying treasury stock (the company's own stock), and repaying debt.

The cash flows from the investing and financing activities are usually balance sheet items. The final section of the statement of cash flows is the **operating-activities** section. This section covers everything that is not investing or financing activities. Daily sport business activity generates operating funds as do most business organizations on interest or dividends earned. Accounts receivable and accounts payable are generally operating activities. Cash flow derived from operating activities typically applies to the cash effects of transactions entering into profit computations. **Cash inflows** from operating activities include:

1. Cash sales or collections on ticket receivables
2. Cash sales or collections on licensed merchandise
3. Cash receipts from returns on loans (interest income) or dividend income
4. Cash received from licensees and lessees
5. Receipt of a litigation settlement (e.g., between city, team, owner, and players)
6. Reimbursement under an insurance policy (e.g., strike insurance)

Cash outflows for operating activities include:

1. Cash paid for raw materials and merchandise for resale
2. Principal payments on accounts payable arising from the purchase of goods
3. Payments to suppliers of operating-expense items (insurance, advertising, supplies)
4. Player and personnel salaries/wages
5. Payment of taxes
6. Payment of interest expense (bonds or loans)
7. Lawsuit payment (collusion settlement)
8. Charitable contributions
9. Cash refunds to customers for merchandise, ticket sales, or services

Current profitability is only one important factor for success in sport. It is essential that current and future cash flows are positive. Inadequate cash flow has possible serious implications because it may lead to declining profitability, greater financial risk, and even bankruptcy. Teams are often sold when their franchise market value increases and cash flow decreases. To demonstrate how important cash flow is to a sport manager, review the financial statements in Table 19-3.

CONCEPT CHECK

Major professional and collegiate sport organizations produce cash very quickly. The revenue streams include ticket sales, concessions, advertising, sponsorship, broadcasting, parking, preferred seating, licensing agreements, and miscellaneous revenues. Cash flow provides relevant information about cash receipts and disbursements of a sport enterprise. The statement of cash flows includes an operating, financing, and investing section. Cash flow is an essential management tool for analysis of financial information.

The balance sheet indicates all the information needed to calculate the statement of cash flows for Sport Enterprises, Inc. for the year 19X5. Additional information is helpful to clearly understand the cash flow statement. Earnings after taxes (net income) were $202,000; depreciation expense was $15,000; and common stock was issued.

Table 19-3 enables us to prepare the statement of cash flows in Table 19-4. It is important to note that preparing a statement of cash flows involves calculating the dollar change in each of the balance sheet items *other than cash.*

It is important to note that Sport Enterprises, Inc. had $202,000 in earnings after taxes, but that there was a $50,000 decrease in cash flow for the year ended 19X5.

The sport manager needs to understand why cash decreased by $50,000. This is accomplished by careful examination of the statement of cash flows in Table 19-4. Cash was primarily decreased by the retirement of $192,000 in bonds. The answer to a cash flow problem is always the change is cash. The difference between 19X4 cash of $280,000 and 19X5 cash of $230,000 equals a $50,000 decrease in cash for the period ending 19X5.

Managing cash flow is essential for the sport administration professional. Cash flow will assist in determining future expansion of facilities, players' salaries and bonuses, and investment opportunities, to mention only a few essential components. The sport business game is managing cash flow. **You must win this game!**

TABLE 19-3   *Sports Enterprises, Inc. Balance Sheet Years ending 19X4 and 19X5 (thousands of dollars)*

Assets	19X4	19X5	Cash increase (decrease)
Current assets			
Cash	$ 280	$ 230	ignore
Accounts receivable	340	380	($40)
Inventory	210	260	(50)
Total current assets	$ 830	$ 870	
Property, plant, and equipment	500	525	(25)
Less accumulated depreciation	(110)	(125)	15
Net fixed assets	$ 390	$ 400	
Total assets	$1,220	$1,270	
Liabilities and stockholders equity			
Current liabilities			
Accounts payable	$ 220	$ 220	0
Taxes payable	80	110	$30
Total current liabilities	$ 300	$ 330	
Long-term liabilities—bonds	432	240	(192)
Total liabilities	$ 732	$ 570	
Stockholders equity			
Common stock	280	290	10
Paid-in-capital	40	50	10
Retained earnings	168	360	192
Total shareholders equity	$ 488	$ 700	
Total liabilities and equity	$1,220	$1,270	

SUMMARY

1. Financing sport-related facilities requires public, private, and joint public/private financing. New construction, expansion, and maintenance of stadiums, arenas, and practice facilities are assets needed to attract and retain professional teams.
2. Professional, collegiate, and interscholastic sport facilities are usually built using public financing instruments, such as general-obligation bonds, revenue bonds, certificates of participation, and tax increment financing bonds.
3. Investors call bond issues municipals (munis) because they are issued by municipalities,

subdivisions of states; they are tax-exempt investment instruments and appeal to high-income investors.

4. Private-sector sport organizations are creating public/private partnerships to finance a few major sport facilities. The financing arrangement must be negotiated between the governmental unit and the team owners. Financing a public/private sport facility provides an opportunity for creative financial agreements between communities and sport owners.
5. The proper financial team should be assembled in order to design, organize, and finance a public, private, or public/private

TABLE 19-4 *Sports Enterprises, Inc. statement of cash flows for period ended 19X5*

Operating activities

Earnings after taxes	$ 202,000
Add depreciation expense	15,000
Increase in accounts receivable	(40,000)
Increase in inventories	(50,000)
Increase in taxes payable	30,000
Net cash flow from operating activities	**$ 157,000**

Investing activities

Increase in plant and equipment	($ 25,000)
Other	0
Net cash used by investing activities	**($ 25,000)**

Financing activities

Payment of dividends	($ 10,000)
Issue of common stock	20,000
Retirement of bonds	(192,000)
Net cash used by financing activities	**($ 182,000)**
Net increase (decrease) in cash	**($ 50,000)**

facility. A successful financial team should include owner, facility manager, feasibility consultant, accountant, financial advisor, underwriters, bond council, and issuer's council.

6. Sport is seasonal and requires proper cash flow analysis. Season tickets may be sold 6–8 months before the season opens, and the business manager or controller needs to use proper cash flow techniques.
7. Cash flow involves knowledge of the balance sheet and income statement. FASB 95 requires a statement of cash flow to be a required financial statement for organizations. Cash flow involves inflows and outflows of cash related to operating activities.
8. Sport business managers must be aware of financial arrangements available for facility construction and how to analyze and manage cash flow.

CASE STUDY I

You are interested in purchasing a AAA baseball team. The team is located in Colorado and requires an infusion of capital. In order to evaluate the purchase price, you need to create financial statements and amortization and depreciation schedules. The financial information is very poor, but what is available follows:

1. There is no balance sheet, income statement, or cash flow statement.
2. The team was created in 1993 and uses the accrual basis of accounting.
3. The team was capitalized (1993) as follows:
   a. It sold 100,000 shares of common stock for $10 per share.
   b. It borrowed $1,000,000 at 8% interest for 7 years.
4. The team incurred certain costs and expenditures in 1993:

a. Equipment	$ 250,000
b. Building	$1,000,000
c. Land	$ 100,000
d. Inventory (at year-end)	$ 20,000
e. Players' salaries	$3,000,000
f. Baseball operations expenses	$ 820,000
g. General and administration expenses	$ 310,000
h. Utilities	$ 100,000
i. Maintenance	$ 125,000
j. Bad-debt expense	$ 12,000
k. Insurance expense	$ 100,000
l. Miscellaneous	$ 115,000

5. The team generated revenue in 1993 as follows:
   a. Ticket sales: 1,000,000 fans at $5/ticket.
   b. Stadium concessions: 1,000,000 fans at $1 per fan.
   c. Parking: $100,000 per year.
6. Depreciation information:
   a. Building: 30-year life using straight-line method.
   b. All other long-term assets over a 5-year life, with straight-line depreciation.
7. Other information:
   a. The baseball team must pay the city **10% for each ticket sold** (license fee).
   b. The team invested in a **certificate of deposit (CD)** on January 1, 1993, for **24 months at 10% compounded daily.** The CD had a **face value of $200,000,** and interest income is recorded at year-end.
   c. Prepaid insurance was $20,000.

d. *Accounts receivable balance is $80,000 at year-end.*

e. *Accounts payable $75,000 at year-end.*

8. *An accrual basis of accounting is observed.*

9. *The income tax rate is 34%.*

10. *Dividend paid: $5 per share of common stock at year-end. Dividend is paid each year.*

11. **Balances (December 31, 1994)**

a. *Inventory*	$ 40,000
b. *Prepaid insurance*	$ 20,000
c. *Accounts receivable*	$ 60,000
d. *Equipment*	$300,000
e. *Accounts payable*	$100,000

12. **Revenues (1994)**

Tickets, concessions, and parking same as 1992. **Don't forget interest income.**

Expenses (1994)

All 1994 expenses are the same, except **depreciation expense.**

REQUIREMENTS FOR CASE STUDY:

1. *Prepare the following financial statements for Sports Properties, Inc.:*

   a. *Balance sheets for 1993 and 1994*

   b. *Income statements for 1993 and 1994*

   c. *Statements of cash flows for 1994*

2. *Prepare corresponding schedules for*

   a. *Loan amortization*

   b. *Depreciation*

   c. *Cash balance "T" account for 1993 and 1994*

3. *Do an analysis of the financial statements and indicate strengths and weaknesses of* **Sports Properties, Inc. Be specific.**

CASE STUDY II

The University of the South wants to increase revenue streams inside the stadium. It has decided to build luxury boxes in the stadium, and it is in the process of evaluating alternative financing arrangements to fund the construction of the boxes. The project includes building 28 corporate boxes with 24 seats per box. The university needs $2.5 million dollars for construction and operation. Compare financing arrangements and discuss the advantages and disadvantages of each.

REVIEW QUESTIONS AND ISSUES

1. Identify and discuss facilities recently constructed for sport organizations in the United States.

2. What public-financing options are available for constructing a stadium or arena?

3. Describe and identify private and public/private financing options available for the construction of major sport facilities.

4. What is the difference between cash flow and cash?

5. Describe how sport is seasonal and the effect this has on cash inflows and outflows.

6. Public-financing instruments are usually tax free. What is the benefit to the investor? The benefit to the community?

7. Why do communities build stadiums for sport organizations?

8. Give examples of private financing of sport facilities.

9. Cash flow requires revenue streams. Discuss and identify the major revenue streams produced by sport enterprises?

REFERENCES

Cooley, P. and Roden, P. (1991). *Business financial management,* ed 2, Hinsdale, Illinois, Dryden Press.

Hurt and others. (1993). *Stadium lease arrangements,* San Antonio, Texas, International City Managers Association, Sports and Special Events Conference.

Regan, T. (1993). *Financing stadiums and arenas in the United States and Europe,* Fourth Annual International Conference on Sports Business, Paris, France.

SUGGESTED READINGS

Zimbalist, A. (1992). *Baseball and billions,* New York, Basic Books.

Staudohar, P.D. and Mangan, J.A. (1991). eds: *The business of professional sports,* Chicago, University of Illinois Press.

Ballpark figures: the Blue Jays and the business of baseball, (1987). Toronto, Ontario, McCelland and Stewart.

Ritter, L.S. (1992). *Lost ballparks,* New York, Viking Penguin.

Gorman, J. and Calhoun, K. (1994). *The name of the game: the business of sports,* New York, John Wiley and Sons.

PART **VII**

Conclusion

CHAPTER 20

Managing Uncertainty

Laurence Chalip and Bonnie L. Parkhouse

In this chapter, you will become familiar with the following terms:

Action research	Structural model	Political model
Applied research	Human resource model	Symbolic model
Basic research		

The literature on sport management, like the literature on management per se, recommends procedures for effective administration. These procedures derive from experience and from voluminous research into sport, management, and human behavior. However, management is rarely as simple as the application of standard routines or strategies. Effective managers do not merely reach into a tool kit of management methods to choose a management tool for the situation at hand. Rather, managers must plan creatively for an uncertain future.

Managers face uncertainty both inside and outside the organization. Inside the organization, employees and the units (e.g., marketing, operations, finance) may respond in unanticipated ways to plans, policies, or conditions. For example, Capital Volleyball (based in suburban Washington, D.C.) shifted its marketing emphasis in 1988 by promoting the club's programs as a means for high school girls to showcase themselves for college scholarships. However, the club's daily operations emphasized preparation of teams for national competition, rather than development of opportunities for individual players to showcase for recruiters. The result was substantial new conflict between coaches, on the one hand, and parents and players, on the other.

Similarly, employee responses to new programs or policies are rarely predictable with certainty, although employee reactions may affect program or policy implementation. Consider, for example, the strike of Major League Baseball players after team owners announced plans for a salary cap (see Chapter 8). Although employee responses are not typically so dramatic, the players' strike aptly illustrates the fact that employees' attitudes and behaviors may have a significant impact on implementation of the organization's strategic plan.

Uncertainties outside the organization further complicate the manager's task. Market conditions, consumer behaviors, competitor responses, and economic conditions are neither fully predictable nor substantially controllable. Consider the following examples of each: Increased demand for minimum-wage labor may reduce the number of teenagers seeking to participate in sports programs. If travelers' leisure preferences shift from passive to active pursuits, the demand for sports in resort communities (and the consequent need for sport facilities) would be likely to rise. A competitor's introduction of new sports programs may erode the organization's market share. If consumer spending declines as a consequence of an economic downturn, ticket revenues may also decline.

If the manager is to manage effectively, the level of uncertainty itself must be managed. Significant resources are often at stake. Consequently, managers seek ways to reduce their level of uncertainty. Plans and budgets are used by managers to minimize internal uncertainty. Forecasts are useful devices for reducing external uncertainty. Research is a key tool for reducing both internal and external uncertainty. Research data may be used as inputs into plans, budgets, and forecasts. However, research data may also be used directly to inform management decisions and choices.

ACTION RESEARCH

Research that is to inform practice is appropriately called **action research** because it is research upon which actions are to be based. In management contexts, action research includes organization assessment (Harrison, 1994), marketing research (Zikmund, 1982; Barabba and Zaltman, 1991), needs assessments (Hudson, 1988), social-impact assessment (Finsterbusch, Llewellyn, and Wolf, 1983), and evaluation research (Rossi and Freeman, 1989). Organization assessments use behavioral-science methods to diagnose an organization's situation and to discover means by which to redress the organization's problems. Marketing research uses the methods of behavioral science to determine the response (or likely response) of consumers to products, services, and marketing campaigns. Needs assessments identify services, programs, or products that are desired by the public and establish criteria for their design and delivery. Social-impact assessments measure a project's or program's likely consequences for the communities and individuals in its vicinity. Evaluation research appraises program effectiveness and locates means to improve program delivery.

Action research is sometimes (incorrectly) referred to as **applied research.** It is often differentiated from disciplinary research, which is sometimes (incorrectly) called **basic research.** Although it is still common to hear that applied research is different from basic research, historians and philosophers of science have discredited the distinction (Chalip, 1985). In many instances, work that began as applied turned out to have profound effects on basic social theory. For example, Lazarsfeld's classic work on status influence began as marketing research for *True Story* magazine. Similarly, work that began for purely disciplinary reasons has often had important practical implications. For example, the study of muscle physiology has helped coaches differentiate aerobic from anaerobic cycles of training.

The distinction between applied and basic research has been detrimental to the practice of action research because it has perpetuated the myth that action research is atheoretical. Because action research is "applied," and therefore motivated by practical rather than academic concerns, some have argued that it need not be informed by social or behavioral theory. However, action research requires substantial theoretical sophistication if it is to be useful (see Chalip, 1990, for a discussion). The practitioner of action research must have a sufficient grasp of fundamental social and behavioral theory to fully interpret the data and communicate their implications to decision makers.

The task of using research data to inform decision making is surprisingly complex (Chalip, 1990; Boggs, 1992). Although research has been shown to have substantial value for decision makers, it is rarely the sole basis for a decision (Weiss, 1980). One reason seems to be that research findings are rarely sufficient, in and of themselves, to determine the optimal choice or decision. Rather, decision makers have to interpret research findings and blend them with their own judgments, experience, and informed opinions (Knorr-Cetina, 1983). Thus, although action research can reduce managers' uncertainty, action research is unlikely to eliminate it.

CONCEPT CHECK

Action research is research upon which actions are based. It is a myth that action research is atheoretical. Since it is "applied," and therefore motivated by practical rather than academic concerns, some have argued that it need not be informed by behavioral theory. However, to be useful, action research requires substantial theoretical sophistication.

USING ACTION RESEARCH

The degree to which the new knowledge generated by action research can enhance decision making depends substantially on ways that knowledge is utilized by the organization (Glaser, Abelson, and Garrison, 1983). It is useful, therefore, for the manager to think about ways in which the organization treats knowledge. Bolman and Deal (1991) suggest that managers should analyze their organization in terms of four models: a structural model, a human resource model, a political model, and a symbolic (cultural) model. Slack (1991) argues that multimodel analyses are particularly useful because "using different approaches to understand the complex and paradoxical nature of sport organizations enables one to better design and manage them." The following analysis employs the models elaborated by Bolman and Deal to provide a framework for probing a sport organization's system for reducing uncertainty.

Structural model

A structural analysis of an organization examines ways that responsibilities are divided among the organization's units and scrutinizes the impact of those divisions on organization function. For example, a college athletics department may separate fund-raising, sport information, compliance, coaching, and academic support into different units. Although this division may be efficient, it might have unexpected side effects. For example, fund-raisers and sport information personnel might find themselves working at cross-purposes. Whereas the sports information staff might be emphasizing positive elements of the department, fund-raisers might want to emphasize inadequacies that warrant new donations. Similarly, compliance, coaching, and academic support staff may need to coor-

dinate their efforts in order to keep athletes with marginal academic skills eligible.

This suggests two analytic tasks. First, determine ways that the organization's structure facilitates or inhibits the flow of information. For example, the institutional research units of universities often generate substantial research on factors affecting student retention and graduation. Although this research might prove useful to athletic personnel seeking to enhance the retention and graduation rates of student athletes, there is rarely any formal channel to facilitate the requisite communication between institutional research and the relevant units of the athletic department (e.g., academic support).

Second, diagnose the ways that rewards or sanctions affect information flow. For example, coaches may learn about an athlete's academic troubles but fear that informing academic support or compliance may generate some conflict over training versus study time. The coach is responding to a different set of expectations than are either academic support or compliance.

Human resource model

The human resource model emphasizes the motivations of personnel and the consequent ways staff interact. Whereas the structural model focuses on formal interactions, the human resource model focuses on informal interactions. The analyst employing this model examines how people feel about their work, the organization, and the ways their work contributes to achievement of the organization's goals.

Consider, again, the problem of relating a university's research on student retention and graduation to the efforts of an athletic department to retain and graduate student athletes. If the university's climate fosters friendly interaction among staff of athletics and institutional research, the likelihood that useful information will be shared is increased, even in the absence of a formal channel for information sharing. If morale is sufficiently high that the staff of both units are strongly committed to the university's academic and athletic goals, then the likelihood that the two units will share information is further enhanced.

This example suggests two analytic tasks. First, explore informal sources of employee interaction, information sharing, and information seeking. Second, scrutinize employee interests and motivation, paying particular attention to ways in which to enhance employee identification with the goals of the organization. By bringing employees' interests into harmony with those of the organization as a whole, the probability of shared problem finding and information sharing is enhanced.

Political model

The analyst using a political framework examines ways that individuals or groups compete with one another for organizational power and resources. For example, Prouty (1988) described ways that members of the board of directors for World Championships, Inc. (cycling) competed with staff for the authority to determine details about ways the world championships would be run. One consequence of the struggle for power was that information was not shared between staff and board, causing the event to lose potential sponsors.

The key task, then, is to determine the effect of potential conflicts over resources (including power) on formal and informal flows of information. In the case of the world cycling championship, individual staff and board members were sequestering information that might have been useful for wooing and winning event sponsors. Information on potential contacts and appropriate means for bringing them into the event became a potential source of influence within the organization. Consequently, the information was not pooled and analyzed in ways that would have made it actionable. The consequent failure to attract sponsors had the further effect of causing the event's title sponsor, Southland Corporation, to scale back its own involvement, jeopardizing the event's feasibility.

Symbolic model

The symbolic model is concerned with culture. It requires the analyst to ask about the beliefs and values that are important to the organization. Using this model, the analyst examines the rituals, ceremonies, stories, and myths that organization members use to convey and interpret information.

McDonald (1988) recounts her experience working for the design department of the Los Angeles Olympic Organizing Committee (LAOOC). She describes ways in which LAOOC's goals came to be symbolized and reinforced through the jokes and stories staff told to one another. These, in turn, solidified staff relations, furthering the sharing of information. Lunches at LAOOC's cafeteria provided daily opportunities for staff from all departments to interact, sharing progress reports, Olympic news, and sports information. The culture of LAOOC facilitated staff identification with the organization's goals and provided daily opportunities for them to share information informally.

CONCEPT CHECK

The degree to which new knowledge generated by action research can enhance decision-making depends on how that information is utilized by the organization. Four models are suggested that managers should utilize in analyzing their organization. The structural model is used to examine ways the responsibilities are divided among units within the organization, and scrutinizes the impact of those divisions on organizational function. The human resource model emphasizes the motivations of personnel and the ways staff interact. The political model is used to examine means by which individuals or groups compete for organizational power and resources. The symbolic model is cultural in nature. Rituals, ceremonies, stories and myths are examined to determine how organization members convey and interpret information.

OVERVIEW AND CONCLUDING OBSERVATIONS

Effective management does not result from the routine application of procedures or prescriptions. Just as situations differ, so will the means for addressing those situations. Managers must manage uncertainties that are ever-changing. Consequently, they must monitor their internal and external environments. That, in turn, requires them to seek information, find creative ways to use information, and to facilitate its flow throughout the organization.

Effective management requires more than applying standard procedures or strategies. This book provides information that facilitates the process of planning for an uncertain future. Fundamentals (Chapters 1-4), Human Resource Management (Chapters 5-8), Issues of Policy (Chapters 9-12), Facilities (Chapter 13), Marketing (Chapters 14-16), and Economics and Finance (Chapters 17-19) are imperative in this endeavor.

Chapter 1 addresses the need for academicians to responsibly ensure quality professional preparation in the field of sport management. That is, coursework and related experiences must be effective in assisting the sport manager to learn to manage ever-changing uncertainties. Chapter 2 focuses on the scope and career opportunities in sport management, including those human resources, technologies, support units, and contextual factors that assist the reader in understanding the work environment of this field. Experiental learning through those field experiences of internships and practica is the focus of Chapter 3. As aforementioned, in addition to traditional courses—such related experiences as fieldwork are an integral part of the curriculum. It is a laboratory experience that affords the opportunity to apply what has been learned from a structured, classroom setting. Given its focus on application, experiential learning is a natural process of being constantly exposed to ever-changing situations. This is an excellent atmosphere in which one can learn to manage uncertainties. Chapter 4 examines the theoretical base, designs, and concepts utilized in sport management research. Research in this field makes a valuable contribution to understanding and improving the practice of sport management. As mentioned earlier, research is a key approach for reducing both internal and external uncertainty.

Chapter 5 describes organizational structure and the various processes that occur within a sport organization; decision making and change are specifically addressed. Although change, in particular, creates uncertainty, organizations cannot remain competitive unless they change to meet the demands of their respective markets. Chapter 6 examines group decision making and problem solving. Human resources are also critical to a strong and effective organization. Management of these resources is the focus of Chapter 7. The traditional, interpretive, and critical paradigms are presented in this endeavor. Both Chapters 6 and 7 offer techniques and/or paradigms for seeking information and finding creative ways of utilizing it in the effort to minimize uncertainties. The focus of Chapter 8 is labor relations—that is, how employer/employee relationships have developed in America's four major professional, team sports: baseball, football, hockey, and basketball. This chapter further addresses a recent case of baseball, which illustrates how destructive the breakdown of labor relations can be when critical questions of the employment relationship are ignored. It's a case in point of crisis management—managing uncertainty ineffectively by not monitoring internal and external environments.

Chapter 9 provides the foundation for a rational application of the principles of ethics to the ethical problems that are encountered in the sport environment. Although it is difficult to determine with precision the relationship between personal and professional ethics, managing uncertainty requires the establishment of clear, unambiguous expectations for the ethical conduct of employees. Sport managers must work diligently to create a climate in which ethical conduct is a matter of habit rather than one of expedience. Chapters 10, 11, and 12 address legal concepts in the areas of tort liability and risk management, contract law, and constitutional and statutory law, respectively. In legal matters it would be ludicrous to suggest that sport managers represent themselves as attorneys. It is, however, important that they are sufficiently informed in order to choose legal counsel wisely and be able to converse with him or her in a knowledgeable manner. Legal issues are dependent upon each party's respective power in negotiating the transition. Although the legal structure inherently provides the basis for managing uncertainty regarding issues of policy, the sport manager has an obligation to facilitate this process.

Chapter 13 describes the various types of facility management and the major components inherent in managing the sport complex. Risk management is one of the most important aspects of facility management presented in this chapter. The function and purpose of risk management is to alleviate liability problems that could result in significant financial loss by providing a safe environment for patrons. Risk management is used by facility managers to minimize internal uncertainty.

Chapters 14, 15, and 16 focus on marketing. Chapter 14 presents concepts relative to sport marketing and discusses the application of these concepts as practiced by sport organizations. Strategic market management, demographics, psychographic analysis, target marketing, and market segmentation, all aspects of marketing research, are critical aspects of this Chapter in terms of reducing internal and external uncertainty. Corporate sponsorship is the focus of Chapter 15. It is premised on exchange theory; that is, sport organizations obtain funds from sponsors to operate their events and programs. It also affords corporations the opportunity to expose their products to the consumer. For the sport marketer, the economic value in the exchange offsets budget-related expenditures which, in turn, minimizes internal uncertainty. The subject of Chapter 16 is sport licensing. Sport organizations grant (license) second parties the right to produce merchandise bearing associated designs or individual likenesses. In return, these organizations receive protection, promotion, and profit, which assists managers in monitoring their internal and external environments.

Economics, accounting and budgeting, and finance are the focus of Chapters 17, 18, and 19. As described in Chapter 17, economics is concerned with the allocation of a limited amount of resources to individuals and other economic agents with unlimited wants. Almost every aspect of sport is susceptible to economic analysis. Economic theory can be used to analyze questions and problems encountered by the sport manager, which, in turn, reduces uncertainty. Chapter 18 discusses principles of accounting, financial statements, computing and interpreting ratios, and types of budgeting. Chapter 19 focuses more generally on cash flow management. Collectively, these two chapters address the issue of managing uncertainty from the financial/economic perspective.

Effective management does not result from the routine application of procedures or prescriptions. Just as situations differ, so will the means for addressing those situations. Managers must manage uncertainties that are ever-changing. Consequently, they must monitor their internal and external environments. That, in turn, requires them to seek information, find creative ways to use information, and to aid its flow throughout the organization. In the opinion of the authors of this chapter, *The Management of Sport: Its Foundation and Application,* 2nd edition, is an excellent resource that sport managers can utilize in the endeavor to facilitate the above process.

SUMMARY

1. Effective management is more complicated than the application of standard routines and strategies. Managers must plan creatively for an uncertain future. They face uncertainty both inside and outside the organization. Internally, the responses of employees and such units as marketing or operations to conditions, plans, or policies are rarely predictable with certainty. Externally, market conditions, consumer behaviors, competitor responses, and economic conditions are neither fully predictable or necessarily controllable.

2. Action research is research upon which actions are based. It is a myth that action research is atheoretical. Since it is "applied," and therefore motivated by practical rather than academic concerns, some have argued that it need not be informed by behavioral theory. However, to be useful, action research requires substantial theoretical sophistication.

3. The degree to which new knowledge generated by action research can enhance decision-making depends on how that information is utilized by the organization. Four models are suggested that managers should utilize in analyzing their organizations. The structural model is used to examine ways that responsibilities are divided among units within the organization, and scrutinizes the impact of those divisions on organizational function. The human resource model emphasizes the motivations of personnel and the ways staff interact. The political model is used to examine means by which individuals or groups compete for organizational power and resources. The symbolic model is cultural in nature. Rituals, ceremonies, stories, and myths are examined to determine how organization members convey and interpret information.

REVIEW QUESTIONS AND ISSUES

1. Managers face uncertainty both inside and outside the organization. What is uncertainty? Describe the differences between internal and external uncertainty, including examples of each.

2. What is action research and why, although it can reduce management uncertainty, is it unlikely to eliminate it?

3. Bolman and Deal (1991) present four models for analyzing organizations. Identify and explain how each facilitates the process of managing uncertainty.

REFERENCES

Barabba, V.P. and Zaltman, G. (1991). *Hearing the voice of the market: competitive advantage through creative use of market information*, Boston; Harvard Business School Press.

Boggs, J.P. (1992). *Implicit models of social knowledge use*, Knowledge: Creation, Diffusion, Utilization 14: 29-62.

Bolman, L.G. and Deal, T.E. (1985). *Reframing organizations: artistry, choice, and leadership*, San Francisco, Jossey-Bass.

Chalip, L. (1985). Policy research as social science: outflanking the value dilemma, *Policy Studies Review* 5: 287-308.

Chalip, L. (1990). Rethinking the applied social sciences of sport: observations on the emerging debate, *Sociology of Sport Journal* 7: 172-178.

Finsterbusch, K., Llewellyn, L.G., and Wolf, C.P., eds. (1983). *Social impact assessment methods*, Beverly Hills, Sage.

Glaser, E.M., Abelson, H.H., and Garrison, K.N. (1983). *Putting knowledge to use: facilitating the diffusion of knowledge and the implementation of planned change*, San Francisco, Jossey-Bass.

Harrison, M.I. (1994). *Diagnosing organizations: methods, models, and processes*, ed 2, Thousand Oaks, California, Sage.

Hudson, S. (1988). *How to conduct community needs assessment surveys in public parks and recreation*, Columbus, Ohio, Publishing Horizons.

Knorr-Cetina, K.D. (1981). *Time and context in practical action: underdetermination and knowledge use*, Knowledge: Creation, Diffusion, Utilization 3: 143-166.

McDonald, P. (1988). *The Los Angeles Olympic Organizing Committee: developing organizational culture in the short run.* In Jones, M.O., More, M.D., and Snyder, R.C., eds, *Inside organizations: understanding the human dimension*, Newbury Park, California, Sage.

Prouty, D.F. (1989). *In spite of us*, Brattleboro, Vermont, Velo-News.

Rossi, P.H. and Freeman, H.E. (1989). *Evaluation: a systematic approach*, Newbury Park, California, Sage.

Slack, T. (1991). Sport management: some thoughts on future directions, *Journal of Sport Management* 5: 95-99.

Weiss, C.H. (1980). *Knowledge creep and decision accretion*, Knowledge: Creation, Diffusion, Utilization 1: 82-105.

Zikmund, W.G. (1982). *Exploring marketing research*, New York, CBS College Publishing.

Index

Page numbers in *italic type* refer to figures. Tables are indicated by *t* following the page number.

Rescission and restitution, in contract law, 188
Research
    action, for uncertainty management, 378-380
    applied, 378
    basic, 378
    ethics in, 56-58
    focus groups for, consent forms in, 57
    framework for sport management, 49-50
    published
        evaluation of, 55-56
        peer-review of, 56
    reliability in, 52, *52*
    in sport management, 48-60
        case studies on, 60
        disciplines of, 51
        new directions in, 58-60
        skills for, 59-60
        work-related functions and, 49
    survey, 55
    on technologies, organizations and, 74-75
    triangulation in, 55
    validity in, 51-52, *52*
Reservation process, in facility management, 227
Reserve clauses, 125, 216
    antitrust and, 138
    of baseball, 129-130
Restitution, rescission and, in contract law, 188
Restoration, in contract law, 188
Restrictive covenant, 190
Retention
    negligent, 172-173
        Haddock v City of New York (1990), 172-173
    in risk management, 176
Return on investments (ROI), sport sponsorships
        and, 291
Revenue
    bonds, 365
    income statements and, 347
    sharing of
        in professional sports leagues, 122
        in publicly financed stadiums, 369t
    streams, 368-370, 369t
        private-sector, sport facility financing and, 366
    v salaries, in baseball, 132t
Reward power, 77
Reynolds v International Amateur Athletic Federation
        (1991), 204-205
RFPs, for facility management, 224-225
Ridgeway v Montana High School Association (1988), 212

Right of first refusal, in professional basketball, 136
Risk assessments, 173
    categories for, 174
    in facility management, 244, *245*
    frequency/severity in, 175, 176
Risk management, 173-177, 181-182
    avoidance in, 173
    facility management and, 244-246, *246*
    implementation of, 177, 181
    operational practices/procedures in, 177-181
    reduction of exposure in, 176
    retention in, 176
    standard operating procedures in, 246
    statements of policy in, 177
    transference in, 173-176
    waivers in, 175-176
Risks
    primary assumption of, 168, 169
    secondary assumption of, 168-169
    unreasonable, 165
Rituals, of organizational cultures, 110
Robertson v NBA (1975), 136
Rodgers v Georgia Tech Athletic Association (1983), 189
ROI, sport sponsorships and, 291
Rollover clause, 190-191
Routine technologies, organizational structure and, 74
Royalties
    audits of, 312-313
    exemptions for, 313
    for licensors, 307-308
Rozelle Rule, 217

S

Safety and medical services, facility management
        and, 229-231
Salaries
    arbitration, final offer, 129
    in baseball
        with free agency, *133*
        v revenue, 132t
    caps in basketball, *v* football, 140t
    in football, *135*
    in professional sports, *139*
Sales
    activity ratios and, 351
    contracts, 192-193
    income statements and, 347, 347t